Critical Heuristics
of Social Planning

Critical Heuristics
of Social Planning

A New Approach to Practical Philosophy

Werner Ulrich

JOHN WILEY & SONS

Chichester · New York · Brisbane · Toronto · Singapore

We cannot, by complaining about the narrow limits of our reason, escape the responsibility of at least a critical solution to the questions of reason.

Immanuel Kant
Critique of Pure Reason

Table of Contents

Part I
Contemporary Models of Rational Discourse

Chapter One
Karl R. Popper's Critical Rationalism: Blind Criticism?

7

Part II
From Kantian A Priori Science to Critical Heuristics

Chapter Five
Kantian A Priori Science and the Process of Unfolding: The Dialectical Turn

Part III
Application

Chapter Six
Toward a "Purposeful Systems" Paradigm of Planning

Chapter Seven
Project Cybersyn: The Chilean Experience with Cybernetics, 1971–73

Chapter Eight
Health Systems Planning:
The Case of the 1976 Areawide Health Systems Plan for Central Puget Sound

List of Figures and Tables

Preface

A the present time there is no adequate philosophical basis, especially no episte-mological basis, of socially rational planning. The main reason for this lack is that the crucial questions in planning are not theoretical or technological questions of know-ing, but practical, i.e., political and moral, questions of willing. Dealing rationally with such questions raises a philosophical problem that has remained unresolved since Immanuel Kant first posed it, two hundred years ago: the problem of practical reason. *How can we rationally identify and justify the normative content of our actions?*

Contemporary practical philosophy examines this problem at a theoretically sophisticated level, but in spite of its sophistication – or perhaps because of it – offers no practicable answer. Much less can it offer adequate heuristic support either to the social inquirer or planner who is willing to question the normative implications of his "rational" activity, or to the citizen who may be affected by this activity and wants to contest its rationality.

Critical Heuristics is an effort to provide planners and citizens alike with the heuristic support they need for confronting the problem of practical reason *in practice* rather than in theory. Its heuristic rather than theoretical orientation is not, however, an excuse for renouncing a self-critical examination and justification of its epistemo-logical foundation. Critical Heuristics finds this foundation in a partial reconstruc-tion of Kantian a priori science and, based on this reconstruction, a critical reinter-pretation of the "systems approach" to planning.

The present study was written while I was an Advanced Research Scholar of the Swiss National Science Foundation (1976–80). During this time I was working with C. West Churchman, Professor of Systems Philosophy and Research Philosopher at the Graduate School of Business Administration, University of California, Berkeley. West's books *Challenge to Reason* (1968), *The Systems Approach* (1968), and *The Design of Inquiring Systems* (1971) had motivated me to move from Switzerland to California, and his latest study *The Systems Approach and Its Enemies* (1979) pro-vided a major source of inspiration for my work. At Berkeley I was fortunate enough to meet other faculty members who shared my interest in the philosophical under-pinnings of a critical systems approach to socially rational planning, both in the public and in the private sector: Professors Henrik L. Blum (School of Public Health), Stephen R. Blum (School of Public Health), Leonard J. Duhl (College of Environ-mental Design and School of Public Health), and Arnold M. Schultz (College of Natural Resources). At a crucial moment during my first year on the Berkeley Cam-pus, Professor Reinhard Bendix of the Department of Political Science supported my project vis-à-vis the Swiss National Science Foundation. Professor Jürgen Habermas, Starnberg, Germany, whose writings helped me to emancipate myself from the epistemological and ideological premises of my own academic background, kindly offered to read Chapter Two of the present study, though his many committments during his stay at UC Berkeley in 1980 did not leave him the time to discuss the chapter with me. Professor Herbert A. Simon was kind enough to agree to the publication of the fictitious debate between himself and C. West Churchman in Chapter Six, in spite of the critical implications of this "debate." Professor Stafford Beer and Mr. Fernando Flores, former Chilean Secretary of Economics in Salvador Allende's cabinet, both provided useful feedback to my case study of "Project Cybersyn" in Chapter Seven, even though they could not agree with my critique. Dr. Joseph Carroll, Berkeley, provided valuable editorial assistance and also contributed many thought-provoking comments.

Portions of this study have been adapted from previously published material. An earlier version of the third section of Chapter Six appeared as "The Design of Problem-Solving Systems" in *Management Science* (1977). A short version of the first section of the same Chapter, "The Metaphysics of Design," was published in *Interfaces* (1980). The entire Chapter Seven, together with the second section of Chapter Six, is taken from my article "A Critique of Pure Cybernetic Reason, " to be published in the *Journal of Applied Systems Analysis* (1981). Finally, for German-speaking readers I should mention that the Introduction to the present study partly overlaps with my "Translator's Introduction" to the German version of C. West Churchman's *The Systems Approach and Its Enemies,* also to be published in 1981.

I dedicate this essay to my little son Dominik, whose happy arrival in February, 1980 has relegated the present study to the number-two spot on the list of items that my wife and I shall take back to Europe.

El Cerrito, California, November 2, 1980   Werner Ulrich

Addition to the Preface (1982)

The two last-mentioned titles have been published in the meantime. In addition, an extended version of "The Metaphysics of Design" has been included for republication in *Metasystems and Metamodels,* to be edited by John P. van Gigch (1984).

I am obliged to the National Research Council of the Swiss National Science Foundation, Bern, for providing a substantial publishing subsidy, without which it might have been impossible to publish the book. My most sincere thanks are due to Dr. Max Haupt of Paul Haupt Academic Publishers, Bern, for offering me a publishing contract without any "ifs" or "buts." Dr. Haupt has unconditionally supported the publication of this book even though it does not conform to current academic fashions and thus may take several years to find its audience. I am all the more grateful to him for giving my book a chance.

I would also like to thank two scholars who have taken the time to read the finished manuscript and to comment on it: Professors Peter B. Checkland, Department of Systems, University of Lancaster, England, and Emil Walter-Busch, Graduate School of Business Administration, Economics and Social Science, St. Gallen, Switzerland. Their comments have been most encouraging to me.

At this place, I would like to remember Dr. Erich Jantsch, Berkeley, who died on December 12, 1980 very shortly before I left Berkeley. His understanding of the systems approach often clashed with mine, but I cannot remember my Berkeley years without remembering him. My thoughts also go to my dear friends at Berkeley, Trudi and Heinz Frei-Bühler; their friendship is among the greatest gains of my Berkeley years.

Finally, a note for those readers who may find it difficult to digest the many philosophical terms used throughout the book and who may wish I had added a glossary: such a glossary always tends to give some arbitrary definitions out of context, and I have therefore preferred to prepare a detailed and thorough subject index.

Bern, Switzerland, November 26, 1982   Werner Ulrich

Introduction
Planning, the Systems Approach, and the Problem of Practical Reason: On the Idea of a Critical Heuristics of Social Planning

This much is certain, that whoever has once tasted critique
will be ever after disgusted with all dogmatic twaddle....
Immanuel Kant, Prolegomena
(1783:A 190, transl. Beck 1951)

Rationality, according to Ambrose Bierce's usually reliable *Devil's Dictionary,* is the quality of being "devoid of all delusions save those of observation, experience, and reflection" (1958:107). Critical Heuristics, or, by its full name, Critical Systems Heuristics, represents a conceptual framework for tracing some of these delusions in the realm of "rational" social planning.

I have chosen the name "Critical Systems Heuristics" for this framework because it seems aptly to suggest three of its main characteristics: its critical intent against present conceptions of "rational" planning, its employment of the systems idea for this purpose, and its heuristic rather than theoretical orientation. I use all three terms – "critical," "system," and "heuristic" – in the sense given to them by Immanuel Kant, the father of critical philosophy. But since I cannot of course presuppose in this introduction the reader's familiarity with Kantian a priori science or even my own partial reconstruction of it, a preliminary explanation of the three terms is in order.

1. *Critical:* To be critical, according to the etymological origin of the word in the Greek *kritike (techne),* "the art of judgement," means to discern or to judge carefully with a view to guarding oneself against error. Such judgement presupposes implicit or explicit standards or *norms* against which to judge something. If in the act of criticizing the presupposed norm itself is not questioned, criticism can be said to serve an instrumental or technical purpose, namely, in the service of established norms. Jurisprudence provides a good example: a law may be worthy of being criticized, but in the act of juridical judgement, the judge has to assume its validity as a norm. Even if the norm itself is criticized, it is by reference to some "higher" norm (law), the validity of which is assumed. This instrumental understanding of criticism underlies the classical concept of criticism as *kritike techne,* as the term itself suggests.

It is only in modern times that "being critical" has come to mean the critical questioning of the norms themselves. With Kant in particular, criticism itself becomes an almost absolute norm "to which everything must be subjected." Criticism in this modern sense no longer serves a merely instrumental purpose in respect to given norms; it now takes on a practical role in determining the norms that are to guide us in all our thinking and acting. "To be critical" then above all means to become self-reflective in respect to the presuppositions flowing into one's own judgements, both in the search for true knowledge and rational action.

In this general sense, Kant speaks of a *Critique of Pure (Theoretical) Reason* and of a *Critique of Practical Reason,* respectively; and it is in this self-reflective rather than in an instrumental sense that we shall employ the term. In the context of applied social inquiry and planning, being critical therefore means to make transparent to oneself and to others the value assumptions underlying practical judgements, rather than concealing them behind a veil of objectivity.

Critical Systems Heuristics, rather than stipulating or simply presupposing some objective standards of rationality, is intended to serve a critical purpose against the objectivist illusion in prevailing concepts of rational planning, rational discourse on planning, or rational criticism of plans. If it succeeds in its purpose, Critical Systems Heuristics will provide planners and concerned citizens alike with an effective tool of reflection and criticism – reflection on the inevitable normative content of all planning.[1] Planning is rational, from the perspective of this study, if the involved planners and the affected citizens make transparent to themselves and to each other this normative content. In the philosophical tradition since Kant, the problem of how we can rationally discuss and justify the normative content of assertions, recommendations, plans or actions is known as the *problem of practical reason.* As is indicated by the quotation from Kant that serves as the motto of this study, we shall, like Kant, aim at a *critical solution* to this problem. A critical solution does not yield any "objective" justification of normative validity claims; it prevents us, rather, from submitting to an objectivist illusion with regard to such claims.

2. *System:* Critical Systems Heuristics finds a powerful tool of critical reflection in the systems idea. This assertion may come as a surprise to many a reader who has become accustomed to associating the concept of system with predominantly technocratic approaches to planning such as, for example, RAND-systems analysis, systems engineering, social cybernetics, General Systems Theory (which is neither general nor theoretical), System Dynamics, Operations Research/Manage-

---

[1] I shall speak of the "normative content" rather than the "underlying value assumptions" of planning because what matters is not only the a priori value judgements (interests, motivations, etc.) but also the a posteriori consequences and side-effects for those who are affected by a plan. The term should also remind us of the fact that all knowledge, in the context of its application, has not only an empirical or theoretical but also a normative content.

ment Science, MIS (management information systems), heuristic programming, artificial intelligence, and other variations of functionalistic "systems science." The critical intent of the present study is partly directed against the objectivistic understanding of rational planning in contemporary systems science.

Again, the key to a critical understanding of the systems idea can be found in Kant. Contemporary systems science, I believe, has failed to understand the critical significance of the systems idea in Kant. Whereas contemporary systems science understands the systems concept merely functionalistically, as referring to a set of variables to be controlled in a context of instrumental action, Kants understands it as referring to the totality of relevant conditions on which theoretical or practical judgements depend, including basic metaphysical, ethical, political, and ideological a priori judgements. Systems scientists often deride Kant's employment of the systems concept as "holistic," meaning that it is of no practical significance because "we never know the whole system." Kant's detractors completely miss the fact that Kant uses the systems concept as a *critical idea of reason,* namely, as an idea that reminds us precisely of the unavoidable incomprehensiveness and selectivity of every definition of a system, and hence of the need for reflecting on the normative content of the a priori whole systems judgements flowing into our systems concepts. No scientistic, "systems-scientific" approach to planning can circumvent or supersede the need for such reflection. The systems idea as we understand it does not presuppose that we can know "the whole system," but only that we can undertake a critical effort to reflect on the inevitable *lack* of comprehensiveness in our understanding of and design for (social) systems. Thus the systems idea, if we do not scientistically misunderstand it, challenges us to make transparent to ourselves and to others the normative implications of our systems concepts and designs.

3. *Heuristics:* In the *Oxford English Dictionary,* we read:
Heuristic, a. (irreg. f. Gr. *heurisk-ein,* to find)
1. serving to find out or discover
2. *spec.* applied to that method of teaching which places the pupil, as far as possible, in the position of a discoverer.

The Oxford definition illuminates two aspects of a heuristic approach but misses two other, crucial aspects.

(a) Heuristics is what helps to discover problem-relevant questions and problem-relevant knowledge: Finding relevant questions for identifying and unfolding problems is the basic task with which the currently prevailing theory of knowledge and model of "rational" inquiry (logical empiricism, Critical Rationalism, analytical philosophy) cannot deal. Since it conceives of "objective" knowledge as "knowledge without a knowing subject" (thus Popper 1972:109), it is helpless in giving the inquirer heuristic support in his task of discovering and unfolding problems. Not surprisingly, it relegates this task to the so-called psychological context, a context that supposedly interests only the psychologist but not the epistemologist. Not surprisingly, too, the "scientific" problem-solving methods of systems science and other disciplines that rely on this theory of knowledge are no problem-solving methods at all, for they prerequire an explicit, complete description of the problem. But if one can give a complete definition of the problem, one has no longer a genuine problem; for a complete definition of the problem is possible only when one already knows how to bound and understand the problem-relevant system (the totality of relevant conditions), that is, when one knows the "solution" to all the crucial questions. In real-world inquiry and design, problems are never "given" like textbook exercices; rather, they must be discovered, unfolded, and defined by someone who is prepared to consider them as problems. Accordingly, by heuristics we understand not a collection of prototypical problem solutions or problem-solving techniques, but rather *the art of making "the problem" the problem.*

(b) Heuristics is what serves to *teach* discovering: One of the most important concerns of Critical Systems Heuristics is the didactic or educational task of preparing citizens, plannings, administrators or managers for their task of critically reflecting upon seemingly given "problems" and "solutions." There are of course limits to the idea of teaching heuristics. But it is certainly possible to provide both citizens and professionals with better conceptual support for critical reflection than is presently available.

(c) Heuristics is what serves to discover deception: This *critical* task of heuristics is not contained in the Oxford definition, and yet it is a necessary complement to its constructive task. At least since Christopher Columbus it has become common knowledge that discovery and deception go together, i.e., that there is no guarantee against deception in discovery. From a critical point of view, the lack of guarantee against deception implies that we have to assume deception. Hence, if we want to support discovery (of problems and solutions), we must also further the planner's reflection on the sources of deception in his "discoveries."

The concept of a *critical heuristics* will seem paradoxical only to those who associate heuristics with "heuristic programming" and other heuristic techniques that are uncritical vis-à-vis their own normative content.[2] The paradox dissolves if we understand the term "heuristic" in a Kantian sense. When Kant designates a

---

[2] To these techniques of "uncritical heuristics," as I am inclined to call them, belong simulation techniques such as System Dynamics (Forrester 1969, 1971, Meadows et al. 1972, Mesarovic/Pestel 1974); analytical techniques such as RAND-systems analysis (Quade/Boucher 1968), cost-benefit analysis, relevance tree and other methods of technological forecasting (Jantsch 1966), and Morphological analysis (Zwicky 1961); intuitive techniques such as Delphi (Helmer 1968), scenario writing, and Bionics (e.g. Papanek 1969, Yeang 1974); and group-dynamic techniques such as Brainstorming (Osborn 1953), Synectics (Gordon 1961, Prince 1970), and Creative Development (Ulrich 1977 e). I have examined some of these techniques in a series of articles (1976 b, c, 1977 a, b, c, e) and on other occasions (1975 a, 1976 a). For critical discussions of systems analysis and System Dynamics, see e.g. Hoos (1972), Berlinksi (1976) and Churchman/Mason (1976).

concept or a principle as heuristic, he means that it represents a merely hypothetical a priori judgement of reason, a judgement whose empirical or theoretical validity is problematic and therefore remains in need of critical reflection. From a Kantian point of view, heuristics cannot serve as a source of discovery unless it is at the same time considered as a source of deception, i.e, as a source of an objectivist illusion.

Since this conjecture is indeed fundamental to our entire study, and specifically to the way in which we shall employ the heuristic tool of the systems idea, it will be sufficient and convenient to speak simply of *critical heuristics* or of a critically-heuristic approach to social planning. This will be less awkward than speaking of a "Critical Systems Heuristics of social planning."

(d) Finally, a heuristic approach is what a theoretical approach is not: All critical philosophies of which I am aware, from Kantian a priori science to Jürgen Habermas' "Critical Theory," seek to attain their critical purpose via theory, i.e., they seek to ground their own critical concepts theoretically. There is nothing wrong with this idea except that it is impractical. We shall find in our study that no theoretical solution to the problem of practical reason can be both critical *and* practicable. An approach to "rational" planning that is both critical and practicable is thereby necessarily a merely heuristic approach, i.e., it cannot theoretically justify its own basic concepts and its own normative content but rather must remain self-reflective with respect to its theoretically problematic and practically normative character. This is why I suggest the program of a critical heuristics of social planning rather than a critical theory of society. Instead of searching for a theoretical justification of its basic concepts, a critically-heuristic approach aims at a strictly heuristic justification – namely, by demonstrating the "heuristic necessity" (a term yet to be defined) of these basic concepts in regard to a critical solution to the problem of practical reason.

Given this preliminary understanding of critical heuristics, let us now try to situate it within the recently developing field of practical philosophy (see Bubner 1975, Riedel 1972–74, Höffe 1979).

The Systems Approach and the Challenge to Practical Reason

Reason is theoretical, according to Kant, when it produces understanding or knowledge of what *is* or what happens; it is practical when it helps us determine what *ought to be* or what ought to be done, i.e., when the problem involves our will (cf. KrV:B iv, 661, 830, and KpV:A 35).[3] Theoretical reason can give us insight into the causal laws and the evolutionary processes of natural systems, but only practical

---

[3] Concerning the style of references to Kant's works see the note appended to the introduction to Chapter 3.

reason can tell us how to use our freedom of choice so as to realize better *human* (social) systems. "By 'the practical' I mean everything that is possible through freedom," says Kant (KrV:B 828).

The challenge to practical reason consists in using this freedom reasonably, that is, in determining the ends and means of one's actions "with reason." We call this effort of rational deliberation on one's use of freedom, on the ends and means of anticipated social practice, *planning*. If planning employs the systems concept as a tool of such normative deliberation, we shall speak of systems planning or *systems design*. Finally, we shall speak of *social* planning (or social systems design) when we want to emphasize the public or societal – especially political and moral – relevance of planning. Planning is politically and morally relevant, and thus "public" rather than "private," if the group of the affected citizens is not identical with the group of the involved planners. It is in this case, particularly, that the inevitable normative content of planning poses a challenge to practical reason: Under what conditions can the involved planners claim rationality for their plan although not all the affected citizens will benefit? How can conflicts of interests between the involved and the affected be resolved by means of reason rather than by resort to power and deception? How, in one word, can planning be *socially* rational?

Since the object domain of social planning is the very complex section of the real world that we call "social reality" or "social practice," many planners have welcomed the idea of a systems approach, i.e., an interdisciplinary and comprehensive approach, to the analysis and unfolding of complex problem situations. The systems concept today enjoys an unprecedented popularity among social planners and "applied" social scientists, a popularity that is well reflected in its becoming a part of everyday language.

The popularity of the systems concept cannot, however, conceal the fact that something has gone awry with its application as an instrument of practical reason. My thesis is that the very popularity of the systems concept in the applied social sciences and particularly in planning literature is symptomatic of what has gone wrong. The problem, I believe, derives not so much from the systems idea itself as from the prevailing scientism by which it has been absorbed.

Scientism identifies the rational with the scientific; it makes the rationality standards of empirical-analytic ("nomological") science the standards of rational practice, thereby reducing practical to theoretical reason. The main underlying fallacy is the narrowing-down of "rationality" to deductive logic, a concept that excludes (self-) reflection. To take a representative and influential example, Popper's "Critical Rationalism" regards deductive logic as the fundamental "organon of critique" (Popper 1962:115, 1972:31). The systems approach has become scientistic – "systems science" – because it has forgotten Kant's early insight that practical reason cannot be derived from theoretical reason but must be grounded in a critically reflected, normative (moral, political) interest. "An interest is that by which reason becomes practical – that is, a cause determining the will." (GMS:B 122, note)

I propose that the time has come to redefine the systems approach as an enterprise of practical reason, and that in order to make a relevant contribution to practical reason, systems thinking must become radical and must, in every application, begin to question its own underlying systems concept in normative terms. To be radical, or to be scientific, is largely the same idea, namely, the idea of going to the root of the matter and questioning the unexamined: political interests and implications, moral assumptions, and theoretical, methodological, and metaphysical presuppositions. Systems thinking that is not *critically normative* in this sense will evade all significant problems of practical reason and thereby fail to be either practical or scientific (cf. Ulrich 1978, 1980, 1981c).

It should be clear from the outset that it is of no avail for the systems planner to seek refuge in the common argument that he "merely" provides tools for those legitimately in control of purposes but is not in any way engaged in social systems design (thus for instance Stafford Beer in a personal reply to my paper "A Critique of Pure Cybernetic Reason," 1981c). In refutation of this argument, we may appeal to the self-evident fact that all design of tools represents *somebody's* solution to *somebody's* problems, and hence has a normative content of its own in need of radical questioning. This is what the challenge to practical reason is all about; practical reason cannot be reduced to instrumental rationality, which is only an application of theoretical reason.

The tools of systems science have traditionally been associated with a claim for "systems rationality" in the sense of comprehensive rationality; but they offer no means for critically reflecting on the normative content of such system rationality. They remain, in other words, at the level of merely instrumental rationality. The present study, in contrast, pursues the idea of a *critical* systems approach to social planning, a systems approach that would offer a conceptual framework for reflecting on the value assumptions and limitations of "systems rationality." Such a systems approach must seek to become self-reflective, that is to say, philosophical rather than scientific. In the domain of social inquiry and design, it is irrelevant if not deceptive to be scientific without being openly and critically philosophical.

The mere call for reflection is not, however, sufficient to make planning self-reflective with regard to its normative content. The social rationality of planning must not depend entirely on the good will and impartiality of planners regarding this task of reflection. Moreover, even if we were to assume that planners are willing to become self-reflective, reflection on the normative content of planning is often a difficult task that requires all the heuristic support that we can possibly provide. Neither systems science nor Kantian a priori science or any of the contemporary approaches of practical philosophy offer such heuristic support.

Kant's conceptual framework is oriented toward the natural science of his epoch and its underlying metaphysics rather than toward the object domain of social inquiry and planning. Accordingly, Kant's reflecting subject is an abstract "transcendental subject" that is removed from the subjective, social and historical, context in which real-world planning takes place. It is, therefore, clear that we cannot immediately go back to Kantian a priori science, although its critical intent is far from being irrelevant to social inquiry and planning. Rather, we must first review the state of contemporary practical philosophy and then seek to reconstruct Kant's framework so as to make it applicable to the object domain of social inquiry and planning without subverting its critical significance.

The contemporary models of practical philosophy no longer start from the assumption of a lonely transcendental subject. They understand practical reason and practical knowledge as the outcome of a *discursive* (or dialogical) process of will-formation rather than a "monological" process of reflection on the part of an isolated subject. Most completely developed and most influential among these models of discursive rationality are Karl R. Popper's model of rational discussion ("Critical Rationalism"), Paul Lorenzen's dialogical logic ("Constructivist Logic, Ethics and Science-Theory"), and Jürgen Habermas' model of practical discourse ("Critical Theory of Society"). These models face, however, a new problem, a problem that arises as soon as one renounces Kant's assumption of a transcendental subject: What are the criteria for distinguishing between a merely factual and a "rational," i.e., genuine or "true," consensus among the participants in a discourse? Without such criteria, practical discourse cannot become a guarantor of practical rationality.

Perhaps because of their preoccupation with this difficulty, none of the three models offers any substantial heuristic support for the task of tracing the normative content of practical statements (recommendations, plans, etc.). Popper explicitly excludes the heuristic problem ("the context of discovery," as he says) from consideration; Lorenzen and Habermas have thus far focused on the requirements of cogent argumentation ("linguistic norms," "communicative competence") while neglecting the equally important task of constructing conceptual frameworks for the heuristic task of rendering intelligible specific object domains such as normative social reality.

In the present study, I have selected Popper's Critical Rationalism, Habermas' Critical Theory, and Kant's Critical Philosophy as the points of departure for developing a new approach to the problem of practical reason, an approach that – although I claim that its critical character *is* justifiable in epistemological terms – nonetheless does not evade the heuristic problem or sacrifice practicability to theoretical ambitions.

The State of the Art in Contemporary Practical Philosophy

Because the contemporary revival of practical philosophy – the philosophical effort to come to grips with the problem of practical reason – is taking place mostly in

German philosophy, many an American reader might welcome a brief introduction to the present state of the discussion.[4]

Basically, we can distinguish two philosophical camps with more or less opposite conceptions of practical reason. On the one hand we have the scientistic position of the logical positivists (Carnap, Vienna Circle) and the critical rationalists (Popper, Albert, Spinner and others); on the other hand we find the anti-scientistic or "dialectical" position of the constructivists (Lorenzen, Schwemmer, Kambartel, Mittelstrass and others) and the critical theorists (Horkheimer, Adorno, Habermas, Wellmer, Offe and others). The two camps polemically address one another as "(Neo-)positivists" and "(Neo-)Marxists," while understanding themselves as "analytical" or "critical" respectively. Their ongoing dispute mirrors the two unresolved methodological debates in German sociology, namely, the *Werturteilsstreit* of the early decades of the twentieth century and the *Positivismusstreit* of the fifties and sixties. The former was the controversy over the role of value judgements in social inquiry and centered around Max Weber's concept of value freedom (e.g. Weber 1947, 1949, 1968); the latter was the dispute on positivism which was sparked by Adorno's critique of the prevailing empiricist logic of the social sciences (1957; all the contributions to this debate among Adorno, Popper, Habermas and Albert can be found in Adorno et al. 1969).

The dispute between the analytical and the dialectical positions appears to go back to Aristotle's division of the *Organon,* his collected teachings on logic, into an "Analytic" and a "Dialectic." The Analytic described the logic for deciding on the truth of theoretical propositions, while the Dialectic represented the appropriate logic for deciding on the rightness of practical assertions. Aristotle thus gave practical philosophy its own genuine logic, thereby emancipating it from the theoretical sciences. We encounter the same terminological distinction again in Kant's division of his "Transcendental Logic" into a "Transcendental Analytic" and a "Transcendental Dialectic," although Kant uses the terms in a different way. In marked contrast to Aristotle, Kant does not associate practical reason with dialectics but instead seeks to found it upon an "Analytic of Pure Practical Reason." I mention this only because it makes understandable why both contemporary schools of practical philosophy, the analytical as well as the dialectical, can see themselves as champions of Kant's challenge to practical reason. In truth, neither side has thus far realized the Kantian program of a practical reason that would critically justify itself. One need not elevate oneself to the status of the arbiter in order to observe that on the one hand the scientists operationalize practical reason by reducing it to theoretical-instrumental reason, while on the other hand their opponents insist on the irreducible character of practical reason without having shown how practical reason can be practiced. It is important that we

---

[4] The following discussion partly overlaps with my introduction to the German translation of C. West Churchman's *The Systems Approach and Its Enemies* (1979), a book that has provided an important source of inspiration for my present effort; cf. Ulrich 1981a.

do not misunderstand this dispute as an exclusively philosophical affair; it is of vital significance for the understanding of "rationality" in all the applied disciplines, such as planning theory, management and organization theory, public administration theory, the so-called policy sciences, decision theory, operations research, etc.

Let us now briefly characterize the two opposite positions, not in order to forestall the detailed discussion in Chapters One and Two, but rather to point to some of the crucial difficulties with which a critical heuristics of social planning will have to come to grips, at least in the sense of a critical solution.

To begin with the critical rationalists, their treatment of the problem of practical reason suffers from an uncritical employment of Kant's theory-practice distinction. Popper designates as "theoretical" all statements, including practical ones, for the simple reason that there is no description of what is or of what ought to be without general, "theory-impregnated" concepts, i.e., concepts that cannot be derived from experience. It is of course true, and by no means a discovery of Popper's, that all experience depends on a theoretical *"horizon of expectations,"* as Popper puts it. Kant already demonstrated that the possibility of knowledge depends on the frame of reference provided by the a priori categories of the understanding, and he therefore conceived of his approach to the task of discovering and validating these categories as "transcendental," that is, it had to transcend the realm of possible experience. Before Kant, Hume had recognized the concept of causality, or cause-effect, to be a necessary a priori category that could not possibly be derived from experience, and this discovery had led him to formulate the basic difficulty of empiricism, the problem of induction.

One can thus agree with Popper's recognition of the theory-impregnated character of all statements; but Popper's use of the term gives rise to a grave misunderstanding. By designating any statement as theoretical, critical rationalists inadvertently pass over the fact that no statement is *merely* theory-loaded but that it is equally value-loaded. It is because there is no room for values in their concept of "theory" that the critical rationalists fall victim to this oversight. The uncritical implications of this oversight come to the fore, for instance, in Popper's treatment of the so-called problem of preference, i.e., the question of how one can rationally choose among alternative theories as possible guides for practical action. Popper's answer is basically this: all practical action presupposes a horizon of expectations and is therefore theory-impregnated; "hence" an action will be rational if it relies on the best-corroborated among the available theories. The *"primacy of theory"* in the sense of a theory-impregnated character of all experience is thus uncritically extended to a "primacy of theory" in the sense of a constitutive role of objective theory for rational practice. Popper tacitly skips over the fact that his procedure for testing the validity of theoretical hypotheses – the so-called falsification method – elevates deductive logic to the sole "organon of criticism" and thus cannot deal with the normative content of the hypotheses in question. The fact that the agent's horizon of expectations is inevitably value-loaded, and that "critically-rational" action proper would have to reflect on this aspect of the horizon of expectations, is simply rationalized away by equating "rational" criticism with deductive logic and with "objectivity" in the sense of value freedom. The choice of values is conveniently referred to an irrational realm of subjective acts of belief, the so-called "psychological context."

Thus, the Kantian concept of practical reason is buried from the beginning, and its place is taken by *decisionism*, a model of the relationship of theory and practice that was first formulated by Max Weber. According to this model, the values or norms guiding practical action cannot be justified with reason, i.e., through rational discourse and reflection; they represent, rather, subjective "decisions" prior to rational activity. Rationality for Popper thus becomes the guardian of the alleged objectivity of critically-rational theory against any infiltrating subjectivity in the form of value judgements.

In effect, then, the critical rationalists replace Kant's critical distinction of practical from theoretical reason with an uncritically employed theory-practice dichotomy: they purchase the alleged objectivity of critically-rational theory at the cost of relegating the normative content of every rational discussion to an extratheoretical realm of merely subjective decisions. Practice appears rational only insofar as it is guided by theory. Theoretical knowledge, to be sure, can explain and predict the causal effects of the employment of available means and thus secure instrumental rationality, i.e., the purposive, effective and efficient use of means in view of given ends; but it cannot secure rational choice among alternative or conflicting ends. "The price paid for economy in the selection of means is a decisionism set wholly free in the selection of the highest-level goals." (Habermas 1973a:265) And even the instrumental rationality thus produced is paid for by unreflected normative consequences of "rational" practice, for every means has inherently the character of an end, i.e., it has a normative content of its own, just as every end except ultimate ideals takes on a means-character in regard to higher-level goals (consider for example the "means" of constructing nuclear power plants for achieving the "end" of satisfying energy demand). We must conclude that rationality in the selection of means cannot be secured by narrowing down Kant's concept of practical reason to instrumental rationality. All that is accomplished in this way is the creation of an objectivist illusion, for an instrumental rationality that is uncritical of its own normative implications is merely an *apparent* rationality. In this respect the critical rationalists resemble the two heroes of Mark Twain, Tom Sawyer and Huckleberry Finn, who recount one of their adventures on the Mississippi River: "When we lost sight of the goal we doubled our efforts." The apparent rationality of means is no substitute for the rationality of ends.

To quote a philosopher who has himself grown out of the tradition of critical rationalism, and who probably won't mind if I mention him in company with a humorist: Paul Feyerabend has recently pointed to the uncritical character of the critical rationalists' talk about the "objectivity of a rational discussion," even where the choice of means is concerned:

The standards of such a discussion are not "objective," they merely *look* "objective" because the group of those who benefit from the application of these standards is not mentioned. (1980:74, my transl.)

This insight is not entirely new for the "dialectical" or "(Neo-)Marxist" position, of course. Let us now turn to the two main representatives of the anti-scientistic position today, Jürgen Habermas' "Critical Theory" and Paul Lorenzen's "Constructivist Logic, Ethics and Science-Theory." Originally used as an epithet for the Critical Theory of the early Frankfurt School (Horkheimer, Adorno, Marcuse and others), the name "dialectical" is no longer entirely suitable for these two contemporary representatives of a genuinely practical philosophy; both are in fact closer to Kant than to Hegel or Marx. As with Popper's critical rationalism, the purpose of the following account is not to introduce the two approaches systematically and to do them justice; I merely wish to point out some of their peculiar difficulties so that the critical intent of the present study becomes clear.

The difficulties in question are of an origin quite different from those of the critical rationalists. Habermas and Lorenzen have this much in common, that they both reject Popper's recourse to a Weberian decisionism. Instead, they both search for a reasonable and rational way of mediating between theory and practice. Therein consists their main dialectical feature. Theory and practice, economy in the selection of means and rationality in the selection of ends, are not to be juxtaposed in an unmediated and irreconcilable fashion; rather, they ought to be dialectically synthesized into a third and higher kind of rationality, namely, practical reason. I say "ought" to emphasize the fact that we are dealing with a research program rather than a solution concept. Both Lorenzen's and Habermas' programs find the medium of such mediation in rational discussion about practice. Lorenzen calls this sort of discussion a "practical deliberation," Habermas calls it a "(rationally-motivated) practical discourse." In distinction to a "critically-rational discussion" in Popper's sense, such a practical deliberation or discourse cannot limit itself to justifying theoretical hypotheses as guides for instrumentally rational action; it also seeks to justify genuinely practical (e.g. ethical or political) statements and to close the gap of rationality between theoretical and practical statements. Both Habermas and Lorenzen suceed to a great degree in realizing this programm, each in his own way. For all their differences in detail, their fundamental conjecture is the same: one cannot disavow the possibility of practical reason without renouncing the claim to theoretical reason, for theoretical statements and theoretical discourses themselves rely on a normative foundation (cf. Habermas 1973c:253; Lorenzen 1974:108 and 1977:passim). In Lorenzen's terms: disciplining one's opinion (by means of theoretical reason) is not possible without disciplining one's will (by means of practical reason), and vice-versa; and the discipline of either must begin with the discipline of one's own speech (cf. 1974:111).

30

Again, the word "begin" is important: the obvious danger of this program is that it exhausts itself in discourse *on* practice, i.e., that rational speech is substituted for rational practice. In contrast to the critical rationalists' scientistic (or technocratic) shortcut from the "primacy of theory" to the primacy of instrumental reason, we here face the danger of a sophistic (rhetorical) shortcut from the primacy of practice to that of discourse *on* practice. Let us examine very briefly how the two models of practical discourse approach the task of disciplining opinion and will.

The constructivists seek to render practical reason teachable by constructing a system of elementary concepts and rules of argumentation, so-called "linguistic norms" (therefore the name "constructivist logic, ethics and science-theory"). In this way they hope to discipline the speaking about practice: the deliberation on ends and the selection of means is to be trained "methodically," as Lorenzen says, so that situations of conflict or want can be resolved "reasonably" (cf. Lorenzen 1974:125, and Lorenzen/Schwemmer 1975:149). "Methodically" means that only those concepts and linguistic norms that are understandable and acceptable to all the participants are to be employed in a practical deliberation. In other words, the participants have to build up a common language, and such a construction Lorenzen designates "methodical" if it proceeds step by step without falling into a vicious circle (cf. 1974:126). To avoid a vicious circle, the language to be introduced must not be presupposed in introducing it: "We begin – like children – without words. But – again like children – we do not begin without some needs. First words are introduced by means of example and counter-example in the context of given needs." (1974:126f)

Once elementary predications of the kind "A is p" (A = a name, p = a predicator) are possible, logical operations ("particles") need to be introduced that allow the transition from one elementary statement to another, e.g. the conjunction ("and"), the implication ("if… then"), the logical quantification ("some," "all"). From these logical operations Lorenzen derives the dialogical rules for attacking and defending statements, i.e., the logical operations according to which proponents and opponents can argue cogently. In this manner a dialogical logic, together with elementary terms such as names and predicators, is to be constructed as the basis for rational practical discourse. With their *Logische Propädeutik,* Kamlah and Lorenzen (1967) have laid a remarkable cornerstone for this program of constructivist logic and ethics, a program that was further pursued in Lorenzen's *Normative Logic and Ethics* (1969) and in Lorenzen and Schwemmer's *Konstruktive Logik, Ethik und Wissenschaftstheorie* (1975; see also Schwemmer 1971 and the collections by Kambartel 1974 and Mittelstrass 1975, 1979).

But even the constructivists have to rely on some presuppositions that they cannot justify within their own framework. This fact becomes apparent by the way in which their term "reasonable" is introduced. An argument for or against a normative validity claim with regard to some practical statement is called "reasonable" if it is "not merely subjective," that is, if it is asserted not merely by reference to given opinions or to factual willing (e.g. the speaker's own needs, inclinations, habits, or emotions). In other words, an argument is said to be reasonable if any listener can reconstruct and accept it as cogent. To speak with Kant, a reasonable argument must admit of generalization. Thus the constructivists introduce the concept of reason by way of a *"principle of transsubjectivity"*: "No subjective arguments!" or "Transcend your own subjectivity!"[5] This principle of transsubjectivity, as the fundamental principle of reasonable argumentation, cannot itself be "reasonably" derived from a still more fundamental and generalizable principle; it can merely be "introduced" by *appealing* to the subjective willingness of the discourse participants to recognize the counter-factual condition of transsubjectivity as a condition that they always already presuppose when they enter into a discourse (cf. Lorenzen 1974:36). We must conclude that the constructivist approach ultimately presupposes what it aims to produce, namely, rationality in the form of "reasonable" practical deliberation. At a crucial point, constructivism falls back into the very decisionism which, in opposition to Popper's critical rationalism, it wanted to overcome: the decision to transcend one's subjectivity when entering into a discourse remains a subjective act of belief, as Lorenzen himself concedes (cf. 1969:74).

It appears that rationalism and decisionism are inseparable siblings: the more consequently all irrational (subjective) elements are kept out of a rational discussion, the more precarious (because fundamental, but not capable of rational foundation) becomes the very first step, the decisionistic act of entering into a "rational" (trans-subjective) discussion. On this first step depends the entire construction. It seems improbable, however, that we can ever persuade a democratic majority of citizens to deny their own natural subjectivity and to discuss their concerns according to the artificial language and the rules of an academic elite. A glance into the (otherwise brilliant) *Logische Propädeutik* suffices to raise doubts about the practical teachability of a thus-constructed practical reason. As a rational planner, for instance, one can hardly impose such linguistic norms upon the man in the street of whom one wishes to know in what way he is affected by a plan. To speak rationally about practice with a view to practice is what we call "planning." But how can planning be rational if rational discussion about practice is defined in such a way that the majority of those who are affected cannot participate in a competent, rational fashion?

Similar doubts are bound to come up with Habermas, who originally presented his program of constructing a model of rational practical discourse under the name of a "Theory of Communicative Competence" (1970d, 1971c). I shall not here anticipate the later discussion in this respect. Let us merely point out a peculiarity by which

---

[5] Cf. Lorenzen 1974:36, 93 f, 129, and Lorenzen/Schwemmer 1975:164. Lorenzen explains: "It is not permissible to employ merely subjective arguments, whereby subjectivity is defined as the claim of a person or a group of persons to being *exempted* from laws or norms instead of their making a general argument for the modification of these laws and norms." (1974:129, my transl.) In a very similar fashion, Lorenzen and Schwemmer define what they call the "moral principle"; see Lorenzen 1974:92 f and, somewhat differently, Lorenzen/Schwemmer 1975:165 ff.

Habermas' model distinguishes itself from all other models of practical discourse and which moves it close to the Kantian program of practical reason: Habermas seeks to make do without any decisionistic "introduction" of a fundamental principle, be it a principle of reason or of morality. In the light of the above-stated suspicion concerning the connection between rationalism and decisionism, his undertaking must be considered as a philosophical experiment that deals with a limiting case – it amounts to an attempt at reducing decisions on normative validity claims entirely to rational argument.

Habermas' solution proposal is original and compelling: the formal structure of a rational discourse itself, rather than the willingness of the participants to transcend their subjectivity, is supposed to make sure that only generalizable validity claims are upheld. These formal properties of discourse that together would secure rational consensus on practical questions are the subject of what Habermas now calls a "universal (or formal) pragmatics" (1979a).

A closer look however, reveals what has to be expected: a conceptual boundary experiment such as Habermas' can clarify the border-line conditions under which the ideal of a self-justifying practical reason is conceivable, but it cannot make the ideal real. Habermas' model is theoretically insightful but impracticable. If it is used as a practical discourse model, it cannot produce rationality, any more than Lorenzen's model can, but must presuppose it. In Habermas' terms, whether or not a factual consensus is to be distinguished as rational can only be determined by reference to an *"ideal speech situation,"* the actual existence of which cannot be verified empirically.

I call a speech situation ideal where communications are not only not hindered by external, contingent influences [such as power] but also not hindered by constraints originating in the structure of communication itself [such as the conceptual framework and linguistic norms employed]. The ideal speech situation excludes systematic distortion of communication. (1973c:255, my transl.)

We shall have an opportunity to examine Habermas' concept of the ideal speech situation, its importance and its implications, in Chapter Two; at this point it may suffice to know that the ideal speech situation for Habermas represents the normative validity basis of rational discourse and consensus, a normative foundation that is as inevitable as it is bound to remain a mere anticipation of ideal conditions of rationality (cf. 1971c:140, and 1973c:258).

Habermas' argument appears *theoretically* convincing in at least two respects. First it is evident that we need a theoretically ideal model of undistorted communication and of comprehensively rational discourse so as to have a critical standard for organizing practical discourses (e.g. among planners and affected citizens) as well as for reflecting on the inevitable lack of comprehensive rationality in such discourses. Second, Habermas' model explains the normative basis not only of practical but also of theoretical discourse, and thus it closes the gap between the two.

Practically speaking, however, Habermas has not yet closed the gap between rational discourse *on* practice and *lived* social practice. While he has, more than most other contemporary philosophers, sought to revive the Kantian ideal of "the comprehensive rationality of reason that becomes transparent to itself" (1971a:3), even he ultimately remains within too narrow a perspective, a "rationalistic" perspective that he shares with both the critical rationalists and the constructivists. By "rationalism" I mean in this context a conception of rationality that in effect sacrifices the practical goal of securing *reasonable practice* to the theoretical interest in showing how the idea of practical reason can be *justified in theory.*

One need not subscribe to a glib antirationalism, or to a more sophisticated "Dadaism" such as that proposed by Feyerabend (1975, 1980), in order to recognize that only that concept of rationality can be *socially* rational which not only makes transparent to itself its own lack of comprehensiveness but which also *comprehends this lack of comprehensiveness – its own self-limitation – as a necessary conditon of reasonable practice.* It is only thus that a concept of rationality can become an effective instrument for bringing reason into an unreasonable world of social practice.

This idea of a non-rationalistic, because self-limiting and self-transcending, conception of rationality is fundamental to the present study. I adopt it from C. West Churchman's *The Systems Approach and Its Enemies* (1979). Although Churchman does not say it in these terms, I believe that in his book the systems approach for the first time has become truly self-reflective with respect to the normative content of its own quest for systems rationality. In Churchman's terms, the systems approach cannot realize its search for the comprehensive rationality of planning so long as it seeks to absorb the "enemies" of such rationality, e.g. politics, morality, religion, and aesthetics. Rather, the systems approach can claim comprehensive rationality if it learns to reflect on its own limitations, namely, by listening to its "enemies" and by understanding them dialectically as what they are: mirrors of its own failure to be comprehensive.

One of the most important consequences of this stipulation is this: those who, because they have to *live* the practical consequences of planning, contest the planner's claim to comprehensive or systems rationality are to be considered as "competent" by virtue of their affectedness rather than by virtue of their "communicative competence." That is to say, we should not require them to voice their concerns in the "rational" terms of the systems approach. Such an opening up of the systems approach must not, however, be misunderstood as renouncing the quest for comprehensive rationality; on the contrary, it should be understood as the pursuit of this quest at a higher level of self-reflection. At this higher level of self-reflection, as I have suggested from the outset, the systems approach ought to be redefined as an effort of practical reason rather than as "systems theory" or "systems science." The present study is an attempt to elaborate the epistemological and heuristic foundations of a critical, or dialectical, systems approach to socially rational planning, a systems approach that aims not at an objective, theoretical solution to the problem of practical reason but only at a *critical solution*. To conclude this introduction, let us come back to Kant (from whom I borrow the concept of a critical solution) and try to give a preliminary explanation of the relation between Kantian a priori science and critical heuristics. This can conveniently be done by explaining the organization of the book.

From Kantian A Priori Science to Critical Heuristics: Toward a Quasi-Transcendental Approach

In *Part I* of this study, we shall examine in detail the two main representatives of the "scientistic" and the "dialectical" concepts of rationality today, the models of discursive rationality advanced by Karl R. Popper and Jürgen Habermas. In *Chapter One,* Popper's model will be examined more because of the wide recognition that it has gained among both philosophers and "applied" social scientists than because of its critical significance for our purpose. Our critique of critical rationalism will, however, provide us with the necessary understanding of the sources of deception in the scientistic, objectivistic approach to social inquiry and design[6], deceptions that a critical approach to the problem of practical reason ought to avoid.

By contrast, *Chapter Two* will examine Habermas' ideal model of practical discourse because it is, in spite of its impracticable character, a rich source of inspiration for such a critical approach. Ultimately, we shall conclude that we cannot hope to find a critical *and* practicable solution to the problem of practical reason without going back to Kant and reconstructing his transcendental approach at least partly; Habermas' approach is nonetheless important to us because it contains some basic ideas for a contemporary "transformed transcendental philosophy."

With Habermas, who himself follows a suggestion by Apel (e.g. Apel 1976–70), I shall subdivide Kant's transcendental question – What are the conditions of the possibility of objective experience or knowledge? – into two "quasi-transcendental" questions:

(a) What are the conditions that are constitutive of meaningful experience? (= problem of the *a priori of experience)*

(b) What are the conditions of the discursive redemption of disputed validity claims? (= problem of the *a priori of argumentation).*

---

[6] The term "social inquiry and design" will be used throughout the book as a summary label referring to a multiplicity of applications of systematic inquiry to improving social reality, e.g. planning, systems design, operations research, action research, empirical social research, applied behavioral science/planned social change, evaluation research/program evaluation, technology assessment, etc.

The term "quasi-transcendental" refers to the fact that Kant's strict apriorism today must be replaced by relying on a merely relative a priori of experience (conceptual framework) *and* an equally relative a priori of argumentation (discourse model). This is because no a priori concepts or discursive principles can be shown theoretically to represent strictly necessary and universal conditions of theoretical or practical knowledge – otherwise there would be no need to reconstruct Kantian a priori science at all.

Taking up the distinction between the two relative a priori problematics, I shall propose a critically-heuristic rather than a theoretical approach to the a priori of experience ("critically-heuristic turn"). Likewise, I shall identify a certain deficiency of dialectic in Habermas' model, due to its underlying Kantian rationalism, and I shall accordingly argue the need for a "dialectical turn" in respect to the a priori of argumentation. Only by means of such a dialectical turn can we hope to come to grips with the crucial difficulty of rational practical discourse, the dialectical interdependence of (practical) reason and (reasonable) practice. Taken together, the "critically-heuristic turn" and the "dialectical turn" will constitute our quasi-transcendental approach to the task of securing a critical solution of the problem of practical reason.

Part II of the book will outline this quasi-transcendental approach. In *Chapter Three,* we shall introduce the basic critical concepts of Kantian a priori science, concepts that have lost nothing of their critical significance in the face of today's prevailing scientism and objectivism. *Chapter Four* will then outline our constructive effort in regard to the a priori of experience. My critically-heuristic solution to this problem will draw on Kant's understanding of the system idea and on the related, crucial problem of boundary judgements. I shall demonstrate the possibility and the structure of "quasi-transcendental arguments" for justifying the critical significance of certain a priori concepts, and I shall derive from the systems idea a set of such concepts for which a quasi-transcendental argument is possible.

Chapter Five, finally, will take up the second of the two quasi-transcendental issues, the a priori of argumentation, and will develop the premises of our "dialectical turn." The basic idea here is that there is no theoretical but only a critical solution to the problem of validating the empirical and/or normative content of (relative) a priori concepts in each application. In such a critical solution, reason must make transparent to itself and to the affected the normative a priori character of its concepts. No a priori concepts of reason can possibly justify the normative consequences of "(systems-)rational" planning for the affected citizens. Reason, by means of its a priori concepts, has only a critical and not an assertive authority. A practicable model of practical discourse cannot therefore be located entirely within the bounds of reason; it must break through them so as to mediate between reason and normative social practice. This is what our envisaged dialectical turn is all about.

Although we shall draw on Hegel's concept of dialectics, Kant will provide the key concept for a model of "rational" discourse that can perform this mediating function and that at the same time gives "ordinary" citizens a relevant role to play; this key concept is that of the "polemical employment of (pure) reason."

Part III, finally, will present an application-oriented framework for social inquiry and design and illustrate this framework by means of two case studies. The framework includes the earlier-introduced critically-heuristic categories and, in addition, a new paradigm of "purposeful systems." In *Chapter Six,* I introduce this new paradigm in critical distinction to the two main contemporary systems concepts, the mechanistic systems concept of early cybernetics, General Systems Theory, and Management Science on the one hand, and the "organic" systems concept of recent cybernetic approaches such as Stafford Beer's "managerial cybernetics" on the other. *Chapter Seven* applies our conceptual framework to an assessment of Stafford Beer's "Project Cybersyn" in Chile 1971–73, a project that represents a unique large-scale application of the tools of systems science to national economic planning and, at the same time, to the problem of democratizing industry. *Chapter Eight* attempts to illustrate the heuristic power and critical significance of our conceptual framework in the field of health systems planning. We shall examine the question of whether the "National Health Planning and Resources Development Act of 1974" (Public Law 93–641) is adequately designed to serve its declared purpose of rendering the American health care system not only more efficient but also more democratic and more responsive to the needs of the socially disadvantaged.

The two case studies will illustrate practically what our "dialectical turn" in Chapter Five suggests theoretically: namely, that the democratic idea of the equality and sovereignty of all citizens is indispensable for a truly critical solution to the problem of practical reason. To be sure, there is no objective justification of the democratic idea. But what matters for a critical solution to the problem of practical reason, as the planner faces it, is this: the normative content of plans must be made transparent to both the involved planners and the affected citizens; and in the light of such transparency, it must be democratically and morally acceptable to the affected. A utopia? Perhaps. But an inescapable challenge to rational planning that is more than what Ambrose Bierce, in his *Devil's Dictionary,* suspects it to be:

Plan, v.t., to bother about the best method for accomplishing an accidental result. (1958:100)

Part I
Contemporary Models of Rational Discourse

Chapter One
Karl R. Popper's Critical Rationalism: Blind Criticism?

Objectivity is the result of an epistemological shortsighted-
ness rather than a philosophical accomplishment.
Paul Feyerabend (1980:149, my transl.)

Introduction

"How can we know? And how can we know that we know?" These are the central
questions of epistemology, and nobody would deny that they are among the great
questions of philosophy ever since the early Greeks. There are probably few people,
however, who would also suppose that they are among the central questions of
heuristics. *Heuristics is epistemology brought down to earth.* Heuristics and epistemology have in common the basic problem which any problem solver will encounter
– the problem of uncertainty. The need for both heuristics and epistemology arises
when one finds oneself lacking any guarantee for the validity of available methods of
inquiry and problem solving. What mainly distinguishes epistemology from heuristics is not its underlying question, but rather its peculiar tendency to withdraw before
the actual problems of inquiry to an abstract, meta-level discussion that too often is of
merely scholarly interest. This may be because epistemologists rarely have been real-
world problem solvers; rather, they have restricted themselves to being philosophers,
and when they condescend to analyze a non-philosophical problem it is usually a
theoretical problem of "hard" natural sciences. But anyone who tries to solve real-
world problems of social concern knows that the epistemological question of "how
can I know that I know?" is nowhere more crucial than in practical, "soft" problems.
It is not in the natural sciences, but in the applied social sciences, and especially in
planning, that the epistemological problem becomes an acute, practical question:
The social systems designer who avoids the epistemological question can claim no
sound or certain basis for his designs. Any planner who seeks such a basis will soon
recognize that he must deal thoroughly with the question of what useful design
knowledge is, and he will recognize that he cannot know very much about social
systems if he has not reflected on how he knows what he knows.

The Idea of Criticism, or: What Does It Mean to Be Rational?

Insofar as the task of epistemological thinking is to reflect on the sources, conditions, and limitations of human knowledge, the idea of *criticism* is necessarily central to all epistemologies. Criticism is the fundamental task of epistemology, and *an epistemology that is not critical is no epistemology at all.* It is not surprising, then, that all epistemologies, from that of John Locke to that of Jürgen Habermas, claim to be "critical." The only question is this: What *kind* of criticism is to be regarded as acceptable criticism? Whatever answer we give to this question will contain an implicit definition of rationality, for it will define what is to be rationally admitted as criticism. In other words, what is admitted as valid criticism is also accepted as part of a rational mode of inquiry and discourse.

Thus, that which really distinguishes different theories of knowledge is the difference in the underlying definition of rationality (i.e., rational criticism). The definition of rationality in turn inevitably depends on metaphysical and psychological assumptions about the nature of inquiry and corresponding concepts of "truth" and "objectivity."

We shall begin our search for a helpful epistemological framework of social systems design by analyzing the assumption and arguments of the prevailing empirical tradition. To establish the relevance of this analysis, it seems reasonable to concentrate on the actual state of the art, as represented by Karl R. Popper's "critical" empiricism, and not to involve ourselves in a lengthy discussion of obsolete British empiricism. It is, however, certainly worthwhile to pause for a moment to recall the philosophical background of all modern epistemology, "naive" empiricism. It is only by considering the so-called naive positions that we can evaluate other positions which claim to be more "critical," and it is only by evaluating these claims that we can ourselves critically transcend Popper's epistemology.

The central ideal of empiricism, from the time of Aristotle to the present, is the attainment of *truth* in the sense of an absolute correspondence of knowledge to "reality"; and the crucial difficulty in this view of truth has been seen to lie in the *problem of induction.* By induction, the early empiricists understood a genetic procedure for gaining universally true statements about reality from particular experiences. Thus, it was assumed that the truth of universal statements could be determined by examining their genesis in the human mind.

It is for this reason that John Locke, in his *Essay Concerning Human Understanding* (1690), proposed a psychological inquiry into the origin of ideas as the clue to solving the problem of induction. By using this approach he became not only the founder of British empiricism, but probably also the first psychologist to suggest a theory of heuristics. Not innate ideas, he argued, but "impressions" (sensations) from the real world are at the origin of ideas: *nihil est in intellectu quod non fuerit in sensu* – "there can be nothing in the mind that was not first in the senses." Consequently, his problem was to show how an inquirer could proceed from first simple "impressions" to general and true ideas.

Here is the famous passage in which Locke outlines his approach:

15. *The Steps by Which the Mind attains several Truths.* – The senses at first let in particular ideas, and furnish the yet empty cabinet; and the mind by degrees growing familiar with some of them, they are lodged in the memory, and names got to them. In this manner the mind comes to be furnished with ideas and language, the materials about which to exercise its discursive faculty; and the use of reason becomes daily more visible, as these materials that give it employment increase. (Book I, chap. II, par. 15; quoted from 1902:142f)

Although at first glance, Locke's concept of the human mind as an "empty cabinet" *(tabula rasa)* may seem naive, it is interesting to note that his approach included not only the *rational* aspect, but also the *social* aspect of inquiry (the need for a community of agreement). It is not his theory of ideas which is naive, but its underlying metaphysical realism: reality is taken for something autonomous "out there" that will manifest itself to the passive (empty) human mind. It is this underlying manifestation theory of truth that had to be overcome by later epistemologists.

In a sense, Locke's empiricism might even be regarded as a truly critical epistemological design. It clearly fulfilled a critical role against its own historical background. Locke did not accept a contemporary explanation of human knowledge as deriving from innate ideas, as, for instance, Leibniz did, but instead proposed "to inquire into the origin, certainty, and extent of human knowledge" (Book I, ch. I, par. 1; 1902:128) and "to consider the discerning faculties of man" (1902:129) in order to explain human understanding. Thus he was truly questioning the prevailing idealist epistemology of his time and so opened the way for a (self-)critical epistemological discussion. Because Locke was critical of the theory of innate ideas, he was forced to choose the only alternative that seemed possible at his time, the mind as an "empty cabinet."

Locke was also critical in a second, perhaps more important sense: he introduced the idea of *self-reflection* as an essential instrument of man's "discursive faculty" (rationality). "By reflection... I would be understood to mean that notice which the mind takes of its own operations, and the manner of them; by reason whereof there come to be ideas of these operations in the understanding." (Book II, ch. I, 1902:207) According to Locke, then, an inquirer can know what he knows only by means of self-reflection, i.e., by using the ideas in his mind to reflect on the other ideas it already possesses.

We can thus say that early empiricism started with an amazingly modern view of criticism as self-reflection, summarized by Locke in the following manner: "Whoever reflects on what passes in his own mind cannot miss it; and if he does not reflect, all the words in the world cannot make him have any notion of it." (Book II, ch. IX, 1902:253) It is one of the paradoxical features of the modern history of epistemology that the "critical" philosophers who uncovered the uncritical side of Locke's empiricism somehow lost its truly critical core.

David Hume was the first to understand the problem of induction as a logical issue of the justification, rather than as a psychological issue of the discovery, of universal statements, and he pointed out the uncritical nature of Locke's empiricism with respect to this issue. His key question was: How can we *logically* infer and justify statements about the future, based on past experiences? His answer created a dilemma: a principle of induction is needed (implied) if empirical statements are to be generalized to statements about the future; but Hume could not find any logical justification for such a principle.

With Hume the induction problem became the central concern of empiricism, because empiricism without a rationally justified induction principle would lose its claim for rationality and truth and become a basically irrational epistemology. Consequently, all epistemological thinking after Hume struggled to regain a rational foundation of human knowledge.

Kant's *"transcendental" criticism* reformulated the problem as the problem of synthetic knowledge *a priori* and resolved it by introducing the a priori categories (a solution which ultimately implied a replacement of the principle of induction by the a priori principle of universal causation).

Rudolf Carnap's *logical empiricism* tried to maintain the induction principle and to justify it by a probabilistic logic of confirmation. His efforts reveal the two tendencies of logical empiricism that finally led to its complete failure: a tendency to reduce epistemology to a branch of formal logic, and a metaphysical naiveté that hardly differs from Locke's naive realism. The fact that logical empiricism failed in its program corresponds to our thesis that only critical epistemologies fulfill the task of epistemological thinking: logical empiricism was not sufficiently critical in any sense.

Finally, Karl R. Popper's *critical rationalism* tried to solve the problem of induction with a deductivist methodology for testing universal statements. Since critical rationalism is the prevailing theory of knowledge today, I shall undertake an extensive critical discussion of its underlying ideas.

1. The Early Popper: The Theory of Falsification

Yes; I have a turn both for observation and for deduction. The theories which I have expressed there, and which appear to you to be so chimerical, are really extremely practical – so practical that I depend upon them for my bread and cheese. Sherlock Holmes in A Study in Scarlet *(Arthur Conan Doyle 1892)*

It may be that the historical credit for the idea of a deductive-empirical method of testing hypotheses should be given to Sir Arthur Conan Doyle's Sherlock Holmes rather than to any epistemologist. Be that as it may – it is Sir Karl R. Popper who claims the credit, and he does so right at the beginning of *Objective Knowledge,* the book that provides the most complete statement of Popper's approach available today:

I think that I have solved a major philosophical problem; the problem of induction. (I must have reached the solution in 1927 or thereabouts.) This solution has been extremely fruitful, and it has enabled me to solve a good number of other philosophical problems. (1972:1)

What is surprising about this claim is not only its defect of modesty but also the fact that it has been written by a philosopher who considers himself "critical" and who likes to call his philosophy "critical rationalism." *How critical is critical rationalism?* The answer to this question will depend on whether we focus our attention on the historical function of critical rationalism in opposing inductivist empiricism, or rather on its underlying concept of criticism; and to some extent our answer will also depend on what we take as the central part of Popper's epistemology, either his early theory of falsification or his more recent, "evolutionary" theory of objective knowledge.

The conjecture behind this distinction is not far-fetched: Popper's theory of knowledge has undoubtedly played an important role within the historical context of its formulation, namely, in its relation to the logical empiricists of the so-called Vienna Circle (Schlick, Carnap) and the analytical philosophers (the early Wittgenstein, Russell, Reichenbach and many others) during the first decades of the twentieth century. All of these thinkers were still occupied with the induction problem, and to appreciate the originally critical function of Popper's theory of falsification within this context will also help us to understand the serious limitations that arise from the context. Critical rationalism today appears to have lost its originally critical function and to be in a mainly defensive position against other critical positions (a situation that the critical rationalists do not seem to appreciate as fully as their critical pretensions might lead one to expect).

1.1. Basic Notions

At the heart of Popper's entire work is his early theory of falsification, a theory which he later imbedded in his general evolutionary theory of knowledge. Though the falsification principle is widely known, it is not always well understood, and even less frequently is it critically examined; indeed, it is difficult to understand how *uncritically* it is accepted not only by scientists but also by epistemologists. Let us therefore begin with a review of its basic assumptions.

1. As a first assumption, Popper redefines Hume's distinction between the genetic and the logical principle of induction by reducing "logic" to *deductive* logic:

   I regard the distinction, implicit in Hume's treatment, between a logical and psychological problem as of the utmost importance. But I do not think that Hume's view of what I am inclined to call "logic" is satisfactory. He describes, clearly enough, processes of *valid inference;* but he looks upon these as "rational" *mental processes.* By contrast, one of my principal methods of approach, whenever *logical* problems are at stake, is to translate all the subjective or psychological terms, especially "belief", etc., into *objective* terms.

   In accomplishing this "translation," Popper adopts not only Reichenbach's well-known distinction between the "context of justification" and the "context of discovery" (Reichenbach 1938:3ff), but also the narrow "logistic" concept of logic common to all members of the Vienna Circle, logical empiricism, and analytical philosophy. In this view, logic is the same as deductive logic, and what is not deductively justifiable is referred to an irrational, merely "psychological," context of discovery – the sum total of subjective states and processes that allegedly are irrelevant for the justification of hypotheses, though they may be relevant for explaining the ways in which these hypotheses are found in the first place. Hume's and Kant's richer concepts of logic (Hume: logic = the rational mental processes of valid inference; Kant: logic = what is *a priori* or transcendental to experience) are abandoned in favor of a purely formal understanding of logic. This formal-deductive concept of logical reasoning offers "objectivity" in the sense of inter-subjective transference: what is deductively valid for one person is also valid for another person. Or, as Popper writes, "What is true in logic is true in psychology." (1972:6)

2. The reduction of logic to formal logic offers another advantage: "From the point of view of deductive logic there is an asymmetry between verification and falsification by experience." (1972:12; similarly 1961:41) General ("universal") statements cannot be logically justified by observational ("singular") statements, but they can be *contradicted* by singular observations.

   Consequently it is possible by means of purely deductive inferences (with the help of the *modus tollens* of classical logic) to argue from the truth of singular

46

statements to the falsity of universal statements. Such an argument to the falsity of universal statements is the only strictly deductive kind of inference that proceeds, as it were, in the "inductive direction"; that is, from singular to universal statements. (1961:41)

3. The main problem with the idea of falsification is that it does not correspond to the practice of inquiry. The inquirer does not work hard in order to gain *false* statements, but rather to gain recognition for his hypotheses; moreover, it is always logically possible to avoid acknowledgement of a falsifying observation by introducing an auxiliary *ad hoc* hypothesis or an *ad hoc* definition that removes the contradiction (1961:42), or even to immunize a theory against refutation from the very beginning (1972:30).

4. Therefore, the basic task of an epistemology that wants to make use of the falsi-fication principle is to make certain that inquirers actively seek to falsify universal statements and are willing to accept falsifications of their theories by incompati-ble singular statements. Precisely this is the purpose of the entire theory of falsi-fication. The theory is thus not a descriptive epistemology, but a normative set of rules in order to increase and guarantee falsifiability. Its chief rule is: "I propose to adopt such rules as will ensure the testability of scientific statements; which is to say, their falsifiability." (1961:49; similarly p. 54)

5. All other norms are derived from this key norm. Together they make up what Popper calls "The Logic of Discovery"; a convention that permits "objective" (purely deductive) decisions about the empirical validity of universal statements, i.e., that permits us to eliminate falsified statements.

6. The first rule to be established is that statements whose empirical validity is not decidable must be eliminated. Such statements are considered to be either tauto-logical or "metaphysical." The problem of distinguishing between empirical (fal-sifiable) and metaphysical (non-decidable) statements is called the *problem of demarcation* (1961:34).

    As a demarcation criterion, Popper establishes the rule: "It must be possible for an empirical scientific system to be refuted by experience." (1961:41) If this con-dition holds, a proposition is said to have empirical content.

7. The *empirical content* of a statement is defined by the number of alternative statements about reality that it excludes, i.e., by the class of its potential falsifiers. "Thus it can be said that the amount of empirical information conveyed by a theory, or its empirical content, increases with its degree of falsifiability." (1961:113)[1]

---

[1] The empirical content of a statement is closely related to its *logical* content, defined as "the class of all non-tautological statements which are derivable from the statement in question. (It may be called its 'consequence class.')" (1961:120)

8. The aim of scientific inquiry is the *growth of knowledge,* which is the same as an increasing number of empirical statements that are increasingly falsifiable.

9. All statements with empirical content, including practical assertions, are said to be "theoretical" in the sense that they presuppose "theory-impregnated" concepts, i. e., concepts that cannot logically be derived from experience. Another term used by Popper in this context is that of a "horizon of expectations":

> At every instant of our pre-scientific or scientific development we are living in the center of what I usually call a *"horizon of expectations."* By this I mean the sum total of our expectations, whether these are subconscious or conscious, or perhaps explicitly stated in some language. Animals and babies have also their various and different horizons of expectations…. The various horizons of expectations differ, of course, not only in their being more or less conscious, but also in their content. Yet in all these cases the horizon of expectations plays the part of a frame of reference: only their setting in this frame confers meaning or significance on our experiences, actions and observations. (1972:345)

Popper accordingly emphasizes "the conjectural and theoretical character of all observations, and all observation statements" (1972:30), and he refers to his falsificationist approach as the method of *Conjectures and Refutations* (thus the title of one of his books, 1963).

10. The conjectural and theoretical character of all statements implies the need for testing their empirical content. The basic instrument for testing the empirical content of statements (theories) is *criticism.* The "organon" of criticism is deductive logic (1962:115, 1972:31); that is, a valid critique must always be based on the demonstration of a logical contradiction.

11. Three test strategies have been established, all of which try to discover logical contradictions:

(a) *Logical analysis:*
Contradictions within statements or theories can be discovered by purely logical analysis. From the demarcation criterion it would follow that self-contradictory statements or theories have maximal empirical content, because they contain their own falsifiers. Therefore *the consistency condition*[2] is added to the falsifiability condition (1961:116).

(b) *Empirical falsification attempts:*
An empirical falsification attempt is made by trying to find an empirically valid falsifier, i.e., an inconsistent singular statement. The problem which then arises is how to establish the truth of a singular statement. This difficulty is called the

---

[2] The consistency condition, since it excludes self-contradictory statements, is traditionally also called "the principle of excluded contradiction."

problem of the empirical basis. (It has not been solved either by Popper or any other philosopher except by recourse to conventionalism, i.e., the agreement of "competent" observers.) If a falsifier is found, the statement or theory is eliminated ("refuted"); if not, the theory is strengthened ("corroborated"). The more falsification attempts a theory has successfully resisted, the higher is its *degree of corroboration.* "Corroboration (or degree of corroboration) is thus an evaluating *report of past performance"* (1972:18); "the degree of corroboration is a means of stating *preference with respect to truth."* (1972:20) However, a high degree of corroboration cannot mean that a subsequent falsification attempt might not be successful: "We must regard *all laws or theories as hypothetical or conjectural, that is, as guesses."* (1972:9)

(c) *Intersubjective criticism:*
Intersubjective criticism is required in order to correct the errors of the individual inquirer (and also his potential immunization attempts!). In order to make rational intersubjective criticism possible, objectivity – in the sense of a linguistic or, even better, a quantitative formulation of conjectures – must be required (1971:31). In order to make intersubjective criticism "rationally" decidable, deductive logic is to be used as the organon of argumentation. Thus, if Popper establishes that the possibility of rational criticism depends on the norm of objectivity, he implies exactly the following definition: *Objectivity is the possibility of intersubjective decidability of statements by means of deductive logic* (a definition avoided by Popper, but logically contained in his conception of intersubjective criticism).

Let us summarize what has been said so far about Popper's theory of falsification. As a consequence of the logical impossibility of verifying universal statements by singular statements, the empiricist claim for truth has been replaced by the claim for "objective," but conjectural knowledge. According to Popper, the conjectural character of all knowledge does not exclude an approximation towards truth by means of criticism. Criticism as the central methodological tool must be "rationally" regulated in order to prevent statements from being immunized against it. This regulation, in turn, requires a methodological convention about the strategies of inquiry accepted as "rational" and "critical." Three strategies of criticism are admitted as rational: logical tests of consistency, empirical falsification attempts, and intersubjective critical discussion. Explicit (linguistic or mathematical) formulation is required to make intersubjective criticism possible; deductive logic is established as the organon of all three strategies of criticism in order to make them "rationally" decidable.

If a discussion on disputed statements satisfies all these methodological requirements of the theory of falsification, it is designated a *critically-rational discussion;* and such a discussion is taken to secure "objective knowledge."

The claim for "objective knowledge" accordingly furnishes the main criterion for evaluating the critical character of a "critically-rational" discussion. From a truly critical point of view, objectivity can be defined only as the complete transparency of all subjective presuppositions, especially value assumptions. In other words, *an inquirer's claim for objectivity implies his effort to emancipate himself and others from any objectivist illusion* with regard to the normative content of the statements in question. It is the task of the following discussion to trace the sources of such an objectivist illusion in Popper's model of a critically-rational discussion.

The main underlying issue of interest to us is of course the problem of practical reason: Does critically-rational discussion represent an adequate model of rational practical discourse on the normative content of the planner's account of social reality, and of his designs for its improvement? In other words, can critically-rational discussion secure the practical rationality of our actions?

Unfortunately Popper and his followers, although they give an affirmative answer to the question above (e.g. Popper 1972:21ff, Albert 1969: Ch. 3 and p. 76ff), hardly ever confront the problem of practical reason. This is understandable because Popper generally denies that there is any essential difference between the logic of natural science (theoretical reason) and that of social inquiry and design (practical reason). In the Introduction to the present study, I have briefly pointed to Popper's effective reduction of practical to theoretical reason; I must now substantiate this allegation by following Popper's arguments for the practical rationality of a critically-rational discussion, and by refuting these arguments. I shall begin with the one argument of Popper's in which he seems to come the closest to confronting the problem of practical reason, the so-called problem of preference: How can we choose among competing theories one theory that will best serve as a guide for rational practical action? This discussion will quite naturally lead us to some of the fundamental difficulties of Popper's model, difficulties such as the so-called problem of the (objectivity of the) empirical basis and the problem of "historicism." We shall find that Popper's solutions to these major difficulties of his approach depend on the exclusion of normative aspects from "critically-rational" discussion.

In Sections 2 and 3 of this chapter, we shall then trace the objectivist illusion contained in the critical rationalists' attempt to apply their model to practical questions, in spite of the unsolved difficulties that have been mentioned above. In the fourth section, we shall examine Popper's recent effort to defend his approach by embedding it within a Neo-Darwinian "evolutionary" framework, an effort that reveals many of the fallacies in the prevailing objectivistic and scientistic understanding of rationality in our society. In the fifth section, finally, we shall summarize the sources of deception identified in Popper's model of critically-rational discussion.

Before undertaking this critical effort, however, let us try to appreciate the originally critical part that Popper's falsification theory has played in its historical role and which, to some extent, it continues to play today.

1.2. Popper's Contribution

In its historical role, critical rationalism can be said to have played a progressive role vis-à-vis inductivist empiricism, including the still popular logical empiricism of the Vienna Circle, by emphasizing the inevitably conjectural character of knowledge. Knowledge or experience is no longer taken to be a passive representation of an immediately manifest reality but is understood to be conditioned by the "horizon of expectations" of an active, knowing subject.[3] "We do not 'have' an observation (as we may 'have' a sense experience) but we 'make' an observation." (Popper 1972:342) Popper has also been the first epistemologist who has systematically (though not entirely) replaced the idea of justification by the idea of criticism. He has worked out a complete set of methodological norms for that purpose, something that no one else had done before. In doing this, he has turned the focus of epistemological and methodological discussions from the unprofitable problem of inductive justification to the *central task of sustaining intersubjective criticism*. How complete his success as a critic of Carnap's inductivism has indeed been is shown by Carnap's explicit adoption of Popper's concept of empirical content (empirical content = class of potential falsifiers = improbability of conjectures, plus actual resistance to falsification attempts) as opposed to his earlier concept of empirical content as inductive *probability* (according to Popper 1972:18).

In respect to its present function as a dominant model of discursive rationality in scientific inquiry, the theory of falsification regulates criticism in at least two positive directions: (a) It liberates the individual inquirer from the obligation of being error-free; (b) it establishes criticism as a social process rather than an individual attitude (though it must be added that Popper's way of dealing with the question of individual attitudes remains completely unsatisfactory).

As to (a), no better comment can be given in favor of Popper's approach than a statement by Sir John Eccles, neurologist and Nobel laureate (whose book *Facing Reality* Popper appreciatively mentions in his preface to *Objective Knowledge):*

> Until 1945 I held the following conventional ideas about scientific research – first, that hypotheses grow out of the careful and methodical collection of experimental data. This is the inductive idea of science deriving from Bacon and Mill. Most scientists and philosophers still believe that this is the scientific method. Second, that the excellence of a scientist is judged by the reliability of his developed hypotheses, which, no doubt, would need elaboration as more data accumulate, but which, it is hoped, will stand as a firm and secure foundation for future conceptual development. A scientist prefers to talk about the experimental data and to regard

---

[3] I have not emphasized this implication of an active, knowledge-constitutive (or, with Kant: transcendental) subject in my presentation of the main lines of the theory of falsification because Popper does not fully appreciate its importance; as we shall see, he later (1972) proceeds to suggest an "epistemology without a knowing subject."

the hypothesis just as a kind of working construct. Finally, and this is the important point: it is in the highest degree regrettable and a sign of failure if a scientist espouses an hypothesis which is falsified by new data so that it has to be scrapped altogether. That was my trouble. I had long espoused an hypothesis which I came to realize was likely to have to be scrapped, and I was extremely depressed about it.... At that time I learned from Popper that it was not scientifically disgraceful to have one's hypothesis falsified.... I was persuaded by Popper in fact, to formulate my electrical hypotheses of excitatory and inhibitory synaptic transmission so precisely and rigorously that they invited falsification – and, in fact, that is what happened to them a few years later.... Thanks to my tutelage by Popper, I was able to accept joyfully this death of the brain-child which I had nurtured for nearly two decades and was immediately able to contribute as much as I could to the chemical transmission story which was the Dale and Loewi brain-child. I had experienced at last the great liberating power of Popper's teachings on scientific method. (Eccles 1970:105)

As to (b), whatever may and must be objected to Popper's deductivist concept of critical discussion, he *has* recognized that objectivity is a matter of a social process of criticism rather than one of the "objective attitude": "It is altogether mistaken to assume that the objectivity of science depends upon the objectivity of the scientist." (1962, in Adorno et al. 1969:112, my transl.)[4] The fact that many critics seem to ignore this position of Popper's (e. g., Mitroff 1974:8ff identifies Popper with the "story-book image of science" which builds on the idea of objective attitude) can only be explained by Popper's own frequent inconsistencies with respect to his alleged rejection of the "objective attitude." He often comes dangerously close to such a requirement, for instance when he characterizes his approach as a "procedure of putting things into the objective or logical or 'formal' mode of speaking" (1972:6), or when he speaks of the need for a "rational attitude" (1972:31).

It is indeed symptomatic of the fallacies inherent in Popper's theory of falsification – and to them we must now turn – that on closer examination there appear to be a great many inconsistencies and "technical" difficulties. They are only the symptoms of underlying deficiencies that we have to consider, such as inadequate metaphysical and psychological assumptions and questionable concepts of truth, objectivity, criticsm, and rationality. Let us then begin our critical effort.

1.3. The Unsolved Preference Problem

How can a critically-rational discussion help an agent or planner to choose between alternative theories or design models as guides for practical action? Among all the difficulties of the falsification theory considered by Popper, this so-called problem of

---

[4] Cf. also: "The so-called objectivity of science consists in the objectivity of the critical method." (in Adorno 1969 et al.:106)

preference perhaps best illustrates the ways in which critical rationalism remains uncritical with regard to the problem of practical reason.

Any attempt to apply Popper's deductivist criterion of empirical content as a preference criterion inevitably leads back to Hume's induction problem: How can we know anything about the future performance of a theory unless we assume the validity of (psychological) induction? Popper, in order to save his deductivist position, is forced to distinguish between "theoretical preference" and "pragmatic preference" for theories. Theoretical preference, he suggests, excludes any reference to (future) practical applications in evaluating a theory. Its criterion is "truth," defined as "correspondence with the facts (or with reality)"; "a theory is true if and only if it corresponds to the facts." (1972:44) Though this construct of Popper's seems to be of little relevance to the actual question of preference in the practice of inquiry, it is revealing to see how Popper tries to defend his approach.

"The theoretician, I will assume, is essentially interested in truth, and especially in finding true theories." (1972:13) Now, according to his own position, Popper must admit that there is no way of establishing the *truth* of a theory, but only its falsity. Therefore, he is forced to construct an *approximation* criterion of truth, which he finds in the idea of *excess empirical content:*

At any time t, the theoretician will be especially interested in finding the best testable of the competing theories in order to submit it to new tests. I have shown that this will at the same time be the one with the greatest information content and the greatest explanatory power. It will be the theory most worthy of being submitted to new tests, in brief *"the best"* of the theories competing at time t. If it survives its tests, it will also be *the best tested* of all the theories so far considered, including all its predecessors. (1972:15)

On the other hand, a theory that does not survive the tests

...poses an important new *problem* for any new explanatory theory. Any new theory will not only have to succeed where its refuted predecessor succeeded, but it will also have to succeed where its predecessor failed; that is, where it was refuted. If the new theory succeeds in both, it will at any rate be more successful and therefore "better" than the old one. (1972:14)

And thus:

The enrichment of the problems through the refutation of false theories, and the demands formulated [above], make sure that the predecessor of every new theory will – from the point of view of the new theory – have the character of an approximation towards this new theory. (1972:16f)

It appears hardly compatible with Popper's claim for being critical that he tacitly implies: when a theory A is preferable to a theory B under the criterion of empirical content, it comes closer to "truth" than B. Accordingly, he later postulates:

And if we fail to refute the new theory, especially in fields in which its predecessor has been refuted, then we can claim this as one of the objective reasons for *the conjecture that the new theory is a better approximation to truth than the old theory.* (1972:81)

And similarly:

I saw that what has to be given up is the *quest for justification,* in the sense of the justification of the claim that a theory is true. *All theories are hypotheses,* all *may* be overthrown. On the other hand, I was very far from suggesting that we give up the search for truth: our critical discussions of theories are dominated by the idea of finding a true (and powerful) explanatory theory; and *we do justify our preferences by an appeal to the idea of truth:* truth plays the role of a regulative idea. (1972:29f)

This is doubly absurd: First, there is no logical justification for such an appeal to truth, as Wellmer (1976:203ff) and Holzkamp (1971, in 1972:184ff) have shown; it can only be a matter of intuitive *belief* ("I am not a belief philosopher; I am primarily interested in ideas, in theories, and I find it comparatively unimportant whether or not anybody 'believes' in them. And I suspect that the interest of philosophers in belief results from that mistaken philosophy which I call 'inductivism'.... This is why... I do not believe in belief." – Popper 1972:25)

As a simple counter-example we may think of a case where a theory A makes use of the same explanation as a theory B, but is better operationalized, i.e., formulated by means of a more precise scale of measurement. In such a case, A's empirical content is higher because it is more precise than B, or, in Popper's terms, B's inaccurate quantitative language is an approximation to A. But does preference for A give any more security that the underlying explanatory hypothesis is "true"? Of course not; Popper's criterion of preference cannot logically justify the belief in an approximation towards truth, because *empirical content has nothing to do with truth,* but only with testability (A may be as false as B). This is the key criticism not only in respect to Popper's treatment of the preference problem but also in respect to many of his claims for universality, rationality, etc., claims that immediately depend on his approximation theory of truth. We can see here how a seemingly minor technical difficulty of critical rationalism is in fact only a surface symptom of a grave epistemological shortcut at the bottom of the theory of falsification.

A second key criticism in this context is that it is simply not true that "truth plays the role of a regulative idea": *not a single methodological principle or criterion can be derived from a logically untenable claim for truth.* Popper concedes that "nothing, of course, can make sure that for every theory which has been falsified we shall find a 'better' successor, or a better approximation – one that satisfies these demands. There is no assurance that we shall be able to make progress towards better theories." (1972:17) In this formulation Popper seems to suggest that only the *heuristic* problem of discovering a better hypothesis is involved, but in fact he should make clear that there is no *logical* principle that could justify his belief in progress towards truth. All of a sudden, Popper "forgets" his own sacred exclusion of the context of discovery and hides his logical difficulty behind a heuristic truism!

A similar attempt at camouflage with respect to this problem can be found in Popper's paper "Truth, Rationality, and the Growth of Scientific Knowledge" (in 1963:215–250), where he introduces the term "verisimilitude" for "approximation to truth": "How do you know that the theory t_2 has a higher degree of verisimilitude than the theory t_1?" (1963:243) Instead of simply admitting that there is no logical way of establishing "verisimilitude," he says:

I do *not* know. I only guess. But I can examine my guess critically, and if it withstands severe criticism, then this fact may be taken as a good reason in favor of it.... A false theory is certainly worse than one which, for all we know, may be true. (1963:234 and 235)

Again in 1972 he writes:

I intend to show that while we can never have sufficiently good arguments in the empirical sciences for claiming that we have actually reached the truth, we can have strong and reasonably good arguments for claiming that we may have made progress towards the truth; that is, that the theory T_2 is preferable to its predecessor T_1, at least in the light of all known rational arguments. Moreover, we can explain the method of science, and much of the history of science, as the rational procedure for getting nearer to the truth. (1972:57f)

This is not only a clear attempt at evasion, suggesting to the reader that critical rationalism can grant "good reasons" or "rational arguments" for believing in progress towards truth; it is also an implicit re-substitution of the psychological problem of induction ("good reasons") for the unsolved logical problem of induction.

Two explanations seem possible for this most uncritical turn op Popper. First, his anti-metaphysical realism might have prevented him from realizing that his approximation theory of truth is not defendable by means of his own falsification theory; second – and this explanation appears more likely – Popper has seen very clearly that admitting the failure of any deductive justification of preference between theories would imply the break-down of the entire edifice – the claim of critical rationalism for securing the growth of knowledge toward truth; its claim for universality; its claim for rationality and objectivity; its claim for having solved the problem of induction without relying on "belief."

Even more precarious is Popper's answer to the question of *pragmatic preference.* In order to answer the question: "Which theory should we prefer for practical action, from a rational point of view?" (1972:21), he is first of all forced to exclude any consideration of *values* (for which there is no place in his deductivist conception of empirical content). He does so not by an explicit statement, but by another attempt at concealment: "Every action presupposes a set of expectations; that is, of theories about the world. Which theory shall the man of action choose? Is there such a thing as a *rational choice?*" (1972:21) This formulation suggests that Popper considers the important role of expectations in practical action, while in fact it reduces expectations to "theories" in the sense of objectively formulated, falsifiable hypotheses, thus tacitly excluding the value-orientation of all expectations. Popper passes over the fact that an agent's "horizon of expectations" is not ónly "theory-impregnated" but also value-laden, and that there is no room in his deductivist concept of rationality for considering this value basis. Only thus can be arrive at the following conclusion:

> We should *prefer* as a basis for action the best-tested theory.... There is no "absolute reliance"; but since we *have* to choose, it will be "rational" to choose the best-tested theory. This will be "rational" in the most obvious sense of the word known to me: the best-tested theory is the one which, in the light of our *critical discussion,* appears to be the best so far, and I do not know of anything more "rational" than a well-conducted critical discussion. (1972:22)

Apart from the fact that this "conclusion" is reached only at the price of ignoring the value problem, it relies on two inconsistencies: (a) the reintroduction of Hume's common-sense concept of rationality which now suddenly serves as an argument for the value of "well-conducted" (i.e., critically-rational) discussion; and (b) the reintroduction of psychological induction; for what is the point of relying on the "best-tested" theory if it is not to be of help in assessing the *future* reliability of the theory?

The second inconsistency in particular has immediate consequences for real-world problem solving and design. *Design is always design for the future,* and hence it is clear that Hume's problem of induction will reappear in any attempt to establish a preference criterion for the choice between alternative design models. Popper argues that design as well as prediction can and should be based on explanatory, universal statements (so-called nomological hypotheses or theories) and cannot be justified otherwise. The argument goes as follows. Design models are nothing other than technological or instrumental transformations of explanatory hypotheses. An *explanation,* according to Hempel/Oppenheim's deductive model of explanation (1948), shows how a given event to be explained (the "explicandum") can be logically derived from a universal hypothesis ("explanans") and given situational constraints ("initial conditions"). The task of explanation is thus to find an appropriate universal statement from which a given event can be deduced under known initial conditions. The task of gaining predictions or instrumental statements is said to be logically based on the same schema. As Popper explains:

> The derivation of predictions proceeds in the opposite direction. Here the theory is given, or assumed to be known (perhaps from textbooks), and so are the specific initial conditions (they are known, or assumed to be known, from observation).

56

What remains to be found are the logical consequences: certain logial conclusions which are not yet known to us from observation. These are the *predictions*. (Popper 1972:352)

In a *technological statement* (the term "technological prediction" is also used), both the situation to be designed and also the theory are assumed to be known, whereas the initial conditions are to be found and realized. In other words, if a theory is known and empirically corroborated, it can be used for gaining predictions and technological statements by mere "tautological transformation" from "if given X, then Y" to "if Y is wanted, then do X." (Them term "tautological transformation" used by critical rationalists stands for the trivial insight that no transformation is really required because the two statements are clearly equivalent.)

From this argument it seems to follow that technological statements that have been derived from a well-corroborated theory are a more reliable or "scientific" basis of planning than intuitively gained *ad hoc* predictions; hence the claim that a design or a design model can be justified as "scientific" if and only if it is based on deductively gained technological statements and predictions. And indeed, this belief is widespread in the literature of prediction and planning. But is it justified?

The answer is a clear *no*. To prefer a design that is based on a technological prediction over another design that has not been based on a theory is – in Popper's own view – the same as choosing a deductively gained prediction instead of an *ad hoc* prediction. Such a preference implies that the deductive derivation makes a prediction more reliable – and this implication is not valid. *Any prediction by definition transcends the given empirical basis.* Therefore, its reliability (its future performance) can only be inductively estimated but by no means deductively justified on the basis of past corroboration. The conclusion may appear surprising: quite in contrast to Popper's widely accepted view, logical deduction must be understood as a *heuristic* means (among other means) for *finding* design models, rather than as a preference criterion that might offer the designer more certainty. To say it even more clearly: *whether or not a design has been logically derived from a theory is quite irrelevant for its justification,* for its derivation from theory cannot clear away the inevitable "induction gap" in future-oriented thinking.[5] If the above conclusion holds, there is no

---

[5] So far as I know, Jürgen Wild, in a paper on the problem of scientific predictions, has been the first to reach a similar conclusion (cf. 1970:553ff). Inspired by Wild, I have used the concept of "induction gap" *(Induktionslücke)* in order to distinguish and assess the various principal approaches to prediction; depending on whether a prediction is gained from historical extrapolation, causal explanation, correlation of interdependencies, simulation, historical analogy, cross-analogy, or "pure" intuition, the "induction gap" will contain in various degrees different sources of deception (Blümle/Ulrich 1972:296ff). Such an assessment might be useful for finding sensible combinations of various prediction techniques that do not multiply but compensate for inevitable sources of deception. Though it is clear that such an assessment must be situational and is a matter of subjective judgement rather than one of logical justification, it might be a first step towards integrating the problem of prediction (Hume's problem of induction) into a general theory of deception such as that proposed by Churchman (1968 b:229, rev. ed. 1979:230).

need for requiring that designs or design models be based on deductively gained technological predictions, i.e., on critically-rational inquiry. Hence, neither is there any need for giving the search for universal explanations (nomological hypotheses) the absolute priority in inquiry; critical rationalism's contention that "growth of knowledge" (i.e., an increasing number of well-corroborated explanatory theories) is a prerequisite for rationally solving design problems cannot be maintained generally. It can be maintained only for those domains of inquiry and design where the "induction gap" is virtually negligible, because the problem-relevant systems may be regarded as completely determined by natural laws; however, hardly any problem in real-world design can be considered as "closed" in this sense.

We have to conclude that Popper has not solved the problem of pragmatic preference but concealed the completed inadequacy of his solution. His solution depends on an uncritical transition from the "primacy of theory" in the original sense of a theory-impregnated character of all experience to a "primacy of theory" in the sense of the constitutive role of objective theory for rational practice. The implication is that practical reason can be reduced to theoretical reason. But since there is no room for the critical consideration of values in Popper's concept of theory we must consider this implication as the source of an objectivist illusion.

Our examination also suggests another conclusion: it is imperative to distinguish between what Popper *says about* his approach and what the methodological rules of critical rationalism actually *imply*. Unfortunately, many ardent defenders of critical rationalism rely on Popper's claims *about* his approach and thereby fail to notice that these claims are not always vindicated by his methodological rules. The same danger is also apparent in Popper's treatment of the so-called problem of the empirical basis, to which we now turn.

1.4. The Unsolved Problem of the Empirical Basis

Refuting a hypothesis (theory) subsequently to a successful empirical falsification attempt makes sense only if the singular statement that is found to falsify the hypothesis is considered to be "true," i.e., empirically valid (within statistical limits of significance). Thus, the logical problem of induction arises anew: How can we justify the truth of a singular statement on the basis of observation? (In this context, the singular statements are also called "basic statements" or "protocol sentences.") It appears that Popper's "solution" to the problem of induction has only shifted the problem to a lower level in the process of theory formation: this is the underlying reason for the constant slipping-back of psychologism into Popper's deductive approach. Popper admits the problem of the empirical basis, but denies its relevance.

First, he refers the problem to the context of discovery and maintains that "all this interests only the psychologist" (1961:99). The context of discovery is assumed to be a problem of psychology rather than of epistemology; "hence" the problem of the empirical basis need not bother the epistemologist.

Second, because it is only too obvious that this does not solve the problem, Popper plays down its practical importance:

For in the practice of scientific research... in connection with singular statements, doubts as to their empirical character rarely arise. (1961:43; I'll ignore the fact that this assertion is more than questionable.)

All of a sudden, reference to the *practice* of inquiry is used as a justification, while originally the aim was to propose a set of normative rules that would exclude the conventionalist practices of inquiry:

The only way to avoid conventionalism is by taking a decision: the decision not to apply its methods. We decide that, in the case of a threat to our system, we will not save it by any kind of conventionalist strategem. (1961:82)

Third, conventionalism at the empirical basis is still inconsistent with Popper's claim "to put forward a concept of *empirical science*... in order to draw a clear line of demarcation between science and metaphysical ideas" (1961:38f), a concept based on a purely "deductive method of testing" (1961:30); because of this claim he is forced to elaborate a *theory of "the objectivity of the empirical basis"* (1961:97ff). There is a clash between Popper's claim that the empirical content of hypotheses can be critically tested according to the "deductive method of testing," and the fact that consensus about basic statements is a matter of *decisions:*

Every test of a theory... must stop at some basic statement or other which we *decide to accept.* (1961:104)

Such a decision cannot be logically justified by experience, as Popper concedes:

Experiences can motivate a decision, and hence an acceptance or a rejection of a statement, but a basic statement cannot be justified by them – no more than by thumping the table. (1961:105)

In order to save the objectivity of the empirical basis against the suspicion of conventionalism, Popper tries to apply the falsification principle to the problem of justifying basic statements; that is, he attempts to transfer his deductivist solution to the induction problem from the level of theoretical (universal) statements to the level of observational (basic, singular) statements. He concedes that the individual inquirer "makes up his mind," i.e., makes a decision, about the truth or falsity of basic statements about "facts" (1972:12); but he maintains that through critically-rational discussion, this merely subjective decision will either be refuted or else become "objective" knowledge. The knowing subject who has "made up his mind," so goes the argument, can then be tacitly forgotten.

However, this attempted solution clashes with Popper's recognition of the primacy of theory. Admitting that all observations are theory-impregnated amounts to saying that there are no subject- and theory-independent facts. The falsification principle, on the other hand, presupposes just that: reality is taken as a subject- and theory-independent world of autonomous "facts" to which observational and theoretical statements should "correspond" (correspondence theory of truth). The simultaneous assumption of a correspondence theory of truth and of a primacy of theory creates a problem of circularity: How can theories be justified (falsified) by facts if the facts are in turn dependent on the theoretical expectations of the inquirer? In order to avoid such circularity between theories and facts, Popper is forced to introduce a new norm of *independent testability* into his original set of methodological rules (cf. 1963:215ff, 1964:74, 1972:192ff).This norm requires that a theory be subjected to independent tests, that is, to tests in the light of "bold" alternative theories that are independent of the theory to be falsified; an idea that has led Paul Feyerabend (1970, 1975) to stress the need for counter-theories ("theoretical pluralism" or, more radically but inevitably, "anarchism" or "dadaism," cf. also Spinner 1974).

However, such independent or counter-theories are ultimately incompatible with the deductivist falsification approach. First of all, they violate Popper's consistency condition (1961:91; cf. p. 52 above). How can we critically-rationally establish the "independence" of two theories except by referring to the inconsistency of the predictions derived from them? And how can we justify any claim for approximation toward truth through the method of conjectures and refutations if the refutation attempts are valid only with reference to the found (bold, alternative) theories? Does this difficulty not show that the context of discovery, like the context of application, cannot be excluded from the context of justification? It is evident that these difficulties originate in Popper's adherence to the classical correspondence theory of truth: "A theory is true if and only if it corresponds to the facts." (1972:44, with reference to Tarski 1956:152ff) The correspondence theory is incompatible with Popper's own critique of positivism. So long as this theory is maintained, the norm of independent testability, and the pluralism of theories it implies, cannot prevent critical rationalism from falling back either on positivism or else on conventionalism, whatever Popper may claim to the contrary.[6]

[6] Imre Lakatos (1970) has tried to overcome Popper's "naive" falsificationism, as he calls it, by suggesting a version of "sophisticated" falsificationism. He renounces the idea of a definitive elimination of isolated theories through confrontation with the facts ("facts" in the light of isolated theories) and suggests instead that we should apply the falsification principle only to an entire succession of theories, a so-called "research programme." According to this approach we should not refute a theory because of its difficulties at any particular moment but rather because its evolution over a long period of time proves unsatisfactory in comparison with the history of rival theories, i.e., because its capacity to predict empirical phenomena is stagnating. It appears that Lakatos' reconstruction of the theory of falsification indeed avoids the problem of the empirical basis; but he pays a high price for this advantage. Lakatos *nolens volens* abandons Popper's goal of providing clear criteria for deciding on when a theory should be eliminated, namely (a) inconsistency or (b) want of excess empirical content of a theory in comparison to its rival or predecessor within the same research programme. But if we are to renounce such clearcut criteria, why then should we adhere to Popper's narrow concept of rational criticism at all?

Jürgen Habermas, in his *theory of knowledge-constitutive (or cognitive) interests* (1964, 1965, 1971a), has advanced an additional and, I believe, convincing argument against Popper's way of establishing the objectivity (value-freedom) of the empirical basis. Habermas takes as his point of departure Popper's concession that basic observational statements can only be established by a decision reached through intersubjective discourse (cf. Popper 1961:97ff). In order to refute Popper's view that such discourse can, when regulated according to the principles of critical rationalism, secure the objectivity of basic statements, Habermas demonstrates that those very principles are at bottom value-laden, that is, selective. It is self-evident that any rational decision presupposes some source of purposefulness, i.e., a criterion for judging the suitability of the decision. The basic criterion of the empirical scientist is the "interest" he has in being able to predict and reproduce the reality in question. This "interest" is obviously contained in such requirements as controlled (reproducible) observation and universal validity of nomological (law-like) hypotheses, and it is on this interest that the meaning of scientific findings depends. As the term "knowledge-constitutive interest" suggests, this interest is not to be understood psychologistically, but rather in a *transcendental* sense,[7] i.e., as referring to a presupposed context of meaning upon which the possibility of intersubjectively meaningful knowledge depends.

The logical structure of admissible systems of propositions and the type of conditions for their corroboration suggest that theories of the empirical sciences disclose reality subject to the constitutive interest in the possible securing and expansion, through information, of feedback-monitored action. This is the cognitive interest in technical control over objectified processes. (1965, in 1971a:309; very similarly 1964, in Adorno et al. 1969:244)

The decision on whether or not to accept a basic statement thus depends upon a hermeneutic prejudgement on what constitutes the meaning of a "fact": namely, its providing us with technical control over causal-analytically determined processes in our environment, particularly with regard to the productive processes on which our material existence depends (cf. also 1963, in Adorno et al. 1969:182). To say it more simply: *what is "fact" and what is "fiction" depends on what is of instrumental use in controlling objectified processes.* And to this precise extent Popper's claim for the objectivity or value-freedom of the empirical basis relies on an objectivist illusion,[8] an

---

[7] The transcendental question, in the sense of the philosophical tradition originating with Kant, is the question of the necessary conditions of the possibility of (objective) experience, i.e., conditions of knowledge that "transcend" (precede) experience.

[8] Habermas characterizes as "objectivistic" an attitude "that naively correlates theoretical propositions with matters of fact" (1971a:307). Regarding Popper's basis problem, "basic statements are not simple representations of facts in themselves, but express the success or failure of our operations.... The facts relevant to the empirical sciences are first constituted through an a priori organization of our experience in the behavioral system of instrumental action." (1971a:308)

objectivist illusion brought about by the inability of critically-rational inquiry to reflect on the normative context on which its possibility and meaningfulness depend.[9]

Habermas does not of course mean to say that empirical science ought to live up to its own claim for value-freedom and to renounce its orientation toward the cognitive interest in instrumental control. Habermas' point is, rather, that there is no knowledge without underlying human interests – "anthropologically deep-seated interests," as Habermas likes to say – and that these interests and their practical consequences must be critically reflected in each case. For the empirical-analytic[10] sciences, the interest in instrumental control is appropriate and constitutive of the intersubjective meaning of empirical-analytic statements.

Habermas thus does not object to the actual research practice of the empirical-analytic sciences but only to their claim for universality. Linked to this claim is the objectivist self-understanding of the empirical-analytic sciences, an understanding that becomes a crucial source of hidden value content and social irrationality in the realm of *social* inquiry and design.

If social inquiry understands itself exclusively in terms of empirical-analytic science ("behavioral science," "social science," "administrative science" etc.); and if, furthermore, social planning or social systems design understands itself in terms of "systems science," then the objectivity of social inquiry and design is bought at the price of eliminating from consideration its proper subject: the social life-world which we call "social reality." The facts of the social life-world are constituted by normative contexts of meaning, not by instrumental control over objectified processes. Overlooking this crucial difference can only lead to an identification of rationality in matters of social concern with "value-neutral" social technology, as Popper demonstrates with his advocacy of "piecemeal social engineering" (cf. 1957:67 and 1966:162f).[11]

---

[9] Critical rationalists usually respond to this charge by associating it with an allegedly "instrumentalist concept of truth" (the true is what functions); cf. Popper's critique of instrumentalism in 1963:111ff and Albert's attempt to refute Habermas' argument by linking it to instrumentalism (1964a, in Adorno et al. 1969:201f). But this is a trivial misunderstanding: the possibility of instrumental control determines the *meaning* of empirical-analytic statements and restricts it to the realm of possible instrumental action, but it does not establish their *truth* (cf. Habermas 1964, in Adorno 1969:246f, and Habermas 1973b:407). The underlying fallacy is the confusion of the (transcendental) a priori of meaningful experience with the a priori of argumentative vindication of truth claims, as we shall see in Ch. 2, Sections 2 and 3.

[10] "Empirical-analytic" is Habermas' term for the empirical and causal-analytic sciences concerned in the production of nomological (law-like) hypotheses with empirical content. Popper, greatly influenced by Max Weber's conception of objective social science (cf. on this Section 2.1 below), conceives of social inquiry almost exclusively in terms of nomological, i.e., empirical-analytic, science.

[11] Cf. in this context Marcuse's critical discussion of what he calls "the internal instrumentalism of scientific rationality," 1964:Ch. 6.

If social inquiry is to be adequate to its subject, namely, the speaking and acting of individuals and their symbolic interaction, it must consider itself not as empirical-analytic but rather as *historical-hermeneutic science,* the constitutive interest of which is not in instrumental control over objectified processes but in intersubjective understanding and consensus:

Hermeneutic inquiry discloses reality subject to a constitutive interest in the preservation and expansion of the intersubjectivity of possible action-oriented mutual understanding. The understanding of meanings is directed in its very structure toward the attainment of possible consensus among actors in the framework of a self-understanding derived from tradition. This we shall call the *practical* cognitive interest, in contrast to the technical. (1965, in 1971a:310, cf. also 1971a:176)

In addition to the practical interest in mutual understanding, Habermas introduces a third knowledge-constitutive interest which is also of importance to social inquiry and design, namely, the *emancipatory interest* of the *"critically oriented sciences"* such as critical social theory. The underlying idea, briefly, is this. When social inquiry has as its purpose not only hermeneutically mediated understanding of social reality but also the prediction, control, and *improvement* of that reality, as is the case with economics, sociology, political science, etc., then it must counter the danger of objectifying the social processes in question. This danger arises with the necessary search for invariant (law-like) regularities and co-variances that make prediction and planned change possible. Rather than making a virtue of the necessity of describing social processes in such objectifying terms, critical social inquiry with a practical intent must consider both the intrinsically normative and self-reflective character of social processes. We can then say (although Habermas does not put it this way) that the idea of the "emancipatory" interest is to combine the "technical" interest in instrumental control with the "practical" interest in mutual understanding, so as to emancipate the inquirer from the seemingly objective (because unreflected) constraints produced by the former, technical, interest. We can now understand Habermas' explanation:

The systematic *sciences of social action,* that is economics, sociology, and political science, have the goal, as do the empirical-analytic sciences, of producing nomological knowledge. A critical social science, however, will not remain satisfied with this. It is concerned with going beyond this goal to determine when theoretical statements grasp invariant regularities of social action as such and when they express ideologically frozen relations of dependence that can in principle be transformed. To the extent that this is the case, the *critique of ideology,* as well, moreover, as *psychoanalysis,* take into account that information about lawlike connections sets off a process of reflection in the consciousness of those whom the laws are about. Thus the level of unreflected consciousness, which is one of the initial conditions of such laws, can be transformed. Of course, to this end a critically mediated knowledge of laws cannot through reflection alone render a law itself inoperative, but it can render it inapplicable.

The methodological framework that determines the meaning of the validity of critical propositions of this category is established by the concept of *self-reflection*. The latter releases the subject from dependence on hypostatized powers. Self-reflection is determined by an emancipatory cognitive interest. Critically oriented sciences share this interest with philosophy. (1971a:310)[12]

We shall deal with Popper's answer to the call for hermeneutic understanding and self-reflection later on in the present chapter (Sec. 4.3); first we shall have to introduce his "epistemology without a knowing subject."

With regard to the problem of the empirical basis, the conclusion is clear. There is only one way in which we can claim "objectivity" – in the general sense of freedom from hidden presuppositions – for our empirical basis of rational discourse: namely, by acknowledging, in each case, the knowledge-constitutive interests on which the validity and meaning of "facts" depend. *To claim objectivity for one's knowledge by referring to the objectivity of one's empirical basis is an impossible undertaking; but to pursue the ideal of objectivity in the sense of emancipating oneself and others from the objectivist illusion is an indispensable idea.*

But if Popper's claim for the objectivity of the empirical basis breaks down, empirical falsification attempts in the sense of critical rationalism are uncritical at the basis. This difficulty is not resolved by applying critically-rational discussion to the problem of the empirical basis, both because such discussion cannot reflect back hermeneutically on the normative contexts of meaning in which it takes place, and because it is inherently restricted to the technical interest in instrumental control over objectified processes. Baron Munchausen cannot pull himself from the quagmire by his own pigtail; the falsification principle cannot save the falsification principle.

1.5. The Problem of "Historicism"

One more obvious difficulty of the theory of falsification must be considered: the assumption that the repetition of potentially falsifying tests is possible. "Only when certain events recur in accordance with rules or regularities, as is the case with repeatable experiments, can our observations be tested – in principle – by anyone. We do not take even our own observations quite seriously, or accept them as scientific

---

[12] Habermas is not of course thinking of contemporary analytical philosophy and critical rationalism, which subject themselves to the objectivist standards of the empirical-analytic sciences and thereby lose their critical function vis-à-vis the seemingly objective constraints produced by the empirical-analytic sciences. Rather, he is thinking of the self-reflective, emancipatory philosophy that reached its culminating point in Kant's call for enlightenment: *"Sapere aude!* Have courage to use your own reason! – that is the motto of enlightenment." (Kant 1784, transl. Beck 1949:286)

observations, until we have repeated and tested them." (1961:45) With this assumption, Popper finally reintroduces a "whiff of verificationism," as he himself admits (1963:248), in order to strengthen his precariously weak "critical approach" to the problem of the empirical basis. The requirement of repetition may raise no serious problem for the laboratory sciences where tests occur under controlled conditions (closed system approach). Repetition of real-world events, however, be they biological, psychological, social or historical, is impossible, for two reasons: such events always change the individual subject from which they originate (phenomenon of individual growth, maturation and self-determination); and the situational conditions of these events cannot be completely controlled (open systems).

It is in order to evade this difficulty that critical rationalism has developed a strong tendency towards *scientism* and its denial of any essential difference between the natural and social sciences. This denial permits the claim for the universality of the critically-rational approach. It also accounts for its anti-"historicism". Historicism, a school of thought pioneered mainly by J. G. Herder in the late eighteenth century and by Wilhelm Dilthey in the late nineteenth century, maintains that historical events are to be understood as processes of individual growth and social evolution rather than as a mere succession of causal events. That is to say, historical events, if they are to become intelligible, cannot be explained in terms of causal relations alone but rather in terms of *meaningful* relationships – between actions and intentions, tradition-bound cultural values and institutions, individuals and social groups. Such meanings obviously cannot be grasped and corroborated by a deductivist falsification approach such as Popper's but only by a hermeneutic (interpretive) approach that is prepared to include in its concept of rationality all sources of human intentionality, all forms of human reasoning and knowing.

In his *The Poverty of Historicism* (1957), Popper first defines historicism in an unusual, if not misleading way – namely, as an approach to the social sciences that sees its principal aim in historical prediction and tries to achieve this aim by establishing the evolutionary "laws" of history[13] – and then proceeds to attack the thus-defined "historicism." In this way he manages to "disprove" the legitimacy of historicism and to retain his claim for the universality of the scientific (critically-rational) method, in spite of the requirement of controlled repeatability. However, because critical rationalism can deal only with events that are subject to universal natural laws and thus repeatable, its application to social-individual events forces Popper to treat these latter events as if they were subject to natural laws: "By choosing explanations in terms of universal laws of nature, we offer a solution to precisely this last… problem. For we conceive all individual things, and all singular facts, to be subject to these laws." (Popper 1972:196) Such a position neglects the fact that individual events are individual (= unique) precisely because they cannot be described by natural laws

[13] The reason for this distorted definition is that Popper wishes to attack Hegel and Marx, rather than Herder or Dilthey, as "historicists."

that would provide for regularity and repeatability. Once again Popper's "solution" to a fundamental difficulty is to exclude from consideration the subjective, normative contexts of meaning on which all rational inquiry and discussion depends. We shall see in Section 4.3 of the present Chapter how Popper tries to answer this charge. At this point we cannot escape the impression that he evades rather than solves the difficulty that the requirement of repeatability poses in the realm of social inquiry.[14]

---

[14] Apart from the epistemological difficulties considered thus far, there are also problems of actual research practice that make it impossible to sustain the falsification principle. The most important ones concern the inevitable use of *ad hoc adaptations* and *ad hoc definitions* to save "falsified" theories, and the procedure of "exhaustion" (Dingler 1923:37), i.e., partial disregard of falsifying evidence by recourse to "unknown disturbing factors" (most obviously in statistical inference). However, other authors such as Holzkamp (1968, 1972) and Feyerabend (1975) have addressed to these rather technical problems critical discussions which need not be repeated here.

2. Implications for Social Planning: Instrumental Reason and Decisionism

In order to facilitate the critical analysis of the theory of falsification we have proceeded thus far without explicit reference to the task of the social planner.[15] It should by now be clear that critical rationalism is sufficiently "chimerical," to use Sherlock Holmes' term, with regard to its claim for being *the* rational method of inquiry. However, it is one of the central claims of critical rationalism that it is of immediate relevance for applied inquiry. Based on the preceding examination of some of its crucial epistemological shortcomings, we must now try to understand fully why critically-rational discussion cannot give the social planner a basis for choosing a design, i.e., deciding on the ends and means of planning, that is in any way better than openly normative debate.

At the bottom of this issue lies the question of the proper relationship between science and society, between technically exploitable knowledge and practical understanding and improvement of the social life-world, between "theory" and "practice."

We have seen how Popper's solutions to all the major difficulties of the falsification theory – the problem of preference, the problem of the empirical basis, the problem of historicism – depend on the exclusion of normative aspects from "rational" discussion. It is thus easy to predict how critical rationalists will conceive of the theory-practice relation. They will be forced to sort out from normative social practice a domain that can be approached in a value-free, but nevertheless "practical" manner, and then to identify this value-free domain with practical rationality (or practical reason) in general so as to maintain the claim for universality. This is indeed the strategy that Popper and his followers have chosen (significantly, it was also the strategy of the earlier positivists whom Popper means to criticize). The considerable success with which they have pursued this strategy is evidenced by the hegemony of scientific expertise over other conceptions of practical rationality in contemporary industrialized societies. Since, however, the positivists have not always enjoyed this hegemony, a short historical excursus may help us to gain a better perspective on the practical implications of critical rationalism for the planner.

2.1. A Historical Excursus: The Rise of Decisionism (From Aristotle to Max Weber)

Until the rise of positivism, Aristotle's view of practice *(praxis)* and practical philosophy as the normative, non-scientific domain of ethics and politics (the order of

---

[15] Except in the case of the problem of pragmatic preference, where the context of justification (on which Popper concentrates) overlaps with the context of application (which Popper generally neglects).

67

the *polis*) was generally accepted. In critical contrast to the Sophists' reduction of good political practice to rhetorical skill or workmanlike technique *(techne)*, practice was carefully distinguished from theoretical knowledge *(theoria)* on the one hand, and from traditional techniques of production *(poiesis)* on the other. Standards of good practice were not to be found in theoretical or technical knowledge but in virtue, justice, excellence, situational prudence, and quite generally in an order of the *polis* that would allow its citizens to lead a *good and just life*. Rational arguments and decisions regarding the proper conduct of life and the order of the *polis* were not to be derived from theoretical-analytical thinking but from what Aristotle called "topical" thinking (from the Greek *topikos* = local, concerning the *topoi* = the commonplaces or commonly used viewpoints for discussing everyday subjects).[16]

The distinction between the topical thinking of practical philosophy and the analytical thinking of theory was developed in the *Organon,* Aristotle's (or his students') collected writings on logic. The *Organon* consists of two main parts, the *Analytic* and the *Topic.* While the Analytic describes a deductive system of logic for deciding on the truth of theoretical (i.e., general) propositions, the Topic focuses on the "logic" of debating and deciding on the "goodness" (virtue) of context-dependent, tradition-bound, normative assertions. An intersubjective discourse was to disclose the range between the extremes of "too much" and "too little," and these extremes were then to be avoided in favor of the balanced middle position characteristic of virtue.[17] The important points for us to note are two: first, that Aristotle's treatment of the role played by topical thinking in unfolding practical problems renders apparent the relative character of possible answers; and second, that Aristotle himself regards this limited degree of precision and completeness as both the only possible and the only adequate goal of practical reason. He clearly understands that only practice itself can complete what reasonable deliberation *on* practice first envisages, and that no rational argument or theory, however precise and complete it may be, can ever reduce good practice to a question of good theory.

It appears strange that our "enlightened" age should have forgotten this insight of early Greek wisdom. And yet, the positivists and critical rationalists have triumphantly championed a theory-practice conception that implies precisely this: that good practice can be derived immediately from good theory.

---

[16] Topical thinking has been reintroduced into jurisprudence by Viehweg (1954) and since then has attracted rising interest by social (esp. political) scientists and philosophers. A helpful short introduction to Aristotle's practical philosophy and the place of topical thinking in it can be found in Höffe 1979:Ch. 2.

[17] Although topical thinking in this sense is an early form of dialectical thinking, it must not be confused with Hegel's dialectic. While Aristotle's topic does not seek to negate the given tension between the alternatives of want and excess but maintains this tension as a necessary condition of finding the virtuous middle, Hegel's dialectic seeks to overcome the contradiction between two incompatible theses by finding a synthesis that advances to a new level of thinking.

The two most important impulses toward this reversal were given by Thomas Hobbes in the middle of the seventeenth century, and by Max Weber in the early twentieth century. Hobbes for the first time systematically conceived of practical questions as questions that could be scientifically solved by dividing them into issues of instrumental control – issues which could be rationalized in terms of causal-analytical laws about human behavior, social interaction and production of goods – and issues of normative decisions which escaped rationalization through causal-analytical science. Thus, simultaneously with this first design for the scientization of politics (practice in the Aristotelian sense), *decisionism* came to see the light of day. Like all "isms," decisionism takes too absolutely a basically correct idea: in this case the idea that genuinely political questions contain an inevitable moment of decision that cannot be rationalized away. In view of the religious disputes of Hobbe's time, decisionism implied tolerance vis-à-vis political and religious convictions that did not coincide with established patterns of political rationality – an idea that has lost nothing of its importance in today's social planning (cf. Lübbe 1978:66). But Hobbes went too far when he employed this idea to bisect practical questions into two neatly separated groups, one containing *merely* purposive-rational issues of technique, the other containing *merely* irrational issues of political decision. In order to make the former accessible to scientific analysis, the latter were dismissed as entirely inaccessible to rational discussion. The implication was that practical questions, to the extent that they could not be reduced to technical questions, did not admit of truth (reasonable justification): *auctoritas non veritas facit legem,* "authority rather than truth makes the law."

With Max Weber's contribution to the *Werturteilsstreit* – the debate over the proper place of value judgements in social inquiry – decisionism found its modern formulation. Since Popper draws heavily on Weber's model of objective social science, I shall discuss it in some detail.

Weber's basic concern was the relation between causal explanation and interpretive (hermeneutic) understanding in the social sciences, a concern which again reflects the theory-practice problem. In the first paragraph of *Economy and Society* (1968, German orig. 1921) he introduces his famous definition of sociology, or social science in general:

Sociology.... is a science concerning itself with the interpretive understanding of social action and thereby with a causal explanation of its course and consequences. We shall speak of "action" insofar as the acting individual attaches a subjective meaning to his behavior.

and similarly:

Statistical uniformities constitute understandable types of action, and thus constitute sociological generalizations, only when they can be regarded as manifestations of the understandable subjective meaning of a course of social action. (Weber 1968:I, 4 and 9, also in Dallmayr/McCarthy 1977:38 and 45)

What makes the subjective meaning of an individual action understandable, and more specifically, *rationally* understandable (= reconstructable)?

The highest degree of rational understanding is attained in cases involving the meanings of logically or mathematically related propositions.... In the same way we also understand what a person is doing when he tries to achieve certain ends by choosing appropriate means on the basis of facts of the situation, as experience has accustomed us to interpret them. The interpretation of such rationally purposeful action possesses, for the understanding of the choice of means, the highest degree of verifiable certainty....

On the other hand, many ultimate ends or values toward which experience shows that human action may be oriented, often cannot be understood completely....

For the purpose of a typological scientific analysis it is convenient to treat all irrational, affectually determined elements of behavior as factors of deviation from a conceptually pure type of rational action. (1968:I, 5f, in Dallmayr/McCarthy 1977:39f)

We can sum up Weber's point in one sentence: The subjective meaning of an action is understandable by *reference to an ideal type[18] of rational action,* namely, purposive-rational action. Thus Weber finds the key for bringing interpretive understanding and causal explanation together in the concept of instrumental or purposive-rationality *(Zweckrationalität),* i.e., the rationality of means (including one's own behavior) in regard to given ends. The identification of rational action with instrumental rationality (or instrumental reason) closes the gap between causal-analytic explanation and interpretive understanding:[19] First, the interpretation of social action becomes unproblematic insofar as this action serves an instrumental function (has means-character) with regard to an identifiable motivating end. When an action can thus be described as the rational pursuit of a motivating purpose, i.e., as purposive-rational, Weber speaks of *motivational understanding (Motivationsverstehen).* Second, such motivational understanding does not by itself represent an explanation so long as it is not empirically tested. To achieve an explanation, the motivational understanding

---

[18] Weber gives this precise definition of an ideal type: "An ideal type is formed by the one-sided *accentuation* of one or more points of view and by the synthesis of a great many diffuse, discrete, more or less present and occasionally absent *concrete individual* phenomena, which are arranged according to those one-sidedly emphasized viewpoints into a unified *analytical* construct *[Gedankenbild].* In its conceptual purity, this mental construct *[Gedankenbild]* cannot be found empirically anywhere in reality. It is a *utopia."* (1949, in Dallmayr/McCarthy 1977:34)

[19] But unfortunately, it also obviates the essential distinction between purposeful action (action that is guided by self-reflective awareness of ends and consequences) and merely purposive action (adequate employment of available means for a "given," but unquestioned, end). Since the notion of purposefulness will be important to my approach, I should like to emphasize here that Weber's use of the phrase "rationally purposeful action" for instrumental rationality is counter to my own use of similar terms through this book.

can be translated into a nomological hypothesis about regularities of social action and then be subjected to empirical testing. To the extent that such hypotheses are empirically corroborated, the social action in question has been *explained,* and in this case Weber speaks of *explanatory understanding.*

Such hypotheses will take the general form of a prediction: "When an individual in a situation S has a purpose X, then the action will be Y."[20] Thus, hypotheses can be formulated without requiring a value judgement on the part of the inquirer; they are objective. Weber concludes that motivational understanding can be part of a value-free, empirical and causal-analytical, social science; in other words, insofar as rational social action can be subsumed under the category of purposive-rational action, an interpretive social science is objectively possible.

This "insofar," however, is a rather big "insofar." It effectively restricts the realm of rational social inquiry to actions that involve no on-going choice of ends or values. The price for an objective, though interpretive, social science such as Weber conceives it is high: it consists in (a) *decisionism* and (b) *the reduction of practical to instrumental reason.*

Re: (a) Under the rationality standards of empirical-analytic science,[21] all those social actions that are not purposive-rational in character become inaccessible to rational discussion and explanation. The empirical content of a nomological hypothesis about a certain pattern of behavior will depend on the degree to which an identified motive or purpose is sufficient for predicting a corresponding (i.e., purposive-rational) action. But precisely this linkage is absent, or at least equivocal, when an action has not merely a means-character in regard to a "given" purpose. Hence, when an action involves on-going choice of ends rather than, or along with, choice of means, it must be dismissed as a merely subjective value judgement, a *decision* which, because it is not value-free, cannot be "rationally" (scientifically) explained.

Even worse, Weber's model does not allow for the possibility that the choice of means for a given end might have a value content of its own. His conception of value-free, interpretive, social science breaks down as soon as one admits this possibility. In order to safeguard his conception, Weber is forced to establish his famous *means-end dichotomy.* With it decisionism stands or falls. This dichotomy implies that value judgements are contained only in (assertions on) ends, but not in (assertions on) means. The latter are treated entirely as questions of fact, such as: how effective and efficient is a certain means in regard to a desired end, how reliable is it, under what conditions and at what costs and risks can it be employed, etc.? To be sure, such questions are unobjectionable as far as they go, but they must not be taken for the only questions that can rationally be asked. Here is the snag. Decisions on means are never questions of fact *only,* for all means are in need of critical exami-

---

[20] We have seen earlier (Section 1.3) that such predictive statements are logically equivalent to causal-analytic statements.

[21] This term includes Weber's model of objective, interpretive, social science. Cf. note 10 to the present chapter.

71

nation with regard to the value implications they themselves contain. Any presumption to the contrary is an uncritical point of departure for social inquiry and design. Weber, as highly differentiated as many of his arguments are, neglects this crucial objection and thereby becomes, at bottom, dogmatic. He simply presupposes that decisions on means are questions of fact only, while decisions on ends are related to questions of values only. This untenable dualism of means vs. ends is analogous to the positivist distinction between "facts" and "values" (standards). On this presumption, decisions on ends can safely be relegated to merely irrational acts of faith, while decisions on means are reduced to "value-free" considerations of purposive-rationality. The implication is that decisions on ends are from the outset withdrawn from rational deliberation and discussion; they can no longer be derived from intersubjective discourse but only from authority. As Hobbes said: *auctoritas non veritas facit legem.*

Fortunately, however, it is quite easy to demonstrate that Weber's basic dichotomy of means and ends is faulty. It presupposes that means and ends are *substantially* distinct categories. As any amateur politician knows, however, decisions on means in view of given ends always have redistributive effects with respect to both benefits and costs/risks, and for that reason are politically just as explosive and value-laden as decisions on ends. The underlying reason is that means and ends are not substantially distinct categories but rather different perspectives for considering hierarchies of goals: what appears as a means from "above" (from the next-higher system level in the goal hierarchy) appears as an end from "below" (subsystem level, cf. Ulrich 1975a:74).

Once this is clearly understood, it seems almost unbelievable how uncritically a majority of contemporary social scientists, led by the logical empiricists and critical rationalists, have adopted the dogma that means and ends are substantially distinct categories, so that only "ends" are supposed to involve value judgements while "means" are understood as value-neutral with regard to "given" ends.[22]

Re: (b) Weber's means-ends schema leads him to believe that once a subjective decision as to the purpose of inquiry has been made – e.g., the purpose of securing purposive-rational action – the inquiry itself, as a means for accomplishing that purpose, can be kept value-free. He thus arrives at his decisionistic model of the relation of science (theory) to practice: decisions on the ends of inquiry are referred to the pre-scientific, pre-rational realm of choosing research *questions,* in the expectation that the *answers* to these questions can then be given without involving additional value judgements, "purposive-rationally," as it were.

---

[22] An early and still rare exception is Gunnar Myrdal's (1933) critique of Weber's means-end dichotomy with regard to its application in economics. A complementary viewpoint was provided by John Dewey (1938). While Myrdal made it clear that in principle all means have also the character of ends (i.e., have a normative content of their own), Dewey pointed out that most ends (except ultimate ideals) have also means-character, i.e., implications with regard to other and higher ends. Accordingly, he introduced the term "ends-in-view" to characterize ends.

But since means and ends are not substantially distinct categories, Weber's attempt to conceive of social inquiry in terms of purposive-rational action does not solve the problem of value judgements. As W. G. Runciman (1963:59, quoted in Habermas 1970a:89) writes:

> Weber's procedure in the face of this situation breaks down not because he fails to concede that a sociological inquiry cannot be framed in value-neutral terms, but because this concession doesn't buy as much immunity from the remaining problems as he thinks. The arbitrariness of standpoints cannot merely be conceded in the original choice of terms, after which, with this sole limitation, the inquiry conducted can be kept value-free. The infection of values cannot all be passed off on to the questions asked and thereby kept away altogether from the answers given.

Because Weber does not see this difficulty in his decisionist model, his approach ultimately loses sight of its declared interpretive goal and "sells out" to an unquestioned interest in instrumental control (purposive-rational action) as the standard of interpretation. Although Weber professes to aim at an interpretive social science that could render understandable the historically transmitted and culturally shared patterns of meaning on which social practice depends,[23] his decisionist model in effect narrows down the scope of interpretive social science to the understanding of purposive-rational action ("motivational understanding"), thereby excluding the historical, socio-cultural, political, etc. sources of meaning that would be crucial to the practical interest in understanding our social life-world. Genuinely practical questions in regard to the proper conduct of life, the just organization of the polis, and so on, questions which in Aristotle's practical philosophy were still the subject of reasonable deliberation and debate, are now relegated to the realm of merely subjective "decisions" or else reduced to technical questions of purposive-rational behavior.

Ultimately, Weber's decisionistic means-end schema is incompatible with the idea that reason can be practical in matters of social concern, for these matters are invariably and essentially subjective, value-laden, concerns. By abandoning the old Aristotelian distinction between *praxis* and *poiesies,* Weber's interpretive sociology inadvertently but inevitably becomes the forerunner of the technocratic consciousness and scientism that culminates in the critical rationalists' assertion: "Nothing is more practical in practice than a correct theory." (Albert 1962:55, my transl.) Let us then finally return to Karl R. Popper's strategy for applying critical rationalism to practical questions.

---

[23] E.g. in 1949:111 (in Dallmayr/McCarthy 1977:37): "Nothing should be more sharply emphasized than the proposition that the knowledge of the *cultural significance* of *concrete historical events and patterns* is exclusively and solely the final end which, among other means, concept-construction and the criticism of constructs also seek to serve."

73

2.2. The Critically-Rationalist Reception

In Popper's terms, the issue of relating "objective" theory to problems of normative social practice is to be considered within the "context of application." That is to say, it is not considered a genuine epistemological or methodological issue but rather a secondary problem, the solution to which can be derived from the basic methodological stipulations made in the context of justification. It is thus clear that Popper needs a model of the theory-practice relation that allows him to rely on his solutions to the problem of preference, to the problem of the empirical basis, and to the problem of historicism. Our earlier discussion of these "solutions" has already led us to predict the way in which critical rationalists[24] will try to approach the context of application: namely, by sorting out from normative social practice a value-free domain, so as to give critically-rational discussion a chance to unfold. What could be more welcome in this situation than a theory-practice model that shows a way to separate, in the realm of normative social practice, questions of fact from value judgements? Weber's decisionistic model can perform exactly this service, and thus the critical rationalists adopt this model without further ado.

Neglecting the more critical part of Weber's conception of an interpretive social science oriented toward understanding historically transmitted patterns of meaning such as the institutional framework of a society, the critical rationalists assimilate nothing but its uncritical core into their own objectivist framework, i.e., Weber's decisionistic means-end schema and the reduction of practical to instrumental reason which it implies. Curiously enough, the dogma that means and ends are substantially distinct categories is adopted without even an attempt at falsifying it empirically. This is hard to understand indeed, for such a falsification attempt would have been relatively easy; one might have tried, for instance, to establish a significant difference of political behavior patterns vis-à-vis "means" and "ends" in real-world planning. Instead, the critical rationalists have apparently preferred to proceed dogmatically in order to demonstrate that instrumental rationality, critically-rationally secured, is the one and only form of practical rationality. This dogmatic effort includes:

(1) an expanded decisionistic model of the relationship between the expert and the politician;

(2) the extension of critical rationalism to a political theory of social rationality (a positivistic version of the "critique of ideology"); and

(3) the elaboration of the falsification principle into a general, "evolutionary" theory of problem-solving within the framework of an "epistemology without a knowing subject."

---

[24] I shall speak of the critical rationalists in general rather than of Karl Popper because the context of application has been discussed extensively by Hans Albert, Hans Lenk, Hermann Lübbe and others whose positions are close to that of Popper.

Strategies (2) and (3) will be critically reviewed in Sections Three and Four of the present chapter. In the remainder of the present section, I shall analyze the critically-rational development of the decisionistic model.

2.3. The Expanded Decisionist Model

With Habermas (1971b:62ff) we can distinguish a decisionistic, a technocratic, and a pragmatistic model of the relationship between questions of "fact" (expertise, theory) and questions of "values" (politics, practice).

The *decisionistic model,* as we have seen, postulates that choice of (technical) means and choice of (political) values are separable. This allows the expert to become a guarantor of purposive-rational design of means and tools for political ends, while the choice of ends themselves is alleged to be non-rational (because not purposive-rational) and consequently referred to a political "decision." Practical questions are thus bisected into a "rational" part that becomes the exclusive domain of expertise – be it in the form of administrative (bureaucracy) or scientific (technocracy) competence – and an "irrational" part remaining to the politician (political power/democracy). For all that, the politician is still given a primary role in comparison to the expert, for *he* determines the needs to be satisfied by the expert's tools; the role of the bureaucrats and technicians remains restricted to advising the politician and executing his decisions.

However, the growth of administrative and scientific tools for rationalizing decisions, exemplified by the development of systems analysis, decision theory, and computerized information processing and cybernetics, has effectively undermined the balance of power between the expert and the politician. In the resulting *technocratic model* of rationalized political practice, the primacy of the politician over the expert is reversed; now the expert's "rational" science determines the *Sachzwänge* (factual restraints, = objective necessity as disclosed by experts) and, implicitly, the criteria of rationality to which the politician must succumb. The political process has no longer a genuine decision-making function but becomes a mere "stopgap in a still imperfect rationalization of power, in which the initiative has in any case passed to scientific analysis and technical planning" (Habermas 1971b:64). Apart from this reversal, the technocratic model shares with the decisionistic model the Weberian asumption of separability of means and ends, and the underlying ideal type of instrumental rationality.

The technocratic model, in effect, has only one distinct advantage over its decisionistic brother: it is increasingly gaining descriptive value in the modern bureaucratic state. As a normative model, however, it has obvious drawbacks. It is possible to criticize these drawbacks from two different viewpoints: from the decisionistic point of view (this leads to a renewed, *expanded decisionistic model)* or from a "dialectical" point of view (leading to a third, *pragmatistic model).*

The first alternative is of course the one corresponding to the "criticist" self-understanding of critical rationalists. Hans Albert in particular has written extensively on the problem of theory-practice mediation and, in the main, insisted on the social rationality of the decisionistic model, that is, defended Popper's dualism of "facts" vs. "decisions" (e.g. Albert 1964a, 1964b, 1965, 1968, 1971, 1978). Of more interest to our discussion is, however, Hermann Lübbe's attempt to develop a *critical decisionism* (e.g. 1962, 1971, 1976, 1978). Lübbe shows that both the decisionistic model and the technocratic model are one-sided in that they either exaggerate or overlook the inevitable decisionistic moment that separates theory or rational discussion from practical action. It is not theoretical competence or rational discussion that gives a decision its normative power, but rather the vote that must follow the discussion.

The counting of votes is the decisionistic act that ends the debate. In the technocratic order, debates and decisions by vote become superfluous. They fall victim to the logic of facts. (1962, in 1978:58, my transl.)

Lübbe's point is well-taken; in opposition to the prevalent technocratic model of rationalization of practice, he gives back to the concept of decision a genuinely rational function, namely that of political legitimation for which neither expertise nor rational discourse are true substitutes. "The decision leaps over a lack of rational grounds of determination. But it is not therefore irrational." (1971:21, my transl.)

But unfortunately, Lübbe's argument does little to explain how decisions can be made and justified in a rational way *without* rationalizing them technocratically away, or else how the assumption that there is, in a given case, a lack of rational grounds of determination can be rationally defended. The insight that decisions fulfill a rational function does not by itself free us from searching for *reasoned* consensus and allow us instead to have recourse to a "showing of hands," as it were. Thus far, Lübbe remains close to Weberian/Popperian decisionism.

On the other hand, Lübbe is more realistic (and critical) than Weber and Popper about the factual reversal of the decisionistic into a technocratic mode of rationalizing political practice. He recognizes the implication of this reversal: namely, that "decisions" on ends are not wholly separable from questions of fact but require expertise and rational deliberation prior to the decision proper. At the same time, however, there remains a genuinely decisionistic (because political) moment that must be defended against a one-sided technocratic model. Combining both insights, Lübbe arrives at an *expanded decisionistic model*. Its two main pillars appear to be the following:

First, against a one-sided technocratic model, decisionism regains a crucial function, i.e., normative (though not descriptive) value. In particular, it serves a critical purpose against the ongoing undermining of the democratic order by expertise, according to Francis Bacon's well-known formula: "Knowledge is power." (Lübbe

1978:40) Expertise may bring "rationality" into political decision-making, but it is no substitute for democratic legitimacy.

Second, to the extent that expertise becomes more and more involved in rationalizing political decisions, the decisionistic model also regains its practical relevance, and thus its descriptive value, with regard to the remaining issues that do not lend themselves to the available tools of expertise. As Habermas comments:

> True, the scope of pure decision has been restricted to the degree that the politician disposes of an augmented and more refined arsenal of technical means and can make use of aids to strategic decision. But within this confined area what decisionism always presupposed has now become true for the first time. Only now has the problem-complex of political decisions been reduced to a core that simply cannot be rationalized any further. (1971b:65)

In effect, then, the prevalence of the technocratic model itself creates a small but genuinely political realm of "decisions" in the decisionistic sense, i.e., questions from which all purposive-rational elements have been eliminated and which must therefore be referred to irrational acts of belief. In this sense, Lübbe actually expands the descriptive and normative range of the decisionistic model by combining it with the technocratic model, a combination that makes room both for the growing range of systems- and decision-theoretic tools for rationalizing politics, *and* also for the genuinely rational function of political "decisions." We may fairly represent Lübbe's critical revision of decisionism as providing the most efficacious of all decisionistic theories, and there is no reason that the critical rationalists should not adopt Lübbe's revision of their approach. At the same time, however, Lübbe's theoretical refinements ultimately confirm the central weakness of decisionism, for his revision offers no challenge to the basic assumption of decisionism. Because of its inability to include value judgements in its deductive-empirical method of error-elimination, critical rationalism, like all decisionistic approaches, necessarily presupposes Weber's concept of rationalization as a process of translating practical into technical questions.[25]

It is precisely this requirement that provides the point of attack for Jürgen Habermas. He suggests a third, alternative model which he calls the *pragmatistic model.* Its basic idea is simple enough. The decisionistic means-end dichotomy does not adequately describe the genuine dialectical interdependence of means and end, the "dialectic of potential and will" *(Dialektik von Können und Wollen,* 1971b:61). This interdependence results from the fact that all means have normative implications of their own (i.e., the character of ends) and all ends except ultimate ideals are them-

---

[25] The critical content of Lübbe's approach, in spite of this remaining Weberian bias, will also be relevant to our later discussion of Habermas' model of rational discourse (Ch. 2), to which we now turn for a preliminary glimpse.

selves also means to other ends, or, as Dewey says, they are ends-in-view.[26] Referring to Dewey, Habermas therefore advocates a "pragmatistic" model in which the inextricable relationship between available techniques and practical decisions is systematically questioned.

In the *pragmatistic* model the strict separation between the function of the expert and the politician is replaced by a critical interaction. This interaction not only strips the ideologically supported exercise of power of an unreliable basis of legitimation but makes it accessible *as a whole* to scientifically informed discussion, thereby substantially changing it. Despite the technocratic view, experts have not become sovereign over politicians subjected to the demands of the facts and left with a purely fictitious power of decision. Nor, despite the implications of the decisionistic model, does the politician retain a preserve outside of the necessary rationalized areas of practice in which practical problems are decided upon as ever by acts of will. Rather, reciprocal communication seems possible and necessary, through which scientific experts advise the decision-makers and politicians consult scientists in accordance with practical needs. (1971b:66f)

The dialectical or "pragmatistic" model thus requires a *model of rational discourse* between experts and political agencies, a model that can guarantee an adequate translation of practical needs into technical questions, and of technical answers into practical decisions (cf. 1971b:70f). The basic requirement for such a discourse is that it be *public;* a second necessary requirement is that it be *"free from oppression,"* that is, not subject to external sources of systematic distortion. We shall examine Habermas' model of rational discourse in Chapter Two, for it is of crucial importance to our search for a socially rational concept of rational criticism. At this point, I only wish to point to its critical implications with regard to the critical rationalists' position.

First, Habermas shows that only a pragmatistic model is truly compatible with democracy (1971b:67ff). The decisionistic model, the technocratic model, and the combined "expanded" decisionistic model all lead to a one-sided reduction of political issues concerning every citizen into questions of expertise, a reduction which effectively serves to exclude the public from participating and to reduce its critical political function to one of mere acclamation.

Second, while the increasing rationalization of political decisions, by means of systems analysis, etc., effectively creates a residual realm of genuinely political questions, this fact does not at all imply that these questions are altogether beyond reasonable discourse (1971b:65, similarly 1973a:276). It is only the underlying means-end dichotomy and the equation of rationality with purposive-rationality that create the impression that value judgements cannot be discussed rationally. In turn, critical

---

[26] Cf. note 22. The expression "genuine interdependence of means and ends" was used by Dewey (1938) in his debate with Leon Trotzky over the moral and political content of the relation of means to ends (not following Habermas).

rationalism is bound to adhere to the dualism of "facts" vs. "decisions" simply because it has no way of including value judgements in its deductive approach. But the consequences of this decisionism disprove its claim for rationalizing practice:

From the mainstream of rationality the pollutants, the sewage of emotionality, are filtered off and locked away hygienically in a storage basin – an imposing mass of subjective value qualities. Every single value appears as a meaningless agglomeration of meaning, stamped solely with the stigma of irrationality, so that the priority of one value over the other – thus the persuasiveness which a value claims with respect to action – simply cannot be rationally justified. (1973a:265)

Against this "positivist isolation of reason and decision" (1973a:163), Habermas advocates an "enlightenment of political will" (1971b:75), i.e., a search for cogent argument and reasoned consensus that goes beyond the reach of instrumental rationality. Critical rationalists usually respond to this call for political enlightenment by referring to Popper's conception of the "open society." Let us see then how Popper defends his decisionistic concept of rationality.

3. Critical Rationalism in Defense (I):
The Theory of the Open Society

Our discussion up to this point has uncovered several crucial weaknesses of the theory of falsification, most importantly the problem of preference, the problem of the empirical basis, the problem of historicism, and the problem of decisionism. It is obvious that these weaknesses bring into question the critical rationalists' claim for the practical applicability and indeed universality of their concept of rationality. This concept of rationality, let us recall, is tied to deductive logic as the organon of criticism and in consequence excludes from "rational" criticism all subjective, social-cultural, historical, political, moral, etc., values and categories insofar as they cannot be reduced to causal-logical relationships. The only exception is represented by purposive-rational action, to which Weber's decisionistic model of objectiv social science and "rationalization" (scientization) of politics can be applied.

However, even a progressively rationalized society, i.e., a society in which an ever-expanding range of practical questions is transposed into technical questions and then "solved" by the experts, still faces genuinely practical (e.g., political, moral, or aesthetic) questions. These questions, on the one hand, cannot be transposed into merely technical questions, and on the other hand, they are too important to be referred to the realm of "subjective acts of belief." In regard to these practical questions, critical rationalism cannot maintain its claim for providing the one and only model of rational criticism without submitting to the charge of *blind criticism:* it becomes a form of criticism that cannot critically deal with its own object, the why and what-for of its existence.[27]

Much of Popper's later[27a] work therefore aims at defending the claim that the critically-rational method of falsification provides *the* general model for rationality within and beyond the realm of science. We have briefly mentioned his two main strategies:

(1) the extension of critical rationalism to a political theory of social rationality, and

---

[27] The term "blind criticism" has been suggested by Klaus Holzkamp (1971, 1972:192). I have found it so well-aimed that I have used it in the title of the present chapter.

[27a] The word "later" is used here to refer to the mainly apologetic purpose of the more recent writings of Popper's, as well as those of his followers, esp. Hans Albert; it is not meant to deny the conjecture that Popper's methodological work from the beginning was influenced by an underlying social philosophy such as his later theory of the "open society." I am obliged to Emil Walter-Busch for drawing my attention to this possible misinterpretation of my meaning. In his study on the philosophy of history underlying neopositivist German sociology (1970), he has found that all neopositivist sociology, contrary to its own self-understanding, relies on a social-philosophical preconception of what a rational society would be. Applying this argument to Popper's work, he suggests that it is his underlying social philosophy which prevented Popper from pursuing the consequences of his own critique of positivism (cf. 1970:25ff).

(2) the elaboration of the falsification principle into a general, "evolutionary" theory of problem solving within the framework of an "epistemology without a knowing subject."

The purposes of both strategies are rather transparent. In the "epistemology without a knowing subject," the major source of Popper's difficulties – the subjective, historical normative character of real-world problems – is to to be eliminated by demonstrating that the critically-rational method is altogether independent of subjective elements for producing rationality. This strategy will be examined in Section Four.

Conversely, the strategy of the "open society" consists in advocating a society in which the conditions of "rationality" would already exist, so that irrational elements could no longer interfere with the universal applicability of the critically-rational approach. But why bother at all to examine these apparently apologetic efforts? The only, but important, reason is this: critical rationalists normally refer to them whenever the social rationality of their concept of rationality is questioned. Especially the notion of an "open society" has proved to be very suggestive and has convinced many people that critical rationalism furnishes an adequate epistemological and methodological basis for socially rational planning and decision making.[28] Therefore, if we want to clear the ground for a truly critical, *socially* rational concept of rational criticism, we have no choice but to point out the crucial sources of deception in the model of the "open society" and the underlying "epistemology without a knowing subject." With regard to the former, fortunately, I can be rather brief.

The strategy of the "open society" is the topic of Popper's books *The Open Society and Its Enemies* (1966, orig. 1945) and *The Poverty of Historicism* (1957). Especially in the two volumes of *The Open Society,* the norm of rational criticism is transferred from the theory of falsification to a general theory of the "open society." An open society is characterized as a political system that makes criticism *possible* and *rational,* where "rational" still means "objective" in the sense of logical decidability, and hence "valuefree." In other words, the "open society" represents the model of a rational society in which all the conditions for applying the critically-rational method would be realized, conditions such as a *"rational attitude"* on the part of every citizen, i.e., the readiness to submit to critically-rational principles of rational discourse, and *"pluralism."* Without going into details, we can immediately note some some crucial weaknesses of such an undertaking.

1. *Utopianism:* Social rationality is simply presupposed, rather than critically-rationally produced. (This observation also reverses the thrust of the standard argu-

---

[28] To give but one striking example, the German Social-Democratic Party has recently (1978) adopted Critical Rationalism as its official philosophy. (It is not the first time, I am tempted to add, that people who believe in democratic socialism have compromised themselves by allying themselves to scientism, beginning with Marx, who misunderstood his philosophy scientistically.)

ment of critical rationalists against their critics, namely, that the latter yield to utopianism and "romanticism.")

2. *Moral decisionism:* Hence, the only way to "introduce" conditions of critically-rational discourse such as the "rational attitude" is by appealing to every citizen's "moral decision" to adopt a "rational attitude." Indeed, Popper on several occasions tries to give "good reasons" as to why the individual citizen "ought" to adopt a "rational attitude," namely because adopting the principles of critical rationalism represents "a moral decision" (e.g. 1966, quoted from the German version 1958:II, 296). Implicitly, every other position now appears not only as inimical to the openness and rationality of society but even as immoral. Similarly, Popper's main disciple in Germany, Hans Albert, argues: "He who adopts it [critical rationalism] does not choose an abstract principle devoid of existential meaning, but a way of life." (1969:78, my transl., cf. p. 40)

3. *Partiality for instrumental reason:* The extension of a concept of rationality beyond its built-in limits (Weber's ideal type of purposive-rationality) does not produce more but less social rationality. The effort to have as many citizens as possible assume a rational attitude cannot produce social rationality so long as that rational attitude itself is inherently restricted to instrumental reason.[29]

4. *Pluralism?* Popper's identification of the "open society" with pluralism cannot deceive us about the fact that the model of the open society has only one, anti-pluralistic, goal: namely, to establish the conditions for the universal application of critical rationalism. Critical rationalism, because its deductivist concept of rational criticism leaves it incapable of critically examining its own why and what-for, necessarily remains centered upon itself. By its own standards of rationality it cannot rationally defend a critical orientation toward any substantive goal, toward an avowedly normative vision of a better society. Instead, it must act as if it could criticize normative social practice from an absolute, value-free standpoint outside the society that it pretends to rationalize. But the real question that a socially rational approach would have to make transparent is always this: Who benefits, and who ought to benefit? When the mask of "pluralism" slips, we discover ideology at war.

5. *Who benefits? (Partiality for the status-quo):* The fact that the model of the open society is not overtly directed toward a substantive ideal but only toward "rational discussion" does not mean that it is in fact free of ideological implications. As Feyerabend puts it, "rationality [critical rationalism] is not an arbiter between traditions but a tradition itself." (1980:68, my transl.) And that means that all the

---

[29] Cf. the remarks concerning a similar claim for rationality linked to the "open systems" approach in the social and behavioral sciences in Ch. 5, Sec. 2.4. The very term by which Popper designates his (incrementalist) concept of practical rationality, "piecemeal engineering" (1957:67, 1966:162f), points to its inherent reduction of practical to instrumental reason.

talk of the objectivity of a rational discussion is, in the context of application, ideological in character: "The standards of such a [rational] discussion are not 'objective,' they merely look 'objective' because the group of those who benefit from the application of these standards is not mentioned." (1980:74, my transl.) The following observations illustrate the point.

6. *"Liberalism"*: Not by accident Popper's model of the open society ensures the support of established political-economic liberalism for critical rationalism – one of the reasons for the strong position that critical rationalism (along with logical positivism) seems to enjoy among the academic elite in universities, government agencies, and business corporations. In return, the orientation of academe toward an "open society" seems to legitimize its autonomy (the autonomy of science) against social control, regardless of the obvious interconnection of science with political and commercial interests. It appears socially rational that science should participate in the "open society" as just one more political force – but with no valid *political* claim.

7. *Socio-political positivism:* The claim to be value-free is always suspect of dogmatism, for there is no such thing as a value-free epistemology or theory of society. Since critical rationalism pretends to furnish a value-free model of rational discourse for an open society, in spite of its apparent conformity with established liberalism, the question must be asked whether it can fulfill the critical epistemological function it claims for itself. A model of rational discourse that does not question its built-in value orientation (however "liberal" and "rational" it may be) cannot credibly fulfill its critical epistemological function but becomes an instrument of socio-political positivism with all its attributes – dogmatism, objectivism, scientism, political status-quo thinking, all of which are inimical to openly normative (e.g. moral) criticism on the part of citizens who care for their society.

8. *Objectivism:* The refusal of critical rationalism, under the pretext of being "rational," to take into account any subjective or openly normative critique, causes a general inability to deal with problems of social concern. Social concerns are basically subjective concerns, and if the latter are excluded from rational discussion, problems of social concern no longer exist objectively. As Roger Poole puts it in his brilliant essay, *Toward Deep Subjectivity:* "The facts of human suffering are non-facts for objectivity, are merely subjective." (1974:47)

9. *Political status-quo thinking:* The critique of a society that is governed by the objective-rational paradigm and understands itself as "open" is necessarily – in the view of the critical rationalists – inimical to rationality, objectivity and openness ("irrational," "unobjective") and thus must not be tolerated. As Roger Poole says in his terse language: "Objectivity does not like to be criticized" (1972:48), "for it is part of the very life-lie of our objectivity that it is totally open to

83

reasoned, even radical (but not revolutionary!) criticism, at all levels, from all corners, at all times." (1972:52)

10. *Positivist critique of ideology:* The refusal to take into account criticism that does not a priori submit to the rationality standards of critical rationalism is staged as a "critique of ideology" (see esp. Albert 1969:Ch. 3 and p. 76ff). The function of this critique of ideology is understood to be that of keeping rational discussion free from any infiltrating value judgements. In effect, however, a critique of ideology thus understood serves to maintain a veil of objectivity and rationality behind which the partiality for instrumental reason, for liberal capitalism and for the status quo can unfold. All value judgements are to be exposed and referred to the realm of "ideological" decision, except those linked to the "rational attitude" of critical rationalists themselves, i.e., to Weber's decisionistic concept of rationalization. Rational discussion of values (of practical statements) is consequently restricted to those questions which can be decided upon deductively:

(a) logical consistency analysis of value premises, and

(b) empirical tests of the realizability of corresponding goals by available means, in conjunction with the prediction of potentially undesirable side-effects of the available means; tests and predictions that operate in a way analogous to the critically-rational examination of theoretical statements about "facts" (cf. e.g., Albert 1969:76ff, critically Habermas 1975:105f).

The moral dimension of practical questions cannot of course be adequately grasped in such deductive and theoretical terms. Instead, Albert introduces a so-called "bridge principle": " 'we cannot' implies 'we ought not' " *(Nicht-Können impliziert Nicht-Sollen, 1969:76).* At a moral level, this principle serves to immunize the status quo against moral argument and relieves it from any effort to incorporate the latter into rational discussion. Searching for rationality in the selection of means is all we can do, hence we need not bother about the challenge to practical reason in the selection of ends. In response to the challenge to practical reason, Popper has only this to say:

> I said so before Hiroshima: there are infinitely many possibilities of local, partial, or total disaster. From a pragmatic point of view, however, most of the possibilities are obviously not worth bothering about because we cannot *do* anything about them: they are beyond the realm of action. (1972:22)[30]

Popper's and Albert's version of a "critique of ideology," oriented at an "open society" of which Weber's ideal type of rationalization is constitutive, here shows its true face: its amoral (I do not say: immoral) character; its being at the service of instrumental reason and scientism, and the established interests behind them.

---

[30] The quotation is from Popper's discussion of the problem of practical preference, i.e., it is *not* out of context here.

To conclude this discussion with a quotation from Habermas that may be aptly matched against Popper's sarcasm: An open society in which practical reason falls between the two stools of instrumental reason and decision "is threatened by the splitting of its consciousness, and by the splitting of human beings into two classes – the social engineers and the inmates of closed institutions" (1973a:282).

4. Critical Rationalism in Defense (II): The Evolutionary Theory of Objective Knowledge and Problem Solving

If Popper's concept of the open society might be called a political strategy of defense, his later theory of objective knowledge must be called a Neo-Darwinian strategy of survival. It is an attempt to extend the falsification principle (a merely *methodological* stipulation) to a general epistemological principle of evolutionary learning and thus to "prove" its universal validity. In *Conjectures and Refutations* (1963), Popper transferred his deductivist approach from scientific inquiry to the "psychological" context of discovery, and human knowledge in general; in the *Open Society* he made it a general standard of social rationality; and finally, in *Objective Knowledge* (1972) he establishes it as the universal principle of biological evolution, i.e., of animal ("organismic") and human ("rational") problem solving. Let us see then how Popper attempts to give the falsification theory and the "open society" an epistemological foundation that might overcome the intrinsic difficulties in both. It is also of some interest to us that Popper views *problem solving* as the fundamental process underlying both human inquiry and natural evolution – a process that is not only basically the same for both but also completely "rationally" explainable. The two central concepts are Popper's concepts of "knowledge" and "problem solving"; the former is explained by Popper's *three-world model of knowledge,* the latter based on D. T. Campbell's *evolutionary model of trial and error.* These two underlying models are now to be examined.

4.1. "Epistemology Without a Knowing Subject"?

The Three-World Model

Popper first introduced his model of the three worlds of knowledge in a paper entitled "Epistemology Without a Knowing Subject" (1968; now in 1972:106-152). This indeed is a significant title. Objectivity of knowledge for Popper means precisely "knowledge without a knowing subject" (1972:109), in contrast to subject-dependent or subjective knowledge – a distinction which he introduced as early as in *The Logic of Scientific Discovery* (orig. 1935). This distinction plays a crucial part in his attempt to establish an "objective" solution to the problem of induction, for only by excluding from consideration the knowing subject can he avoid the psychological problem of induction (cf. the discussion of the problem of the empirical basis in Sec. 1.4 above). In a second step, Popper then established the principle of the "primacy of theory" in order to extend the "critical approach" (the falsification principle) to the problem of the empirical basis. Both the exclusion of the knowing subject and the primacy of theory are necessary conditions for Popper's "solution" to the problem of induction; and both stand or fall with his contention that knowledge in the subjective sense is irrelevant for epistemology (1972:108, 111).

In a final step towards dropping the knowing subject altogether, the three-world model suggests the existence of an autonomous "third world" of objective knowledge standing apart from the worlds of physical bodies (world 1) and of subjective knowledge (world 2). The justification for this thesis is found in the Neo-Darwinian principles of natural selection.

Let us now examine this model in some detail, for it is of crucial importance for our understanding of both the potential usefulness and the essential faultiness of an objectivist epistemology in general; it is, moreover, a decisive element in the meaning of "problem solving" and "understanding" in such a framework. *Figure 1/1* gives a diagram of the three-world model proposed by Eccles (1970:165, see also Popper's account in Popper/Eccles 1977:36-50).

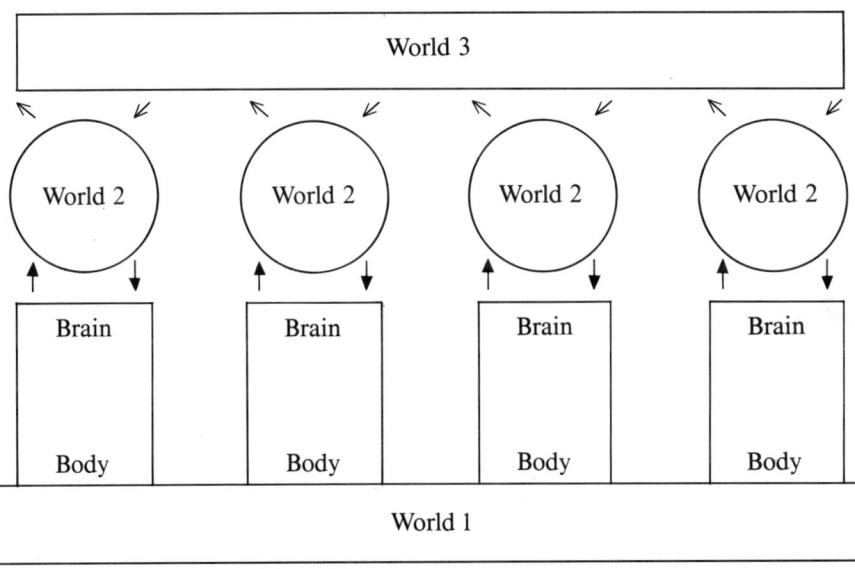

Figure 1/1: The three-world model

World 1 includes everything that has a physical reality, such as inorganic objects, the bodies of living organisms, humans, as well as the products of their behavior such as the net of a spider or a piece of art – insofar as they are physical. Popper also uses Plato's term for world 1: it contains the *visibilia,* i.e., everything that is visible (1972:154). It corresponds to Popper's metaphysical (or should we rather say: *anti-*metaphysical) realism that he views world 1 as an autonomous "real-world," as a world of given facts, and accordingly he regards the task of inquiry as gaining objective knowledge of these facts.

87

World 2 represents knowledge in the subjective sense, i.e., the "mental states" of humans and animal organisms. "Knowledge in its various subjective forms is dispositional and expectational. It consists of dispositions of *organisms.*" (1972:71) World 2 thus contains what Popper refers to as the "context of discovery": psychological states and processes allegedly irrelevant for the epistemologist, including both subjective consciousness and unconscious behavioral dispositions. Popper does not deny the reality of human subjective consciousness, but he places it on the same level as "organismic dispositions." It is apparent that such a concept of subjective knowledge is largely a *behavioristic* one, though Popper claims quite the contrary ("I am not a behaviorist," 1974:110). Typically, it "forgets" its own subjective a priori: How else could Popper have found the epistemological irrelevance of World 2 but through a "mental state" (an "organismic disposition")? It is indeed significant of all positivist thought that it *must* forget the constitutive subject of knowledge as soon as this subject has "made up its mind" (1972:12). It must do so because in its own epistemological world-3 framework it cannot "know" of the constitutive part of world 2: "It is a subjective conviction that subjective convictions are irrelevant for epistemology." (Nordhofen 1976:188, my transl.)

World 3 stands for knowledge in the objective sense. It alone is epistemologically relevant for Popper, for it alone can be dealt with critically once world 2 has been dismissed in terms of "organismic dispositions." World 3 contains the products of the human mind insofar as they are linguistically (or mathematically) formulated, "a world of articulated knowledge... independent of knowing subjects" (Lakatos 1970:180). What distinguishes them from world 2 is that they are criticizable and that they exist independently of the human inquirer who first articulated them. In Popper's words:

> The common-sense theory of knowledge, and with it all philosophers until at least Bolzano and Frege, mistakenly took it for granted that there was only one kind of knowledge – knowledge possessed by some knowing subject.... Now I wish to distinguish between two kinds of "knowledge"; subjective knowledge (which should better be called organismic knowledge, since it consists of the dispositions of organisms); and objective knowledge, or knowledge in the objective sense, which consists of the logical content of our theories, conjectures, guesses (and, if we like, of the logical content of our genetic code). Examples of objective knowledge are theories published in journals and books and stored in libraries [e.g., Popper's critical rationalism!]; discussions of such theories; difficulties or problems pointed out in connection with such theories; and so on. (1972:73)

Popper associates his world 3 with what Plato called the *intelligibilia,* the world of immutable ideas (cf. 1972:154). But in contrast to Plato's *intelligibilia,* the conjectures of Popper's world 3 may be false; they are intelligible not because they are universally true but because they are logically decidable. This is so, Popper asserts, because the objects of world 3 are in *logical* relationship to each other, whereas the contents of world 2 are "only" in psychological relationships. However, Popper here overlooks the fact that world 3 will contain as many logically incompatible theories as there are subjective world-views and convictions in world 2. Explicit formulation does nothing to assure us of the objective (logical) decidability of competing world-views, traditions, ideologies, etc. Unperturbed by such doubts, Popper argues:

The decisive thing seems to me that we can put objective thoughts – that is, theories – before us in such a way that we can criticize them, argue them. To do so, we must formulate them in some more or less permanent (especially linguistic) form. A written form will be preferable to a spoken form, and printing may be better still. And it is significant that we can distinguish between the criticism of a mere formulation of a thought – a thought can be formulated rather well, or not so well – and the *logical* aspects of the thought in itself: its truth, its truthlikeness in comparison with some of its competitors, its compatibility with certain other theories. (1974:145, italics mine)

The three worlds, though autonomous, are of course interacting with each other; world 2 has a linking function between world 3 and world 1. But – and this is Popper's new argument for an objectivist theory of knowledge – "every subjective act of understanding is largely anchored in the third world," and "consists in the main of operations with third-world objects: we operate with these objects almost as if they were physical objects." (1972:163) Despite the fact that explicit formulation cannot secure objective decidability, one might be inclined to follow Popper thus far in his preference for explicitly formulated statements. What remains unspoken, however, is that the explicitness of Popper's third world is not really meant to render explicit its normative and ideological content – the purpose that a properly defined requirement of explicitness ought to serve. Instead, it effectively serves to conceal the exclusion of subjective and normative elements behind a veil of objectivity. The explicitness of statements cannot provide for a rational discussion of their normative content so long as deductive logic remains the "organon of criticism."

It is thus very questionable whether Popper's three-world model represents an appropriate epistemological basis for a general theory of problem solving. Nevertheless, Popper has convinced thousands of fellow philosophers and scientists of the validity of his evolutionary theory of objective knowledge and problem solving based on the three-world model, and many social scientists have espoused related objectivist ideas of scientific or rational problem solving without bothering about the epistemological justifiability of these ideas. A critical discussion of the objectivist model of problem solving is therefore necessary. To this end, the principle of trial and error on which it relies must now be examined.

The Principle of Trial-and-Error and Campbell's "Evolutionary Epistemology"

Popper assumes that the principle of trial and error operates in all three worlds and is both necessary and sufficient to explain processes of learning and problem solving in all three. This assumption would support the claim that the method of conjecture and refutation, or falsification, is universally valid and is moreover the *only* method – "the method of trial and error elimination" (1972:16, 24f, 119ff, 242f, etc.).

In order to support this argument, Popper adopts Donald T. Campbell's "evolutionary epistemology" in which Campbell tries to demonstrate the non-trivial, universal character of the trial-and-error principle (Campbell 1960a, 1960b, 1965, 1974). It is significant that Campbell is one of the most fervent representatives of behaviorist-associationist learning psychology, a psychology which has been largely based on laboratory experiments with cats, rats and other animals, beginning with the landmark work on trial-and-error learning by Edward L. Thorndike (1898) and later followed by behaviorists such as Clark Hull (e.g. 1952) and B.F. Skinner (e.g. 1966). It is also significant that Campbell is one of the outstanding representatives of a cybernetic theory of problem solving, a theory that reduces any form of problem solving to a cybernetic adaptation process. Clearly the behaviorist principle of trial and error, the cybernetic feedback paradigm, and Darwin's process of mutation and natural selection contain the same logical (a priori) model of learning as a purely adaptive process – adaptive with respect to the "autonomous" real world. This similar if not identical metaphysics explains the striking tendency of cyberneticians towards a behavioristic trial-and-error conception of problem solving and of man in general, as well as the tendency of positivist epistemologists towards an evolutionary epistemology. It is the goal of both to explain (and design for) problem-solving processes without reference to insightful, purposeful or teleological behavior, for *insight or purposefulness cannot be grasped in an objectivist framework.* Therefore, trial and error is proclaimed to be not only one possible method of problem solving among others, but the only possible one. The principle of trial and error is thus taken as both necessary and sufficient for explaining any goal-directed learning process; and from this then it seems to follow that biological evolution, cybernetic adaptation and human problem solving must obey one and the same underlying "law" of learning – the method of conjecture and refutation adopted by the critical rationalists. Hence it becomes the task of an "evolutionary epistemology" to show how the trial-and-error method of learning works at all three levels of knowledge – the biological adaptation of organisms (world 1), the development of dispositional subjective knowledge (world 2), and the growth of objective knowledge (world 3).

In his paper "Evolutionary Epistemology" (1974), Campbell has undertaken this task of demonstrating the empirical validity of the trial-and-error principle in a hierarchical model of evolution. (Hierarchy is another significant part of the behaviorist-cybernetic-objectivist paradigm in that it is indicative of its reductionistic world-view.) Campbell distinguishes ten different levels of evolution and tries to show that trial and error is necessary and sufficient for explaining each level; he generally follows the formula "what cannot be false (by definition) has to be (empirically) true." A brief review of this ten-level model is necessary; it will help not only in understanding Popper's theory of problem solving, but also in uncovering the pitfalls of objectivist epistemology and cybernetic modelling when they are applied to social systems design.

1. Campbell begins at the lowest level of his trial-and-error hierarchy with one-celled animals such as amoebae or slipper-animalcula (paramecium). He shows how *blind* locomotor activities are used as "trials" until an adequate environment is found that resolves the amoeba's problem (e.g., hunger). If all its trials fail, it will die: an absolute form of error elimination.

2. At the second level, vicarious locomotor devices (e.g., tentacles, eyes) are substituted for direct locomotor trials; this represents a first level of non-fatal error-making. Only if a successful substitute trial is found does the organism go on and "select" a corresponding safe direction. This process is taken as a first piece of empirical evidence that "teleological" behavior is brought about entirely by trial-and-error learning. The substitute trials are necessarily *blind;* but through selective retention of successful blind trials the organism can "select" its behavior. Campbell therefore uses the terms "vicarious selector" for the substitute trial devices (1974:419), and "blind variation and selective retention" for trial and error (1974:427).

3. Each following level then introduces some "higher" form of substitution for the previous one and thus develops selectivity for previously blind trials. At the third level, the substitution is accomplished by habits; at the fourth by instincts; and at the fifth by "visually supported thought": "With the environment represented vicariously through visual search, there is a substitute trial and error of potential locomotions in thought." (1974:427)

4. The sixth level is characterized by "mnemonically supported thought," i.e., substitute trial and error in a memorized model of the environment. "The net result is the 'intelligent', 'creative', and 'foresightful' product of thought, our admiration of which makes us extremely reluctant to subsume it under the blind-variation-and-selective-retention model." (1974:427)

5. At the seventh level, Campbell introduces the substitute of social imitation ("socially vicarious exploration," 1974:431); at the eighth level he finally considers *language* as a substitute for actual trial and error. Popper's objectivity criterion is tacitly introduced here, because only falsifiable linguistic representation of problem situations can substitute for actual trial and error. In Campbell's view, Popper's objectivity criterion is here given a biological legitimation.

6. At the ninth level, socio-cultural evolution is explained by a yet higher substitute for actual trial and error: linguistic trial and error is completed by (blind) development and selective survival of socio-cultural institutions, a process that Campbell calls "cultural cumulation" (for a detailed account see Campbell 1965).

7. The tenth level finally is the level of objective science, characterized by Popper's norms of testability. These norms represent an ultimate substitution for the actual elimination of the "carrier" of an erroneous conjecture, because tentative "objective knowledge" can be refuted (allegedly) without any destructive real-world consequences.

The whole model fits in nicely with Popper's theory of falsification – not by chance, but because it is Campbell's purpose (!) to extend his blind-variation-and-selective-retention model to the socio-cultural and scientific level, and thus to demonstrate its explanatory power with respect to Popper's falsification theory. We have already seen that Campbell's and Popper's world-view is largely the same: objectivist, behaviorist, cybernetic – and hence *antiteleological.* Campbell explicitly refers to Popper's antiteleological position:

> Popper has spoken for that emerging position in biology and control theory which sees the natural selection paradigm as the universal nonteleological explanation of teleological achievements, of ends-guided processes, of "fit." (Campbell 1974:420)

It is important to understand the fallacies of such a position with respect to inquiry and design for problem-solving processes in social systems:

1. It seems correct to admit that indeed many complex biological adaptation processes can be explained by non-purposeful or non-insightful behavior. And as far as such processes can be *completely* reduced to and understood by hierarchically organized trial-and-error processes, there is no need to speak of purposeful or insightful problem solving.

2. The crucial question, however, is not whether the same principle of trial and error can be found in primitive and complex forms of learning, but whether it is *sufficient* to explain all forms of purposeful human action. In other words: do we need the category of purposefulness (or teleology) in order to understand human action? At this point, two basic observations must suffice. (a) The issue is at least in part a *metaphysical* problem and thus cannot be dealt with in the framework of critical rationalism. (b) The issue is also to be understood as a *pragmatic decision* that an inquirer and designer of social systems cannot avoid. As a pragmatic question, we will not reject the idea of purposefulness *a priori,* that is without thorough evidence that it is of no use at all in explaining and designing complex problem solving processes.

3. Such evidence is not given by Campbell's model nor by any other trial-and-error research. As for instance Davis (1973:43ff) has argued, trial-and-error experiments (typically with cats or rats put into mazes) are organized so as to give the animal no other choice but blind trial-and-error behavior, because no insightful association of the outcomes of available response alternatives is possible. These experiments may

prove that trial-and-error learning by selective retention takes place *under such circumstances;* but they cannot prove that the principle of trial and error is sufficient to explain human purposefulness. In other words, they cannot falsify the conjecture that purposefulness is a necessary complement to trial and error, at least *at a socio-cultural level of organization.*

4. Even if such a reduction to trial and error were *in principle* possible, the fact remains that at present we are very far from a successful understanding of human problem solving in terms of trial and error. Nevertheless we have to design better problem-solving processes in social systems *today* and therefore must look for *pragmatically* useful conceptions of problem solving.

5. Even if the preceding objections are neglected, Campbell's demonstration of the universal character of trial and error is not convincing. It is empirically deficient and logically *suspect of circularity.* The "universality" of trial and error is in effect presupposed in Campbell's and Popper's behavioristic definitions of problem solving. If problem solving is first defined as a (cybernetic) process of adaptation to a non-equilibrium situation (e.g., hunger) by means of trial and error elimination, it is entirely pointless to elaborate a sophisticated model in order to find that "indeed" every form of problem solving can be reduced to trial and error and nothing but trial and error. This is circular in the same way as Darwinian evolutionary theory runs great risk of becoming tautological (and tautologies may be used to prove anything): By definition those tentative problem solutions (organisms, theories) that fit best survive, while other trials do not survive; "hence" those who have survived must be empirical examples for the validity of trial and error. Popper himself concedes the danger (1972:69, 24f), but nevertheless takes Campbell's work as "empirical" evidence that trial and error is the only method of problem solving in natural evolution and human knowledge production.

6. Moreover, it is not only a logical tautology but also a *heuristic truism* that any kind of problem solving cannot help "learning from our mistakes" (Popper 1963:216); for there is no certainty of knowledge. Only if there were such a thing as certain knowledge would error and error-elimination not necessarily be a part of problem solving. It is only because Popper has originally (and mistakenly) excluded the context of discovery from the problem of justification, that he must now reintroduce what is heuristically trivial; namely, that the context of discovery ("trials," "mistakes," "conjectures") is inseparably linked to the context of justification ("error elimination," "falsification"), and that error elimination is meaningless without bold imagination and challenge of the given. Just as well could we conclude that "dialectic" is the only method of problem solving: what else is dialectic than trial (thesis) and challenge (antithesis) in order to gain new bold conjectures (syntheses)?

Thus, if Popper "concludes": "The process of learning, of the growth of subjective knowledge, is always fundamentally the same. It is *imaginative criticism*" (1972:148), this is a mere tautology without any empirical content, to use his own terminology. If "imaginative criticism" is to mean "*blind* variation and selective retention", it is a pragmatically helpless a priori definition of heuristics based on circular argumentation; if however the attribute "blind" is to be dropped (against Campbell's underlying model), "variation and selective retention" remains as an absolute heuristic truism which tells us nothing except that errors should not be retained. How they are discovered, and how new "imaginative" conjectures are to be found by the "critical method," remains obscure. Nevertheless, Popper contends that his truism explains the method of Einstein as well as the method of the amoeba (the former standing for world 3, the latter for world 2):

> The difference between the amoeba and Einstein is that, although both make use of the method of trial and error elimination, the amoeba dislikes to err while Einstein is intrigued by it: he consciously searches for his errors in the hope of learning by their discovery and elimination. The method of science is the critical method. Thus evolutionary epistemology allows us to understand better both evolution and epistemology so far as they coincide with scientific method. It allows us to understand these things better on logical grounds. (1972:70)

If Popper were not a very serious writer whose evolutionary epistemology has been accepted by an increasing part of the scientific community, one might laugh at the carefree naiveté of the argument. However, the fact is that even in the domain of social systems design, attempts to elaborate a "scientific" methodology of societal problem solving have largely been based on the cybernetic-behavioristic paradigm with its tendency to create models in which human consciousness is eliminated. This reductive tendency is a serious source of failure in approaches such as heuristic programming (Newell/Simon 1972), cybernetic modelling (Klir/Valach 1967, Beer 1972, Gomez/Malik/Oeller 1975), computer simulation and gaming (Hoggatt/Balderston 1963), RAND-systems analysis (Quade/Boucher 1968), "system dynamics" (Forrester 1969), systems engineering (Chestnut 1966), and educational cybernetics (Smith/Smith 1966, Skinner 1968, Frank 1969, OECD-CERI 1971). All these approaches are completely compatible with (if not explicitly based on) Popper's theory of problem solving. Let us take the final step and consider Popper's schema of problem solving, as it results from his three-world model of knowledge and Campbell's trial-and-error hierarchy.

4.2. Popper's Model of Rational Problem Solving

Popper introduces his schema in the following way (in 1972:243):

> Using "P" for problem, "TS" for tentative solutions, "EE" for error-elimination, we can describe the fundamental evolutionary sequence of events as follows:
>
> $$P \rightarrow TS \rightarrow EE \rightarrow P$$
>
> But this sequence is not a cycle; the second problem is, in general, different from the first: it is the result of the new situation which has arisen, in part, because of the tentative solutions which have been tried out, and the error-elimination which controls them. In order to indicate this, the above scheme should be rewritten:
>
> $$P_1 \rightarrow TS \rightarrow EE \rightarrow P_2.$$
>
> But even in this form an important element is still missing: the multiplicity of the tentative solutions, the multiplicity of the trials. Thus our final schema becomes something like this:

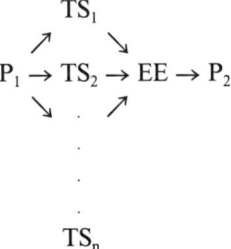

Background Knowledge

This then is the general schema of problem solving that Popper applies to all three worlds. What in world 1 is a "mutation" is a tentatively formulated conjecture in world 3; "natural selection" in world 1 corresponds to falsification in world 3 (1972:242). The main difference between world 1/2 and world 3 is the substitution of complete elimination (of organisms) by *criticism,* which has become possible through the evolution of language. The objectivity of world 3 in the form of autonomous linguistic existence is seen as the condition of this substitution, and thus of the "critical method." *Rational* criticism is possible in world 3 only, because its objects are characterized by *logical* relationships instead of physical or psychological relationships.

To come back to Popper's favorite metaphor: the method of problem solving is the same for the amoeba (world 2) and for Einstein (world 3), with the only difference that Einstein can be *rational* because he can *logically* examine and eliminate his world-3 trials. As to the trials, they "occur" to him as they occur to the amoeba, if one is to believe Popper – namely, as "cloud-like trials":

I admit that there is a difference: even though their methods of almost random or cloud-like trial-and-error movements are fundamentally not very different, there is a great difference in their attitudes towards error. Einstein, unlike the amoeba, consciously tried his best, whenever a new solution occurred to him, to fault it and detect an error in it: he approached his own solutions *critically*.

I believe that this consciously critical attitude towards his own ideas is the only really important difference between the method of Einstein and that of the amoeba. It made it possible for Einstein to reject, quickly, hundreds of hypotheses as inadequate before examining one or another hypothesis more carefully, if it appeared to be able to stand up to more serious criticism. As the physicist John Archibald Wheeler said recently, "Our whole problem is to make the mistakes as fast as possible." This problem of Wheeler's is solved by consciously adopting the critical attitude. This, I believe, is the highest form so far of the rational attitude, or of rationality. (1972:247)

No further comment is necessary, except that we can now explicitly state critical rationalism's underlying concept of rationality: *Rationality is implied to be trial-and-error operation with world-3 objects and their logical interrelations, and their confrontation with the "facts" of world 1.*

Apart from the preceding objections against Popper's antiteleological interpretation of the trial-and-error procedure, his belief in its universality, and its subsequently becoming a heuristic truism, two big question marks remain:

1. How does the conception of trial and error elimination, in the sense of the consistency condition and confrontation with the "facts," go together with Popper's original acknowledgement that all observations of facts and all conjectures ("trials") are conditioned by the knowing subject's "horizon of expections"? The recognition of the active, knowledge-constitutive (transcendental) role of the subject ("We do not 'have' an observation... but we 'make' an observation," 1972:342) would imply that a model of rational problem solving includes a critical discussion of the constitutive – and possibly deceptive – function of the subject's expectations, normative and theoretical presuppositions, categorical apparatus, etc., in comparison to alternative frames of reference. But of course, the notion of a deductive-empirical justification of *objective* knowledge would then become illusory. Hence, Popper shrinks from pursuing the consequences of his own insight – the need for a renewed epistemological focus on the "transcendental" function of the knowing subject – and instead simply eliminates the constitutive function of the subject altogether.

2. The elimination of the knowing subject also brings up again the problem of hermeneutics. How can a world-3 centered (i.e., objectivist) epistemology deal with world-2 problems such as understanding subjective human action and normative social practice?

4.3. The Problem of Hermeneutics and Popper's Concept of "Situational Analysis"

Popper does not ignore the above question, but instead tries to demonstrate that rational understanding of human actions can and must rely on world-3 objects. "This," he himself admits, "is a radical departure from the fundamental dogma accepted by almost all students of the humanities (as the term indicates), and especially by those who are interested in the problem of understanding. I mean of course the dogma that the objects of our understanding belong mainly to the second world, or that they are at any rate to be explained in psychological terms." (1972:16) Let us say beforehand that this position of Popper's is *partly* correct and merits a closer examination. It is correct insofar as it argues that world 3 is *necessary* in order to understand human action (world 2); it is incorrect insofar as it presupposes that world 3 is *sufficient* to do so.

These are Popper's basic assumptions concerning understanding:

(1) That every subjective act of understanding is largely anchored in the third world;

(2) that almost all important remarks which can be made about such an act consist in pointing out its relations to third-world objects; and

(3) that such an act consists in the main of operations with third-world objects: we operate with these objects almost as if they were physical objects.

This, I suggest, can be generalized, and holds for every subjective act of "knowledge"; all the important things we can say about an act of knowledge consist of pointing out the third-world objects of the act – a theory or proposition – and its relation to other third-world objects, such as the arguments bearing on the problem as well as the objects known. (1972:163)

Two conclusions are drawn from these assumptions – the first trivial, the second of interest to us. First: Understanding subjective events follows the general schema of problem solving by conjecture and error elimination ($P_1 \rightarrow TS \rightarrow EE \rightarrow P_2$), where TS now means tentative interpretation, and EE a critical revision of the tentative interpretation through critically-rational discourse. Second, subjective events always take place against a world-3 *background* consisting at least of language and corresponding theoretical assumptions, and probably also of other objective constraints that can be demonstrated.

It is only against a background like this that a problem can arise. A problem together with its background (and perhaps together with other third-world objects) constitutes what I call a *problem situation.* (1972:165)

Thus, the task of understanding subjective events can indeed rely on a rational examination of the "objective" problem situation, and it is also correct to contend that it *must* do so in order to be rational. In the case of historical events, the problem situation must be reconstructed in terms of the historical background of knowledge. This is what Popper calls a *situational analysis:*

> By a situational analysis I mean a certain kind of tentative or conjectural explanation of some human action which appeals to the situation in which the agent finds himself. It may be a historical explanation: We may perhaps wish to explain how and why a certain structure of ideas was created. Admittedly, no creative action can ever be fully explained. Nevertheless, we can try, conjecturally, to give an idealized reconstruction of the *problem situation* in which the agent found himself, and to that extent make the action "understandable" (or "rationally understandable"), that is to say, *adequate to his situation as he saw it.* This method of situational analysis may be described as an application of the rationality principle. (1972:179)

We easily recognize Weber's conception of motivational understanding in this account (cf. Section 2.1 above): the relation of an action to the situation is logically decidable to the extent that it can be explained (predicted) as a means-end relation, i.e., in terms of instrumental or purposive-rationality. When such a "logical" relationship between the situation ("problem background" in world-3 terms) and a subjective action ("problem solution") can be presumed, Popper accordingly speaks of a "logic of the situation" or *situational logic* (e.g. 1972:179, 1962:120). Similarly to Weber, he acknowledges that a presumable reconstruction (understanding) of the situational logic must and can be empirically tested before it acquires the status of an explanation, and that as a rule such explanations of the situational logic are mere approximations toward the real situation (cf. 1962:121) – with Weber: complete purposive-rationality is an ideal type that is hardly ever realized.

Also similarly to Weber, Popper concludes that there can be an objective social science:

> An objective, interpretative *[objektiv-verstehende]* social science can be developed independently of all subjective or psychological ideas. It consists in sufficiently analyzing the *situation* of the acting subject so as to explain the action in terms of the situation without any further psychological support. Objective "understanding" means that we see that the action was *adequate to the situation.* In other words, the situation is analyzed to such an extent that the seemingly psychological elements, e.g. desires, motives, memories and associations, are transformed into situational conditions. The man with certain desires thus turns into a man whose situation includes the pursuit of certain objective *ends.* And the man with certain memories or associations turns into a man whose situation is characterized by certain theories or information [i.e., *means*] that are at his disposal. That allows us to understand his actions in the objective sense of saying: Personally I have other ends and other theories... but if I had been in his situation... I... would have acted in the same way. (1962:120f, my transl.)

We can conclude that Popper's solution to the problem of hermeneutic understanding of social practice relies on essentially the same presuppositions, and will have the same drawbacks, as Weber's (cf. my earlier discussion). The most remarkable difference is a change in terminology ("situational logic" instead of "purposive-rationality") which shifts the focus from world-2 to world-3 aspects of the situation. This shift of focus is a useful complement to Weber's model but does not of course overcome its blindness for rationality in other than purposive-rational terms.

Still, insofar as social practice can actually be grasped in purposive-rational terms, it makes sense that one should examine the situational logic with regard to the always-present world-3 background *before* turning to a psychological analysis of the world-2 background by means of empathy, or sympathetic re-enactment of the agent's situation, as Collingwood (1946:283) has called it. In this sense we might even agree with Popper that the a priori neglect of the "logic of the situation" (world 3) is a form of psychologism (1972:162).

However, we cannot follow Popper in his attempt to establish a third-world approach to situational analysis as the *only* rational and sufficient way of understanding:

Even some of those who admit the need to analyze the final state of (subjective) understanding in terms of third-world objects will, I fear ... [believe] that we cannot do without such subjective procedures as sympathetic understanding... or the attempt to put ourselves into another person's situation by making his aims and his problems our own.

As against this view my thesis is this. Exactly as a subjective state of understanding finally reached, so a psychological process which leads up to it must be analyzed in terms of the third-world objects in which it is anchored. In fact it can be analyzed *only* in these terms. (1972:163f)

The world "only" is crucial. If the assumption behind this "only" does not hold – namely, the assumption of complete (purposive-) rationality, and thus logical decidability – then one has to admit that the world of subjective knowledge (world 2) must be included in the concept of rationality (and accordingly cannot be reduced to "organismic dispositions"). Popper escapes this objection by referring to his earlier-mentioned *principle of transference*:

What is true in logic is true in psychology. (An analogous principle holds by and large for what is usually called "scientific method" and also for the history of science: what is true in logic is true in scientific method and in the history of science.) (1962:6)

Here it becomes clear that *logicism* cannot do without inherent psychologism and even historicism: it simply claims the validity of logical rules for both psychology and history. This assumption was already underlying Popper's very first step in redefining Hume's problem (cf. above) and is a crucial assumption throughout his epistemology.

It becomes clear then that Popper's vehement attacks against epistemological psychologism and historicism, because they rely on epistemological and psychological logicism, inadvertently turn against Popper's own position.

A final observation to Popper's situational analysis is this: the fact that he gives it so much importance represents an implicit concession that the crucial difficulty of problem solving is *to define the problem situation.* This, however, is the central concern of *heuristics,* or (in Popper's terms) the context of discovery. What should have been clear from the very beginning – and, by the way, already appeared in the title of Popper's first book, *The Logic of Scientific Discovery* – is now at last admitted: the context of discovery is not "relatively irrelevant" but in fact crucial to epistemology, because problems are not just there, waiting for an inquirer. Problems must be discovered, developed, defined by someone who ist prepared to consider them as problems; a trial-and-error model of problem solving, however, is "blind" with respect to this issue. Popper's answer to this "metaproblem" is accordingly helpless:

> Thus my answer to the metaproblem "How can we learn to understand a scientific problem?" is: by learning to understand some *live* problem. And this, I assert, can be done only *by trying to solve it, and by failing to solve it.* (1972:181)

The helplessness of that answer is significant. In order to solve the epistemological problem in an objective way, critical rationalism has excluded one half of the problem and by doing this fails in its critical task. Habermas' well-known phrase is to the point: critical rationalism is "positivistically bisected" *(positivistisch halbiert,* 1964).

5. Conclusions: The Sources of Deception
in Critical Rationalism

A minimal list of the sources of deception in critical rationalism must include the following underlying assumptions:

1. Underlying Metaphysical Assumptions

(a) Critical rationalism wants to avoid metaphysics and thereby ignores the fact that no description or theory of "reality" can ever be completely free of metaphysical assumptions. In the context of application, an inquirer's metaphysics may have important normative implications that ought to be made transparent.

(b) Precisely because it means to avoid the metaphysical question, critical rationalism relies on a strong metaphysical bias which might be called anti-metaphysical realism. It is to be called *naive realism* insofar as it is unreflected realism.

(c) The consequences of this naive realism appear in the following crucial assumptions of critical rationalism: the correspondence theory of truth, the untenable claim for approximation towards truth, and the alleged autonomy of facts. Popper's correspondence theory of truth has not yet overcome the obsolete manifestation theory of truth. Both presuppose a universe of subject-independent facts to which knowledge "corresponds." This *autonomy of facts* is also a necessary condition for the validity of the falsification approach; therefore it is maintained although it is in obvious contradiction to the recognized theoretical ("theory-impregnated") character of all observation.

2. Underlying Psychological Assumption

(a) Critical rationalism considers itself progressively critical of psychologism; that is, it fights the reduction of epistemology to psychological analysis. It is in fact correct to say that psychological analysis is not sufficient for explaining or criticizing human knowledge; however, this cannot mean that it is not *necessary*. Popper's critique of psychologism is too simple because it avoids both the psychological and the metaphysical component of knowledge. The result is *epistemological logicism.* But neither psychology nor metaphysics are irrelevant: Popper's own concept of a "horizon of expectations" implies that they are both necessary in order to reflect critically on the knowledge-constitutive presuppositions of knowledge.

(b) Popper's extreme antipsychologism leads to an *implicit psychologism* of critical rationalism. And because this implicit psychologism is not questioned or even denied, it must be called a naive psychologism. Its sources are behaviorism and cybernetics. The underlying *behaviorism* is most obvious in Popper's equation of subjective with organismic knowledge; the *cybernetic paradigm* appears in Campbell's trial-and-error model of problem solving. Cybernetics itself is clearly behavioristic in that it applies to the explanation of purposeful human action the same objectivist and reductionist framework which behavioristic psychology uses. Insofar as the cybernetic paradigm is uncritically applied to epistemology in order to avoid the problem of human purposefulness, one might speak of metaphysical-psychological "cybernetism."

(c) Because epistemological logicism, behaviorism and "cybernetism" are insufficient to account for the psychological components of knowledge, critical rationalism must establish the so-called *principle of transference:* "What is true in logic is true in psychology." This is a case of *psychological logicism.*

(d) Based on the allegedly "psychological" principle of transference, the logical (cybernetic) principle of trial and error is extended to a psychological theory of heuristics. The empirical support for this transfer is circularly based on Darwinian evolutionism. Apart from its logical and empirical weaknesses, a trial-and-error theory of problem solving is pragmatically helpless: it conceptualizes the crucial step of the discovery and formulation of problems in terms of "blind variation."

(e) Ultimately, the weakness of trial-and-error behaviorism is rooted in its incredibly *poor image of man.* It regards the central qualities of being human as "irrelevant": uniqueness, emotionality, subjective meaningfulness, insight and purposefulness, creativity, self-reflection, and so on. The underlying fallacy is behaviorism's impoverished concept of objectivity, a concept which refuses to consider subjective and unquantifiable qualities of man. As Roger Poole (1972:65) would say: "It is not surprising that behaviorist psychology never tells us anything that we could not have observed for ourselves on the bus."

3. Underlying Scientism and Decisionism

(a) The underlying behaviorist-objective paradigm of critical rationalism is closely connected with its *scientism.* Critical rationalism is scientistic because of its claim for the universal applicability of the scientific method, as regulated by the falsification approach, even to problems of social concern where a hermeneutic understanding of social reality is required (so-called situational analysis). Along with this claim goes an even further-reaching *methodological monism:* the contention that there is only one method of problem solving and inquiry, which is the critically-rational method of trial and error elimination (by comparison with the "facts").

(b) Even within the domain of empirical-analytic inquiry, critical rationalism cannot solve the *preference problem:* How should we rationally choose between alternative theories or design models? Popper's contention: "We do justify our preferences by an appeal to the idea of truth" provides no criterion of preference, for it relies on an untenable *equation of truth with empirical content* of statements.

(c) With regard to the *problem of the empirical basis,* Popper similarly substitutes "objectivity" for "justification" of decisions about basic statements. But the objectivity of the empirical basis turns out to be an *objectivist illusion,* for meaningful basic statements are inevitably embedded in a context of meaning, i.e., a value-laden context of action or experience. With Habermas, we have characterized critical rationalism's basic orientation as one directed toward instrumental control.

(d) The above charge is confirmed by the critical rationalists' recourse to Weber's *decisionistic model* of theory-practice mediation. This model serves to extend the range of the "objective," i.e., critically-rational, method to practical questions, but only at the price of reducing them to technical questions. Practical reason, and rationality in general, is measured against the ideal type of purposive-rationality.

(e) Quite apart from the decisionistic consequences of this ideal type, the tacit supposition that there is only one reasonable definition of rationality is always suspect of ideology. It conceals the fact that some will benefit and others will lose by the practical application of this definition. Popper's appeal to pluralism and to the *"open society,"* and the positivistic version of a "critique of ideology" or "critique of values" advocated by Albert, do not help to overcome the ideological character of critical rationalism so long as its concept of rationality is regarded as value-free.

4. Underlying Value Assumptions

(a) Critical rationalism pretends to be *value-free.* As a consequence it ignores not only the value implications of the problems and theories it deals with, but also the underlying value assumptions of its own epistemological framework.

(b) This is necessarily so because its *concept of criticism* is based on deductive and hence formal logic. But criticism and self-criticism with respect to values requires more than the critique of logical form: it requires a critique that has regard to the material contents of statements (e.g. psychological, moral or social-political implications). "Truth" is not a formal-logical category only; it is logical *and* metaphysical *and* psychological *and* moral *and* social, etc. By its own standard of value-free inquiry, critical rationalism is bound to miss its aim, "approximation toward truth"; and by its own definition of criticism, critical rationalism is bound to be uncritical with respect to its value orientation.

(c) The value orientation underlying critical rationalism is clearly influenced by John Stuart Mill's *liberalism.* The socio-political idea of free competition and concurrence is applied to epistemology and subsequently extended to a concept of social rationality in general (model of the open society). To be sure, such a value orientation is not bad in itself; but it is a source of ideological deception insofar as it is not critically reflected in the framework of critical rationalism. On the contrary, it is linked to a moral claim for uncriticizability and a corresponding refusal to take into account its own critics. *Critique of critical rationalism is a priori considered irrational* and hence irrelevant.

(d) Another consequence of the exclusion of values is critical rationalism's focus on *social technology* or "piecemeal social engineering" (Popper 1957:67, 1966:162f) where social problems are concerned (e.g. social cybernetics, behavior modification, management information systems etc.; in general, design of tools rather than prevention of problems, "technological fix" rather than change of values). This tendency arises because technological or instrumental statements are believed to be objectively decidable insofar as they are derived from nomological hypotheses (so-called tautological transformation), a possibility that is falsely taken for a guarantor of practical reason. Thus, "rational" design for social systems can only deal with what is technologically verifiable; it cannot deal with such categories as quality, aesthetics, religion, politics, or the moral or emotional aspects of social planning. As a result, "practical reason" inadvertently creates a technological imperative which it cannot sufficiently reflect within the framework of critical rationalism.

5. Underlying Concept of Rationality

(a) Critical rationalism employs a completely inadequate concept of rationality. It is inadequate because it implies that the fundamental task of inquiry, the challenge of improving the human condition, cannot be met rationally. Improvement is always improvement in regard to value assumptions and subjective preferences; by referring them to the realm of merely psychological "acts of belief," *critical rationalism immunizes these presuppositions of purposeful problem solving against the efforts of practical reason.*

(b) Critical rationalism's inadequate concept of rationality is explicitly defined in its establishment of *deductive logic as the organon of criticism.* This concept of criticism implies that only what is logically decidable will be admitted as rational criticism. What is not logically decidable is thus considered irrational and excluded from rational inquiry; this category includes not only emotional arguments, but also pragmatic, normative, moral, and religious considerations (among others) insofar as they are inseparably linked to the subjective life-worlds of individuals, i.e., insofar as the principle of transference does not hold (the condition of intersubjective logical decidability).

(c) By reducing rational problem solving to trial-and-error operation with world-3 objects, critical rationalism not only abstracts from the knowing subjects on whose "horizons of expectations" the meaning of problems and solutions depends, but also from the *institutional context* in which these knowing subjects work. It is bound to ignore institutional sources of deception as well as its own contribution to the preservation or creation of those very sources of deception. Worse still, *it identifies such ignorance of institutional conditions, barriers, and consequences of knowledge production with rationality itself* (cf. Bendix 1975:357).

(d) And finally: Defining rational criticism in terms of deductive logic and objectivity offers no help to the inquirer in reflecting on the normative premises of a critically-rational discussion, and upon the practical implications of its results in the context of application: *critical rationalism's concept of criticism cannot be applied to critical self-reflection.* This is why critical rationalism has become so uncritical of itself. And because it is uncritical of itself, it ignores or even denies its own underlying assumptions and hence becomes a source of deception wherever these assumptions are inadequate.

As a result of its concept of rationality, critical rationalism both fails its critical task as an epistemology and is heuristically helpless as a methodology.

What can be preserved from critical rationalism are only those regulative ideas that are not necessarily linked to its concept of rationality, namely:

(1) there is no guarantee for (or ultimate justification of) knowledge;

(2) hence, the idea of justification must be replaced by the idea of criticism;

(3) hence, immunization against criticism is to be avoided; and

(4) interpersonal criticism is a major source of knowledge.

These principles cannot be sustained without three additional principles at least:

(5) criticism without metaphysics is blind just as metaphysics without criticism is empty;

(6) there can be no guarantee for (or ultimate justification of) critical rationality by means of explicit rules; and hence,

(7) self-reflection is a necessary constitutent of "rational" inquiry.

The challenge arising from our review of critical rationalism is to find a broader, more adequate concept of rational criticism, or rationality – "adequate" in view of the challenge to practical reason that the social planner has to face. No better comment can be found to conclude this chapter than what Nicolai Hartmann has written in another context (in an essay on Kant):

The signs of the times are increasing that there must also be an awakening from the criticist slumber, no less than from the "dogmatic" one. For the epistemological problem has shown itself to be basically a metaphysical problem. (1924:160f; my transl.)[31]

---

[31] Hartmann is referring here to Kant's famous remark (in the *Prolegomena:* A 13) that David Hume aroused him from his "dogmatic slumbers."

Chapter Two
The Critical Theory of Jürgen Habermas:
Toward a Transformed Transcendental Approach

That we disavow reflection is positivism.
Jürgen Habermas (1971a:vii)

Introduction

Our review of critical rationalism has led us to the conclusion that it falls back upon logical positivism – or logical empiricism, which is the same thing – because it lacks an adequate concept of rational criticism. For the social planner who does not want to avoid the crucial question of how he can know what constitutes the social reality he struggles to improve, the empiricist strategy is of little help, for it excludes from critical consideration half of the relevant reality (e.g., moral, metaphysical, and political-institutional presuppositions). It is not, of course, the case that the search for an empirical basis is of no importance to the planner's knowledge of social reality. The trouble with logical empiricism and critical rationalism is that they rely on a naive, deceptive conception of what the "empirical" basis of social inquiry and design ought to be.

In the age-old debate between epistemological empiricism (originally: sensualism) and idealism (intellectualism), the pendulum has once again reached the point where it must start to swing back toward the idealist side – not in order to renounce the search for an empirical basis of knowledge altogether, but in order to reflect once more on the sources of deception in the empiricist model, and through this reflection to reconstruct a new, richer, and truly critical concept of what it means to be "empirical."

Such an undertaking cannot shun the fundamental epistemological question that Kant has called the *transcendental question:* What are the conditions of the possibility of (objective) experience? It is obvious that this question cannot be answered, as the positivists answer it, by referring to an independent empirical basis, i.e., a universe of "positive" facts; rather, an answer must show how such facts can positively be established. Popper has meant to detach himself from positivism by asserting that all "facts" are "theory-impregnated" and hence must be treated as mere hypotheses. But his falsificationist methodology falls back into positivism by making those same "facts" the "critical instance" for falsifying theories.

Popper shrinks from pursuing the consequence of his own critique of positivism: namely, the need for questioning the metaphysical and normative presuppositions that inevitably flow into the standards or theories (the "horizon of expectations") on which we rely for establishing the "facts." Such questioning is what transcendental criticism is all about. If our envisaged critical heuristics of social planning is to merit the epithet "critical," it must overcome the positivistic remainder in critical rationalism. It is in regard to this task that we shall attempt, in the later chapters, to develop our heuristic approach through a dialogue with Kant.

The notion that we should go back to Kant in order to develop a non-positivistic systems approach to planning is bound to raise two immediate questions:

1. Has contemporary philosophy as a whole not long since overcome the Kantian transcendental approach?
2. Is there really no contemporary school of philosophy that can offer a viable alternative to Popper's model of rational criticism?

The answer to both questions, I think, is at best a hesitant "yes, but...": yes, but this does not spare us the trouble of going back to Kant and seeking to reconstruct his transcendental criticism.

Re: 1. Yes, it is indeed true that Kant's transcendental method has long since been found to be impossible. There is simply no absolute, i.e., invariant and objective, standpoint from which to oversee and verify the totality of conditions of possible experience in general. One's standpoint is one's blind spot: this everyday insight holds true also for the transcendental approach, for it cannot help relying on a first frame of reference which it cannot itself validate. (In the case of Kant, the underlying frame of reference is evident for instance in his taking Newtonian physics as a general model of science, and in his subsequent neglect of the normative presuppositions of social science.) But the fact that transcendental questioning raises a genuine philosophical difficulty does not of course mean that such questioning is critically irrelevant and that it may safely be disregarded.

Re: 2. The preceding "but" furnishes the central point of attack against positivism for the "critical theory of society" of the Frankfurt school. Among its early members were Max Horkheimer (e.g. 1937 a–b, 1941, 1967), Theodor W. Adorno (e.g. Adorno et al. 1969, Horkheimer/Adorno 1947), Herbert Marcuse (e.g. 1964), Erich Fromm (e.g. 1941, 1947) and others.[1] Among the contemporary critical theorists are Albrecht Wellmer (e.g. 1967, 1970), Claus Offe (e.g. 1972) and others, but the outstanding figure – outstanding in terms of both the range and depth of his work – is of course Jürgen Habermas (e.g. 1957, 1962, 1963, 1964, 1965, 1970 a, 1971 a, 1971 b, 1971 c, 1971 d, 1973 a, 1973 c, 1975, 1979 a, 1981).[2] Habermas has been among the most persistent critics of positivism in general, and of critical rationalism in particular. Not by acci-

---

[1] For a detailed history of the Frankfurt school cf. Martin Jay (1973).
[2] For a comprehensive, though hardly critical, account of Habermas' work cf. McCarthy (1978).

dent has he based his criticism on the observation explained above, namely, that positivism cuts off the "transcendental-logical inquiry into the conditions of possible knowledge" (1971a:67), and that "Popper does not take the way back to the transcendental dimension, though this way is called for in consequence of his own criticism." (1964, in Adorno et al. 1969:242, my transl.)

Before entering upon our dialogue with Kant, it is therefore worthwhile to consider what Habermas' critical theory (of society) can contribute to the development of a critical heuristics (of social planning) that would not ignore the transcendental question. Of particular interest to us is Habermas' attempt to construct a model of rational discourse, for such a model might answer our quest for a concept of rationality that would merit the title "critical." Moreover, this model takes a systematic place in Habermas' bold conception of a "transformed transcendental philosophy," a conception that is of obvious interest for any non-objectivistic approach to rational criticism.

Due to the considerable scope and intrinsic difficulty of Habermas' work; due also to the fact that his work is still very much in progress, the task of reviewing any portion of this work is not an easy one. In the rather lengthy discussion which follows I have sought to clarify the nature and significance of his work by focusing on three of his themes that promise to be of systematic importance for our own effort: (1) his conception of a transformed transcendental philosophy and the role of the "theory of cognitive interests" in it; (2) his model of oppression-free discourse and the underlying approach toward a "universal pragmatics" or "theory of communicative competence," and (3) the application of this model to the problem of practical reason and morality. In a fourth section of the present chapter, we shall attempt to draw the necessary conclusions from this discussion for our program of a critical heuristics.

Let me point out from the start that this last section is crucial to the entire book. The main benefit to be derived from the following discussion of Habermas' work should be that it will help us to clarify our own purpose and standpoint in critical distinction to his. Although there is much to be learned from Habermas' insights into the scope and difficulties of the theoretical task which he has mapped out for himself – the task of constructing a model of critical social inquiry that would not cut off the transcendental question – the reader should keep in mind that the purpose of the present study is heuristic rather than theoretical. The first two sections of the chapter mainly serve as a preparation for the third and fourth section, where I examine the difficulties and the unpractical nature of Habermas' model of discursive rationality and, on this basis, define the crucial requirements for a heuristic approach that is to avoid these drawbacks without circumventing the transcendental question.[3]

---

[3] The reader who wishes to gain a somewhat more detailed picture of what we are going to learn from Habermas before he reads the chapter should turn to Section Four and read the brief introduction to that section.

1. The Conception of a Transformed Transcendental Philosophy, and the Role of the Theory of Cognitive Interests in It

Rational criticism in the sense of critical theory distinguishes itself from critical rationalism and logical positivism by the reflection on its own presuppositions and implications with regard to social practice. Positivism[4] narrowly equates practical rationality with instrumental reason – an approach that can understand itself as value-free only because it conceals from itself both its own dependency on normative social practice and the repercussions it has on that practice. In opposition to positivism, critical theory maintains the Kantian ideal of "the comprehensive rationality of reason that becomes transparent to itself." (Habermas 1971a:3) In *Knowledge and Human Interests* (1971a), Habermas traces the dissolution of the Kantian ideal, and with it the metamorphosis of epistemology into methodology of science, "over abandoned stages of reflection." (1971a:vii) Habermas describes this work as a "historically oriented attempt to reconstruct the prehistory of modern positivism with the systematic intention of analyzing the connections between knowledge and human interests." (1971a:vii) Since this work represents the origin not only of his theory of cognitive interests but also of his conception of a transformed transcendental philosophy, and of the subsequent turn to an "universal pragmatics," I shall begin with a very brief review of the main line of Habermas' thought in this work.

1.1. Knowledge and Human Interests: Toward a Renewed Transcendental Approach

The "natural" starting point that would have seemed to offer itself for Habermas' search for a comprehensive, non-objectivist concept of rationality is Kant. Through Kant's transcendental criticism, "epistemology first became conscious of itself and thereby entered its own singular dimension." (1971a:3) In Kant, the previously separated currents of British empiricism (Locke, Hume, Berkeley) and German rationalism (Leibniz, Wolff) came together to produce an epistemological approach whose philosophical level of (self-) reflection was and remains unique.[5] In Habermas' view, the post-Kantian development of philosophy, beginning with Hegel's critique of Kant and Marx' subsequent metacritique of Hegel, could not maintain this reflective level. Hegel recognized the unrealistic and unacknowledged presuppositions in Kant's abstract construct of the knowing subject as an absolute, self-contained origin of knowledge, i.e., a "transcendental unity of consciousness." He therefore tried to

---

[4] Because critical rationalism has been shown to fall back on the logical positivism it means to criticize, I shall use the label "positivism" as a convenient name for both logical positivism and critical rationalism wherever their shared shortcomings are concerned.

[5] I shall deal in Chapter 3 with the ways in which both British empiricism and German rationalism failed their epistemological tasks and thus stimulated Kant to his seminal synthesis of the two currents.

radicalize Kant's transcendental criticism by turning to a phenomenological and dialectical self-reflection of the knowing subject, *The Phenomenology of Mind* (1807). Marx pursued this radicalization of Kant's transcendental criticism by introducing the "social turn" into epistemology. He was the first to recognize clearly that the conditions of possible knowledge cannot be located entirely within the (self-reflective) knowing subject but are rooted in the empirical and historical structure of social practice, particularly in the contingent material conditions of work, or, as Marx liked to say, of the self-reproduction of the human species. The decisive dialectic for him was therefore not in the self-reflective process of the knowing subject (who thereby becomes its own subject) but rather in the process of work, in which human subjectivity – the realm of the "spiritual" – and the objective forces of nature and human society – the realm of the "material" – meet and coproduce human consciousness, interest and knowledge.[6]

Both Hegel's critique of Kant and Marx' metacritique were necessary and insightful steps toward a radicalization of the transcendental question. But paradoxically, each in his own way contributed to the subsequent self-abolition of epistemology in favor of a positivist methodology of science. Hegel's phenomenological self-reflection of the knowing subject did not lead to a more reflective or realistic account of the a priori conditions of empirical knowledge but to a philosophy of "absolute spirit," a philosophy that misunderstood itself as a science of absolute knowledge and thus could not perform a critical epistemological function vis-à-vis the progressing empirical sciences. As for Marx, his insight into the necessity of a "social turn" in epistemology enabled him to overcome both Kant's and Hegel's artificial constructions of the knowing subject as a transcendental consciousness or a self-reflectively forming absolute spirit; but he too failed to pursue the radical implications of his insights for social epistemology and instead understood his work as a science of the "laws" of the evolution of (capitalist) society.

The result of this self-abolition of critical epistemology was the triumph of positivism. In the light of the striking progress of the natural sciences, epistemological reflection appeared more and more as just another part of "mother philosophy" from which the sciences had finally emancipated themselves. Epistemology had to be replaced by a logic or methodology of science that was to be developed within the framework of the natural sciences. Logical positivism and Popper's critical rationalism accordingly replaced Kant's "transcendental logic" with deductive logic as the "organon of criticism" (cf. Ch. 1). This is precisely what we mean by "positivism": the denial of the very possibility of a transcendental reflection on the conditions and meaning of knowledge, and the elevation of the procedures of empirical-analytic science itself to a guarantor of meaningful knowledge. "That we disavow reflection *is* positivism." (Habermas 1971a:vii)

---

[6] For the development of Marx' "social turn" cf. particularly his early writings from the doctoral dissertation of 1840 to the *Communist Manifesto* of 1848, collected in Siegfried Landshut's edition (Marx 1953).

There were, however, three thinkers who, in Habermas' interpretation, made important first steps toward a revival of epistemological (transcendental) self-reflection from *within* the boundaries of positivist science: Charles S. Peirce (1839–1914), the founder of pragmaticism[6a]; Wilhelm Dilthey (1833–1911), the pioneer of the historical-hermeneutic sciences *(Geisteswissenschaften);* and Sigmund Freud (1856–1939), the founder of psychoanalysis. Habermas associates with these three thinkers his three forms of science: empirical-analytic, historical-hermeneutic, and "emancipatory" or critically oriented science. In his view, however, each of these thinkers succumbed to a "scientistic self-misunderstanding" of his respective approach. Here we have the original point of departure for Habermas' conception of a transformed transcendental philosophy: he conceived of the plan to reconstruct the critical epistemological implications of the work of Peirce, Dilthey, and Freud in such a way as to overcome their scientistic self-misunderstanding. Habermas established the basic framework for this reconstruction in his theory of cognitive, or "knowledge-constitutive," interests.

I have given a brief sketch of this theory in the context of my critique of the objectivist illusion in Popper's solution to the problem of the empirical basis. There is no need for repeating the argument here, but it is perhaps useful to recall its conclusion. To quote Habermas:

Orientation toward technical control, toward mutual understanding in the conduct of life, and toward emancipation from seeingly 'natural' constraint establish the specific viewpoints from which we can apprehend reality as such in any way whatsoever. (1965, in 1971a:311)

We should now begin to understand the systematic place of the theory of cognitive, or "knowledge-constitutive," interests in Habermas' quest for "the comprehensive rationality of reason that becomes transparent to itself." In ascribing a "transcendental" function to the three basic interests (e.g. in 1971a:194), Habermas avoids the problem of an absolute starting point for transcendental reflection without giving up the Marxian conception that the knowledge-constitutive (transcendental) categories must be sought in the basic historical categories characterizing the social life-world, without however succumbing to Marx' reduction of social practice to production, i.e., to instrumental action. Thus the technical, practical, and emancipatory interests are given a constitutive role as three basic "starting points" for transcendental reflection on the conditions and meaning of possible knowledge. They refer to the "transcendental limits" of objective knowledge, limits that are rooted in the three basic modes of social organization: work (instrumental action), language (communicative action, mutual understanding), and power (ideological and institutional barriers to emanci-

---

[6a] Habermas speaks of *pragmaticism* rather than *pragmatism* because his understanding of historical-hermeneutic science has nothing to do with the common understanding of American pragmatism (Peirce, Dewey, James) according to which "true is what works." Rather, he seeks to incorporate into his epistemology contemporary *pragmatics* which is dealing with the pragmatic aspect of communication processes. Cf. note 8 to Chapter Four (p. 240).

pation from oppression).[7] Although no form of inquiry or rational discourse can ever "outwit" these transcendental limits, it is always possible to reflect back on them as conditions on which meaningful description of "reality" depends (cf. Habermas 1965, in 1971a:311, 313).

In the form of these "interests," then, comprehensive rationality makes transparent to itself its own dependency upon anticipated social practice. In opposition to the "utopia" of instrumental control over historical social practice implied in the positivistic concept of rationality (cf.1973a:275), comprehensive rationality proposes a utopia that would consist of emancipating man from domination by man and machine. The realm of validity of instrumental reason is restricted to its proper object domain, i.e., the realm of objectified processes in the context of instrumental action. Practical reason is entrusted with the task of maintaining, against instrumental reason's claim to universality, the utopia of the good life and the just, oppression-free, society (mutual understanding and emancipation).

Let us now turn to the notion of a "transcendental" status of Habermas' knowledge-constitutive interests (or the underlying historical utopiae). Thus far it has been presented as a mere presumption which remains to be justified. Can a theory of knowledge-constitutive interests satisfactorily resolve the dilemma posed by Kant's impossible, but unavoidable transcendental analysis of the necessary (subjective) conditions of possible (objective) knowledge?

The broad international discussion following the publication of *Knowledge and Human Interests* revealed numerous difficulties and doubts regarding the "transcendental" status of the technical, practical, and particularly the emancipatory interests. They are of course not transcendental in the full Kantian sense of absolute a priori categories, i.e., they do not stand for strictly universal conditions of possible knowledge that would go beyond (transcend) any empirical or historical contingencies. As Habermas himself writes,

these conditions are no longer a priori *in themselves,* but only *for the* process of inquiry.... [They] have a transcendental function, but they determine the architectonic of processes of inquiry and not that of transcendental consciousness as such.... They have a transcendental function but arise from actual structures of human life: from structures of a species that reproduces its life both through learning processes of socially organized labor and processes of mutual understanding in interactions mediated in ordinary language. (1971a:194)

In this peculiar position, somewhere between empirically contingent and strictly transcendental conditions of knowledge, lies both the strength and weakness of Habermas' idea of cognitive interests – strength, because they overcome the Kantian abstraction from those historical and social contexts of discovery and application that

---

[7] Cf. also Habermas' definition of the term "interest": "I term *interests* the basic orientations rooted in specific fundamental conditions of the possible reproduction and self-constitution of the human species [the knowing subject, that is], namely, *work* and *interaction.*" (1971a:196)

alone give practical meaning to knowledge; weakness, because they can no longer serve as an absolute ground of determination of *knowledge* but only as guides to *critique,* i.e., reflection on the contingent and systematic sources limiting the validity and meaning of possible knowledge.

However, it seems to me that one should not accuse Habermas, as some of his critics have done, of those consequences of his approach that are necessarily involved in any attempt at a post-Kantian renewal of transcendental reflection. There are genuine philosophical difficulties raised by the transcendental question, difficulties that Kant could avoid only at a price that we are no longer willing to pay, namely, the abstraction from the social and historical context on which meaningful inquiry and criticism depend. On the other hand, there are of course other difficulties that are not necessarily consequences of the transcendental question but rather depend on Habermas' specific understanding of critical social theory. These difficulties require critical examination well beyond the scope and intent of the present book. I shall, however, attempt to highlight some of those basic difficulties in Habermas' approach which our own "heuristic" approach should consider and perhaps even resolve. But let us postpone these critical comments until we have thrown at least a summary glance at Habermas' own response to the difficulties of the theory of cognitive interests, and until we have examined in some detail his model of rational discourse.

1.2. The A Priori of Experience vs. the A Priori of Argumentation

In a postscript to *Knowledge and Human Interests,*[8] Habermas (1973b) introduces a distinction which is not yet contained in *Knowledge and Human Interests* but which helps to clarify many of the difficulties of a post-Kantian approach to transcendental reflection.[9] Referring to Karl-Otto Apel's (1967–70) distinction between "constitution of meaning" *(Sinnkonstitution)* and "reflection on validity" *(Geltungsreflektion),* he proposes to distinguish two types of "transcendental" questions that a transformed transcendental philosophy, as he calls it, would have to consider:

(a) the question of the "a priori of experience" *(Erfahrungsapriori),* and
(b) the question of the "a priori of argumentation" *(Argumentationsapriori,* also called "a priori of communication" by Apel 1972; cf. Habermas 1973b:382–293).

The *a priori of experience* takes up one intention of Kant's transcendental question: What are the conditions that precede (are a priori to) the constitution of objects of experience and give it meaning? The *a priori of argumentation* concerns a second

---

[8] The *Postscript* (1973b) is contained in the appendix to the German pocket book edition of *Erkenntnis und Interesse* but not in the English edition *Knowledge and Human Interests.* A translation of the *Postscript* has appeared in *Philosophy of the Social Sciences* 3 (1975):157–189. I quote from the original.
[9] This same distinction is anticipated, though not yet fully developed, in Habermas 1970b:126f.

intention of the transcendental question: What are the conditions for justifying the truth claims of statements about objects of experience, i.e., assertions of "facts"? (The same question also applies to validity claims of statements about values, i.e., assertions of "norms.") Because Kant still assumed that the transcendental approach, taking as a point of departure an abstract transcendental subject, could yield universally necessary and sufficient conditions of objective experience, "objectivity" and "truth" implied each other and the a priori of experience was congruent with the a priori of argumentation. This is no longer the case once we have recognized the limited, normative character of any viewpoint from which we can apprehend reality or assert the validity of statements about "facts" and "norms." The *objectivity* of experience then becomes a question of sharing intersubjectively the categories or *conceptual frameworks* that are constitutive of our experience, whereas the *truth* (validity) of assertions becomes a question of establishing mutually binding standards of valuation by means of intersubjective *discourse.*

The *objectivity* of an experience means that everyone can count on the success or failure of certain actions;[10] the *truth* of a proposition asserted in a discourse means that everyone can be motivated by reasons to acknowledge the validity claim of the assertion as justified. (1973b:389, my transl.)

If the validity claim in question concerns the assertion of "facts," Habermas calls the discourse required a *theoretical discourse;* if however the validity of norms (e.g. standards of evaluation, rules of action) is asserted, he speaks of a *practical discourse* (cf.1973b:391).

It should be apparent that the *theory of cognitive interests* responds only to the problem of the *a priori of experience:* it investigates the fundamental conditions of the possibility of "objective" (intersubjectively shared and meaningful) experience. That is, it is a basic contribution to a *constitution theory of experience.* But it does not address itself to the other question: What are the conditons of the possibility of intersubjective vindication of validity claims, i.e., the conditions of "true" consensus about assertions? This latter question concerns the *a priori of argumentation.* It requires a *consensus theory of truth,* that is, a theory of truth that demonstrates how theoretical and practical statements can be discursively validated so that we know a factual consensus about them is not merely contingent but can be justified with good reasons. In reference to this requirement, Habermas speaks of "rational consensus" and of "rational discourse." Hence, a model of rational discourse becomes a crucial part of Habermas' program of a "transformed transcendental philosophy." Before we turn to a detailed examination of Habermas' model of discourse, *Table 2/1* gives an overview of his conception of a transformed transcendental philosophy and the place both of the theory of cognitive interests and of a model of discourse in it. (Table 2/1

---

[10] (My annotation) A trivial example may be helpful: if I describe to my wife a tie I have seen in a shop so that she can go and buy precisely this tie as my birthday present, our experience of the tie is "objective" in the sense intended here.

114

anticipates some of the issues that we shall have to clarify in the following discussion, thus the reader should not worry if everything does not seem clear to him at this point; but he may want to turn back to this table later on, lest he get lost in details.)

Kant's Transcendental Question

A Priori of Experience:	*A Priori of Argumentation:*
Requires a *constitution theory of experience* that would clarify the conditions of intersubjectively meaningful experience → "objectivity"	Requires a *consensus theory of truth* that would clarify the conditions of argumentative justification of controversial validity claims → "truth"
Deals with the constitution of *objects* of possible experience ↓	Deals with the discursive redemption of validity claims, i.e., assertions of *facts* or *norms* ↓
1. Contexts of experience and action on which the meaning of experience and "objectivity" depends 2. Conceptual frameworks, i.e., categories that are constitutive of our experience within such contexts	1. Types of validity claims involved in theoretical and practical statements 2. Rules of rational discourse that can guarantee "true" (rational) consensus about such validity claims
Apel: "constitution of meaning"	Apel: "reflection on validity"

Previous Approaches

Peirce: pragmatic a priori	Apel: the a priori of communication
Dilthey: communicative a priori of experience	

Contributions by Habermas

Theory of cognitive interests	*A model of rational discourse*
(responds to problem 1. above, defines three basic contexts of experience and action: instrumental, communicative action and self-reflection, and corresponding object-domains of empirical-analytic, historical-hermeneutic, and critically oriented science)	(responds to problems 1. and 2. above) theoretical practical discourse discourse (on "facts") (on "norms")

Table 2/1: Basic issues in a transformed transcendental philosophy

115

2. A Model of Oppression-Free Discourse

With regard to the a priori of argumentation, the basic issue is the need for a consensus theory of truth. Such a consensus theory is intended to fulfill two major critical tasks.

First, it is to overcome the uncritical correspondence theory of truth that is at the bottom of critical rationalism's failure to furnish an adequate model of rational criticism. The uncritical aspects in question are mainly these:

(a) The ontological or objectivist illusion arising from the unquestioned assumption of a fixed reality, a universe of subject-independent "facts" that could be recognized as such.

> *Any* transcendental approach from the very first excludes the notion that there can be a fidelity of assertions vis-à-vis empirical reality *[Wirklichkeitstreue]* in the sense of realism. Correspondence theories of truth amount to a hypostatization of facts as entities in the world; uncovering an objectivist illusion in this view belongs to the intent and logic of any epistemology that reflects on the conditions of the possibility of experience in general. (1973b:408f, my transl.)

(b) The correspondence theory of truth, because it ignores the distinction between the a priori of experience and the a priori of argumentation, confuses objectivity (of experience) and truth (of assertions). In Chapter One (Sec. 1.3, p. 53f) we found that Popper's theory of falsification indeed depended on the equation of empirical content or testability (= objectivity) with approximation to truth. It was one of our chief criticisms that empirical content, as defined by the falsification approach, has nothing to do with truth, only with intersubjective testability (objectivity) and precision.

> The conditions of objectivity of experience can be clarified in a *theory of the constitution of objects;* they are not identical with the conditions of argumentation, which can be clarified in a *theory of truth* unfolding the logic of discourse, though they are connected with the latter through the structures of linguistic intersubjectivity. (1973b:389, my transl.)

As soon as this distinction is recognized, it becomes clear that the truth of assertions can only be discursively established, regardless of whether the assertions in question concern "facts" or norms (values, standards, purposes, etc.).

> Experiences *support* the truth claim of assertions.... But a truth claim can be redeemed only through argumentation. A claim *founded* in experience is by no means a *justified* claim. (1973c:218, my transl.)[11]

Second, not every consensus necessarily represents a justified validity claim. It is therefore the second major task of a consensus theory of truth to establish criteria for distinguishing "true" consensus from "false" consensus, i.e., merely factual, contingent, consensus. If every consensus were regarded as a source of validation for practical assertions, this would amount to reintroducing the very decisionism from which critical rationalism suffers. Against this danger, Habermas posits as his basic assertion that "practical questions admit of truth." (1975:111; "truth" is to be read here in the general sense of "justification.") It is important to keep this basic assertion of Habermas in mind, for it implies that we shall be dealing with a conceptual boundary experiment that can succeed only under ideal conditions. This is so because the problem of reducing decisions to rational argument remains today an unresolved philosophical task – there is always an inevitable decisionistic remainder in the process of validating claims, as we have seen in our discussion of the problem of decisionism in Chapter 1. Such a boundary experiment, even though it may fail, is an important step toward a critical understanding of the sources of deception in all consensus. But let us keep in mind that it might itself become a source of deception, namely, if we expect it to yield a model of discourse that could do without any decisionistic remainder.

Let us now examine Habermas' attempt to construct a model of both theoretical and practical discourse, a model that would operationalize and vindicate the idea of a consensus theory of truth. This construction attempt, it must be noted, is still in progress. The thus-far most important publications in this direction have been a paper written in Habermas' debate with Luhmann on social systems theory, "Vorbereitende Bemerkungen zu einer Theorie der kommunikativen Kompetenz" (1971c); two chapters in the book *Legitimation Crisis* (1975, German orig. 1973) entitled "The Relation of Practical Questions to Truth" and "The Model of the Suppression of Generalizable Interests"; and the three articles "Towards a Theory of Communicative Competence" (1970d), "Wahrheitstheorien" (1973c) and "What is Universal Pragmatics?" (1979a) – the latter two providing the most complete statement of Habermas' approach available today. What follows is an attempt to review in some detail the basic premises and conclusions contained in these writings.[12]

---

[11] A "justified" claim is one for which good reasons are provided. Thomas McCarthy, in a note to his introduction to Habermas' *Legitimation Crisis* (1975:145, note 17), explains:

> I have translated *begründen*... as 'justify'. This has, perhaps, connotations in English that it need not have in German, as Karl Popper and his followers have equated justification with deductive proof and attacked it as an unattainable goal even for the natural sciences. But... Habermas rejects this identification. As he employs the term, *Begründung* is a matter of providing good grounds or reasons *(Gründe)* for a claim; it is a pragmatic rather than a syntactical notion.

[12] According to an oral communication by Habermas (February 5, 1980), his long-awaited book *Wahrheit und Diskurs (Truth and Discourse)* will not appear for the time being. Habermas is presently working on a theory of communicative action. (Postscriptum 1982: After completion of my manuscript, the two volumes of Habermas' *Theorie des kommunikativen Handelns* were published [1981]. As far as I can see, the new work does not question the basic premises of Habermas' discourse model such as they are contained in the above-mentioned earlier publications; rather, the new book aims to develop a communication-theoretic paradigm for a critical social *theory* that would conceive of "rationalization" not only in terms of Weber's ideal type of purposive-rational action, as do traditional social theory and cotemporary systems theory of society, but also – and primarily – in terms of communicative action.)

2.1. The Principle of Publicity

The question "How can we distinguish a true from a false consensus?" can be given the more basic form: "When do we call an assertion true?" Since this question is not to be answered in terms of correspondence between that which is asserted and a hypostatized, fixed reality, there remains only one principal possibility: instead of referring to "reality," one can refer to the judgement of others about the assertion in question. The more persons judge and agree, the more an assertion will become credible. The first premise of a consensus theory of truth is therefore: "The condition of the truth of assertions is the potential agreement of *all* others." (1971c:124 and 1973c:219; note again that we are dealing with a boundary case.)

The underlying principle is the *principle of publicity* or *general accessability:* any other person must be able to convince himself that my assertion is warranted by reasons that are publicly acceptable and that it does not merely conceal private motives. In his Habilitation thesis *Strukturwandel der Öffentlichkeit* (1962), Habermas gave an in-depth analysis of the rise and fall of the liberal model of the public domain in the bourgeois-capitalist state. This model is based on the idea that publicly relevant decisions ought to be made by public processes of discursive will-formation rather than by the arbitrary political rule of established authorities, as is the case in the absolutist state. Political dominion is to be "dissolved" into discourse, and the medium of this dissolution is the public domain (1962:101ff). This "fiction of a discursive formation of the will that dissolves political rule" (1973a:4) is at the bottom of the classical liberal model of the public domain; it is the exact opposite of the model of decisionism. Decisionism assumes that *"auctoritas non veritas facit legem"* (Hobbes, power rather than truth makes the law). The principle of publicity aims at the reversed case in which *"veritas non auctoritas facit legem"* (cf. 1962:104f, 110f).

In a functioning public, competing private interests are subject to rational argument, and conflicts are decided not by power but by the *better argument*. But the liberal model presupposes two necessary conditions that are no longer warranted in the contemporary bourgeois state:

(a) Public processes of will-formation, if they are to merit the title "public," must be completely transparent and accessible to every citizen.

The bourgeois [model of the] public domain stands and falls with the principle of general accessibility. A public from which definable groups are excluded is not merely incomplete but is no public at all. (1962:107, my transl.)

(b) The liberal model presupposes a strict separation between the sphere of (competing) private interests and the sphere of government, so that the public can function as a mediator between the two and legitimize the latter (cf. 1962:211). Today, however, organized group interests in the form of political parties, trade associations, unions, private corporations, pressure groups, etc. have established themselves between the private and government spheres so that these two spheres are no longer separate.[13] This undermines the functioning of the public domain as a meeting place of equal and sovereign citizens. The intended substitution of the better argument for political power becomes illusory and decisionism, in the form of internal and external sources of governmental selectivity that are not publicly transparent,[14] is effectively reintroduced into the process of will-formation.

In order to meet condition (a), Habermas must insist that a discourse can produce rational consensus only when "all others," i.e., all citizens, are admitted to participate in the discourse. Since this condition can never be practically fulfilled, it seems reasonable to restrict "all others" to "all those actually or potentially affected by a decision or a plan." Of course, this raises the question of how we can know the group of those who are or might be affected. And since in many cases the only critical answer will be that we cannot know for sure, the restriction is not particularly helpful. Perhaps for this reason Habermas uses it rarely. He does use it mainly in *Legitimation Crisis,* where the emphasis is more on political than on epistemological aspects of the problem of practical reason:

The appropriate model [for validating normative assertions] is rather the communication community of those affected, who as participants in a practical discourse test the validity claims of norms and, to the extent that they accept them with reasons, arrive at the conviction that in the given circumstances the proposed norms are 'right'. (1975:105)

Moreover, even where it is possible to determine the group of those affected, the restricted condition (a) remains counterfactual, for rarely are all those affected able to participate in a rational discourse. Think of those who are not there to argue and vote because they are too young, unborn, or handicapped by other reasons; or of those who are not willing or able to formulate their concerns "rationally." We shall draw the necessary critical conclusions later on (Section 4). Still, I prefer the restricted form, for although it is hardly more "operational" to speak of the affected rather than of the citizens in general, this formulation has the advantage of pointing to the crucial moral issue: How can we justify the possibility that somebody belongs to the group of those affected without at the same time belonging to the group of those *involved?* The "restricted" formulation can thus serve as a critical reminder of the normative content of every possible consensus about what social reality is or what it ought to be.

[13] Cf. in this context John Kenneth Galbraith's (1975:139) concept of the "bureaucratic symbiosis" between government and group interests, esp. in the form of an easy and permanent exchange of personnel, and his consequent call for an "emancipation of the state" from organized private interests.

[14] Cf. Claus Offe's (1972:65ff) theory of governmental selectivity (briefly explained in Section 3.4, note 33 of the present chapter) and Habermas' analysis (1962:217ff) of how the originally critical, political, function of the principle of publicity has been perverted, in the bourgeois-capitalist state, into a demonstrative and manipulative function ("public relations," "public opinion polls," "publicity" in the modern sense of advertising).

Condition (b), in Habermas' model of rational discourse, takes the form of an "oppression-free" discourse, i.e., a discourse that must not be subject to empirically contingent constraints such as power, ideological and institutional constraints, for these constraints might systematically distort the communication among participants and thus undermine the force of the better argument. This requirement leads us to the second major supposition of Habermas' model of discourse, the "ideal speech situation."

2.2. The Ideal Speech Situation and the Four Validity Claims

I call a speech situation ideal where communications are not only not hindered by external, contingent influences but also not hindered by constraints *[Zwänge]* originating in the structure of communication itself. The ideal speech situation excludes systematic distortion of communication. More precisely, the structure of communication produces no constraints if and only if there is a symmetrical distribution of the chances of all participants in the discourse to select and perform speech acts. From this general requirement of symmetry we can derive specific requirements [of symmetry] for the different classes of speech acts. (1973 c:255, my transl.; cf. also 1970 c:131 and 1971 c:137)

In order to understand Habermas' requirements with regard to the "structure of communication itself," we must first introduce the term "spech acts." Speech acts are the elementary units of linguistic communication, e.g. making a statement, asking a question, giving a command, etc. Important contributions to a theory of speech acts have been provided by John L. Austin (1962) and John R. Searle (1969). By referring to the elementary units of discourse as speech acts rather than as words or sentences, we make it clear that we are concerned not so much in the grammatical (syntactic) or semantic structure of well-formed sentences but in the *pragmatic* structure of cogent argumentation. "To argue" means situating (or "embedding," as Habermas says) well-formed sentences in specific relations to reality (1979:29). In every speech act, we communicate *with* somebody *about* something and thereby also express our *own* subjectivity.[15] Accordingly, Habermas distinguishes three pragmatic functions that speech acts can serve (1979 a:66f):

1. Speech acts can refer to the "external world," i.e., the objectified segment of reality which is accessible to sensory experience and about which we can make "true" or

---

[15] Habermas speaks of a "double structure of speech": every speech act moves (a) at the "level of intersubjectivity on which speaker and hearer, through illocutionary acts, establish the relations that permit them to come to an understanding with one another, and [(b)] the level of propositional content which is communicated." (1979 a:42) The "illocutionary force" of a speech act, according to Austin (1962:99, 147), is its capacity to move the listener to enter into a communicative relationship and to recognize the speaker's intent as sincere; "We can also say that [it] consists in fixing the communicative function of the content uttered." (1979 a:34, cf. also 1971 c:104f)

"false" statements. Habermas calls such speech acts *"constative"* speech acts, for they serve to "state" (assert) facts; e.g., descriptions, accounts, predictions, negations, etc. (cf. 1971c:111f, 1979a:53).

2. Speech acts can refer to "our social world" of shared cultural patterns and norms, i.e., the symbolically prestructured segment of reality that is accessible to "communicative experience" (experience mediated through language) and with the normative content of which we can either conform ("right") or disagree ("wrong"). The pragmatic function of such speech acts is *"regulative,"* for they serve to "regulate" interpersonal relationships through the assertion of legitimate norms: e.g. recommendations, commands, prohibitions, excuses, promises, refusals, etc. (cf. 1971c:112, 1979a:54).

3. Finally, speech acts can refer to "my own inner world," i.e., that segment of reality to which the speaker has a privileged access – his feelings, intentions, wishes, etc. – and which he can either express "truthfully" or else conceal or express "untruthfully." In this case we have *"expressive"* speech acts, for they serve to "express" the speaker's subjectivity; e.g. confessions, disavowals, wishes, hopes, etc. (cf. 1971c:112, 1979a:58).[16]

We can then apply the general symmetry requirement to each of these three pragmatic functions of speech acts. Unfortunately, Habermas' specification of these requirements is less systematic than what we are accustomed to from this brilliant writer. The different elements must be brought together from various pieces in 1971c, 1973c, and 1979a. It seems to me that the following requirements are essential to Habermas' concept of the ideal speech situation:

1. All potential participants in a discourse must have the same chance to speak *at all,* that is, to initiate an argument and to perpetuate it through argument and counterargument (cf. 1971c:137, 1973c:255). This requirement excludes *external constraints* such as power and institutional barriers.

2. With regard to *internal constraints* – those constraints that originate in the structure of communication itself – all participants must have the same "chance" to employ *constative, regulative,* and *expressive* speech acts. In Habermas' words:

> All participants in the discourse must have the same chance to establish assertions, recommendations, explanations and justifications, as well as to question *[problematisieren],* prove or disprove the involved validity claims, so that no prejudgement will remain unreflected and unchallenged for long. (1973c:255, my transl., cf. similarly 1971c:137)

---

[16] In this case Habermas also speaks of "representative" speech acts (e.g. in 1971c:112, 1973c:256). But since in 1979a he also says of constative speech acts that they serve a "representative" function – they "represent facts," cf. 1979a:67, 68 – I prefer to use only the terms "constative" and "expressive" respectively.

These first two requirements are relatively "trivial"; they simply require "equal distribution of the chances to employ speech acts." The first requirement implies a *"virtualization* [i.e., a temporary suspension] *of the constraints of action* [and experience]" in which all speech acts are embedded (1971c:117). The second requires the *"virtualization of validity claims"* which we always link to our speech acts, "so that all motives except that of a cooperative search for mutual understanding are rendered inoperative (1971c:117, my transl., similarly 1973a:18).

3. But such virtualization, and the equality of chances to employ speech acts, remain meaningless if there is no assurance that the participants are effectively and equally competent to argue convincingly, i.e., to substantiate the validity claims they raise by their arguments. I shall explain these validity claims in a moment; the point here is that a rational discourse cannot come about if the participants do not ascribe to each other the competence to substantiate or "make good" their speech-act-immanent validity claims. The third basic requirement of the ideal speech situation, then, consists in a *mutual imputation of accountability:*

> When we encounter a discussion partner *[ein Gegenüber]* as a subject rather than an object that we can manipulate, we (unavoidably) impute to him accountability *[Zurechnungsfähigkeit].* We can enter into an interaction with him, that is to say, meet him at the level of intersubjectivity, only if we suppose that he could account for his actions when asked to do so. We cannot help assuming... that he would be able to explain why in a given situation he behaves the way he does. (1971c:118, my transl.)

This general expectation of accountability of course implies not only that a speaker is capable of substantiating his claims but also that he is willing to do so without deceiving the others about his true intentions; it implies an expectation of *truthfulness* (cf. 1971c:131, 138; 1973c:256).

4. The fourth requirement consists in the *freedom of all participants to move from a given level of rational discourse to a higher, more "radical" one* (metalevel). For instance, if there is an exchange of argument and counterargument and a consensus arises about which one is the "better" argument, then a participant may wish to question the selectivity of the conceptual framework on which the discussion has thus far relied. This requirement must await further explanation in connection with the formal structure of argumentation ("logic of discourse") yet to be introduced.

We shall return now to the problem of validity claims immanent in every speech act. If the situation of discourse is such that there is no effective equality of the chances and competences to initiate and pursue an argument, a consensus resulting from the discourse is suspect of being not the result of the "better argument" but rather the result of distorted communication – "distortion" meaning that motives other than that of a cooperative search for understanding and truth have determined the consensus, e.g. motives of power, competition, ideology, etc. This suspicion can be refuted only if each participant in the discourse is prepared (willing and able) to substantiate all the validity claims he raises. Habermas mentions *four basic types of validity claims,* corresponding to the three above-mentioned functions of speech and, in addition, to the need for understandable language as the medium of speech:

1. *Comprehensibility:* "The speaker must choose a comprehensible *[verständlich]* expression so that speaker and hearer can understand one another." (1979 a:2)
2. *Truth:* "The speaker must have the intention of communicating a true *[wahr]* proposition (or a propositional content, the existential presuppositions of which are satisfied) so that the hearer can share the knowledge of the speaker." (1979 a:2)
3. *Truthfulness:* "The speaker must want to express his intentions truthfully *[wahrhaftig]* so that the hearer can believe the utterance of the speaker (can trust him)." (1979 a:2f)
4. *Rightness* (in the sense of normative, e.g. moral, appropriateness): "Finally, the speaker must choose an utterance that is right *[richtig]* so that the hearer can accept the utterance and speaker and hearer can agree with one another in the utterance with respect to a recognized normative background." (1979 a:3)

These four basic claims constitute the universal, normative "validity basis of speech," i.e., "what we must necessarily always already presuppose in regard to ourselves and others as normative conditions of the possibility of understanding; and in this sense, what we must necessarily always already have accepted." (Apel 1976:210); read "understanding" as "rational consensus.") Of course, this validity basis of speech can come about only through the expression of commitment and trust on the part of speakers and listeners; but it is not therefore irrational, a mere "act of belief":

> With their illocutionary acts [i.e., the relationship-establishing component of speech, in contrast to its propositional content, cf. note 15 above], speaker and hearer raise validity claims and demand they be recognized. But this recognition need not follow irrationally, since the validity claims have a cognitive character and can be checked.... [Since] the speech-act-typical commitments take on the character of obligations to provide grounds or to prove trustworthy, the hearer can be rationally motivated by the speaker's signaled engagement to accept the latter's offer [to provide grounds]. (1979 a:63)

Habermas goes on to elucidate this obligation to provide grounds for the three claims: of "truth" (of the propositional content of one's utterances), of "rightness" (of the normative content of one's utterances), and of "truthfulness" (of the speaker's expressed intention).[17]

---

[17] The fourth claim, comprehensibility of utterances, is not at issue in this context. "Naturally there can be no mode of communication in which the intelligibility of an utterance is thematically stressed; for every speech act must fulfill the presupposition of comprehensibility in the same way." (1979 a:57)

1. With regard to the propositional content or the "constative" function of speech acts,

the speaker proffers a speech-act-immanent *obligation to provide grounds [Begründungsverpflichtung]*. Constative speech acts contain the offer to recur if necessary to the *experiential source* from which the speaker draws the *certainty* that his statement is true. If this immediate grounding does not dispel an ad hoc doubt, the persistingly problematic truth claim can become the subject of a theoretical discourse. (1979 a : 63f)

2. With regard to the normative content or the "regulative" function of speech acts,

the speaker proffers a speech-act-immanent *obligation to provide justification [Rechtfertigungsverpflichtung]*. Of course, regulative speech acts contain only the offer to indicate, if necessary, the *normative context* that gives the speaker the *conviction* that his utterance is right. Again, if the immediate justification does not dispel an ad hoc doubt, we can pass over to the level of discourse, in this case of practical discourse. In such a discourse, however, the subject of discursive examination is not the rightness claim directly connected with the speech act, but the validity claim of an underlying norm. (1979 a :64)

3. With regard to the expressive content of the "expressive" ("representative") function of speech acts,

the speaker also enters into a speech-act-immanent obligation, namely the *obligation to prove trustworthy [Bewährungsverpflichtung]*, to show in the consequences of his action that he has expressed just that intention which actually guides his behavior. In case the immediate *assurance* expressing what is *evident* to the speaker himself cannot dispel ad hoc doubts, the truthfulness of the utterance can only be checked against the consistency of his subsequent behavior. (1979 a :64)

The demarcation of these three modes of employing speech acts, and of meeting the obligations involved, is of course only ideal-typical; as a rule, all kinds of validity claims come into play in a rational discourse. Habermas therefore adds:

I am not claiming that every sequence of speech actions can be unequivocally classified under these viewpoints. I am claiming only that every competent speaker has in principle the possibility of unequivocally selecting one mode because with every speech act he *must* raise three universal validity claims, so that he *can* single out one of them to thematize a component of speech. (1979 a :58f)

In analogy to Chomsky's distinction between (ideal) "linguistic competence" and (actual) "linguistic performance" (1965:par. 1&2), Habermas attributes *"communicative competence"* to the ideal speaker who is able to employ speech acts according to the requirements of the ideal speech situation and, in particular, to redeem the validity claims involved in these speech acts (cf. 1971c:101, 117ff; 1979a:26, 29). The *ideal speaker* is thus a necessary counterpart to the ideal speech situation. Taken together, the development of the model of the ideal speech situation (an ideal model of discourse) and of the ideal speaker (a theory of communicative competence) make up a "research program aimed at reconstructing the universal validity basis of speech." To this research program Habermas gives the name of *universal pragmatics,* for it is concerned with reconstructing universal and pragmatic – rather than grammatical – competences (1979a:1, 5); more recently he has preferred the name "formal pragmatics" (cf. 1979a:1, note 1). It is the purpose of this research program to develop a *general theory of undistorted communication,* as the necessary background against which to understand and improve everyday forms of distorted communication.

Habermas does not of course ignore the counterfactual character of his model of undistorted communication:

> We know that institutionalized actions *[discourses]* do not as a rule fit this *model of pure communicative action,* although we cannot avoid counterfactually proceeding as if the model were really the case – on this unavoidable fiction rests the humanity of intercourse among men who are still men. (1971c:120, my transl.)

Even more important is another objection, as Habermas acknowledges: we cannot empirically verify to what extent the ideal speech situation obtains in a given case, and to what extent it does not.

> In retrospect we can often enough determine when we have failed to meet [the conditions of] the ideal speech situation. We lack, however, an external criterion [for measuring the extent to which we have done so]; thus we can never be certain, in a given situation, whether we are conducting a discourse proper or whether we are rather acting under constraints of action and feigning an apparent discourse. (1973a:257, my transl., similarly 1973d:381)

We must thus conclude that the conception of the ideal speech situation does not provide us with a criterion in regard to the question from which we departed: How can we distinguish "true" or "rational" consensus from "false", or merely contingent, consensus?[18]

What then is the use of this conception? There are three other functions that the conception of the ideal speech situation can fulfill:

---

[18] In 1971c:122 Habermas apparently overlooks this implication when he writes: "In each discourse we are required to suppose an ideal speech situation.... Specifically, we must suppose an ideal speech situation in order to gain a sufficient criterion for distinguishing true from false consensus." Likewise, his formulation in 1973c:258 might be misleading:

> This anticipation [of the ideal speech situation] alone is the warrant that permits us to link to an actually attained consensus the claim to a rational consensus. At the same time it is a critical standard against which every factual consensus can be called into question and tested as to whether it stands for a justified consensus.

First, according to Habermas the ideal speech situation is operatively effective in communication even where it is completely counterfactual. It represents an unavoidable "as if" that each participant in a discourse has to suppose. The ideal speech situation is "the normative foundation of communicative understanding [sprachlicher *Verständigung*]," and as such "it is both anticipated and effective as anticipated basis." (1971c:140, 1973c:258) A theory of undistorted communication must take into account this normative basis of rational discourse, regardless of whether or not there is a criterion for verifying it empirically.

Second, the critique of systematically distorted discourse is possible only against the background of an ideal speech situation that would make possible undistorted, or oppression-free, discourse. In the language of the present book, in order to understand the potential sources of deception in "rational" discourse, we must first have a clear conception of the ideal case where such deception is excluded. A merely descriptive model of "real" (rather than ideal) discourse could serve no critical epistemological function in distinguishing genuine from illusory consensus, or practical reason from practical unreason. In epistemological issues, a merely descriptive account of what is "normal" cannot be substituted for a genuine "norm," i.e., a standard against which to evaluate and improve the "normal." Specifically, four basic sources of potential deception are indicated by the four unavoidable validity claims explained above.

Third, the ideal speech situation can serve as a general guideline for organizing actual speech situations in such a way as to minimize systematic sources of deception. Though in retrospect it is difficult to verify the degree to which the conditions of the ideal speech situation have actually obtained, we know at least toward what ideal we should work when making social arrangements for institutionalized discourses (e.g., in the realm of community planning). ("It is recommendable to separate issues of consensus-theoretic introduction of the concept of discourse from issues of [practical] institutionalization of discourses." (1973d:382, my transl.) We note here a peculiar feature of a model of an oppression-free discourse that is tied to ideal conditions of rationality: it is at once a means and an end, an "ideal form of life." (1971c:139) We easily recognize in this model the *emancipatory interest* of the critically oriented sciences and the underlying *emancipatory utopia* of a society free from unjustified domination. Communication free from domination (undistorted discourse) is to be the means for realizing or approximating the utopia, for dissolving arbitrary domination into discursive will-formation. But there need not be a vicious circle in this. Habermas defends the double function of his model of rational discourse as both a social utopia and a means for realizing it by referring to history. In the historical evolution of society the *institutionalization of domain-specific discourses* has played a key role in the development of civil liberties (emancipation from domination of men over men) as well as for the unfolding of productive forces (emancipation from natural constraints). As the three most "dramatic" examples, Habermas mentions:

(a) the institutionalization of discourses in which the validity claims of traditional myths and religious dogma were systematically called into question; this development characterizes the beginning of philosophy and academic teaching in classical Greece;

(b) the institutionalization of discourses in which the validity claims of traditional crafts and trades were systematically called into question; it marks the beginning of the modern empirical sciences;

(c) the institutionalization of discourses in which validity claims linked to practical questions and political decisions were *intended* to be questioned continually; this development characterizes the beginning of the bourgeois "public domain" and liberal democracy in Renaissance Italy, seventeenth century England and the USA. (1973a:25f, similarly 1973d:282f)

These examples, though only roughly sketched out by Habermas, demonstrate – quite convincingly, I think – that the social institutionalization of domain-specific, approximately ideal speech situations is indeed an effective means for replacing political authority (decisionism) by discursive will-formation (practical reason), and that this means is intrinsically identical with the emancipatory utopia of democratization of all domains of social practice. In order to carry on the three preceding evolutionary institutionalizations of discourse – in particular, in order ot make the third a social reality rather than a fiction – such democratization of all domains of political decision-making and planning should now become the goal of a fourth stage of institutionalizing discourses. In view of the steadily increasing gap between the liberal-democratic model of the public domain and the realities of interest-group liberalism[19] and technocratic social planning,[20] the traditional objection against this call for democratization, the reproach of «utopianism»,[21] is no longer justifiable: the utopia becomes the only means today for maintaining the democratic achievements of the past.

2.3. The Logic of Discourse (1): Partiality for Reason

The ideal speech situation as sketched out above represents only the necessary condition under which rational discourse on controversial claims can unfold, but it does not by itself produce rational consensus, i.e., agreement based on cogent argu-

---

[19] Cf. Lowi 1969:55ff. The term refers to the interconnection of organized private interests with public government, a connection that interferes with that proper functioning of the public domain which is so fundamental to the liberal model of democracy.

[20] I mean apolitical and amoral planning under the cover of scientific expertise, e.g. "systems science," "administrative science," "management science," "behavioral science", etc.

[21] A reproach voiced by Robert Spaemann in an article entitled "The Utopia of Freedom from Domination" (1972) and answered by Habermas in his brief reply, "The Utopia of the Good Ruler" (in 1973d:378–388).

ment. It is the task of a consensus theory of truth to explain the sufficient conditions of such genuine consensus. In Habermas' research program, the consensus theory of truth takes the form of a general *logic of discourse* (we might also say, a logic of argumentation). Before entering upon any details, let us clarify some basic presuppositions.

(a) *Habermas' "language-analytical turn."* – Habermas' conception of a consensus theory of truth shares with Charles S. Peirce's consensus theory of truth the basic idea that truth is not a matter of individual certainty or of "correspondence" between statements and a fixed reality, but rather a matter of possible reference, within a theoretically infinite community of inquirers, to the judgement of others. In Peirce's famous formulation:

> The opinion which is fated to be ultimately agreed to by all who investigate, is what we mean by truth, and the object represented in this opinion is the real. That is the way I would explain reality. (Peirce 1878:par. 407)

There are, however, two essential differences in Habermas' approach. (1) He distinguishes between the a priori of experience and the a priori of argumentation and associates consensus with the latter only. (2) He shifts the focus from Peirce's community of "scientific investigators" to the community of "competent speakers":

> In order to distinguish true from false statements, I refer to the judgement of others – more precisely, to the judgement of all others with whom I could ever enter into a dialogue (among whom I counterfactually include all the dialogue partners I could find if my life history were coextensive with the history of mankind).... As a matter of fact, of course, I can test my assertion always only by referring to the agreement of a few persons. This factual agreement of a few others... will be the more likely to meet with agreement on the part of further judges *[Beurteiler]* the less we and others have reasons to doubt their competence. I can therefore restrict my counterfactual condition of truth to this: I can assert p [a predicate] of X [an object] if every other competent judge would agree with me. (1971c:124f, my transl.; see also 1973c:219)

This shift from "scientific" to "communicative" competence corresponds to the linguistic or language-analytical turn that has occurred in philosophy since Peirce's time: the critique of language has replaced the traditional (Kantian) critique of consciousness as the key to understanding both the a priori of experience and the a priori of argumentation (cf. also Habermas 1970a:220). For this reason, Habermas cannot return immediately to Peirce's logic of inquiry but instead takes contemporary language analysis as a starting point for his logic of discourse.

(b) *Toward a pragmatic logic of discourse.* – In contrast to the prevailing logical and structuralist approaches to the analysis of language since Carnap, Habermas does not intend to reduce the scope of his analysis to the syntactic and semantic levels of speech. "The logic of discourse is a pragmatic logic. It examines the formal properties of contexts of argumentation." (1973 c:241, my transl.) We have already noted Habermas' reference to the works of Austin (1962) and Searle (1969). In addition, his logic of discourse will draw heavily from Stephen Toulmin's analysis of *The Uses of Argument* (1964).

(c) *The necessity of a formal logic of discourse.* – The pragmatic logic of discourse envisaged by Habermas is necessarily a formal one. That is to say, it cannot establish any material criterion of rationality (rational discourse, rational criticism, rational consensus), but must restrict itself to explicating the formal properties of rational discourse. This is so because any substantial criterion of rational consensus (discourse) would in turn depend for its validity on a rational consensus (discourse). An infinite regress or a vicious circle could only be avoided by justifying the basic criterion of discursive rationality in other than consensus-theoretic terms, i.e., by renouncing the idea of a (self-sufficient) consensus theory of truth. The implication of this renunciation would be that a consensus or discourse theory of truth cannot replace, but only complement, some form of a non-positivistic correspondence theory of truth.[22] But this conclusion would of course not correspond to Habermas' purpose, which is to develop a model of rational discourse that might overcome the narrow concept of rationality in logical positivism and critical rationalism. Habermas therefore maintains that a general logic of discourse must explain the criteria of rational consensus solely in terms of the *formal* (though pragmatic rather than syntactic) *properties of discourse:*

The consensus theory of truth claims to explain the peculiarly unforced force of the better argument in terms of formal properties of discourse, rather than in terms of logical consistency of sentences... or empirical evidence that enters the argumentation from outside, as it were. The result of a discourse cannot be decided upon either by logical or empirical force alone but rather by the 'force of the better argument'. This force we call *rational motivation.* It must be explained within the framework of a logic of discourse. (1973 a:240, my transl.)

When speaking of rational motivation, Habermas has in mind the Kantian concept of enlightenment,[23] a concept that we need to maintain as a critical idea against the contemporary prevalence of decisionism and instrumental reason. Rational motivation is, in Habermas' words, "the only universalizable partiality – the interest in reason itself.» (1975:142)

---

[22] In fact, this implication will be of some importance to our "dialectical turn" in Chapter 5.
[23] "Enlightenment is man's release from his self-incurred tutelage. Tutelage is man's inability to make use of his understanding without direction from another. Self-incurred is this tutelage when its cause lies not in lack of reason but in lack of resolution and courage to use it without direction from another. *Sapere aude!* 'Have courage to use your own reason!' – that is the motto of enlightenment." (Kant, "What Is Enlightenment?" 1784, in Beck 1949:286)

(d) *Discourse vs. communicative action.* – "Partiality for reason" (1975:142) requires of course that all external pressures and constraints, such as political pressure and the "objective necessities" disclosed by the experts, be temporarily suspended:

> Discourse [ought to] serve the examination of problematic validity claims of opinions (and norms). The only force permitted in discourse is that of the better argument, and the only permissible motive is the cooperative search for truth. (1973b:386, my transl.)

And similarly:

> What *rationally motivated recognition* of the validity claim of a norm of action means follows from the discursive procedures of motivation. Discourse can be understood as that form of communication that is removed from contexts of experience and action and whose structure assures us: that the bracketed validity claims of assertions, recommendations, or warnings are the exclusive object of discussion; that participants, themes and contributions are not restricted except with reference to the goal of testing the validity claims in question; that no force except that of the better argument is exercised; and that, as a result, all motives except that of the cooperative search for truth are excluded. (1975:107f)

Entering into such a discourse clearly requires a "stepping out" of everyday forms of interaction. A logic of discourse must therefore begin by clearly distinguishing "rationally motivated" discourse from other types of communication.

In his new introduction to the fourth edition of *Theory and Practice* (1973a:1-40), Habermas therefore introduces a distinction between "communicative action" and "discourse," a distinction he had not yet developed in *Knowledge and Human Interest*:[24]

> In the investigations up to this point I have brought out the interrelation between knowledge and interests, without making clear the critical threshold between communication (which remains embedded within the context of action) and discourses (which transcend the compulsions of action). (1973a:19, similarly 1973b:397)

The critical threshold in question concerns the calling into question of the four basic validity claims on which the possibility of mutual understanding and rational consensus rests: the claims for comprehensibility, truth, truthfulness, and (moral, etc.) rightness.[25] In everyday communication, the validity of these claims is "assumed

---

[24] The distinction is briefly mentioned first in 1971c:115.

[25] More generally speaking, we could also say that the critical threshold consists in the transition from an unreflected to a self-reflective level of discourse. Seen in this light, Habermas' distinction is reminiscent of Kant's distinction between reason (which remains tied to the contingencies of action contexts, e.g., to unreflected motives or needs) and *pure* reason (which frees itself from any contingent interest except the interest in pure reason itself). In analogy to Kant, we might understand Habermas' concept of discourse as a case of "pure communication."

130

naively" (1973:18), that is, the purpose of the discussion consists in the exchange of information but *not* in the examination of the underlying validity claims. In this case, Habermas proposes to speak to *communicative action* (in contrast to strategic action, i.e., use of force and/or deception, etc.), for such communication "remains embedded within the context of action." (1971c:115, 1973a:19) If for some reason the validity of the basic claims becomes problematic, normal communicative action breaks off and the participants are then confronted with the following alternative: they can either switch to strategic action, renouncing the search for mutual understanding altogether, or they can attempt to settle the controversial claims argumentatively, so as to reestablish the lost consensual basis for communicative action (cf. 1979a:3f). In this latter case, Habermas now speaks of *discourse* rather than communicative action:

> In actions, the factually raised claims to validity, which form the underlying consensus, are assumed naively. Discourse, on the other hand, serves the justification of problematic claims to validity of opinions and norms. Thus the system of action and experience refers us in a compelling manner to a form of communication in which the participants do not exchange information, do not direct or carry out action, nor do they search for arguments or offer justifications. Discourse therefore requires the virtualization [suspension] of constraints on action. This is intended to render inoperative all motives except solely that of a cooperative readiness to arrive at an understanding. (1973a:18, cf. 1971c:115, 117; 1973b:386; 1973c:214; 1979a:1, note 2c)

The importance of the distinction between communication which remains tied to the context of experience and action, and discourses which transcend the constraints of experience and action, should become apparent in the following section.

2.4 The Logic of Discourse (II): Its Relation to the Theory of Knowledge-Constitutive Interests

The idea that we might identify and reconstruct universal conditions of possible understanding in terms of a general logic of discourse is very much reminiscent of the Kantian transcendental program of establishing the universal a priori conditions of possible (objective) experience. But we have seen that Kant's program, because it presupposes an absolute starting point in the form of an abstract "transcendental subject," can no longer be carried through today. We can no longer conceive of knowledge as independent of the empirically contingent, social and historical, standpoint of the knowing subject. Habermas' theory of knowledge-constitutive interests has undermined the Kantian assumption that one set of a priori concepts can constitute all objects of experience in general. Rather, a priori concepts are related to specific domains of objects, i.e., different contexts of experience and action, and hence the meaning of knowledge or experience is domain-specific. At first glance, we must then suspect that Habermas' own program of a "universal" pragmatics or a general logic of discourse is at odds with his insight into the "differential meaning-constitution of object domains." (1973b:393)

What is at stake is, in Kantian terms, the "unity of reason" – with Habermas: the unity of argumentation – vis-à-vis the different object domains of the theoretical, practical, and emancipatory interests (the contexts of instrumental action, communicative action, and self-reflection, respectively). Habermas is of course keenly aware of this issue. His answer is of interest to us because it takes up again the question of the relationship between the a priori of experience and the a priori of argumentation, a question that will be of fundamental importance for our own program of a critical heuristics.

Basically, the suspicion of incompatibility between a general logic of discursive vindication of validity claims (esp. "truth") on the one hand, and object-domain-specific constitution of meaning on the other, is tied to the old confusion of truth with objectivity.[26] Objectivity means intersubjectivity of the constitution of the objects and meaning of experience by virtue of shared categories or conceptual frameworks; it applies to the *a priori of experience*. Truth, on the other hand, means intersubjectively warranted assertability of statements *about* objects of experience, i.e., assertions *of* "facts"; it applies to the *a priori of argumentation*. Facts are not to be confused with objects: [27]

> Facts are what statements (when true) state; they are not what statements are about [i.e., objects, or ontological entities]. They are not, like things or happenings [objects] on the face of the globe, witnessed or heard or seen, broken or overturned, interrupted or prolonged, kicked, destroyed, mended or noisy. (Strawson 1964:38, partly quoted by Habermas in 1973b:384 and in 1973c:215)

That is to say, "facts" cannot be experienced (whether objectively or not), just as objects of experience cannot be asserted (cf. Habermas 1973c:215). Consequently, the truth of "facts," of statements about objects of possible experience, cannot be established without recourse to the a priori of argumentation, i.e., to the discursive procedures by which we decide on disputed validity claims such as truth or rightness. Truth is a matter of the logic of discourse, not of the constitution of experience. On the other hand, the objectivity of a *theoretical* statement (or the propositional content of a constative speech act) cannot be established discursively, but only through cumulative corroborations in the context of experience and action (cf. 1973b:391). This distinction is less important for *practical* statements: the objectivity of their

---

[26] With Habermas, I shall use truth here as representative of the other validity claims, esp. rightness.

[27] Such confusion is characteristic of Popper's correspondence theory of truth: true statements are supposed to "correspond" to facts (confused with objects), while in fact they can only correspond to other statements about objects. Facts do not "exist" independently of statements. Cf. also Kamlah/Lorenzen 1967:135f, 139.

content does not concern facts but norms, and these norms can ideed be called objective when they are intersubjectively assertable, i.e., when their claim for rightness has been discursively established. The relationship of the a priori of argumentation to the a priori of experience is therefore problematic only in the case of theoretical statements:

> The a priori of experience (the structure of objects of possible experience) is independent of the a priori of argumentation (the conditions of possible discourse). But *both* confine the validity [or define the boundaries, *begrenzen]* of empirical scientific theories.... Theories can only be constructed and developed *under the conditions* of argumentation and, at the same time, *within the limits* of prior objectification of possible experience *[des erfahrbaren Geschehens].* "Under the conditions of argumentation" means: in the form of discursively examined systems of propositions. "Within the limits of prior objectification of possible experience" means: in a theoretical language whose fundamental predicates remain tied to independently constituted objects of possible experience. Theoretical languages... can *interpret* and in a certain sense even reformulate the structures of pre-scientific object domains; but... they cannot *transform* them into the conditions of another object domain (1973b:392, my transl.).

That is to say, the "objectivity" of the empirical content of theoretical proposition – and more generally, their meaning – will always remain confined to a domain-specific a priori of experience, i.e., to domain-specific cognitive interests and categories; but when it comes to the discursive validation of these propositions, the domain-specific restrictions of the a priori of experience are irrelevant and only the a priori of argumentation, i.e., the logic of discourse, is relevant. The linkage of the proposition in question to a context of experience and action is temporarily suspended or "bracketed"; but once the truth claim of the proposition is argumentatively settled, its meaning will again be linked to the same context of experience and action in which it originated (now no longer the context of discovery, but the context of application). In this merely temporary suspension of the domain-specific constraints of experience and action consists the *transcendental link between knowledge and human interests;* but in the fact that such temporary suspension is possible and necessary with regard to the discursive vindication of validity claims consists the *unity of argumentative reason.*

The unity of argumentative reason manifests itself in two major ways: (1) The same logic of (theoretical or practical) discourse applies to all three basic forms of sciences; and (2) regardless of the object domain concerned, all four basic types of validity claims come into play.

Re: (1) "True" propositions (or "facts") represent a research goal for empirical-analytic science as well as for historical-hermeneutic or critically oriented science. Similarly, propositions in all three sciences are in need of critical examination with regard to their normative content, although this content ist linked to a specific object domain as the context of application. Regardless of whether the emphasis is on a theoretical discourse about "facts" or on a practical discourse about "norms," the logic of discourse (the a priori of argumentation) is invariable for all object domains. This is different from the a priori of experience, where not only the basic conceptual framework but also the research procedures – the logic of inquiry – remains tied to a specific object domain. In this regard, the unity of argumentation reflects the "critical threshold" between communicative action and discourse (cf. above): the a priori of experience remains embedded within everyday contexts of instrumental or communicative action, but the a priori of argumentation – the logic of discourse – transcends the constraints of experience and action.

Re: (2) Regarding the a priori of argumentation, we have seen earlier that the validity basis of speech always comprehends the four claims, "comprehensibility" (of utterances), "truth" (of propositional content), "rightness" (of normative content), and "truthfulness" (of the speaker's expressed intention). As Habermas explains:

> In every instance of communicative action the system of all validity claims comes into play; they must always be raised simultaneously, although they cannot all be thematic at the same time. (1979a:66)

At this point we are threatened with a new source of confusion between the a priori of experience and the a priori of argumentation. Leaving aside the claim to comprehensibility, it appears that each type of validity claim refers to a specific domain of reality: "truth" refers to statements about the empirical world of objects and events, "rightness" refers to norms regulating the realm of social practice, and "truthfulness" refers to the inner world of self-consciousness. This impression is correct, but we must resist the shortcut of associating "truth" exclusively with empirical-analytic science (instrumental action), "rightness" with historical-hermeneutic science (mutual understanding), and "truthfulness" with critically oriented science (emancipatory self-reflection). Despite the suggestive character of that association, it would make us fall behind the level of differentiation we have reached with the separation of the two a priori problematics. It is apparently for this reason, though he does not explicitly say so, that Habermas has recently (1979b:66ff) suggested the terms "external nature," "society," and "internal nature" to designate the segments of reality to which the three validity claims refer. (Comprehensibility in this scheme refers to language as a segment of reality *sui generis,* cf. 1979a:67.) Since in a discourse all of these segments of reality come into play, regardless of the domain-specific a priori of experience concerned, we need some labels to refer to them; the use of different labels will then make it clear whether we are referring to the a priori of argumentation or to the a priori of experience. (Correspondingly, I have used the terms "external world," "our social world," and "my inner world" in characterizing the pragmatic functions of speech acts above, cf. p. 120f.)

However, since the introduction of new distinctions generates more complexity for the student who is trying to follow Habermas, let us try to clarify somewhat the correlations in question.

(a) "Truth" is not the exclusive affair of the empirical-analytic sciences. Rather, "truth" means the discursively warranted assertability of "facts," i.e., statements about the objectified segment of reality to which we refer from a third-person viewpoint, as "the" world of external objects and happenings.

(b) "Rightness" is not the exclusive affair of the historical-hermeneutic sciences. Rather, "rightness" means the discursively warranted assertability of "norms," i.e., statements about the symbolically prestructured segment of reality to which we refer, from an ego-alter viewpoint, as "our" world of society, and with which we either do or do not conform.

(c) "Truthfulness" is obviously not the exclusive affair of the critically oriented sciences such as critical social theory, despite the considerable role that emancipatory self-reflection plays in them. Rather, "truthfulness" concerns a speaker's expressed or concealed subjectivity, to which he refers, from a first-person viewpoint, as "my" inner world of feelings, intentions, etc.

(d) Insofar as every statement can be critically discussed with regard to its propositional content ("truth"), its normative content ("rightness"), and its expressive content ("truthfulness"), we can say that every speech act in a discourse invokes all three segments of reality. Correspondingly, the speaker's obligation to substantiate these validity claims can be met only by recourse to "facts," to underlying "norms," or to the speaker's readiness to act according to his expressed intentions (cf. Habermas 1979a:63ff). *Table 2/2* attempts to give an overview.

We can now understand Habermas' assertion, in the *Postscript,* that

the *unity of argumentation* is compatible with the *differential meaning-constitution of object domains.* In all the sciences argumentation is subject to the same conditions for the discursive redemption of truth claims. (1973b:393, my transl.)

On the other hand, the claim of critical rationalists and logical positivists for the unity of scientific method is incompatible with the differential meaning-constitution of object domains and must not be confused with the unity of argumentation. Hence, Habermas concludes, the "conditions of a rationality that is not scientistically restricted" can be reconstructed within the framework of a general logic of discourse for *all* domains of inquiry (cf. 1973b:393). As far as the validity claims subject to rational discourse are truth claims, we need a logic of *theoretical* discourse; as far as claims to rightness are thematic, we need a logic of *practical* discourse. Let us now turn to a comparative analysis of the logic of cogent argumentation in theoretical and practical discourse.

135

A Priori of Argumentation   *A Priori of Experience*

(1) Segments of reality	(2) Modes of communication: basic attitudes	(3) Validity claims	(4) Pragmatic functions of speech acts	(5) Speech-act-immanent obligations	(6) Types of discourse required	(7) Forms of science (contexts of action)
"The" world of external nature	Cognitive: objectifying attitude	Truth	Representation of facts (constative speech acts)	Obligation to provide grounds (by recourse to facts)	Theoretical discourse (about fact or fiction)	Empirical-analytic science (instrumental action)
"Our" world of society	Interactive: conformative attitude	Rightness	Establishment of legitimate interpersonal relations (regulative speech acts)	Obligation to provide justifications (by recourse to underlying norms)	Practical discourse (about right or wrong)	Historical-hermeneutic science (communicative action)
"My" world of internal nature	Expressive: expressive attitude	Truthfulness	Disclosure of speaker's subjectivity (expressive speech acts)	Obligation to prove trustworthy (by virtue of behavior)	(consistency of subsequent behavior)	Critically oriented science (emancipatory self-reflection)
(Language)		Comprehensibility	(Speech as such)			

Table 2/2: Correlations between validity claims and related segments of reality, modes of communication, functions of speech-act-immanent obligations, and types of discourse *within* the a priori of argumentation; their applicability to each object domain of the a priori of experience (columns 1 to 4 adapted from Habermas' table in 1979a:68)

2.5 The Logic of Discourse (III):
Levels of Argumentation in Theoretical and Practical Discourse

We have up to now discussed the basic presuppositions of Habermas' conception of a general logic of discourse: the principle of publicity and oppression-free discourse; the ideal speech situation and the four unavoidable validity claims; the supposition of communicative competence; the formal and pragmatic (rather than syntactic) character of a logic of discourse; the partiality for reason or "rationally motivated" consensus and the related distinction between communicative action and discourse; and finally the compatibility of the idea of a general logic of discourse (the unity of argumentation) with the theory of knowledge-constitutive interests, and the underlying distinction between the a priori of experience and the a priori of argumentation. We are now prepared to turn to the more practical question: How can a theoretical discourse actually establish the truth of a statement with regard to its propositional (theoretical) content? And how can a practical discourse vindicate the rightness of a statement with regard to its normative (practical) content?

First of all, Habermas makes it clear that the possibility of cogent argumentation does not rest on deductive logic as the organon for linking sentences, as the critical rationalists assume; for argumentation does not in the first place consist of a chain of sentences but of a chain of speech acts (cf. 1973c:241). To construe cogent argument in terms of propositional logic would mean to reduce it to a syntactic level of speech; but the argumentative power of speech acts can only be grasped at the pragmatic level of speech. That is to say, the power of an argument (a chain of speech acts) is not a matter of deductive-logical modalities such as consistency/contradiction or necessity/impossibility, but rather of the pragmatic modality of *cogency*.

We have already seen that the possibility of cogent argument, at the pragmatic level of speech, rests on the speaker's obligation and ability to substantiate the speech-act-immanent validity claims. We have also seen how a speaker can make good these claims. The only question that remains concerns the formal structure of a cogent chain of speech acts, i.e., the question: What kind of speech acts must follow each other in what order for an argument to be cogent? In order to answer this question, Habermas now relies on Stephen Toumin's analysis of *The Uses of Argument* (1964). Toulmin represents the formal structure of argument by the following scheme:

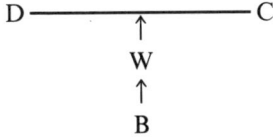

Fig. 2/3: The formal structure of argument according to St. Toulmin
D = Data   C = Conclusion   W = Warrant   B = Backing

Toulmin gives the following example (in Habermas 1973 c:242). The conclusion C "Harry is a British subject" is explained by referring to the fact D "Harry was born in Bermuda." If this explanation is challenged, the connection between the data and the conclusion must be demonstrated by a warrant W such as "A man born in Bermuda will generally be a British subject." W represents a general rule or premise that can in turn be questioned; in this case, a backing B for the warrant must be furnished, such as "W holds on account of the following statuses and other legal provisions...."

This scheme of argumentation is formally similar to the Hempel/Oppenheim scheme of explanation, where C = explanandum, D = initial conditions (in classical logic called the minor premise), W = law or nomological hypothesis (major premise), and B = the empirical basis for W (basis statements). W and D together are also called the explanans. The step from B to W raises the problem of induction. But the Hempel/Oppenheim scheme remains, of course, at the syntactic level of speech, that is, it considers an explanation as the logical deduction of a sentence C from a nomological hypothesis W (another sentence) and an observational statement describing the initial conditions D. There is no place for pragmatic considerations regarding the (propositional, normative, and expressive) content of the statement in question.

When we move to a pragmatic level of speech, we must distinguish between theoretical discourse (with regard to propositional content) and practical discourse (with regard to normative content). C, D, W and B stand then for the following speech acts: *(Table 2/4)*

Speaking at a syntactic level of speech, an argument is logically *necessary* (i.e., conclusive) if W permits the deduction of C from D *and* if W can be inferred from B. This condition can obviously not be met unless there is no "induction gap"[28] between B and W. An approach that remains at the syntactic level of speech, such as Popper's model of rational discourse, must therefore from the outset renounce the possibility of discursive vindication of the truth of statements that are not merely tautological but have empirical content; hence the recourse to a correspondence theory of truth and the falsification approach to the problem of induction. The situation is different, however, for a universal-pragmatic approach such as Habermas'. At the pragmatic level of speech, an argument is *cogent* not if it is logically conclusive (necessary) but if the step from B to W is logically possible (=necessary condition) and if the discourse participants can be rationally (cognitively) motivated, by virtue of B, to accept W as plausible (= sufficient condition) (cf. Habermas 1973 c:243).

The step from B to W is not a merely analytical one; it involves interpretation of B's and W's empirical (propositional) and normative (practical) *content.* This implies that rationally motivated discourse will have to question and possibly revise the conceptual framework within which the discourse takes place – for this framework of course influences the way in which "facts," "norms" and basic statements (backings) are interpreted. Otherwise, a factual consensus remains open to the charge of being

---

[28] This term is not used by Habermas; cf. my note 5 to Chap. 1.

	Theoretical discourse	*Practical discourse*
C	Assertion (proposition)	Recommendation/ evaluation
Controversial validity claim	Truth	Rightness (or appropriateness)
Speech-act-immanent obligation to substantiate claims	Obligation to provide grounds (explanation)	Obligation to provide justification
D	Recourse to "facts": causes (for events), motives (for explaining purposive-rational actions)	Recourse to underlying "norms": reasons (for justifying the choice of ends or norms)
W	Reference to nomological hypotheses (description of empirical regularities or covariances in "the" external world)	Reference to general norms of action/evalua-. tion (e.g. moral principles of "our" social world)
B	Observations (findings of empirical-analytic, historical-hermeneutic, or critically oriented science)	Indication of interpreted needs (values), consequences and potential side-effects

Table 2/4: The structure of cogent argument (adapted from Habermas 1973 c:243)

merely contingent – namely, on the unreflected content and selectivity of the underlying (previously internalized) frame of reference. The question must be posed: Is the conceptual framework employed "adequate" to the segment of reality it is to describe? Specifically, in what way is it selective, compared to alternative frameworks?

In a theoretical discourse, the theory-language influences the meaning of "facts" and basic observations; hence a "metatheoretical discourse" on alternative theory-language is necessary. Likewise, in a practical discourse the conceptual system determines the interpretation of "norms" and basic statements about related needs and consequences; hence a "metaethical" or "metapolitical discourse" must take place. Such considerations lead Habermas to distinguish *four levels of radicalization* of discourse:

Level 1 – the step from communicative action to discourse: given controversial validity claims, the involved parties enter into a discourse rather than switching to strategic action.

Level 2 – meeting of speech-act-immanent obligations: claims are explained and substantiated by virtue of argument according to the structure of cogent argumentation, i.e., by putting forward D, W, and B (cf. Table 2/4).

Level 3 – metalinguistic (metatheoretical or metaethical) *discourse:* the conceptual framework employed is called into question, critically examined with regard to its relative adequacy, and possibly modified (= substantial critique of language).

Level 4 – critique of knowledge: the normative question is raised: What *ought* to count as knowledge? The normative fundament of all (theoretical as well as practical) knowledge is reflected upon: namely, the basic life-practical interests on which knowledge depends and which it serves (cf. Habermas 1973 c:252ff).

A discourse will merit its title "rational" only to the extent that the participants are free to raise the level of critical self-reflection from a given to a more radical level. Habermas therefore establishes what we have earlier designated the fourth requirement of the ideal speech situation: the formal properties of discourse must be such as to guarantee to every participant, at all times, the freedom to move from one to another level of argumentation (cf. 1973 c:250). "The consensus-producing power of an argument rests on the fact that we can move to and fro among the various levels of discourse, until a consensus develops." (1973 c:254, my transl.) Applied to either theoretical or practical discourse, the four levels of argumentation will take the following forms:

As Table 2/5 suggests, the fourth level of argumentation bursts the boundaries of both theoretical and practical discourse: the practical question of what we *ought* to will is dependent on what we *can* will, and the theoretical question of what we *can* know depends on what we *ought* to count as knowledge. At this level, then, theoretical and practical discourse become clearly interdependent and complementary. (I have therefore included in Table 2/5 a reference to the "dialectic of potential and will," cf. Habermas 1971 b:61; Habermas refers instead to "critique of knowledge" in the case of theoretical discourse and to "research-political will-formation" in the case of practical discourse.)

A question that Table 2/5 is bound to raise is this: Why should cogent *practical* arguments require *theoretical* justifications, as Habermas seems to suggest for the second level of argumentation? This question brings us back, at the end of our introduction to Habermas' approach, to the one underlying issue that is of central interest to us: the problem of practical reason.

Level of argumentation (radicalization steps)	Theoretical discourse	Practical discourse
1. Entry into discourse (speech acts)	Assertions (propositions)	Recommendations/ evaluations, commands/ prohibitions
2. Substantiation of validity claims (cogent argument)	*Theoretical* explana- tions D ——— C ↑ W ↑ B	*Theoretical* justifica- tions D ——— C ↑ W ↑ B
3. Metalinguistic discourse (substantial critique of language)	*Meta*theoretical	*Meta*ethical/ *meta*political
	modification of language	
4. Critique of knowledge	Reflection on what *ought* to count as knowledge	Reflection on what *ought* to count as need or interest
	in view of the dialectic of potential and will	

Table 2/5: Levels of progressive radicalization in theoretical and practical discourse (= levels of argumentation) (adapted from Habermas 1973c:254)

3. Practical Discourse and Morality

Reason is practical when it gives us cognitive guidance in practical action. In other words, practical reason is to provide us with cogent *reasons* for selecting normative criteria of improvement, so that we can distinguish them from other criteria because they are reasonable, or rationally justified, norms. At the bottom of this issue lies not the instrumental question of what we *can* do – a question subject to theoretical discourse – but the *moral* question of what we *ought* to do. It is now time to consider Habermas' ethics, and the way in which his model of practical discourse can deal with moral problems.

3.1. From "Monological" to "Communicative" Ethics

Traditionally, the moral question has been dealt with by individualistic or "monological" approaches, that is to say, from the point of view of a solitary, abstract, moral consciousness rather than from the point of view of a community of acting and speaking subjects. Accordingly, moral philosophers have sought to "deduce" universal criteria of moral action in some objective fashion, e.g. from empirical concepts of good and evil or from ontological principles regulating the organization of the world. The most oustanding among these monological approaches is probably Kant's "transcendental" deduction of a highest moral principle, the "moral law."

Habermas' model of practical discourse, to the extent that it can help us decide rationally on practical questions of moral concern, opens up a new, dialogical rather than monological, approach to ethics. Habermas speaks of "communicative ethics" (1975:89), or sometimes of "cognitivist linguistic ethics" *(Sprachethik,* 1975:110). The program of a communicative ethics is for us perhaps the most important part of Habermas' research program, for it promises to provide a way to incorporate the moral idea into the concept of rationality from which it has been excluded since the rise of positivism. The question for us is this: can the program of a communicative ethics, embodied in a model of practical discourse, become a practical – i.e., practicable – reality or must it remain a mere program?

The very term "practical discourse" is symptomatic of the ambiguity that surrounds this question, for this term tacitly equates discourse *on* practical (moral) questions with a discourse that transcends the realm of theory and becomes itself a piece of practice. At the same time, however, we have seen that Habermas speaks of a "theoretical" justification of practical arguments (cf. Table 2/5 above). He also likes to assert that "practical questions admit of truth" (1975:111). Moreover, there is the connection of his discourse model with an anticipated ideal speech situation; these and other peculiarities of Habermas' position are apt to raise doubts about the practical status of "practical discourse."

We must view this issue against the background of Habermas' underlying purpose. His purpose is not, in the first place, a heuristic one, i.e., to develop some practicable arrangement for institutionalizing discourses, but a critical (epistemological) one – critical against the positivism, scientism and decisionism of the contemporary philosophy of science. In opposition to the decisionistic relegation of moral questions to the realm of irrational acts of belief, he maintains that moral questions admit of rational treatment and can be decided "with reason" (1975:102, 105). Setting himself against the reduction of practical to instrumental reason, he advocates the "comprehensive rationality of reason that becomes transparent to itself." (1971a:3) The key to such a comprehensive concept of rationality, as he sees it, is a reconceptualization of the relationship between theory and practice; and this reconceptualization takes for Habermas the form of a model of practical discourse.

A very brief summary may be helpful at this point. Habermas finds the normative fundament of discourse in four unavoidable validity claims – truth, rightness, truthfulness, and comprehensibility – each of which comes into play in every instance of discursive rationality, though they cannot all be redeemed simultaneously. If this is so, it is obviously impossible to isolate practical reason from the sphere of rational discourse. In fact, rightness claims as well as truth claims admit of rational, cognitive treatment: both are linked to a speech-act-immanent obligation to substantiate them, if challenged, by cogent argument. We have considered the structure of cogent argumentation in both cases: basically, it consists in the theoretical justification of a conclusion C by recourse to a data basis D, a warrant W, and a backing for the warrant B. The critical step in this chain of argument is the step from B to W, for it connot be justified logically – at a syntactic level of speech – but only "with reason," i.e., at a pragmatic level of speech. If the step can be made successfully and meets with rationally motivated consensus, it can still be challenged by calling into question the presupposed conceptual framework (metalinguistic discourse) and by calling into question the underlying life-practical interests (critique of knowledge). The requirements of the ideal speech situation are intended to guarantee to every participant in the discourse that he can raise the discussion to these more radical levels of criticism, and thus to exhaust all possibilities for rational treatment of normative validity claims.

This then is the situation in which Habermas must attempt to incorporate the moral idea into his approach. With Kant he insists on the idea that a moral will is the same as a "rational will" (1975:108). He goes beyond Kant, however, in that he pursues the idea of a communicative ethics. In opposition to the non-cognitivist treatment of moral questions in analytical philosophy, he insists on the possibility of a "cognitivist linguistic ethics." In order to support this claim, he must seek to locate the sufficient conditions of moral will-formation in the proposed formal properties of discourse. And against the decisionist "auctoritas non veritas facit legem," he must show in what way "practical questions admit of truth."[29]

3.2. The Principle of Generalization

Basically, one might see in Habermas' emphasis on the truth-relatedness of rightness claims simply a way of pointing to the fact that both validity claims can be redeemed by cogent arguments of similar (though not identical) structure. The following quotation corresponds to this "weak" interpretation:

> If rightness as well as truth can qualify as a discursively redeemable validity claim, it follows that right norms must be capable of being grounded in a way similar to true statements.... I suppose that the justification of the validity claims contained in the recommendation of norms of action or of evaluation can be just as discursively tested as the justification of the validity claims implied in assertions. But of course the grounding *[Begründung]* of right recommandations and evaluations differs in the structure of argumentation from the grounding of true statements. The logical conditions under which a rationally motivated consensus can be attained in practical discourse are not the same as those in theoretical discourse. (1973c:226, my transl.)

The logical conditions in question concern the logical possibility of the step from B to W, a step which earlier was said to be the necessary (though not sufficient) condition of cogent argument. This step is not a deductive one; it represents an "induction gap." The only way to close an "induction gap," we have argued, is by moving from a syntactic to a pragmatic level of speech, and to do this we must consider both the empirical-theoretical (propositional) and practical (normative) content of this step. On the one hand, we encounter here indeed a systematic relation of practical questions to *theoretical* claims for *truth*. On the other hand, it is also clear that theoretical considerations alone cannot close the "induction gap" between B and W.

Insofar as *theoretical* considerations are concerned, the crucial induction gap between B and W consists in the generalization of particular observational statements to universal, "law-like" (nomological) hypotheses. In moral issues, such observational statements are involved in the explanation and prediction of the *consequences* and potential *side-effects* (e.g., social costs, ecological risks) that a norm might produce if

---

[29] "If the capacity of practical questions for truth could be disputed, the position I defended would be untenable." (1975:101) After the earlier strict distinction between theoretical claims to truth and practical claims to rightness, this strong formulation comes as a surprise. It does not mean that the earlier distinction becomes irrelevant, but that practical and theoretical discourse are inseparable at bottom because rightness claims are truth-related, and vice-versa. The following Section 3.2. is meant to clarify this issue.

144

it gets implemented. If we want to describe or predict the possible consequences and side-effects of a proposed norm, we must refer to past experiences with comparable norms and thus generalize observational statements. We can reasonably say that the induction gap involved is acceptable if the propositional content of this generalization is subject to rational discourse and if a rational consensus is reached that does not constitute an effective source of deception. The requirements of the ideal speech situation are the sufficient (though unattainable) conditions that would permit us to consider the induction gap as entirely closed.

But the *practical* (normative) content of the generalization from B to W cannot even approximately be closed by recourse to observational (empirical) statements. Basically this is so because in moral questions, "facts" alone never constitute good reasons. All too often norms that meet with factual recognition cannot be justified by cogent argument, just as norms that can be so justified do not necessarily meet with factual recognition. The implication ist that *in practical discourse, unlike the case in theoretical discourse, the step from B to W has an intrinsically critical character with regard to empirical reality;* hence it cannot be based on the very reality it ought to regulate critically. Applying this insight to the issue at hand, it becomes clear that the normative and critical content of our theoretical considerations about the *consequences* of norms must be elucidated by an additional generalization: the generalization of particular to universal *needs* or *interests.* Only in the light of life-practical needs or interests of the people affected can the empirical consequences of norms acquire normative acceptability or rightness. This becomes evident if one considers that "norms regulate legitimate chances for the satisfaction of needs." (Habermas 1973c:251)

The task of *practical* discourse is then clear. It must secure rational consensus on (a) what needs or interests ought to be given a legitimate chance for satisfaction, and (b) what negative consequences or side-effects can rightfully be imposed on those whose needs are not served. It is obvious that this is the permanent and fundamental moral issue that any social planner has to deal with. Less clear is the question of how practical discourse can fulfill this task. It is at this point that we need an interpretation, stronger than the "weak" interpretation given above, of Habermas' basic assertion: that "practical questions admit of truth."

A "strong" interpretation would require that Habermas' communicative ethics, just like Kant's "monological" ethics, be buttressed with a very strong assumption. It must suppose that the critical induction gap in practical discourse can be closed, at a pragmatic level of speech, by analogy to theoretical discourse. That is to say, it must rely on an "induction principle" in the form of a *principle of generalization.* The implication is that only those needs or interests are to be considered as rationally justified which can be shown to be *generalizable.* Needs and interests, or the corresponding norms, are generalizable only if "everyone affected agrees (or would agree) without constraint if they enter into (or were to enter into) a process of discursive will-formation." (1975:89) In effect, then, the rightness of a norm can be justified to the extent that the needs or interests that will benefit are shared by every one who might be affected by the consequences. Only then can we say that the (potentially negative) consequences of the norm, as established by theoretical discourse, are morally acceptable (because practically generalizable).

In order to render the argument up to this point a little clearer, it may be helpful to consider its implication for either monological or communicative ethics. In *monological* approaches, the concerned agent will have to be required to put himself into the position of those affected and test whether he would then still want the norm in question to be recognized as right. This is why Kant, with his famous *categorical imperative,* requires the agent to consider himself as a universal legislator: "So act that the maxim [underlying norm] of your will could always hold at the same time as the principle of universal legislation." *(Critique of Practical Reason,* 1778:A54, transl. Beck 142, Abbott 119).

In a *dialogical* approach, the discourse among those affected takes on the critical function of the categorical imperative. But of course it can do so only if every one who is potentially affected can participate in the discourse and be motivated to agree without recourse to political power or deception. Since this condition will always remain counterfactual – one need only think of the future generations who might be affected by today's actions – *the only way to make certain that everyone affected can agree is by requiring that the needs or interests behind the proposed norm be generalizable.* Negatively put: the needs that the proposed norm gives a legitimate chance for satisfaction must not merely be the particular needs of those actually *involved* but rather the common needs of all those potentially *affected.* Hence, it would seem as if we still need to introduce some sort of categorical imperative, a moral appeal to the involved to put themselves into the situation of those affected but not involved, that is, to apply the generalization principle. But that would mean to rely on moral decisionism: whether or not those involved heed the appeal is decided by an "act of faith" on their part.

Habermas' answer to this potential objection is original and quite distinct from other approaches to ethics that have recourse to the generalization principle contained in Kant's categorical imperative.[30] What is new in Habermas' communicative ethics is not the fact that he relies on the principle of generalization, but the fact that he does not "introduce" this principle by an appeal to the moral responsibility of the involved; instead, he locates it within the formal properties of discourse, i.e., the necessary structure of cogent argument. Still, the problem of moral decisionism is important enough to warrant some further considerations as to whether Habermas really succeeds in overcoming it. First, however, I would like to quote Habermas at some length, since my discussion thus far has only paraphrased his writings concerning the logic of discourse. The following quotation may thus serve as both a confirmation and a summary of the preceding argument.

[30] E.g. Baier 1958, Singer 1961, Lorenzen 1969, Rawls 1971, Schwemmer 1971 and Lorenzen/ Schwemmer 1975.

Since in practical discourses we do not have recourse to the experience of an external, objective reality... a consensus theory of rightness does not encounter the same objections as a consensus theory of truth [namely, objections concerning the objectivity of the empirical content of discursively vindicated propositions]. It seems obvious that practical questions regarding the selection of norms can be decided upon only by a consensus among all the involved and all those potentially affected.... A consensus theory of rightness runs however the risk of raising doubts as to whether practical questions really admit of truth, i.e., whether the rightness of commands or prohibitions is a discursively redeemable validity claim at all or whether it is not rather something merely subjective. In fact, this conviction underlies non-cognitivist ethics. In this context the principle of universalization gains central importance, a principle according to which only those norms are admitted that can find general recognition. The principle of universalization in fact serves to exclude, as not admitting of censensus, all norms whose content and range of validity are particular. Insofar as such non-generalizable norms can also meet with consensus, we are dealing with a compromise between particular interests rather than an argumentatively reached consensus. Compromises are the results of prudent action and negotiation, not of discourses. Like induction, universalization plays the role of a bridge principle that is to explain why we can make plausible a proposed norm of action by referring to the consequences and side-effects that the application of the norm may have in regard to accepted needs. This step is plausible if the casuistic evidence [i.e., the backing B for the warrant W] can rely on *generally* accepted needs. (1973c:250f, my transl.)

We can then define precisely the function of practical discourse implied in Habermas' model: Practical discourse is to test whether the interests that motivate a contingent consensus on norms, or a disputed claim for rightness, are generalizable and hence admit of rational consensus. If they are not generalizable, the consensus is at best a compromise among negotiated particular interests, or else it is a mere cover for the result of strategic action, i.e., conflict involving deliberate deception and/or recourse to unrestrained force. In other words, practical discourse about matters of moral concern serves the discursive realization of the principle of generalization, as "the only principle in which practical reason expresses itself" (1975:108).

There remain two essential questions. They concern the suspicion of moral decisionism and the possible suppression of generalizable interests.

3.3. The Problem of Moral Decisionism

As a rule, approaches to ethics that rely on the principle of generalization have one important drawback: they ultimately fall back on moral decisionism. Moral decisionism is typical of the non-cognitivist ethics that relegate moral decisions to the realm of irrational – and implicitly, private – acts of belief. By contrast, the principle

147

of generalization is intended to establish a link between morality and rationality: those norms are moral which can be justified as being generalizable.

But unfortunately, this link is not sufficient to overcome moral decisionism, for the principle of generalization itself must be introduced in the form of a "moral law" or "moral principle." The problem of moral decisionism is thus merely shifted to another level; but we must still make a decisionistic start and appeal to the moral responsibility of agents, planners or discourse participants.[31] This is well illustrated by Kant's categorical imperative, which gains its normative power only if we can convince planners to adopt it. The same is true of Lorenzen's "constructivist" model of rational discourse, a model that is in some respects similar to Habermas'.[32] Lorenzen "introduces" the moral principle in the form of a "principle of transsubjectivity": "Transcend your subjectivity!" or: "No subjective arguments!" where subjectivity is defined as the claim of a person or a group for exemption from being subject to norms that stand for generalizable interests (e.g. 1974:92ff, 129; Lorenzen/Schwemmer 1975:164ff). In order to "introduce" this principle, Lorenzen, as he himself recognizes, must appeal to a decisionistic "act of faith" on the part of those involved (1969:74).

Not so Habermas. Overcoming decisionism is his declared purpose, for decisionism immunizes ideologically motivated claims (including the claim to "pluralism of values") against the efforts of practical reason (cf.1975:107). Habermas' model avoids falling back on moral decisionism by making the formal properties of rational discourse the guarantor of generalizability:

The problematic that arises with the introduction of a moral principle is disposed of as soon as one sees that the expectation of a discursive redemption of normative-validity claims is already contained in the structure of intersubjectivity and makes specially introduced maxims of universalization superfluous. In taking up a practical discourse, we unavoidably suppose an ideal speech situation that, on the strength of its formal properties, allows consensus only through *generalizable* interests. A cognitivist linguistic ethics *[Sprachethik]* has no need of principles. It is based only on fundamental norms of rational speech that we must always presuppose if we discourse at all. (1975:110, similarly 1976:344)

---

[31] Nietzsche, for example, would point out that the normative content of this decisionistic start consists in an egalitarian orientation, and we would hardly be able to move him "with reasons" to accept such an orientation.

[32] The main concern of this approach is to construct a system of basic terms and rules – "linguistic norms" – that will render practical discourse a teachable subject (therefore the name "constructivism"). Constructivism shares with Habermas' model the need to appeal to counterfactual conditions of ideal rationality. Cf. Kamlah/Lorenzen 1967:118f, Lorenzen 1974:129, Lorenzen/Schwemmer 1975:161ff. The basic exposition of this approach is Kamlah/Lorenzen 1967 and, in English, Lorenzen 1969. Other sources include Schwemmer 1971, Kambartel 1974, Lorenzen 1978, Mittelstrass 1975 and 1979.

But since we know that the presupposed ideal speech situation is counterfactual and non-verifiable, what then is the point of replacing the appeal to a moral principle by the appeal to utopian conditions of rationality? Epistemologically speaking, Habermas' point is of course that we need an ideal model of undistorted discourse as a background against which to arrange for real-world discourses. Heuristically speaking, however, it appears that Habermas'model cannot avoid falling back on moral decisionism so long as it must admit that the ideal speech situation remains counterfactual. We shall return to this problem in the concluding section.

3.4. The Problem of the Suppression of Generalizable Interests

The remaining question is this: What if interests are not generalizable at all? As Habermas recognizes, his solution to the problem of moral decisionism depends on the generalizability of interests:

> The limits of a decisionistic treatment of practical questions are overcome as soon as argumentation is expected to test the generaliz*ability* of interests, instead of being resigned to an impenetrable pluralism of apparently ultimate value orientations (or belief-acts or attitudes). (1975:108)

When interests are not generalizable, the "second-best" way to legitimate normative validity claims is by *compromise*. A compromise, according to Habermas, is "a normed adjustment between particular interests... if it takes place under conditions of a balance of power between the parties involved." (1975:111) From a democratic point of view, such compromise is clearly preferable to merely strategic action. But, on the other hand, there arises the danger that generalizable interests are suppressed by a compromise from which only the involved parties benefit, but not the larger community of all those who share the same needs and who may be negatively affected by the side-effects of the compromise. In this case, Habermas speaks of a *pseudo-compromise (Scheinkompromiss,* 1975:112). Pseudo-compromises withdraw legitimate, because generalizable, validity claims from public discussion and therefore threaten to narrow the range of application of Habermas' model of practical discourse. Critical theory must counter this danger by working toward a *model of the suppression of generalizable interests,* i.e., a theory that would explain the ways in which generalizable interests are suppressed in various social systems. As an example, Habermas refers to Claus Offe's theory of governmental selectivity (Offe 1972:65ff). With Offe (but in a more systems-theoretic terminology) we can distinguish four principal leverage points for identifying institutional sources of the suppression of generalizable interests: (a) input selectivity, (b) internal selectivity, (c) output selectivity, and (d) complementary selectivity, i.e., selectivity of information intended to conceal systematic selectivity of the other types.[33]

In order to distinguish justified from pseudo-compromise Habermas establishes the rule:

> A compromise can be justified as a compromise only if both conditions are met; a balance of power among the parties involved and the non-generalizability of the negotiated interests exist. If even one of these general conditions of compromise formation is not fulfilled, we are dealing with a pseudo-compromise. (1975:112)

Habermas' concern about the suppression of generalizable interests is understandable, for such suppression considerably narrows the applicability range of his discursive model of rationality. On the other hand, it seems that this range of applicability is even more restricted by the fact that strict generalizability of disputed interests is the exception rather than the rule. If this is true, we should be equally concerned about the danger that interests are presented as being generalizable when they are in fact particular interests. We might speak of *pseudo-rationality* in this case, that is, of ideologically motivated apparent generalization of interests in terms of "the common good," "the public interest," and "pluralism of values." Habermas is of course aware that such ideologically distorted "generalization" of interests is a prevalent source of deception in democratic decision-making processes (cf.1975:112).[34]

Against the danger that practical discourse might become a cover for ideological partisanship, Habermas advances his own advocacy role for practical discourse, the before-mentioned "partiality for reason." (1975:142) To him,

> The advocacy role of the critical theory of society would consist in ascertaining generalizable, though nevertheless suppressed, interests in a representatively simulated discourse between groups that are differentiated (or could be non-arbitrarily differentiated) from one another by articulated, or at least virtual, opposition of interests. (1975:117)

[33] I can only give a brief explanation in the present context. Offe defines as *selectivity* "the non-contingent, i.e. systematic, restriction of a range of possibilities [for rational decision making]" (1972:78). If for instance the U.S. Department of Energy derives its information about the production and distribution of oil from the very oil industry it is to regulate, we are surely dealing with a case of input selectivity (of information). If there is a frequent exchange of experts between the nuclear industry and the regulating federal agency, the Nuclear Regulatory Commission, this is a symptom of internal selectivity (cf. Galbraith's "bureaucratic symbiosis, 1975:139). If there are frequent compromises or "gentlemens' agreements" between an industry to be regulated (e.g., the aviation industry) and the regulating agency (e.g., the Federal Aviation Agency), we have a case of output selectivity. And finally, if the same agency conceals in its public statements its own selectivity, i.e., the lost chances for rational public decision-making and the "non-events" of suppressed but generalizable interests, it is relying on complementary selectivity. In all these cases it must be suspected that generalizable interests are suppressed by pseudo-compromises.

[34] As a case in point, cf. also my discussion of Popper's conception of the "open society" in Ch. 1, Sec. 3. The notion of an "open," "liberal," and "pluralistic" society all too often serves as an excuse, if not a cover, for generalizing particular interests.

One may have doubts about whether such a partisanship for reason is not bound to end up as covertly ideological partisanship, be it only because the partisanship for reason is and will remain a critical ideal rather than a generalizable interest. It will always be a minority of citizens that can be moved "with reason" to follow Habermas' appeal to the partiality for reason, and even they will not thereby become bloodless beings renouncing all but generalizable needs and interests. But again, such considerations can by no means derogate from the theoretical significance of Habermas' model in general, and his attempt to avoid a decisionistic start in particular. Only against the background of Habermas' ideal model of oppression-free discourse can we hope to understand both the possibilities for institutionalizing real-world discourses and the inevitable sources of deception involved in them. The practical task of discovering these sources of deception, in each case, is what our conception of a critical heuristics of socially-rational planning is all about. In regard to this task, we shall now undertake a critical appreciation of Habermas' approach and try to draw the necessary conclusions for the conception of a critical heuristics.

4. Conclusions: Critical Theory or Critical Heuristics?

To begin with, I wish to emphasize that I find much of Habermas' work extraordinarily well-argued and well-aimed and that I generally share his critical intentions against scientism, positivism and decisionism. Habermas' attempt to reconceptualize the theory-practice problem in terms of a model of practical discourse and to move it back into the center of social epistemology from where it had been removed by the analytical and neopositivist philosophers; his critique of the positivist reduction of practical to instrumental questions and of the objectivist illusion in that reduction; his defense of self-reflection and hermeneutic reflection as indispensable parts of social science; his conception of a transformed transcendental philosophy; his reconstruction of the linguistic turn in post-Kantian philosophy in terms of a universal pragmatics; his attempt to revive the tradition of the liberal model of the public domain as a basis for institutionalizing discourses in new areas of social practice; his partisanship for communicative rather than strategic resolution of conflicts; the conception of a dialogical rather than a monological ethics – these and other aspects of his work seem to me to provide important contributions to the long-standing task of developing a critical social epistemology.

But no great philosophical system can probably ever answer all the questions which it discovers. Appreciation for Habermas' immense contribution – which moreover is far from being at an end – need not therefore prevent us from searching for a position that might provide us with practicable answers to some of these questions, without at the same time renouncing Habermas' basic insights. I propose to concentrate on two fundamental issues.[35] The first concerns Habermas' conception of a transformed transcendental philosophy. This conception seems of fundamental importance for any critical approach to social inquiry, but it leaves open the difficult question of the quasi-transcendental status of the cognitive interests and categories that make up the a priori of experience. I shall argue that this question calls for a "critically-heuristic turn," and I shall try briefly to explain my conception of critical heuristics. (Section 4.1)

The second issue concerns the a priori of argumentation, the other half of a transformed transcendental approach. The problem that appears crucial in this regard, particularly from a heuristic point of view, is the practical status of a "practical discourse" tied to utopian conditions of rationality. It seems to me that Habermas'

---

[35] For critical discussions of other aspects of Habermas' work cf. among other sources: Maurer's comprehensive and often brilliant critique of what he calls "Jürgen Habermas' Abolition of Philosophy" (in German language, 1977); the "Review Symposium on Habermas" in *Philosophy of the Social Sciences* 2 (1972):193–270, with articles by Lobkowicz, Dallmayr, Lenhardt, Hill and Nichols (all 1972); the collection *Materialien zu Erkenntnis und Interesse,* edited by Dallmayr (1974).

model of practical discourse does not really mediate between reasonable discourse *on* practice and practice itself but rather substitutes the former for the latter. I shall argue that we need a more genuinely dialectical perspective on the relationship between reason and social practice, or a "dialectical turn." (Section 4.2)

4.1. Toward a "Quasi-Transcendental" Approach: The Critically-Heuristic Turn

Habermas' and Apel's distinction between problems of the constitution of meaningful experience (the a priori of experience) and problems of the rational justification or criticism of the validity of statements (the a priori of argumentation) appears to me an indispensable step toward a renewal of Kant's transcendental criticism. As I have pointed out briefly, the basic difficulty of such an undertaking lies in the fact that Kant's presupposition of an absolute starting point in the form of an abstract transcendental subject of knowledge is philosophically no longer respectable. This is so because this sort of objectivist starting point circumvents the crucial epistemological problem of accounting for the empirically contingent, social and historical context on which both the meaning and the validity of possible knowledge (and deception) depend.

In comparison to the difficult implications of this insight, Kant's problem looks almost simple. He termed "transcendental" an investigation of those conditions of experience and empirical science which are not themselves empirical but which by necessity precede experience. Since he presupposed an objective and abstract starting point, he did not have to distinguish the a priori of argumentation from the a priori of experience: the a priori conditions of objective experience were to him also the a priori conditions of true knowledge. He could still conceive of a "monological" approach to establishing knowledge-constitutive or transcendental categories, and since an objective starting point made it also unnecessary to distinguish between different object domains with specific categories, this monological approach could even be expected to yield universally valid categories. Establishing these categories could take the form of a "transcendental deduction." With his transcendental logic, Kant created a logic that was every bit as rigorous and universal as deductive logic but which was incomparably richer because it incorporated the systems idea. We shall deal with Kant's transcendental "systems approach" in the following chapters; at this point it is sufficient to have a general notion of the complex situation from which we must start out to reach once again Kant's unique level of epistemological reflection.

The reader will have noticed at least two large omissions in my account of Habermas' work: there is no reference to the role of the systems approach in Habermas' conception of a transformed transcendental philosophy, and there is no elaboration of knowledge-constitutive categories that might be useful for the social inquirer. In fact, Habermas has not – or at least, not yet – formulated a systematic and critical role for the systems approach in a transformed transcendental philosophy, although (or perhaps rather, because) he has provided an important contribution to the critique of the prevailing technocratic understanding of "systems theory" (cf. Habermas 1971 d). The fact that he does not seriously embark on a critical revision of systems-theoretic categories cannot be explained by his critical stance vis-à-vis systems theory; his critique could, indeed, enable one to undertake such an effort.

A more likely explanation, it seems to me, can be found in Habermas' relative neglect of the problem of a constitution theory of experience (concerned in the a priori of experience) in favor of a universal pragmatics (concerned in the a priori of argumentation). Although a renewed transcendental approach requires both research programs, Habermas thus far has attempted to locate the conditions of rational criticism and justification of truth claims entirely within the a priori of argumentation. Not surprisingly, such an attempt can hope to succeed only under ideal conditions – and this insight throws some new light on Habermas' need to suppose an ideal speech situation. Habermas had solid reasons for concentrating his efforts first on the a priori of argumentation – among them of course the historical neglect of this issue and the need to counter Popper's narrow model of rational discourse with a more critical model of practical discourse. But there is another reason, a reason that Habermas himself has never mentioned, but which represents a decisive assumption of the present work: *a constitution theory of experience is, I believe, possible today only by way of a heuristic approach.* A heuristic approach is incompatible with critical theory's search for a theoretically justifiable status for its basic categories. The categories a heuristic approach might yield cannot of course be justified theoretically (i.e., by demonstrating their necessity) but only heuristically, i.e., by referring to their empirically contingent usefulness. This implication does not however exclude the possibility that such categories can at least be "derived" or "discovered" systematically (e.g., from a critical understanding of the systems idea), though it does mean that a rational criticism that relies upon these categories can no longer claim the status of a critical theory (of society) but only that of a *critical heuristics* (of social planning). Nor does it exclude the possibility that we can systematically reflect on the sources of potential deception in our heuristic categories; for although we may not be able positively to justify their validity, we may still be able to understand why we are not able to do so. An outstanding example has been provided by Kant in the context of his attempt to establish the "objective" validity of the basic moral category of a practical "law" or categorical imperative. In his *Groundwork of the Metaphysic of Morals* (1786), Kant justifies his famous conclusion:

> And thus, while we do not comprehend the practical unconditioned necessity of the moral imperative, we do comprehend its *incomprehensibility.* This is all that can fairly be asked of a philosophy which presses forward in its principles to the very limit of human reason.[36]

[36] Last two sentences of the book, p. B 128; transl. Paton 1964: 131.

To the best of my knowledge, Habermas has not drawn such a conclusion thus far, in spite of the fact that his contribution to a constitution theory of experience has hardly advanced beyond the early theory of cognitive or "knowledge-constitutive" interests. Habermas ascribes to these "knowledge-constitutive" interests a quasi-transcendental status:

[They] express anthropologically deep-seated interests, which direct our knowledge and which have a quasi-transcendental status. These interests of knowledge [cognitive interests] are of significance neither for the psychology nor for the sociology of knowledge, nor for the critique of ideology in any narrower sense; for they are invariant.... The technical and practical interests of knowledge are not regulators of cognition which have to be eliminated for the sake of the objectivitiy of knowledge; instead, they themselves determine the aspect under which reality is objectified, and can thus be made accessible to experience to begin with. They are the conditions which are necessary in order that subjects capable of speech and action may have experience which can lay a claim to objectivity. (1973a:8f, cf. also 1971a:194)

Strictly speaking, however, Habermas' cognitive interests are not at all constitutive of knowledge but only of the three object domains related to instrumental action, communicative action, and emancipatory self-reflection. To be very precise, they establish a "transcendental link between experience and action" (1973b:396) and accordingly differentiate the a priori of experience into a pragmatic, a communicative, and a self-reflective a priori of experience (to which correspond the following modes of experience: sensory experience or observation of objects and events; "communicative experience" or linguistically mediated experience of interacton and mutual understanding; and "inner experience" or self-consciousness, cf. Habermas' preliminary sketch in 1973b:394ff). This differentiation serves a critical purpose against the scientistic claim for the unity or universality of science. In addition, the cognitive interests may be said to serve a critical purpose against false validity claims and objectivist illusions where the interpretation or application of statements about objects of experience transgress their appropriate object domain. But they have in fact no (quasi-) transcendental function in constituting specific objects of experience *within* the object domains they constitute. Accordingly, Habermas at present has not furnished any conceptual framework for the social inquirer who is to work within the object domains of the hermeneutic-historical and the critically oriented sciences. And yet it is only such a conceptual framework that could transform critical theory from a mere research program into a practical tool of critical social inquiry and design.

There is a difficulty that might help explain why Habermas has not taken the "critically-heuristic turn" which I propose. It concerns his declared aim of keeping the epistemological foundation of critical theory free of metaphysics.[37] *As soon as one recognizes the merely heuristic character of "quasi-transcendental" categories, the only way to keep a conceptual framework free of unreflected metaphysical presuppositions is to understand and examine them critically not only as a quasi-transcendental but also as quasi-metaphysical concepts.* Any form of criticism that is not strictly transcendental is subject to the conclusion we reached in the context of our critique of critical rationalism: criticism without metaphysics is as blind as metaphysics without criticism is empty. It is clear of course that once we give up the notion of an absolute starting point, metaphysics can no longer be understood as "first philosophy" but takes on a new, heuristic function which I propose to call "quasi-metaphysical," by analogy to "quasi-transcendental." Heuristic categories are to be reflected as *metaphysical* in the sense that they contain a hermeneutic prejudgement about the structure of the real world to which they are applied: e.g., is the underlying worldview a reductionistic or a holistic one, is real-world complexity understood in mechanistic or organic metaphors, etc. (cf. Ulrich 1979, 1980). Heuristic categories are merely *quasi*-metaphysical, however, insofar as there is no way of establishing them by means of metaphysical or ontological speculation. They can be validated only by recourse to their heuristic fruitfulness in promoting mutual understanding and critical discussion – in one word, reasonable practice.

Let me sum up the thrust of what has been said thus far.

1. A "quasi-transcendental" constitution theory of experience appears to be conceivable today only as a heuristic approach.

2. The transition from a strictly trancendental to a *quasi*-transcendental approach entails not only the need for quasi-transcendental criticism but also for quasi-metaphysical criticism. (These two tentative concepts will be developed in the course of our "dialogue" with Kant; at this point I can only give preliminary definitions.)

---

[37] Habermas justifies his search for a metaphysics-free critical theory by referring to the historical fact that traditional metaphysics shares with traditional theory the ontological illusion and the illusion of "pure theory," i.e., the illusion of presuppositionless, interest-free, self-justifying theory. The traditional name for metaphysics, "First Philosophy," captures this illusion. Indeed, both traditional theory and First Philosophy conceal from themselves the presuppositions in their own claim for presuppositionless self-justification: "pure" theory is pure only by virtue of abstracting from its pre-scientific basis in the world of social practice, and from the repercussions of "pure" theory on that social practice. Cf. Habermas 1965, in 1971a:307, 315. With Adorno, Habermas asserts: "It is time not for First Philosophy, but for the last philosophy." (1957:435) Critical theory is to be "last philosophy" because it is to become practical itself (cf. 1957:412, 424, critically Maurer 1977:16f). But as much as one can sympathize with Habermas' critical intent against the pretensions of First Philosophy, it seems to me that the notion of a metaphysics-free critical theory represents an over-reaction that loses sight of the impossibility (and therefore, uncritical character) of "metaphysics-free" theory or epistemology. The opposition of metaphysics and criticism is not a critical but a positivist concept which Habermas strangely seems to share with critical rationalists.

3. By *quasi-transcendental criticism* I mean an argument that does not explain the necessary a priori conditions of empirical knowledge (such as transcendental criticism is supposed to do) but rather the sources of possible deception contained in the unavoidable a priori component of all knowledge and thought.

5. Similarly, by *quasi-metaphysical criticism* I mean the reflection on the real-world implications of our conceptions of (social) reality, with special regard for the "subjective" concerns of those who live the social reality in question. The precise difference between quasi-transcendental and quasi-metaphysical criticism can be explained only within the dialectical framework of the later chapters; basically it is a difference of emphasis with respect to the "critical instance" to which cogent criticism must refer – rational argument and discourse in the first case, lived social reality in the second.

5. Taken together, the two forms of critical reflection represent the necessary critical part of a heuristic approach. To the extent that we succeed in incorporating them into a heuristic approach, we can speak of a *critical heuristics.* There is of course a dialectical tension, if not a paradox, in the notion of a critical heuristics. *Heuristic* concepts aim at discovering questions or problems and reconstructing basic frameworks for inquiry. In short, they ought to help us reflect on the *sources of discovery,* i.e., of possible knowledge. *Critical* concepts, on the other hand, aim at reflection on the *sources of possible deception* in inquiry, design, or discourse. But at least since Christopher Columbus it has become popular knowledge that discovery and deception go together, or that there is no guarantee against deception in discovery. Hence, if we want to provide inquirers and planners with conceptual support for the discovery of relevant questions and answers, we must also further their reflection on the sources of deception in all inquiry and design.

Let us now examine the basic lessons that, from our discussion of Habermas, we can learn for the program of a critical heuristics.

1. First of all I wish to prevent a possible misunderstanding: I do not mean to confine the "critically-heuristic turn" to the problem of a constitution theory of experience. The a priori of experience and the a priori of argumentation are closely and inextricably interrelated – an aspect thas has partly been lost from view in Habermas' universal pragmatics. Moreover, one of the major motivations for the proposed critically-heuristic turn is that it ought to help us in coming to grips with the problem of the a priori of argumentation *without* having to resort to utopian conditions of rationality.

2. If one seeks to substitute a universal (= formal) pragmatics for the unfeasible undertaking of a metaphysics-free, quasi-transcendental, constitution theory of experience, one must indeed explain the material content of discursively validated statements by referring to an "always already" presupposed context of "social

reality," and to ordinary language (ordinary communication) as the source of our conceptual framework. This is exactly what a heuristic approach practices from the very beginning, but without paying the price of an unavoidable recourse to the ideal speech situation ("pure communication"). The conception of the ideal speech situation makes sense as a theoretical construct and critical idea for a theory of undistorted communication; but it cannot serve as a practical criterion of rational (as opposed to merely factual) consensus. The conclusion is this: The attempt to locate the quasi-transcendental conditions of rational consensus within a universal pragmatics (i.e., within the a priori of argumentation) is a theoretically important boundary experiment, but it cannot yield a practical model of practical discourse. *Only an approach that strikes a balance between the a priori of experience and the a priori of argumentation can accomplish this; and such an approach can be "quasi-transcendental" only in a heuristic sense.*

3. Although Habermas thus far appears to have maintained a strict claim to a research program ("universal pragmatics") that, if successful, would yield a theoretical justification of the necessary and sufficient conditions of discursively validated knowledge, he has nevertheless prepared the ground for a critically-heuristic turn. Above all, he has been the first to demonstrate in detail the fundamental role of the a priori of discursive argumentation for a renewed transcendental criticism. He has made the important *step from Kant's "monological" toward a dialogical approach to the problem of transcendental criticism,* a step which seems of special significance for a heuristically useful solution to the problem of practical reason.

4. On the other hand, it appears that Habermas' universal pragmatics is still a rather "monological" program – it remains bound to the notion that necessary and sufficient conditions of knowledge can be derived from theoretical considerations. In this respect, the idea of a dialogical approach seems capable of radicalization. A critical heuristics must take up Habermas' contribution and try to radicalize it: *a renewed transcendental approach will also have to be a renewed dialectical approach* (cf. to this Section 4.2 below).

5. Habermas has clearly stated the basic assumption on which we rely, even though he has not as yet pursued all its implications:

> I see it as the task of a non-objectivistic theory of knowledge [literally: science-theory, *Wissenschaftstheorie*] to demonstrate in detail that the logic of inquiry *is* the logic of the connection between the a priori of experience and the a priori of argumentation. (1973b:397, my transl.)

It would be altogether presumptuous to imply that we shall be able to explain the logic of this connection *theoretically* in a more complete way than Habermas. Nor is this our purpose. However, it is an unavoidable task to come to grips *practically* with the link between the constitution of meaningful experience and the discursive

158

redemption of validity claims. This task will be the central concern of Chapter Five.

6. Finally, Habermas has made some interesting observations with regard to the quasi-transcendental status of a universal pragmatics. Provided that we keep in mind Habermas' theoretical rather than heuristic perspective, they may help us better understand what so far is a rather tentative and vague concept, namely the meaning of a "quasi-transcendental" approach. He asks:

> What is the relation of universal-pragmatic reconstruction of general and unavoidable presuppositions of possible processes of understanding to the type of investigation that has, since Kant, been called transcendental analysis? (1979 a:21)

Obviously this relation is even more precarious with regard to the a priori of argumentation than it is with regard to the a priori of experience with which Kant was mainly concerned. It is therefore of interest for us to see how Habermas answers his question.

First of all, the distinction between the two a priori problematics makes it clear that

> the relation between the objectivity of possible experience and the truth of propositions looks different than it does under Kantian premises. In place of a priori demonstration [of knowledge-constitutive categories] we have transcendental investigation of the conditions for argumentatively redeeming validity claims that are at least implicitly related to discursive vindication. (1979 a:23)

The next question is: Can such an investigation still be called "transcendental," once we have dropped Kant's focus on the a priori of experience? In contrast to Apel, who speaks in this context of a "transcendental hermeneutics" or a "transcendental pragmatics" (e.g. 1976), Habermas hesitates to adopt the transcendental terminology and instead speaks of "reconstructive (or formal) analysis" and of the "reconstructive sciences" (cf. 1979 a:8f, 15, 23; 1973 b:413). He mentions two main reasons, the first and basic one concerning the a priori of experience, the second the a priori of argumentation.

Re: the a priori of experience. Reconstructive analysis, for want of a strictly transcendental deduction of basic categories, must rely on empirical research. Such research is not however empirical in the sense of the empirical-analytic or nomological sciences; its object is not perceptible reality (sensory experience) but symbolically prestructured reality, i.e., "objects" of communicative experience (= the conceptual frameworks that make possible the intersubjective sharing of experience, cf. 1979 a:10). As a prototype of such research, Habermas refers to Jean Piaget's cognitive developmental psychology (e.g. 1965, 1971). He also frequently refers to Lawrence Kohlberg's studies of moral development, studies which rely on Piaget's approach (e.g. Kohlberg 1969, 1971, cf. Habermas' article on "Moral Development and Ego Identity" in 1979 b:69–94), and to Noam Chomski's theory of linguistic competence (1957, 1965). These studies have in common a cognitive-developmental perspective on the knowing subject, and they can thus fill in the gap left open by Kant's abstract transcendental subject. Piaget indeed has understood his research as an empirical verification of Kant's categorical framework for sensory experience (substance, space, time and causality) and has suggested the research program of a "genetic epistemology" (Piaget 1970). It is characteristic of this type of reconstructive analysis that it moves somewhere between the realms of strictly transcendental and empirically contingent concepts and that this distinction between the two becomes blurred (cf. Habermas 1979 a:24). On the one hand, reconstructive analysis is concerned in the a priori conditions of possible experience, i.e., categories that are presupposed in all experience. On the other hand, these categories are developed and applied under empirically contingent conditions and thus admit of empirical analysis. In other words, we are still dealing with *a priori* conditions of possible experience, but these conditions can no longer be understood and reconstructed as an absolute but only as a *relative a priori of experience* – relative with regard to the cognitive developmental stages reached by individuals, cultures, and the human species in general (phylogenetic and ontogenetic development), and of course also with regard to the specific object domains that are constituted by the "anthropologically deep-seated" cognitive interests (cf. 1979 a:22).

In consequence, Habermas partly agrees with the analytical reception of Kant's transcendental philosophy (he mentions Strawson 1964 as an example, cf. 1979 a:21). Analytical philosophy has broken with Kant's strong apriorism in favor of a weaker interpretation of the transcendental:

Every coherent experience is organized in a categorical network; to the extent that we discover the same implicit conceptual structure in any coherent experience whatsoever, we may call this basic conceptual system of possible experience *transcendental.* This conception renounces the claim that Kant wanted to vindicate with his transcendental deduction; it gives up all claim to a proof of the objective validity of our concepts of objects of possible experience in general. The strong apriorism of Kantian philosophy gives way to a weaker version. From now on, transcendental investigation must rely on the competence of knowing subjects who judge which experiences may be called coherent experiences in order to analyze this material for general and necessary categorical presuppositions. Every reconstruction of a basic conceptual system of possible experience has to be regarded as a hypothetical proposal that can be tested against new experience. As long as the assertion of its necessity and universality has not been refuted, we term *transcendental* the conceptual structure recurring in all coherent experiences. In this weaker version, the claim that that structure can be demonstrated a priori is dropped (1979 a:21f).

160

The consequence of this recognition would seem to me the necessity of a critically-heuristic approach: if conceptual frameworks cannot be validated a priori, they can be established only tentatively, that is, as heuristic categories that are in need of both empirical (a posteriori) validation (are they fruitful for discovering relevant questions or real-world aspects?) and permanent critical reflection (in what way are they deceptive, i.e., selective or inadequate with respect to the object of inquiry?). Habermas, as we have seen, is not prepared to draw such a conclusion but instead turns to the a priori of argumentation.

In opposition to the analytical Kant reception, Habermas maintains that

> the reservation regarding a strong apriorism in no way demands limiting oneself to a logical-semantic analysis of the conditions of possible experience. If we surrender the concept of the transcendental subject... this does not mean that we have to renounce universal-pragmatic analysis of the application of our concepts of objects of possible experience.... (1979a:22)

Here Habermas implies another conclusion that is of obvious importance for a heuristically oriented approach: while Kant's transcendental categories were tailored to the needs of empirical-analytic science, we shall have to search for categories that can grasp the essential *pragmatic* dimension of historical-hermeneutic and critically oriented inquiry.

Re: the a priori of argumentation. Along with the adoption of the "weak" version of transcendental philosophy, Habermas considers using the concept of "communicative experience" as a bridge concept that might make plausible an extension of the transcendental terminology to the a priori of argumentation:

> Something like a transcendental investigation of processes of understanding seems plausible to me as long as we view these under the aspect of processes of experience. It is in this sense that I speak of communicative experience; in understanding the utterance of another speaker... the hearer (like the observer who perceives a segment of reality) has an experience.... Just as we analyze our a priori concepts of objects in general – that is, the conceptual structure of any coherent perception – we could analyze our a priori concepts of utterances in general – that is, the basic concepts of situations of possible understanding, the conceptual structure that enables us to employ sentences in correct utterances. (1979a:23f)

Habermas concludes, however, that the term "transcendental" is inadequate to characterize the research program and basic concepts of a universal pragmatics. He mentions two main reasons:

(a) The use of Kantian terminology might conceal Habermas' shift of focus from the a priori of experience to the a priori of argumentation.

(b) Likewise, the term "transcendental" might conceal the transition from Kant's strong apriorism to a weaker apriorism (cf. 1979a:24).

161

However, although the transition to a weak apriorism is compelling, Habermas' shift of focus from the a priori of experience to the a priori of argumentation appears to be too one-sided. It would seem to me, as I have briefly suggested above, that Kant's *strong* apriorism can only be replaced by *both* a *relativized* a priori of experience *and* a *relativized* a priori of argumentation, and that the conditions of possible understanding (rational discourse and consensus) cannot be located entirely within the a priori of argumentation. It is, then, not sufficient to refer the problem of the a priori of experience to empirical-developmental studies of the kind pioneered by Piaget. If the conditions of possible understanding include the conceptual frameworks that are constitutive of intersubjectively meaningful experience – both sensory and communicative experience – then the ultimate test of such frameworks is not to be found in the empirical explanation of their phylogenetic and ontogenetic development but in their heuristic usefulness for the intersubjective exchange of experience and arguments. Even in the abstract realm of quasi-transcendental reflection, the final test of the much-touted pudding consists in the eating.

We cannot escape facing the question of priorities: Do we want to reconstruct the conditions of possible understanding in such a way as to justify or explain them theoretically, or do we want to provide heuristic support for practical inquiry and design "out there" in the world of social practice? If our goal is theoretical, we must, with Habermas, undertake a reconstruction of the necessary and sufficient ("universal") cognitive-linguistic competences of speakers, and such an undertaking entails both the formal analysis of the ideal speech situation and the empirical analysis of the development of the required competences and concepts. But if our goal is practical, we must first of all provide the social inquirer with helpful conceptual tools for grasping normative social practice. With regard to the a priori of argumentation, the corresponding task is then not to explain the sufficient conditions of perfectly rational discourse, but rather to guide the discourse participants toward reflection upon the inevitable lack of perfect rationality. That is to say, we face not so much a task of theoretical *explanation* as one of practical *design* – design for conceptual frameworks and social arrangements that together might provide heuristic support to inquirers in their search for discovery and deception. In view of this task, the expression *"quasi-transcendental"* gains a new, critical, meaning: understanding heuristic concepts as "quasi-transcendental" is to remind us that we do in fact substitute them as relative a priori categories for Kant's absolute a priori categories, and hence that they can become a useful source of discovery only if we also reflect on them as sources of possible deception.

4.2. Toward a Practical Model of Practical Discourse: The Dialectical Turn

In addition to the critically-heuristic turn, a "dialectical turn" appears as the second key to making Habermas' model of practical discourse truly practical. In

162

particular, this goal requires that we give Habermas' purely formal model ("universal pragmatics") its materially pragmatic dimension, i.e., an access to the historical and normative content without which practical discourse remains not only unpractical but empty.

I have already hinted that Habermas' shift of focus from a monological to a discursive concept of rationality seems capable of radicalization. By "radicalization" I mean in this context a stronger committment to the dialectical idea that the challenge to practical reason requires a *mediating third* between reason and practice, and that this mediating third is to be found in practical discourse. *As important as Habermas' ideal model of practical discourse is theoretically, practically it cannot play the role of a mediating force between reason and practice, for it is itself located entirely within the boundaries of reason.*

From this perspective, the usual association of Habermas and the Frankfurt school with the "dialectical" (as opposed to the analytical) position conceals what appears to be a deficiency of dialectic in Habermas' conception of rational criticism and practical discourse. In spite of his shift to a discursive approach and his professed orientation toward a reconstruction of Marx' historical materialism (cf. the title of his book of 1976), his model of discourse is today much closer to Kant and the analytical tradition than it is to Marx. Kant is a very rich source of reflection for any epistemologial or heuristic effort, but this must not make us forget that his transcendental approach was a pre-dialectical one – which is why Habermas has justly characterized it as monological. Here, it seems to me, lies the root cause of why Habermas' model of practical discourse is not quite as practical as its title claims but has thus far had little impact on the social practice at which it is aimed. In the following, I should like to limit our discussion to what I see as the two basic sources of the deficiency of dialectic in Habermas' practical discourse: (1) the dialectic between the a priori of experience and the a priori of argumentation, and (2) the dialectic between a priori and a posteriori concepts of practical reason.

The Dialectic Between the A Priori of Experience
and the A Priori of Argumentation

1. Habermas' retreat to a merely formal analysis of the conditions of possible understanding leaves no room for considering the necessary dialectical interplay between experience and reflection in practical discourse, and for the corresponding possibility of basing the conditions of rational consensus on both the a priori of experience and the a priori of argumentation rather than on the latter alone. Only in this latter way can we hope to avoid falling back on an ideal speech situation which entirely abstracts from the material a priori of experience as a source of mutual understanding and practical reason.

2. As we have seen, Habermas conceives of rational discourse as "pure communicative action" (1971c:120) that is removed from constraints of action and experience

(cf. 1973a:21; 1973b:387; *handlungsentlastet und erfahrungsfrei)* and in which "problematic validity claims are thematic but no informations are exchanged." (1971c:115, my transl., similarly 1973a:18, 1973b:381, 1973c:214) Habermas' theoretical reasons for developing such a "model of pure communicative action" (1971c:120) are plausible; but it is equally clear that practical discourse in the proper sense will always remain dependent on the exchange of informations about the context of experience and action that is to be regulated by the norm in question. How else could "rational" discourse consider the practical implications of controversial validity claims and decide on the cogency of related arguments? In this regard the conception of "pure" communication is strikingly reminiscent of Kant's concept of "pure" (practical) reason. Kant's own conclusion applies:

> How can reason, without other motives taken from elsewhere, be practical by itself? That is, how can the mere *principle of the universal validity of all its maxims...* provide a motive for itself without any material (object) of the will in which one might take a prior interest?... In other words, *how can pure reason be practical?* All of human reason is entirely incapable of explaining this, and all effort and labor to find an explanation of it is in vain. (Kant 1786:B 124f, quoted by Habermas in 1971a:202)

3. A parallel observation is indicated with regard to the ideal speaker required by the ideal speech situation (which in turn is required in order to locate the conditions of possible understanding within the a priori of argumentation). In the form of the ideal speaker, Kant's abstract "transcendental subject" seems to slip back in, though it does so only through the back door of the principle of generalization. The "competent" participant in a practical discourse is expected to give up normative validity claims with regard to personal needs or interests insofar as their generalizability cannot be argumentatively demonstrated. I do not mean to question the principle of generalization as such, but rather its location within the ideal speech situation (i.e., within the formal properties of the a priori of argumentation): it seems to me that individuals who abstract from their particular (non-generalizable) needs lose their identity, and that subjects without identity cannot reasonably negotiate about their conflicting needs, interests, and values. *If practical discourse is to become a practical – and moral – reality, we must look for a model that gives the individuality of both those involved and those affected a relevant role to play.*

Specifically, the moral idea cannot be located exclusively within the formal properties of discourse (the a priori of argumentation) unless one is willing to exclude from moral argument the moral experience of those who are affected by a norm in question but who may not be able to argue their moral concerns in rational terms. This price seems altogether too high for a practical discourse that ought to be both a practicable and a relevant tool of socially-rational planning.

4. A similar conclusion has been drawn by Reinhart K. Maurer who notes that

generalization is a procedure for testing norms but not for creating them. Quite apart from the problem of its universal applicability *[Berechtigung]* it requires contents to which it can be applied.... A *creatio ex nihilo* is not possible for man. (1977:65, my transl.)

Indeed, whether we understand the problem of practical reason in discursive or monological terms is irrelevant with regard to the fact that reason by itself cannot tell us what our needs are; only life-practical experience and moral consciousness can.

5. Still another question must be raised concerning Habermas' association of the moral idea with the a priori or argumentation. The underlying motivation, we have seen, is to overcome *moral decisionism:* instead of "introducing" a moral principle by an appeal to moral responsibility, Habermas incorporates it into the formal properties of practical discourse. But does this device not merely shift the problem of moral decisionism to the decision, in the face of value conflicts, to enter into a discourse? It does indeed seem that Kant's categorical imperative and Habermas' imperative to enter into a discourse both gain their practical, normative power through a decisionistic act of an individual who decides to accept the imperative rather than to switch to strategic action. It appears as if the problem of moral decisionism – it too – cannot be theoretically resolved within a logic of rational discourse, and hence that our only hope of handling it practically lies in unfolding the unavoidable dialectic between the a priori of (moral) experience and the a priori of (moral) argumentation.

6. As a last observation, the attempt to locate the conditions of possible understanding within the a priori of argumentation is responsible for a circularity in Habermas' definitions of "truth" (or "rightness") and "rational consensus." Rational consensus is defined by the formal properties of a discourse that can vindicate truth claims, while truth is defined in discursive terms.[38] Without ignoring the critical content of Habermas' consensus theory of truth vis-à-vis Popper's objectivistic correspondence theory of truth, it seems that we cannot break through this circle except by including the a priori of experience in a consensus theory of truth. Otherwise, what epistemological assurance of reality (and linked to it, practicality) is there in a rational consensus that is defined entirely in terms of the formal properties of discourse? Clearly, a consensus is always a consensus *about* something, which means that *a consensus theory of truth cannot obliterate but only redefine the question of the "correspondence" between the consensus and the real*

---

[38] This has also been noted, among others, by Otfried Höffe (1979:272):
The concept of consensus is not suitable as a criterion or a guarantor of truth because with Habermas this concept itself can only be defined by reference to truth.... (my transl.)

world of social practice.[39] In consequence, we must search for a *dialectical concept of "true" consensus* (or else of "truth"), one that would combine elements of a non-objectivist correspondence theory of truth (as far as the a priori of experience is concerned) with a consensus theory (as far as the a priori of argumentation is concerned). As Höffe notes:

> As soon as a discourse is to establish not only the correspondence of statements with systems of statements but also their relation to reality, we must complement the [consensus-theoretical] approach by the correspondence-theoretical approach. (1979:266, my transl.)

So long as we do not ignore the dialectic between the a priori of experience and the a priori of argumentation, there is no danger that such a perspective should have us fall back on an objectivist correspondence theory of truth such as Popper's.

The Dialectic Between A Priori and A Posteriori Concepts of Practical Reason

1. As important as it is, from a quasi-transcendental point of view, fully to unfold the dialectic between the a priori of experience and the a priori of argumentation, this is not in itself sufficient. Quasi-transcendental or heuristic a priori concepts situate themselves in a dialectical relationship with a posteriori (empirical) concepts. That is to say, the dialectic between experience and reflection, between the constitution of meaning and the discursive vindication of validity claims, is not merely a matter of the (quasi-) transcendental link between the two a priori problematics; it unfolds into a more general dialectic between the quasi-transcendental realm of the strictly rational and the empirical realm of the partly irrational, that is, between *rational* search for (theoretical or practical) knowledge and *lived* social reality or social practice. As far as the problem of practical reason – the search for practical knowledge and mutual understanding with regard to normative social practice – is concerned, we can therefore speak of a *dialectic between a priori and a posterori concepts of practical reason,* whereby "a priori concepts" stand for the heuristic or quasi-transcendental frames of reference by which we approach social reality, while "a posteriori concepts" can be understood to mean the life-practical knowledge and moral experience of those who live the social reality in question.

I should like to concretize in three steps what I mean by the dialectic of a priori and a posteriori concepts of practical reason.

2. The first concretization concerns the *inevitable dialectic between (practical) reason and (reasonable) practice.* In Habermas' conception of practical discourse, the gap between rational discourse *on* practice and social practice itself is not always sufficiently considered. His model of discourse succeeds in bridging the gap between

---

[39] Lorenz 1972:117 emphasizes that the opposition between correspondence and consensus theories of truth is inadequate because it leads to one-sided concepts of "truth," concepts that do not sufficiently consider the justified objections of the other side.

theoretical and practical discourse but remains helpless with regard to the problem of bridging the gap between practical discourse and practical action. Particularly in his logic of discourse (cf. Section 2.5 above), Habermas convincingly demonstrates the normative presuppositions of theoretical discourse. But the trouble is that closing the epistemological gap between theoretical and practical discourse does nothing to close the gap between practical discourse and social practice itself; in fact, it sometimes serves to blur this second gap. This is why I have suggested above that Habermas' model of discourse does not really mediate between the realms of argumentative reason and lived social practice but remains bound to the former. The underlying trap is almost exactly opposite to the one in the decisionistic model: Habermas seeks to locate "rational" practical discourse entirely within the boundaries of reason. As an epistemological boundary experiment, this attempt makes sense; but it cannot free us from the necessity of developing a practicable, heuristic, approach to the problem of making reason practical. For all practical purposes, the problem of rational criticism and consensus bursts the framework of pure reason or "pure communication." Let me mention only a few examples.

(a) First, there is the problem of moral decisionism. Habermas' own boundary experiment seems to indicate that the problem cannot be solved within the boundaries of argumentative reason (cf. point 5 above). We are left with the conclusion that this problem can be adequately dealt with only by comprehending it as a case of the dialectic of reason and practice.

(b) Then there is the problem of "rational motivation." Only a minority of people can ever be expected to meet the formal requirements of rational argumentation, but that need not mean that what the majority have to say is (socially and individually) irrational. One can ask whether it is rational at all to identify relevant criticism with criticism that subjects itself to an established concept of rationality. However comprehensive this established concept of rationality may be, such a conception of rational criticism ultimately retains a rationalistic bias: "admitted to the discourse," as Habermas furmulates (1973c:256), are only those who are "competent" to argue their case rationally (i.e., according to the requirements of the ideal speech situation). Human suffering or concerns on the part of citizens who are not willing or able to meet the formal criteria of rational argument constitute no valid criticism. Formal rationality in this sense threatens to militate against *social* rationality. Socially rational is what leads to an improvement of the human condition, i.e., the "quality of life" within a defined community of citizens; I can see no reason why such improvement should come about only by means of formally rational discourse.

(c) It must even be questioned whether locating criticism within the bounds of reason is compatible with the democratic idea of publicity. We can exclude from the exercise of their profession those professionals who do not submit to, and do not meet, professional standards of excellence or rationality; that is to say, we can deny to them the status of experts in technical matters. But in a democracy, we cannot exclude *citizens* from exercising their status as sovereign and experts in *political* matters solely because they are not willing or "competent" to argue their case "rationally." If we do so exclude them, we effectively treat practical (political, moral) questions – questions in wich everybody is an "expert" – as technical questions in which only professionals are experts. This undermines not only the democratic idea but also the idea of discursive rationality, for it reintroduces a positivistic source of systematic distortion into practical discourse: it *presupposes* rationality (in the form of communicative competence) instead of *producing* it (in the form of social rationality).

There is indeed a striking parallel between Habermas' insistence on "rational motivation" and Popper's call for a "rational attitude." However, if the challenge to practical reason is taken seriously and is to include the democratic idea, the only rational stance that represents an absolute presupposition is this: *everybody who is potentially affected by the outcome of a practical discourse must be admitted to the discourse and considered competent by virtue of his affectedness,* regardless of whether or not he is able to argue his case rationally. And since it is rarely the case that all those affected can actually become involved – the unborn never can – *the involved are fully rational or competent only to the extent that they place themselves in the "irrational" positions of those who cannot argue their concerns rationally.* (Cf. to this also point 3 below.)

(d) Another parallel between Habermas' and Popper's models of rational criticism is perhaps not entirely accidental. As we have briefly noted (cf. footnote 37 above), they both pursue a concept of metaphysics-free criticism. Quite apart from the question of its practicality, such a concept of criticism ultimately retains a conservative bias. Paul Feyerabend's distinction between anticipatory and conservative criticism is relevant here. He calls "conservative" a critique that meets existing standards of acceptable criticism, while an "anticipatory" critique depends on not yet accepted, i.e., anticipated, standards. "An anticipatory critique always sounds somewhat odd, and conservative critics have no difficulty in proving its absurdity. The success of rationalistic arguments rests mainly on this circumstance." (1980:47, my transl.) The requirement of metaphysics-free criticism is motivated, among other reasons, by the desire to render criticism rationally or objectively decidable; but it effectively serves to exclude anticipatory criticism. The reason is easy enough to see: anticipatory criticism is rooted in new ways of considering the given universe of "facts," in new visions or world-views, and that is to say, it involves a new metaphysics of problems. An example that comes readily to mind is the "holistic health" movement; the metaphysical basis of anticipatory criticism in this case is the holistic world-view of the systems approach, which clashes with the existing analytical metaphysics of contemporary Western medicine and its corresponding tendency to treat the sick like defective machines.[40] Other instances of anticipatory criticism may be based on Eastern metaphysics, etc. In all these cases, criticism cannot a priori be dismissed as "irrational" simply because its source of inspiration is metaphysical. In fact, all criticism is rooted in metaphysical presuppositions, although we tend to forget the metaphysical character of long-familiar world-views. The neglect of the dialectic between criticism and metaphysics can thus be understood as just another symptom of the rationalistic and undial-ectical outlook of contemporary discourse models.

3. Let us now turn to the second step of concretization regarding the suggested dia-lectic between a priori and a posteriori concepts of practical reason. Within the realm of social planning, this same dialectic reappers in the *opposition between the planner and the planned-for,* between "experts" and citizens, between the involved and those who are not involved but only affected. A really practical concept of practical discourse might do well to consider the planner's conceptual frameworks and his corresponding "maps" of social reality (or designs *for* social reality) as heuristic *a priori concepts* of practical reason. That is to say, these "maps" or designs should be regarded as depending for their validity on *a posteriori concepts* of practical reason. The only source of such a posteriori concepts lies in those who know the social reality in question because they *live* it – those planned-for and those affected by the planner's conception of reality. Considerations (a) and (b) above fully apply to the problem of unfolding this dialectical interdependence between planner und citizen.

4. Finally, we can find this same dialectic at an even more specific level, I mean the social planner's specific conceptual tool that we call the "systems approach." The technocratic character of contemporary systems theory, RAND-systems analysis, systems engineering, social cybernetics and related approaches all too well attests to the need for a *dialectical systems approach* in which systems designers and citizens are given complementary roles to play. We find such a dialectical framework in C. West Churchman's *The Systems Approach and Its Enemies* (1979). In this book, Churchman presents a dialectical approach to the unfolding of the unavoidable conflict between the systems planner who strives for whole-systems rationality and the "enemies" of whole-systems rationality who are concerned with their "pri-vate," subjective rationality – e.g., political, religious, moral or aesthetic concerns. The provocative term "enemy" is meant to connote the irreconcilable conflict between the "rational" systems approach and the "irrational" citizens who are not willing to subject themselves to the standards of "systems rationality," even though the systems planner may claim to plan for them. They are in this sense the "deadly enemy," i.e., the dialectical negation, of the systems approach. But the systems planner, even though he understands himself as planning from the superior view-point of the whole system in question, cannot ignore his "enemies." Rather, he is in

[40] I have given another example in my paper on "The Metaphysics of Design" (1980) where I compare Herbert A. Simon's analytical systems approach and C. West Churchman's dialectical systems approach with regard to their metaphysical presuppositions. Cf. Ch. 6, Sec. 1.

a dialectical relationship with them, a relationship in which every side depends on the other for securing improvement. The planner depends on the "enemies" partly because a plan cannot be successfully implemented if it is not accepted by those planned-for, partly because those who are affected will usually know more about the social reality in question than does the planner, so that he is dependent on them for his "data basis." In this interdependenc between systems-oriented planner and citizens who contest the alleged systems rationality of the systems planner, a dialectical systems approach finds the best possible guarantor of socially rational planning. We shall have sufficient opportunity to meet the "enemies" of the systems approach in later chapters; at this point I introduce them only as a source of a posteriori concepts of practical reason.

5. Once we have understood the general meaning of the dialectic between a priori and a posteriori concepts of practical reason, several specific difficulties of Habermas' model of practical discourse can be clarified. I shall limit myself to two of them: the quasi-transcendental status of the principle of generalization (problem of moral decisionism), and the danger of a new sophism.[41]

Regarding the *principle of generalization,* the concept of the "enemies" raises some doubts about the generalizability of the generalization principle. It is hard to see why only those needs and interests which are generalizable should be legitimate or reasonable. Such a position would require that we adopt a whole-systems point of view as the only legitimate one – in the light of the preceding discussion an untenable "monological" concept of rationality. However, Habermas' model does in fact identify rational with generalizable interests and maintains that "the only principle in which practical reason expresses itself [is] the principle of universalization." (1975:108) But the notion that generalizability of interests should define the range of possible rational consensus on controversial validity claims has paradoxical implications. It effectively limits the range of application of Habermas' practical discourse to merely *apparent* conflicts of values, that is, to cases where conflicting validity claims turn out to be linked to one and the same underlying interest and hence are illusory (resting on self-deception) rather than genuine.

---

[41] I should like to point out, as a side-remark, that the dialectic between a priori and a posteriori concepts of practical reason also provides an answer to the long-standing charge on the part of positivist critics that "dialectical" approaches cannot be rationally reconstructed and hence that "the whole dialectical method is merely a license for 'speculative' arbitrariness." (Lobkowicz 1972:198, similarly Albert 1979:54f) This argument rests on a mistaken identification of dialectics with the self-reflection of a subject that is removed from the constraints of experience and action. Dialectical reasoning remains arbitrary – if it is arbitrary in the first place – only so long as it is an unfinished dialectic, i.e., one located entirely within the boundaries of reason. Our conception provides for a very concrete and practical method of (re-)constructing dialectical reasoning in a non-arbitrary way: namely, by arranging for a discourse between planners and citizens, or the involved and the affected, as the sources of a priori respectively a posteriori concepts of practical reason.

When value conflicts are genuine, however, then rational consensus is bound to be illusory, for conflicts between particular (non-generalizable) values can at best be mediated by compromise under conditions of a balance of power. There is an obvious danger that such a view does not help practically the cause of practical reason but immunizes genuine value conflicts against the efforts of practical reason – at the price of falling back into decisionism and strategic action.[42]

The underlying root cause of this difficulty lies in Habermas' association of legitimate needs with the traditional liberalist notion of the *"common good."* There are however alternative positions with regard to the generalizability of interests. One is represented by Marx' concept on the *class interest:* interests are at most generalizable into two or more conflicting classes of socio-economically determined interest groups. The other position is provided by contemporary liberalism's *pluralistic* model: there is a plurality of conflicting interests which are all justifiable in their own right. None of the three models seems entirely unproblematic. Habermas correctly points to the immunizing effect of the prevailing pluralistic model against the efforts of practical reason. Contemporary liberalism is equally correct in criticizing Marx' two-class model as simplistic and untenable in the light of actual sociological knowledge. The model of the common good, finally, is as simplistic and sociologically untenable as the class model. In addition, planning for the common good or "public interest" all too easily succumbs to an objectivist illusion and forgets to reflect on its own redistributive effects (not everyone can equally benefit). From a critical point of view, it seems more desirable that planning openly assume an advocacy or partisanship position. It would then have to understand itself as inevitably serving some interests better than others. The classical statement of this position is Paul Davidoff's paper on "Advocacy and Pluralism in Planning" (1965). Davidoff suggests that public planning can be kept honest not by seeking to plan for the "public interest" but rather by taking on an advocacy role on behalf of an explicitly defined client group. This position contrasts with Habermas' view of critical theory as assuming an advocacy role in ascertaining generalizable but suppressed interests (1975:117, cf. also Section 3.4 above).

The question then presents itself: In what way can we understand the generalization principle as a quasi-transcendental, i.e., necessary and universal, criterion of practical (moral) reason? A dialectical model of practical discourse can help us find an adequate answer: the principle of generalization can reasonably claim general validity and necessity only as an *a priori* concept of practical reason, e.g. as a part of the social planner's heuristic framework. But as such it must remain open to critical reflection and challenge on the part of those who have to *live* its implications. That is, it has no privileged status whatsoever as an *a posteriori* concept of

---

[42] My formulation is meant to allude to Habermas' parallel statement: "The empiricist and/or decisionist barriers, which immunize the so-called pluralism of values against the efforts of practical reason, cannot be overcome so long as the power of argumentation is sought only in the power of refuting deductive arguments." (1975:107)

practical reason. These few remarks can of course only hint at the kind of "dialectical" strategy that a critical heuristics of socially rational planning will have to pursue; they must await further elaboration.

6. As a last observation, the danger of a new *sophism*. In ancient Greece, the sophists were rightly attacked by Plato and Aristotle for reducing practical reason to a question of rhetorical skill. Does Habermas' theory of communicative competence not threaten to reduce once more the problem of practical reason to a question of discursive technique? Does it not replace the Aristotelian practical question of the good and just order of the *polis* and the proper conduct of life by the sophists' question of proper speech? A strong argument can be made for this view, and it has been made, e.g. by Rüdiger Bubner (1969:208f, 1976:227ff, cf. also 112) and by Reinhart Maurer (1977:62f). It appears that this argument is justified at least insofar as Habermas' basic goal of providing for discursive mediation between theory and practice has been replaced by the mediation between theoretical and practical *discourse* (cf. point 2 above). Although it seems basically sound to seek in practical discourse the mediator between theory and practice, we must not fall into the trap of making rational discourse a guarantor of socially-rational practice. Only practice itself can secure socially-rational action. Bubner says it well: "Action must itself care for its purposes." (1976:114, my transl.) Practical philosophy – and a model of rational discourse *on* practice remains a piece of practical philosophy – cannot replace the practice into which it wants to bring reason. Rather, it is to make room for practice so as to come to grips with the intrinsic dialectic of (practical) reason and (reasonable) practice. It can do so by renouncing the notion that we can or should locate the conditions of practical reason within a priori concepts of practical reason. If practical philosophy is to merit its title, it must take the "dialectical turn" toward unfolding the dialectic of a priori and a posterori concepts of practical reason – however precarious the task may prove to be for the practical philosopher himself.

Part II
From Kantian A Priori Science
to Critical Heuristics

Chapter Three
Introduction to Kantian A Priori Science

All philosophy before 1781 seems to flow into Kant's great system, and little that has appeared since cannot be traced back to his influence. It has been truly observed that in the modern world, one can philosophize against Kant or with him, but never without him.
Robert Paul Wolff (1967:ix)

Introduction

In this second part of our study (Chapters Three to Five), I propose that we go back to Kant and examine with him the possibilities and limitations of reason in dealing with the unsolved problem of practical reason. It was in fact Kant who introduced the term "practical reason" into philosophy. Reason is practical, in the Kantian sense, if it provides us with "good reasons" (cogent arguments) for asserting or questioning normative validity claims. In other words, the problem of practical reason is the problem of how we can "reasonably" deal with the normative content of our concepts of social reality, or with the planner's recommendations for changing that reality.

Let us begin by briefly reviewing our preliminary conclusions regarding this problem. In Part I of this study, we have examined two of the leading contemporary models of discursive rationality. Popper's "critical rationalism" is representative of the scientistic position in the newly revived discussion about the problem of practical reason, while Habermas' "critical theory" stands for the opposite, so-called dialectical, position. We have found that Popper's model relies on an inadequate, objectivist concept of rationality, and that it has therefore no way of coming to grips with its own normative implications. The underlying reason for this lack of self-reflectiveness seems to be that Popper seeks to avoid the Kantian transcendental question, the question of how reason can establish the conditions of the possibility of (objective) experience and knowledge. We agree with the critical rationalists and with the analytical Kant critics in general that Kant's strictly transcendental approach is no longer possible today; but at the same time, we maintain with Habermas that a critical approach to social inquiry and design cannot excise the challenge to self-reflection posed by the transcendental question. Habermas' own model of rational practical discourse is a valuable theoretical contribution because it can serve as a critical standard for reflecting on the sources of deception contained in any factual consensus. It cannot, however, serve as a practical discourse model for the planner, for it depends on utopian conditions of complete rationality. In this regard, Habermas' model demonstrates the conceptual boundary character of the search for a theoretical solution to the problem of practical discourse. Such a solution can show the conceptual boundary conditions that would enable us to justify a factual consensus as "rational," conditions such as Habermas' "ideal speech situation"; but it cannot make these conditions real. The following conclusions appear inevitable:

1. No theoretical solution to the problem of practical reason can at the same time be practicable.
2. No practicable solution to the problem of practical reason can be located within the bounds of reason in general; instead, it must seek to mediate between reason and practice so as to make reason practicable, and practice reasonable. We might say that no "internal" justification of (practical) reason is sufficient to make practice reasonable, and hence that reason must not elevate itself to the arbiter between practice and itself.
3. In consequence of (1) and (2), there can be only a *critical* solution to the problem of practical reason. By a "critical solution" I do not mean an approach that would establish universal conditions excluding all possible sources of selectivity or deception in our concepts of social reality, or in the planner's recommendations for changing that reality. I mean, rather, an approach that would help us to recognize and reflect upon these sources of deception. I intend to show that Kant, although he aims at the former task, falls back, at a crucial point in his philosophy, upon a merely critical solution in this sense, and that we can therefore learn from him what the implications of a critical solution are. For this reason I have chosen his remark, in the *Critique of Pure Reason,* as a motto of this entire study: "We cannot, by complaining about the narrow limits of our reason, escape the responsibility of at least a critical solution to the questions of reason." (B 508, my transl.; concerning the style of references to Kant's writings, see the note appended to this introduction.)
4. Precisely because it does not presuppose ideal conditions of complete rationality, a merely critical solution to the problem of practical reason can hope to contribute to the practical "enlightenment" of social inquirers, planners or decision makers, that is, to help them become self-reflective with regard to the normative implications of any standard of rationality on which they may rely.
5. On the other hand, because such a critical solution cannot claim a theoretical, but only a heuristic status, it will always run the risk of becoming a source of deception itself. That is to say, it remains in need of critical reflection as a source of possible deception, and such reflection cannot circumvent the Kantian transcendental question. It is only by conceiving of the ideal conditions of complete rationality that we can see through the actual conditions of incomplete rationality.

6. With Apel and Habermas we agree that the transcendental question today can be posed only by subdividing it into two "quasi-transcendental" questions:

(a) What are the conditions that are constitutive of meaningful experience? (a priori of experience)

(b) What are the conditions of a discursive redemption of disputed validity claims? (a priori of argumentation)

The term "quasi-transcendental," as we have seen, refers to the fact that Kant's strict apriorism must be replaced by relying on a merely relative a priori of experience *and* an equally relative a priori of argumentation. The a priori concepts and discursive principles in question are merely "relatively" a priori because no a priori concepts or principles can be shown theoretically to be strictly necessary and hence to be universally applicable.

7. The models of discursive rationality examined in Part I take into account only the a priori of argumentation. But the problem of practical reason cannot be solved within the context of the a priori of argumentation. *Instead of searching for a theoretical solution to the problem of practical discourse, we need to search for a merely critical solution to either of the two a priori problematics, and these two solutions will depend on each other.*

8. For the purpose of achieving the above task, I have suggested

(a) the need for a "critically-heuristic turn" in regard to the a priori of experience, and especially in regard to the difficult question of the "quasi-transcendental" status of the basic categories on which the planner is to rely; and

(b) the need for a "dialectical turn" in regard to the a priori of argumentation, especially the problem of how practical discourse can mediate between reason and practice so as to help the planner *practice* practical reason.

The two turns imply each other; hence we can use the label *"critical heuristics"* for our envisaged critical systems approach, although of course it will have to embody both turns. The label seems apt in that it expresses two basic assumptions of our effort: (a) a practicable solution to the problem of practical reason can claim no theoretical but only a *heuristic* status, and (b) such an approach must be constructed as a merely *critical* solution to the problem – no more, no less.

It is the task of the following chapters to unfold the meaning of these preliminary conclusions. In Kantian language, the two a priori problematics pose the following challenges to reason. In regard to the search for a priori concepts that are constitutive of our (the planner's) experience of the "real world," reason faces a challenge to *transcend (go beyond) the boundaries of possible experience.* Obviously we cannot derive such a priori concepts, even if they are not strictly necessary or universal, from the world of "facts," for we are asking for the conditions that enable us to establish "facts" in the first place. In other words, relatively a priori concepts, understood as heuristic concepts, are to make "facts" intelligible and for this reason cannot presuppose them. And of course, concepts that make the "given" intelligible – meaningful –

do not thereby establish its reality, i.e., attain a theoretical status. Thus a Kantian reformulation of the first a priori problematic immediately points to the need for a critically-heuristic turn.

Regarding the a priori of argumentation, I have argued that "rational" discourse and criticism, if it is to become practical, cannot be located entirely within the boundaries of reason. Rather, reason must break through its own boundaries and open itself up to the objections of the social practice into which it wants to bring reason. In Kantian terms, by analogy to the above formulation, we might say that the challenge here is *reason's self-transcendence of its own boundaries;* self-transcendence does not mean self-abolition but rather self-reflection, self-comprehension, and as a result of this perhaps self-limitation.

We can, then, determine the task of the following chapters as follows:

Chapter Three will give an introduction to Kantian a priori science. *Chapter Four* will deal with the first of the two quasi-transcendental issues, the a priori of experience. Basing my arguments on the conjecture that Kant himself falls back on a merely critical solution to the strictly transcendental problem, I shall attempt to show in what way Kant's approach is relevant to our envisaged critically-heuristic turn. In other words, this chapter should prepare us for the transition from Kant's transcendental a priori concepts to critically-heuristic a priori concepts. The *system idea* will play an important part in this transition. This is why the title of Chapter Four refers to the "systems approach." Let me anticipate here only so much: the systems idea allows us to make the transition from Kantian "a priori science" to critical heuristics *without* thereby giving up the claim for at least a critical solution to the problem of the a priori of experience. The systems idea can play this part because Kant himself uses it both in a heuristic and in a critical fashion.

Chapter Five will take up the second of the two quasi-transcendental issues, the a priori of argumentation, and will outline the premises of our envisaged dialectical turn. The underlying idea here is that Kant's undertaking, though presented in a monological fashion, is essentially a dialectical undertaking, for it requires that reason become its own object of study, i.e., that it become self-reflective. "Pure reason is in fact occupied with nothing but itself." (KrV:B 705) In our dialogue with Kant, we shall attempt to bring this basic dialectic to the surface and to examine the unavoidable implication: reason must comprehend itself as furnishing *a priori* concepts of practical reason only, and it therefore remains inextricably dependent on "irrational" social practice as the source of *a posteriori* concepts of practical reason. This conjecture will provide the key to a model of practical discourse that breaks through the boundaries of reason and can thus hope to perform a mediating function between reason and practice.

Note Concerning References to Kant

(a) *Pagination:* A and B refer to the pagination of the original editions of Kant's writings (A = 1st ed., B = 2nd ed.). "Ak" refers to the pagination according to the Akademie edition (cf. point c below); the roman figure following Ak indicates the volume. In the case of the *Prolegomena,* references are frequently to paragraphs rather than to pages. "Refl." followed by a number refers to the numbered fragments *(Reflexionen)* as originally numbered in the Akademie edition.

(b) *Original editions:* The following abbreviations will be used:

KrV = *Critique of Pure Reason* (Kritik der reinen Vernunft, A 1781, B 1787)

KpV = *Critique of Practical Reason* (Kritik der praktischen Vernunft, A 1788)

Prol. = *Prolegomena to Any Future Metaphysic* (Prolegomena zu einer jeden zukünftigen Metaphysik, die als Wissenschaft wird auftreten können, A 1783)

GMS = *Groundwork of the Metaphysic of Morals* (Grundlegung zur Metaphysik der Sitten, A 1785, B 1786)

Other writings by Kant will be cited by giving their full title.

(c) *Complete editions of the collected works in German language:* I have generally used the edition of Kant's collected writings by Wilhelm Weischedel, 12 volumes, Frankfurt 1968. The Akademie edition mentioned above has been published by the Königliche Preussische Akademie der Wissenschaften, Berlin, 28 vols. 1910ff.

(d) *English translations:* Translations for the KrV are those by Norman Kemp Smith (1965), for the KpV by Lewis White Beck (1949), and for the GMS by H. J. Paton (1964). Translations from other works are mine if not otherwise indicated. In the case of the KpV, Beck's pagination is given in addition to the original pagination of the first ed., for Beck does not use the latter. And since the same holds true of Abbott's translation (1949), I have included references to his pagination for those readers who want to compare his translation of relevant passages (e.g.: KpV:A 110, Beck 171, Abbott 154). In the case of the GMS, I have occasionally preferred Liddell's translation (1970) where it simplifies without sacrificing content.

1. Historical Roots: The "Unavoidable Problems of Reason" and Kant's "Copernican Revolution" of Metaphysics

1.1. The Unavoidable Problems of Reason

Human reason has this peculiar fate that in one species of its knowledge it is burdened by questions which, as prescribed by the very nature of reason itself, it is not able to ignore, but which, as transcending all its powers, it is also not able to answer. (KrV:A vii)

Thus begins the preface to the first edition of the *Critique of Pure Reason*. It could hardly have a more significant beginning. In this very first sentence, Kant introduces his basic concern with the inevitable metaphysical content of all human knowledge and thought. We designate as "metaphysical" those presuppositions of empirical knowledge which account for its intelligibility, but the validity or appropriateness of which we cannot establish either empirically or logically, i.e., by means of empirical-analytic science. For example, the concepts of substance and causality (in the natural sciences) or the systems idea (in the so-called social sciences and in planning) represent such presuppositions. There is no such thing as a "system" or a "substance" among the objects of possible experience to which we could point our finger and say: "Look, a system!" or "Look, a substance!" Rather, such concepts are instruments of thought by means of which we make intelligible to ourselves the objects of our experience and the interrelationships among them.

Before examining Kant's systematic interest in the transcendental function of such metaphysical concepts for empirical knowledge, it is perhaps useful to consider his *historical* interest in these concepts. Since no great philosopher – and indeed, no thinker of any stature – can be understood apart from the historical context of discovery in which he works, I shall take the first sentence quoted above as providing us with an opportunity to examine the intellectual situation with which Kant had to deal.

The three most important philosophical questions of Kant's time were:

1. What could be known about the existence of *God?* ("theological question"). This question had led to a longstanding debate on the different proofs of God's existence, none of which seemed quite acceptable.
2. What could be known about *Man,* in particular, about the immortality of his soul and the freedom of his will? ("psychological question"). The latter question had sparked the famous debate on free will in the sixteenth century between Erasmus of Rotterdam and Martin Luther (cf. Erasmus/Luther 1961). The question remained a central philosophical issue throughout the seventeenth and eighteenth centuries.

3. What could be known about the *World,* that is, about the order and moving forces in nature? ("cosmological question"). Ever since Newton had led the mechanistic-causal explanation of nature to its triumph, there was a need for explaining how man's free will and God's existence were possible at all in a world of universally valid causal laws, i.e., in a deterministic world. Discussion of this issue naturally directed itself toward attempting to determine what the limits were to the mechanistic-causal explanation of the world.

Kant was keenly interested in all three issues, as we may see in his early contributions to cosmology (Kant-Laplace theory of the origin of the solar system), and his life-long attempts to find a proof of God's existence and to explain the possibility of freedom. These are in fact the issues that, in his first sentence quoted above, he refers to as "questions that human reason is not able to ignore." Historically speaking, it was philosophy which could not ignore them if it wanted to claim a legitimate place at the side of Newtonian physics. Kant accordingly refers to them, throughout the *Critique,* simply as the "unavoidable problems of reason" (B 7, passim).

Now, it appears that the outstanding philosophers of all times have in common not only the great questions with which they deal but also the fact that their historical context of discovery provides an important "enemy" against which to develop a new argument. For instance, in order to understand Plato one needs to know that he developed his arguments in opposition to those of the Sophists. Aristotle, in turn, "needed" Plato as an adversary against whom to develop his great philosophical system. Kant too would not have become Kant had he not faced a challenge from two important adversaries at once. They were the two great philosophical schools of the time: *German rationalism* (Leibniz, Wolff) on the one hand, and *British empiricism* (Locke, Berkeley, Hume) on the other. Both schools tried to solve the "unavoidable problems of reason," and both failed.

German rationalism failed in the task because it relied on *dogmatism.* That is to say, it assumed that speculative reason can produce knowledge about metaphysical subjects "without previous criticism of its own powers." (KrV:B xxxv) It was only on this basis that Leibniz succeeded in constructing a rationalist-metaphysical system – the "Monadology" – that could maintain the possibility of God's existence and of human individuality (soul, free will), and could reconcile this possibility with Newton's teaching that the world could be described in terms of universal causal laws. Leibniz's explanation ultimately relied on the idea that human reason was indeed able to recognize the principles of nature because these principles themselves were established by the world's divine author according to a rational plan. This Leibnizian dogma of the "prestabilized" or "preestablished harmony" gained wide popularity through the writings of Christian Wolff, whom Kant called "the greatest of all the dogmatic philosophers" (B xxxvi); although dogmatically established, it did much to reinforce the rationalist's belief in the power of reason – a belief standing in remarkable contrast to the self-doubts by which the empiricists, on the other side of the English Channel, were plagued.

British empiricism, indeed, failed in its epistemological task with respect to the three "unavoidable problems" because it inevitably led to skepticism. We have seen earlier that the founder of British empiricism, John Locke, summarized his credo in the statement *nihil est in intellectu quod non fuerit in sensu* – "there can be nothing in the mind that was not first in the senses" (cf. the Introduction to Chapter 1). George Berkeley extended the implications of Locke's philosophy by concluding that nothing could be known that was not perceived by a *subject,* and hence that a "real world" independent of human perception and consciousness did not exist. If one subtracted from a body all its qualities given by sense impressions, what remained? Locke had said: its substance. But Berkeley showed that this answer was inconsistent and that the only possible answer was: nothing. The famous formula in which Berkeley summarized his subjective idealism, *esse est percipi,* meant that "the real is what is perceived," or "external objects do not subsist by themselves but exist only in mind." Such a conclusion was not of course very helpful for answering the questions about God, Man, and the World. Berkeley himself found "solutions" to these questions, but very few of those who recognized the cogency of his subjectivist inferences from Locke were willing to grant the cogency of his positive hypotheses. The net effect of Berkeley's work was to render the three questions more remote than ever from any acceptable solution. In a famous note to the Preface to the second edition of the *Critique,* Kant referred to this failure as "a scandal to philosophy and to human reason in general." (B xl, note)

The third great British empiricist was David Hume. We have already seen how Hume pointed out the uncritical nature of Locke's empiricism in respect to the problem of induction. He recognized that a principle of induction was necessary if particular observational statements were to be generalized to statements about the future or to universally valid theories; but he could not find any justification for such a principle. In particular, he showed that a principle of universal causality could not be justified by reference to sensuous experience, the only source of knowledge according to Locke. Hume also shared Berkeley's critical view of Locke's use of the concept of substance. Hence he could not help concluding that the two basic metaphysical presuppositions of Locke's empiricism – "substance" and "causality" – were only dogmatically introduced and that Lockean inquiry could not be critically justified, i.e., that empiricism could not provide certain knowledge. This skeptical conclusion was directed not so much against common sense or natural science as against the fact that both the empiricist and rationalist epistemologies remained uncritical with respect to their inevitable metaphysical premises.

It is because of this telling insight into the problem of metaphysical premises that Hume's critique of empiricism had a decisive influence upon Kant, even though in his early "precritical" writings he had adopted the German rationalists' point of view. Strongly influenced by the Leibnizian-Wolffian metaphysics, he too believed in the power of reason to solve the "unavoidable problems." Why precisely they were and still are unavoidable problems of reason, we shall understand when we come to deal with Kant from a systematic (rather than historical) point of view. At this point it may be sufficient to note that for Kant, as for Leibniz, it was simply a necessary assumption that the world was organized according to some reasonable plan if it was to be intelligible at all. In his time, there was no alternative to the idea that an intelligible plan of nature had to be due to God's authorship; the principle of self-organization which holds that nature's organization is not necessarily consciously designed ("prestabilized") but rather the result of systematic conditions of its development, i.e., "poststabilized," had not yet been discovered (on the issue cf. Riedel 1975, Jantsch 1980). The principle of self-organization does not, however, conflict with Kant's basic argument that reason is in need of some a priori ideas – systems ideas, as we shall come to see – which must always remain problematic. He maintains and pursued this conviction in a unique movement of thought from his early dogmatic (precritical) through his critical and postcritical writings.

When Kant became aware of Hume's skeptical argument, he awoke from his "dogmatic slumbers," as he states in a famous passage in the *Prolegomena to Any Future Metaphysics* (A 13). Torn between dogmatism and skepticism, neither of which seemed acceptable to him, it became clear to Kant that he had to search for a third approach to the three great philosophical questions of his time, an approach that would rely neither on rationalism nor on empiricism but would, rather, attempt to combine the two in some critical fashion. As he sums up in the last paragraph of the *Critique of Pure Reason,*

those who adopt a *scientific* method ... have the choice of proceeding either *dogmatically* or *skeptically;* but in any case they are under obligation to proceed *systematically*. I may cite the celebrated Wolff as a representative of the former mode of procedure, and David Hume as a representative of the latter, and may then, comfortably with my present purpose, leave all others unnamed. The *critical* path alone is still open. (B 884)

Kant found the key to the envisaged " critical path" in a shift of perspective which he considered as his "Copernican" revolution of metaphysics, by analogy with Copernicus' revolution of astronomy.

1.2. The Copernican Hypothesis and the Distinction Between Phenomena and Noumena

Before Copernicus, it was thought that the reality to be explained was what appears as the movement of the sun and the planets around the earth. Copernicus, by attributing the planets' irregular movement around the earth to our own perception (as a mere appearance) rather than to reality itself, overcame the difficulties resulting from the older view and brought astronomy on the "secure path of a science" (KrV:B vii). In metaphysics, the assumption that knowledge conforms passively to an independent reality (manifestation theory of truth) produced similar difficulties. Metaphysical objects do not reveal themselves to us as a physical reality against which to test the ideas we make us about them. Should it not be possible, Kant thought, to effect a similar change of view in metaphysics, in order to bring it on the secure path of a science? This is the famous passage from the preface to the second edition of the *Critique:*

> Hitherto it has been assumed that all our knowledge must conform to objects. But all attempts to extend our knowledge of objects by establishing something in regard to them *a priori,* by means of concepts, have, on this assumption, ended in failure. We must therefore make trial whether we may not have more success in the task of metaphysics, if we suppose that objects must conform to our knowledge. This would agree better with what is desired, namely, that it should be possible to have knowledge of objects *a priori,* determining something in regard to them prior to their being given. We should then be proceeding precisely on the lines of Copernicus' primary hypothesis. (B xvi)

Note the complete reversal which this suggestion implied for Kant: in order to demonstrate that the World was indeed rationally designed by God and thus intelligible to the human mind, he had to assume just the opposite idea, namely, that "reason has insight only into that which it produces *after a plan of its own."* (B xiii, italics added) It was to the a priori ideas conceived by reason "after a plan of its own" that the objects of our experience had to conform, rather than vice-versa.

Of course, such a change of perspective required a distinction corresponding to Copernicus' distinction between the apparent and the real planetary motions: the former belong to the *phenomenal* world of the objects of possible sensuous experience *(phenomena),* the latter to the *noumenal* world of objects of thought that go beyond limits of sensuous experience *(noumena;* cf. B 306, A 248f). Kant also calls the phenomena "appearances," while the noumena are "things in themselves."[1] The important point to understand is that phenomena and noumena are not different physical (ontological) entities but rather two sides of one and the same thing: its phenomenal "surface" as it appears to our senses from a certain standpoint, and its noumenal "essence" as we comprehend it by reflection. The *critical intent* of the distinction lies in the insight that every phenomenon is "really" a noumenon, i.e., that we have not comprehended its essential nature as long as we do not go beyond the fragmentary, because standpoint-dependent, appearance of it. We can thus define a *noumenon* as that part of an object of experience which is not itself appearance; it is

---

[1] The distinction is parallel to Plato's distinction between the "visibilia" and the "intelligibilia"; Kant therefore also likes to refer to noumenal reality as "the intelligible world," in contrast to the "sensible world" (e.g. Prol.:par. 34, KrV:A249, B312, 566). Cf. however the subsequent remarks concerning the danger of a dogmatic metaphysical dualism contained in such language.

not given to the intellect through the senses but can only be thought; and it *needs* to be thought in order to see through the objectivist (or ontological) illusion in our experience of appearances.

It is useful to think of the distinction between phenomenal and noumenal reality in terms of a famous statement by semanticist Alfred Korzybski (1958:58, 750): "A map is *not* the territory." The "territory" is the noumenal reality that we cannot grasp as such; the "map" represents the phenomenal reality that appears to us from a given standpoint. The essential critical point in Korzybski's as in Kant's distinction is the limited, perspectival character of all our experience and knowledge. In Korzybski's terms: *all our knowledge is in terms of maps.* Whoever forgets this insight submits to the objectivist illusion: he confuses maps with reality, which implies that he is no longer aware of the selective character of his – of any – standpoint, i.e., the metaphysical and normative presuppositions flowing into the maps in terms of which we "see" the territory.

Now let us turn back to Kant. The distinction between appearance and reality in itself was to become fundamental to his critical enterprise, for it led him from dogmatic metaphysical realism (from which Hume had awakened him) to *critical ("transcendental") idealism.* The basic hypothesis of idealism is that experience does not represent a subject-independent reality but that the principles of order in our experiences are themselves a priori ideas. This need not mean that nothing is real "out there" (as in the case of Berkeley's subjective idealism); rather, it means that the reality behind our phenomenal experience must remain problematic. Insofar as an idealist position reflects upon this, it can be called *phenomenalism,* or, closer to Kant's terminology, *critical* or *problematic idealism.*[2] Critical idealism is a sound basis for any epistemology insofar as it forces both empiricists and rationalists to renounce any pretension to an immediate grasp of "reality" and requires instead a self-critical search for deception in the form of an objectivist or ontological illusion –

[2] Kant speaks of "problematic idealism" in his second-edition refutation to Berkeley's subjective (and dogmatic) idealism (B 274); while in the first-edition refutation he calls his own standpoint "transcendental idealism," explaining that "by transcendental idealism I mean the doctrine that appearances are to be regarded as being, one and all, representations only, not things in themselves...." (A 396) I prefer the more general term "critical idealism" because it points to the essential critical intent of such a non-subjectivist idealism. N.K. Smith, in his commentary on the first *Critique* (1962:274), suggests, for similar reasons, the term "phenomenalism" as a label for Kant's standpoint. This label has the advantage of pointing to the underlying distinction between phenomena and noumena; it has, however, two disadvantages as I see it: first, a number of other philosophical standpoints name themselves "phenomenalism"; and second, the term seems too narrow. It correctly characterizes the critical intent of the "Transcendental Analytic," where Kant demonstrates that knowledge is possible only within the boundaries of phenomenal experience, but it does not point to the equally (if not more) important critical intent of the "Transcendental Dialectic," where Kant shows that critical thought (reason) can and must go beyond the boundaries of the phenomenal and ask for the unconditional, the noumenal reality behind it – indeed, it is only in this way that we can comprehend the distinction between appearance and reality in the first place. (On this topic cf. the later sections of the present chapter.)

and that is what epistemology is about. In Korzybski's terms, the basic message of critical idealism is: *Mind the map-territory relation!*

Let us briefly illustrate the critically-idealist perspective in terms that the social planner will understand. There is for example the difficult problem of values in social inquiry and design. The Kantian *Critique* can be meaningfully applied to this problem only on the critically-idealist assumption that there is no social reality except by mediation of normative presuppositions, i.e., value judgements. The social reality which we can grasp in terms of empirical-analytic science is only the map, a standpoint-dependent, phenomenal reality. In order to avoid deception, we must mind the map-territory relation, that is, reflect on the normative (because selective) implications of our own standpoint vis-à-vis the territory, the lived social and individual reality which we cannot objectively grasp as such. Similarly, considering the fact that social planning is always design for the future, the critical idealist will maintain that a social reality that is not seen in the light of the future is a distorted reality. Likewise, with respect to the no-longer given (the past), social reality cannot be understood except in terms of its historic development. Again, to the critical idealist the empirically "given" social reality is only a phenomenal reality that cannot be grasped except by transcending that which is, the given, towards that which is not, the no-longer given and the not-yet given. As a last example, with respect to that which is not otherwise given but collectively (e.g., the political), critical idealism suggests that a social reality that is not seen as a political reality is no reality at all; and this again poses the question of how we can critically go beyond the given (the map) in order to understand the political reality behind it (the territory).

As we consider these examples, however, a word of caution is in order. Let us not forget the merely critical intent of the distinction between phenomena and noumena! This intent forbids the hypostatization of phenomena and noumena as ontologically distinct entities. Accordingly, the examples are not meant to convey the impression that the normative (historical, political, moral, etc.) aspects of social reality are noumenal *only*. Rather, they have both a noumenal and a phenomenal side, just as is the case with the spatiotemporal aspects that can become the object of our "external" senses. We cannot of course "see" as such the value judgements that are contained in all social reality; but they have phenomenal expressions such as redistributive effects, moral feelings of social or individual injustice, political expression of voters at the ballot-box, social and ecological costs imposed on third parties and so on, and nothing in principle precludes the possibility that such phenomenal expressions can become objects of the planner's "maps" of social reality. We shall return to this issue; the point of the examples above is merely that we need to reflect on the normative presuppositions that are constitutive of all our maps of social reality, lest we take these maps for the territory, i.e., for a "given," fixed social reality.

Kant was not concerned with problems of social mapping but rather with the problem of how metaphysics could become a science; nevertheless, the problem of metaphysics is epistemologically equivalent to the problem with which the social

186

inquirer and planner is confronted: How can we, by means of reason, go beyond our maps of phenomenal reality and validate the noumenal concepts that are *a priori* to our maps, and hence constitutive of either knowledge or deception? To the extent that such a priori concepts flow into our maps, we cannot validate these maps empirically or logically, i.e., we are dealing with the inevitable metaphysical content of our maps (the territory which we cannot grasp as such); and this is so regardless of whether the territory in question is spatiotemporal or moral, political, religious, etc. The contemporary social planner may not be interested in Kant's "unavoidable" problems, but he needs nevertheless to take the Kantian step from unreflected realism to critical idealism, according to Kant's lesson: "reason has insight only into that which it produces after a plan of its own." (B xiii, quoted above) If the planner recognizes that all his maps of social reality are dependent on the "plan" in terms of which he perceives (constructs) that reality, he will also come to recognize the "unavoidable" metaphysical content of his maps. Since we are dealing here with the noumenal side of social reality rather than with traditional speculative metaphysics, we shall henceforth speak of the planner's "metaphysics of social problems" or his "metaphysics of social design"; the first term refers to the a priori component in the planner's *maps* of the problem situation he wants to improve, while the second term refers to the same a priori component insofar as it flows into his social *designs* and determines the way he plans. For the sake of convenience, the shorter term "social metaphysics" can be used in both cases.

As a critical idealist, the planner will keep in mind that he cannot hope to be epistemologically critical (i.e., know what he knows) if he is not first of all metaphysically critical (in regard to the social metaphysics constitutive of his social maps and designs). Heuristics, as we have said, is (or better, ought to be) epistemology brought down to earth. Epistemology, we may now add, should be (social) metaphysics brought up from the level of blind assumption to the level of critical awareness. Let us, then, turn from this brief review of the historical roots of Kant's critical (and transcendental) idealism to the systematic structure of Kantian "a priori science."

2. Systematic Structure of Kantian A Priori Science

Figure 3/1 provides an overview of the architectonic of Kantian a priori science as far as the a priori of experience is concerned. Let us try to grasp the basic structure of Kant's argument in the *Critique of Pure Reason* by following this schema, lest we lose ourselves in the enormous complexities of Kant's work.[3]

2.1. A Priori and A Posteriori Concepts

First, there is the distinction between the *a priori* and the *a posteriori* component of knowledge. Kant explains this distinction in the Introduction to the *Critique,* along with the other important distinction between *analytic* and *synthetic* judgements.

"There can be no doubt that all our knowledge begins with experience," Kant writes in the beginning of the Introduction. "But though all our knowledge begins *with* experience, it does not follow that it all arises *out of* experience." (B 1, italics added)

What makes the difference between the empiricist "out of" and the Kantian "with" is that which Kant calls the a priori component of all knowledge. With this classical distinction, Kant resolves once for ever the old debate between the empiricist "tabula rasa" position ("We know nothing except what the senses tell us") and the rationalist credo of innate ideas ("We can know without experience because we are given innate ideas"). Kant's cogent reply is "neither of the above," and with this "neither of the above" he dismisses the Age of Enlightenment's simple appeal to reason (in the case of the rationalists) or to the presuppositionless observation of nature (in the case of the empiricists) as guarantors of truthful knowledge. Neither can experience alone provide us with the general categories of spatiotemporal perception, nor can mere speculation independent of all experience (pure reason) provide any knowledge of what "really" is. For example, the statement "If two men are fighting, and one kills the other, then there will be only one man left," necessarily entails the application of the a priori categories of quantity, quality, relation and modality (cf. Figure 3/1). At the same time, the concepts "man," "fighting," and "kill" are not given a priori but

---

[3] A noted Kant scholar has this to say about the difficulty of surveying Kant's work:
> The difficulty of Kant's doctrines makes mastering even one of the *Critiques* a mind-stretching task. To master them all in depth and then to trace out the underlying logical relationships among their principal theses is more than Kant himself was able to do. The result is that the literature on Kant has somewhat the air of a multitude of reports from the blind wise men who encountered the elephant. Each one tells of the part on which his hands happen to fall, but a careful reader might fail to recognize the beast from their descriptions. (Wolff 1967:xvii)

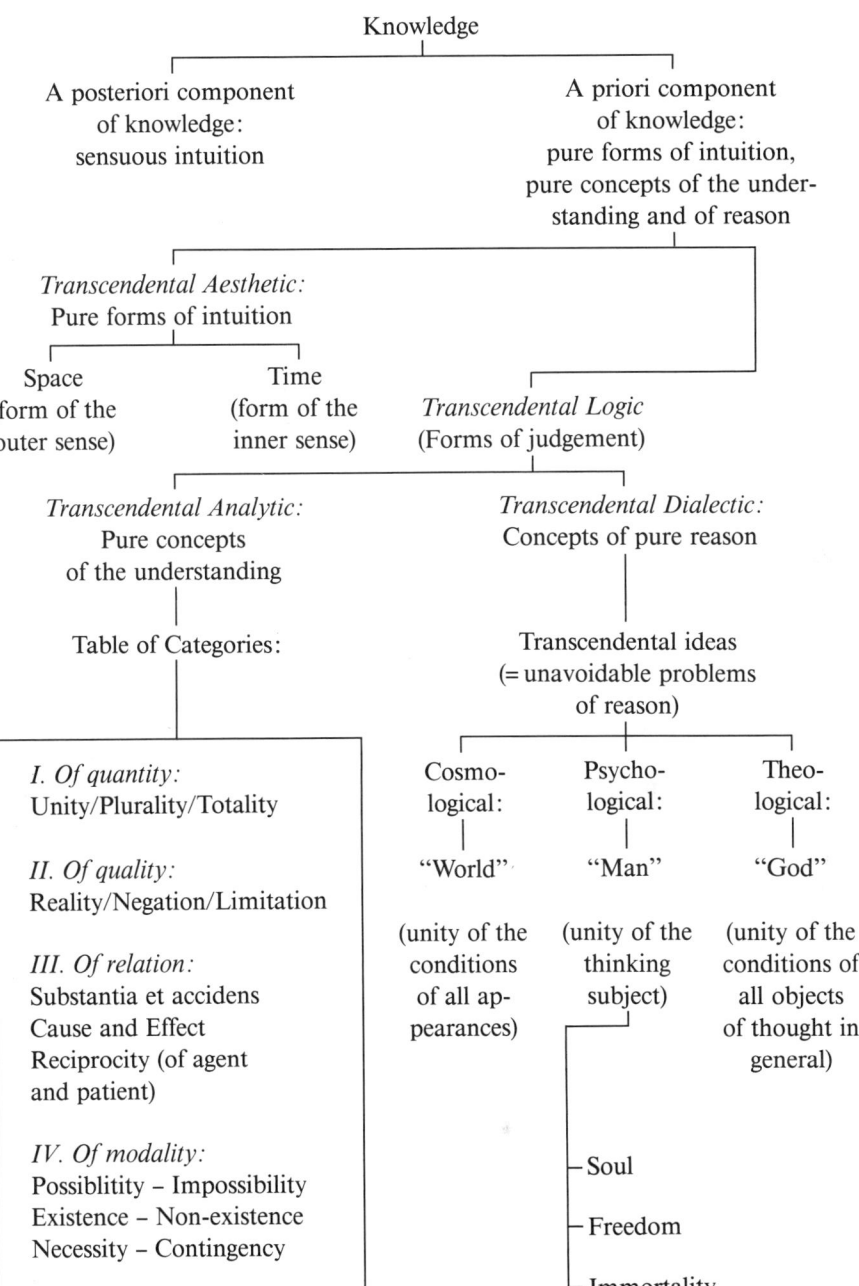

Figure 3/1: The architectonic of Kant's metaphysics of experience

depend on a posteriori perception of the senses. Experience is blind without guidance by general, organizing concepts such as "cause" and "effect" ("if... then"), while concepts without empirical content remain empty:

> Thoughts without content are empty, intuitions [Kant's term for sensuous experience] without concepts are blind. It is, therefore, just as necessary to make our concepts sensible, that is, to add the object to them in intuition, as to make our intuitions intelligible, that is, to bring them under concepts. These two powers or capacities cannot exchange their functions. The understanding can intuit nothing, the senses can think nothing. Only through their union can knowledge arise. But this is no reason for confounding the contribution of either with that of the other; rather it is a strong reason for carefully separating and distinguishing the one from the other. (B 75)

Well then, let us see how Kant distinguishes his terms. I shall deal with these terms at some length, for they are basic to our own constructive effort in the later chapters.

The general meaning of the term *"a priori"* is fairly obvious: it refers to that which goes "prior to," or is presupposed in, an observation or a thought. This "prior to" may be understood in two ways, either temporally or logically. Although both meanings are contained in Kant's "a priori," logical apriority is more important to him than temporal apriority. Thus, an *a priori concept* is one that is logically presupposed in, rather than derived from, an experience (or is presupposed in a thought insofar as the thought has empirical content). For example, noumenal concepts such as "soul," "immortality" or "causal law" are clearly a priori. (All noumenal concepts are necessarily a priori, but not all a priori concepts necessarily refer to noumenal objects, as will be seen shortly.) An *a posteriori concept,* in contrast, is one that *is* derived from experience, which is to say, it is abstracted from a number of particular, but similar, perceptions. We have already mentioned the concepts "man" (as a phenomenal being, not to be confused with the noumenal idea of Man as a being with an immortal soul and a free will), "fighting," and "killing" as examples, other typical examples are concepts of colors, plants or animals.

In order to give a more precise definition of the term "a priori," and in order to employ the term carefully, we must distinguish between absolute and relative a priori concepts. *Absolute* a priori concepts, in contrast to relative ones, represent not merely "knowledge independent of this or that experience, but knowledge absolutely independent of all experience." (B 3) To say that a concept is absolutely independent of experience means that it has no empirical content. Kant expresses this by saying that absolute a priori concepts are "pure" or derived from "pure reason." (In B 3, Kant defines "pure" as meaning "there is no admixture of anything empirical." That is to say, "pure" simply serves as a convenient adjective for describing something as being absolutely a priori or as derived from reason alone; e.g. "pure concepts of reason" or "concepts of pure reason," "pure knowledge" and even "pure intuition.") Pure concepts obviously do not refer to any possible object of experience; they merely serve to *organize* objects of actual experience (i.e., particular perceptions) into *meaningful* experiences (i.e., empirical concepts). To paraphrase Kant, when we apply an absolute a priori concept, we impose it upon the objects of our experience "according to our own plan" and thereby produce a new, conceptual object.

Relative a priori concepts, on the other hand, are independent not of all possible experience in general but only of possible experience *in a given situation.* Such a concept can be given empirical content, though this empirical content must be determined prior to the situation in question. As an example, let us take the systems concept. When Kant uses the term, he does so in an *absolutely* a priori sense, that is, he thinks of a (noumenal) totality of conditions, a totality to which no possible object of experience corresponds. In critical heuristics, however, we shall use the same term in a *relatively* a priori sense, i.e., we shall use it as a convenient tool to refer to some phenomenal reality that may be of interest to the social planner. Such a use for the systems concept requires that we define a *boundary criterion;* everything within the boundary can then be said to belong to the system, while everything outside the boundary belongs to the system's "environment." Without such a conceptual boundary, the systems concept remains an emtpy concept. For instance, when a planner refers to a section of social reality as a social system S, his implicit boundary criterion may be: "everybody who is either involved in the planning process or affected by its outcome belongs (should belong) to S." Or, when we refer to certain phenomena as parts of an "energy system," the implicit boundary judgement may be: "everything that is involved in the production and distribution of energy in this country and in the OPEC countries belongs to the system." Determining the system in question, it should be noted, is not a matter of arbitrary definition; apart from value judgements, it takes empirical knowledge to draw the boundary in a meaningful way. Such a boundary judgement amounts to both a theoretical and a practical (normative) proposition about the real-world context in question. Because such a judgement is constitutive of the empirical and the normative content of the systems concept in a given situation, it must be made *before* the systems concept can meaningfully be applied to describe the situation. Hence, both the boundary judgement and the systems concept it defines must be regarded as being relatively a priori to any empirical statement about the system in question.

We can now understand Kant's own definition: he speaks of a *relative* a priori concept (or judgement) when "we do not derive it immediately from experience, but from a universal rule – a rule which is itself, however, borrowed by us from experience." (B 2) Clearly, a "rule" like the above boundary criterion for determining the planner's client system – the notion that third parties affected by a plan should be included within the social system to be improved – is derived from planning experience, e.g. from the experience that plans do not get implemented or do not produce the desired results if those affected are not included. Kant's own example implicitly uses the empirical rule "bodies are heavy" as a boundary criterion. We "know" that a house built on the surface of the earth will collapse if its foundation is destroyed because we judge relatively a priori that it is within the reach of the earth's force of gravity:

> Thus we would say of a man who undermined the foundations of his house, that he might have known *a priori* that it would fall.... But still he could not know this completely *a priori*. For he has first to learn through experience that bodies are heavy, and therefore fall when their supports are withdrawn. (B 2)

The example of the systems concept also suggests the close interrelation between a priori concepts and *a priori judgements:* applying an (absolute or relative) a priori concept implies making an (absolute or relative) a priori judgement, and vice-versa. (*"Judgement"* is Kant's preferred term for "proposition" because the very term "judgement" suggests that subjective presuppositions – a priori concepts that cannot be derived from experience – flow into all propositions with empirical content, and hence that we cannot hope to justify propositions unless we reflect on the a priori judgements they imply.)

When Kant speaks of a priori concepts or a priori judgements, he usually employs the term in the absolute sense. As Norman Kemp Smith explains in his *Commentary,* however, "it is not true that the relative a priori falls outside the sphere of the Critical inquiry. Such judgement ... demands a transcendental justification no less urgently than the absolutely a priori." (1962:55) Perhaps the best way of putting it is to say that Kant is dealing with a *limiting case* (the absolute a priori), a case that is crucial to an understanding of the general case, the relative a priori. It is true that relative a priori concepts and judgements are not independent of experience; but it does not follow that they are derived entirely from experience. A critically-heuristic approach therefore needs to reflect on the absolute a priori concepts (e.g. "totality") that may be presupposed in its relative a priori concepts (e.g. "system S"), so as to discover the sources of possible deception in its reliance on relative a priori concepts. Critical heuristics cannot escape the responsibility of at least a critical solution to the Kantian problem.

Now, as complex as the limiting case is with which Kant deals, it has the one advantage that he can define two clear-cut criteria for recognizing (absolute) a priori concepts or judgements: *necessity* and strict *universality* (B 3f). Neither of these two features can be derived from experience, and each implies the other. As examples Kant gives the proposition "every alteration must have a cause" (B 5) and the concept of substance (B 6). Almost needless to say, these two criteria will not apply to the a priori concepts of a critical heuristics, at least not in the sense intended by Kant. When Kant speaks of "necessity," he means "necessary in order to *justify* the *validity* (or 'objective reality') of a concept or proposition." There is, however, another kind of necessity on which Kant also relies and which will be of central interest to us. This is what we might call *heuristic necessity,* that is, necessity of a concept or principle in the sense of its being a necessary, though hypothetical, *presupposition for critical reflection on the sources of deception* in all empirical knowledge. In this case, we cannot justify the empirical content of a concept but only its unavoidability as a critical standard for reflection. In Chapter Four, I shall attempt to show that Kant's "transcendental method" relies on precisely such a concept of "necessity" to justify what he calls the "(a priori) concepts of pure reason." In the present context it suffices to note that Kant is dealing with a limiting case, but that this does not preclude the possibility that we can learn from his boundary experiment. In fact, his purpose is not so far apart from our own as one might at first assume. Having said so much, I shall now proceed to introduce the basic structure of Kant's metaphysics of experience without constant references to our own approach; before beginning our own reconstructive effort, we need to listen to Kant without, as it were, interrupting him on every occasion. Our present purpose is to clarify our position in a way that would be impossible without Kant's work: "Who we are" is how we understand (and question) Kant.

2.2. Synthetic A Priori Judgements and the "Tribunal of Reason"

What has been said so far implies that we cannot know what we know *a posteriori* (the empirical content of our knowledge) without knowing what we assume *a priori* (the metaphysical content of our concepts). The question then poses itself: How can we demonstrate that the a priori component of our knowledge is a valid source of knowledge rather than a source of deception? Note that we do not ask how a judgement "A is B" is *derived,* but how it is *justified* (or, alternatively, ruled out). This second issue involves (with Habermas) the "a priori of argumentation" rather than the "a priori of experience," or (with Popper) the "context of justification" rather than the "context of discovery." (I introduce it here only insofar as it is necessary for understanding "Kant's problem.") In regard to this issue of justification, Kant introduces the distinction between *analytic* and *synthetic* judgements:

In all judgements in which the relation of a subject to a predicate is thought ... this relation is possible in two different ways. Either the predicate B belongs to the subject A, as something which is (covertly) contained in this concept A; or B lies outside the concept A, although it does indeed stand in connection with it. In the one case I entitled the judgement analytic, in the other synthetic. (B 10)

Instead of analytic judgements, Kant also speaks of "explicative" judgements, for they merely explain a concept in terms of its defining characteristics. Likewise, he uses the term "amplicative" instead of "synthetic," for synthetic judgements amplify a concept by some predicate not contained in its definition (cf. B 11). Analytic propositions are today called tautologies: they are true by definition, at the price of not adding anything to our empirical knowledge. (To have knowledge means for Kant to have concepts with empirical content.) The negation of a tautology is necessarily

193

self-contradictory. *We can thus be certain we are dealing with a synthetic judgement if its negation is not a contradiction in terms,* i.e., if its negation is possible.

Let us illustrate this criterion with Kant's own examples (cf. B 11). "All bodies are extended" is an analytic judgement, for its negation is a contradiction in terms. "All bodies are heavy," on the other hand, must be synthetic, for its negation is possible. While we "know" (understand) by definition that all bodies are extended, it is not clear before empirical testing whether a certain body is heavy – an example familiar to the age of space exploration.

Analytic judgements are necessarily a priori. Since they have no empirical content (they "add no information") they can be justified purely logically, according to the principle of excluded contradiction. The answer to the problem of justification is less clear in the case of synthetic judgements. The logical positivists, from Hume to Carnap, have defined a meaningful proposition as one that is either analytic or empirical (derived from experience). By implication, metaphysical propositions are meaningless, for they are neither analytic nor empirical. Kant's point is that the positivist classification is too narrow and confuses the distinctions "a priori vs. a posteriori" and "analytic vs. synthetic." (Kant here comes closest to an explicit distinction between the two a priori problematics; unlike Popper after him, he does not confuse "empirical content" with "truth" – cf. in the present study Chapter One, Section 1.3.) The dichotomy of empirical and analytic propositions excludes the possibility that a judgement might represent more than a mere tautology and still be a priori. Judgements that are neither analytic nor empirical (a posteriori) may still be meaningful. In point of fact, the inevitable a priori component in our knowledge implies that empirical judgements are not possible without a priori judgements about the empirical reality in question. (As we have seen, applying an a priori concept to some object of sense-experience implies making an a priori judgement, and vice-versa.) Every meaningful synthetic judgement thus implies both a synthetic a priori judgement and an a posteriori judgement:

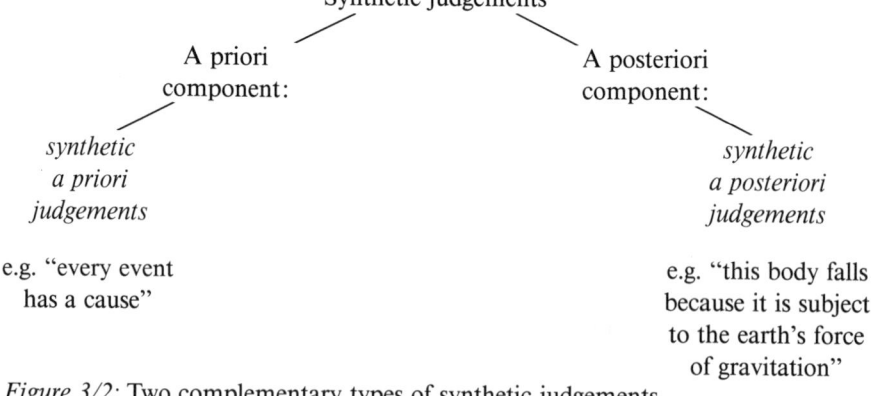

Figure 3/2: Two complementary types of synthetic judgements

From the Kantian point of view, then, the positivist Kant-interpreters are mistaken in identifying synthetic judgements with empirical (a posteriori) judgements. The correct reading of Kant's classification is this: whenever a meaningful judgement cannot be justified (or ruled out) logically, regardless of whether it is a priori or a posteriori, it is synthetic. A judgement cannot be justified logically, as we have seen, if its negation is not self-contradictory. But that a meaningful judgement cannot be justified logically does not imply that it can be justified empirically. Synthetic judgements can be validated by reference to experience only if they are a posteriori; but to the extent that they are a priori to meaningful experience, they can be justified only by reference to *good reasons,* i.e., by theoretical or practical reason (cf. to the latter distinction Section 1.2 of Chapter Four).

We now have in hand three basic distinctions of Kant's, by means of which we can characterize a judgement such as "this body is now heavy" in three ways: (a) as referring to phenomenal rather than noumenal reality, (b) as being a posteriori, and (c) as being synthetic. "Kant's problem" derives directly from these three distinctions. Before examining Kant's central problem, let us therefore be sure to distinguish carefully:

(a) the pair *phenomena* vs. *noumena* is a metaphysical distinction with critical (rather than dogmatic) intent;

(b) the pair *a priori* vs. *a posteriori* is an epistemological distinction referring to the context of discovery (the "a priori of experience," to use Habermas' terms);

(c) the pair *analytic* vs. *synthetic* is an epistemological distinction referring to the context of justification (the "a priori of argumentation").

We can now reformulate in a more precise way the problem posed at the beginning of this section: we cannot know what we know by means of synthetic *a posteriori* judgements without understanding what we presuppose in terms of synthetic *a priori* judgements. Hence, Kant's central problem is: *"How are a priori synthetic judgements possible?"* (KrV:B 19, Prol.:A 41)

Since Kant is dealing with the limiting case of *absolutely* a priori concepts and judgements, examples of synthetic a priori judgements are of a problematic character. Kant maintains that the fundamental principles of mathematics (arithmetic, Euclidian geometry) and of natural science (Newtonian physics) are synthetic a priori in an absolute sense. Perhaps the best examples are the three synthetic principles that he proposes for natural science (he calls them "Analogies of Experience," cf. KrV:B 218ff):

1. "In all change of appearances substance is permanent; its quantum in nature is neither increased nor diminished." (B 224, cf. Prol.:A 73) Kant calls this synthetic a priori judgement the "principle of permanence of substance"; it is essentially equivalent to today's principle of the conservation of matter-energy.

2. "All alterations take place in conformity with the law of the connection of cause and effect." (KrV:B 232, cf. Prol.:A 73f) This is the still familiar principle of

causality, also known as the principle of universal causation or the principle of sufficient reason.

3. "All substances, insofar as they can be perceived to coexist [i.e., exist at the same time] in space, are in thorough-going reciprocity." (KrV:B 256) This is the "principle of coexistence according to the law of mutual interaction" (my transl.). A familiar version of this principle is Newton's gravitational law, with which Kant was familiar; a more recent application is the cybernetic principle of mutual causality.[4]

These propositions are all *a priori* insofar as their supposed universality and necessity cannot be inferred from experience; nothing in the phenomenal realm of experience is strictly universal or necessary. They are *synthetic* rather than analytic because their negations are not self-contradictory. For Kant, then, the question is not whether synthetic a priori judgements exist, but only how they can be justified. Because they are a priori, they cannot be justified *empirically;* and because they are synthetic, they cannot be justified *logically*. We have thus the two defining characteristics of "metaphysical" propositions; i.e., those presuppositions that may account for the intelligibility of meaningful experience but the validity of which we cannot establish either empirically or logically, i.e., by means of empirical-analytic science.[5]

---

[4] In the systems literature, the principle of mutual causality is usually ascribed to Magoroh Maruyama (1963). He introduced it into cybernetics, apparently unaware of the fact that Kant already assigned to it the same epistemological status as to the principle of "linear" causality. What is really new in Maruyama is only his demonstration of the deviation-amplifying effects of mutual causality in feedback-monitored systems. It is thus not quite correct if Maruyama claims that the concept of mutual causality signals an "epistemological transition" from traditional Western thought (of which Aristotle and Kant are the most influential representatives) to a non-linear and non-hierarchical systems view of the world (1976:198f). I mention this because systems theorists and cyberneticians tend to assume that modern systems theory has long outgrown Kantian a priori science and that Kant, because there is no place in his philosophy for the cybernetic concept of mutual causality (as they assume), is irrelevant to "modern" systems philosophy. Far from it!

[5] The reader will also note that Kant, with his question of how synthetic a priori judgements are possible, actually reformulates Hume's problem of induction (cf. the introduction to Chapter One of the present study). The step from particular to general synthetic *a posteriori* judgements cannot be justified without reference to synthetic *a priori* judgements. The problem of induction *is* the problem of metaphysics – and this has too often been neglected by the empiricists – for "induction" means to transcend the given, the particular, the manifold that makes up our phenomenal experience and to describe it in the light of the not-given, the general, the a priori concepts standing for the noumenal side of the content of our experience. This observation explains why Popper's alleged solution of the problem of induction is not critically tenable: he has wrongly formulated the problem of induction as a seemingly metaphysics-free problem of empirical testing. Compare in this context Kant's famous remark in the *Prolegomena:* "Hence critique [a critical theory of knowledge] necessarily contains the entire plan, and indeed all the means for its accomplishment, according to which metaphysics is possible as a science...." (A 189, my transl.)

196

Again, let us keep in mind that Kant is dealing with a limiting case: as a practical matter, such metaphysical presuppositions cannot of course be expected to account for the intelligibility of *all* possible experience. Kant's own fundamental principles of natural science cited above are obviously "necessary" for Newtonian physics only. In most everyday experience of natural phenomena and instrumental action, the metaphysical presuppositions of Newtonian science can indeed be relied upon *"as if"* they were necessary. In the realm of social inquiry and planning, however, other synthetic a priori judgements will be necessary to render intelligible the nature of social reality and to allow for mutual understanding and socially-rational planning. In this relative sense, *some* synthetic a priori judgements can indeed be said to be necessarily presupposed in all coherent experience and thought. Neither the existence nor the meaningfulness of such judgements can be disavowed, on critical grounds, just because they are metaphysical.

I have briefly alluded to the implication of this insight in the introduction to the present chapter: reason faces an unavoidable challenge to *transcend* (go beyond) the boundaries of possible experience. Since we cannot justify synthetic a priori judgements either logically or by reference to phenomenal experience, we can only validate them by reference to reason (or, as we have said earlier, to good reasons). We cannot escape the question of how we can deal *reasonably* with the metaphysical content of our knowledge: How can we, by means of reason, go beyond the phenomenal realm of the given, the particular, the manifold objects of possible experience, so as to determine the "facts" in the light of the not-given, the general, the a priori concepts constitutive of these "facts"?

The positivist Kant-interpreters have tried to avoid this question by reformulating Kant's problem as the "problem of demarcation" (so Popper 1961:34), i.e., the problem of defining the borderline beyond which reason must not go. But the task of demarcating the borderline is of interest to Kant only as a necessary preparation of the unavoidable task of critically transcending that borderline. If metaphysical presuppositions flow into all our experience and knowledge, how can we avoid questioning their theoretical or practical implications and trying to deal with them reasonably? Had Kant's interest been only that of keeping phenomenal (empirical-analytic) science free from "meaningless" metaphysical considerations, as the positivists assume, he would hardly have needed to write some of the greatest and most complex works in the history of philosophy. He could have stopped right at the point we have now reached and contented himself with an (hypothetical) answer such as this: "We cannot gain knowledge of that which is not phenomenal; for noumenal concepts would have to be derived from pure reason (a priori) and thus could have no empirical content. But though it is true that knowledge never does come *out of* experience alone, it is nevertheless true that it must agree *with* experience – which by definition is impossible for noumenal concepts." (Cf. the formulation in B 1 quoted above, Section 2.1.)

The positivist Kant-interpretation espouses this hypothetical answer as the essential lesson to be learned from Kant. But Kant did not, in fact, stop here, for not only is this conclusion trivial insofar as it is implied in the very definition of knowledge as "concepts with empirical content"; it is also self-defeating: he who admits that knowledge does not solely come *out of* experience must also grant that, due to its partly noumenal character, it can never simply "correspond" or "agree" *with* experience. Kant dit not, therefore, stop at this point, but went on to examine his "transcendental" question: "How are a priori synthetic judgements possible?"

To conclude, let us reformulate this question in such a way as to render explicit its continued critical significance in the face of a still prevalent positivism in our contemporary standards of scientific excellence and expertise: *In as much as all empirical knowledge presupposes a priori concepts or a priori judgements the validity of which we cannot establish either logically or empirically, how can we justify such knowledge at all? And if we cannot ultimately justify it, how can we accomplish at least a critical solution, i.e., make sure that we do not succumb to an objectivist illusion?*

This reformulation is meant to suggest two things. First, it does not imply, as Kant's original formulation does, that synthetic a priori judgements can be shown to be "necessary" in any absolute sense. Instead it assumes that they are "necessary" only in the relative sense that *some* synthetic a priori judgements are necessary conditions of consistent thought about certain object domains and for certain purposes. Second, the question is relevant not only in respect to the metaphysical content of all empirical propositions, but also in respect to their *normative* content, i.e., their inevitable value premises and, in the context of application, their normative implications. Normative presuppositions, just like metaphysical ones, cannot be validated either logically or empirically (in terms of empirical-analytic science); neither what is logically consistent nor what is empirically given can tell us what *ought* to be. In this respect, normative and metaphysical propositions are epistemologically equivalent; metaphysical propositions state what world-views *ought* to be presupposed theoretically, normative propositions what purposes or interests *ought* to be presupposed practically. *Some* metaphysical presuppositions and *some* normative presuppositions necessarily flow into all social inquiry; if we do not reflect on the fact that neither of the two kinds of a priori judgements can be justified logically or empirically, we submit to an objectivist illusion.[6] Thus, far from being of a merely historical interest,

6 From the first two chapters of the present study it should be sufficiently clear that the usual distinction between metaphysical and normative presuppositions, according to which the latter are taken to be necessary only for planning but not for inquiry, is untenable. We cannot define and understand a problem (a section of social reality) without a priori judgements about what *ought* to be considered as a problem (whose problem is it?), what purpose the inquiry *ought* to serve, what *ought* to be regarded as the totality of problem-relevant conditons vs. the "problem-environment," what kind of rationality criterion *ought* to be employed to decide among alternative problem views, etc. In other words, "theoretical" inquiry cannot be kept free from practical assertions, just as practical design cannot be kept free from theoretical assumptions.

Kantian a priori science goes right to the heart of the really crucial issues in the social planner's challenge to practical reason.

As to Kant's own formulation of his basic question, *its* critical significance can be seen in the fact that it condenses these issues into an almost "hopeless" boundary question. The very fact that he formulated his problem in such a hopeless way demonstrates that he was not a positivist but a critical idealist – notwithstanding the efforts of many of his alleged successors to turn him into a positivist against his will. With his basic question, Kant designs a *"tribunal of pure reason"* in which the burden of proof – that we *can* reasonably deal with the inevitable a priori component in our knowledge – is entirely on the side of pure reason. Kant is himself well aware of the difficulty of his undertaking, and his own description of it both suggests the reason for the abstruse complexity of his thought and at the same time gives the lie to the common opinion that his writing style is dry and clumsy:

> It is a call to reason to undertake anew the most difficult of all its tasks, namely, that of self-knowledge, and to institute a tribunal which will assure to reason its lawful claims, and dismiss all groundless pretensions, not by despotic decrees, but in accordance with its own eternal and unalterable laws. This tribunal is no other than the *critique of pure reason*. (KrV:A xif)

Let us see, then, how Kant seeks to realize this tribunal of reason. As Figure 3/1 suggests, Kant organizes the trial into three major parts, the "Transcendental Aesthetic," the "Transcendental Analytic" and the "Transcendental Dialectic." In each part of the trial, reason is questioned about the a priori component it contributes to one of the following, complementary sources of knowledge (or deception): sensation, pure understanding, and pure reason. The following section will take up these three parts of the "tribunal of pure reason."

2.3. The Transcendental Aesthetic

In order to understand the purpose of the Transcendental Aesthetic (B 33–73), we need first to understand its name.

1. *"Transcendental"* is a term introduced by Kant in critical distinction to the similar term "transcendent." While "transcendent" refers to what is "beyond" (transcends) the phenomenal realm of objects of possible sense-experience, "transcendental" refers to what is necessarily presupposed in experience. "Transcendental" and "a priori" are not identical: "a priori" (even in the absolute sense) refers to everything that is prior to experience, "transcendental" only to that which is a necessary condition of the possibility of a certain experience. Consequently, referring to certain ideas as a priori does not exclude the possibility that there are alternative a priori ideas that might allow for one and the same experience; refer-

ring to an idea as transcendental, however, does exclude this possibility (cf. B 80, also Bubner 1974:22ff). It is the task of the "transcendental method" to demonstrate that a certain a priori idea or principle is necessarily presupposed in an empirical concept or proposition. As we have said earlier, the transcendental method, if it is to yield such "transcendental proofs," presupposes a presuppositionless starting point in the form of an abstract, transcendental subject; it is therefore less a method than a conceptual boundary experiment.

Here is Kant's own definition of the term:

I entitle *transcendental* all knowledge which is occupied not so much with objects as with the mode of our knowledge of objects insofar as this mode of knowledge is to be possible *a priori.* (B 25)

Probably the clearest explanation of the distinciton between "transcendent" and "transcendental" can be found in a footnote to the *Prolegomena:*

The word transcendental... does not signify something that transcends all experience, but what (a priori) precedes it in order to make it possible. If these concepts transcend experience I call their use transcendent, in distinction to their immanent use which is restricted to experience. (Prol.:A 204 note, my transl.)

We can thus say that the transcendental use of nomunenal concepts (which are always a priori) is *immanent,* in contrast to their transcendent use, whereby the point of reference is the realm of possible experience. The *transcendent* use of noumenal concepts is uncritical, for the critical intent of the distinction between phenomena and noumena forbids the hypostatization of noumena as distinct objects "outside this world of ours." "The metaphysical [or noumenal] is immanent in our knowledge; the transcendent is merely a name for this immanent factor when it is falsely viewed as capable of isolation and of independent treatment." (Smith 1962:livf) The *transcendental* use of noumenal concepts accordingly aims at the *explanation of the possibility of experience,* an explanation that requires reflection on the immanent metaphysical content in every experience.[7]

To sum up, we might perhaps say that *transcendental questioning* in its intent (though not its form) is essentially *Socratic questioning.* Socrates does not ask his listeners what they know of things but rather what they know of their own knowledge. "Know yourself!" he demands of his listeners, and of himself he says: "I know that I don't know." Socratic questioning, in other words, does not aim at knowledge of things but rather at making us conscious of our ignorance with regard

---

[7] Unfortunately, Kant does not always carefully distinguish between immanent and transcendent metaphysics. Strictly speaking, his transcendental criticism allows one to conceive of metaphysics only as immanent metaphysics, in the sense in which we have used the term "social metaphysics" (namely, as referring to the unavoidable metaphysical content of experience and knowledge). Especially when speaking of the unavoidable idea of God, however, Kant frequently adheres to the traditional, transcendent concept of metaphysics.

to the conditions of possible knowledge. If by "immanent metaphysics" we understand what is not known and is yet presupposed in our phenomenal maps of the "real world," we can usefully think of Kant's transcendental approach as a more precise (though monological) reformulation of Socratic questioning.

2. The term *"Aesthetic"* is used by Kant in its original sense, which derives from the Greek *aisthanesthai,* to perceive. "Aesthetic" for Kant thus means "theory of sense-perception" rather than "theory of the beautiful" or "criticism of taste."[8] According to his traditional use of the term, Kant defines: "The science of all principles of *a priori* sensibility I call *transcendental aesthetic."* (B 35) Its task consists in determining "the possibility of all things as appearances" (B 188), and its method is described by Kant in the following way:

> In the transcendental aesthetic we shall, therefore, first *isolate* sensibility, by taking away from it everything which the understanding thinks through its concepts, so that nothing may be left save empirical intuition. Secondly, we shall also separate off from it everything which belongs to sensation, so that nothing may remain save pure intuition and the mere form of appearances, which is all that sensibility can supply *a priori.* (B 36)

Kant discovers two *pure forms of intuition,* as he calls the "mere forms of appearances"; *space* and *time.* They have in common the following defining features:

1. Space and time are not concepts derived from experience but are necessary a priori representations preceding all experience. "We can never represent to ourselves the absence of space, though we can quite well think it as empty of objects. It must therefore be regarded as the condition of the possibility of appearances and not as a determination dependent upon them." (B 38f, similarly said for time in B 49f)
2. Neither space nor time represent things in themselves; they do not belong as attributes to things in themselves; and nothing experienced in space and time can be known as a thing in itself. In this respect, Kant ascribes to space and time *"transcendental ideality"* rather than transcendent reality (cf. B 44, B 52).
3. On the other hand, space and time are attributes of all objects of experience; objects as appearances are "side by side in space" (B 43) and "[one after the other] in time" (B 52).[9] In this respect, Kant ascribes to space and time *"empirical reality,"* i.e., they have "objective validity in respect to all objects which allow of ever being given to our senses." (B 52, cf. B 44)

---

8 The latter meaning had been adopted only thirty years before Kant's first *Critique* by the German philosopher Alexander G. Baumgarten in his work *Aesthetica* (2 vols., 1750–58). In a footnote to the Transcendental Aesthetic (B 35), Kant protested against Baumgarten's misuse of an old philosophical term. However, Baumgarten's use of the term became popular in German and then, according to the *Oxford English Dictionary,* "appeared in English after 1830, though its adoption was long opposed."

9 Strictly speaking, the assertion that all things appear "side by side in space" of course holds only for the objects of the "outer sense" (the five external senses), while time also applies to the objects of the "inner sense," that is, "the intuition of ourselves and of our inner state" (B 49).

4. Kant therefore asserts, at the same time, the empirical reality *and* the transcendental ideality of space and time (B 44, B 52). We meet here a first and clear symptom of the inherently dialectical character of the Kantian undertaking: it presupposes the *dialectical complementarity of realism and idealism,* a theme that will be important for our discussion of the a priori of argumentation in Chapter Five.

At this point, I should like to add only three comments in regard to our later task of formulating our own basic "mapping dimensions" for social mapping and design.

1. Using Korzybski's terminology, Kant's "pure forms of intuition" represent nothing other than the basic mapping dimensions in terms of which all physical (spatiotemporal) appearances are to be identified and described. The essence of these two dimensions is *extension,* or extensity: extension in space allows us to identify the existence and form of appearances in terms of "here and there"; extension in time allows us to order appearances ("events") in terms of "now and then." Mapping extension in space leads to the concept of quantity, mapping extension in time to the concept of causality.
2. Nowhere in the *Critique of Pure Reason* or in Kant's other critical writings is there a proof that space and time are the *only* forms of intuition available to the human mind. Kant merely shows them to be necessary conditions of the possibility of mathematical judgements that are to be synthetic a priori (cf. Prol.:par. 10). Kant's focus on spatiotemporal mapping appears to be the result of his orientation toward the model of natural science provided by Newtonian physics rather than a necessary consequence of his critical standpoint.[10]
3. It is not hard to see the additional dimension that is required for adequate mapping of *social* reality: the pragmatic dimension ("pragmatic" in the semiotic sense). The essence of this dimension is intension and *intentionality* rather than extension. I shall introduce this "third dimension" after the present introduction to Kantian a priori science.

2.4. The Transcendental Analytic

While it is the task of the Transcendental Aesthetic to isolate the a priori component in sense-perception, it is the task of a "Transcendental Logic" (B 74ff) to isolate the a priori component in *thought* (cf. B 87). Kant distinguishes transcendental from formal (or general, as he says) logic. The latter "abstracts from all content of knowledge, that is, from all relation of knowledge to the object, and considers only the logical form in the relation of any knowledge to other knowledge" (B 79). By contrast, transcendental logic does not entirely abstract from the content (objects) of knowl-

---

[10] In a passage added to the second edition of the first *Critique,* Kant admits that he has no proof for his contention that space and time are the only forms of intuition (cf. B 145).

edge. By analogy to the transcendental aesthetic, which deals with pure (rather than empirical) intuitions, transcendental logic concerns itself with "pure thought of objects," i.e., with "concepts which relate *a priori* to objects" (B 81, cf. B 80). In other words, transcendental logic is to establish the conditions of the possibility of *a priori* concepts of possible objects of experience. It is to clarify the constitutive part they play, together with sense-perception, for the possibility of knowledge.[11]

Kant subdivides the "Transcendental Logic" into a "Transcendental Analytic" and a "Transcendental Dialectic" (cf. *Figure 3/1* above). The former deals with the employment of a priori concepts by the *understanding,* the latter with the employment of a priori concepts by *pure reason:*

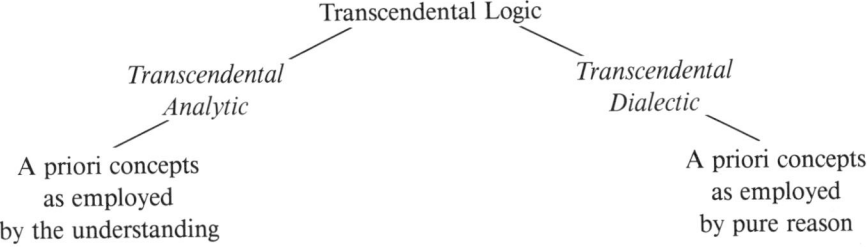

Figure 3/3: The structure of the Transcendental Logic

Reason and the Understanding

I belong to the generation that *as yet* distinguishes between the understanding and reason. Seen from such a perspective, space exploration is a triumph of the understanding, but a tragic failure of reason.

This remark by nuclear physicist Max Born (quoted from Lorenzen 1974:102, my transl.) illustrates the one Kantian distinction that is perhaps most important for us: the distinction between reason *(die Vernunft)* and the understanding *(der Verstand).* Before examining this distinction, it should be noted that Kant here employs the term "reason" in a narrower sense than, for instance, it is employed in the title of the *Critique of Pure Reason* or than when he speaks of the "tribunal of reason." In the

---

[11] The fact that Kant deals with "transcendental" rather than "general" logic corresponds to our earlier interpretation, in Chapter Two, that his transcendental philosophy addresses itself mainly to the problem of a constitution theory of meaningful experience (the problem of the a priori of experience). It is only because he does not yet clearly distinguish from this problem the other a priori problematic – the a priori of argumentation – that he can nevertheless call his transcendental logic a "logic of truth" (B 87, 170). For the same reason, Kant's distinction between "general" and "transcendental logic" remains somewhat unclear and is, in fact, subsequently neglected by him, as we shall see shortly.

latter, general sense, reason includes all a priori sources of knowledge, to which belong not only the pure forms of intuition but also the understanding and reason (in the narrower sense) insofar as they are pure, i.e., contribute a priori concepts.

The *understanding* is that power of the mind which connects ("synthesizes") the manifold perceptions gained by the senses to intelligible, meaningful experiences (cf. B 362, 672, 692). More specifically, it is the task of the understanding first to "bring the manifold of intuition under concepts" (B 362) and then "to bring it under empirical laws" (B 692) by connecting the concepts to meaningful propositions ("judgements") according to the rules of (general) logic. Kant accordingly speaks of the understanding as the "faculty of concepts" (A 126, B 199), the "faculty of judgement" (B 94, A 126), or the "faculty of rules" (A 126, B 356), in distinction to reason, which is the "faculty of principles" (B 356). The basic concepts of the understanding are represented in Kant's famous *Table of Categories* (B 106, cf. *Fig. 3/1* above). Because they precede all experience and hence have no empirical content, Kant also calls them "pure concepts of the understanding" (B 104f). In addition to pure concepts, the understanding contains within itself a priori rules, the rules of formal logic which are for Kant "the absolutely necessary rules of thought" (B 76).[12]

The understanding *(Verstand)* as Kant intends it has only appearances as its object, in contrast to the other important power of the mind, (pure) reason. It is not difficult to see Kant's critical purpose in this narrow use of the term *Verstand:* by contrasting *Verstand* and *Vernunft,* he reminds us that we are not to confuse phenomenal with noumenal knowledge, the map with the territory. The understanding produces maps; reason, at least in a critical sense, aims at the territory (which is not to say that it reaches its aim). The mapping activity of the understanding finds its most systematic form in the empirical-analytic sciences; reason's effort gains its most systematic expression in critical, philosophical reflection on the metaphysical presuppositions flowing into the maps of the understanding. We can postpone a thorough explanation of Kant's concept of reason to the next chapter, for first we should familiarize ourselves with the basic results and difficulties of the Transcendental Analytic as far as they are of concern to us.

According to his definition of the understanding, Kant divides the Transcendental Analytic into two parts. The first deals with the *concepts,* the second with the *principles* of pure understanding (cf. B 90):

---

[12] By *Verstand* Kant thus does not intend the hermeneutic idea of *Verstehen* ("understanding" in the every-day sense), but rather the analytic faculty of mind that Popper refers to when he speaks of the "organon of logic." In contemporary language, "intellect" would probably be a better translation than "the understanding." Indeed, Kant himself used *Verstand* as the German correlative to the Latin "intellectus" which he originally employed in his dissertation in Latin, *De Mundis Sensibilis Atque Intelligibilis Forma et Principiis* (1770:A$_2$ 1, passim). The term "understanding" is, however, the normal translation throughout the literature and shall therefore be used in the following, except where the danger of confusion necessitates the use of "intellect." (As far as I know, Hannah Arendt is the only writer who has used "intellect" instead of "understanding," cf. her comment in 1978:13f.)

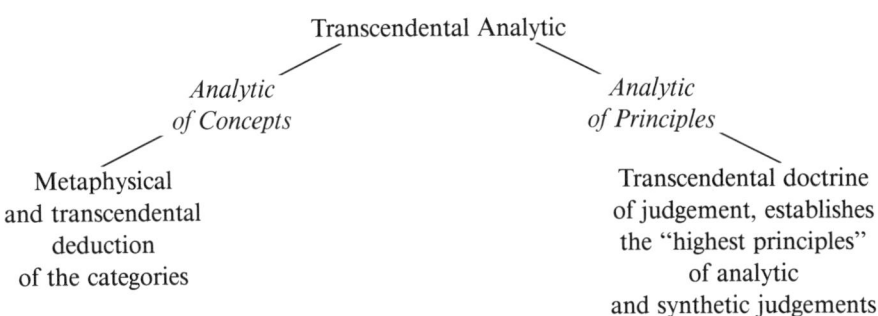

Figure 3/4: The structure of the Transcendental Analytic

The Analytic of Concepts

In the "Analytic of Concepts" (B 91–169), Kant introduces his *Table of Categories* (B 106). Categories are for Kant the *absolutely* a priori concepts that are constitutive of all our empirical concepts and of knowledge in general. In order to establish a list of absolute a priori concepts, Kant faces *two systematic questions:*

1. *How can the categories be systematically* discovered, so that one can be sure to have a *complete* and systematically organized list? ("Metaphysical deduction" of the categories).
2. How can the strict *necessity* and *universality* of these categories be proved, that is, their validity as absolute a priori concepts? ("Transcendental deduction" of the categories).

The second question is crucial for Kant, but irrelevant for us, since our heuristic approach renounces any claim for a theoretical justification of its basic categories and treats them as merely relative a priori concepts. But this renunciation need not imply the complete arbitrariness of a conceptual framework that claims for itself only a heuristic status. We therefore have to face, like Kant, the first of the two questions above. Indeed, this first question becomes the more important in that the *systematic* character of a heuristic framework depends, to a large extent, on the systematic introduction of basic concepts. (It should however be noted that the same does not hold true regarding the *critical* character of a heuristic approach: from a heuristic point of view, the critical character of our maps of (social) reality is determined not so much by the way in which we *introduce* our basic concepts as by the way in which we *employ* them.)

It seems advisable, therefore, to consider how Kant attempts to attain complete-ness in his list of categories. Let me anticipate this much: Kant's claim for complete-ness is theoretically untenable, but indeed yields a heuristically useful idea as to how one can systematically "discover" basic (even though relative only) a priori con-cepts.

Kant's "clue" for the systematic discovery of the categories consists in deriving them from the logical forms of judgements. His argument (B 91ff) is less than lucid, but it seems to rely on the following assumptions:

(a) In contrast to the pure forms of intuition, the categories, as the pure concepts of the understanding, are not to be abstracted from perception but rather from thought, as the faculty of concepts. ("Besides intuition there is no other mode of knowledge except by means of concepts." B 92f)

(b) "Concepts are based on the spontaneity of thought, sensible intuitions on the receptivity of impressions." (B 93) That is to say, *the ways in which we gain our concepts are dependent on the ways in which we form judgements.* Whenever we subsume an object of possible experience under a concept, this amounts to a judgement in which different representations (attributes) are judged to be related to an object.

(c) The converse also holds true: concepts are possible predicates in judgements ("S is P," S = subject, P = predicate), hence *there must be as many pure concepts of the understanding as there are possible forms of judgements.*

(d) The possible forms of judgement, as the basic principles of discursive thinking, have long been established in classical logic. The rules of formal logic have remained basically the same from Aristotle to Kant's day; Kant takes this fact as evidence for their final character (cf. B viii, Prol.:par. 39).

(e) Since we can give a systematic and final list of the forms of judgement, the best way to gain a complete list of categories is by strict analogy to the forms of judgements. To each form of judgement there corresponds a basic way of forming concepts, that is, a pure concept of the understanding by means of which we can form empirical concepts (cf. B 94, 104f). Kant gives the following *Table of Judgements,* which indeed is closely parallel to the Table of Categories:

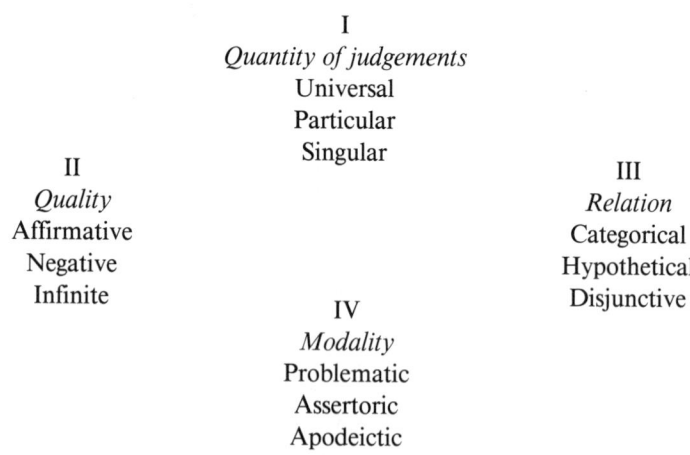

I
Quantity of judgements
Universal
Particular
Singular

II
Quality
Affirmative
Negative
Infinite

III
Relation
Categorical
Hypothetical
Disjunctive

IV
Modality
Problematic
Assertoric
Apodeictic

Figure 3/5: Kant's Table of Judgements (KrV:B 95)

The specifics of these forms of judgements need not be explained here; in order to understand their meaning, it will be sufficient to compare them with the kind of basic concepts to which they give rise according to the Table of Categories (cf. *Fig. 3/1).* More important to us is the question of whether Kant's argument for the completeness of his Table of Categories is acceptable, and what we must conclude if it is not. Again we need not examine the many specific difficulties in Kant's argument that have been uncovered by Kant scholars (cf. for instance Smith 1962:175–186, Ewing 1974:136–144). The following comments are sufficient for our purpose.

1. Kant relies on the principles of *analytic* judgement (i.e., on *formal logic)* in order to derive the categories constitutive of *synthetic* judgement *(transcendental logic).* This is inconsistent with his earlier distinction of the two.

2. It is only natural that every systematic approach to inquiry, Kant's transcendental one just like our own heuristic approach, will strive for as much completeness of its conceptual framework as it can attain; on the other hand, it appears just as natural that human thought can never demonstrate the completeness of such frameworks, neither a priori (in the case of the transcendental approach) nor a posteriori (in the case of heuristics). If this conjecture holds true, the transition from transcendental to merely heuristic a priori concepts would appear less problematic, for even Kantian a priori concepts have then, strictly speaking, only heuristic status: Kant might have conceived of a priori concepts other than those he gives in the Table of Categories, and his table can claim merely heuristic adequacy for the purpose he had in mind – natural science according to the model of Newtonian physics. Just as naturally, our own purpose (of providing the social planner with heuristic support in mapping complex, and normative, social reality) will require another set of basic categories.

3. For the purpose of deriving systematically the central categories adequate to social mapping, Kant's "clue" remains nevertheless useful. *We can find a somewhat systematic and complete list of "mapping categories" by considering what kind of (a priori) judgements social mapping typically involves.* I shall attempt to explain the crucial types of judgements involved in social mapping below, where we examine on the one hand the role of Kant's "concepts of pure reason," and on the other that of the systems idea, for we shall conceive of the planner as a system designer. At this point it suffices to note that we shall not of course derive our basic categories from the formal-logical judgements required in social mapping (they are the same as in all cogent argument) but rather from the critically-heuristic (quasi-transcendental) judgements constitutive of social maps and designs. From the systems point of view, these judgements need to be reflected as *whole systems judgements;* and such judgements clearly involve an a priori component (the whole system is the territory, not the map). It is this a priori component that we need to open up to critical reflection by bringing it under concepts – the planner's basic "mapping categories."

The Analytic of Principles

In the "Analytic of Principles" (B 169-315), Kant undertakes a long and difficult examination of the question of how, by means of categories, we can arrive at synthetic a priori judgements. The problem is this: granted that the categories are necessary conditions of possible knowledge, how then can we actually use them to bring appearances under concepts that will serve as predicates of possible synthetic judgements, given the fact that the categories are "pure"? It is obvious that the categories, because they lack empirical content, cannot immediately serve as predicates for synthetic judgements. (In fact, they describe only the forms of possible judgements. This is especially apparent in the case of the categories of relation – e.g. causality – and of modality, e.g. possibility-impossibility. For instance, the category of causality describes the *form,* not the content, of hypothetical judgements ("if-then," cause-effect).)

In order to solve the problem, Kant first "operationalizes" his abstract categories, as it were, by associating them with what he calls *schemata* (B 176ff). To give but two examples: the schema of the category of "plurality" is number, the schema of the category of "causality" is succession according to a rule (cf. B 182 and B 183).[13] Next, Kant must try to show what principles guarantee the truth of judgements by means of the schematized categories. By analogy to the highest principle of purely analytical judgements – the principle of excluded contradiction (B 189ff) – he seeks to establish a *"highest principle of all synthetic judgements"* (B 193ff, esp. 197). This principle is to explain how it is possible at all that a priori concepts can "correspond" to empirical objects. It does so by postulating an identity between the cognitive conditions (a priori judgements and concepts) accounting for the *intelligibility* of experience and the ontological conditions accounting for the *reality* of the empirical objects in question. Kant does not say it in these words, but his way of stating the principle amounts to such an identity thesis, as Nicolai Hartmann (1924:185ff) has demonstrated. We can postpone the discussion of this principle and the implications it has for us until Chapter Five, for it concerns the problem of the a priori of argumentation and is of interest to us only in regard to our "dialectical turn." For the same reason, I have not included the "Analytic of Principles" in the architectonic given in Figure 3/1.

Let us conclude this introductory account of the Transcendental Analytic by pointing to its chief implications – implications that are essential to understanding the critical significance of the subsequent *Transcendental Dialectic.* The purpose of the following comments is thus to prepare the ground for my attempt, in Chapter Four, to show that the Transcendental Dialectic holds the key to a critical transition from Kantian a priori science to critical heuristics of social planning.

---

[13] The schemata can be regarded as interpretations of the categories in the dimension of time, which is the form of the inner sense, the universal form of all possible intuition (cf. B 181, 185).

Conclusions from the Transcendental Analytic

1. Kant succeeds in demonstrating that our experience would be unintelligible without the pure concepts (or forms) of the understanding, i.e., the categories, in addition to the pure forms of intuition. This confirms his "Copernican hypothesis," according to which "reason has insight only into that which it produces after a plan of its own." (B xiii)

2. However, Kant's critically-idealist standpoint – a standpoint which we have seen to be a necessary consequence of the distinction underlying the Copernican hypothesis, the distinction between appearances and reality in itself – requires him to restrict the validity of the categories to the realm of phenomenal experience. Since the categories have no empirical content, they can yield knowledge only in conjunction with sensuous experience, which in turn is always merely phenomenal:

> From all this it undeniably follows that the pure concepts of understanding can *never* admit of transcendental [here = transcendent] but *always* only of *empirical* employment, and that the principles of pure understanding can apply only to objects of the senses under the universal conditions of a possible experience.... Accordingly the Transcendental Analytic leads to this important conclusion, that the most the understanding can achieve a priori is to anticipate the form of a possible experience in general. And since that which is not appearance cannot be an object of experience, the understanding can never transcend those limits of sensibility within which alone objects can be given to us. (B 303)

This is the main conclusion that Kant himself draws from the Transcendental Analytic. It seems to call into question his program of an a priori science that would provide answers to the "unavoidable problems of reason" and allow us to deal "scientifically" (which for Kant is still the same thing as "critically") with the metaphysical content of all our experience and thought.

3. A closer look shows, however, that Kant's conclusion in fact opens up new perspectives for just that program, although it does so partly because of a flaw in the conclusion itself. First of all, the limitation of knowledge to the phenomenal realm of possible experience does *not* exclude but indeed *requires* our going beyond the limits of sensuous experience. It is precisely because all our knowledge is knowledge of appearances that we need to remind ourselves of the non-phenomenal reality behind our phenomenal maps. Although we cannot know noumenal reality, we can at least "know" (understand) that we do not know it, and in this way we can avoid an objectivist illusion. As Kant himself states:

> Though we cannot *know* these objects as things in themselves, we must yet be in a position at least to *think* them as things in themselves; otherwise we should be landed in the absurd conclusion that there can be appearance without anything that appears." (B xxvi; cf. also the notes to this passage and to B 166, and further A 245)

This is an important distinction. In a famous passage in the Preface to the second edition of the *Critique,* Kant remarks: "I have therefore found it necessary to deny *knowledge,* in order to make room for *faith."* (B xxx) Obviously, Kant here thinks of noumena such as God, freedom, and the immortal soul, i.e., of transcendent (speculative) rather than immanent metaphysics (on this distinction cf. note 7 above). With regard to the problem of immanent metaphysics, which is the only problem of critical interest to us, the more important achievement is really that he has *made room for reasonable thought,* by separating *knowledge* from *thinking* (cf. Arendt 1978: 14, 63). What he has "denied" is not so much knowledge but rather the *unreflected identification of the limits of knowledge with the limits of reason.* This, I believe, is the first way in which the negative result of the Transcendental Analytic opens up the way to reason's transcendence beyond the universe of established "facts," and beyond the boundaries of possible experience in general.

4. A second way is the following. The restriction of the understanding to the limits of sense-experience (i.e., experience in space and time) concerns only the scope of *theoretical knowledge* or understanding, insofar as sense-experience is a necessary a posteriori source of such understanding. But it does not apply to what Kant calls *practical knowledge,* namely, understanding of what ought to be rather than of what is (cf. B 661). This is because the a posteriori sources of practical understanding are of quite different nature – e.g. moral, religious, political or aesthetic experience. For all practical purposes – including the application of theoretical knowledge – we can and need to know the phenomena in terms of which the moral, religious, political or aesthetic side of social reality reveals itself to us. To prevent any possible misunderstanding, the issue here is not whether moral, religious, political and aesthetic reality is phenomenal or noumenal – it is either both at once or it is non-existent. Of course, we can *know* only the phenomenal expressions of moral reality, etc., but we can yet *think* its noumenal side and recognize it as that which it is: an immanent part of the total reality that we can know *as* appearances. At issue here is the *mistaken identification of the limits of sense-experience with the limits of moral, religious, political and aesthetic experience.* The former limits define the scope of possible theoretical knowledge, the latter that of practical knowledge. Both such phenomenal knowledge and such noumenal insight as we can gain in the realm of the practical goes beyond the boundaries of sense-experience.

Let us take as an example the practical (rather than transcendent) idea of freedom, an idea which is of immediate relevance to the planner. It does not belong to the phenomenal world of sense-experience and hence cannot be known or explained theoretically. Practically speaking, however, the fact that freedom cannot be an object of sense-experience makes room for recognizing its true character: it is the noumenal idea of an unconditional condition of our moral experience and action. Because the planner can *think* himself as free, he can view himself as a morally responsible actor. But apart from such insight, he can also experience and *know* himself as being free, namely, in terms of the phenomenal expressions that freedom may have. For instance, the experience of uncertainty with regard to value judgements that are required in planning is a clear phenomenal symptom of the planner's freedom to choose. So is his sense of moral obligation vis-à-vis those affected but not involved in his planning, or his experience of doubt in regard to his role as an expert vis-à-vis a sponsor and decision maker whose values or goals he does not share. Such phenomenal expressions of freedom, as the necessary condition of possible moral experience and action, are also distinctive of those other subjects for whom, or perhaps against the interests of whom, he plans. Only, in this case the planner has no privileged access to inner (though phenomenal) experience and must rely on external symptoms, such as social costs or risks imposed upon third parties, to find those who have such access and may be willing to share it with him in communication.

5. Kant's summary of his conclusions in the Preface to the second edition of the *Critique* confirms the above "positive" interpretation of the "negative" result of the Transcendental Analytic:

> So far as our Critique limits speculative reason, it is indeed *negative;* but since it thereby removes an obstacle which stands in the way of the employment of practical reason, nay threatens to destroy it, it has in reality a *positive* and very important use. At least this is so, immediately we are convinced that there is an absolutely necessary *practical* employment of pure reason – the moral – in which it inevitably goes beyond the limits of sensibility. (B xxv)

However, the formulation "going beyond the limits of sensibility" should not make us identify practical knowledge with noumenal knowledge. Kant at times seems to do just that and to assume that moral (or religious) experience actually provides an access to things in themselves (cf. Schrader 1967:183f). Such an association of moral or religious experience with noumenal reality is not of course tenable on critical grounds. All our practical knowledge is in terms of maps, just as is theoretical knowledge. In either case, the reality behind our maps may be theoretically intelligible but is not theoretically knowable. From a critical point of view, things in themselves are not separate ontological entities "beyond this world of ours"; rather, they can be known *as* appearances. The content of our moral or religious experience is therefore no less and no more phenomenal (standpoint-dependent) than the objects of our sensuous experience (cf. similarly Schrader 1967:181f).

6. In reading anew the chief conclusion of the Transcendental Analytic quoted under point 2 above ("From all this it undeniably follows…" B 303), we now discover a serious positivistic shortcut in it. The trap lies in the phrase about the "limits of sensibility within which alone objects can be given to us." The tacit implication is

that objects that do not appear to us in space and time are noumenal and therefore cannot be known. Here Kant moves on uncritical grounds. He neglects the critical intent of his own distinction between phenomena and noumena, which forbids – as we have noticed several times already – the hypostatization of noumena as entities separate from the objects that we know *as* appearances. It is true, objects that do not appear to us in space and time are, like spatiotemporal objects, theoretically unknowable; but they may still be objects of moral (or religious, political, aesthetic) experience, and we can then know them *as* appearances. (For instance, if a plan causes social costs to people who are not involved in the planning, we may consider these social costs, along with the vocalized protest of those affected, as a phenomenal expression of an underlying moral reality.) Let us recall that nowhere in the *Critique* is there a proof that space and time are the only possible forms of intuition (or mapping dimensions, in the language of critical heuristics). Provided that we do not a priori restrict our social maps to spatiotemporal terms, there is no reason why the moral, religious, political and aesthetic reality that is an integral part of what we call social reality should not become a possible object of social mapping.

Let us then avoid the positivistic shortcut by restating the chief conclusion of the Transcendental Analytic in the way required by Kant's *critical* standpoint:

> Accordingly the Transcendental Analytic leads to this important conclusion, that the most the understanding (whether in its theoretical or practical employment) can achieve *a priori* is to anticipate the form of a possible experience in general. And since that which is not appearance cannot be an object of experience (neither spatiotemporal nor moral, etc.), all our knowledge is in terms of appearances. We experience and understand reality *as* scientist, *as* moral being, *as* morally responsible planner, *as* artist, etc. In the theoretical as in the practical employment of the understanding, our empirical basis is inevitably selective, perspective-bound, phenomenal; it is the critical intent of the distinction between phenomena and noumena – and in fact, its only justification – to remind us of this fact and thereby to prevent us from submitting to the objectivist or ontological illusion. (My hypothetical formulation, cf. B 303 quoted above)

This critical reformulation should make it even more clear that the result of the Transcendental Analytic *requires,* rather than forbids, an effort on the part of reason to go beyond the limits of the phenomenal, the conditioned, the empirically contingent, and to reflect on the noumenal, the unconditioned which alone makes intelligible the phenomenal objects of our experience and their interrelationships. It is the task of the next main part of the *Critique,* the Transcendental Dialectic, to examine how reason – now to be distinguished from the understanding – can become the critical judge of the knowledge of the understanding, its validity and meaning, without itself falling victim to an objectivist illusion.

2.5. The Transcendental Dialectic (Preliminary Remarks)

The Transcendental Dialectic (B 349–732) is best known for the "antinomies of pure reason" with respect to the cosmological idea of the World (B 432ff). Kant demonstrates that reason, if it is taken for a source of *knowledge* of that which lies beyond the phenomenal world, must become a source of transcendental illusion. The "transcendental illusion" is more or less the same thing that we have thus far called "objectivist" or "ontological illusion"; Kant defines it as "a merely deceptive extension of *pure understanding*" (B 352) in distinction to empirical (e.g. optical) or logical illusion (formal fallacies). Transcendental illusion arises whenever the implication of the Transcendental Analytic is neglected, namely, that the categories and principles of pure understanding allow only of empirical (immanent) and not of transcendent employment (cf. B 352f). Kant tries to demonstrate that reason in its transcendent employment is bound to get entangled in antinomies, i.e., in contradictions. To this purpose, he proceeds "dialectically"; he first "proves" a thesis (e.g.: "The world has a beginning in time and is also limited as regards space"), then "proves" the antithesis ("The world has no beginning, and no limits in space; it is infinite as regards both time and space" – B 454). The point is that neither proof is adequate, for we cannot possibly *know* the unconditioned, noumenal reality that lies behind the conditional, phenomenal objects of our experience. The dialectical method is thus for Kant a mere "logic of illusion" (B 349). The positivist Kant-interpreters have therefore tended to regard the Transcendental Dialectic as a relatively uninteresting appendix to the Transcendental Analytic, as a mere call to "demarcation" (B 352) – demarcation, that is, between possible empirical and impossible metaphysical statements.[14]

However, our conclusions from the Transcendental Analytic suggest that there is another, more important side to the Transcendental Dialectic. The real question, as we have noticed on various occasions in this study, is not whether or not we want to deal with metaphysical issues that we cannot decide either empirically or logically; the question is only, whether or not we want to do so *critically*. The possibility of dealing critically with the metaphysical content of our knowledge ("immanent metaphysics") has been opened up by the Transcendental Analytic insofar as it "denies knowledge" to make room for reasonable *thought*. In the Transcendental Dialectic, Kant takes up this implication and shows that reason not only is capable of thinking beyond the limits of what can be known, but that its own nature in fact requires it to do so.

Kant's concept of *reason* is of importance for our own effort because of both its critical and its constructive side. In critical distinction to the understanding, *reason's task is not to produce knowledge of the phenomenal world but rather to produce insight*

---

14 Characteristically, Karl Popper has gone so far as to define the Kantian problem as the "problem of demarcation"; cf. in the present study Ch. 1, Sec. 1.1, point 6 and the remarks about the false opposition of criticism and metaphysics in Ch. 2, note 37.

into the meaning, and the potential deceptiveness, of such knowledge. In order to fulfill this critical task, reason needs its own conceptual tools, similarly to the pure concepts of the understanding. Kant calls them "concepts of pure reason" or "transcendental ideas" (B 368). In addition, pure reason also has its own "principle of reason," as we shall see.

There is thus good reason to expect that the Transcendental Dialectic contains concepts and principles that are of great heuristic value for a critical approach to social inquiry and planning. Since the following discussion goes beyond a mere introduction to Kantian a priori science, and since it deals with what I consider to be central issues to a critically-heuristic approach, I have assigned it to the next chapter. In this chapter, we shall begin our own constructive effort.

Chapter Four
Kantian A Priori Science and the Systems Idea: The Critically-Heuristic Turn

Reason is impelled by a tendency of its nature to go out beyond the field of its empirical employment, and to venture in a pure employment, by means of ideas alone, to the utmost limits of all knowledge, and not to be satisfied save through the completion of its course in [the apprehension of] a self-subsistent systematic whole. Is this endeavor the outcome merely of the speculative interest of reason? Must we not regard it as having its source exclusively in the practical interests of reason?
Immanuel Kant (KrV:B 825)

Introduction

In the previous chapter we have familiarized ourselves with Kant's critically-idealist, "transcendental" approach as it is developed mainly in the Transcendental Aesthetic and in the Transcendental Analytic of the *Critique of Pure Reason*. In the present chapter, we must begin our own constructive effort. Our starting point will be the a priori of experience, and our tactic for dealing with this topic will be to take the "critically-heuristic turn." As I intend to demonstrate, the *Transcendental Dialectic* holds the key to a *critical* transition from transcendental to *heuristic* concepts, for it introduces two central concepts: Kant's *principle of reason* and the *systems idea.*

In the first section of the chapter, I shall seek to uncover the basic critical significance of these two concepts. Then, in the second section, we can examine the kinds of *"quasi-transcendental" arguments* that the two concepts make possible, i.e., arguments that justify the transition from Kant's absolute a priori concepts of pure reason to the merely relative a priori concepts of critical heuristics.

The principle of reason will provide the clue to this transition at the level of the (quasi-) transcendental ideas, while the systems idea leads us to the corresponding clue at the level of the categories. In the latter case, we shall examine the crucial role of *boundary judgements* in defining some section of the real world as a (social) system. "Kant's problem," the problem of how we can justify synthetic a priori judgements, is immediately relevant here, for these boundary judgements must be understood as synthetic, relatively a priori judgements. They are synthetic rather than analytic in that they cannot be justified purely logically; they are (relatively) a priori rather than a posteriori in that they cannot be justified empirically.

Finally, there is the level of what Kant calls "pure forms of intuition," space and time. Leaving apart the question of whether space and time are a priori intuitions or a priori concepts, I shall argue that they do not have an absolute a priori status any more than do the categories or the ideas, and I shall try to outline the kind of quasi-transcendental argument by means of which we can justify an additional, relatively a priori "mapping dimension."

Our conceptual framework, like that of Kant, will thus comprise three levels: the level of "unavoidable" ideas, the level of categories, and the level of mapping dimensions. In the third and final section of the chapter, I shall introduce the "pragmatic" mapping dimension, twelve categories of pragmatic mapping, and three "unavoidable" (quasi-transcendental) ideas, all of which will be regarded as being relatively a priori to any effort of social mapping or design. Accordingly, the basic clue to their systematic discovery will be that they ought to satisfy the conditions established in Section 2 for a quasi-transcendental argument at the respective level of relative a priori concepts.

The purpose of this chapter is thus to develop our critical solution to the problem of the a priori of experience, as a necessary element of a critical solution to the problem of practical reason. The result of this effort will consist in a basic conceptual framework for critical social inquiry and design, a framework for which we can claim a quasi-transcendental status. The framework will be somewhat parallel to Kant's framework of absolute a priori concepts, and as in the case of Kant, the systems idea will play an important part in it. The essential difference from Kant's strictly transcendental approach will be this: while the transcendental status of absolute a priori concepts is established by demonstrating their *theoretical* necessity, the *quasi*-transcendental status of relative a priori concepts is established by demonstrating their *heuristic* necessity in regard to a critical solution of the problem of practical reason. They cannot claim theoretical validity but only *critical significance* within the context of a practical discourse about normative validity claims of social maps and designs. The problem of how such a discourse is to be organized concerns the a priori of argumentation and will be examined in Chapter Five. This much is certain: since there is no objective, theoretical solution to this practical problem, the power of a critical solution to it will depend, to a large extent, on the critical significance of the conceptual framework that we are about to introduce.

1. Kant's Concept of Reason and The Systems Idea

1.1. The Principle of Reason

Kant's critical standpoint forbids him to introduce his concept of reason, as distinguished from the understanding, simply by stating that reason has as its object noumenal rather than phenomenal reality. Kant originally hoped that by showing how reason could respond to its own "unavoidable problems" he could eventually establish, by means of the "critical path," the existence of the World, of Man's immortal soul and the freedom of his will, and of God. But of course, the Transcendental Analytic made it clear that the "critical path" does not allow of a positive, i.e., transcendent, use of such noumenal concepts. The concept of the noumenon can only serve a critical purpose. Kant aptly summarizes this consequence of his critical standpoint in the formula of the *Noumenon im negativen Verstande.*[1] By contrast, a "noumenon in the positive sense" (B 307) would be a noumenon in the uncritical sense of a hypostatized entity separate from the phenomenal world.

> The concept of a noumenon is thus a merely *limiting concept,* the function of which is to curb the pretensions of sensibility; and it is therefore only of negative employment.... The division of objects into phenomena and noumena is therefore quite inadmissible in the positive sense.... Nonetheless, if the concept of a noumenon be taken in a merely problematic sense, it is not only admissible, but as setting limits to sensibility is likewise indispensable. (B 310–312)

After ruling out the hypostatization of noumena and phenomena, Kant finds, in the Transcendental Dialectic, a more elegant way to define the critical intent of his concept of reason:

> Reason has, therefore, as its sole object the understanding and its effective application. Just as the understanding unifies the manifold in the [phenomenal] object by means of concepts, so reason unifies the manifold of concepts by means of ideas, positing a certain collective unity as the goal of the activities of the understanding. (B 672)

The reader may wonder whether a sharp distinction between reason and the understanding does not itself represent an unallowed hypostatization of two seemingly distinct noumenal (psychological) entities that are taken in the positive sense. The only critical response to this objection is to say that reason and the understanding do not refer to separate psychological entities but rather to two sides of one and the

---

[1] B 307. The English translation "noumenon in the negative sense of the term" does not capture the double meaning of the original: "im negativen Verstande" means not only "in the negative sense" but also "in the critical employment of the understanding."

same thing, namely, the human ability of thinking. This distinction, too, is intended to serve a merely critical purpose. Thus, *whenever we speak of reason, we do not intend some miraculous part of the human mind, the existence of which might be doubted; we merely refer to a perceived need for critical reflection on the conditioned nature of our understanding.* That this interpretation conforms to Kant's critical intent will become apparent in the following discussion. And if we are asked for proof that we are capable of such reflection, what better evidence could we offer than the existence of Kant's own critical writings!

But let us go back to the above-quoted definition. The key terms in this characterization of reason are "unity" and "ideas." Reason needs some ultimate standard to assess critically the meaning and validity of the empirical concepts (maps) of understanding. Kant finds such a standard in the idea of *unity.* More precisely, the transcendental idea in question is that of the *unity or totality of the conditions that are constitutive of our experience and thought.* Totality, Kant explains, is nothing else than plurality considered as unity, i.e., in its completeness (cf. B 111). The critical significance of such a standard is obvious: in order to reflect on the partiality and deceptiveness of our knowledge, we must ask in what way it is conditioned by conditions that we do not know. Since we never *know* the totality of conditions, such reflection is absolutely *unavoidable* from a critical point of view; but at the same time, since we can only *think* the unconditioned reality behind our conditioned knowledge, the conception of the unconditioned must remain *problematic.*

This consideration quite naturally leads us back to the "unavoidable problems of reason." It is now easy to see their significance even though we have ruled out their transcendent use and hence can use them only in the sense of immanent metaphysics. They are simply three different expressions of the underlying idea of unity: the World is the unity of the conditions of all appearances. Man stands for the unity of the thinking (and acting) object, and God is the unity of the conditions of all objects of thought in general (cf. B 391). Because the three "unavoidable problems," thus interpreted, "operationalize" reason's basic standard for reflecting on the conditioned knowledge of the understanding, Kant finds in them the *transcendental ideas*[2] he envisaged (cf. B 379, 391).

We are now at a key point regarding the relevance of the *Critique* for the program of a critical heuristics. Let us therefore be sure to comprehend the linkage between Kant's notion of a totality of conditions and his transcendental ideas of pure reason. The notion of a totality of conditions implies (a) that there is something conditioned (typically, an appearance); (b) that there is a series of conditions preceding the conditioned; and (c) that there is a first, or better, an unconditioned condition. To speak with Kant, "if the conditioned is given, the whole series of conditions, subordinated

---

[2] "I understand by idea a necessary concept of reason to which no corresponding object can be given in sense-experience. Thus the pure concepts of reason, now under consideration, are *transcendental ideas.*" (B 383)

218

to one another – a series which is therefore itself unconditioned – is likewise given." (B 364) Instead of saying that the totality of conditions includes an unconditioned "first" condition, it is equivalent to say that *the totality of conditions is always itself unconditioned.*[2a]

From the proposition of an unconditioned condition follows what Kant calls the *principle of reason in general:* "to find for the conditioned knowledge obtained through the understanding the unconditioned whereby its unity is brought to completion." (B 364) While it is the task of the understanding to "understand" (know) the conditioned (an appearance) by *explaining* it as the result of a series of conditions, it is the task of reason to "reflect" on the conditioned, empirically contingent, phenomenal character of the knowledge of the understanding by *conceiving* of the totality of conditions (the unconditioned) that alone could fully explain the conditioned. "Concepts of reason enable us to *conceive,* concepts of [the] understanding to *understand."* (B 367)

As heuristic guides to such reflection, reason can employ its transcendental ideas, for each of them represents nothing other than the idea of a totality of conditions:

The transcendental concept [here = idea] of reason is, therefore, none other than the concept of the *totality* of the *conditions* for any given conditioned. Now since it is the *unconditioned* alone which makes possible the totality of conditions, and, conversely, the totality of condition is always itself unconditioned, a pure concept of reason can in general be explained by the concept of the unconditioned, conceived as containing a ground of the synthesis of the conditioned. (B 379)

Why can reason, by means of its transcendental ideas, only *conceive* of the unconditioned, and cannot *explain* it anymore than can the understanding? This is the case because we cannot explain anything except by indicating a condition preceding it, which in the case of the unconditioned is excluded by definition.

We might compare in this context Edmund Husserl's pertinent observation: "One must finally achieve the insight that no objective science, no matter how exact, explains or ever can explain anything in a serious sense." (1970:189) Take for example the quest of astronomers to explain the origin of the universe, e.g. in terms of the "big bang" theory. The discovery of the phenomenon of the 3° K background radiation has been welcomed by many (including, it seems, the Nobel Prize Committee which in 1978 awarded the most prestigious scientific award to the astronomers involved) not only as a proof of this theory but also as evidence that cosmology has finally emancipated itself from philosophical (metaphysical) speculation and has become scientific. This view overlooks the fact that the philosopher's (Kant's) cosmological question of whether or not the world has an absolute beginning in time and limits in

---

[2a] In a note to B 445, Kant explains the two ways of conceiving of the unconditioned: we can either conceive of it in terms of a finite series of conditions, the first condition being unconditioned, or we can conceive of it in terms of an infinite series of conditions that is itself an unconditioned totality. Cf. also the citation from B 379 below in the text.

space remains unanswered and will never be answered by empirical-analytic science. The latter can answer only the scientist's "surrogate questions," but never man's real question about the origin of the universe. Philosophical reflection cannot answer the question either; but at least it makes us recognize the fact that and the reason why we do not know, and thereby prevents us from falling victim to deception.[3]

The principle of reason, then, must be understood as a *critical* one only. To speak with Kant, the principle of reason is a *regulative* rather than a constitutive principle, "regulative" meaning that it serves as a rule for critical reflection:

> The principle of reason is thus properly only a *rule,* prescribing a regress in the series of conditions of given appearances [toward the unconditioned], and forbidding it to bring the regress to a close by treating anything at which it may arrive as absolutely unconditioned. It is not a principle of the possibility of experience... and therefore no principle of the understanding.... Accordingly I entitle it a *regulative* principle of reason, to distinguish it from the principle of the absolute totality of the series of conditions, viewed as actually present in the object (that is, in the appearances), which would be a constitutive cosmological principle. (B 536f)

To sum up, the principle of reason formulates a merely critical, but crucial role for reason. Reason can "complete" the fragmentary knowledge of the understanding only in the critical sense of making us conceive of the totality of conditions that such knowledge must presuppose. In this way reason, although it cannot establish the reality of these conditions, helps us "realize" the inevitable *lack* of totality in the knowledge of the understanding – its phenomenal, standpoint-dependent character, its partiality, its normative implications. To the extent that we do not "realize" the selective nature of our knowledge, it becomes a source of deception rather than a source of mutual understanding or rational action. The principle of reason is therefore the fundamental principle of what we call, in the language of the present study, reflection on the sources of deception.

The statement that reason can "complete" (or "realize") the totality of conditions only conceptually calls for a qualification, however, for the principle of reason has different implications for theoretical and practical reason.

1.2. Theoretical vs. Practical Reason

Reason is theoretical if it secures critical understanding of *what is;* it is practical if it secures critical understanding of *what ought to be* (cf. B 661, 830). Both in the realm of

---

[3] The same conclusion holds true in regard to the search of nuclear physicists for "elementary" particles, to mention another prominent example. Kant's question, in the Second Antinomy (B 462ff), of whether the world is ultimately made up of simple parts cannot be decided by phenomenal science, for it concerns "first" conditions.

the theoretical and of the practical, reason strives to find unconditioned conditions for all that is empirically conditioned. However, this task does not mean the same thing in the two cases.

In regard to that which *is,* the unconditioned is inaccessible to our experience and we can only conceive of it and critically reflect on the potential deceptiveness of our knowledge in this regard. Not so in regard to that which *ought* to be: as human beings with an intrinsic freedom of choice, we cannot only conceive of that which ought to be, but we can also *realize* it through our actions – "realize" in the two meanings of "making it happen" and, thereby, of experiencing it as real. For example, when I conceive of the idea of a "categorical" (= unconditional) moral law, I can "realize" this law by acting according to it. Practical reason, in distinction to theoretical reason, can thus actually bring about the "first" or "unconditioned" principles which its concepts contain.[4] Or, as Kant also says, practical reason "has causality" in respect to our will (cf. KrV:B 385, 835, GMS:B 109, KpV:A 116).

In the practical employment of reason it is thus mistaken to say of a pure concept of reason that "it is only an idea"; for although reason, by means of such ideas, does not have causality vis-à-vis nature, it can indeed exercise causality in respect to our free will:

Pure reason, then, contains, not indeed in its speculative employment, but in that practical employment which is also moral, principles of the possibility of experience.... [But] although moral principles of reason can indeed give rise to free actions, they cannot give rise to laws of nature. Accordingly it is in their practical, meaning thereby their moral, employment, that the principles of pure reason have objective reality. (KrV:B 385f)

This difference is in fact constitutive of Kant's theory-practice distinction: "By 'the practical' I mean everything that is possible through freedom." (B 828)

This is not of course the place to examine Kant's practical (moral) philosophy in any detail; at this point, only two conclusions are of immediate concern.

(a) In addition to the three transcendental ideas of reason mentioned earlier, "a special kind of systematic unity, namely the moral, must likewise be possible." (B 835) The *moral idea* represents for practical reason what the psychological, cosmological and theological ideas represent for theoretical reason: a necessary standard by which reason can assess the lack of unity or totality in the empirically conditioned

---

4 Of course, the principles of practical reason are "unconditioned" only from the practical point of view of an *agent,* not from the theoretical perspective of a *spectator.* A behaviorist might well say that the "moral law" is conditioned by heredity, cultural and environmental factors; the point here is merely that as a free and self-responsible agent, I cannot explain away the moral responsibility for my action by referring to its theoretically conditioned character. In this practical sense, the moral law is unconditioned; my action may violate it, but it becomes not thereby invalidated. The doctrine of these two standpoints is an important part of Kant's moral philosophy, see GMS:B 105ff and KpV:A 116, Beck 174, Abbott 157. On this topic cf. also Beck's study, *The Actor and the Spectator* (1975).

(practical) knowledge of the understanding. As is the case with the ideas of pure theoretical reason, the validity ("objective reality") of the moral idea cannot be established theoretically, for that would mean to explain the possibility and reality of *freedom* (free will), as the unconditioned condition of moral action. Practically speaking, however, the moral idea gains reality to the extent that it determines (motivates) the human will.

Now, insofar as the same can be said of the pure concepts of theoretical reason (e.g., the religious idea of God gains reality to the extent that it determines the actions of the faithful), it is similarly mistaken to say that "they are only ideas." Kant therefore hints that "concepts of reason may perhaps make possible a transition from the concepts of nature [= theoretical concepts] to the practical concepts." (B 386) The following consideration (b) strengthens this expectation.

(b) In respect to the "unavoidable" concepts of pure reason, among which we now also count the moral idea, theoretical reason has, as a consequence of the previous remarks, no advantage over practical reason. That is to say, the dichotomy between theory and practice – or between theoretical and practical reason – serves no critical purpose in this respect. In the *Critique of Judgement* (1970:par. 76), Kant makes clear what he has already suggested in the earlier *Critiques,* that there is only one reason, and that this one reason fulfills the same function in two different applications. This function consists in the search for the unconditioned conditions that account for all empirical conditions; it is the constitutive principle of reason both in its theoretical and practical employment and is, therefore, constitutive of the unity of theoretical and practical reason.

Since the dichotomy between theoretical and practical reason does not remind theoreticians of the practical (normative) content of all theory but rather makes them oblivious of it, we shall replace this dichotomy by a *complementary* view: all theoretical concepts have practical (normative) implications, just as all practical concepts have theoretical (speculative) implications. In the present context, this view suggests that all concepts of pure reason, whether theoretical or practical, can be treated in the same way: each has theoretically problematic implications, each has, nevertheless, heuristic and critical importance for the practice of social inquiry and planning, and each also has normative implications when used for heuristic and critical purposes.

We are now ready to establish the link between Kant's transcendental concepts of reason and our own critically-heuristic approach. The mediating third between the two is the *systems idea.*

1.3. The Critical Significance of the Systems Idea

Kant does not frequently use the concept of system; more commonly he uses the concept of totality which we have introduced above. Both concepts refer to the whole set of relevant conditions in a given situation of inquiry. The essential difference is this. When Kant speaks of a totality of conditions, he thinks of the entire series of conditions that precedes a given appearance and hence must also be assumed to be given, accordingly to his principle quoted earlier: "if the conditioned is given, the whole series of conditions... is likewise given." (B 379) On the other hand, when Kant speaks of a system, he tends to think of the *result,* rather than the presupposition, of reason's reflection on the totality of conditions determining the knowledge of the understanding; that is to say, he intends the systematic unity, or coherence, of our knowledge. "The systematic unity (as a mere idea) is, however, only a *projected* unity, to be regarded not as given in itself, but as a problem only." (B 675) In other words, the systems concept is just another name for the critical standard formulated in the general *principle of reason,* according to which it is the task of reason to "bring to completion" the unity of the understanding by reflecting on the totality of conditions flowing into it.

Here is the passage in which Kant is most explicit about the intrinsic connection between the systems idea and his general principle of reason:

If we consider in its whole range the knowledge obtained for us by the understanding, we find that what is peculiarly distinctive of reason in its attitude to this body of knowledge, is that it prescribes and seeks to achieve its *systematization,* that is, to exhibit the connection of its parts in conformity with a single principle [the principle of reason]. This unity of reason always presupposes an idea, namely, that of the form of a whole of knowledge – a whole which is prior to the determinate knowledge of the parts and which contains the conditions that determine *a priori* for every part its position and relation to the other parts. This idea accordingly postulates a complete unity in the knowledge obtained by the understanding, by which this knowledge is to be not a mere contingent aggregate, but a *system* connected according to necessary laws. (B 673, italics added to "system")

Of course, such an understanding of the systems idea is rather different from the use of the term in contemporary "systems science" ("General" Systems Theory, cybernetics, RAND-systems analysis, Operations Research/Management Science, etc.). In contemporary systems science, the systems concept is understood merely functionalistically, as referring to a set of variables to be controlled in a context of instrumental action (cf. to this Habermas 1970a:10ff, also in Adorno et al. 1969:156ff). The systems literature is replete with references to the allegedly "scientific" character of the functionalistic systems concept as against the "unscientific" use of the concept in philosophy; systems scientists typically scorn Kant's use of the term as "holistic." What seems to elude them is the normative content of their "scientific" systems concept in every application, and, to the extent that this normative content is not exposed and critically considered, the uncritical character of the reduction of Kant's holistic systems concept to a merely functionalistic systems concept.

223

"Knowing the whole system," so goes the anti-holistic argument, is impossible, "hence" the idea of comprehensiveness contained in the systems idea is of no use or relevance for the practice of inquiry but merely amounts to a "trap of holism." In its stead, the *incrementalist* approach is advocated as a "practically attainable" strategy for inquiry and design (cf., as representative of many others, Bryer 1979:221, against whom our argument in Churchman/Ulrich 1980 was directed; see also Bryer's reply 1980 and my reply 1981 b). Incrementalism assumes that comprehensive understanding of whole systems is not only impossible (which it is) but also unnecessary (which it is not). Breaking up complex problems into small segments will make it possible, so goes the argument, to define clear criteria for small ("incremental") but "satisfactory" improvements of the systems in question, for such a strategy allows us to be relatively comprehensive in our efforts to map and design small subsystems. The incrementalist position has found its most important formulation in Braybrooke's, Dahl's and Lindblom's concept of "disjointed incrementalism" (Dahl/Lindblom 1953, Lindblom 1959, Braybrooke/Lindblom 1963), but it is also inherent in many other concepts of contemporary systems science, such as Herbert A. Simon's concepts of "bounded rationality," "satisficing" and "near-decomposability" of social systems (Simon 1945, 1957, 1962) and Karl Popper's concept of "piecemeal social engineering" (Popper 1957:67, 1966:162f).

From a critical point of view, however, the conclusion is quite the opposite: if we take the systems idea seriously for what it is, namely, an unavoidable critical idea of reason, we must conclude that our maps and designs are deceptive to the extent that we do not critically reflect on the *whole systems judgements* that inevitably flow into them, i.e., our (reflected or unreflected) prejudgements about the relevant totality of conditions that we can never know as such. The fact that we never know "the whole systems" does not imply that we should keep the scope of inquiry within arbitrary boundaries and treat the environment as a "given," as the incrementalists conclude; rather, it implies that we cannot know anything unless we reflect upon our ignorance of the totality of relevant conditions and the normative content of the boundary judgements by which we separate the problem-relevant system from the whole (the "environment").

It is of no avail for the incrementalists to argue that they do not "in principle" deny the desirability of the systems idea but merely adopt the incrementalist approach as a "practical guide for action" (cf. again Bryer 1979:222); for in methodological issues the *"normal"* (practical, feasible) becomes the *norm* without the investigator's being aware of it. Thus the "normal" becomes the standard against which the scientific character of inquiry is judged (e.g. "peer review" in judging the quality of research proposals).

In conclusion, the systems idea, understood as an "unavoidable" critical idea of reason, does *not* presuppose that we can know "the whole system" (i.e., that we can reach comprehensiveness of our maps) but only that we undertake a critical conceptual effort to reflect on the inevitable *lack* of comprehensiveness in our maps, by conceiving of the unknown totality of conditions that might distort them. Kant says it very accurately:

As is easily seen, what pure reason alone has in view is the absolute totality of the synthesis *on the side of the conditions…;* it is not concerned with absolute completeness *on the side of the conditioned.* For the former alone is required in order to presuppose the whole series of conditions, and to represent it *a priori* to the understanding. Once we are given a complete (and unconditioned) condition [a whole systems judgement!], no concept of reason is required for the continuation of the series; for every step in the forward direction from the condition to the *conditioned* is carried through by the understanding itself. The transcendental ideas thus serve only for *ascending,* in the series of conditions, to the unconditioned, that is, to principles. (B 393f)

Once we have understood the critical significance of the systems idea in connection with the principle of reason, it is no longer possible to associate it, as the incrementalists do, with a "holistic trap." The anti-holistic argument mistakenly assumes that the systems idea *causes* the difficulty of which it reminds us, the inevitable lack of comprehensiveness in our maps and designs.[5] It seems to me that such an argument is no more intelligent than accusing the messenger who brings the bad news of having caused it. Killing the messenger, or rejecting the critical message of the systems idea, does not make our maps and designs any more objective or helpful, but only deceptive (cf. Ulrich 1981 b).

We are now ready to turn to the crux of our transition from Kant to critical heuristics, the *problem of boundary judgements.* This problem represents both a fundamental methodological difficulty in the quest for practical reason and a very practical problem in social inquiry and design. In this one problem, much of what we have learned from Kant comes together: the unavoidable problems of reason (the question of the "whole system" of all relevant conditions); the problem of synthetic a priori judgements; the difference between knowledge and thinking; the principle of reason; and the critical significance of the systems idea.

1.4. The Crucial Problem of Boundary Judgements

Whenever we apply the systems concept to some section of the "real world," we must make very strong a priori assumptions about what is to belong to the system in question and what is to belong to its "environment." We call such judgements *boun-*

---

[5] Representative of many others, cf. Bryer's (1980) comment on our plea for a critical understanding of the systems approach (Churchman/Ulrich 1980):
My critics accuse me of misunderstanding the systems approach because I do not appreciate "the genuine philosophical difficulties" which it raises. I *do* and that is why I find it unhelpful.

dary judgements. And since such a priori judgements are constitutive of our maps of real-world systems and of our conception of the nature of the relevant section of the "real world," we can also call them *whole systems judgements* (cf. Churchman 1970a). It is not the reality "out there" (the territory, to use once more Korzybski's helpful terminology) that determines the boundary between the system and the environment, but rather the inquirer's standpoint, the purpose of his mapping effort, his personal preconceptions of the reality to be mapped and the values he associates with it. To paraphrase Kant, the inquirer determines the systems boundaries "according to his own plan." For us this means that *all boundary judgements, and the systems maps or designs of which they are constitutive, have a normative content in need of critical reflection.*

In contemporary "systems science," the problem is either entirely ignored (typically in textbook exercises and case studies) or else it is discussed in terms of formal criteria of modelling, rather than in terms of the normative content of boundary judgements. Frequently, models of "systems" are presented as if the boundaries were objectively given, and the model itself does not tell us whether the boundaries in question have been adequately chosen. If the problem is discussed at all, it is seen merely from a modelling point of view: so as to facilitate the modelling task, boundaries are determined according to the availability of data and modelling techniques.[5a] But even from a merely technical modelling point of view, this way of dealing with the problem of boundary judgements is inadequate. First, the implicit criterion is that everything that cannot be controlled or is not known falls outside the boundaries of the model, so that the model itself looks neat and scientific. In point of fact, the reverse criterion should be applied: we cannot understand the meaning of the model (and hence, the system in question) if we do not understand the model-environment. Hence aspects that are not well understood ought to be considered as belonging to the system in question rather than to its environment, at least until their significance has been studied. Second, such studying of boundary questions must not be restricted to the *"is"* but must always include the *"ought".* Whether or not a certain boundary judgement is rational depends less on what boundaries are presently established than on what the boundaries should be, given the purpose of the model (the systems map or design). The normative content of the answer to the question of what the boundaries should be cannot be justified by referring to data availability, to presently accepted boundaries, or to the success of instrumental action. The norma-

[5a] It appears symptomatic of the unreflective character of much of today's systems-science and planning literature that the implicit reversal of perspective is rarely noted: modelling was originally intended as a tool for better understanding problems, but in practice problems now tend to be defined so as to fit the requirements of the tool. As a result, the original, normative, question of how a problem ought to be bounded (and how the related boundary judgements ought to be justified) has been replaced by technical questions of modelling – another example for the reduction of practical to instrumental reason in contemporary systems science. One rare author who has noted the problematic implication of the wide-spread retreat to modelling questions is Donald A. Keller (1980:164–166).

tive content can be justified only through the voluntary consent of all those who might be affected by the consequences.

The planner can thus only aim at a *critical solution to the problem of boundary judgements,* i.e., it is his responsibility *to secure the transparency of the boundary judgements on which he relies and to trace their possible normative consequences;* at the same time, he depends on some kind of practical discourse with those affected to secure the social rationality (i.e. above all, the moral and democratic legitimacy) of his maps and designs. Our entire effort is directed toward such a critical solution. As far as the a priori of experience is concerned, the task is to develop a conceptual framework that offers heuristic support in tracing the normative content of boundary judgements. We cannot hope to find a practicable, critical solution to the problem of rational practical discourse (a priori of argumentation) without giving the discourse participants the best possible heuristic support in identifying the normative validity claims in question. The systems concept can play an import part in developing such a heuristic framework, *provided* that we give it back its original, critical sense which it has lost in contemporary "systems science." This is why we have associated it with Kant's transcendental idea of a totality of conditions and with the pertinent principle of reason.

Why then not simply speak of "totality" and leave the systems concept to the "systems scientists"? One advantage of the systems concept has been mentioned: it reminds us that we are not dealing with a "given" totality of conditions but rather with a *projected* unity, i.e., with a problematic idea (problematic if it is taken as a theoretical rather than a practical and heuristic concept). This is the reason for Kant's distinction between totality and system, as we have seen.

A second advantage concerns the problem of boundary judgement, as the crux of the transition from Kant's absolute a priori concepts (his strictly transcendental approach) to the merely *relative* a priori concepts of critical heuristics (as a quasi-transcendental approach). The critical significance of the systems concept for such a transition is this. Like the concept of totality, the systems concept refers to the critical idea of a whole of relevant conditions, a whole that we cannot possibly *know,* although we can and must nevertheless *think* it. But unlike the concept of totality, with its implication of an unconditioned, transcendent reality (the totality of conditions is always itself unconditioned), the systems concept has the advantage of reminding us of the *relative* character of every system of which we can meaningfully speak. It does so because it is clear that what belongs to the "whole system" is entirely a matter of the inquirer's choice of the conceptual boundary that separates the "system" from the "environment." Thus, whenever we speak of a system it is clear that we do not speak of transcendent reality (the total, unconditioned reality behind our maps, the territory) but that we are dealing, whether willingly or unwillingly, with *immanent* metaphysics: with implicit boundary judgements that cannot be validated either empirically or logically. To use Kant's terms, boundary judgements are *not* a posteriori (they cannot be derived from experience), and they are *not* analytic (their negations are not self-contradictory); we have thus an important case of *synthetic a priori judgements* in social inquiry and planning (cf. the discussion of this in Section 2.2. of Chapter Three). Boundary judgements are not *absolutely* a priori, that is, they must be made (or for that matter, are implicitly made) before the relevant section of the real world can be mapped. Some typical examples of boundary judgements (whole systems judgements) will help us to see both the relative a priori character and the normative content of such judgements.

1. What is/should be considered as a *problem?* That is, what or who belongs/ought to belong to the section of social reality that is to be studied? (What belongs/ought to belong to the social "system" to be mapped or designed, and what to the system's "environment"?)

2. What *purpose* does/should the study serve? That is, who will/ought to belong to the group of those who are to benefit from the project? (What is/ought to be the inquirer's or planner's "client"?)

3. What is/ought to be the totality of conditions that define the client's *standard of success* for the study to be undertaken? (What is/ought to be the measure of "improvement" of the social system in question?)

4. What is/should be the *time horizon* with respect to the "relevant" conditions in the future? For instance, should the *future generations* be included within the problem-relevant client system? Is intergenerational transfer of costs or risks acceptable? Are irreversible consequences acceptable? (To what extent is the future to be part of the system, and to what extent part of the "environment"?)

5. What is/should be the time horizon in respect to the "relevant" conditions in the *past?* (Should the past generations – e.g. their goals and dreams, the traditions we inherited from them – belong to the problem-relevant system?)

6. Who is/might be *affected* by the project (by a change in the social system in question) although he does not belong to the client, i.e., to those who are involved and benefit from the planning effort? Under what conditions can we assume it is legitimate that some people are affected although they cannot belong to the client system? How do we draw the boundary between the affected and the unaffected in the case of long-term risks such as radiation or cancer? (Who among the affected is/ought to be involved in the project?)

7. Who does/should *plan* and who belongs/ought to belong to the *decision-making body?* (Who belongs/ought to belong to the "experts" and "decision makers"?) etc.

Such questions are clearly normative, and they clearly need to be decided upon before the real-world section of interest can be mapped or (re-)designed. Earlier, we have found that making an (absolute or relative) a priori judgement implies using an (absolute or relative) a priori concept, and vice-versa (cf. Ch. 3, Sec. 2.1.). Hence, to say that the answers to boundary questions such as the above represent relatively a priori, synthetic judgements implies that we cannot help relying on some set of relative a priori concepts. A critical solution to the problem of the a priori of experience must render explicit these concepts. Regarding the a priori judgements in question as whole systems judgements provides us with a clue to the task of identifying the relative a priori concepts that are implicit in our systems maps and designs. We can recognize them by asking: What kinds of boundary judgements (whole systems judgements) are necessary for adequately defining (mapping or designing) a system? Let us say that *a definition (map, design) of a system is "adequate" if it makes explicit its own normative content.* Our question then reads: *What are the whole systems judgements that are constitutive of the normative content of a systems map or design?*

If we can find a systematic way of answering this question, we shall also have established the *heuristic necessity* of the corresponding, relative a priori concepts – "heuristic necessity" in the sense that they are indispensable for making explicit the normative content of a systems map a design, and thus for a critical solution to the problem of practical reason. In other words, we ascribe "heuristic necessity" to a relative a priori concept if it is not possible for a planner to claim value transparency for his design unless he has made explicit the whole systems judgement to which the a priori concept in question refers. Kant's strictly transcendental (and monological) approach, because it does not yet distinguish between the a priori of experience and the a priori of argumentation, must justify its absolute a priori concepts by demonstrating their *theoretical* necessity (their "objective reality," as Kant characteristically says). A critically-heuristic (and dialogical) approach such as ours, however, can and needs to justify only the critical significance of its relative a priori concepts in the above sense, i.e., it needs only to show their *heuristic* necessity; the validity of their empirical and normative content in each application cannot be established a priori but remains the subject of a practical discourse.

We shall take up this requirement of "heuristic necessity" in the following section of the chapter. Before, let us summarize what we have said about the critical significance of the systems idea as compared to Kant's idea of totality on the one hand, and the functionalistic and incrementalist systems concept of contemporary systems science on the other hand.

1. Fundamental for a critical understanding of the systems idea is the Kantian *principle of reason.* The principle of reason in turn presupposes the distinction between knowing and thinking. Although we can never *know* the totality of relevant conditions, we can and need to *think* it.

2. Whenever we refer to a certain section of the real world as a (problem-relevant) *"system,"* we thereby imply the unknown totality of relevant conditions behind the phenomenal reality that can become an object of our maps and designs. We remind

ourselves of the synthetic *a priori* judgements (boundary judgements) that are constitutive of our maps and designs, and of the fact that we cannot justify their normative content either empirically or logically. There is no objective solution but only a critical solution to the problem of boundary judgements.

3. Compared to the Kantian concept of totality, the systems concept has the advantage of reminding us of the *relative*, rather than absolute, character of the synthetic a priori judgements in question; for the choice of system boundaries is largely a matter of the inquirer's or planner's standpoint and purpose.

4. Compared to the functionalist-incrementalist systems concept, our "holistic" systems concept has the advantage of maintaining the *critical intent* of Kant's concept of totality. It is because we cannot reach comprehensiveness in our maps or designs that we need to maintain the practice of reflecting on the unknown totality of conditions behind our phenomenal maps and designs. In other words, it is because a lack of comprehensiveness is *"normal"* that we need to understand the systems idea as a *"norm"* that can give us critical distance to the normal. This understanding presupposes, however, that we do not elevate the normal to a norm, as the incrementalists do.[5b]

5. Rejecting the systems idea because of the problem of which it reminds us, the crucial *problem of boundary judgements,* is no more helpful than killing the messenger who brings the bad news. The problem is unavoidable, and the systems idea can help us in dealing critically with it. The systems idea can help us to determine a basic set of relative a priori concepts for tracing the normative content of the boundary judgements that are constitutive of our social maps or designs.

We have now taken the first step toward a critical transition from Kantian a priori science to critical heuristics. Let us now try to describe the structure of "quasi-transcendental" arguments – arguments that should help us to justify the heuristic necessity of the different kinds of relative a priori concepts required for a critical heuristics.

[5b] I have discussed this issue a little further in my "Introduction" to the German translation of West Churchman's *The Systems Approach and Its Enemies,* see Ulrich 1981a:30–32.

2. The Structure of Quasi-Transcendental Arguments

How can we justify the critical significance of relative a priori concepts, i.e., of critically-heuristic concepts? (It should be clearly understood that we are not concerned here with the validation of the empirical and normative content of the planner's maps and designs of which these a priori concepts are constitutive; such validation is the task of a practical discourse. At present we are still concerned with the a priori of experience, i.e., with the critical significance of a priori concepts in mapping, and designing for, social reality.) In contrast to Kant's "transcendental deduction" of absolute a priori concepts, we cannot of course aim to demonstrate the strict (theoretical) necessity and universal applicability of critically-heuristic concepts. Rather, our goal is to establish the *heuristic* necessity of such concepts in regard to a *critical* solution to the problem of practical reason.

We shall call an argument that achieves this task "quasi-transcendental." Let us try to develop the basic form of such arguments with regard to the three levels of our conceptual frameworks:

1. Relative a priori ideas (by analogy to Kant's transcendental ideas)
2. Relative a priori concepts (categories)
3. Relatively a priori mapping dimensions (pure forms of intuition)

Because the transition from strictly transcendental to merely quasi-transcendental argumentation is least problematic at the level of the ideas, I shall begin at this level and then work downwards toward a quasi-transcendental justification for critically-heuristic categories and mapping dimensions.

2.1. Critically-Heuristic Ideas as Quasi-Transcendental Ideas

Kant's transcendental ideas, because they stand for the idea of an unconditioned totality of conditions, cannot be justified by means of a "transcendental deduction." As we have seen, the transcendental ideas serve only for *ascending* in the series of conditions toward the unconditioned, according to the regulative principle of reason. Deducing them would, by contrast, require a *descending* to the conditioned (cf. B 394). Kant is therefore forced to admit: "No *objective deduction,* such as we have been able to give of the categories, is, strictly speaking, possible in the case of these transcendental ideas." (B 393)

The qualification "strictly speaking" is important. Although we cannot demonstrate the objective necessity of such ideas, we can nevertheless attempt to show their *heuristic* necessity for critical social inquiry and design. Such an attempt makes sense because Kant's admission that there is no objective deduction of his transcendental ideas amounts to saying that they have a merely heuristic status. We have therefore no reason to despair about the merely heuristic character of *relative* a priori concepts. The "strictly speaking" leaves open the possibility of a quasi-transcendental argument for their heuristic necessity. Furthermore, it leaves open the possibility of a "metaphysical deduction," i.e., a systematic discovery of relative a priori concepts that can be shown to be heuristically necessary. The clue to such a systematic discovery of relative a priori concepts can be expected to be closely related to the structure of possible quasi-transcendental arguments for their heuristic necessity. But the fact that in a merely quasi-transcendental approach the two issues are interdependent is no reason to confound them; the present section is concerned mainly with the possibilities for a critical justification of relative a priori concepts, while the following section will focus on the clues to their systematic introduction.

In the "Appendix to the Transcendental Dialectic" Kant explains the heuristic character of his transcendental ideas by means of the phase *"as if."* Thus, the psychological idea of Man requires us to "connect all the appearances, all the actions and receptivity of our mind, *as if* the mind were a simple substance which persists with personal identity"; the cosmological idea of the World demands that we explain nature *"as if* the series of appearances were in itself endless, without any first or supreme member"; and the theological idea of God tells us to "view everything that can belong to the context of possible experience… *as if* the sum of all appearances (the sensible world itself) had a single, highest and all-sufficient ground beyond itself.…" (B 700) Kant's particular formulations here are less important for us than his use of the *"as if."* Understanding the meaning of this "as if" is so important for an adequate understanding of Kant's work that Hans Vaihinger has justly characterized Kant's philosophy as *The Philosophy of "As If"* (1924). (My own discussion is not, however, based on Vaihinger's "idealistic positivism.")

The "as if" is to remind us of the fact that the transcendental ideas are not *constitutive* of objects of experience (as are the categories), nor are they *abstracted* from experience (as are a posteriori concepts); hence they cannot be used to describe the empirical content of our perceptions or thoughts. But, at the same time, the "as if" indicates that although the ideas do not refer to objects of possible *knowledge,* they nevertheless refer to objects of possible *thought,* objects such as the totality of relevant conditions for explaining a phenomenal experience or for defining a social system S. They are, in fact, necessary presuppositions of systematic and self-critical thinking according to the principle of reason. *According to the principle of reason, it is the essence of reasonableness not to cut reflection at an arbitrary point but to take reflection always one step further than what we can explain.* This consideration can indeed be said to amount to a quasi-transcendental argument: the "as if" is a necessary condition of the possibility of critical reflection on the selective character of our maps and designs *according to the principle of reason.* Kant himself, apparently thinking of just such an argument, contradicts his earlier remark that "no objective deduction… is, strictly speaking, possible in the case of these transcendental ideas" and concludes:

If, then, it can be shown that the three transcendental ideas (the psychological, the cosmological, and the theological), although they do not directly relate to, or determine, any object corresponding to them, nonetheless... lead us to systematic unity... and that they thus [as heuristic guides] contribute to the extension of empirical knowledge... we may conclude that it is a necessary maxim of reason to proceed always in accordance with such ideas. This, indeed, is the *transcendental deduction* of all ideas of speculative reason, not as constitutive principles for the extension of our knowledge to more objects than experience can give, but as regulative principles of the systematic unity of the manifold of empirical knowledge in general, whereby this empirical knowledge is more adequately secured within its own limits and more effectively improved than would be possible, in the absence of such ideas, through the employment merely of the principles of the understanding. (B 699, italics mine)[6]

The interpretation of the phrase "strictly speaking" in the original conclusion is then clear: although a transcendental deduction of the ideas is not possible in respect to their *theoretical* necessity, it is indeed possible in respect to their *heuristic* necessity. With regard to their theoretical implications, we need only to make certain that the ideas in question (their objects) are possible, i.e., that they are not in contradiction with what we theoretically know (cf. B 798). If their possibility cannot be ruled out by reference to existing empirical knowledge, "he who denies their possibility must do so with just a little knowledge [of their impossibility] as we can have in affirming it." (B 701) Strictly speaking, we should not call such a combined argument for the theoretical possibility and the heuristic necessity transcendental, for a strictly transcendental argument always establishes the theoretical necessity of a concept or principle. This is why I have suggested the term quasi-transcendental.

We have thus a precise *definition of a quasi-transcendental argument:* provided a (relative) a priori concept is theoretically possible, an argument for its validity is quasi-transcendental if it demonstrates not its theoretical but its heuristic necessity in regard to a critical solution to the problem of practical reason.

I have thus far merely shown that Kant's own transcendental ideas admit, strictly speaking, of a quasi-transcendental argument only – no more, no less. The remaining task is thus to reformulate Kant's three ideas in such a way as to render them more

---

[6] Of course, since Kant develops his argument in the first *Critique,* he thinks of the ideas of theoretical (speculative) reason rather than of practical reason. This does not however question the validity of his argument in regard to the problem of practical reason; as we have seen in Section 1.2 above, within a critically-heuristic framework we can treat the ideas of theoretical reason in the same way as the moral idea: both kinds of ideas remain theoretically problematic, both have non the less heuristic and critical significance in connection with the "principle of reason in general," and both have normative implications when used as critically-heuristic ideas. The crucial distinction in this context is not that between theoretical and practical reason but that between *knowledge* and reasonable *thought* (cf. the conclusions we have drawn from the Transcendental Analytic in Chapter 3, Section 2.3).

immediately relevant to the planner's task of social mapping and design, without however abandoning the possibility of a quasi-transcendental argument. In other words, the condition of the possibility of a quasi-transcendental argument for relative a priori ideas – the possible reference to their being implied by the principle of reason – will be our basic clue to the systematic discovery of such ideas. Before turning to this issue, however, we should examine the question of whether a quasi-transcendental argument is possible also for relative a priori concepts at the level of the categories.

2.2. Quasi-Transcendental Arguments for Critically-Heuristic Categories

At the level of the categories, we cannot rely on Kant for a critical justification of merely relative a priori concepts. Kant claims to give a strictly transcendental deduction of his table of categories, i.e., to establish their absolute theoretical necessity and their universal applicability; such a "deduction" by definition is excluded in the case of merely relative a priori concepts. One might be tempted to fall into the opposite extreme and renounce any *a priori* justification of categories in favor of an a posteriori validation; the criterion of validity (or applicability) of categories would then be seen exclusively in their heuristic fruitfulness, i.e., their usefulness for mapping social reality. Although heuristic fruitfulness is of course a relevant criterion for heuristic concepts, it is not sufficient. To maintain that it is sufficient would imply that we rely on some kind of metaphysical pragmatism, for whatever categories we may choose will be constitutive of our maps of the "real world," and ultimately of our world-views. To accept this implication would be to renounce the critical point of Kant's "a priori science" altogether. If we are to avoid an objectivist illusion, we have no alternative but critically to examine and somehow to justify the a priori component that conditions our maps of reality. This a priori component, since it represents the metaphysical basis of our knowledge, cannot be justified by reference to established "facts" and world-views but only by a critical solution prior to or simultaneous with the establishment of "facts." An a posteriori validation of relative a priori concepts can thus only complete but not replace an a priori justification. Such a justification need not establish the theoretical necessity of categories; it can consist in demonstrating their heuristic necessity. It seems to me that there is indeed a way to demonstrate the heuristic necessity of certain categories, and in this way to justify them by a quasi-transcendental argument. My demonstration of this possibility rests on the following four considerations.

1. We have earlier identified the proposition that *applying a (relative) a priori concept implies making a (relative) a priori judgement, and vice-versa* (cf. Chapter 3, Sec-

234

tion 2.1 and the discussion of Kant's clue to the discovery of the categories in Section 2.4).

2. While ideas can be applied only in a regulative manner, we "apply" a category by using it in a *constitutive* manner. That is to say, applying a category also implies making a *synthetic* judgement. The two statements (1) and (2) are compatible because a synthetic judgement implies both a synthetic, relative *a priori* judgement and a synthetic a posteriori judgement.

3. *An a priori justification of categories is therefore possible to the extent that we can demonstrate that certain synthetic, relative a priori judgements are constitutive of possible knowledge in certain object domains.* With regard to the purpose of this study, we can formulate this important conclusion thus: a quasi-transcendental argument for critically-heuristic categories is possible to the extent that we can show certain synthetic, relative a priori judgements to flow necessarily into the planner's maps of, or designs for, social reality. We have thus found a clue to the a priori validation of categories (understood as relative a priori concepts) that is somewhat parallel to Kant's clue to the systematic discovery of his categories. The reader will recall that Kant's clue consisted in deriving his table of categories from the table of judgements. The parallel is limited, however. While Kant was referring to the forms of *analytic* judgements, I propose to examine the necessary forms of *synthetic* a priori judgements that are constitutive of the planner's maps or designs. It is because of this essential difference that we can draw on this clue not only for a systematic discovery of our categories but also for a quasi-transcendental argument with respect to their validity, i.e., their constitutive character for social mapping and design.

4. We have already encountered the crucial type of synthetic, relative a priori judgements constitutive of social maps and designs; namely, *boundary judgements* or *whole systems judgements.* Our task, then, is simply to examine what kinds of whole systems judgements inevitably flow into every adequate social map or design. "Adequate," the reader will recall (cf. Section 1.4), means that a systems map or design is to make explicit its own normative content. Hence we may fulfill the above task by posing the following question: What kinds of boundary judgements need we critically reflect upon in order to discover the sources of deception in social maps and designs, i.e., their lack of comprehensiveness, their selectivity, their normative content? To answer this question is to discover systematically the relative a priori concepts for which a quasi-transcendental argument is possible. This task will accordingly be accomplished in the next section; the point of the present section is only to establish the possibility and structure of quasi-transcendental arguments *before* introducing the conceptual framework of critical heuristics. This task has now been fulfilled for the two levels of critically-heuristic ideas and categories; there remains the level of mapping dimensions.

2.3. Quasi-Transcendental Arguments
for Critically-Heuristic Mapping Dimensions

By "Mapping dimensions" I mean those dimensions in terms of which we define our basis of experience, i.e., the planner's "data base," and in terms of which we accordingly map some phenomenal reality of interest to us. To paraphrase Kant, mapping dimensions represent the "mere forms of appearances" (B 36). Kant insisted that these "forms of intuition" were not a priori concepts but rather "pure intuitions"; for our purpose, we need not argue with him about this issue. What matters is the fact that mapping dimensions, be they understood as a priori concepts or as pure intuitions, have a heuristic rather than theoretical status: they do not refer to any objects of possible experience; they are heuristic tools for identifying and mapping certain object domains. As such they again pose the problem of whether we can demonstrate the heuristic necessity of certain mapping dimensions.

We have seen that Kant defined his basis of experience in terms of the two dimensions *space* and *time,* without proving or even contending that they are the only forms of intuition available to man. We have also noted that the essence of these two dimensions is *extension:* spatiotemporal mapping allows us to identify phenomena "side by side in space" and "one after the other in time" (B 43, 49). Furthermore I have suggested that Kant's restriction of the empirical basis to spatiotemporal mapping is not a necessary presumption of his critically-idealist standpoint but rather a result (a) of his tacit identification of phenomenal reality with objects of *sense*-experience, and (b) of his orientation toward the model of Newtonian natural science, or in other words, toward the object domain that can be described in terms of physical determinism.

We have no reason to reject Kant's conclusion that space and time are necessary mapping dimensions for the object domain of Newtonian natural science. The question is only whether the object domain called "social reality" does not require a mapping dimension other than space and time. What mapping dimension(s) is (are) heuristically necessary to map social reality?

The heuristic significance of this question can be expressed by reformulating it like this: *What kind of differences in the social reality to be mapped should make a difference in the planner's map?* Thus posed, the question clearly has normative implications; we must consider the purpose that the planner's map is to serve, and implicitly we must ask ourselves *what ought to count as knowledge,* i.e., as a valid representation of social reality. Generally speaking, the purpose of the planner's map is to help him identify and understand the relevant section of the complex, and normative, social reality with which he should concern himself; and the criterion for an adequate understanding may be located in his capacity to design effectively for the *improvement* of that reality.

"Improvement" is again a normative concept, that is to say, it is meaningless to speak of improvement without asking "improvement for whom?" In other words, improvement is always relative to the purposes (interests, values) of individuals. In socially rational planning, there are basically two groups of individuals on whom the meaning of "improvement" depends in any given case:

(a) those who are *involved* in the planning process, among them the planner, the "experts," political decision makers, and presumably the representatives of those who are to be served; and

(b) those who are *affected* but not involved, that is, all those who will have to live the "improved" social reality in question without having a say in the planning process, e.g. the future generations who are not there to express their concerns, those who are not considered "competent" to argue their cause, those who contribute taxes without benefitting from the project in question, those who might suffer unintended side-effects such as social and ecological costs, health risks, moral unjustice, or any kind of reduction in their quality of life.

As far as the planner is concerned, these are the actors on the stage of planning who define what "social reality" is and what it ought to be. The characteristic feature that accounts for the complex and normative nature of the object domain "social reality," and accordingly of the planner's mapping task, is the integral, constitutive role played by human (self-)consciousness, self-reflectiveness and self-determination, in one word, by human *intentionality*. In contrast to the object domain of Newtonian natural science, which can be roughly described as the realm of physical determinism, the object domain of social inquiry and planning is better characterized as the realm of *mental* determinism.[7] This statement must not be misunderstood as a relegation of social reality to a merely "psychological," subjective, or even noumenal status. That would be to repeat what we have identified as Kant's positivistic shortcut in the Transcendental Analytic, where he falsely equates reality that does not appear to us in space and time (e.g., moral reality) with noumenal reality. The human intentionality that is constitutive of social reality – of political, ideological, moral, religious, aesthetic reality, etc. – *does* have phenomenal expressions that are as much a part of the total "real world" as are the phenomenal expressions of physical determinism. Moreover, the idea underlying the concept of mental determinism – the idea of freedom, of a free human will – is no more and no less noumenal than is the idea of a causal law that leads to the concept of physical determinism. All I am saying is that *the idea of mental determinism is crucial for understanding the "facts" of social reality in much the same way that the idea of physical determinism has been crucial for the success of the natural sciences in understanding the "facts" of nature.* The concept of human intentionality (mental determinism) does not refer to a transcendent reality "beyond this world of ours" any more than does the concept of causality (physical determinism); rather it refers to an immanent part of the "real world", a part that has both a

---

[7] The fact that the natural sciences themselves are today steering away from the mechanistic-causal world-view of Newtonian physics does not question but rather supports my argument here.

noumenal and a phenomenal side.[7a] As far as it is *noumenal,* we are dealing with what we have called immanent (rather than transcendent) metaphysics, just as in the case of the concept of causality. As far as it is *phenomenal,* there is no reason to exclude the phenomenal expressions of human intentionality from our definition of the planner's basis of experience; on the contrary, if it is true that human intentionality is a constitutive, immanent part of social reality, a corresponding mapping dimension is *heuristically necessary* for mapping that social reality.

We need not look far to discover such phenomenal expressions of human intentionality and to realize their immediate relevance to the planner. Almost every act of mental determination that really "makes a difference" to the planner will also produce phenomena that can make a difference in his maps of social reality. To these phenomena belong not only the subjective (moral, etc.) experiences of individuals – phenomena to which only one individual has an immediate access but which he can share with the planner by means of communication – but also the comparatively "objective" symptoms of human selectivity, phenomena which we usually describe in terms of interests and purposes, means and ends, costs and benefits, social costs and risks imposed on third parties, political power and "expertise," social classes and minorities, etc. For all practical purposes, it makes little sense to consider these phenomena as "facts" produced by the causal determinism of nature; if we want to understand them in such a way that we can eventually change them, we must understand them as "facts" produced by the working of human intentionality. Again, this has nothing to do with relegating such "facts" to a merely subjective status; rather, the point is that we must take the idea of objectivity seriously enough to take into account the subjective intentionality that is constitutive of it.

We have, then, accomplished the task of clarifying the structure of a possible quasi-transcendental argument for mapping dimensions that are adequate to the task of social mapping: the *heuristic necessity* of such mapping dimensions can be demonstrated by *reference to the constitutive role of human intentionality for the social reality to be mapped.* Since the intentionality that is constitutive of the planner's

[7a] Gregory Bateson, in *Steps to an Ecology of Mind,* has reached a similar yet different conclusion: "The cybernetic epistemology which I have offered you would [that] the individual mind is immanent but not only in the body. It is immanent also in pathways and messages outside the body; and there is a larger Mind of which the individual mind is only a subsystem. This larger Mind is comparable to God and is perhaps what some people mean by 'God', but it is still immanent in the total interconnected social system and planetary ecology." (1972:461) And: "In sum, what has been said amounts to this: that in addition to (and always in conformity with) the familiar physical determinism which characterizes our universe, there is mental determinism. This mental determinism is in no sense supernatural. Rather it is of the very nature of the macroscopic world that it exhibit mental characteristics. The mental determinism is not transcendent but immanent and is especially complex and evident in those sections of the universe which are alive or which include living things." (1972:465)

Unlike Bateson, I do not associate mental determinism with nature and the universe in general but only with the social life-world, i.e., the complex social reality that makes up the object domain of social inquiry and design.

238

object domain (and of the meaning of its "improvement" through planning) cannot be grasped in terms of extension in space and time (spatiotemporal mapping) alone, an additional mapping dimension is heuristically necessary. The planner needs to identify the phenomena of social reality not merely in terms of their location and extension in space and time, but rather in terms of their *meaning,* i.e., their location and significance in the spectrum of intentionality defined by the concerned actors, the involved and the affected. The meaning in question is not merely semantic but also, and essentially, *pragmatic* ("pragmatic" in the semiotic sense): in what ways does the plan "matter," or "make a difference" to those concerned, especially the affected? A precise definition of this pragmatic dimension will be given in the next section.

We have thus indeed been able to demonstrate the possibility and basic structure of quasi-transcendental arguments for the three levels of a critically-heuristic framework: relatively a priori ideas, relatively a priori categories, and relatively a priori mapping dimensions. *Table 4/1* gives an overview that may be helpful later on for quick reference.

Level of relative a priori concepts	Basic structure of quasi-transcendental arguments
Quasi-transcendental *ideas* of critical heuristics	Heuristic necessity established by reference to the *principle of reason*
Critically-heuristic *categories* of pragmatic mapping	Heuristic necessity established by reference to the *boundary judgements (whole systems judgements)* constitutive of social maps and designs
Pragmatic *mapping dimension*	Heuristic necessity established by reference to the *constitutive role of human intentionality* for the social reality to be mapped

Table 4/1: The structure of quasi-transcendental arguments for *relative* a priori concepts (note that the term "heuristic necessity" refers to a genuine a priori argument and not merely to the a posteriori heuristic fruitfulness of relative a priori concepts)

3. Introduction of the Basic Conceptual Framework of Critical Heuristics

The basic clue to a systematic "discovery" (introduction) of critically-heuristic concepts is this: the different structures of quasi-transcendental arguments for the validity (heuristic necessity) of critically-heuristic ideas, categories, and mapping dimensions must be taken as the fundamental clues to their systematic discovery. In this way, we shall be sure to introduce only such relative a priori concepts as we can demonstrate to be heuristically necessary for a critical solution to the problem of practical reason. Of course, additional clues may be required at the three levels of our conceptual framework; but the possibility of a quasi-transcendental argument is in any case the necessary condition for a critical, and systematic, transition from absolute to relative a priori concepts.

While the systematic introduction of our pragmatic mapping dimension and of our quasi-transcendental ideas poses no special new difficulties, it is at the level of the categories that our basic clue will have to prove its fruitfulness. Since quasi-transcendental arguments for categories require the possible reference to the constitutive role of certain boundary judgements (as synthetic, relative a priori judgements) for the planner's maps and designs, the challenge for us is to find a systematic way of discovering the pertinent boundary judgements.

I shall this time begin with the definition of our "third," pragmatic mapping dimension and then proceed to the categories that are heuristically necessary for pragmatic mapping; finally, I shall define the three quasi-transcendental ideas that are required for critical reflection on the pragmatic maps thus produced, their normative content and their potential deceptiveness.

3.1. The Pragmatic Mapping Dimension

Before defining the pragmatic mapping dimension in a way parallel to the definition of space and time in the Transcendental Aesthetic, let us make certain that we understand the meaning of the term "pragmatic." The term should be associated here not with the common understanding of American *pragmatism* (Peirce, Dewey, James) according to which "true is what works," but rather with the theory of signs, for which Charles W. Morris (1938, 1946) has introduced the name *semiotics*.[8] Semi-

---

[8] In order to do justice to the founder of pragmatism, Charles S. Peirce, I should add that his work provided an important cornerstone to the later theory of signs. The significance of this contribution becomes clear if one considers his famous "pragmatic maxim," which still is an excellent formulation of the perspective that is constituent of the pragmatic aspect of semiotics: "Consider what effects, that might conceivably have practical bearings, we conceive the object of our conception [a sign, a word, a communication] to have. Then, our conception of these effects is the whole of our conception of the object." (1878:par. 402, Vol. V of the Collected Papers) This maxim can immediately be translated into contemporary semiotic terms: the pragmatic meaning of a sign consists in the practical implications that the receiver conceives it to have. It is for this reason that Habermas regards Peirce as the pioneer of historical-hermeneutic science and of his "pragmaticism" (cf. p. 111).

otics comprises three branches studying three different aspects of the use of signs (symbols, language): syntactics, semantics, and pragmatics. Syntactics deals with the formal relationships of signs to one another apart from their meaning; semantics deals with the relationships of signs to the objects or ideas to which they refer, i.e., their connotations; and pragmatics, finally, deals with the relationships of signs to their users. This distinction is well known, I explain it here merely because it is often neglected in the systems literature (in fact, I shall argue in Chapter 6 that it is *systematically* ignored in the contemporary systems paradigm of cybernetics and "systems science," and I shall trace the consequences of this neglect in the case study about the Chilean experience with cybernetics, Chapter 7). The three aspects just explained can be understood to refer to three different levels of communication. Thus, a series of *signs* constituting a message is said to be *syntactically well-formed* if it follows a certain code or "grammar" known to both the producer and the receiver, so that the receiver can "read" the message.

A message is *semantically meaningful* if the receiver can not only read it but also "understand" its *signification,* i.e., that which it signifies; it is *pragmatically meaningful* to the receiver if it has also practical *significance* for him, i.e., if it "matters" to him practically in the sense of changing his purposeful orientation. The syntactic aspect of communication processes can be handled by information processing machines; the semantic and pragmatic meaning of messages only by self-conscious humans.[9]

The interdependency of semantic and pragmatic meaning may cause some confusion. It is not a coincidence that the Latin root word *intensio,* as opposed to *extensio,* means both "intension" (= semantic meaning) and "intention" (= pragmatic meaning). The relationship between the two is asymmetric: pragmatic mapping usually includes the semantic dimension, while semantic mapping excludes, by definition, the pragmatic dimension. It is for this reason that I suggest speaking of semiotic "levels"; the pragmatic level is the highest in that it presupposes the others. (A similar asymmetric relationship can be found in the case of spatial and temporal mapping; the latter usually presupposes the former but not vice-versa.)

Clearly, the phenomenal expressions of the human intentionality that is constitutive of social reality cannot be adequately grasped at the syntactic or even at the semantic levels but only at the pragmatic level. This is why I have spoken of "pragmatic mapping." I should note, however, that it is somewhat dangerous to associate the label "pragmatic mapping" with the object domain "social reality," for *every* adequate mapping process must, of course, be considered at all three semiotic levels. For this reason, I usually prefer the term "social mapping" (or "social mapping and

---

[9] This explains why contemporary information theory characterizes communication processes and information systems in terms of a machine, and why it must ignore the fact that this very characterization implies that there is some purpose which the "machine" is to serve and which cannot be grasped at the syntactic level but only at the pragmatic level. For a detailed philosophical argument cf. Beck 1975:Ch. 1.

design") and tacitly imply that the pragmatic dimension is essential to social maps and designs.

This last remark gives me an opportunity to define explicitly the difference between "social mapping'" and "social design." What the two have in common is that they are both supposed to determine complex and normative social reality, a task that requires that we include the pragmatic dimension in the definition of our basis of experience. If the task is to determine ("realize" in the sense of "understand") *actual* social reality, i.e., the *problem* situation, we speak of "mapping"; if the task is to determine ("make real") *future* social reality, we speak of "design." Of course, at the pragmatic level the distinction is not sharp, for "determining" reality, as the term suggests, is in any case a normative task and hence requires us to go beyond the given universe of "facts." Mapping the problem-relevant reality in such a way as to understand the problem implies an answer to the normative question of what *ought* to be considered as a problem, and *whose* problem it is. Moreover, as Rittel and Webber have shown in their well-known paper "Dilemmas in a General Theory of Planning" (1973:161), "the information needed to *understand* the problem depends upon one's idea for *solving* it.... To find the problem is thus the same thing as finding the solution; the problem can't be defined until the solution has been found." We can thus say that social mapping implies social design, just as social design presupposes social mapping. The two terms are useful to replace the sharp and often misleading dichotomy of "theory" and "practice" by a "softer" differentiation, one that does not imply that there is such a thing as value-free description, or theory-free design, of social reality.

A last comment is in order before defining the pragmatic mapping dimension. Although we define the planner's basis of experience as including the spatiotemporal dimensions of space and time as well as the pragmatic dimension, I shall concentrate on the latter. The fact that we understand space and time as being *relatively* a priori only does not require any changes in the explanation given in Chapter Three, except that we now regard them as merely complementary rather than sufficient for the purpose of social mapping. It makes sense for the planner to identify the phenomenal expressions of human intentionality in space and time only if he has already identified their pragmatic meaning, or if spatiotemporal mapping will help him to do so. Let us then attempt to define the pragmatic mapping dimension analogously to space and time (cf. Section 2.2 of Chapter 3):

1. The key concept with which we associate the pragmatic dimension is the concept of human intentionality, or purposefulness, or simply "purpose."[10] On critical grounds, we can never assume the absence of purpose from our maps of social reality, just as "we can never represent to ourselves the absence of space [and

---

[10] I shall speak of "human intentionality" when thinking of the noumenal concept of free will, while the term "purpose" is rather meant to be associated with the phenomenal expressions of such intentionality, phenomenal expressions that are an integral part of social reality.

time]" in our maps of physical reality (cf. KrV:B 38f). Defining "purpose" as a mapping dimension analogous to "space" and "time" is thus *not* to "introduce" value judgements into social mapping but rather to include in our basis of experience the value judgements that are always already there, as constituent elements of both social reality and our maps of it. Unlike "space" and "time," "purpose" is thus also a critical concept, that is, it will also serve as a critically-heuristic category of social mapping. But that must not wrongly lead us to locate it only at the level of the understanding (or of the categories); since it is an essential part of the phenomenal social reality to be mapped, we must introduce it in the definition of the planner's empirical basis, i.e., at the level of mapping dimensions.

2. Purposes do *not* represent things in themselves, and of course nothing mapped in the pragmatic dimension of purpose can be known as a thing in itself. In this respect, we can ascribe to purpose *"heuristic ideality"* rather than transcendent reality, that is, it serves a necessary heuristic function in making intelligible the complex phenomenal object domain which we call "social reality," but it does not give us access to noumenal reality any more than do space and time. (The term "heuristic ideality" replaces the Kantian term "transcendental ideality" because the pragmatic dimension of purpose is not said to be universally applicable or necessary in any absolute sense.) This definition effectively answers any possible objection as to an alleged "teleological fallacy" in ascribing purposes to social systems.

3. All *phenomena* belonging to the object domain "social reality" must be considered as being related to human purposes, i.e., as having a normative content, as pointing to the sources and consequences of human intentionality, and implicitly, of selectivity. In this respect, we can ascribe to purpose *"empirical reality,"* or, to avoid confusion with Kant's strictly transcendental terminology, *"pragmatic reality";* that is, for all practical purposes the planner must recognize the normative character of his "data basis." While the objects of spatiotemporal mapping stand to each other "side by side in space" and "one after the other in time," the objects of pragmatic mapping are to be ordered in relations of "means" and "ends" (whereby the two are not, of course, to be hypostatized as distinct ontological entities).

4. We therefore assert, at the same time, the heuristic ideality *and* the pragmatic reality of purpose as a relative a priori representation. Pragmatic mapping in terms of means and ends (purpose) is required both as that which makes social reality *intelligible* (a priori of experience) and as the basis of experience for a practical discourse about the *"reality"* (validity) of statements about social reality (a priori of argumentation).

If this "quasi-transcendental" definition of our pragmatic mapping dimension appears indigestible to the reader, he should not dwell on its details but simply note that we have introduced the pragmatic dimension in accordance with the critical intent of Kant's fundamental distinction, the distinction between phenomena and noumena. We have shown that it is indeed possible to reconstruct Kant's Transcendental Aesthetic in relative a priori terms and to introduce the pragmatic dimension of purpose analogously to space and time. This reconstructive "experiment" also serves as the epistemological basis for the next, and crucial, step in our constructive effort: namely, the systematic introduction of our categories of pragmatic mapping. Since these categories are to conceptualize the pragmatic mapping dimension, they will "automatically" serve to elucidate its meaning.

3.2. Twelve Critically-Heuristic Categories of Pragmatic Mapping

According to our basic clue, we want to introduce a set of categories for which a quasi-transcendental argument can be made. Such an argument has been shown to be possible, in the case of the categories, by reference to the boundary judgements that are constitutive of social maps and designs. In regard to these boundary judgements, we have identified three propositions:

1. The boundary judgements in question are to be regarded as *synthetic, relatively a priori judgements,* that is, they cannot be justified either logically (as can analytic judgements) or empirically (as can synthetic a posteriori judgements). Only a critical solution to the validation problem is possible in this case, which means that the planner must trace the normative implications of alternative boundary judgements (i.e., alternative conceptualizations of the planning problem) and make these implications transparent to those concerned.

2. Making a relative a priori judgement (such as a boundary judgement) implies *"applying"* a relative a priori concept (a category), and vice versa. Since categories, unlike ideas, are "applied" in a *constitutive* manner, we must ask to what kind of empirical objects they ought to refer. In this respect, we can say that the categories ought to conceptualize those phenomenal aspects of the real world that are crucial to understanding the complex and normative nature of *social reality.* We have associated these aspects with the pragmatic mapping level.

3. The boundary judgements in question are to be understood as *whole system judgements.* Regarding the social reality to be mapped as a social system that is to be bounded reminds us of the fact that we are dealing not with a given totality of conditions but with a projected unity, and that this projection is dependent on the planning purpose and on the planner's own standpoint vis-à-vis the system. In this respect we can conclude that the envisaged set of categories must be understood to represent a general conceptualization of any planning situation, namely, as a social system (or a social process) of which the planner is a part. More specifically, this conceptualization ought to cover all the essential sources of the normative content of any systems design.

244

All three considerations point to the same clue to a systematic discovery of the boundary judgements that are constitutive of social maps and designs, and of the corresponding categories: we ought to look for the crucial sources from which the normative content of any social map or design derives. We have earlier found that *human intentionality* is the constitutive element accounting for the complex and normative nature of the object domain "social reality." We have also identified two basic groups of social actors who define what "social reality" is and what it ought to be, namely, the *involved* and the *affected* (cf. Sec. 2.3 of the present chapter). Hence our *clue* is this: *we can determine the boundary judgements that are constitutive of social maps and designs if we can give a systematic list of the social actors to whom the planner must refer in order to understand the normative content of his maps and designs.*

Two clarifications are called for immediately. First, the term "actors" refers to social *roles* (such as planning) rather than to individuals. In any concrete case it is of course necessary to make specific boundary judgements as to what individuals ought to be considered as representatives of these social roles; but at present we are concerned only with the *"forms" of constitutive boundary judgements,* that is, with the social *roles* to be categorized. Second, in order to help the planner grasp the normative content of his activity, the categories of course must conceptualize not only the social *roles* in question but also their essential *concerns* in respect to the social system to be improved, or in other words, the kinds of information and considerations that they can contribute to the planner's "data base."

Before trying to apply our clue and to determine a systematic list of social roles that the planner must invariably consider, I should point to an earlier conceptualization attempt to which the present effort owes a good deal of its inspiration, C. West Churchman's list of defining systems characteristics as presented in his book *The Design of Inquiring Systems* (1971:43). The basic idea of Churchman's list is that social systems are teleological (in the language of the present study: purposeful) entities, and that there is such a thing as a minimal "anatomy of systems teleology," i.e., a necessary set of conditions that must be fulfilled for a system S to be capable of purposeful activity. Here is Churchman's original list of 1971, comprising nine necessary conditions (he gives a similar list of eight postulates in 1979:106):

1. S is teleological
2. S has a measure of performance [i.e., an integrating standard for measuring and aggregating improvements]
3. There exists a client whose interests (values) are served by S in such a manner that the higher the measure of performance, the better the interests are served, and more generally, the client is the standard of the measure of performance
4. S has teleological components which coproduce the measure of performance of S

5. S has an environment (defined either teleologically or ateleologically [e.g. social and ecological environment]), which also coproduces the measure of performance of S
6. There exists a decision maker who – via his resources – can produce changes in the measures of performance of S's components and hence changes in the measures of performance of S
7. There exists a designer who conceptualizes the nature of S in such a manner that the designer's concepts potentially produce actions in the decision maker, and hence changes in the measures of performance of S's components, and hence changes in the measure of performance of S
8. The designer's intention is to change S so as to maximize S's value to the client
9. S is "stable" with respect to the designer, in the sense that there is a built-in guarantee that the designer's intention is ultimately realizable (1971:43)

Implied in this list of necessary conditions are nine categories. We can rearrange their order, as Churchman did in *The Systems Approach and Its Enemies* (1979:79f), into three groups of three categories, so that the first category of each group stands for a social role and the two others point to the essential concerns distinctive of these roles:

I
Client
Purpose
Measure of Performance

II
Decision Maker
Components
Environment

III
Planner
Implementation
Guarantor

In *The Systems Approach and Its Enemies* (1979:80), Churchman added a fourth group of categories, one that can be understood to conceptualize the self-reflective dimension of his conceptualization attempt:

IV
Systems Philosophers
Enemies of the Systems Approach
Significance

246

In three case studies (two of which are included in Part III of the present study). I have attempted to apply these categories to the task of tracing the normative content of systems designs in the realms of national economic planning, public health planning, and environmental design. I found that the categories number 1-7 and 9 were of great heuristic value for this task, while the others, though far from being irrelevant, seemed less immediately helpful. Their significance, I believe, consists in helping us to reflect upon our basic philosophy of planning rather than to map some section of social reality, that is, they serve a critical rather than constitutive role. They point to issues such as the meaning of "systems rationality," the systems paradigm and the model of practical discourse to be presupposed, etc.; issues that arise in connection with all other categories and that are obviously fundamental to this entire study. In our own conceptual framework, they ought to be defined at the level of ideas rather than at the level of mapping categories. We shall indeed find, in Section 3.3. below, that the concerns behind these concepts (systems philosopher, enemies, implementation and significance) seem to be essentially the same as those behind our three ideas derived from Kant's "transcendental ideas."

Be that as it may, for our present purpose we are in the fortunate position of having a well-defined criterion for deciding on the heuristic necessity of any of these categories. This makes it unnecessary to base our list of categories merely on personal experience or preference, or even on the mere desire to develop a different list for the sake of difference. Instead, we shall make our basic clue – the requirement of a possible reference to constitutive boundary judgements – the criterion by which to judge what categories – those of Churchman or of anyone else – deserve to be granted a quasi-transcendental status, and to judge what other categories may seem necessary for a systematic list.[11]

Let us see, then, whether we can determine a systematic list of social roles and corresponding concerns, and can relate them to necessary boundary judgements. Our first systematic consideration needs no further explanation:

In order to bound a social system S, the planner has to trace the normative content of the necessary boundary judgements. In order to do so, he must refer to the group of those social actors who ought to define what the social reality in question is and what it ought to be. There are basically two grounds on which anyone can claim to belong to this group: (a) because he lives, or will have to live, the social reality in question,

---

[11] For the sake of completeness, I should mention Peter B. Checkland's conceptualization attempt (1972, cf. also Smyth/Checkland 1976 and Checkland 1981:223ff). His basic list of eight "formal systems properties" is explicitly based on Churchman's original list of 1971, though he prefers a somewhat different terminology and arrangement. It seems to me that the only significant difference lies in Checkland's strictly functionalistic interpretation of the guarantor category in terms of "[systems] continuity"; it was not Churchman's intent to associate this category with the characteristic orientation of functionalistic systems theory toward systems maintenance. To do justice to Checkland's effort, let me add that he situates his categories within a larger framework of "soft" systems methodology, a framework that is free from the scientistic pretensions of "general" systems theory or functionalistic systems science.

i.e., because he is actually or potentially *affected* by the outcome of the planning effort; or (b) because he has some kind of resources to contribute to the effort (be it expertise, political or financial support, etc.), i.e., because he is factually *involved* in the planning process.

The social
system S
to be
bounded
$\left\{\begin{array}{l}\text{Social actors}\\\text{defining}\\\text{the normative}\\\text{content of S}\end{array}\right.$
$\left\{\begin{array}{l}\text{Those } \textit{involved}\\\text{in the planning of S}\\\\\text{Those } \textit{affected} \text{ by S}\\\text{but not involved}\\\text{in its planning}\end{array}\right.$

From this first basic distinction we can derive the necessity of two basic kinds of boundary judgements, as the following Venn-diagram shows:

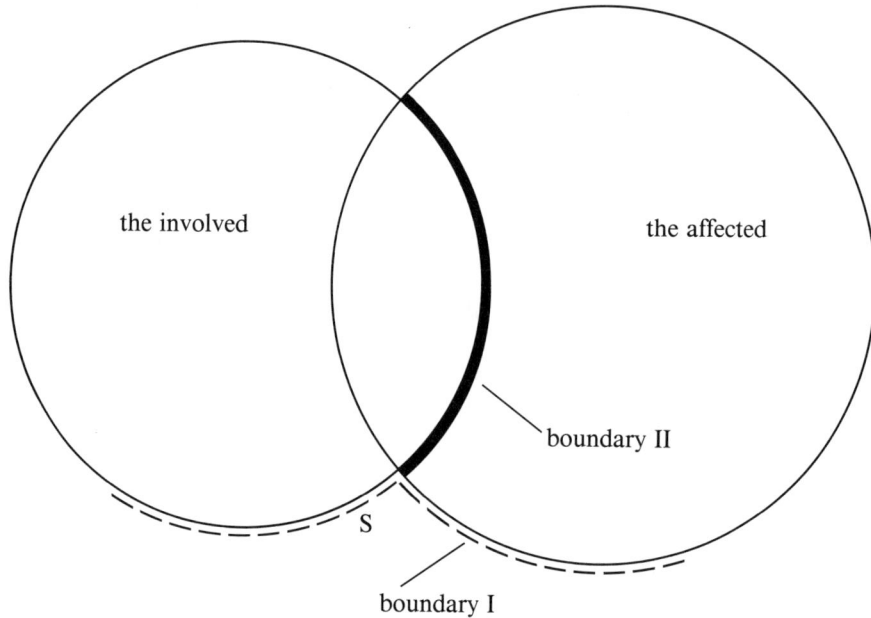

the involved

the affected

boundary II

S

boundary I

Figure 4/2: Two basic kinds of boundary judgements
I: the social system S to be bounded vs. its environment
II: the affected vs. the involved

In order to define the two basic boundary judgements, we need first to define the two overlapping terms "involved" and "affected" and their interrelationship.

(a) Generally speaking, to be *"involved"* means to *have input,* that is, to have a say in the process of will-formation. The spectrum of participation ranges all the way from being given an opportunity to voice one's concerns to an immediate decision competence. On the other hand, being *"affected"* will be understood here in a rather narrow sense, namely, as having to *live* the social reality in question, and hence personally to bear at least some of the consequences of the planning outcome. If we would define "affected" in looser terms, e.g. as having any kind of interests at stake, such as one's professional reputation as a planner or expert, being involved would virtually become congruent with being affected. This would blur the essential distinction between those affected *and* involved on the one hand, those affected but *not* involved on the other. This distinction is important to the planner in tracing the sources of a design's normative content because those affected *and* involved can voice their concerns in the same way as those involved but not affected, while those affected but *not* involved cannot do so.

(b) Because of the previous consideration, the term *"the involved,"* where not otherwise stated, will be meant to include those affected *and involved.* Typically (though not necessarily) those who are to be served by a planning effort will belong both to the affected and to the involved.

(c) The term *"the affected"* will be used to refer to the group of *those affected but not involved.* That is to say, when we contrast "the involved" with "the affected," the crucial boundary judgement concerns boundary II in Figure 4/2.

(d) The total group (i.e., the union) of those to be involved and/or affected is what we term *"the social system S."* The problem of bounding the social reality to be mapped and improved thus refers to boundary I in Figure 4/3, which in turn is composed of the two boundary judgements concerning the affected and the involved. Conversely, the problem of bounding the two groups of the affected and the involved can be understood to imply the two boundary judgements I and II:

I: How to draw the boundary between S and its environment? or: What belongs to the problem (the problem-relevant system S) and what to the problem-environment?

II: How to draw the boundary between the involved and the affected?

Usually, the two judgements I and II will be the *result,* rather than the point of departure, of the process of unfolding an ill-structured and unbounded problem. But although the planner can hardly ever start out with one-shot judgements about boundaries I and II, he must not forget that they are the crucial boundary judgements toward which he must work. As a rule, the planner will begin with a tentative definition of the essential planning purpose and try to bound the two groups of the involved and the affected by breaking them down into manageable *subgroups.* We are looking for the categories that will guide him to the relevant subgroups that are constitutive of each group.

Let us first turn to the problem of specifying the group of the involved. There are three basic sources of influence in terms of which we can analyze the involved:

1. *Sources of motivation:* Who contributes (ought to contribute) the necessary sense of direction and "values"? Or: Whose purposes are to be served? Given a tentative planning purpose, whose purpose is it?
2. *Sources of control:* Who contributes (ought to contribute) the necessary means, resources and decision authority, i.e., "power"? Who has (ought to have) the power to decide?
3. *Sources of expertise:* Who contributes (ought to contribute) skills and necessary knowledge of "facts"? Who has (ought to have) the know-how to do it?

These three sources of influence closely correspond to the three prototypical roles which were categorized in Churchman's list of conditions. We can understand the *"client"* as the group of all those whose purposes (values, interests) are (ought to be) served. Similarly, the *"decision maker"* conceptualizes all the sources of control that influence (ought to influence) the effective outcome of the planning effort, that is, whether the intended client is actually served or whether a surrogate client (such as the decision maker himself) is served. Finally, the *"planner"* can be understood as the prototype standing for all the experts who are (ought to be) involved because of their professional or personal skills and knowledge, i.e., because they serve as a source of necessary expertise.

Note that each of these three roles will usually comprise a complex of persons, and that the boundaries defining such a complex of persons are rarely identical with given organizational or institutional boundaries such as they are established by organizational diagrams, public law, etc. To use a sociological phrase, the groups of social actors in question are usually "informal groups" rather than "formal groups," that is, they extend beyond formal boundaries.

As a second important note, every role needs to be considered both as an "is" problem (Who *is* the client?) and as an "ought" problem (Who *ought* to be the client?). As far as the problem of a priori boundary judgements is concerned, we are dealing with the "ought" problem, for these judgements cannot be justified by reference to what is empirically the case. Of course, answering the "ought" question implies anticipation of "is" answers, but the latter can only be empirically validated by mapping the social system S *after* ist has been bounded.

We have then three basic categories for the purpose of specifying the group of the involved:

The involved
$\left\{ \begin{array}{l} 1. \text{ "Client" (sources of motivation)} \\ 2. \text{ "Decision Maker" (sources of control)} \\ 3. \text{ "Planner" (sources of expertise)} \end{array} \right.$

Of course, nothing in what we have said implies that the three subgroups are or ought to be mutually exclusive; they are, however, to be understood in a sense that is wide enough to cover the entire group of the involved, i.e., they are intended to be exhaustive with respect to that group.

Turning now to the second major group of social actors defining the normative content of S, the group of those *affected* but not involved, it is obvious that this group is less easy to specify. To name only two reasons, this group is potentially very large, and its members do not "qualify" as such by making some well-defined contribution. Their "contribution" may consist in suffering unwanted side-effects and risks, or in paying some other costs that are not borne by those who benefit. Accordingly, a systematic attempt to dissolve this group into subgroups would have to rely on a general taxonomy of the costs of social planning imposed on the uninvolved, e.g.:

1. socio-ecological costs
   - quality of individual life
   - quality of community life
   - quality of the natural environment
   - etc.

2. socio-economic costs
   - redistributive effects at the community level (e.g. among individuals, among social classes)
   - redistributive effects at the state level (among communities)
   - redistributive effects at the federal level (among states)
   - redistributive effects at the international level (e.g. among developing and "developed" countries)
   - intergenerational transfers (costs imposed on future generations)
   - etc.

3. socio-political costs
   - undermining of civil rights (e.g. need for a police state in the case of nuclear power plants)
   - undermining of the democratic process
   - undermining of government through private interests
   - undermining of the "free" market (e.g., through government subventions or corporate concentration)
   - creation of structural conflicts ("jobs vs. health," "inflation vs. recession," "market rationality vs. social rationality", etc.)
   - etc.

This very insufficient list already demonstrates the complexity of such an undertaking, both heuristically and theoretically. Heuristically speaking, such a taxonomy tends to become so extensive and complex that it is of little heuristic value in guiding the planner to the affected groups of individuals. Theoretically speaking, the affected groups can rarely be bounded, for knowledge about the potential side-effects and long-term risks of interventions into social and ecological reality is usually insufficient; one needs only to think of the unknown ecological effects of many chemicals, of the carcinogenic effects of low-level radiation, quite apart from the socio-psychological effects of any intervention into social reality. And even where it is possible to trace all potential effects, the group of those affected will often enough include individuals to whom the planner cannot turn for hearing their concerns, be it because they are unborn, too young, or handicapped by other reasons. The conclusion is inevitable that for all practical purposes, the affected can only be represented vis-à-vis the planner, and the involved in general, by a limited number of social actors; and it is of course not the involved (the planner) but the affected themselves who will determine who is to represent them.

We come back to the problem which we have already encountered in discussing Habermas' model of practical discourse (Chapter 2, Section 2.1). The theoretical validity of the underlying consensus theory of truth – of "rational" consensus, that is – depends on the premise that the discourse is accessible to all those concerned, be they involved or only affected. ("The condition of the truth of assertions is the potential agreement of *all* others." – Habermas 1971c:124) Practically speaking, however, such a theoretical stipulation evades the crucial task of a model of rational discourse: namely, to show how a discourse can be rational *even though not everyone affected can become involved.* This problem will be the subject-matter of the next chapter; awaiting an eventual practical solution to this problem, the best we can do is to give the planner a category that captures the essential *role* played by those who, in a practical discourse, will argue the case of the affected. The essence of their role, it seems to me, is that of a *witness:* by virtue of their own affectedness, they can bear witness to the ways in which all those who cannot voice their concerns may be affected – their feelings, their suffering, their moral and political consciousness, their ways of expressing dissent, their ways of *living* the social reality in question, their vision of their own future.

Rather than pretending that we can adequately grasp such issues by means of a detailed list of heuristically necessary categories, I suggest that we limit the claim for heuristic necessity to the one essential category of the *"witness."* This much at least we can tell for certain: the planner cannot adequately trace the normative content of alternative boundary judgements regarding the social system S to be mapped without referring to *some* social actors playing the role of a witness.

Summarizing what has been said up this point, our schema now looks thus:

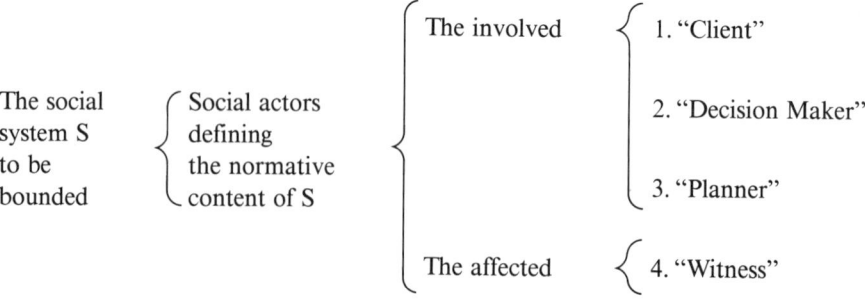

Of course, thus far we have only asked the question: *"Who* should have input in the map of S?" (question 1). We have not as yet any categories in terms of which the planner can conceptualize the essential inputs he needs from each of the four groups. In order to categorize these inputs, we need to complement the "who?" question by two auxiliary questions, namely "what?" and "so what?":

(2) What are the role-specific *concerns* which each of the four groups will wish to communicate to the planner, and which the planner needs to know?

(3) Given tentative answers to questions (1) and (2), what then is the *crux* for the planner in regard to a critical solution to the necessary boundary judgements? In particular, are there implicit a priori judgements which the concerned social actors may not be willing or able to make explicit but which are crucial for the planner's understanding of their concerns?

The best way to explain these two questions is to apply them to each of the four groups of actors. Before introducing, in this way, our entire set of categories, let us just summarize our "combined" clue to this task:

1. Basic clue:

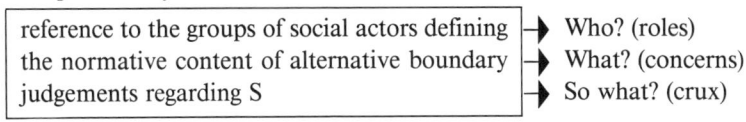

2. Complementary clue:

Table 4/3: The "combined" clue to the systematic introduction of the categories

Let us now see where this "combined" clue leads us. (Since the case studies of Part III will illustrate the application and the critical significance of our categories, the present account really is only to "introduce" the categories to which our clue leads us, not to explain them.)

1. In regard to the *client,* the "what?" question is not difficult to answer. The client will try to communicate to the planner his *purposes,* i.e., his interests, his values, his preferences with respect to what would be an "improvement"; for only to the extent that he succeeds in doing so can he become a major source of motivation for the planning process. To say the same thing from a critical point of view, "purpose"

and "client" are the categories that make intelligible the sources of *power:* "Power is the ability of an individual or a group to impose its purpose on others." (Galbraith 1975:88) The issue of power, I believe, is as fundamental to social inquiry and planning as is the concept of force or energy to natural science (cf. Russell 1938:12); the essential difference between the two is that power is linked to the intentionality of human agents, while the forces of nature are nonintentional. "Forces make things happen. Power makes things happen according to an intention." (Ogilvy 1979:22)

The crucial difficulty for the planner ("so what?" question) lies in the fact that the client is not usually a homogeneous group of people united by one common and clear-cut purpose. Usually there are several purposes conflicting with each other, so that they cannot be ordered in a simple hierarchy. How then can the planner identify the client's purposes? The crux lies in formulating a trade-off principle that reflects the client's true preferences with respect to "improvement." As Churchman (1971:47) suggests, "the designer seeks to find the underlying principle behind the client's trade-offs by estimating a 'measure of performance' which enables him to assign numerical values to possible futures." Leaving apart the requirement of numerical form, as Churchman himself has done in *The Systems Approach and Its Enemies* (1979:85), we can say that *some* measure of performance is implied in every systems design, though the planner may not always be aware of it or able to define it in an explicit way. In any case, it is not possible for him to claim value transparency for his design without making transparent the kind of trade-off principle he ascribes to the design's client, and thus the notion of "improvement" presupposed in the design. The "so what?" question therefore suggests that mapping the client and his purposes requires a category such as Churchman's *measure of performance,* defined as "the underlying principle behind the client's trade-offs."

There is, however, a terminological difficulty. Referring to a system S_1, we can speak of its "measure of performance" when the system to be improved is *not* S_1 but a second system S_2. For instance, we can say that a proposed change in the health care system (S_1) of a community (S_2) increases the measure of *performance* of S_1, or we can say that it increases the measure of improvement of S_2. The question, in other words, is what we take as the point of reference for defining "improvement." The terminological distinction is necessary to avoid the trap of inadvertently making S_1 the reference point for measuring improvement, and thereby unintentionally making S_1 a surrogate client. To avoid this trap from the beginning, we should speak of "measure of performance" *only* when the system to be designed is *not* the one to be improved; we should speak of "measure of improvement" whenever the system in question *is* the one to be improved. The second measure is a fundamental prerequisite to the first, for establishing a measure of performance prerequires the existence of a measure of improvement.

Of course, in social planning there is rarely a completely satisfactory, explicit measure of improvement, but this deficiency does not alter the fact that some such measure is implied in every social design, and that the existence of such a measure is a heuristic necessity. The long-standing discussion about quality of life indicators illustrates both the difficulty and the unavoidability of the problem.

2. Let us now turn to the second group of actors, the *decision maker.* The decision maker can be defined as the complex of persons who can produce and control changes in S's measure of improvement (cf. Churchman 1971:43). Making a reasonable boundary judgement as to *who* ought to belong to the decision maker presupposes judgements about *what* means or conditions are necessary to serve the client's purpose, i.e., to increase the measure of improvement, and who is in control of these means or conditions. From the systems point of view, the conditions controlled by S's decision maker can be called S's *components,* in contrast to the *environment* of S. Churchman defines the components as "aspects of reality that the decision maker can change" and the environment as "aspects of reality that the decision maker cannot change" (1979:89). The latter should more precisely be termed *"decision environment,"* for we are not referring here to the common-sense concept of the environment of a planning problem as that which is "irrelevant" for solving the problem. We are referring to those means or conditions that are necessary for improving S *although* they are not under the control of S's decision maker. Another precise way of defining components and environment is to say that both coproduce the measure of improvement of S, but only the components are controlled by S's decision maker.

   We can therefore associate the problem of determining the environment with the "so what?" question: given the planner's knowledge of what means or conditions are needed, the *crux* lies in tracing the sources of control that are (ought to be) beyond the control of S (i.e., in the environment) and to take account of the ways in which the improvement of S depends on them.

3. Regarding the third group of actors, the *planner,* the "what?" question must aim at the sources of expertise required for mapping and improving S, and at the appropriate relationship between "experts" and "decision makers." Although expertise is of course a resource, we do not treat it as a component under the control of the decision maker, for that would mean to presuppose, from the outset, a decisionistic model in which the "rational" effort of planners and experts are bound by the "decisions" of those who happen to be in control of resources. For this reason, we need a category such as "expertise" in addition to "components."

   However, the term "expertise" should not be understood here in the narrow scientific sense that it has acquired both in Academe and in politics. As the term is intended here, whoever has some relevant knowledge, experience or skill to contribute to the planning process is to be considered an "expert." In other words, we do not onesidedly associate the term with instrumental reason, but instead consider an expert as somebody who has something to contribute to the planner's quest for *practical reason.*

Why then distinguish between "planner" and "expertise"? The planner is a special case in that his crucial skill consists in bringing together all the people whose expertise is needed, not in replacing any of them. It is because we do not simply presuppose that the planner is *the* source of expertise that we need to give him a category for tracing the necessary sources of expertise wherever they are to be found. For instance, in a given case an appropriate boundary judgement about the "planner" might be that the client ought to be congruent with the planner, a boundary judgement which cannot reasonably be meant to imply that the client is the only source of expertise required for improving S.

The *crux* in determining the necessary sources of expertise lies in the fact that there is no guarantee that "expertise" will secure improvement. How can the planner ever know that the experts' skills, experience, or tools are not a source of deception rather than a source of guarantee that improvement will result? The "so what?" question therefore should have the planner trace the implicit sources of guarantee on which the experts rely – be it the computer, scientific "data," cybernetic modelling, consensus among specialists, intuition, ideological/political consciousness, moral conscience, religious faith or whatever. Only to the extent that he examines these "built-in" guarantors as possible sources of deception can he avoid deception later on, when it comes to decision making and implementation of a plan. One major guarantor that always must be determined is the kind of consultation model to be presupposed, i.e., the appropriate relationship between "expertise" and "practice" (cf. the discussion of this in Section 2.3 of the first chapter); for such a model is always implicit in the expert's understanding of his own expertise. Churchman's *"guarantor"* category perfectly embodies the intent of the "so what?" question in this context. It encompasses the two questions of the consultation model and of the conditions preventing implementation failure, and I shall not therefore introduce a special category "implementation," as does Churchman; instead, our "what?" question has suggested the category of "expertise" as a necessary complement to the category of the planner.

4. Finally, there is the fourth group of actors, that of the *witnesses.* What kind of concerns ought they to represent? While the previous three roles have been associated with the sources of motivation, of control, and of expertise, the witnesses represent the crucial *source of legitimation.* They do not contribute resources or expertise, nor do their purposes motivate the planning effort; their contribution cannot be grasped in the functionalistic terms of systems teleology. By arguing the case of the affected vis-à-vis the involved, they remind the latter of their moral responsibility for all the practical consequences of their planning effort. This responsibility goes beyond the effective "functioning" of a systems design which secures improvement for the client; it extends to the costs and risks imposed on all

those who do not belong to the client. In a democratic society in which every citizen is sovereign, only the voluntary consent of those affected but not involved can possibly legitimize the costs and risks imposed upon them. This assertion again points to the importance of institutionalizing practical discourses in which the involved must publicly secure the consent of the affected.

The essential point is that the affected must be given the chance of emancipating themselves from being treated merely as means for the purposes of others. I therefore suggest that we conceptualize the essential concerns of the witnesses by the category "emancipation." Other terms such as "legitimation" might stand for the same concept, but "emancipation" seems to hit the nail on the head: it reminds us that social mapping and design is not merely a matter of instrumental orientation toward some purpose (as functionalistic "systems science" seems to assume), but that for *socially* rational planning it is essential that the planner initiate a *process of emancipatory self-reflection on the part of the affected.*

The *crux* in this context, I believe, lies in the fact that the different concerns of the involved and the affected may be fundamentally conflicting because they may be rooted in different *Weltanschauungen* ("world-views"), i.e., in different visions of what social reality and human life in it ought to be. In order to account for this fact, the planner must trace the different visions that possibly separate the affected from the involved. The last of my twelve categories for which I think a quasi-transcendental argument can be made is therefore *"Weltanschauung."*

Table 4/4 summarizes our twelve categories of pragmatic mapping.

3.3. Three Quasi-Transcendental Ideas of Critical Heuristics

The circle is closing; we finally come back to Kant's three "transcendental ideas" with which we began this chapter. We have already seen that strictly speaking even Kant's ideas can claim only a heuristic status. We have also established the necessary condition for ascribing heuristic necessity (i.e., quasi-transcendental validity) to them, namely, the possible reference to the principle of reason as the source of such necessity.

The additional clue required for a critically-heuristic reformulation of Kant's ideas is almost self-evident: it is to construe the ideas in terms of *immanent* rather than *transcendent* metaphysics. The term "immanent metaphysics" refers to the (inevitable) metaphysical content of our phenomenal knowledge, while the term "transcendent metaphysics" designates classical, and uncritical, metaphysics with its vain search for explaining a transcendent reality "beyond" this world of ours.

Categories	Central issues covered
1. *Client* 2. Purpose 3. Measure of improvement }	Sources of *motivation* (of S) ⎫
4. *Decision Maker* 5. Components 6. Environment }	Sources of *control* (of S) ⎬ The involved ⎫
7. *Planner* 8. Expertise 9. Guarantor }	Sources of *expertise* and implementation (of S) ⎭ ⎬ The social system S to be bounded
10. *Witness* 11. Emancipation 12. Weltanschauung }	Sources of *legitimation* (of S) } The affected ⎭

Table 4/4: Basic categories for describing the normative content of systems maps and designs (and hence of the boundary judgements, or whole systems judgements, that are constitutive of such maps or designs). The first category of each group refers to a social role, the second to role-specific *concerns,* and the third to the related *crux* in regard to the boundary judgements in question. The first category of each group is basic, while the two others serve an auxiliary function.

Kant's ideas, as we have seen, closely correspond to the three "unavoidable problems" of classical metaphysics – the existence and limits of the World, Man's immortal soul and freedom of the will, and God. What made them unavoidable was the principle of reason, according to which reason has to reflect upon the unconditioned totality of conditions on which any knowledge of the understanding depends. But it is certainly not unavoidable that we understand the ideas in terms of transcendent metaphysics, as Kant does; rather, the social planner needs to understand them as critical standards for reflection on the normative content and potential deceptiveness of his maps of social reality. Such a reinterpretation will strengthen, not weaken, the practical significance of the principle of reason. Indeed, only as critical ideas of *immanent* metaphysics are Kant's "unavoidable problems of reason" really unavoidable.

In a famous passage of the *Critique,* Kant formulates the three basic questions that motivate man's search for knowledge:

> All the interests of my reason, speculative as well as practical, combine in the three following questions:
> 1. What can I know?
> 2. What ought I to do?
> 3. What may I hope? (B 832f)

The three questions seem strikingly parallel to the three ideas, although Kant does not explicitly refer to this parallel. He usually associates all three ideas of the first *Critique* – the cosmological, psychological and theological ideas – with transcendent reality, i.e., with the "unavoidable problems" of speculative reason only.[12] If however we interpret the three ideas strictly in terms of immanent metaphysics, it is quite obvious that their critical significance relates to the three quoted questions (or interests) of *both* theoretical *and* practical reason. The "cosmological" idea of the World, as the unity of the conditions of all appearances, yields a critical standard for reflecting on the deceptiveness of our *knowledge;* the "psychological" idea of Man, which in the practical employment of reason becomes the moral idea, and which thus far can be understood to refer to the unity of the thinking *and acting* subject, yields a critical standard for reflection on the moral imperfection of our *actions;* and the "theological" idea of God, as the unity of the conditions of all objects of thought in general, yields a critical standard for reflecting on the deceptiveness of our *hopes* or beliefs, namely, if we make them the unreflected guarantors of improvement. I would like, therefore, to redefine the three ideas by relating them to the three questions.

1. "The first question," Kant explains, "is merely speculative." (B 833) Since we are redefining his ideas in terms of immanent metaphysics, it is more appropriate to say that this first question characterizes the interest of theoretical reason. And since

---

[12] He questions this association, however, in a passage which I have made the motto of this chapter.

furthermore we have found, in Section 1.2 of the present chapter, that all the ideas of reason – whether theoretical or practical – have *both* theoretical (metaphysical) *and* practical (normative implications, we can simply say that the first question characterizes the planner's interest in *mapping social reality,* and comprehending the conditioned character of the maps. Maps represent phenomena only, hence the relevance of Kant's "cosmological" idea of a totality of conditions of all appearances. We have earlier introduced the *systems idea* as the relative a priori concept corresponding to the absolute a priori concept of a "given" totality of conditions (cf. Sections 1.3ff of this chapter). The systems concept, as we understand it, maintains the critical intent of Kant's concept of totality, but it has the advantage of not raising any associations with an absolute, transcendent reality. It merely refers to a relatively a priori set of relevant conditions that are constitutive of our maps of reality, and it thereby reminds us to reflect on the boundary judgements that inevitably flow into our maps.

We can thus say that the systems idea provides the necessary standard for reflection on the deceptiveness of social maps in accordance with the principle of reason. It meets both requirements established by our clues: a quasi-transcendental argument as to its heuristic necessity is possible, and it refers to immanent rather than transcendent metaphysics.

Given these two conditions, we can safely go back to Kant's explanation of the ideas by means of the phrase "as if". We can now associate the systems idea with the following heuristic principle:

"In order to discover the sources of deception in your maps, look for comprehensiveness on the side of the conditions[13] and reflect on the inevitable *lack* of comprehensiveness in your maps, *as if* there were a completely intelligible whole system (totality of relevant conditions)!"

To sum up, the systems idea stands for the ideal of comprehensiveness on the side of conditions, and because such comprehensiveness is *only* an ideal, it implies a lack of comprehensiveness of all our maps. It implies, in other words, the need for critical reflection on the underlying whole systems judgements; our list of categories is intended to help the planner conceive of all the whole systems judgements in question.

2. The second question, "What ought I to do?", is, according to Kant, "purely practical" (B 833); in the language of critical heuristics, it concerns the planner's interest in *designing for a better social reality,* and comprehending the imperfect character of his designs. From the point of view of practical reason, we can replace Kant's "psychological" idea (Man, esp. his freedom of will) by the *moral idea.* It is easy to see that the moral idea is indeed the practical equivalent of the systems idea, in that it requires an agent to reflect on the total group of individuals who might be affected by his action. Here again the inevitable boundary judgements flowing into

[13] Cf. KrV:B 393 and p. 225 of the present chapter.

any social design are in need of critical reflection according to the principle of reason. As in the case of the ideal of comprehensiveness (systems idea), the ideal of moral perfection, because it is an ideal, implies the *moral imperfection* of all our designs, and hence the need for reflecting on the sources and potential consequences of such imperfection.

The pertinent heuristic principle reads: "Design for improvement of the human condition, and reflect on the inevitable *lack* of moral perfection of your designs, *as if* those affected by your designs were self-responsible moral beings!" And of course, this idea again implies the need for reflection on the underlying whole systems judgements, namely, with regard to their moral implications.

3. The third question, according to Kant, "is at once practical and theoretical" and can be restated more precisely: "If I do what I ought to do, what may I then hope?" (B 833) Translated into the planner's language, the question reads: Provided the involved planners and decision makers pursue their plans in a morally responsible way, what are the sources of guarantee on which they (ought to) rely to make certain that improvement will actually come about?

This third question aims not only at the conditions of adequate social mapping and design but also at the conditions of successful *implementation* of these conceptual efforts. In this respect, the "unavoidable problem of reason" to be considered is that there is *no guarantee for improvement through planning.* Precisely because this is so, the planner must strive to incorporate into his design effort as many sources of (imperfect) guarantee as possible, e.g., by involving a large spectrum of both experts and witnesses, by building a basis of oncensus between the involved and the affected, by presupposing an appropriate consultation model, etc. But such sources of guarantee are bound to become sources of deception as soon as the planner forgets that they might be false guarantors and that in any design there is necessarily a built-in *lack* of guarantee. The critical idea called for is thus the (problematic) notion of a *guarantor of design,* a source of guarantee presupposed in each design effort (including any designs for inquiry, as Churchman 1971:22f has argued).

In Kant's time, the only conceivable guarantor was God; for the contemporary planner, the guarantor idea may also take other forms such as the "emancipatory interest" (Habermas 1965), "intrinsic control" (the cybernetic design ideal) or "design for purposefulness" and "intrinsic motivation" of social systems (Ulrich 1977 d:1101). The notion underlying the "modern" guarantor idea is search for a *"guarantor within,"* in contrast to Kant's divine guarantor "without."

The guarantor *idea* is not to be confused with the guarantor *category,* although the two are of course closely related; the former is applied in a critical (regulative) manner – in the sense of the principle of reason – while the latter is applied in a constitutive manner, i.e., als referring to the phenomenal expressions of the (false) guarantors that are presupposed in a design.

The pertinent heuristic principle standing for the guarantor idea is: "Design for guarantee, and reflect on the inevitable *lack* of guarantee in your designs, *as if* there were a built-in guarantor of design!"
Table 4/5 gives an overview.

Metaphysical problems		Quasi-transcendental ideas		Heuristic principles
Kant	Our terms	Kant's terms	Our terms	
"World"	Whole system	Unity (or totality) of the conditions of all appearances	*Systems idea* = ideal of comprehensiveness (on the side of the conditions)	Look for comprehensiveness on the side of the conditions, and reflect on the *lack* of comprehensiveness in your maps, *as if* there were a completely intelligible whole system!
"Man" Immortal soul Free will (+ "The moral law within me")	Individual Future generations Self-responsibility	Unity of the thinking (and acting) subject	*Moral idea* = ideal of moral perfection of design (with respect to the total group of those affected)	Design for improvement of the human condition, and reflect on the moral *imperfection* of your designs, *as if* those affected were self-responsible moral beings!
"God"	Guarantee	Unity of the conditions of all objects of thought in general	*Guarantor idea* = ideal of securing implementation of improvement	Design for guarantee, and reflect on the *lack* of guarantee, *as if* there were a built-in guarantor of design!

Table 4/5: The three quasi-transcendental ideas

Concluding Comment: Toward a "Dynamic" Interpretation of the Ideas

The three quasi-transcendental ideas just introduced can serve as critical standards for reflection and argumentation about the sources of deception in alternative maps or designs. The planner will first employ them "monologically," i.e., he will use them to improve his understanding of his maps and designs and to eliminate deficiencies prior to submitting them to public scrutiny. The three ideas help the planner to critically "transcend" (go beyond) his given understanding of maps and designs by reminding him of the potential deceptiveness of the underlying whole systems judgements (systems idea), implied normative validity claims (moral idea), and presupposed guarantors of successful implementation (guarantor idea). But the ideas can of course also be used discursively, as reference points for cogent argumentation in a practical discourse. The witnesses, for instance, can question the normative validity of maps or designs by pointing to the arbitrariness of built-in boundary judgements (systems idea), to the moral inadequacy of value premises and consequences (moral idea), or to the likelihood of implementation failure because of resistance on the part of the affected (guarantor idea). The three ideas will therefore play a basic role in our attempt, in the next chapter, to come to grips with the unsolved problem of practical discourse (a priori of argumentation). Our critical solution to this difficult problem will partly depend on the critical significance of the three ideas. We shall understand the practical discourse among the social actors on the stage of planning – the involved and the affected – as a process of unfolding the critical implications of the three ideas. I borrow the term "process of unfolding" from Churchman (1979:80, 82, passim). He uses it to characterize the dialogue among what he calls the "goal planner," the "objective-planner," and the "ideal-planner," three subcategories of the planner category that can be understood to stand for an increasingly wider conceptualization of the planner's role. I find the term especially suitable because it points to the need for a "dynamic" interpretation of the three ideas. We might thus say that the systems idea stands for a *process of unfolding* (namely, the "whole system"); the moral idea can be associated with an *ethical process* (rather than a body of moral theory); and the guarantor idea can be interpreted to stand for a *process of dis-illusionment*. In the case of the moral idea, one might also think of what C.G. Jung calls "the process of [moral] individuation" (cf. 1953:e.g. par. 373). Similarly, we shall interpret the process of dis-illusionment as a "process of democratization" in which the affected citizens emancipate themselves from the premises and promises of the experts. In socially rational planning, the three processes converge in one and the same discursive process between the involved and the affected. For the sake of convenience, we shall usually speak of the "process of unfolding" in a wide sense that encompasses all three ideas.

The basic presuppositions of the process of unfolding will be the subject matter of the next chapter. Let us conclude this chapter with a graphic outline of our entire set of relative a priori concepts. Such an outline can be analogous to that given earlier of the architectonic of Kant's metaphysics of experience *(Figure 3/1);* the present chapter has, I hope, sufficiently stressed the crucial differences between Kantian a priori science and critical heuristics to forestall an uncritical understanding of such an analogy. (See *Figure 4/6.)*

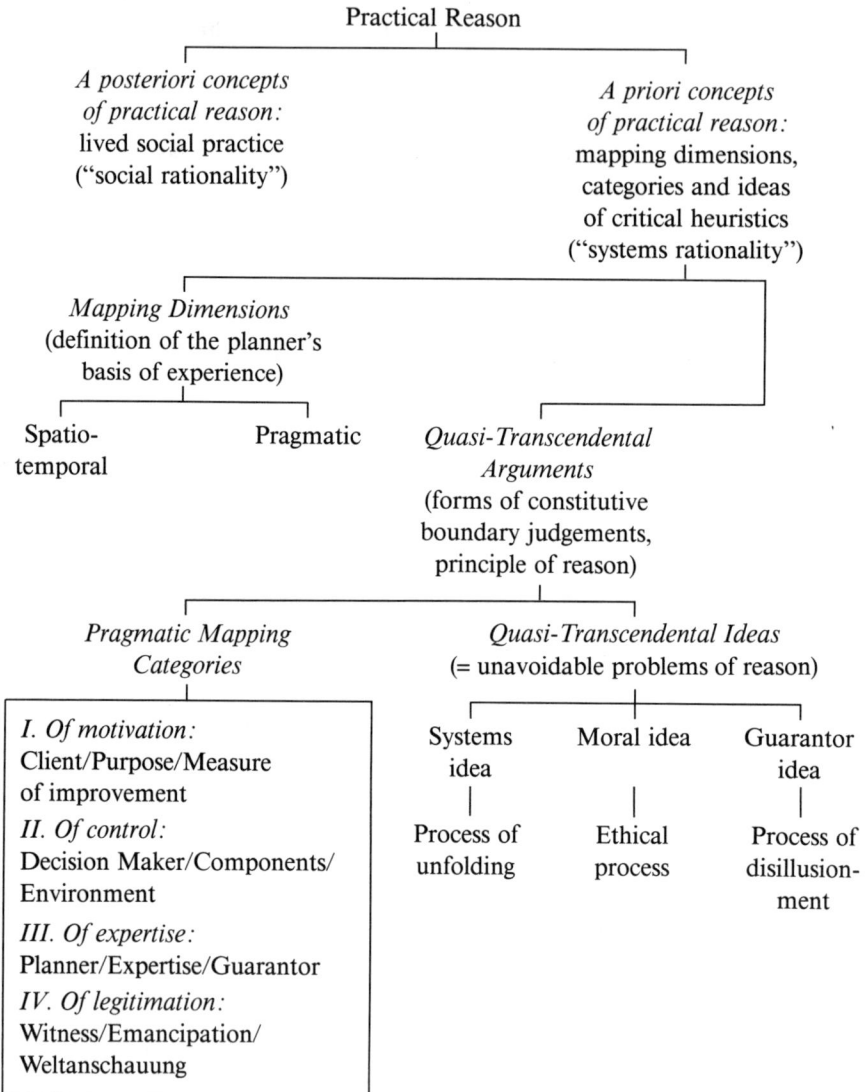

Figure 4/6: Basic conceptual framework of critical heuristics (a priori concepts of practical reason, = immanent metaphysics of social mapping and design). Cf. Figure 3/1 on p. 189 for the structure of Kant's metaphysics of experience.

Chapter Five
Kantian A Priori Science and the Process of Unfolding: The Dialectical Turn

How can reason, without other motives taken from elsewhere, be practical by itself? ... In other words, how can pure reason be practical? All of human reason is entirely incapable of explaining this, and all effort and labor to find an explanation of it is in vain.
Immanuel Kant (GMS:B 124f)

Introduction

Of the two a priori problematics posed by the problem of practical reason, we have thus far dealt with the a priori of experience. We must now turn to the a priori of argumentation and seek to conceive of a *critical* solution to the unsolved problem of "rational" practical discourse. The problem is unsolved in that philosophers thus far have been unable to come up with a theoretically justified model of rational practical discourse that would also be *practicable*. It appears that no such model is possible, for we are dealing with the Kantian *ideal* of "the comprehensive rationality of reason that becomes transparent to itself" (Habermas 1971a:3), which suggests that any theoretical solution will have to refer to *ideal* conditions or standards of rationality. We have encountered this difficulty in the chapter on Habermas' model of practical discourse, and our main conclusion there was the need for a "dialectical turn." The "monologue" of the involved ("competent" speakers, systems planners or experts) is to be replaced by a dialogue among the involved *and the affected*. In such a dialogue the rationality standards of the involved ("systems rationality") do not have an a priori privileged status. We must avoid presupposing that the affected are "competent" only to the extent that they adopt the monologically established rationality standards of the involved, be these standards defined in terms of "rational attitude" (Popper), "rationally motivated consensus" (Habermas) or "systems rationality." A really dialectical approach to the problem of practical discourse must give both parties an equal role to play – those striving for, or asserting, the "whole systems" rationality of their systems designs, and those bearing witness of the social irrationality of those designs. For the sake of convenience, I shall refer to the former as "planners" (although all the involved may belong to this group) while referring to the latter as "witnesses" (namely, of the ways in which the affected may be affected by the established standards of rationality).

I have already hinted at the basic consideration on which the present chapter is to rely: a truly dialectical approach will seek to mediate between conceptualized systems rationality and lived social practice by understanding the former as a source of *a priori concepts of practical reason only.* A priori concepts of practical reason are intrinsically dependent for their content and validity on "irrational" social practice, as the source of *a posteriori concepts of practical reason.* In other words, the challenge faced by reason (the systems approach) in this context consists in its own self-transcendence – "self-transcendence" not in the sense of reason's abolishing itself, but in the sense of its becoming transparent to itself, i.e., its seeing through the normative implications of its own "rational" concepts in every application. This challenge requires that reason become its own subject of study – or better, of questioning – and thus that it become self-reflective, dialectical. Since we do not want to rely simply on a decisionistic appeal to self-reflection on the part of the planners, we need to give the witnesses a crucial role to play in securing the self-reflectiveness of planners. We need to conceive of an institutional arrangement in which planners and witnesses become mutually dependent for realizing their goals, so that they can mutually challenge one another to reflect on the normative content of their viewpoints, their maps and designs of social reality, and particularly the underlying boundary judgements (whole systems judgements). We call this dialectical interplay between planners ("systems rationality") and witnesses (lived social practice) the *process of unfolding.* The process of unfolding is intended to represent our critical, and practicable, solution to the problem of practical discourse. It cannot claim to represent an objective, theoretical solution to the problem; rather, it claims a critically-heuristic status, i.e., it is to embody the heuristic principles that are indispensable for adequate reflection on the sources of partiality and deception in a "rational" design. As in the context of the a priori of experience, a "critical solution" to the a priori of argumentation represents only the negative half of a solution, as it were; it prevents us from falling victim to an objectivist illusion (in this case with regard to the "objectivity" of our rationality standards), but it does not serve to establish a positive claim for the generalizability of any specific rationality criterion.

I propose to focus on three fundamental principles that seem heuristically indispensable for such a critical solution:

(1) the *principle of "dialectics";*
(2) the principle of what Kant calls *"the polemical employment of reason";*
(3) the *democratic principle* of the sovereignty and equality of all citizens, be they involved or "merely" affected by planning.

The chapter is divided in three main sections and a brief concluding comment (Section 4). The *first* section examines the development of the principle of dialectics from Socrates to Kant and Hegel and draws some necessary conclusions in regard to our own effort. The *second* section leads us back to Kant and to what we can learn from him about the eternal dialectic of idealism and realism, of the intelligibility *and* the reality of our concepts and judgements. No effort of argumentative reason can supersede the dependency of practical discourse on an empirical basis that furnishes the material for cogent argumentation and makes certain that such argumentation remains in touch with lived social practice. We shall discuss the ways in which reason can and must transcend its own boundaries to become practical. In the *third* section, we shall draw on Kant's concept of the polemical employment of reason to give reason, in its critical but not in its assertive employment, an important mediating function between planners and witnesses. We shall find that it is indeed possible to define a criterion of cogent argumentation on the part of the witnesses that does not require their "competence" or willingness to submit to the rationality standards of the involved. On this basis, the democratic principle can become an integrative part, and indeed a guarantor, of rational practical discourse. The necessary conditions of such mediation between argumentative reason and democratic practice are not only epistemological, however, but also institutional. In the brief *fourth* section we shall make some concluding comments with respect to the institutional issue.

1. On Dialectics

The word "dialectics" today is frequently associated with two tendencies: rigidly schematic thinking in terms of the triad thesis-antithesis-synthesis, and dogmatically metaphysical or ideological thinking. Dialectical reasoning is, in point of fact, the exact opposite of all schematic and dogmatic thinking: it is self-reflective, self-critical, self-transcendent thinking *par excellence.* I should like to illustrate this claim by introducing some key historical figures whose thinking was thoroughly dialectical: Socrates, Plato, Kant, Hegel, and the early Marx. In doing so I shall be very brief except for Hegel, whose thought is of particular importance for our "dialectical turn."

1.1. Dialectical Reasoning as Critical Reflection: From the Socratic Dialogue to the Kantian Critique of Reason

The term "dialectics" comes from the Greek *dialektike (techne),* the dialectical art, which in turn derives from *dialegesthai* = talking together, holding a dialogue (*dialogos,* from *dia-* = through, across, between, also thorough; and *logos* = word, speech, reason). Etymologically, dialectics thus means the art of unfolding the meaning of a word or idea through a debate in which two or more persons argue pro and contra. Dialectics in this original sense is embodied in the *Socratic dialogue,* the art of reflecting together on the fact that "I know that I know nothing."

In contrast to formal-logical reasoning, which proceeds in a linear and unreflective manner and which simply elaborates on the implications of its own premises, dialectical reasoning breaks through the given premises, unfolds their limited and selective character and frees us to overcome our fixed patterns of thinking – and our being contented with them. In this sense, dialectical thinking is "open" and "dynamic," while formal-logical thinking is "closed" and "static."

The Socratic art of dialogue is also to be distinguished from the rhetorical art of the Sophists; it is not the rhetorical form but the *content* of arguments that counts, and the aim is not to confuse the other and to "talk him over" but to comprehend the essential nature of things and the inadequacy of one's own knowledge of them.

After Socrates, Plato is the greatest dialectician, as the Platonic dialogues attest. In critical distinction to the Sophists, he links the dialogical form of unfolding an idea to the philosophical task of justifying binding *standards* for human thinking and action, and he finds such standards in what he calls the *ideas* (in constrast to mere appearances). By "idea," Plato means the essential content of our concepts, that which experience cannot show us in perfection but at best in a fragmentary way. He finds the highest idea and organizing principle of all reality in the idea of "the good."

Dialectics thus becomes the art of discriminating the ideas that are or ought to be constitutive of our experience, thought and action, so as to guide us in the proper conduct of life and in the just organization of the *polis.*

In Plato, philosophical reflection and reasonable social practice are still thought of together; only with Aristotle do theory and practice become separated. It is hardly a mere coincidence that Aristotle also divides the dialectical art into two branches, the *Analytic* (syllogistics, classical formal logic) and the *Topic* (dialectics). Formal logic thus becomes the exclusive method for establishing the truth of theoretical propositions, while dialectics is restricted to reflection on the goodness of practical propositions. The original intent of Aristoteles' double distinction may have been a critical one; but the subsequent triumph of instrumental reason and decisionism, and the concordant downfall of the idea of practical reason in what today we call the "age of enlightenment," teach us that the dichotomy has uncritical consequences (cf. the discussion of these consequences in Section 2.1 of Chapter 1).

It is only with Kant that reason recovers its dialectical dimension, at least partly. He undertakes the basically dialectical task of making reason reflect upon its own limits; and in the course of this undertaking, he rediscovers the forgotten insight that theoretical reason is fundamentally dependent on practical reason, and vice-versa. In the *Critique of Practical Reason,* he establishes his famous postulate of the "primacy of practical reason (KpV:A 215ff, Beck 223ff, Abbott 216ff). But Kant, in spite of having rediscovered the theory-practice dialectic, fails to rediscover the dialectical art itself and instead persists in his "monological" approach to the critique of reason's claims, both in the realm of theoretical reason and in the realm of practical reason. Kant's approach to practical philosophy is not dialectical at all. Dialectics to him remains a mere source of deception, a "logic of illusion" (KrV:B 349).

It is Hegel who finally reintroduces dialectical reasoning into epistemology and thereby radicalizes its self-reflective dimension. Let us now turn to Hegel.

1.2. Dialectical Reasoning as Radical Self-Reflection: Hegel's "Exertion of the Concept"

I have asserted at the beginning that dialectical reasoning is self-reflective, self-critical and even self-transcendent rather than schematic and dogmatic as is commonly believed. The foremost dialectician of modern times, Georg Wilhelm Friedrich Hegel, is not entirely free of responsibility for the sad fate of the art of dialectical reasoning in our age; but the metaphysical language which he speaks should not distract us from the critical and critically-heuristic significance of his philosophy.

Hegel's *Phenomenology of Mind* (1807, engl. 1910) unfolds dialectics as a process in which the thinking subject (the mind) becomes its own object, that is, conscious of itself, self-reflective. As to the charge of schematic thinking in terms of thesis-antithesis-synthesis, Hegel rarely ever used these terms.[1] They are in fact Fichte's terms and are wrongly ascribed to Hegel. It is true, Hegel did use the dialectical triad "affirmation-negation-negation of the negation" as well as other triads such as "in itself – for itself – in and for itself"; but he never intended the triad as a lifeless schematism and indeed attacked those who (like Fichte and Schelling) employed it in a formalistic and mechanical manner. For example, in the Preface to the *Phenomenology* we read:

> It is equally obvious that we must not consider scientific that use of this form [the dialectical triad] which reduces it to a lifeless schema.... This formalism supposes it has comprehended and expressed the nature and life of a form when it merely ascribes to it as a predicate some determination of the schema; e.g., subjectivity or objectivity, or magnetism, electricity, etc., contraction or expansion, east or west, *et al.* This sort of thing can be multiplied *ad infinitum* because in this manner every determination or form can be used again as a form or moment of the schema when it comes to another, and each can perform the same service for another. But in this circle of reciprocity one never learns what the matter itself is – neither what the one nor what the other is.... Instead of the inner life and the self-movement of its existence, such a simple determinateness is taken from intuition, which here means the knowledge of the senses, and expressed according to a superficial analogy, and then this external and empty application of a formula is called construction. (Hegel 1807:48f, transl. Kaufmann 1977:74ff)

Ironically, Hegel even ridicules the formalistic thinking with which his dialectics has frequently been associated:

> The trick of such wisdom is learned as quickly as it is easy to master it [the formula]; its repetition, once it is known, becomes as insufferable as the repetition of a sleight of hand one sees through. The instrument of this monotonous formalism is no more difficult to handle than a painter's palette on which there are only two colors, say, red and green, one if an historical piece is wanted, the other for landscapes. (1807:50, transl. Kaufmann 1977:78)

Against the association of dialectics with schematizing formalism, Hegel poses his own understanding of dialectical reasoning: it is *"the exertion of the concept" (die Anstrengung des Begriffs,* 1807:56, transl. Kaufmann 1977:88). What does Hegel mean by this phrase? The German expression "Anstrengung des Begriffs" sounds as odd as the English translation, but it has the advantage of reminding us of the underlying verb "begreifen" (comprehend). Hegel contrasts "formalistic thinking that argues back and forth in unactual thoughts" *(formales Denken, das in unwirk-*

---

[1] According to Kaufmann, Hegel "never once used these three terms together to designate three stages in an argument or account in any of his books." (1966:154) And according to Findlay, "the terms 'thesis', 'antithesis' and 'synthesis', so often used in expositions of Hegel's doctrine, are in fact not frequently used by Hegel: they are much more characteristic of Fichte." (1958:69f)

lichen Gedanken hin und her räsoniert) with "thinking that comprehends" *(begrei-fendes Denken,* 1807:56, transl. Kaufmann 1977:88 and 90). Formalistic thinking produces "unactual thoughts" because it relies on abstractions like formal logic and the dialectical triad, and it imposes these fixed abstractions on the concrete content rather than taking the concrete real world for what it is – a continuous movement from that which is given to that which is not given, a movement of opposites, a process of becoming, a process of change driven by the internal contradictions within all things, in society and nature as well as in thought. Instead, "the content should be made to move itself by virtue of its own nature." (1807:56, transl. Kaufmann 1977:88) Thinking cannot be reasonable (or "scientific," as Hegel could still say, for in his day the meaning of the term had not yet been corrupted by scientism) if it finds its logic only in empty abstractions but has no way of grasping and *comprehending* the contradictoriness (or contrariness) within the concrete reality which it claims to explain. The "exertion of the concept" is thus to be understood as an exertion of conceptual analysis ("attention to the concept," as Hegel says) that strives to comprehend the content of a concept by unfolding it according to its own inner logic, however contradictory the latter may be.

The word "comprehend," like its German counterpart "begreifen," has two root meanings. First it means grasping a thing (mentally) so as to make it comprehensible, i.e., to be able to identify and recognize its *essential* nature. This meaning is uppermost when we speak of "comprehension." Second, its root meaning also includes what we refer to as "comprehensiveness": comprising the *totality* of all aspects that make up the concrete reality (both the essence and the appearance) of that which is to be comprehended. One aspect belonging to this totality is the thinking subject itself: thinking that comprehends the concrete reality is necessarily self-reflective thinking, i.e., thinking that comprehends *itself* as a constitutive part of its own content. We can then understand the key ideas in Hegel's "exertion of the concept" by means of the following equation:

the exertion of the concept
= "attention to the concept"
= "thinking that comprehends"
= thinking that is moved by its content rather than its form
= thinking that strives for comprehensiveness
= self-reflective thinking

"Thinking that comprehends" is an "exertion" precisely because it cannot hope to attain comprehension without at the same time striving for both comprehensiveness and self-reflectiveness.

The question thus poses itself: What power of the mind is there to which we can entrust this exertion of comprehensiveness and self-reflectiveness? At this point we come back to the critical distinction between the understanding *(Verstand)* and reason *(Vernunft),* a distinction which Hegel borrows from Kant. Hegel associates "formalistic thinking" with Kant's concept of the understanding, while ascribing "thinking that comprehends" to reason.

What then does it mean to say that reason should be moved by the content rather than by the form of the understanding? The moving force that Hegel has in mind is the *contradiction* that is present in the process of development of all things, as he sees it. The term "contradiction" is certainly a key term of dialectics, but rarely is it well understood. Let us therefore clarify this concept.

It is often said that dialectics rejects the fundamental principle of formal logic, the *principle of excluded contradiction,* and that this rejection renders dialectics "a license for speculative arbitrariness" (Lobkowicz 1972:198, similarly Albert 1969:54f, cf. note 41 to Chapter 2 of the present study). Karl Popper, in his well-known paper "What Is Dialectics?" (1940), explains: "If two contradictory statements are admitted, any statement whatever must be admitted; for from a couple of contradictory statements any statement whatever can be validly inferred." (in 1963:317) This widely accepted characterization of dialectics misses the point. It reveals less about dialectics than about the unreflectiveness of the critic – what the dialectician Ernst Bloch ironically describes as "the art of never thinking dialectically, never learning to philosophize." (Bloch 1977:110f) The charge betrays unreflective thinking because it does not see its own one-sidedness, the fact that it simply presupposes what it means to prove – namely, that formal logic with its principle of excluded contradiction is the only possible "organon of critique." The very distinction between formal-logical and dialectical reasoning is interpreted in terms of formal logic, i.e., as a formal-logical contradiction. Hence, because formal logic is tacitly made the arbiter between two seemingly incompatible traditions, dialectics appears as "speculative arbitrariness." Just as easily a dialectician could assert that it is arbitrary to interpret the distinction between the two modes of reasoning as a formal contradiction, and that the distinction itself has in fact to be interpreted in dialectical terms. Of course, neither of the two arguments is adequate by itself. The crucial point to be understood is that dialectics does not (and cannot) mean to *negate* the formal-logical principle of excluded contradiction but rather wants to *complement* it by an additional principle, the *dialectical principle of universal contradiction.*

The *principle of excluded contradiction* applies only to cases where two opposites exclude each other *and* exhaust the universe of possible choices, i.e., there is no third possibility. For example, all animals are either male or female, and roses are either red or not red; one of the two must be true in each case. Classical logic designates this formal contradiction "contradictory opposition." In contemporary symbolic logic it is called "contravalence" (Jpg, also p)–⟨g, "exactly one of the two holds," i.e., the falseness of the one implies the correctness of the other). Mao Tse-tung, in an essay that is a small classic, "On Contradiction" (1968:68ff), speaks of "antagonistic contradiction."

The dialectical *principle of universal contradiction,* on the other hand, applies to cases where two opposites exclude each other but do *not* exhaust the universe of possibilities. For example "blue" and "green" are two predicates that exclude each other in the sense that they cannot describe the same thing at the same time, but they do not exhaust the universe of possibilities. In classical logic this case is called "contrary opposition." In symbolic logic it is termed "exclusion" (Dpq, also p|q, "not p and q at the same time"). Mao speaks in this case of "non-antagonistic contradiction."

Now dialectical reasoning agrees that the former case of formal contradiction must be excluded in reasonable discourse; one cannot at the same time assert both (or neither) of two exclusive predicates that exhaust the universe of possibilities. If one knows that two incompatible possibilities exhaust the totality of possibilities and still denies that exactly one of the two must be correct, then the contradiction lies in the assertion (the "concept," as Hegel would say) rather than in its object ("content") – the assertion (concept) does not adequately describe (comprehend) its object (content). Here we see why Popper is mistaken when he assumes that Hegel denies the necessity of avoiding such contradiction. What Popper does not grasp is that it is because of the necessity of avoiding *formal* contradiction (contradictory opposition) *in thought and speech* (in the "concept") that dialectical reasoning must recognize the *material* contradictions (contrary oppositions) that are present in *reality* itself (in the "content"). In that sense dialecticians speak of the "principle of universal contradiction"; the intent of this principle is not dogmatic-metaphysical but rather critical, i.e., it reminds us not to mistake a formal-logical rule of thought (the principle of excluded contradiction) for an ontological principle.

The original author of formal logic, Aristotle, succumbed to precisely this danger of ontologizing a cognitive principle when he assumed that reality itself had to be free from contradiction. Western thought today is still under the spell of this assumption – so much so that we perceive it as common sense rather than a questionable piece of metaphysics. Hegel is perhaps the first, but certainly the profoundest non-Aristotelian thinker that Western civilization has produced since Plato. By *"non-Aristotelian thinking"* I mean thinking that rejects the ontologization of the principle of excluded contradiction without rejecting the principle itself. Far from rejecting, or offending against, this principle as a rule of thought, Hegel merely frees it from the dogmatic-metaphysical interpretation which it inherited from its original author. He does so by *complementing* the principle with the dialectical principle of universal contradiction. As Andries Sarlemijn finds in his study on *Hegel's Dialectic* (1975:109f),

Hegel acknowledges the value of formal logic for everyday experience, for the non-philosophical sciences, and even for the form of presenting dialectical-logical thought.... In fact, Hegel rejects only the transferring of this rule [of excluded contradiction] from the domain of formal logic to that of ontology. The rule of thought pertaining to the understanding is not a law of being.... The principle of non-contradiction *as* a formal-logical rule is not at all refuted or touched by the assumption of irrational [contradictory] structures in objective reality.

It is truly ironic that Hegel is so often accused of "speculative arbitrariness" and metaphysical dogmatism by those who still adhere to Aristotelian thinking; for it is Hegel himself who demonstrates the metaphysical unreflectiveness, if not dogmatism, of those who are raising the charge.

Of course, Hegel has contributed to the sad fate of his insights by his often dark language. In particular, one may regret that he speaks of "contradiction" both in the case of contradictory opposition and in the case of contrary opposition, although he does clearly distinguish between contradiction in the realm of thought and contradiction in the realm of being. As a rule, contradiction in the realm of thought stands for contradictory opposition, while contradiction in the realm of being refers to contrary opposition (cf. under point (a) below).

Let us now consider some epistemological and heuristic implications of the principle of universal contradiction, as the cornerstone of non-Aristotelian thinking (I shall take up the question of the metaphysical implications of this principle when we come to define our normative systems paradigm, in Chapter Six). Its two main implications, I believe, are (a) the need for complementary thinking and (b) the need for maintaining contradiction in the sense of contrary opposition.

(a) *Complementary thinking:* When we are dealing not merely with formal-logical expressions but with real-world objects and events, we rarely can be certain that we see the totality of possibilities. As a rule we cannot assert, therefore, that our concepts exhaust the universe of possibilities. From a critical point of view we should therefore assume that we are dealing not with contradictory but with contrary oppositions, although there may be some cases where one can empirically establish the exhaustiveness (and hence, contradictoriness) of two opposites (e.g. positive-negative charge of particles in the absence of uncharged particles). Accordingly, dualistic thinking in terms of "either p or q" (exactly one of the two, i.e., the correctness of the one implies the falseness of the other) must be replaced by complementary thinking in terms of "p as well as q" or "neither p nor q" (the correctness of the one does not imply the falseness of the other). The old Chinese saying quoted by Mao Tse-tung (1968:68) captures the essence of complementary thinking: "Things that oppose each other also complement each other."

Thus, when we are dealing not with the form but with the content of our thinking, we should never rely on the principle of excluded contradiction in the sense of taking it for an ontological principle. Non-Aristotelian thinking is necessary especially with respect to the many dichotomies we have inherited from centuries of Aristotelian thinking: subjectivity vs. objectivity, idealism vs. realism, rationalism vs. empiricism, theory vs. practice, theoretical vs. practical reason, "facts" vs. "values," the concrete vs. the general, incremental vs. synoptic planning, "means" vs. "ends", etc. Regarding such dichotomies, "thinking that comprehends (itself)" will critically consider the ways in which the one alternative is presupposed in, or inseparable from, the other, what are the normative presuppositions of the involved boundary judgements, etc. This leads us to the second implication.

(b) *Maintaining the contradiction:* In order to break through the one-sidedness and incomprehensiveness of our concepts, the dialectician maintains that we should hypothetically *negate* them. That is to say, he does not content himself with a simple call to reflection but offers us some heuristic guidance in the form of the dialectical triad: affirmation-negation-negation of the negation. According to this formula, adequate dialectical negation of the given understanding of our concepts must negate itself, by *negating the negation* – it must reflect back on its own partiality, on the normative content of both the affirmation and the negation of our concepts, according to that deepest of Hegel's insights:

The true is the whole. But the whole is only the essence perfecting itself through its development. Of the absolute [which the whole represents] it should be said that *it is essentially result,* that it is only in the end what it is in truth....

...

It is therefore a misapprehension about reason when reflection is excluded from the true instead of being comprehended as a positive moment of the absolute. *It is reflection that makes the true a result.* (Hegel 1807:24 and 25, transl. Kaufmann 1977:32, italics mine)

This insight, rather than the dialectical triad itself, is the key to dialectical reasoning: what is "given" in thought and experience is never the whole and hence never true, for the whole includes the not-yet given and the no-longer given. "Truth, then, includes the negative as well – that which might be called the false if it could be considered as something from which one should abstract." (Hegel 1807:46, transl. Kaufmann 1977:70)

Hegel's formulation of the triad has the advantage over Fichte's ("thesis-antithesis-synthesis") in that it explicitly reminds us of the importance of maintaining the negation. Still, there is the danger of its being imposed on the content of our thinking in an external and schematic manner. For our purpose, we can just as well renounce the ritual of the dialectical triad and instead adopt some critical reminder that can guide us in the process of unfolding the normative content of our systems concepts (maps and designs), e.g.:

1. "The true is the whole, and the whole includes its own negation." (paraphrasing Hegel)
2. "We have to maintain the contradiction or else we allow ourselves to be overwhelmed by the consistent." (Churchman 1968 b:229, rev.ed. 1979:230)
3. "The fool never notices that everything has two sides." (Bloch 1977:121)
4. "Make the weaker argument the stronger." (the basically correct maxim of the Sophists)
   or simply
5. "I know that I know nothing." (Socrates)

Each of these observations is thoroughly dialectical, but I shall prefer the second once because it is most explicit about the trap to be avoided – the trap of no longer negating that which is seemingly given, i.e., consistent with the established universe of "facts" or with one's own internalized patterns of thought. Of course, since we must distinguish between contradiction as contradictory opposition (in the realm of thought) and contradiction as contrary opposition (in the realm of being), the imperative to "maintain the contradiction" is no license for inconsistent argument or speculative arbitrariness but rather a call to undogmatic thinking: it demands that we seek to eliminate contradictory oppositions in our thought *not* by ignoring but by taking account of the contrary oppositions that may be present in the objects of our thought.

1.3. Dialectical Reasoning as the Self-Transcendence of Reason: The Process of Unfolding the Reason-Practice Dialectic

For all its merits, Hegel's understanding of dialectics suffers from a major shortcoming. Although Hegel locates the contradictions that drive the dialectical process in the real world rather than in the thinking subject, his dialectic does not mediate between the realms of concepts and practice but *only between concepts.*[2] (The term "practice" can be defined without further explanation: it refers to *lived* social reality, as opposed to merely conceptual efforts such as mapping social reality, holding a discourse *on* practice, or writing a book on practical reason; such conceptual efforts remain at least partly "theoretical" in that they are *not* to be substituted for practice itself.) Here, I believe, lies the root cause that Hegel ends up with a science of absolute spirit or absolute knowledge. Hegel pursues the consequences of his approach radically enough to accept their thoroughly undialectical character. The implication for us is not that Hegelian dialectics is self-contradictory (that it offends against the

---

[2] Superficially, it may seem as if Hegel's dialectic worked fine without any necessary reference to practice. On closer examination, however, it becomes clear that Hegel's attempt to seek the whole ("the true") in a theoretical absolute has undialectical consequences – not by mere coincidence does Hegel's dialectic turn into a "science of absolute spirit" or of "absolute knowledge." As I explain below in the text, it seems to me that an extension of Hegel's dialectic to a reason-practice dialectic is logically necessary. My argument in the present section does not, however, depend on this rather bold claim; my purpose is not to propose a logically necessary correction of Hegel's dialectic *per se,* but rather to adapt it to the task of developing a critical solution to the problem of practical reason. (In the same way, we have adapted Kantian a priori science to social planning: our reconstruction of Kantian categories does not claim to be a logically necessary correction of Kant but only a heuristically necessary adaption in respect to the planner's quest for practical reason.) With regard to the problem of practical reason such as the planner faces it, reference to practice is indeed a necessary correction of Hegel's dialectic. In distinction to Hegel, we cannot seek the whole or "the true" in a theoretical or rational absolute but only in a synthesis of the conceptual and the "practical" ("real"), a synthesis that remains necessarily imperfect and in which there is no rational absolute.

principle of excluded contradiction) but rather that Hegel has not yet rediscovered the one and only point of reference in relation to which dialectics originated and in relation to which it is meaningful: the *inevitable dialectic of concepts and practice in all efforts of reason*. In the present study, this dialectic is reflected in the opposition between *systems concepts* (the whole systems judgements of the planner) and *social practice* (the testimony of the witnesses). Rather than associating the two sides with the misleading theory-practice dichotomy, we understand systems concepts as a source of a priori concepts of practical reason, while considering social practice as a source of a posteriori concepts of practical reason; only together can they secure practical reason.

It is not a necessary implication of Hegel's radicalization of the Kantian self-reflection and self-limitation of reason that in the end this self-reflection does not make room for concrete social practice but for a philosophically abstract "absolute spirit." What wonder that Marx, in the Introduction to his *Critique of the Hegelian Philosophy of Right* (in Marx 1953:215) objects: "You cannot abolish philosophy without realizing it," and "[you cannot] realize philosophy without abolishing it." The early Marx here grasps what Hegel and the later Marx neglect: namely, that *the dialectical process cannot be located only within either the realm of reason (concepts) or the realm of practice without loosing its dialectical character at the very basis*. The dialectical process can be unfolded only as a mediating process between *conceptual* (systems) rationality and *lived* (social) practice, or between *a priori* and *a posteriori* concepts of practical reason. In this process either side "feeds" on the other by negating it in the threefold sense of the German verb *aufheben* (sublate, or, in Kaufmann's translation, sublimate – cf. 1977:16): to negate, to preserve, to elevate onto a higher level of comprehension. Otherwise, the dialectical process will soon have nothing more to negate and will succumb to the trap of consistency, as both Hegel and Marx have illustrated in their own way. Hegel's dialectic, because it moves only within the realm of concepts, ends up as life-less and undialectical metaphysics of absolute spirit, a metaphysics that misunderstands itself as a "science of absolute knowledge"; and Marx' dialectic, because it moves only within the material (economic) "substructure," ends up as a linear and deterministic metaphysics of the "laws" of historical progress, equally misunderstanding itself as a science.

Let us therefore be very clear about our use of the term "dialectics." Whenever we speak of the dialectical relationship between a priori and a posteriori concepts of practical reason, theoretical and practical reason, or between rationalism and empiricism, idealism and realism, holism and incrementalism, systems rationality and social rationality, the involved and the affected, etc., we refer to two positions that are complementary because the one represents the realm of concepts, the other the realm of practice; *by virtue of their contrariness, they can prevent each other from succumbing to the trap of consistency*. Either side must appear "irrational" or "arbitrary" from the other's viewpoint; each represents in this way the necessary negation of the other's understanding of rationality; and either can become fully rational only to the extent that it breaks through the consistency of its own rationality and opens itself up to the other side.

The underlying principle is this: the only way in which planning can bring practical reason into social practice is to go beyond (transcend) the bounds of any given (a priori) concept of "rationality" in a planning situation. *The rationality of planning cannot be secured rationalistically in terms of a "systems rationality" that justifies itself monologically,* namely, by reference to its own a priori concepts of practical reason. Rather, planning must rely on a *non-rationalistic concept of rationality,* as it were. As "rationalistic" I designate in this context a conception of rationality that pursues the theoretical goal of explicating, operationalizing and justifying the idea of practical reason at the price of effectively sacrificing the practical goal of making it actual, of practicing it (cf. Ulrich 1981a). Our review of Popper's and Habermas' models of discursive rationality suggested that both must be called rationalistic in this sense (cf. Chapters 1 and 2). A non-rationalistic concept of rationality will rely on the dialectical notion that *rationality is a process of mediation between a priori and a posteriori concepts of practical reason,* whereby the former are associated with the realm of (systems) concepts and the latter with the realm of (social) practice. The medium of such mediation must be a discourse, a discursive process of unfolding the normative content of both the a priori and the a posteriori concepts in question.

In this process, each side will have to be responsible for the rationality and formal consistency of its own position, but neither can claim normative validity for its arguments without the approval of the other side, for "the true is the whole," and the whole "includes the negative as well." Of course, comprehensive rationality can thus no longer justify itself *theoretically;* but perhaps in this way comprehensive rationality can be *practiced,* in the sense that practice, instead of justifying its rationality by reference to theoretical concepts, becomes morally and democratically self-responsible. Practice is self-responsible when those who *live,* or will have to live, the social reality in question establish on their own accord the democratic and moral legitimacy of disputed normative validity claims.

Such self-responsibility of practice requires, of course, its critical awareness as to its own normative content, i.e., its actual and potential consequences for all those affected by it. Knowledge of such consequences may require expertise. Again we encounter the inevitable reason-practice dialectic: in order to become self-responsible with respect to its consequences, practice cannot ignore the findings of theoretical reason, just as theoretical reason, in order to justify itself, cannot ignore its own practical (normative) content. Thus, whenever we speak of a dialectical relationship or a dialectical process, this will be the crucial idea: one side serves as the source of theoretical (a priori) concepts of rationality for the other, while the latter serves as the source of practical (a posteriori) concepts of rationality for the former. In this sense we shall speak of a dialectic between *"systems rationality"* and *"social rationality."* Reason, as the source of the former, must recognize its basically negative character vis-à-vis practice, i.e., it has only critical but no assertive authority; and practice, as the source of the latter, must recognize that it depends on this critical power of reason for its own enlightenment, its emancipation from the given universe of "facts."[3] This consideration will finally lead us back to Kant and his concept of the "polemical employment of reason."

---

[3] To prevent any misconception, I should perhaps emphasize that my association of reason with the planners, and that of practice with the witnesses, is not meant to divide society into thinkers (planners) and feelers (affected citizens). Rather, the interpretation of the relationship between planners and citizens as a reason-practice dialectic is to serve a critical purpose: our approach must avoid requiring the affected to be "thinkers" in order to be admitted to discourse. Many concerned citizens representing the affected may be just as intellectual and self-reflective as are the planners, but we do not want to exclude those citizens who are not so intellectual. Moreover, the term "affected' has been defined as "having to bear the consequences without being involved," it is not intended to signify emotionality or lack of thinking in the first place.

2. The Dialectic of A Priori and A Posteriori Concepts of Practical Reason

Let us now return to Kant. What can we learn from him about the appropriate place of reason in the process of unfolding the normative content of systems concepts and judgements, a process that is to come to grips with the reason-practice dialectic? How can we, in a Kantian perspective, secure at least a critical solution to the problem of the a priori of argumentation?

The two basic Kantian considerations in this regard are these:

(1) No effort of reason (e.g. on the part of the planner) can supersede its dependency on an empirical basis that furnishes the material for reasonable thought (e.g. the testimony of the witnesses).

(2) In validating its empirical basis, reason has no assertive but only critical authority; it has assertive authority at best in establishing the a priori component that it contributes to the construction of an empirical basis.

Kant captures thesis (2) in his phrase of the "polemical employment of reason," and we shall deal with it under the same heading (Section 3). First, however, we need to examine the meaning and applicability of thesis (1) within our own framework. I would like to discuss the first thesis by means of the following list of dialectical opposites (I indicate the most important sources of inspiration for my discussion in parentheses):

Subsection	A priori vs. a posteriori concepts		
2.1	1. A priori concepts vs. or judgements	a posteriori concepts or judgements	(Kant 1781)
	2. Intelligibility	vs. reality	
2.2	3. Standpoint	vs. problem	(N. Hartmann 1924)
2.3	4. Rational structure	vs. surrational structure	(Bachelard 1940)
	5. Systems approach	vs. enemies of the systems approach	(Churchman 1979)
	6. Quasi-transcendental reflection	vs. quasi-metaphysical reflection	(Critical heuristics)
2.4	7. Systems rationality	vs. social rationality	
	└→ Process of unfolding ←┘		

Table 5/1: The dialectic of a priori and a posteriori concepts of practical reason – different aspects to be unfolded in the process of unfolding.

2.1. The Dialectic of Idealism and Realism, or: The Struggle for Intelligibility and Reality

The fact that Kant's approach is analytical ("monological") rather than dialectical (dialogical) does not imply that there is nothing we could learn from him about reason's appropriate place in the process of unfolding. Both in an analytical and in a dialectical perspective, reason cannot produce reality out of itself. Only a source that is essentially independent of reason can assure us of keeping in touch with reality. This fundamental dialectic of a priori and a posteriori concepts is the common basis of both Kant's monological and our dialogical approach, and we can therefore expect that Kant has something to say about reason's appropriate role in the unfolding of this dialectic.

There is, however, a crucial difference that might prevent us from drawing any analogies to Kant. The two sources of knowledge with which Kant is concerned are "pure understanding" and "sensibility" (= perception that is yet to be brought under the pure concepts of the understanding to become experience, cf. Prol.:par. 22). His critical effort is directed against dogmatic empiricism (which makes perception the only source of knowledge) and against dogmatic rationalism (which makes the understanding the only source of knowledge). Kant is critical of both dogmas because they both fail to recognize the principle enunciated in the Transcendental Analytic:

Unterstanding and sensibility, with us, can determine objects only when they are employed in conjunction. When we separate them, we have *intuition without concepts,* or *concepts without intuition* – in both cases, representations which we are not in a position to apply to any determinate objects. (KrV:B 314, italics mine)

It is the basic critical purpose of Kant's transcendental criticism to forestall the objectivist (or "transcendental") illusion that occurs when the interdependency of a priori and a posteriori sources of knowledge is not adequately considered.

Our own critical effort is similarly directed against empiricism and rationalism, but these two terms now refer to other sources of knowledge (or deception) and accordingly gain another meaning. The problem with contemporary empiricism (logical positivism, critical rationalism) is not that it ignores the importance of the understanding but rather that it disavows Kant's distinction between the understanding and *reason.* Not by accident has modern science-theory (which is basically empiricist) served an uncritical function in immunizing science against the efforts of practical reason. On the other hand, the trouble with contemporary rationalism, as we have defined it in Section 1.3 above, is not that it ignores the importance of sense-experience; the problem is rather that it locates *practical* reason within the boundaries of reason instead of trying to mediate between reason and "irrational," lived social practice. Hence the two sources of knowledge (or deception) with which we are mainly concerned are not pure understanding versus sensibility but rather reason (in the wider sense including the understanding) versus lived social practice.

By analogy with Kant's insight that it is impossible to locate the sources of knowledge either in sensibility or in pure understanding, we rely on the critical assumption that practical reason (or practical knowledge) cannot be located either in the realm of reason (rational discourse) or in the realm of practice; *otherwise we have reason without practice, or practice without reason.*

For us as for Kant, reason is the source of a priori ideas and of the a priori categories of the understanding. We differ from Kant, however, in one crucial respect. By renouncing Kant's tacit identification of phenomenal with spatiotemporal reality, we have enlarged the empirical basis that furnishes the necessary a posteriori concepts (cf. Section 3.1 of Chapter 4). Such a reinterpretation is, as I have argued, in accord with the critical intent of Kant's fundamental distinction between phenomena and noumena; far from rendering Kant's critical insights inapplicable, it makes them relevant guides for critical social inquiry and planning. Nevertheless, the question must be raised whether the analogy between Kant's dialectic of pure understanding vs. sensibility and our own dialectic of the conceptual efforts of reason vs. lived social practice is valid. I believe that this is indeed the case, because both dialectical relationships are, at bottom, expressions of one and the same fundamental dialectic – the old and eternal *dialectic of idealism and realism.*

Reason's a priori concepts and judgements are meant to render reality intelligible; but what is the use of the highest degree of *intelligibility* if there is no assurance of *reality* linked to it? This difficulty is in fact an inevitable consequence of Kant's critically-idealist standpoint, according to which "reason has insight only into that which it produces after a plan of its own." (B xiii, cf. the discussion of the "Copernican hypothesis" in Section 1.2 of Chapter 3.) In Kant's formulation, the difficulty is "how subjective conditions of thought can have objective validity, that is, can furnish conditions of the possibility of all knowledge of objects." (B 122) The subjective conditions of thought that Kant has in mind are synthetic a priori judgements. The subjective conditions of thought with which critical heuristics is concerned are the boundary judgements that inevitably flow into our social maps and designs (see the examples given in Section 1.4 of Chapter 4). "Kant's problem" is relevant to us because these boundary judgements, just like synthetic a priori judgements, cannot be validated either logically or empirically; they remain theoretically problematic but are practically indispensable. This is why we have considered them as relatively a priori, synthetic judgements.

The question of how we can validate such boundary judgements represents the crux of our envisaged critical solution to the problem of practical discourse. We might state the question by analogy to our reformulation of "Kant's problem" in Chapter Three (Section 2.2):

282

In as much as all validity claims for social maps or designs presuppose boundary judgements that cannot be justified either logically or empirically, how can we justify such judgements at all? And if we cannot objectively justify them, how can we accomplish at least a critical solution, i.e., make sure that we do not succumb to an objectivist illusion?

Boundary judgements, or whole systems judgements, represent the "idealist" (a priori) component of our approach; our question asks for the "realist" (a posteriori) component. Kant's question of "how subjective conditions of thought can have objective validity" is his way of confronting the same basic issue: How can a critically-idealist approach, as much as it does for clarifying the conditions of intelligibility (the a priori of experience), assure us of the reality of that which it renders intelligible? Within Kant's monological framework, there is only one possibility: a critically-idealist account of the conditions of intelligibility must in itself contain the conditions of reality. Kant is forced to demonstrate that his account of the a priori of experience represents at the same time an account of the conditions for the truth of theoretical judgements. Of course we already know today that the problem of the a priori of argumentation cannot be reduced to that of the a priori of experience. Kant's conceptual boundary experiment is nevertheless of interest to us, for it offers an important lesson with regard to a critical solution to the problem of rational practical discourse.

Kant deals with the problem in that very difficult section of the "Analytic of Principles" where he seeks to establish *"the highest principle of all synthetic judgements"* (B 193ff). In the preceding section, he showed the principle of excluded contradiction to be "the highest principle of all analytic judgements" (B 189–193). This task presented no special difficulty, for analytic judgements by definition are true if they are not self-contradictory. The principle of excluded contradiction is not sufficient, however, to account for the truth of synthetic judgements, for their truth implies that they somehow "correspond" to something that lies beyond them.

> In the analytic judgement we keep to the given concept, and seek to extract something from it.... But in synthetic judgements I have to advance beyond the given concept, viewing as in relation with the concept something altogether different from what was thought in it. This relation is consequently never a relation either of identity or of contradiction. (B 193f)

Thus far this is fairly straightforward and certainly no news. But at this point comes the problem: *How then* can we validate a synthetic judgement? What is the correlative for synthetic judgements of the consistency condition for analytic judgements? Kant fails to outline a corresponding methodological principle. His answer remains unusually vague because on the basis of his critically-idealist standpoint the problem cannot be solved. He must break through his standpoint, but does not yet fully recognize this requirement:

If knowledge is to have objective reality, that is, to relate to an object, and is to acquire meaning and significance in respect to it, the object must be capable of being *in some manner* given. Otherwise the concepts are empty. (B 194, italics added)

With this "in some manner" Kant starts to open up his original standpoint and to acknowledge that the demand of the problem (namely, access to reality) is simply overriding the demand of the standpoint (which excludes an immediate intuitive grasp of reality without the mediation of a priori concepts). He must show how the intellect with its a priori concepts can adequately anticipate the content of real-world objects not yet given to it. There is only one way to resolve the dilemma: the principles governing the structure and processes of the real world must be the same as those governing the intellect. Hence Kant formulates his famous "highest principle of all synthetic judgements":

We then assert that the conditions of the *possibility of experience* in general are likewise conditions of the *possibility of the objects of experience,* and that for this reason they have objective validity in a synthetic *a priori* judgement. (B 197)

Since Kant originally defined synthetic judgements, in distinction to analytic judgements (= tautologies), as those in which the connection of the predicate with the subject "is thought without identity" (B 10), we are not surprised that the notion of identity here is reintroduced at a higher level, as it were. It is identity at this "higher" (ontological) level which legitimates the "connection without identity" at the "lower" (cognitive) level. Since in synthetic judgements the mind is to connect a concept with a non-identical or non-tautological predicate, on what other basis could the validity of that connection rest but on the prior connection of the principles or categories of the judging mind with those of the reality to be judged? In this respect, the human mind is in the same situation as the computer: neither can take in, store and adequately process incoming "data" unless it has been given both the basic mapping dimensions in terms of which the data is to be recognized, and the principles according to which it is to be connected with other data into WFF's ("well-formed formulae").

What can we learn from Kant's "highest principle"?

Unlike traditional idealist or realist solutions to the problem of truth, Kant's solution does *not* postulate an immediate identity of subject and object, thinking and being, but only an identity of the principles that govern them. In fact, this solution depends on the dualism (non-identity) of the two sources of knowledge, as the sources of a priori vs. a posteriori concepts. That is to say, Kant's solution is independent of either his critically-idealist or an alternative realist standpoint: the demand of the problem, the struggle for intelligibility *and* reality, cannot be solved on the basis of either standpoint but requires a dialectic between both.

C. West Churchman has further unfolded this theme of the idealist-realist dialectic in his *Challenge to Reason* (1968a:Ch. 14). His basis thesis is that idealism and realism are always two aspects of one and the same thinking process, and hence that we cannot approach the question of the "reality" (validity) of our systems concepts without going through the opposition between the real and the ideal (the intelligible). Thus any critically-idealist standpoint, be it a strictly transcendental or a quasi-transcendental approach, needs to open up itself to the arguments of the other, realist position; otherwise it is not critical enough. Any approach runs the risk of becoming uncritical if it insists on consistency with itself *à tout prix.* Being critical in the full sense of the word means to question all the assumptions or a priori concepts presupposed in one's standpoint, and to carry this questioning far enough so that the original standpoint becomes – at least temporarily – irrelevant for the conclusion. *Any truly critical position should have consequences independent of that position.*

This implication of Kant's "highest principle" is perhaps the most fundamental lesson in critical thinking that we can learn from Kant. It is Kant's way of formulating the *principle of dialectics: we must maintain the contradiction or else we submit to the trap of consistency* (cf. Churchman 1968b:229 and Section 1.3. above). By hindsight, it is easy to see that the dialectical principle is indeed the counterpart of the principle of excluded contradiction (as the "highest principle of all analytic judgements"), the very counterpart for which Kant searches in his "highest principle of all synthetic judgements." Kant could easily have discovered it, had he not been blinded by his own preconception of dialectics as a mere "logic of illusion" (B 86). Thus it remained for Hegel to comprehend the dialectical negation of identity (or consistency) as the highest principle of synthesis: a synthetic judgement that does not say "no" to some previous synthetic judgement has no information content and is no synthetic achievement at all.

We now gain a deeper understanding of the dialectical principle. *Regardless of how "critical" our standpoint may be, we need to maintain the contradiction, for no standpoint is ever sufficient in itself to validate its own implications:* the synthetic judgements to which it gives rise do not represent synthetic achievements at all, they are problematic a priori judgements that can be validated only through a confrontation with standpoint-independent a posteriori judgements.

The importance of this conclusion for the problem of the a priori of argumentation is obvious. No consensus theory of truth – or better, of rational discourse about normative validity claims[4] – can be self-sufficient; only embedded in some kind of a non-objectivistic "correspondence" theory can practical discourse put us in touch with reality. In the chapter on Habermas, we already found that his consensus theory of truth could not obliterate but only redefine the problem of correspondence; we now find that Kant's *Critique* can indeed help us to understand the meaning of this

---

4 This formulation is more adequate because the question is: What *ought* to count as a valid description (map) of social reality? Neither in validating maps of social reality nor in validating social designs is there such a thing as value-free truth claims.

earlier conjecture. "Correspondence" is not of course to be understood in the sense of the naive empiricist manifestation theory of truth; "correspondence" for us simply refers to some source of a posteriori concepts on which our a priori concepts and judgements (and the maps or designs of which they are constitutive) depend for their validation. Our earlier requirement that this source be largely independent of reason does not imply that we have to look for a fixed, subject-independent territory, or for an autonomous universe of "facts." There is no theoretical reason why we should not consider "irrational," lived social practice as such a source; there are, rather, very sound reasons speaking *for* such a perspective, as I have argued above (see Section 1.3 above). By regarding social practice as the necessary source of a posteriori concepts for the planner, we acknowledge its autonomous character vis-à-vis reason, or vis-à-vis the rationality standards of the involved: reason has no authority over those who *live* social practice except by their own free choice.

Let us now try to concretize our basic conjectures up to this point. How should the planner understand and unfold the dialectic of idealism and realism, of a priori and a posteriori concepts, so as to secure the rationality ("intelligibility") *and* the normative validity ("reality") of his maps and designs?

2.2. The Dialectic of Standpoint and Problem

Let us practice what we have preached above, namely, approaching the question of "reality" (the a priori of argumentation) by going through the opposition between the real and the ideal. Since our effort is inspired by Kant's critical (transcendental) idealism, let us invite to our discussion a critical *realist,* Nicolai Hartmann (1924, 1949), and listen to his case.

In his paper "Diesseits von Idealismus und Realismus" (1924), Hartmann argues that many of the difficulties and apparent inconsistencies in Kant's writings – e.g. the unclear status of the "noumenon in the positive sense" or the rather obscure justification of the "highest principle of all synthetic judgements" – are due to the fact that Kant in these cases pursues the consequences of his problems rather than those of his standpoint. Thus Hartmann develops one of his most interesting themes, the *dialectic between the consequences of the problem and the consequences of the standpoint.*

Problems resist being forced into limits such as the choice of a standpoint always sets them. They have their self-will, they lead a life of their own. That is also true of Kant's problems. (Hartmann 1924:162, my transl.)

Only a perfect or infinite mind, Hartmann writes, could oversee all the remotest consequences of his problem at the time of formulating the standpoint from which it wants to approach the problem. Such a mind alone could lay out a comprehensive conceptual system so that every aspect of the problem would find its proper place in it. A finite, human mind will never fully succeed in reconciling all the consequences of the standpoint with all those of the problem. Its conceptual systems designs can only be anticipations of problems that it has not yet completely penetrated (cf. 1924:163).[5]

It is not difficult to see the realist-idealist dialectic in this basic argument of Hartmann's. A "standpoint" is a conceptual construct by virtue of which a problem is to be rendered rationally *intelligible;* the "problem" is taken to exist independently of the standpoint insofar as it resists complete rational penetration and in that sense "leads its own life," claims its independent *reality. (On pense comme on se frappe* says the French poet Paul Valéry – "one thinks as one bumps one's head.")

Nor is it difficult to see that such a dialectic of standpoint and problem exists in Kant's *Critique* right from the beginning. "Kant's problem" – of how reason could establish the objective reality of its own unavoidable ideas, i.e., the existence of God, of the World, of Man's immortal soul and free will – originated in his deep personal conviction that the world had been designed by a divine creator and that humans were indeed endowed by him with freedom of the will and immortality of the soul. But in order to demonstrate the validity of these ideas, Kant had to assume a "Copernican," critically-idealist standpoint, according to which reason had insight only into what it produced "after a plan of its own." (B xiii) His standpoint required that noumena be admitted only "in the negative sense," while his problem originated in the assumption that "noumena in the positive sense" such as God and the soul existed. Throughout his critical writings, Kant struggled with this tension between the demands (or consequences) of his problem and those of his standpoint.[6]

A majority of Kant's interpreters have been inclined to dismiss Kant's positive use of the thing in itself as occasional blunders that are of no significance for his systematic thought and can safely be disregarded. George Schrader, a noted Kant scholar of Yale University, may here represent this view:

> If one considers Kant's private views, it is not difficult to understand the reason for this inconsistency. In his private views, he was a confirmed realist throughout his critical period.[7] Apparently he could not resist the temptation to offer a defense of realism, and employed the concept of the thing-in-itself to that end. However, this

---

5   In his book *Grundzüge einer Metaphysik der Erkenntnis* (1949:12), Hartmann similarly speaks of a "metaphysics of problems": because no conceivable standpoint can make reality as such (the territory) accessible, there is always a rationally impenetrable "metaphysical remainder" in problems. Hartmann's recognition of this "metaphysics of problems" is the critical realist's way of admitting that there is no such thing as complete "correspondence" between subjective (standpoint-related, a priori) concepts and "objective" reality as such. In other words, it is the realist's way of being self-critical and of opening up his standpoint to the arguments of the idealists.

6   The same tension between standpoint and problem is evident, for instance, when Kant refers to the thing in itself as the "cause of appearances" (e.g. KrV:B 344, 523; Prol.:A 104) – a hypostatization of the thing in itself that violates his standpoint but corresponds to his original problem.

7   Cf. KrV:Bxli (note), B 236, A 51, A 380, B 524 (references by Schrader).

represents a dogmatic employment of the concept. Such passages must be dismissed as reflecting Kant's private views, but as of little significance for his critical position. (Schrader 1967:174)

One can easily agree with Schrader that Kant's association of the concept of a noumenon with the causes of appearances or with the divine creator of the world bursts the framework of his critical, systematic standpoint. Our previous considerations suggest, however, another explanation. It seems reasonable to assume that Kant consciously accepted and maintained the tension between standpoint and problem because he was critical enough to see the limitations of his own standpoint as compared to the demands of his problem. In support of this interpretation, we may cite some evidence that is quite independent of our own argument: Kant's thesis, in the Transcendental Aesthetic (B 44, 52), of the "transcendental ideality" *and* the "empirical reality" of space and time. By putting that thesis at the head of the first *Critique,* he forced himself to work consiously and permanently with the dialectic of problem and standpoint. If such an interpretation is not entirely mistaken, Kant's readiness to put up with inconsistency may be said to contain an important lesson in rational criticism, a lesson that Hartmann formulates as follows:

What is in the deepest sense critical in Kant is this: that he frequently violates the consequences of the system (his idealism), but rarely or never the concequences of the problem. (1924:167)

Of course, Hartmann does not mean to imply an opposition between critical and systematic, standpoint-related thinking. Thinking must always presuppose some standpoint; but thinking that remains the prisoner of its presupposed standpoint is bound to become dogmatic. Problems that do not fit in its conceptual framework do not exist for such thinking. In other words, *critical thinking is not standpoint-free thinking but rather standpoint-transcendent thinking:* it breaks through the standpoint whenever the demands of the problem are inconsistent with those of the standpoint. The point is that critical thinking should neither let the standpoint dictate the problem nor should it allow the problem to dictate the standpoint. Because no conceptual standpoint is ever sufficient to render intelligible the totality of problem-relevant conditions *and* to establish their reality, *critical thinking must unfold and work with the dialectic of standpoint and problem.*

2.3. The Dialectic of Expertise and Emancipation

What does the above conclusion mean for the social inquirer or planner? It means that no (self-)critical systems approach to social mapping and design must elevate itself to the position of the arbiter who determines what ought to be considered as a planning problem. It means that the people who *live* the social reality in question, although they may not be able to formulate the problem in the rational terms of the systems approach, represent as indispensable a source of practical reason (and practical knowledge) as do the professionals who are planning on their behalf. The task of unfolding the dialectic of standpoint and problem must therefore be operationalized as the task of organizing a practical discourse between planners (the involved) and witnesses (the affected), a practical discourse in which each side challenges the other to make transparent the normative consequences of its position (the conceptual standpoint of the systems planner vs. the lived social practice of the witnesses).

What are the adequate roles of planners and witnesses in this process of unfolding? Again Kant's basic consideration applies: no effort of reason (on the part of the planner) can supersede its dependency on an empirical basis that furnishes the material for reasonable thought (the testimony of the witnesses). Reason can produce a rational conceptual structure such as the systems approach or critical heuristics; but it would be absurd if rationality itself wanted to take the place of the unstructured that is to be structured (cf. Bubner 1976:192 who reaches a similar conclusion in discussing the interdependence of reason and norms). The unstructured that must be presupposed if rationality is to fulfill its proper role is "irrational" social practice as it is lived by the affected and represented by the witnesses. The planner is dependent on the witnesses because he must presuppose social practice in at least three ways: (a) as the precondition of any effort of practical reason, (b) as its subject matter, and (c) as its purpose.[8]

Practice is *precondition* in that the process of unfolding does not begin with rational and systematic but with vital practical presuppositions voiced by the witnesses. Practice is *subject matter* in that the rational planner cannot understand his effort as a value-free means in the service of "given" purposes; he must, rather, question both the purposes that are already built into the social practice of which he becomes a part, and the values that his planning effort itself introduces. Such critical reflection again depends on the witnesses' testimony about the normative implications of alternative maps of the planning problem and designs for improvement. Finally, to say that social practice is the *purpose* of planning means that planning – and the effort of reason behind it – must be kept a *means*. Planning is to be a means for giving people control over the social practice they have to live; it must not treat *them* as means for the purpose of "rational" planning.

All three considerations suggest that a critical systems approach to planning must not be allowed to make itself the judge of what is "rational" and what is "irrational." Rather than requiring the witnesses to submit to its a priori standards of rationality, a critical systems approach ought to recognize them as representatives of alternative, though no less partial, "rationalities" – e.g. the political rationality of power, the

---

[8] Aristotle, whose *Nikomachian Ethics* represents an early highpoint of the tradition of practical philosophy, already emphasized that practice (ethical experience and action in the *polis*) is not only the subject matter of practical philosophy but also its inevitable precondition and purpose (cf. for instance Höffe 1979:8, 38ff).

moral rationality of conscience, or the aesthetic rationality of "quality of life." If we give a privileged status to the rationality of the systems approach, "rational" systems design is likely to become an end in itself instead of remaining a means for *socially* rational planning. *Under the guise of rationality and expertise, the involved make themselves the client while treating the affected as means.* It is only by giving an equal status to the different rationalities of the involved and the affected that we can prevent the former from making themselves the judges who define the measure of improvement. In short, the affected must be helped to emancipate themselves from the rationality of the involved, from the premises and promises of the "experts." Thus, if the process of unfolding is to be a means for keeping planning a means, it must embody a *dialectic of expertise and emancipation,* of professional competence and democratic participation of citizens.

It is the shared role of planners and witnesses to unfold this dialectic, though the two sides will have different criteria of rational planning and of improvement. Going back to *Table 5/1,* we can conceptualize the two roles in terms of three overlapping dialectical relationships:

1. rational vs. surrational structures (Bachelard 1940)
2. systems approach vs. enemies of the systems approach (Churchman 1979)
3. quasi-transcendental vs. quasi-metaphysical reflection (as suggested in Chapter 2, Section 4.1 of the present study).

1. The French epistemologist Gaston Bachelard develops his theme of the *dialectic of rational and surrational structures* in his book *La Philosophie du Non.*[9] One of his basic observations concerns the contemporary significance of Kant's a priori concepts and synthetic a priori principles. Because they apply only to the object domain of Euclidian geometry and Newtonian science, they can no longer be regarded as necessary conditions of possible knowledge, though they may still represent sufficient conditions for the two specified domains (cf. Bachelard 1978:125). Therefore, Bachelard argues, the philosophy of the "as if" (Kant) must today become a philosophy of the "no," i.e., analytical (transcendental) deduction must be complemented by dialectical negation (cf. 1978:162).

Bachelard's dialectic, unlike Hegel's, does not move within the realm of a priori concepts. Since a priori concepts are merely "as if's" that make up the accepted rational structures or paradigms of inquiry at a certain stage of knowledge,[10] critical inquiry must strive to "open up" (one of his key terms) the given rational structures by negating some of their essential features and by replacing them with their

[9] Literally: The Philosophy of the "No" (1940). I have used the German translation entitled *Die Philosophie des Nein* (1978).
[10] Bachelard does not use the term "paradigm," but the closeness of his meaning to Thomas Kuhn's concept of the paradigm (1962) is obvious. Outside France, Bachelard has only recently begun to be recognized as one of the early representatives of a non-evolutionary, i.e., "revolutionary," theory of knowledge.

dialectical opposites, according to the motto: "why not?" He calls these opposite "as if's" *surrational* structures, for they do not (yet) belong to the established rational structures of a domain but may belong to it some day, so that they cannot simply be dismissed as "irrational" (cf. 1978:49, 155, 157). For instance, historically established rational structures such as Aristotelian logic, Euclidian geometry, Newtonian physics or the phlogiston theory of combustion in chemistry may, at some point in the development of the respective disciplines, become "epistemological obstacles" (another of Bachelard's key terms) to the progress of knowledge and must be replaced by opposite or conflicting structures such as non-Aristotelian logic, non-Euclidian geometry, Einsteinian physics or the oxydation theory of combustion in chemistry.

In Bachelard's perspective, Kant "opened up" classical empiricism by demonstrating once for all the need to transcend experience; but his rationalism remained closed (cf. 1978:24f, 43). Opening up Kantian rationalism requires our going beyond the "as if's" that underly it, namely Aristotelian logic and Newtonian physics, and thus must lead to a dialectical and non-mechanistic paradigm of inquiry. The rational structures that determine coherent experience are thus themselves rooted in metaphysical, "surrational" structures, and there is accordingly no objective solution but at best a critical solution to the problem of justifying them. As Bachelard puts it,

> Coherent experience is a product not of architectonic but of polemical reason. Surrationalism, by its dialectic and its criticism, constitutes sur-objects, as it were. The sur-object is the result of a critical objectification, of an objectivity that retains of an object only that which it has first subjected to criticism. The atom as it appears in contemporary physics embodies a sur-object.... The model of the atom that Bohr developed a quarter of a century ago has served as a useful image: nothing more has in fact remained of it. But it has provoked so many *no*'s that it retains an indispensable pedagogical function for any introduction [to nuclear physics]. Those *no*'s have worked together so well that they indeed make up contemporary microphysics. (1978:159f, my transl.)

Bachelard develops his "philosophy of the 'no'" within the context of the history of natural science; but its relevance for our own context of social inquiry and planning is evident. In social inquiry and design just as in natural science, "surrational" or metaphysical structures are an indispensable source for the opening up of rationalism – or, as we have earlier phrased it, for reason's self-transcendence. Only, we are now dealing with *metaphysics of social practice* rather than with metaphysics of nature (therefore my term "quasi-metaphysical," cf. point 3 below; remember also that "metaphysical" for us entails the idea "not logically or empirically justifiable").

The rational structure that needs to be opened up in our case is made up by the a priori systems concepts and judgements underlying the planner's maps and designs; and the "surrational" structures that may effect this opening up are embodied in the concerns and in the "private" rationality standards of the witnesses.

2. C. West Churchman's study *The Systems Approach and Its Enemies* (1979) offers a conceptual framework for elaborating this dialectic of rational and "surrational" structures. Churchman is concerned about the technocratic and elitist character of the rational structure that we call the "systems approach" and that claims for itself comprehensive rationality. The "enemies" of the systems approach are those who do not accept this claim for comprehensive rationality but rather maintain their "private," subjective standards of rationality – political, moral, religious, and aesthetic standards. As I have explained earlier (section 4.2 of Chapter 2), the provocative term "enemy" is meant to connote the irreconcilable conflict between the "rational" systems approach and the "irrational" citizens who are not willing to subject themselves to the standards of "systems rationality." They are in this sense the "deadly enemies," i.e., the dialectical negation, of the systems approach. Precisely for this reason the planner depends upon them in his quest for comprehensive rationality: he cannot claim the comprehensiveness of his "rational" planning effort without opening up his understanding of rationality to the objections of the enemies. Thus a self-critical and dialectical systems approach finds the best possible guarantor of comprehensive rationality in those citizens who contest its claim for such rationality; they are in this respect its friends-enemies. That is to say, *rationality can become comprehensive and practical only if it does not strive to "absorb" its enemies by means of rational argument but instead respects them as indispensable partners in the quest for practical reason.*

This conclusion implies that the "enemies" are to be considered as "competent" participants in a practical discourse *without* requiring them to voice their concerns in the "rational" terms of the systems approach. At the same time, however, this opening up on the part of the systems approach must not be misconstrued as its renouncing the quest for comprehensive or systems rationality; rather, it should be understood as the pursuit of this quest at a higher level of self-reflection. At this higher level of self-reflection, the systems approach recognizes that "no problem can be solved simply on its own basis." (Churchman 1979:5) In the terms of our previous discussion, no conceptual standpoint, however comprehensive it may be, is sufficient to grasp all the consequences of the problems that it is to render intelligible; hence the systems standpoint's own claim to comprehensiveness requires it to break through its own framework.

This then is the important lesson that we can learn from *The Systems Approach and Its Enemies:* a truly rational systems approach must neither make itself the only judge of rationality (by "absorbing" its enemies) nor simply renounce the quest for comprehensive rationality by adopting the viewpoints of the enemies of comprehensive rationality. It must, rather, strive to unfold the conflict between the two sides in such a way that each side, by questioning the rationality of the other, becomes the guarantor of the other's self-reflection and self-transcendence.

3. Finally, there is our earlier, tentative distinction between *"quasi-transcendental"* and *"quasi-metaphysical"* reflection or criticism. When we first envisaged our critically-heuristic turn, I suggested that the only way to keep our quasi-transcendental categories and ideas free of unreflected metaphysical presuppositions was to understand and examine them not only as quasi-transcendental but also as quasi-metaphysical concepts, i.e., as concepts that contain a hermeneutic prejudgement about the social reality to which they are applied (cf. Chapter 2, Section 4.1). In Chapter Six, where we define our own systems paradigm, I shall discuss some of the metaphysical presuppositions underlying critical heuristics. At this point, we are still trying to characterize the role-specific viewpoint and standards of planners and witnesses in terms of the dialectic of a priori vs. a posteriori concepts. To this end, I would like to subsume quasi-transcendental reflection under the planner's tasks, while associating "quasi-metaphysical" reflection with the testimony of the witnesses. We can distinguish the two kinds of critical reflection in the following way.

Since all maps or designs are standpoint-dependent, cogent criticism can take two forms. It can refer either to standpoint-*internal* or to standpoint-*external* standards. *Quasi-transcendental* criticism relies on internal standards. The basic internal standard to which a quasi-transcendental argument refers is the principle of reason, from which we have derived three quasi-transcendental ideas: the systems idea, the moral idea, and the guarantor idea. Accordingly, quasi-transcendental reflection means reflection on the inevitable lack of comprehensiveness in our maps and designs with regard to the underlying whole systems judgements, moral generalizations, and guarantor assumptions. Quasi-transcendental reflection leads the planner critically to transcend his a priori understanding of the planning problem, his value premises, and the guarantors built into his designs.

Quasi-metaphysical criticism, on the other hand, refers to external standards such as the subjective, life-practical experience of the social reality in question on the part of witnesses. The witnesses draw attention to the normative content of social maps and designs "on the side of the conditioned," as it were: they point to the real-world implications of planning such as they appear to the affected who have to *live* them. To the affected, the internal standards of the systems planner appear abstract, his claim for comprehensivenes an insult to their political, moral, religious, or aesthetic convictions. The planner who takes serious his quest for comprehensiveness must face the reality of which the enemies of such comprehensiveness bear witness: "What's really happening in the human world is politics, or morality, or religion, or aesthetics." (Churchman 1979:53) As Hartmann would say, the objections of the witnesses are quasi-metaphysical in that they represent the "metaphysics of problems," i.e., those aspects of the planning situation that resist rational penetration from the systems standpoint of the planner but are nonetheless a very real part of the situation. Or, to use Bachelard's term, we might say that the witnesses provide the necessary *"no's"* that will prevent the *"as if's"* making up the planner's rational structure from becoming the source of an objectivist illusion.

In conclusion, we rely upon the *planner* for quasi-transcendental reflection on the a priori judgements flowing into his maps and designs, for such reflection is in his own interest – he wishes to avoid deception (e.g. implementation failure) and to demonstrate his professional competence. But upon the *witnesses* we have to rely for securing quasi-metaphysical reflection on the normative consequences of "competent" planning – otherwise the rationality of the involved might become the end of planning rather than serving as its means. The participation of the witnesses in the process of unfolding is meaningful only if they are allowed to refer to their own, external standards of criticism and to use them for polemical purposes against the systems planner's internal standards. This is where Kant's concept of the "polemical employment or reason" comes in (cf. Section 3 below).

2.4. The Dialectic of Systems Rationality and Social Rationality

To be reasonable is to conceive of order-systems, real or ideal.
Josiah Royce (1913:107)

Up to this point, we have frequently put the word "rational" in quotation marks. The marks were intended to forestall an objectivist illusion with regard to the normative character of any assertion of rationality. What holds true for concepts such as "problem," "solution," "improvement," etc. is also true for "rationality": one always ought to ask, *whose* rationality?

This is so because of the earlier-discussed, constitutive role of human intentionality for the object domain of social inquiry and design: "rationality," like "improvement," etc., is always relative to the purposefulness of individuals. It is meaningless to speak of the rationality of natural events or natural laws; only human actions, plans, recommendations or other utterances are rational or irrational, i.e., operate logically according to some human standard or goal. Of course, human purposefulness has to take into account the causal laws of nature. But it is essentially grounded in *contexts of meaning* made up of intersubjectively shared values, beliefs, ideals, attitudes, social roles or role expectations, traditions, institutions, world views, etc. It is only in respect to such contexts of meaning that actions can be judged to be rational or irrational.

Our preceding discussion of the idealist-realist dialectic suggests that comprehensive rationality must always consider two dialectically opposed contexts of meaning, the one corresponding to the "idealist" side, the other to the "realist" side of the dialectic. We can now define the two terms "systems rationality" and "social rationality" by associating each with its corresponding context of meaning.

On the idealist side, it is reason's a priori ideas, particularly the systems idea, which furnish the point of reference for asserting the rationality of a map or design; we therefore speak of *systems rationality.* Typically, but not necessarily, it is the involved who are employing the systems point of view to pursue their planning purpose and who therefore claim systems rationality for themselves.

On the realist side, the point of reference is lived social practice, that is, the subjective, especially the democratic and moral acceptability of a map or design to the affected citizens who have to account with their daily lives for the a priori judgements behind "systems rationality." When rationality is asserted in respect to this context of meaning, we speak of *social rationality.*

Systems rationality is an a priori concept of practical reason; social rationality is an a posteriori concept of practical reason. Systems rationality relies on internal standards of criticism which can be employed in monological fashion by systems designers and experts; social rationality considers external standards which can be employed only in intersubjective discourses in which the involved (represented by the planner) face the affected (represented by the witnesses) according to democratic rules of participation. The critical validity of internal standards is justified by reference to the principle of reason; that of external standards, as I shall explain in a moment, by reference to the democratic principle of the sovereignty and equality of all citizens.

Both concepts of rationality may give rise to some objections.

(a) Regarding "systems rationality," does a systems planner who steps outside the scope of rationality defined by his own systems point of view not still remain within the realm of reasonable argumentation? Is it therefore not misleading to equate the systems point of view (or "systems ratonality") with the principle of reason in general? This objection would be quite correct if the systems point of views were to be understood in the scientist sense of funtionalistic "systems science."[11] However, we have defined the systems idea in the critical sense it was given by Kant, namely, as the problematic but unavoidable notion of a totality of relevant conditions – a totality that we cannot possibly *know,* although we can and must nevertheless *think* it. The

[11] Habermas, for instance, uses the term "systems rationality" in this sense when he associates it with the systems-theoretic "paradigm of self-regulated systems" or of "systems maintenance," as opposed to the "communication-theoretic" (or consensus-theoretic) "paradigm of will-forming discourse" underlying his own concept of practical rationality (cf. 1975:139f). In our dialectical framework, monological "systems rationality" (according to Kant's principle of reason) and discursive "social rationality" (according to the democratic principle) are both necessary constituents of practical reason.

critical significance of the systems idea is that it reminds us of the need to reflect on the conditioned character of our maps or designs (boundary judgements!) *according to the principle of reason* (cf. the discussion in Chapter 4, Sections 1.3 & 1.4).

Moreover, not only the systems idea but also the moral idea and the guarantor idea have been derived from the principle of reason. Thus, when we speak of the "systems point of view" or of "systems rationality," we intend the use of all three a priori ideas for critical reflection on the relevant totality of conditions.

It is important, of course, to keep in mind that "systems rationality" is to be understood as an a priori concept of practical reason only; the moral idea in particular has a quasi-transcendental status (and thus can be associated with systems rationality) merely as an a priori idea. As such it has no normative but only critical validity. This is different from its use as an a posteriori concept. As an a posteriori concept, the term "morality" (we do not spek in this sense of the "moral idea") refers to the moral testimony of the witnesses who contest the systems planner's claim for systems rationality because they have to bear its normative consequences. This difference explains why in the preceding discussion we could associate moral reasoning both with reason's (the systems planner's) quest for comprehensiveness and with the "private" rationality of the enemies of such comprehensiveness. The moral point of view has a place both in "systems rationality" and in "social rationality."

(b) Regarding the concept of "social rationality," a parallel objection may be raised: How can one equate "rationality" with "democratic and moral acceptability" any more than one can equate rationality with "the divine authority of kings" or with "the historical inevitability of the dictatorship of the proletariat" or with "the theoretical competence of experts"? It seems to me that there is indeed a big difference. Resuming the previous argument, in a democratic society we have good reasons to regard the democratic principle of majority vote among the concerned citizens as a legitimate concretization of the guarantor idea. Although reason cannot demonstrate a priori the theoretical necessity of the democratic principle, it shows at least the unavoidability of assuming a posteriori *some* guarantor such as God or kings or experts or the people.

More importantly, the democratic principle can be distinguished from all other guarantor assumptions by the closeness of its underlying ideal to the ideal of rational practical discourse. The ideal of democracy is the *identity of rulers and ruled* – "government of the people, by the people, for the people." The ideal of rational practical discourse is the *identity of the involved and the affected* – every affected citizen ought to have access to the discourse by virtue of his affectedness (cf. Habermas' postulate of general accessibility as discussed in Section 2.1 of Chapter 2).[12]

As a practical matter, truly rational planning has to take into account its own inevitable lack of comprehensiveness, that is, its inevitable selectivity and hence its *deficit of legitimation* vis-à-vis the affected. The democratic principle can fill this legitimation gap, for it makes every affected citizen, regardless of his theoretical or communicative competence, a sovereign with equal voting power. Of course this legitimizing function of the democratic principle depends on a functioning public domain, i.e., a public domain that is not controlled by organized special interest groups. As we have seen with Habermas (1962:107), "A public from which definable groups are excluded is not merely incomplete but is no public at all." But the institutionalization of domain-specific, democratically organized, practical discourses among involved planners and affected citizens need not therefore be an entirely utopian idea, as is shown by examples such as neighborhood self-government, workers' self-management, citizens' initiatives, and some cases of direct democracy in Switzerland and other countries. In any "enlightened," i.e., non-totalitarian, society the democratic consensus of affected citizens is a mandatory source of legitimation for "rational" planning *whenever the involved and the affected are not identical.*[13]

12 Of course, there ultimately remains a rationally unverifiable (decisionistic) value judgement in this ideal. We have earlier seen, with Lübbe (1971, 1976, 1978), that there remains a genuinely decisionistic (because political) moment in rational practical discourse. Recognizing this political element serves a *critical* purpose against the on-going undermining of the democratic process by expertise; it need not mean that we fall back into an *uncritical,* Weberian decisionism (cf. Section 2.3 of Chapter 1 on Lübbe's "critical decisionism"). The point is that *any* concept of rationality has a value basis; hence we have no reason to conceal from ourselves that our concept of "social rationality" takes the democratic ideal to be an appropriate value basis. (As to our concept of "systems rationality," its value basis consists in what Habermas [1975:142] calls the "partiality for reason" – the Kantian ideal of the "comprehensive rationality of reason that becomes transparent to itself" [1971a:3].) Admitting this value basis has nothing to do with relegating practical judgements or decisions on ends to an entirely irrational domain of "subjective acts of belief," as do Weber and the critical rationalists. Their decisionism is uncritical because it leads them to *exclude* the subjective from their understanding of rationality, while our own acknowledgment of a value basis, especially in "social rationality," effectively serves to *include* the subjective within our understanding of rationality. It is not at all decisionistic – in the uncritical sense of the term – to acknowledge the inevitable value basis of one's concept of rationality; rather, it would be decisionistic to immunize this value basis against the efforts of practical reason by *not* acknowledging it. In our dialectical systems approach, this necessary effort of practical reason is embodied in the fact that we understand *"rationality" as a process of mediation between systems rationality and social rationality,* which precludes any one-sided association of social rationality with practical reason. Our residual "decisionism" can thus hardly be said to immunize claims to social rationality (on the part of the witnesses) against the critical efforts of reason. Rather, it secures the freedom of the witnesses to question any claims to comprehensive rationality on the part of the involved ("systems rationality"). In Section 3 of the present chapter, we shall operationalize this function of the democratic principle by means of the "polemical employment of reason," and we shall find that the polemical employment of reason on the part of the witnesses is compatible with both democratic participation by the affected *and* cogent, rational, argumentation.

13 The discrepancy between the involved and the affected represents a precise criterion for distinguishing between "private" and "political" (or politically relevant) planning and decision making. For instance, "private" economic activity becomes political when it imposes external affects (e.g. air pollution) upon uninvolved citizens who can evade these effects not as individuals but only collectively (e.g. through citizens' initiatives, organized consumer boycotts, government intervention etc.). On the political relevancy of "private" economic activity and the concept of the political cf. Chamberlain 1973:71.

Similar considerations can be made with respect to "moral acceptability." Just as "democratic acceptability" can be understood as an a posteriori concretization of the a priori guarantor idea of reason, "moral acceptability" can be understood as a necessary counterpart of the moral idea of reason, i.e., of the a priori principle of moral generalization (cf. Section 3 of Chapter 2). The moral idea, since it has a merely quasi-transcendental status, acquires normative validity only through an ethical process (a practical discourse) in which the moral conscience of affected citizens is given a relevant role to play. Unfolding the dialectical relationship between the moral idea of reason and the moral testimony of the witnesses has nothing to do with falling back into an uncritical Weberian decisionism; it does not serve to immunize moral claims on the part of the witnesses ("social rationality") against the critical efforts of reason, but only to render transparent the moral implications of "systems rationality" (cf. note 12 above).

Let us return now to the main argument regarding the dialectic of systems rationality and social rationality. *In the ideal of practical reason, systems rationality and social rationality converge.* An ideal systems map or design, according to the ideal type of *systems rationality,* would make fully transparent its own conditioned character (and thus its normative content) by showing all the a priori systems judgements constitutive of it. In Korzybski's terms: an ideal map would have to include a map of itself.[14] The ideal type of *social rationality,* as we have just seen, would be realized if a democratic decision-making process were actually completely transparent and accessible to all the affected, i.e., if all the affected – including the future generations – were there to vote. The two ideals converge because a systems map or design that makes transparent its normative implications is the best possible basis for a fully transparent process of democratic will-formation.

So much for the ideal. In practice, systems rationality and social rationality do not so easily converge. More often than not they conflict. But perhaps this is to the good: by virtue of their contrariness, the "systems rationality" of the involved and the "social rationality" of the affected prevent each other from succumbing to, or purposely creating, an illusion of comprehensiveness and objectivity. Neither side can claim comprehensive rationality without the approval of the other. In consequence, comprehensive rationality can hardly ever be asserted, which corresponds to the fact that we are dealing with an *ideal* of practical reason – as Habermas formulates it, "the comprehensive rationality of reason that becomes transparent to itself." (1971a:3) But it is in any case more rational to make transparent the inevitable *lack* of comprehensive rationality, and hence the normative content, of any specific concept of rationality – be it a monological or a discursive one – than to maintain a veil of comprehensiveness and objectivity. The opposition of systems rationality and social

---

[14] Because the map-territory relationship obtains at every mapping level, Korzybski's precise statement reads: "An ideal map [of the territory] would contain the map of the map, the map of the map of the map, etc., endlessly. This characteristic was first discovered by Royce [(1913)]. We may call it self-reflexiveness." (Korzybski 1958:751, similarly 58).

rationality is meant to serve this critical purpose: it is of no help for asserting the comprehensive rationality of a proposed action or plan, but it *is* helpful for examining such a claim and for making transparent its normative content. It compells us, in other words, to ask the emancipatory question: *whose* rationality?

The dialectic between the two concepts of rationality can be described in terms of the six earlier-discussed pairs of opposites: a priori vs. a posteriori concepts or judgements, intelligibility vs. reality, standpoint vs. problem, rational vs. surrational structure, systems approach vs. enemies of the systems approach, quasi-transcendental vs. quasi-metaphysical reflection. These pairs of opposites need not be reconsidered here; it will suffice that we associate systems rationality with the a priori side, social rationality with the a posteriori side of the dialectic.

If we were to describe the dialectic between the two concepts of rationality in a single sentence, we might perhaps say that the one (systems rationality) is at its best when the task is to find *rational questions,* i.e., to make intelligible the normative content and potential deceptiveness of social designs, while the other (social rationality) serves an essential critical purpose in *questioning the rational,* i.e., in opening up the given understanding of rationality.

This characterization has the advantage of emphasizing the complementarity of the two rationalities. Less optimistically put, it points to the dangers immanent in any one-sided reliance on either concept of rationality. To conclude this discussion, let us briefly examine two of the dangers in question.

A major trap associated with a systems rationality that remains unchallenged by social rationality is this: as soon as the systems point of view is no longer questioned but taken as the only point of reference for assessing the rationality of a design, the *critically-heuristic purpose of systems thinking* threatens to be perverted into a mere *heuristics of systems purposes.* This means that it is no longer "the system" and the boundary judgements constitutive of it that are considered as the problem; instead, the problems of the system are now investigated (cf. Narr 1972:171). In the terms of our earlier discussion of the dialectic of standpoint and problem, the standpoint is allowed to dictate the problem. The bounded system, instead of being a means for investigating social reality, becomes the reality to be investigated and to be improved as if the underlying boundary judgements were objectively given; accordingly, "rational" is what furthers given systems purposes and secures systems maintenance.

The danger is well illustrated by the wide-spread belief that "open" systems models are more conducive to socially rational designs than are "closed" systems models. "Open," in contrast to "closed," systems models consider the social environment of the system; but so long as the system's own purposes remain the only point of reference, the consideration of environmental factors does nothing to increase the social rationality of a systems design. In fact, if the normative orientation of the system in question is socially irrational, "open" systems planning will merely add to the socially irrational effects of "closed" systems planning. For instance, when applied to the planning of private enterprise, the open systems perspective only increases the private (capital-oriented) rationality of the enterprise by expanding its control over the environmental, societal determinants of its economic success, without regard for the social costs that such control may impose upon third parties.

On the other hand, exclusive reliance on "social rationality" may entail a bottomless ethical relativism. The different social actors who have a stake in a certain planning project are likely to champion different causes that are grounded in conflicting views of the good and just order of society. For the planner who cannot escape the challenge of dealing reasonably with the problem of boundary judgements, the wide-spread cry for a "pluralism of values" is of little help. Pluralism of values is a decisionistic principle, not a principle of reason. Therefore, if "social rationality" is not to immunize moral decisionism (and democratic majority rule) against the efforts of practical reason, the planner needs some heuristic guides and critical standards for problematizing and assessing the "given" pluralism of values. It is at this point that the "unavoidable" ideas of pure reason for which we have made a quasi-transcendental argument become truly indispensable, namely, as a priori ideas that have no assertive but only critical power.

Thus both systems rationality and social rationality, when made the exclusive standard of rationality, tend to subvert the critical purpose of practical discourse; but taken together, they can drive the dialectical process of unfolding the normative content of any "rational" design.

3. The Polemical Employment of Reason

Our discussion up to this point has relied and elaborated on the notion that rationality is a process of mediation between a priori and a posteriori concepts of practical reason, or between systems rationality and social rationality. Such mediation cannot be the exclusive privilege of reason, for the two sides embody the underlying reason-practice dialectic, and reason can hardly be the sole arbiter between itself and practice. Nor can practice be the arbiter between its own concerns and those of reason. It follows that there is no easy way, i.e., no single standard, for mediating between the two sides. There is, in other words, no objective solution to this task of mediation, but at best a critical solution. A critical solution can only aim to unfold the dialectic between the two sides in such a way that each side challenges the other to make transparent its normative presuppositions. Only such value transparency can prevent either side from claiming rationality, objectivity or expertise when in fact it is dogmatic, interest-bound or incompetent.

In this third section we shall try to identify the manner in which reason can be made to contribute to the mediation between itself and practice, namely, through what Kant calls its "polemical" employment. As to practice, it does contribute to the polemical employment of reason by furnishing its (normative) content. Another, more specific contribution concerns the problem of a "stopping rule" for the process of unfolding: when should the discourse *on* practice stop and practice itself begin? In the concluding comment to this chapter (Section 4), I shall briefly argue that there is no epistemological (or heuristic) but only an institutional solution to this problem.

3.1. The Conflicting Demands of Cogent Argumentation and Consensus

We have thus far associated reason mainly with the planner's quest for comprehensiveness, or for systems rationality. Systems rationality depends upon critical (quasi-transcendental) reflection on the sources of deception contained in the inevitable *lack* of comprehensiveness of any systems map or design, given the necessity of a priori boundary judgements. Such reflection requires the capability to think and argue cogently according to the principle of reason, a capability that we can expect from the planner but that we do not want to prerequire from the witnesses. (We have therefore associated the witnesses with quasi-metaphysical rather than quasi-transcendental reflection.) It would not be a good idea, however, to leave such self-reflection entirely to the planner. Not only is he human and thus subject to error, but he is also under the pressure of the interest groups that pay him or on which his professional ambitions may depend, quite apart from the fact that he has his own world-views and values. We need therefore to rely on the witnesses, as the representatives of the affected, for making certain that the normative content of the planner's maps and designs is brought to light.

It is easy to say that the planners have to confront the witnesses in a practical discourse, but it is less easy to show how an eventual consensus between the two sides can be distinguished as "rational" or "true" from merely factual consensus. The difficulty originates in the conflicting demands of cogent argumentation and democratic participation: cogent argumentation requires knowledge and a certain ability of abstraction, while democratic participation demands that every affected citizen has equal access and influence regardless of whether or not he has expertise and is capable of quasi-transcendental reflection.

The contemporary discourse models (of Popper, Lorenzen and Habermas) are quite correct in assuming that the validation of practical propositions is not a matter of demonstrating their logical or theoretical *necessity,* as Kant still thought, but rather a matter of pragmatic *cogency,* i.e., cogent argumentation at a pragmatic level of speech. But they remain close to Kant's monological approach in that they first make the speaker's "rational attitude" or "communicative competence" a prerequirement of cogent argumentation and then proceed to make cogent argumentation the guarantor of rational consensus. It is quite obvious that these models do not succeed in mediating between the two conflicting demands of cogent argumentation and (democratic) consensus; because they admit to the discourse only "competent" speakers, they are inherently elitist and non-democratic.[15]

The challenge for us is thus to find a criterion of cogent argumentation or criticism (on the part of the witnesses) that does not depend on any kind of special competence except such use of reason and information as is attainable by every adult citizen. Since we are searching for a *critical* solution to the problem of practical discourse only, such a criterion need not serve to validate the empirical and/or normative content of practical propositions but only to prevent an objectivist illusion in dealing with such validity claims.

We have seen that every map or design depends on a set of boundary judgements which, because they are relatively a priori rather than empirical, and synthetic rather than merely analytic, admit of no objective justification. The obvious danger is that the involved planners and experts, trying to defend their maps or designs against the objections of the witnesses, will not stress this fact but will instead emphasize "objective necessities" such as factual (e.g. technical, legal or institutional) constraints, empirical evidence, common sense, and their own professional competence and credibility. Implicitly they will thus tend to employ the boundary judgements in question *dogmatically* rather than critically.

---

[15] For somewhat different reasons, Höffe (1979:262) also concludes that the two demands of cogent argumentation and consensus conflict in Habermas' model. He argues that consensus is a historical, situation-dependent event that is partly dependent on non-argumentative and in that sense non-rational elements, whereas argumentation means to free the recognition of validity claims from such contingencies as manipulation, deception, power etc. In his view, Habermas takes the demands of argumentation so seriously that there remains no room for genuine processes of consensus-formation.

Such dogmatic assertion of the "objectivity" or "rationality" of presupposed boundary judgements is of course incompatible with a critical solution to the problem of practical discourse. Against this danger, we must strengthen the case of the witnesses and give them an instrument to "discipline" the employment of boundary judgements on the part of the involved.

I believe that Kant offers us such an instrument in a chapter of the much-neglected last main part of the *Critique of Pure Reason,* the "Transcendental Doctrine of Method." The chapter is entitled, significantly, "The Discipline of Pure Reason" (B 737–822), and the instrument of discipline proposed by Kant is what he calls "the polemical employment of pure reason" (B 767ff). I intend to show that Kant's concept of the polemical employment of reason yields a criterion of cogent criticism that does not rely on any kind of special "competence" and hence can serve a mediating function between reason (with its demand for cogent argumentation) and democratic social practice (the demand for participation and consensus). But let us follow Kant.

3.2. The Need for a "Discipline of Pure Reason"

Both terms, "discipline" and "polemic," today as in Kant's time, raise strongly negative associations. Kant therefore begins his account with the following words:

> Owing to the general desire for knowledge, negative judgements, that is those which are such not merely as regards their form but also their content, are not held in any very high esteem. They are regarded rather as the jealous enemies of our unceasing endeavor to extend our knowledge, and it almost requires an apology to win for them even tolerance, not to say favor and high repute. (B 736f)

And with regard to the notion that reason needs to be disciplined, he concedes:

> That reason, whose proper duty is to prescribe a discipline for all other endeavors, should itself stand in need of such discipline may indeed seem strange. (B 738)

Kant explains his claim:

> But where the limits of our possible knowledge are very narrow, where the temptation to judge is great, where the illusion that besets us is very deceptive and the harm that results from the error is considerable, there the *negative* instruction, which serves solely to guard us from errors, has even more importance than many a piece of positive information by which our knowledge is increased. (B 737)

Kant is thinking of the illusion that is caused by the transcendent employment of reason, as a subsequent passage makes clear:

Where neither empirical nor pure intuition keeps reason to a visible track, when, that is to say, reason is being considered in its transcendental [here = transcendent] employment, in accordance with mere concepts, it stands so greatly in need of a discipline, to restrain its tendency towards extension beyond the narrow limits of possible experience and to guard it against extravagance and error, that the whole philosophy of pure reason has no other than this strictly negative utility. (B 739f)

Now we are not concerned, in critical heuristics, about the transcendent employment of absolute a priori concepts such as "God" or "soul" but rather about the dogmatic assertion of the objectivity or rationality of boundary judgements on the part of systems designers or experts. The two cases are, however, analogous: the transcendent employment of absolute a priori concepts is impermissible because it amounts to dogmatism – it depends on synthetic a priori judgements that cannot be justified either logically or empirically, just as is the case with the planner's boundary judgements. Both kinds of judgements admit only of a critical employment in which their *"as if"* character and their normative implications are made transparent, otherwise their use is dogmatic.

This close parallel explains why Kant's description of the circumstances so strikingly applies to the planning situation: "The limits of our possible knowledge are very narrow" – for the planner is concerned with a normative task of determining complex social reality rather than describing a given universe of "facts." "The temptation to judge is great" – there is no way to circumvent the need for boundary judgements prior to mapping and designing social reality, and the temptation is great, of course, for the involved to judge according to their own criteria and to make these criteria seem more objective than they are, rather than to problematize them publicly. For instance, they might tend to determine the boundaries so as to facilitate the mapping task (according to the availability of data and tools), to serve their interests while imposing the costs on third parties, to avoid political opposition or to accomodate institutional "givens," to enhance their own status as experts, etc. "The illusion that besets us is very deceptive" – it is hard indeed for the uninvolved citizens to see through the objective appearance of the involved, who usually have an advantage of information and can display an impressive array of "scientific" statistics, computer charts, modelling techniques, expert opinions, etc. to support their claims. And finally, "the harm that results from the error [from this objectivist illusion] is considerable" – social and economic costs may be imposed on the uninvolved, ecological costs and risks transferred to future generations, the democratic process is undermined, and citizens who ought to belong to the planning client my be used as mere means for the purposes of others.

Let us see, then, what we can learn from Kant about the critical power and the validity of the polemical employment of reason.

3.3. The Polemical Employment of Boundary Judgements

Here is Kant's definition of the polemical employment of (pure) reason:

> By the polemical employment of pure reason I mean the defense of its propositions as against the dogmatic counterpositions through which they are denied. (B 767)

It is important for our purposes not to misread this definition. The dogmatic counterpositions that deny reason are in our case *not* the "irrational" objections of the witnesses against the "objective necessities" disclosed by the experts in the name of reason; they are, rather, the dogmatically asserted boundary judgements underlying the expert's validity claims. Those who defend the rightful claims of reason are in this case the witnesses, even though they are concerned with their own "private" rationality rather than with reason's quest for comprehensiveness.

The point I wish to make is this. The witnesses, if only they understand the power of the polemical employment of reason, can expose the dogmatic character of the expert's "objective necessities" *through their own subjective arguments,* without even having to pretend to be "objective" or to be able to establish a true counterposition against the expert's "objective necessity." Therein, I believe, lies the enormous significance of Kant's concept of the polemical employment of reason for a non-objectivist approach to rational planning, an approach that would actually mediate between the conflicting demands of reason (cogent argumentation) and those of democratic social practice (consensus).

The crucial point in Kant's polemical employment of reason is that it entails no positive validity claims and hence requires neither theoretical knowledge nor any other kind of special expertise or "competence." A polemical argument is advanced merely in hypothetical fashion, to show the dogmatic character of the opponent's (the "expert's") pretension of knowledge. For this merely critical purpose, it is quite unnecessary to prove or even to pretend that a polemical statement may not be false or merely subjective. What matters is only that no one can demonstrate the objective impossibility (and hence, irrelevance) of a polemical statement any more than its proponent can demonstrate its objective necessity (cf. B 767f). It is easy to see where this requirement is fulfilled with absolute certainty: in the case of all judgements that cannot be validated or falsified either logically or empirically. Both the absolute a priori judgements of reason with which Kant is concerned and the relative a priori judgements with which we are dealing in critical heuristics correspond to this criterion.

> As reason is incompetent to arrive at affirmative assertions in this field [of a priori judgements], it is equally unable, indeed even less able, to establish any negative conclusions in regard to these questions. (B 781)

Once again, then, the relatively a priori boundary judgements that we have found to be constitutive of social maps and designs provide the key for applying a piece of

Kantian a priori science to the realm of social planning. Kant's formula of "the polemical employment of pure *reason*" thus means for us *the polemical employment of boundary judgements.*

When an expert, by reference to his theoretical knowledge, defines "the problem" at hand or determines "the solution," he must always presuppose such boundary judgements. To define the problem means, in fact, to map the social reality (or the social system) to be dealt with; to determine the solution means to design a better social reality (or social system). And since every map or design depends on previous boundary judgements (or whole systems judgements) as to what is to be included in it and what is to belong to its environment, it is clear that no definition of "the problem" or "the solution" can be objectively justified by reference to theoretical knowledge. It can only be critically justified by reference to both the transparency of values and the consent of all the affected citizens.

The first implication is trivial: *no amount of expertise (theoretical knowledge) is ever sufficient for the expert to justify all the judgements on which his recommendations depend.* When the discussion turns to the basic boundary judgements on which his exercise of expertise depends, the expert is no less a layman than are the affected citizens.[16]

The second implication is less trivial, in that it seems to contradict common sense: *no expertise or theoretical knowledge is required to comprehend and to demonstrate that this is so.* The necessity of boundary judgements can be intuitively grasped by every layman: since no one can include "everything" in his maps or designs, he cannot help presupposing some boundaries. It is equally understandable to every citizen that such boundary judgements depend on values or interests rather than on theoretical knowledge alone, and that no amount of expertise but only the consent of the affected citizens can justify the practical consequences of the expert's value judgements. Finally, at least some of the twelve kinds of boundary judgements the heuristic necessity of which we have earlier established (cf. *Table 4/4*) appear immediately plausible to common sense; I think of the boundary judgements concerning the categories of client, purpose, decision maker, components vs. environment, and witnesses. (The other categories can be popularized, e.g., "measure of improvement" can often be read as "quality of life.") Anybody who is able to comprehend the

---

[16] I find an interesting addition to this conclusion in Paul Feyerabend's new introduction to the revised German version of *Science in a Free Society* (1980:20). He observes that experts are often quite unable to justify routine procedures and routine arguments on which their claim for rationality depends; in discussing the assumptions underlying these procedures, they are indeed laymen. Our concept of boundary judgements suggests one possible explanation: the expert's routine procedures and arguments embody the basic boundary judgements by means of which problems are bounded in such a way that they fit his domain of competence. What falls outside this domain is relegated to an "irrelevant" or "irrational" ("merely subjective") status. The subjective, indeed dogmatic, character of such boundary judgements is then concealed behind a facade of routine procedures and professional authority ("all experts agree that this is the way to do it," or "we dont't know any other way to do it").

meaning of these specific boundary judgements is also able to see through the dogmatic character of the expert's "objective necessities" with respect to these same categories. He can then easily expose such dogmatism by hypothetically asserting the validity of an alternative boundary judgement, confident that no amount of expertise can either defend the objective validity of the expert's boundary judgement or else demonstrate the objective invalidity of his own.

Perhaps we should consider an example. Let us assume, for instance, that a nuclear power station is planned and that this project meets with the resistance of local citizens. At a certain stage of the complex decision-making process, the responsible government agencies, under pressure from both proponents and opponents of the project, announce that the decision for or against a construction permit will depend on whether or not the involved public utility company can establish the factual necessity of additional energy production. A public hearing is scheduled at which the experts of the utility company ("planners") confront the representatives of the concerned citizens ("witnesses"). The experts display an impressive array of statistics and computer charts demonstrating the ever-increasing consumption of electrical energy in the affected community. By means of some statistical extrapolation technique, they project the demand for the years ahead and compare it to the projected energy production without the power plant under consideration. They thus establish their definition of the problem: there will be a gap between "is" and "ought," and since it is the task of a public utility to produce the energy demanded by the public, they conclude that there is an objective necessity to construct the nuclear power plant.

One need not be an energy expert to expose the dogmatic character of such an account of the planning problem. It suffices that we understand the a priori character of the implied client judgement, for instance, to make a cogent argument against the experts' claim. Any layman can ask himself what is really the client group served by the experts' definition of the problem, i.e., who is likely to benefit and what kind of costs will be imposed on the community. He might begin by realizing that a public utility is really a private company and hence is its own surrogate client (its actions are dictated by the needs of capital realization, not by those of the local community). Next he might conjecture that this surrogate client secures its economic success by collaborating with other surrogate clients such as the producers of nuclear equipment or local industries that depend on additional energy for increased rationalization of their production. This conjecture would point to the fact that the lion's share of the economic benefits of the plant will be exported out of the affected community to those communities where the involved corporations have their headquarters, while the lion's share of social and ecological costs will be imposed on the local community (e.g. in the form of higher utility rates, fewer local jobs, long-term health risks, lower property values, etc.). And so on. We need not pursue this chain of common-sense reasoning to see that any of these considerations can serve as the inspiration for a cogent, though merely polemical, counterargument against the experts' "objective necessity."

Here are some examples of polemical boundary judgements on the part of the witnesses:

(1) "Your account of the problem is not objective – you tell us that we, the public, are going to benefit, while in fact we are going to pay the bill for private interests. Your true client is corporation X and community Y rather than our community."

(2) Or: "Your prime client is outside our community. If you discount the energy consumed for the benefit of outside interests, our community needs no additional power plant."

(3) Or: "If we are to be the client, as you proclaim, we shall be better served by less, not more, central energy production, that is, by promoting energy conservation and conversion to decentralized solar energy installations." Etc.

The witnesses cannot of course establish the validity of their boundary judgements any more objectively than the experts can justify theirs. But what matters is only that the normative basis of the experts' "objective necessity" of an additional power plant becomes apparent. The experts, of course, will be quick to point out that the objections of the opponents are "merely subjective" or "ideologically motivated" and that they are incompatible with the "facts." But such a reply, justified as it may be, does nothing to prove that the experts' "facts" and "objective necessities" are any less subjective than those of the witnesses. The witnesses can reply with the same right that no amount of "facts" or "expertise" can justify the experts' claims to present an objective account of the problem. Once it has become transparent that defining the problem is at bottom a subjective political act, the experts indeed disqualify themselves by their own claim for objectivity.

If the above example appears trivial to the reader, it should. *Polemical arguments need not demonstrate the sophistication of the speaker but only the embarrassment of his opponent.* Such embarrassment is created when it becomes plain that the expert is unable to justify *within* the bounds of his theoretical knowledge the basic premises of his maps and designs, premises such as the planning purpose and the client to be served. Polemical argumentation is not required to produce any knowledge, its importance lies in its ability to initiate a *process of dis-illusionment* in the course of which the affected citizens emancipate themselves from the premises and promises of the involved experts.

How can planning produce "solutions" if "problems" remain unquestioned? The "problem" predetermines all the a priori whole systems judgements on which the normative content of the "solution" will depend. *Experts may be able to contribute to the task of anticipating the practical consequences of alternative boundary judgements; but they cannot delegate to themselves the political act of sanctioning the normative content of these consequences.* A truly rational *and* truly democratic planning process must therefore start with a practical discourse among the involved and the affected *in which the "problem" itself is the problem,* and in such a discourse the witnesses who represent the affected must not be required to submit to the rationality standards of the involved but must be entitled to argue polemically.

308

Let us *summarize* our conclusions. Our task in this section was to provide the witnesses with a tool for confronting the planner's advantage of information and expertise, so that they can "discipline" the planner's use of boundary judgements. Since the latter represent a priori whole systems judgements, we can reformulate our solution thus: *A critical employment of the systems concept is possible without the critic's knowing everything about the system in question.* All that counts is that the critic can demonstrate to the systems designer or to the expert that the latter's theoretical knowledge is insufficient to claim objectivity or systems rationality for his definition of the problem-relevant system. Such a demonstration is always possible with respect to the whole systems judgements presupposed in any systems map or design, for those judgements cannot be justified or falsified by reference to experience (to the theoretical knowledge of the expert).

The importance of such a polemical employment of reason (of boundary judgements) is twofold:

1. It is accessible to every affected citizen and to the witnesses representing him vis-à-vis the involved. It gives him an advantage over the experts, as it were, so long as he uses it for critical purposes only. (It would give him no advantage over the expert if he wanted to claim to *know* better than the expert.) Kant has given an excellent description of this practical advantage of merely polemical argument (I shall make bracketed insertions in order to show the relevance of Kant's account for the witnesses):

> Reason has, in respect of its *practical employment* [by the witnesses], the right to postulate what in the field of mere speculation it can have no kind of right to assume without sufficient proof.... In the practical sphere reason has rights of possession [boundary hypotheses], of which it does not require to offer proof, and of which, in fact, it could not supply proof. The burden of proof accordingly rests upon the opponent [the planner].... For he [the witness] is at liberty to employ, as it were in self-defense, on behalf of his own good cause, the very same weapons that his opponent employs against that cause, that is, hypotheses [boundary judgements]. These are not intended to strengthen the proof of his position, but only to show that the opposing party has much too little understanding of the matter in dispute to allow of his flattering himself that he has the advantage in respect to speculative insight [expertise]. (B 804f)

We have earlier pointed to the conflict between reason's demand for cogent argumentation (according to the principle of reason) and the practical demand for consensus (according to the democratic principle). We can now conclude that the polemical employment of reason meets the second demand. It is *inherently democratic* because its critical power does not depend on any theoretical knowledge beyond common sense. Thus it helps the citizen to emancipate himself from the experts who by their "objective necessities" undermine his democratic status as sovereign.

2. The polemical employment of boundary judgements also meets the demand for *cogent argumentation.* Boundary judgements can never be demonstrated to be objectively (theoretically) necessary; it is precisely for this reason that the polemical employment of boundary judgements *against* dogmatic claims for their necessity is always cogent. "The burden of proof accordingly rests upon the opponent." (B 805)

We have thus indeed found a criterion of cogent argument (or more precisely, cogent criticism) that does *not* depend on "competence"; there is no need to require the witnesses to meet the rationality standards of the involved.

In addition, the polemical employment of boundary judgements even enables the witnesses to demonstrate cogently to the planner why *his* rationality cannot invalidate *theirs:* namely, because no rational argument can ever prove the objective necessity of any boundary judgement. That, I think, is what C. West Churchman means when he thus characterizes the "strategy of the enemies" (of the systems approach): "[They] use reason to show why reason can't absorb them." (1979:116)

We can thus conclude that the polemical employment of boundary judgements, because it is both cogent as well as democratic, is an important force of mediation between the two demands and thus between the two sides of the underlying reason-practice dialectic. It can advance the unfolding process toward both systems rationality and social rationality: it makes "the system," i.e., the planner's presupposed boundary judgements and his corresponding definition of the "problem," the problem of all the concerned citizens (social rationality), and it thereby also makes the systems planner reflect on the conditioned nature of his assertion of systems rationality. Kant, to give him the last word, captures both demands, that of democracy and that of reason, in his beautiful formula of the *veto of free citizens* to which reason must always subject itself:

> Reason must in all its undertakings subject itself to criticism; should it limit freedom of criticism by any prohibitions, it must harm itself, drawing upon itself a damaging suspicion. Nothing is so important for its usefulness, nothing so sacred, that it may be exempted from this searching examination, which knows no respect for persons. Reason depends on this freedom for its very existence. For reason has no dictatorial authority; its verdict is always simply the agreement of free citizens, of whom each one must be permitted to express, without let or hindrance, his objections or even his veto. (B 766f)

310

4. Concluding Comment: The Institutional Challenge

In the present chapter we have tried to achieve the basic goal that we set ourselves when we first envisaged our "dialectical turn." This goal was to give "rational" discourse an access to the historical and normative social reality that it cannot produce out of itself and without which it remains not only unpractical but empty (cf. Section 4.2 of Chapter 2). Let us briefly recall some of our earlier premises and compare them with our results.

1. If practical discourse is to become a practical reality, I suggested, we must look for a discourse model that gives the individuality of both the involved and the affected a relevant role to play (rather than require them to transcend their subjectivity and to become "ideal speakers" according to such criteria as "communicative competence" or "rational attitude").
2. Since a consensus is always a consensus *about* something, we conjectured that a consensus theory of truth cannot obliterate but only redefine the question of the "correspondence" between the consensus and the real world of social practice.
3. Neither Popper's nor Habermas' model of rational practical discourse appeared capable of playing the role of a mediating force between reason and practice, for we found that both are themselves located entirely within the boundaries of reason. But such mediation is the very crux of the problem of practical reason: How can reason become practicable, and practice reasonable?
4. We also quoted the negative conclusion that Kant draws from his monological approach to the problem of practical reason:

   How can reason, without other motives taken from elsewhere, be practical by itself? That is, how can the mere principle of the universal validity of all its maxims... provide a motive for itself without any material (object) of the will in which one might take a prior interest?... In other words, *how can pure reason be practical?* All of human reason is entirely incapable of explaining this, and all effort and labor to find an explanation of it is in vain. (GMS:B 124f, italics partly omitted)

5. In a democracy, we said, we cannot exclude citizens from exercising their status as sovereign and expert in political matters solely because they are not willing or able to argue their case "rationally." Even if we do not presuppose the democratic idea, the requirement of communicative competence subverts the purpose of practical discourse: it *presupposes* rationality (or a rational stance) instead of producing it. The only rational stance that represents an absolute presupposition of the quest for practical reason, I argued, is this: everybody who is potentially affected by the outcome of a practical discourse must be admitted to the discourse and considered competent by virtue of his affectedness.

6. Since it is rarely the case that all the affected can actually become involved, we added the following conclusion: the involved are fully rational and competent only to the extent that they place themselves into the "irrational" positions of those who cannot argue their concerns rationally.
7. Our last premise that I would like to recall here was this: in the interdependency of systems-oriented planner and citizens who contest the alleged systems rationality of his maps or designs, a dialectical systems approach finds the best possible guarantor of socially-rational planning.

All of these premises stated in Chapter Two suggested the importance of unfolding the underlying reason-practice dialectic. We undertook this task in the second section of the present chapter. Let us now briefly examine the question: To what extent does our concept of the polemical employment of boundary judgements, as proposed in Section 3 of this chapter, answer to our original premises? To what extent can it actually mediate between reason and practice so as to make reason practicable, and practice reasonable?

1. Regarding the first premise, the polemical employment of boundary judgements does indeed give a relevant role to the individuality of the affected; for it offers them a way to argue their case cogently without having to pretend to be objective.
2. Considering the second premise, the question of how the validity of some practical propositions can be positively asserted remains unanswered; the polemical employment of reason serves only a critical but not an assertive purpose.
3. With respect to the third premise, the polemical employment of boundary judgements does indeed mediate between the demands of reason and those of democratic social practice; it is compatible with both cogent argumentation and democratic participation. Thus it helps to make reason practicable, and practice reasonable.
4. As regards Kant's attempt to make the a priori principles or "maxims" of pure reason (i.e., synthetic a priori judgements) the ground of validity for practical propositions, we do not follow him. The polemical employment of boundary judgements serves to expose the dogmatic nature of any validity claims that are based on a priori judgements, it does not serve to establish such claims.
5. Regarding the fifth premise, the polemical employment of boundary judgements draws its power from the fact that experts are no less laymen than the affected citizens when it comes to the basic normative presuppositions of their work. Disputes about boundary judgements are disputes among laymen, no special competence beyond common sense is required.
6. In respect to the sixth premise, the polemical employment of boundary judgements on the part of the witnesses does indeed incite the involved to place themselves in the "irrational" positions of those who cannot argue their concerns "rationally."

How else could the planner hope to show himself able to counter the objections of the witnesses, and to anticipate future objections?

7. Finally, with regard to the seventh premise, the polemical employment of boundary judgements in fact enables the witnesses to play the guarantor role, for it enables him to question the systems rationality of the planner without knowing everything about the systems in question, simply by questioning the underlying whole systems judgements.

Taken together, it appears that the polemical employment of boundary judgements really constitutes a major step toward the unfolding and critical resolution of the reason-practice dialectic. Only the second premise, regarding the need for a non-objectivistic "correspondence" theory of truth, remains unfulfilled. It is easy to see why: according to our own premise, there can be not objective (theoretical) but only a critical solution to the problem of justifying practical propositions. A critical solution assures us that the involved will make transparent to themselves and to the affected the normative presuppositions and consequences of their validity claims; it prevents the experts from withdrawing such claims from public discussion, and it gives the affected an effective tool for reopening the discussion when it has been dogmatically stopped by the experts. But it does not provide a *stopping rule,* that is, a criterion for deciding when the discussion *on* practice ought to stop and action should begin. In other words, a critical solution can guard us against the ever-present danger of an objectivist illusion; but it cannot secure actual consensus. There is no epistemological (or heuristic) but only an *institutional* answer to the question of the stopping rule: only the institutionalization of domain-specific, participatory decision-making processes can guarantee that discussion about disputed practical propositions stops and practice begins. All that an epistemological and heuristic study such as the present one can contribute to this institutional challenge is to show *that* the democratic participation of affected citizens need not be an obstacle to rational planning and decision making but is actually an indispensable part of it, and to show *how* the demands of cogent argumentation and democratic participation can be made compatible.

Regarding the task of institutionalization, there are basically only two alternatives: institutional arrangements can be elitist (an elite decides on behalf of all others) or they can be democratic (all the affected vote according to democratic majority rule, regardless of "expertise" and "competence"). If we do not want to rely on the elitist alternative, we need a normative conception of planned (or self-planning) democracy as basis. It cannot of course be the task of the present study to develop an adequate theory of planned democracy. The established political and administrative sciences have not as yet accomplished this task, perhaps because they one-sidedly conceive of planning and administrative processes in terms of the involved (as for instance the German political scientist Fritz W. Scharpf conceded, cf. 1973:34, note 8). Perhaps this task too is mainly a practical one for which there is no theoretical solution. There is now a growing awareness among citizens everywhere in the United States and in other countries that they have to take into their own hands the issues that were formerly believed to be the exclusive province of government and expertise (cf. the environmental movement, the holistic health movement, the anti-nuclear movement, the industrial democracy movement, etc.); ideas such as grassroots democracy and citizens' initiatives, decentralization of government, community self-planning, neighborhood self-sufficiency and workers' self-management are gaining ground.[17] Our conception of rational practical discourse as a process of unfolding the dialectic of reason and practice anticipates this growing movement, but it cannot replace it.

Practical philosophy almost by definition must remain incomplete so as to make room for actual practice: the question is only whether it makes room for a democratic practice in which citizens together with experts resolve their conflicts through processes of mutual learning (and mutual disillusionment) according to institutionalized rules of discourse and majority vote, or whether it makes room for a practice in which conflicts are decided by resort to power and deception.

The present chapter cannot claim to furnish a complete "model" of practical discourse; but at least it can claim to leave room for the practice of democracy, and for the practice of critical reason by democratically minded citizens.

---

[17] As my examples should make sufficiently clear, I am not advocating a reprivatization of issues that have become government controlled because of their political relevance. The citizens' movements of which I speak *are* examples of public control over politically relevant affairs. The point is that government and administrative planning is all too often controlled by special, i.e., private, interests (cf. on this point Offe's theory of governmental selectivity, 1972:Ch. 3, and Galbraith's concept of a necessary "emancipation of the state" from private interests, 1975:Ch. 24). Thus, Henrik Blum is quite justified in observing, approvingly, that (for instance)

> health care is moving into the public sector because the parties to what once was purely a private transaction could find no way to deal happily with one another.... Decision making as a private matter is now further giving way to the public arena. (1974:496)

It is because the public arena is not identical with the government or with administrative planning that citizens have to take back into their own hands politically relevant affairs such as health planning, environmental design, urban renewal, energy planning, and many other issues that have increasingly become the exclusive province of government. Grassroots democracy is certainly not a universal remedy for the selectivity and other inadequacies of government-controlled administrative planning; but in a dialectical framework such as ours, it is an important source of emancipatory self-reflection on the part of affected citizens, and it thus contributes to the necessary emancipation of politically relevant planning from special interests in control of government and expertise.

Part III
Application

Chapter Six
Toward a "Purposeful Systems" Paradigm of Planning

If the only tool you have is a hammer, you tend to treat everything as if it were a nail.
Abraham H. Maslow (1969)

Introduction

If the only systems concept we have is a mechanistic one, we tend to treat everything as if it were a machine. Similarly, if biology furnishes the root metaphor in terms of which we conceive of systems, we tend to regard social systems as if they were biological organisms.

The concept of "root metaphors" has been suggested by Stephen C. Pepper in his book *World Hypotheses* (1942:84ff). He uses it to designate those basic analogies, taken from common-sense experience, the structural characteristics of which furnish the paradigms for describing and explaining the complex real world. "Concepts which have lost contact with their root metaphors are empty abstractions." (Pepper 1942:123) The systems concept remains an empty abstraction so long as it is not linked to some root metaphor such as the machine (classical cybernetic systems concept), the biological organism (contemporary cybernetic and ecological systems concept), the social group (sociological systems concept), or the historical event (hermeneutic systems concept).

The question is not whether we should rely on such common-sense metaphors; the question is whether we do so critically. Let us recall one of the conclusions of Chapter One: criticism without metaphysics is blind just as metaphysics without criticism is empty. This is why we must begin the present chapter, in which we want to formulate an application-oriented, normative paradigm of planning, with metaphysical considerations. The reader who has followed me up to this point may be assured, however, that the present chapter is concerned solely in *practicing* the critically-heuristic approach for which we have laid the epistemological foundations in Parts I and II. The task, quite simply, is to offer the planner an openly normative systems paradigm so that he need not fall back on the seemingly value-free, mechanistic and organicist paradigms of contemporary systems science.

In the first section of the chapter, we shall highlight some of the metaphysical implications of the mechanistic paradigm, of which systems scientist Herbert A. Simon is a leading advocate. In the second section, we shall examine some of the pitfalls of the "organic" systems paradigm of contemporary cybernetics, represented by Stafford Beer's work. In critical distinction to the "organic" paradigm, I shall introduce a list of central assumptions on which our own, "purposeful systems" paradigm is to rely. In the third and final section, we can then define the concept of a purposeful system and briefly consider some of the viewpoints it suggests for the design and assessment of social systems. Since the application of our conceptual framework will be illustrated – at least insofar as the a priori of experience is concerned – in the case studies of Chapters Seven and Eight, our discussion of the purposeful systems paradigm will be rather brief.

1. The Metaphysics of Design

The task of our generation, I have no doubt, is one of meta-physical reconstruction.... We are suffering from a meta-physical disease, and the cure must therefore be metaphysical.

E. F. Schumacher (1975:101)

At least since the Apollo Project of NASA, the systems concept has been associated by the public with the management of complex decision-making and planning processes. It has hardly been noticed, however, that the systems concept presupposes a metaphysical preconception of the nature of "complexity." Without some previous understanding of the nature of complex social reality, the systems concept cannot help us to comprehend and manage this reality.

Systems scientist Herbert A. Simon was awarded the 1978 Nobel prize for his contribution to the understanding and management of complex decision-making processes in social systems (see esp. Simon 1945, 1957, 1960, 1962, 1969; also Newell/Shaw/Simon 1958, 1966; Newell/Simon 1972). Especially in his paper on "The Architecture of Complexity" (1962), Simon has given its most elegant formulation to the model of complexity that underlies contemporary management and planning thought. But the elegance of the formulation is not necessarily a guarantee of the validity of the content. Let us therefore take the first Nobel award for systems science as providing us with an opportunity to reflect on the metaphysical content of the prevailing systems concept. In what way is its underlying model of complexity a source of hidden value content and/or practical irrelevance of contemporary management and planning theories?

A fictitious debate between Herbert A. Simon and another outstanding philosopher of systems management, C. West Churchman, may help us to reflect on the metaphysical content of Simon's systems concept. At the same time, this "debate" will serve to clarify some basic metaphysical presuppositions of our own conception of social systems design, a conception that is close to Churchman's philosophy of social systems design.[1]

Before entering into the debate, let us briefly introduce the two debaters and their views of complexity. The two standpoints represented in our debate can be labelled by the titles to two of their works: Churchman's *The Design of Inquiring Systems* (1971) and Simon's "The Architecture of Complexity." Two labels also used by the authors are "(The Philosophy of) Social Systems Design" (Churchman 1979) and *The Sciences of the Artificial* (Simon 1969).

[1] Earlier versions of the following discussion have been published in the Swiss journal *Die Unternehmung* (1979) and in the TIMS/ORSA journal *Interfaces* (1980). Both Professor C. West Churchman and Professor Herbert A. Simon have kindly agreed to the publication of the fictitious "debate" between them.

Simon (1962:468) calls a system "complex" when "the whole is more than the sum of the parts, not in an ultimate, metaphysical sense, but in the important pragmatic sense that, given the properties of the parts and the laws of their interaction, it is not a trivial matter to infer the properties of the whole." This "pragmatic" definition is, however, ambiguous with respect to its metaphysical content. From what has been said above it is clear that Simon cannot avoid a metaphysical prejudgement in applying his systems concept. At a closer look one finds indeed in Simon's writings assertions that betray the metaphysical content of his seemingly metaphysics-free, if not antimetaphysical, systems concept. A good example is his reliance on "in-principle reductionism": "In the face of complexity, an in-principle reductionist may be at the same time a pragmatic holist." (1962:468) It is obvious that even a pragmatically disguised reductionism will determine the ways in which a planner tries to understand and master complex real-world problems.

By *complexity* we therefore have to understand not so much a "given" attribute of a particular system but rather an individual strategy for dealing with ill-structured problems. That is to say, a model of complexity is nothing other than an inquirer's way of confronting a lack of knowledge – the lack of empirical or logical decidability that is characteristic of all metaphysical assumptions.

Such a concept of complexity is of course quite different from the definition offered by the *Oxford English Dictionary:*

complex, a. (f. *com-* together + *plexus* plaited...)
1. Consisting of or comprehending various parts united or connected together; formed by combination of different elements; composite, compound. Said of things, ideas, etc. (Opposed to *simple,* both here and in sense 2.)
2. *esp.* Consisting of parts or elements not simply co-ordinated, but some of them involved in various degrees of subordination; complicated, involved, intricate; not easily analyzed or disentangled.

This definition neglects virtually all those aspects of complexity that are crucial to a planner. A heuristically useful concept of complexity ought to consider the root causes of lacking decidability, e.g., the inseparability of systems components for the purpose of planning (design-nonseparability); the uniqueness of systems (and hence their design-nonfeasibility); the intrinsic autonomy and self-motivation of systems; the perspectival character of any standpoint from which the planner may apprehend a system (e.g., the dependency of any definition of a system on an interest); etc. The *Oxford* definition is obviously based on the Aristotelian, analytic-reductionistic tradition of thought which is so familiar to Western thinking that it is identified with common sense, even though it depends on very questionable (because metaphysical) assumptions about complexity. Herbert Simon is an outstanding representative of this tradition, a tradition that has built its enormous success on Caesar's old principle: *divide et impera!* – translated into the language of systems science: decompose and control!

C. West Churchman's philosophy of social systems design, on the other hand (see esp. 1968a, 1971, 1974, 1979, 1981; also Churchman/Nelson/Eacret 1977, Churchman/ Ulrich 1980 and Churchman/Cowan/Ulrich 1983), is closer to the other great tradition of Greek philosophy, the nonobjectivist and antireductionistic tradition of thought of which Plato is representative. To avoid the derogative meaning with which the dominant Aristotelian tradition has associated the term "Platonic," it may be advisable to speak of "dialectical" or simply non-Aristotelian rather than "Platonic" thinking.[1a] This tradition has recently gained new attention because it promises more help in dealing with design-nonseparability, uniqueness, and other essential difficulties encountered by the social planner.

For the planner who understands himself as a systems designer, the two positions represent more or less opposite answers to crucial questions such as wholeness or decomposability of systems, the "spirit" of social systems, the role granted to subjectivity in one's understanding of "rational" design, etc. Opposite need not imply incompatible; indeed, the most significant difference between the two positions might be that the one (Simon) *in principle* denies their compatibility whereas the other (Churchman) does not. Churchman has argued that either position becomes absurd, if taken as absolute; both are needed for rational thinking about the reality of systems (cf. 1968a:Ch. 14).

The stage is set; enter the two debaters.

Position: *Represented by:*	"Sciences of the Artificial" H. A. Simon	"Philosophy of Social Systems Design" C. W. Churchman
Subjectivity is	*avoided:* excluded from the definition of objectivity; objectivity has no way to deal with the spirit of social systems	*not avoided:* must be included in the definition of objectivity; the designer must consider the spirit of individuals and whole systems in his design
Complexity is	*hierarchical:* complex systems are built up from hierarchies of subsystems	*not hierarchical:* systems are complex because they cannot be described as hierarchies of components
Wholeness of systems (holism) is	*denied except in a pragmatic sense:*	*critically considered:* there are wholes that

[1a] Cf. the definition of non-Aristotelian thinking in Section 1.2 of Chapter Five, where I have also discussed some of its epistemological and heuristic implications.

	the whole is not more than the sum of the parts, though its analysis is not trivial; regarding complex systems as wholes does not help explain them	cannot be dealt with as sums of parts; regarding complex systems as wholes serves the critical purpose of reminding us of the limits of our understanding
Reducing complexity of systems to "simple" subsystems (reductionism) is	*a source of knowledge:* every system has components which are simpler systems; systems can be understood as black boxes, and the inquirer's task is to make them transparent (reductionistic systems approach)	*a source of irrelevance:* what really matters is systems that are individuals; the inquirer's problem is to account for the individual aspects of systems (antireductionistic systems approach)
The purposeful character of systems (teleology) is	*denied:* ascribing purposes to social systems is a source of deception (teleological fallacy)	*critically considered:* ascribing purposes to social systems serves a necessary critical purpose against hidden value assumptions (teleological imagery is needed in addition to causal-analytic terms)
The *decomposability principle* is	*accepted:* near-decomposability of complex systems (the decomposability principle for artificial systems is applied to social systems)	*rejected:* design-nonseparability of the components of complex systems (the design-separability of components of artificial systems does not hold for social systems)
The *description of systems* must	*focus on redundancy:* by making use of the world's redundancy, complex systems can be described simply (e.g., in terms of simple	*focus on uniqueness:* every system has not only redundancy but also uniqueness; to the extent a system is unique, it is its own sim-

	process descriptions standing for redundant state descriptions)	plest description (description of uniqueness matters as much as description of redundancy)
The *crucial design task* to be solved is	*problem decomposition:* how to decompose a complex system into simple systems that are easy to be controlled? Or: how to design and control complex hierarchies? ("*Divide et impera!*" standpoint; control problem)	*problem identification:* how to describe unique systems, and especially: how to identify the whole system on the one hand, the smallest system (individual) on the other? ("*Ethics of whole systems*" standpoint; boundary problem)
The designer's *main tool* is	*objectivity:* semantic precision of concepts, model building, causal-analytic explanation: mathematical analysis, empirical research, computer simulation, heuristic programming; scientific rigor, "programmed decision making" (*Science of the Artificial*, 1969)	*subjectivity:* reflection on the sources of knowledge and deception: social practice, community, interest and committment, ideas, esp. the moral idea, affectivity, faith; ongoing debate and self-reflection, "process of unfolding" (*The Artificiality of Science*, 1970b)

Table 6/1: A fictitious "debate" on the metaphysics of systems design (adapted from Ulrich 1980:36ff)

Some Implications

From a design point of view, the major difference emerging from the debate concerns the authors' view of what constitutes the crucial lack of knowledge, i.e., the complexity of real-world problem solving and decision making. For Simon it is objective *explanation,* for he identifies the limits of rational design with those of rational (= objective) explanation. For Churchman it is the *consideration of and design for the inexplicable,* because design that does not consider the whole system invites deception.

The underlying motivation is sincere and valid in both cases, so long as no claim for generality is linked to it. Herbert Simon attempts to apply the objective approach of natural science to the domain of social inquiry and design. In Simon's terminology, all systems designed by man are called artificial, in contrast to nondesigned natural systems; hence the name "Sciences of the Artificial." The underlying assumption is that we cannot design subjective social systems. This is true from an objective point of view. It is, however, irrelevant from a critical point of view: man cannot escape his freedom to design *for* the social systems of which he is an integral part. And it is a source of deception, for it fails to consider the fact that all design (of artificial systems) is design for some subjects to be served.

C. West Churchman's philosophy of social systems design, on the other hand, is an attempt to overcome the gap between subject and object wherever it prevents the planner from dealing with the subjectivity of the systems for which he plans. Churchman tries to include the subjectivity of systems in his concept of objectivity rather than to avoid it.

To make it very clear: the question is not whether one can objectively explain and design social systems as whole, unique systems. The question is whether or not we want to design *for* them to become more whole, unique, self-motivated, etc. The first question implicitly reduces the problem of rational social design to one of *theoretical* (or instrumental) reason, while the second seeks to understand it as a problem of *practical* reason.

The first rather than the second question has been addressed by Simon's theory of complexity. That may explain, to a large extent, why it has become a major source of irrelevance – if not deception – in designing *for* social systems: General Systems Theory, RAND-systems analysis, systems engineering, managerial cybernetics, artificial intelligence, heuristic programming, MIS design, Management Science/Operations Research, incrementalist planning approaches, behaviorist learning theories, administrative and policy sciences *all suffer from a common inability to deal critically with the very social reality which they ought to improve.* Langdon Winner (1975) has traced a bit further the limited rationality of these systems-scientific approaches to social complexity. According to Winner, they rely on four typical assertions:

(1) "The first prescription for [dealing with] complexity is always the same. Simplify. In modern practice this usually means 'control as much as possible of that which is changing in the system'." (1975:64)

(2) "Technology caused the problems. Technology must solve them." (1975:65) The progress of computer *hardware* and software (which in fact is rather "hard"!), together with systems analysis, is the supposed remedy for complexity.

(3) Another remedy has been found in the functional *redundancy* of complex systems which is taken for a guarantor of complexity control (cf. Landau 1969). "By implication this argument gives us one reason why failure to understand complex

systems may not be all that important as a practical matter. As long as the complication of an organization includes sufficient redundancy, the organization will be protected from serious errors and breakdowns. Complexity in this sense contains its own saving remnant." (1975:69)

As a comment on this, it may suffice to point to the nuclear incident at Three Mile Island near Harrisburg, Pennsylvania, in April, 1979. In the design of nuclear power plants, technical redundancy of emergency systems has increasingly been substituted for subjective and social rationality as a guarantor of complexity control.

(4) Finally, the idea of disjointed *incrementalism* is often inherent in this position, although the notion as such is now in disrepute (see Section 1.3 of the fourth Chapter). "All that a decision maker needs to understand is the specific context of the activities of the particular choice before him. Knowledge of the activities of the whole system is irrelevant except as it bears directly on the incremental step at hand." (1975:71)

Incrementalist thinking is presupposed in Simon's principle of "near-decomposability" and many other concepts currently used in planning, from cybernetics to interest-group pluralism. The problem of incrementalism is clear: it simply avoids the moral and political question of how a better whole will result from incremental improvement of small and separate subsystems; it leaves that question to the market as a surrogate planner – and to the interest groups that control it as surrogate clients.

The second of the above questions – of how we can design *for* social systems to become more whole, unique, etc. – is addressed by Churchman's theory of complexity. He associates the planner's unavoidable lack of knowledge with the unique and nondecomposable character of social systems. The crucial task then is not one of providing analytic tools such as social indicators, simulation models, etc., but rather dialectic tools to help the planner reflect on his designs, and enter into reasonable discourse with the affected. In his book *The Systems Approach and Its Enemies* (1979), Churchman accordingly presents a dialectical approach to the unfolding of the unavoidable conflict between the systems planner who strives for systems rationality and the "enemies" of such rationality who are concerned in their private, subjective rationality – an issue that we have discussed in Chapter Five. The point is that no systems approach for handling real-world complexity can be rational unless it makes room for the (self-)critical reflection of free *citizens;* for these alone know what social reality is and what it ought to be like. The systems approach may yet have a great future, if only it begins to understand that the "enemies" are really its allies.

2. Toward a Concept of Purposeful Systems

Much of present-day "systems science" relies on a *cybernetic* systems concept, not necessarily on the mechanistic systems concept of early cybernetics (Wiener 1948, Ashby 1956), but rather on the so-called "organic" systems concept (Pask 1958, Beer 1972, Varela/Maturana/Uribe 1974, implicitly also von Foerster 1960, Nicolis/Prigogine 1977, Jantsch 1980). The organic paradigm claims to overcome the narrowness of the machine paradigm by taking account of the intrinsic capability of complexity absorption, self-regulation and self-organization ("organic control") that is characteristic of biological, ecological, and social systems.

The proponents of the organic paradigm, as different as their approaches are, have in common that they introduce their basic systems concepts at the biological level of organic self-regulation rather than at the physical level of information-processing machines. They also share a common hope of contributing significant conceptual tools for the design and management of complex *social* systems. But is this hope justified? Although one can easily agree that the step from a mechanistic to an organic paradigm represents a progress, it appears doubtful whether the organic systems concept is adequate within a critically-heuristic framework. Above all, conceiving of social systems in analogy to biological systems leaves out the crucial role played by human purposefulness and self-reflectiveness at a sociocultural level of systems organization.

In the following discussion, I shall introduce the premises of an alternative "purposeful systems" paradigm that would take account of the constitutive role of human intentionality and, at the same time, offer the planner a conceptual platform for coming to grips with the problem of practical reason. I shall do so by contrasting this "purposeful" to the "organic" systems concept; in this way the sources of deception contained in the organic paradigm will become transparent and can be avoided. This discussion will also serve as a theoretical basis for the case study in Chapter Seven, where we shall apply our new paradigm, together with the earlier-introduced conceptual framework of critical heuristics, to an assessment of Stafford Beer's "Project Cybersyn" in Chile, 1971–73. In order to present the premises of our purposeful systems paradigm in as concise a way as possible, I shall begin with four critical distinctions that are fundamental to my argument. These distinctions will also help us to understand some of the pertinent insights provided by the Habermas-Luhmann debate (1971) on social cybernetics and systems theory of society, to which I shall refer in defining the premises of our paradigm.[2]

---

[2] The following Sections 2.1 and 2.2 are adapted from the theoretical part of my study "A Critique of Pure Cybernetic Reason" in the *Journal of Applied Systems Analysis* (1981).

2.1. Four Critical Distinctions

1. My first critical distinction is this: the organic systems concept of cybernetics appears to be oriented toward the idea of *intrinsic control* rather than *intrinsic motivation*. Intrinsic control means the capability of a system, independently of an external controller, i.e., by means of internal complexity control, to maintain its stability (e.g. its structure, its boundaries, and particularly a given goal state) across a range of environmental or internal variations. The idea is that the *sources of control* are "spread through the architecture of the system" (Beer 1972:35) rather than localized within a separate system: the controller and the controlled are inseparable.[3] The primary example of such a system is the brain; its remarkable capability of complexity control is distributed throughout the central nervous system and hardly any of its functions (e.g., the memory) can be localized within a single unit of control.

   By analogy, we can introduce the term "intrinsic motivation" to refer to a system's *source of purposefulness* (source of motivation) when this source cannot be localized within an external decision maker but is distributed throughout the system itself. *Intrinsic control does not imply intrinsic motivation:* just because a system is capable of maintaining a given goal state by means of intrinsic homeostatic control, it is not necessarily self-responsible with regard to the purposes it serves. If the question of the source of motivation is not raised in addition to the question of control, homeostatic system maintenance or "survival" tends to be substituted for an openly normative definition of the system's purposes (which are always *somebody's* purposes).

2. A second critical distinction is well known, but nonetheless systematically neglected in the cybernetic paradigm: the distinction between the syntactic and the semantic-pragmatic levels of communication. As we have seen (Section 3.1 of Chapter 4), the syntactic aspect of communication processes can be handled by information processing machines, the semantic and pragmatic aspects only by people.[4]

   Within the theoretical framework of information theory and cybernetics, information is defined at a purely syntactic level, that is, its significance can only be identified by its statistical improbability. This focus on the syntactic level is often neglected in discussions about the meaning of cybernetic's basic principle of complexity control, Ashby's *law of requisite variety:* "Only variety can destroy variety."

---

[3] Since purely intrinsic control is a limiting case which rarely obtains in real-world (i.e., open) systems, some authors (Pask 1958, Beer 1959, Gomez 1977, Malik et al. 1977) use the term "organic control" to refer to the combined case of partly intrinsic and partly extrinsic control. Likewise, purely intrinsic motivation is of course only a limiting case and we are normally dealing with partly intrinsic motivation ("partial autonomy," as I have suggested in 1977:1100f), as opposed to merely extrinsic motivation.

[4] See also note 9 to Chapter Four.

(1956:110) Variety is an information-theoretic measure of complexity; it refers to the number of distinguishable states that a system or its output variables can assume at the syntactic level.

In managerial cybernetics, Ashby's theorem is generally interpreted as a criterion for "rational" management of complexity. Cybernetically rational is then what helps a system to generate requisite control variety or else what reduces its need for control variety by destroying environmental perturbation variety (cf. similarly Beer 1975:110). Since this principle is taken to apply to machines as well as to organisms, to extrinsic as well as to intrinsic (organic) control; and since the concept of organic control is applied to social systems, we must conclude that a syntactic criterion of rationality is effectively substituted for a pragmatic, openly and critically normative, criterion of "good" management or design. We shall trace the consequences of this substitution in our case study in Chapter Seven.

3. My third critical distinction is that between *purposiveness* and *purposefulness.* Purposiveness refers to the effectiveness and efficiency of means or tools, purposefulness to the critical awareness of self-reflective humans with regard to ends or purposes and their normative implications for the affected. Cyberneticians usually claim that their discipline enables them to explain and design goal-directed systems without recourse to teleological concepts such as purposeful behavior (e.g. Rosenblueth/Wiener 1950, critically Churchman/Ackoff 1950). Teleology, they say, can be reduced to causal concepts of feedback-monitored behavior, i.e., to "teleonomy." Hence, they conclude, ascribing purposes to a system represents a "teleological fallacy." But this conclusion is a non sequitur, for it is based on the confusion of intrinsic control with intrinsic motivation (cf. above). The charge of the "teleological fallacy" is the more dubious in that it is advanced by cyberneticians and behavioral scientists who, by their own epistemological or methodological standards, have no way of dealing with human purposefulness *within* their theoretical frameworks. To them, the semantic and pragmatic aspects that are mandatory for grasping motivation and complexity at the sociocultural level of systems organization always remain extrinsic and irrational categories, for they must consider systems purposes and boundaries as "ascribed" or "given" to the systems they deal with. This is so because teleonomy cannot deal with the important capability of social systems to change their goal state and structure in a stable environment, that is, without extrinsic motivation. Hence teleonomy is inherently limited to the problem of systems maintenance. It can explain the purposiveness but not the purposefulness of a system's selective accomplishments. Finally, not only is the assumption that one can reduce the category of purposeful choice (i.e., free will) to causal-cybernetic principles philosophically untenable, but it also has uncritical practical implications with regard to the normative content of all systems designs. It evades one of the crucial epistemological difficulties of social systems theory, and along with it the challenge to practical reason. In real-world problem solving and planning we *are* faced with the problem of purposeful choice; it will not help very

much to explain the problem away. In cybernetic's own terms: a cybernetic approach that from the outset excludes relevant variety from consideration in order to reduce its own internal complexity will thereby fail to generate the *relevant* kind of variety required for its self-set task of rational complexity management in social systems.

4. Finally, my fourth critical distinction results from the preceding ones: from the point of view of practical reason, the social planner must reflect upon his activity as an effort in *social systems design* rather than mere *tool design*. By "tool design" I mean a problem-solving attitude that takes problems and purposes as given and refers decisions on them to "irrational" (because value-laden) acts of belief on the part of political decision makers; this seemingly enables the designer to become an expert of "scientific" (purposive-rational) systems design for "given" ends. In other words, tool design relies on a decisionistic model of the relation of science to politics, social systems design on a pragmatistic model. This difference, I believe, is at the bottom of the wide-spread but rarely well-defined distinction between "hard" and "soft" systems thinking: hard systems thinking is any systems thinking that adopts Weber's decisionistic means-end schema.[5] In terms of the previous distinctions, tool design

(1) substitutes intrinsic control for intrinsic motivation;

(2) defines its basic concepts and its principle of complexity control at a syntactic rather than a pragmatic level; and

(3) reduces teleology to teleonomy and thereby excludes its own normative content from critical consideration within its framework of "rational" complexity management.

In contrast, regarding problem solving or planning as social systems design implies recognition of the fact that any such effort amounts to an intervention into a social system – i.e., normative social reality – and hence has a normative content of its own. Social systems design distinguishes itself from tool design by anticipating and questioning its own normative implications; that is to say, it understands itself as an effort of practical reason rather than of systems science.

We are now ready to understand the meaning and relevance (and maybe, fairness) of a "purposeful systems" assessment of social designs. It is to give a social inquirer or planner the heuristic support (the conceptual framework) he needs to reflect upon the normative implications of a plan. It is to bring out into the open those issues of effective and democratically acceptable systems design that cybernetics and "systems science" cannot critically consider within their own conceptual framework – espe-

---

[5] As far as I know, Peter B. Checkland is the only author in the entire systems literature who has clearly recognized this defining feature of all variations of hard systems thinking, e.g., systems engineering, RAND-systems analysis, Operations Research/Management Science, managerial cybernetics, etc. See Checkland's discussion of "The Origin and Nature of 'Hard' Systems Thinking" (1978) in the *Journal of Applied Systems Analysis* which he edits and which is one of the very few systems journals today oriented toward "soft" rather than "hard" systems thinking.

cially the (semantic) question of meaning and the (pragmatic) question of motivation: Where does the meaning in "information" come from? Where do the purposes of systems come from, whose purposes are they? What are their normative implications for those affected, both inside and outside the social system in question? What is the meaning of "control" and "participation" in social-cybernetic designs? How can a social system become purposeful and self-responsible?

2.2. A List of Central Assumptions

With the preceding critical distinctions and questions in mind, we can now easily understand the central assumptions that distinguish our purposeful systems concept from the organic systems concept of cybernetics:

1. Social systems are constituted by *subjects,* not merely by functional organs.
2. Therefore, the *internal variety generation* of social systems is inextricably rooted in the semantically and pragmatically meaningful experience of subjects.
3. The boundaries, structures and goal states of social systems are not defined physically, as is the case with organisms, but rather by *contexts of meaning.* Hence, their viability and productivity depends less on the elimination of physical variety than on what Luhmann (1971a:11f, 1973:176) calls *"sinnvermittelte Selektivität"* – conscious anticipation and choice of alternative actions within contexts of meaning.
4. Because such contexts of meaning are the basis of sensible orientation or selectivity vis-à-vis a complex world, they represent a desirable kind of variety that is not to be reduced or "destroyed," but rather to be maintained and interpreted as a potential source of new selections. "In comparison to purely organic selection it is significant of conscious experience that... the complexity of alternative possibilities is constituted and *maintained* in the subject itself." (1971b:33, my transl.)
5. We can thus say that at the semantic and pragmatic levels of social (sociocultural rather than sociobiological) systems, the cybernetic problem of complexity control takes on the new sense of *selectivity without variety destruction.* Thereby "variety" becomes a function of the observer's semantic and pragmatic context of meaning and is not an absolute, observer-independent measure of complexity (cf. Habermas 1971d:157f and Rivett 1977:34).
6. "The function of *meaning* is thus not that of *information,* i.e., the reduction of a system's state of uncertainty about the world; hence it cannot be measured in the terms of information theory." (Luhmann 1971b:34, my transl.)
7. Even such basic cybernetic concepts as "homeostasis," "survival" or "viability" become blurred at the sociocultural systems level. Speaking of "survival," etc. of social systems becomes a merely metaphorical way of referring to a social sys-

330

tem's potential for the purposeful coping with problems (cf. Churchman/Ackoff 1950:33 and Habermas 1971d:151).

8. In consequence of the above-mentioned characteristics distinguishing the problem of complexity control at the sociocultural level from that at the organic level of systems organization, *Ashby's law of requisite variety loses its status as a general criterion of systems rationality.* Its principle that "only variety can destroy variety" is helpful only so long as there is merely one kind of variety, namely a physical (or physiological) variety that can be reduced to information-theoretic terms. The underlying reason is of course that we are dealing with a mapping process: the informational terms of cybernetics stand for a syntactic map which can be accurately related to the mapped world only insofar as that world is one-dimensionally physical.

9. *Whether cybernetics employs a machine model or an organic systems concept is irrelevant to the one-dimensionality of its implicit rationality criterion.* A rationality criterion based on merely syntactic mapping cannot produce rational social praxis, or practical reason, in a world where semantic and pragmatic aspects are constitutive. To the extent that this is neglected, social-cybernetic design becomes a source of social irrationality. The fallacy committed might be termed the *syntactic fallacy.*

10. In comparison to the older machine paradigm of cybernetics, the organic systems concept represents a progress because it adds the idea of intrinsic control, that is, homeostatic regulation ubiquitously distributed within a self-organizing system, to the older idea of a merely external controller. But it is important to keep in mind that *intrinsic control in the cybernetic sense is not identical with intrinsic motivation, that is, purposefulness.* It is the latter idea which provides an adequate design ideal for social systems.

11. Thus, the organic systems concept, despite its grasp of the idea of intrinsic control, appears to be inadequate to social systems design, for it is still oriented toward a *merely extrinsic concept of motivation.* The fact that such a system may be given some built-in choice (a "program") is largely irrelevant; for such choice is exercised merely in *re*action to externally determined inputs (namely, purposes "given" to the system, and environmental "perturbations" to be eliminated). When, for instance, Klix (1971:33, 37) considers an information processing machine as capable of "motivated output of information," this simply diverts us from the main issue, a lack of true intrinsic (human) purposefulness. In practice, it leads to a neglect of pragmatic (particularly political and moral) issues of information systems, a consequence sufficiently illustrated in the MIS-debate.[6]

When applied to problem solving in social systems, any systems concept that does not include the idea of intrinsic purposefulness ultimately falls back upon a machine model of social systems. That is to say, what we now call "social systems design" because it is a planned intervention into social systems, is reduced to mere "tool design."

12. The design ideal implied in cybernetic tool design is the *purposiveness* of self-regulating systems, but not their intrinsic *purposefulness*. Even if it were granted that we cannot "design" purposefulness (which is true *if* one tacitly identifies "design" with "design from without" rather than self-design), this would not dispense us from respecting, and designing *for,* the individual purposefulness of those affected by our planning. The true fallacy lies not in looking for the intrinsic purposes of social systems, as those speaking of the "teleological fallacy" assume, but rather in ignoring them by reducing teleology to teleonomy *(reductionistic fallacy).*

13. As a guide to critically normative reflection on the sources of practical irrationality in cybernetic's organic systems concept (and the syntactic and reductionistic fallacies linked to it), we shall establish the following regulative principle: *In real-world problem solving and design, purposiveness (of tools) depends on purposefulness (of people using tools).*

Table 6/2 provides a synopsis of the premises of our purposeful systems paradigm in comparison to those of the mechanistic and organic paradigms.

---

[6] The field of Management Information Systems (MIS) provides a case in which the failure of nonradical, scientist systems design is similar to that of managerial or social cybernetics. Significantly, most authors explain MIS failures as a psychological or organizational problem, i.e., a problem of inadequate "acceptance" of MIS by the intended users (cf. Argyris 1971, Swanson 1974, Lucas 1975, Dickson et al. 1977, Zmud 1979). From this assumption, the conclusion is drawn that "more" behavioral-science research on the psychological needs, types, and cognitive styles of users can save the MIS conception; the underlying design ideal (e.g., "rationalization of management") remains unquestioned. Those rare authors who do question this ideal nevertheless content themselves with raising issues of mere tool design, such as alternative modes of information presentation in response to psychological types or problem classes (e.g. Mason/Mitroff 1973). This approach is not radical enough because it evades the normative content of any MIS design and so cannot secure social rationality for MIS designs.

Paradigm	Original cybernetic paradigm	Contemporary cybernetic paradigm	Suggested purposeful systems paradigm
Level of systems organization	physical	biological	sociocultural
Corresponding systems concept	"machine"	"organic system" (organism)	"purposeful system"
Frequently used model	servo-mechanism	brain	social group (*polis*)
Criterion of systems rationality	Ashby's law (syntactic)	Ashby's law (syntactic)	purposefulness in inquiry, action, and valuation (semantic and pragmatic)
Problem-solving perspective	tool design (decisionistic)	tool design (decisionistic)	design for social systems (pragmatistic)
Implied design ideal	purposiveness in respect to given purposes	viability in view of externally determined perturbations and purposes	purposefulness (self-reflectiveness and self-responsibility) in respect to a design's normative implications
Implied concept of control	extrinsic control	intrinsic and extrinsic control = "organic control"	intrinsic and extrinsic control = "partial autonomy"
Implied concept of motivation	extrinsic	extrinsic!	intrinsic

scientistic-antiteleological position   critically normative position

Table 6/2: Comparison of three major systems paradigms (adapted from Ulrich 1981c)

3. Design and Assessment of Purposeful Systems

3.1. Definition of a Purposeful System

Our approach regards the crucial source of deception in systems design as originating in a system's built-in design ideal. This ideal is not determined by the designer's declared purpose but rather by the systems concept or paradigm on which he relies. The systems concept a designer employs will determine how he conceives of the *social* systems for which and with which he plans, specifically

(a) whether he considers himself a mere tool designer or a social planner, and

(b) what role he gives to subjective (self-)reflection in his designs as well as in his own thinking: Is the systems idea for him a critical idea that reminds him of the limits of his understanding, and of the normative content of his designs (whole systems judgements)? Does he design for critical reflection on the part of those who will have to work and live with his designs? Does he think of those who do not belong to the client of his systems designs?

In applying the categories and ideas of critical heuristics for the design and assessment of social systems, our guiding question *will be whether a system S is adequately designed to become a purposeful system;* for if it is not, it is likely to serve purposes and people other than those intended (or pretended) by the planner.

Definition: We designate a system S a *purposeful system* if S is self-reflective with respect to its own normative implications, seen from the point of view not only of the involved but also of the affected, and if S has at least partial autonomy in determining its client, its purposes, etc. "Partial autonomy" precludes the possibility that a system is purely extrinsically motivated; it means that the system can exercise its own will in choosing its goals.[7]

---

[7] Ackoff and Emery (1972) have been the first to present a book-long, systematic conceptualization of social systems in terms of purposeful systems. Their work is based on previous attempts by Singer (e.g. 1959), Sommerhoff (e.g. 1969), Churchman (1948:198ff, 1971:42ff), and Churchman/ Ackoff (1950) to integrate the causal-mechanistic and the teleological explanations of goal-directed systems into one concept of systems functionality or systems teleology. Unlike Rosenblueth and Wiener (1943, 1950), Ackoff and Emery avoid the reduction of teleology to teleonomy (see the discussion under point 3 of Section 2.1 above). Unfortunately, however, their effort is oriented toward behavioral science rather than practical philosophy; they seek "to define the concepts of *function, goal-seeking,* and *purpose* with all the rigor of the [causal-mechanistic] concepts used in the physical sciences" (1972:15) so as to "facilitate consideration of behavioral variables in the evaluation and design of social systems" (1972:10). As rigorous as their conceptualization of purposeful systems is, its predominantly behavioristic and frequently mathematical language offers little help to the planner in dealing with the problem of practical reason. I suggest that we understand purposefulness as a concept of practical philosophy rather than of behavioral science, i.e., as referring to the intentionality and self-reflectiveness of an agent (agent's point of view) rather than to systems behavior as observed from a spectator's point of view.

334

Let us briefly highlight the most important implications of this definition when it is used as a design ideal or assessment criterion.

1. Purposefulness is a merely formal design ideal or assessment criterion, "formal" in the sense of not prescribing any material purposes but rather calling for their open and critical introduction. Its application thus requires for each assessment question both an "is" and an "ought" question: e.g., What *ought* to be a system S's source of control (its decision maker)? What *is* S's actual, built-in concept of control? Who *ought* to belong to S's client, as compared to those actually served? etc. It is because of this requirement of value transparency that I have distinguished our paradigm from the seemingly value-free mechanistic and organic paradigms by characterizing it as "openly normative" (e.g. in the Introduction to this chapter).

2. Since only human individuals are self-reflective and autonomous in the sense intended here, it is clear that purposeful systems are made up of groups of purposeful individuals who are united by the convergence or interdependence of *some* of their purposes, though their interests may otherwise conflict. This is why I have suggested, in Table 6/2, the social group or the Greek *polis* as a root metaphor of purposeful systems.

3. Lest our term "social systems design" make us inadvertently fall back on an inadequate mechanistic or organic systems concept, let us be clear about our reading of the term: when we speak of the planner's task as one of social systems design, we do not mean to imply that social systems can be designed, as can machines, according to some functional criteria of purposiveness. Rather than reading social systems design as "design *of* social systems," we ought to read it as "design *for* social systems," i.e., design *for* the purposefulness of the individuals or partly autonomous groups belonging to the system in question. Insofar as the systems concept is used in a constitutive sense (as a relative a priori category), we associate it with our newly defined "purposeful systems" paradigm rather than with the organic or mechanistic paradigms; insofar as it is used in a critical sense (as an a priori *idea* of reason), we associate it with the Kantian principle of reason and with the challenge to practical reason rather than with "systems science."

3.2. A Taxonomy of Problem-Solving Dimensions for the Design and Assessment of Purposeful Systems

As a consequence of the previous considerations, the fundamental design task of the social planner is to design for the development of intrinsic motivation and critical reflection on the part of those who will have to work and live with his designs. This task applies to each of the three basic kinds of complementary problem-solving processes that a purposeful system S, and each of its purposeful subsystems, must inevitably perform (Ulrich 1975c:206ff, 1977d:1102ff):

1. *Inquiry:* A purposeful system S must produce meaningful knowledge in respect to its purpose (S ought to become a purposeful inquiring system).
2. *Action:* S must secure the purposeful use of this knowledge (S ought to become a purposeful action system).
3. *Valuation:* S must responsibly evaluate its production and use of knowledge from the standpoint of both the client and those who do not benefit but might be negatively affected (S ought to become a purposefull, morally responsible, valuation system).

For each of these three complementary (i.e., design-nonseparable) dimensions, our guiding question – of whether a system is adequately designed to become a purposeful social system – yields a basic assessment criterion:

1. What kind of an *inquiring system* is S? That is, what concept of information (or knowledge) is built into the design of S? Does it make S a purposeful inquiring system?
2. What kind of an *action system* is S? That is, what concept of action (what use of knowledge or expertise) is built into the design of S? Does it give security that S is a purposeful action system?
3. What kind of *valuation system* is S? That is, what concept of values (what capacity for judging and modifying S's normative content) is built into the design of S? Does it make S a purposeful (morally responsible) valuation system?

Note that in all three questions we ask for the degree of purposefulness as it is revealed by the system's design, *not* by its designer's intentions or claims.

In reflecting upon these questions, it will be especially important to consider the system's sources of motivation, as opposed to its sources of control: Is S's motivation mainly intrinsic or merely extrinsic? Let us therefore conceptualize both an intrinsically motivated system and an extrinsically motivated system for each of the three problem-solving dimensions. We thus gain a taxonomy of six ideal-typical systems concepts that may help the planner to reflect on the design ideal built into a design: *(Table 6/3)*

Problem-solving dimension	Sources of motivation	Complementary view-points	Design ideal	Necessarily imperfect examples that might serve as root metaphors	Related conceptualization attempts
Valuation	Intrinsic + Extrinsic	"Ethical system"	"Responsible"	Polis (or political community)	Churchman 1968 a: "Ethics of whole systems"
	Extrinsic	"Ecosystem"	"Self-sustaining" ("viable") ←	Ecological community (organism)	
Action	Intrinsic + Extrinsic	"Social system"	"Purposeful"	Autonomous work group (or worker-controlled factory)	Ackoff/Emery 1972: "Purposeful system"
	Extrinsic	"Operating system"	"Purposive" ←	Servo-mechanism	
Inquiry	Intrinsic + Extrinsic	"Inquiring system"	"Reflective"	Human inquirer (or community of inquirers)	Churchman 1971: "Inquiring system"
	Extrinsic	"Fact finding system"	"Responsive" ←	Information processing machine (computer)	

Table 6/3: A taxonomy of problem-solving dimensions for the design and assessment of purposeful systems (adapted from Ulrich 1977 d:1103); arrows indicate internalization of motivation

Let us briefly characterize each of the six ideal types.

1. An *extrinsically motivated information system* is capable of constructing "fact nets," i.e., of not only storing but also interrelating and combining, cataloguing and retrieving data. If it is given the necessary algorithmic and heuristic routines, it can also perform various tests to make sure that its inputs are syntactically well-formed and statistically plausible; it can extrapolate new facts from given fact nets, receive and identify inquiries and "answer" by putting out corresponding fact nets, etc. (cf. on the concept of "fact nets" Churchman 1968 b:106, 1971:29ff). But it cannot recognize and question the semantic and pragmatic meaning of these fact nets, it has no knowledge of what it knows and why it knows what it knows. The classical example of such an information system is the library; the contemporary example is provided by the computerized information system. Contrary to Newell, Shaw, and Simon (e.g. 1958, 1960, 1972), who were the first to demonstrate that the heuristic capabilities of information processing machines can achieve the same results that have been associated with human intuition, we cannot consider such a system as a valid model of human problem solving; for it remains at a merely syntactic level and thus avoids the crucial problems of cognitive-affective organization, self-reflectiveness, interests, etc. characteristic of human problem solving. Instead, we understand it only as an auxiliary, complementary viewpoint for the design and assessment of inquiring systems.

The design of extrinsically motivated information systems – "fact finding systems," as we might call them – must be oriented toward the crucial problem of securing communication between the fact finding system and its external user. The only design ideal that makes sense for a fact finding system is maximum responsiveness to the language and the problems of its external motivator.

2. An *intrinsically motivated information system* must include at least one human inquirer, for purposefulness exists only where human reflection can recognize and question facts. Such questioning is imperative because no design for inquiry (and hence for a "responsive" information system) can possibly offer complete guarantee gainst deception. As Churchman (1971) has shown in his discussion of "classical" designs for inquiry – by Leibniz, Locke, Kant, Hegel, and his own teacher, Edgar A. Singer – every conceivable design will run into some particular difficulties. A good design for inquiry will have to consider this fact and its consequence: namely, that an information system can produce meanigful knowledge only to the extent that it makes its user reflect both on the sources of deception that might prevent his inquiry from serving its purpose, and also on the sources of deception that might be contained in the purpose itself. Churchman's term "inquiring system" refers to such a design that includes the self-reflectiveness of human inquirers as a mandatory component of a purposeful information system.

3. An *extrinsically motivated action system* is oriented toward the *purposive* use of knowledge in respect to given ends. We designate such a system "operating sys-

tem." It may possess the capability of intrinsic control, as does a servomechanism, i.e., a feedback-monitored control system. But of course, the purposes that an operating system serves are determined externally, and the system remains uncritical and unresponsible in respect to these purposes. Again we regard this ideal type as a merely complementary one for the design of purposeful action systems; only if it is embedded within a purposeful *social* system can an operating system secure purposeful action. This assertion may sound more trivial than it is in practice: in Chapter Seven we shall examine a case in which a social system was actually designed as an operating system, Stafford Beer's design of a real-time regulatory system for the nationalized sector of the Chilean economy under Salvador Allende.

4. An *intrinsically motivated action system* does not only operate purposively; it acts purposefully. There is no need for restating the defining features of a purposeful system here (cf. above). A partly autonomous working group in a manufacturing plant (e.g., in Norwegian chemical plants and in Swedish automobile plants) provides a prototypical (though somewhat restricted) example of what we intend by a purposeful action system (see the work by Emery and Thorsrud, 1969).

5. An *extrinsically motivated valuation system* is represented here by the ideal type of the naturally self-regulating ecological community, e.g., the ecosystem of a pond, a forest, a desert, etc. (the underlying root metaphor is that of the organism). Viable ecosystems are intrinsically controlled, though they need not attain a stable equilibrium state; there is now a new nonequilibrium ecology developing which complements the classical concept of homeostasis by the new concepts of "resilience" of ecosystems (Holling 1976) and "order through fluctuation" (Nicolis/Prigogine 1977). Ecosystems are, however, extrinsically motivated in the sense that nature does not develop new motivations of its own; that is, we do not assume that nature is purposeful. Nature provides a source of orientation and values for social systems design insofar as mankind, at least in the long run, cannot impose its own purposes on nature without regard for the needs of ecosystems. It is not possible, however, to found an ethics of planning solely on ecological concepts; for although it is true that man cannot live without nature, he must nevertheless face his freedom to organize – and change – society "after his own plan" (to paraphrase Kant). For instance, it is not possible to defend a hierarchical and unequal order of society by referring to the hierarchical organization of nature; man, the *zoon politicon,* cannot delegate the responsibility for a good and just order of society (of the *polis)* to nature. Thus we find again that the extrinsically motivated systems type furnishes only a complementary, but as such necessary, viewpoint for the design and assessment of purposeful systems.

6. An *intrinsically motivated valuation system,* finally, would be a social system with an internalized "ethics of whole systems." The concept of an "ethics of whole systems" was suggested by Churchman (1968 a) to refer to the fact that the ethical value of a design or action cannot ultimately be measured except in terms of the

improvement of the whole relevant system: "The problem of systems improvement is the problem of the ethics of the whole system." (1968a:4) Since we understand "the whole system" to include all those affected by the design or action in question, it is clear that the underlying idea is Kant's principle of moral generalization (see Chapter 2, Section 3.2). Kant's *categorical imperative* requires the planner or agent to consider himself as a universal legislator: "So act that the maxim of your will could always hold at the same time as the principle of universal legislation." (KpV:A 54, Beck 142, Abbott 119) That is to say, the planner must place himself in the position of all the affected rather than treating them as means only. The same idea applies to the decision maker (intrisic controller) of any purposeful system insofar as its (partly autonomous) decisions affect third parties. The problem of designing for purposeful valuation systems is essentially the problem of internalizing an ethics of whole systems; and such internalization, as we have seen, cannot rely on a mere appeal to the moral responsibility of the involved but must consist in giving the witnesses representing the affected a relevant (i.e., "competent") role to play. In other words, the term "internalization" must not be misunderstood psychologistically – from the point of view of social systems design, it is first of all a term referring to the institutionalization of practical discourses.

Our prototypical example here is the Greek *polis,* or more generally, any form of political community that relies on rationally-motivated practical discourses for reconciling private concerns with public authority, and for legitimizing such authority.[8]

As a final comment on the proposed taxonomy of ideal types for the design and assessment of purposeful systems, I should point to Ivan Illlich's conceptual framework for the social assessment of systems in the domains of education, public health care, transportation, etc. (see Illich 1973, and especially 1977). This framework is remarkably akin to our taxonomy (which I first conceived in 1975 before becoming aware of Illich's work). Illich's terminology is different, but his intent is not so different from ours. Not only does his normative orientation toward self-reliance and "autonomous coping" closely correspond to our general design ideal of intrinsically motivated, purposeful systems; but his three levels of institutional counterproductivity in today's health care systems – clinical, social, and cultural iatrogenesis (medically caused illness) – can be understood to refer to the extrinsically motivated sys-

---

[8] Reinhard Bendix has proposed a definition of the concept of a "political community" that appears to come close to our intent:

Where each individual or group takes the law into their hands until checked by the momentarily superior force of an opponent, anarchy reigns and a *political community* does not exist. Some subordination of private interest to public authority is the *sine qua non* of such a community. Governments vary greatly with regard to the subordination they demand and the rights they acknowledge. The term "political community" may be applied wherever the relations between rulers and ruled involve shared understandings concerning this "exchange." These understandings concern the *legitimacy* of public authority. (1970:184)

tems types in our taxonomy. In fact, counterproductivity in Illich's sense [9] is nothing else but that paralysis of purposeful coping on the part of the affected which results from the one-sided design of a system in terms of tool design rather than social systems design. Thus clinical iatrogenesis means the medically induced damage produced by a system of medical diagnosis and treatment that treats the sick as the passive object of a fact finding system rather than as an active, purposeful participant in an inquiring system. Social iatrogenesis is the "expropriation of health" caused by a health care delivery system designed as a purposive operating system rather than a purposeful social system. And cultural iatrogenesis, finally, refers to the paralysis of socio-cultural patterns and values of personal coping with, and interpersonal sharing of, sickness, suffering, and death by a medicine that understands itself as value-free and transforms pain and sickness into merely technical problems (cf. 1977:xvif, 24f, 33, 121). We shall have an opportunity to take up some of these issues in the case study of Chapter Eight; at this point I would merely like to suggest that our taxonomy might be useful for tracing the sources of conterproductivity in systems designs. Whenever a system's built-in design ideal is onesidedly defined in terms of tool design (extrinsic motivation), we must suspect counterproductivity.

Before turning now to our case studies, let us simply remind ourselves of the overall structure of our critically-heuristic approach to the design and asssessment of purposeful systems: *(Table 6/4)*

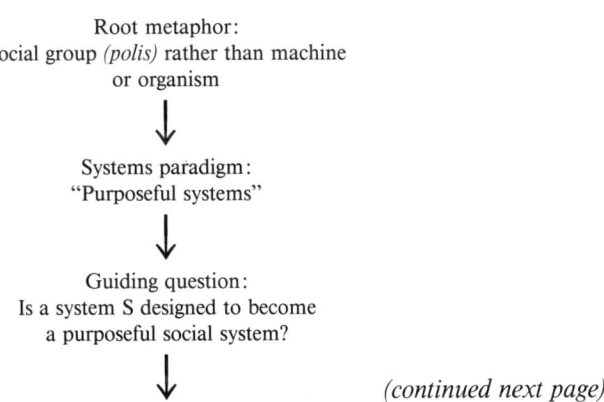

Root metaphor:
Social group *(polis)* rather than machine
or organism

Systems paradigm:
"Purposeful systems"

Guiding question:
Is a system S designed to become
a purposeful social system?

(continued next page)

---

[9]   Illich gives this explanation of counterproductivity:
It exists whenever the use of an institution paradoxically takes away from society those things the institution was designed to provide. It is a form of built-in social frustration.... Fundamentally it is due neither to technical mistakes nor to class exploitation but to industrially generated destruction of those environmental, social, and psychological conditions needed for the development of non-industrial or non-professional use-values. Counterproductivity is the result of an industrially induced paralysis of practical self-governing activity. (1977:209)

(continued from p. 34)

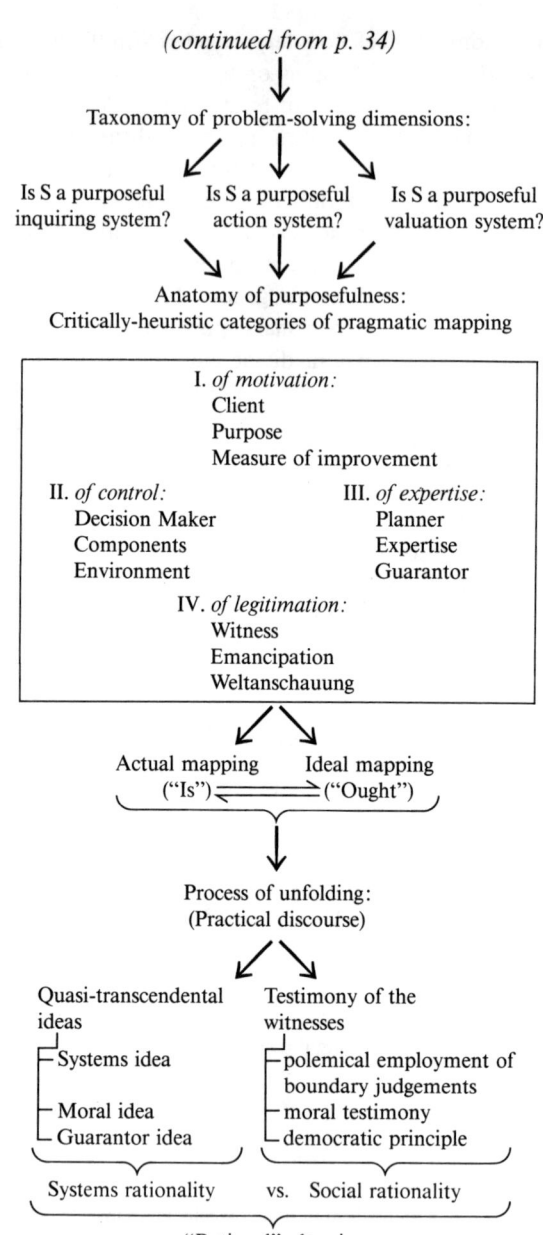

Taxonomy of problem-solving dimensions:

Is S a purposeful inquiring system?   Is S a purposeful action system?   Is S a purposeful valuation system?

Anatomy of purposefulness:
Critically-heuristic categories of pragmatic mapping

I. *of motivation:*
 Client
 Purpose
 Measure of improvement

II. *of control:*   III. *of expertise:*
 Decision Maker   Planner
 Components   Expertise
 Environment   Guarantor

IV. *of legitimation:*
 Witness
 Emancipation
 Weltanschauung

Actual mapping   Ideal mapping
 ("Is") ⇌ ("Ought")

Process of unfolding:
(Practical discourse)

Quasi-transcendental   Testimony of the
ideas   witnesses
 ⌐ Systems idea   ⌐ polemical employment of
                               boundary judgements
 ⊢ Moral idea   ⊢ moral testimony
 ⌊ Guarantor idea   ⌊ democratic principle

 Systems rationality   vs.   Social rationality

"Rational" planning

Table 6/4: Overall architectonic of our critically-heuristic approach to the design and assessment of purposeful systems

Chapter Seven
Project Cybersyn:
The Chilean Experience with Cybernetics, 1971–73

The capacity for <u>control</u> *made possible by the empirical sciences is not to be confused with the capacity for* <u>enlightened action</u>*.... The scientific control of natural and social processes – in one word, technology – does not release men from action. Just as before, conflicts must be decided, interests realized, interpretations found – through both action and transaction structured by ordinary language.*
Jürgen Habermas (1971b:56)

Introduction

Stafford Beer's "Project Cybersyn" (from *Cyber*netics and *Syn*ergy) was a truly unique application of the tools of cybernetics to democratic government. It represented a large-scale attempt to provide the nationalized sector of the Chilean economy under Salvador Allende with an information and decision system, or, in Beer's own words, "an attempt to provide a real-time regulatory activity vis-à-vis the social economy which would embody the political purposes of the government" (personal communication). It should be made quite clear at the beginning that the political purpose which Cybersyn was to serve is *not* the subject of my critique. It is not my intent to question the social and democratic ideals that both Salvador Allende and Stafford Beer associated with the project; but I am afraid that an approach to national complexity management that does not openly and critically consider its own normative content is more likely to work against those ideals than toward them. The subject of my critique is the scientistic, i.e., positivist, apolitical epistemology that has taken possession of the systems idea and thereby prevented it from becoming a tool of practical reason.

Beer's work in Chile has not yet met with extensive discussion. This may be due to the difficulty of obtaining complete information about Cybersyn after its premature end in the Chilean *coup d'état* of September, 1973. Because of the lack of reports by independent observers, the following review has to rely on Beer's own reports (1973a, 1974, 1975); his theoretical basis presented mainly in *Brain of the Firm* (1972), but also in *Decision and Control* (1966) and *Platform for Change* (1975); on Hermann

343

Schwember's detailed report (1976); on some rather superficial if not distorting comments in the journal *New Scientist* (Grosch 1973; Hanlon 1973 a, b) along with Beer's replies (1973 b, c); on two lectures delivered by Fernando Flores, former Secretary of Economics in Allende's cabinet, to the Institute of International Studies, Berkeley, in Spring 1978; and on the personal feedback that I received from Fernando Flores as well as from Stafford Beer. Finally, since the premature end of the Chilean project in the 1973 coup creates some difficulty in the verification of my account, I am obliged to an anonymous reviewer who was involved in the project and who has confirmed the accuracy of my account.[1]

---

[1] The following case study, together with Section 2 of Chapter Six, has been adapted from my article "A Critique of Pure Cybernetic Reason" (1981 c). The reader is advised to read Section 2 of Chapter Six as a theoretical introduction to the present Chapter.

1. Project Cybersyn: The Design

Salvador Allende's Chile was in an economically precarious situation when Stafford Beer arrived in Santiago, in November, 1971. The two main problems of the economy were probably (a) the brain drain of qualified managers and professionals subsequent to a rapid introduction of nationalization and worker participation; and (b) a serious shortage of foreign credits, technical aid, and spare parts as a result of a virtual economic blockade by other nations. Both industrial and agrarian production were insufficient; inflation and internal political opposition were rapidly increasing and put the government under time pressure to improve production and political stability (according to Mr. Flores).

The administration of the nationalized sector of the economy was entrusted to CORFO, the state-controlled *Corporation for Nationalized Industries* which, operating in a fashion similar to that of the IRI in Italy, had served the Chilean governments preceding Allende in fostering the industrial development of the country by developing state-owned public utilities and basic industries. When Allende became President, CORFO supervised about 30 to 35% of industrial production; Allende's nationalization program meant that CORFO hat to incorporate another 40% of the Chilean industry, or about 200 newly nationalized factories (figures by Mr. Flores). Two main difficulties faced CORFO at that time. First, there was an acute lack of the management tools that would render CORFO a more effective instrument of economic coordination than that provided by the centralized bureaucracies of the communist countries (cf. *Figure 7/1*).

Second, there was a shortage of managerial expertise *within* the factories to be controlled by CORFO because most of the former managers and business owners had left the country. The *workers' committees* that had taken their place were not only relatively unskilled but had also been promised active *participation* in management by Allende. Each of these committees was headed by a so-called intervenor appointed by the government. But neither the intervenors not the workers knew what the crucial bottlenecks were and what exactly was going on in the nationalized industry as a whole (cf. Beer 1974:4, 1975:423f).

In this situation, Fernando Flores, then a high official in CORFO, invited Beer to advise CORFO in developing the managerial tools for the support of the worker's committees as well as for the government itself. Beer was appointed scientific director of the project. The challenge he faced was the combination of active workers' participation (which was an important part of Allende's political program) and more effective national planning of the economy (which was indispensable for economic survival). "Cybersyn" was to provide the nationalized part of the Chilean economy with a "nervous system" that would link workers' committees, CORFO, and the government so as to render all three more effective.

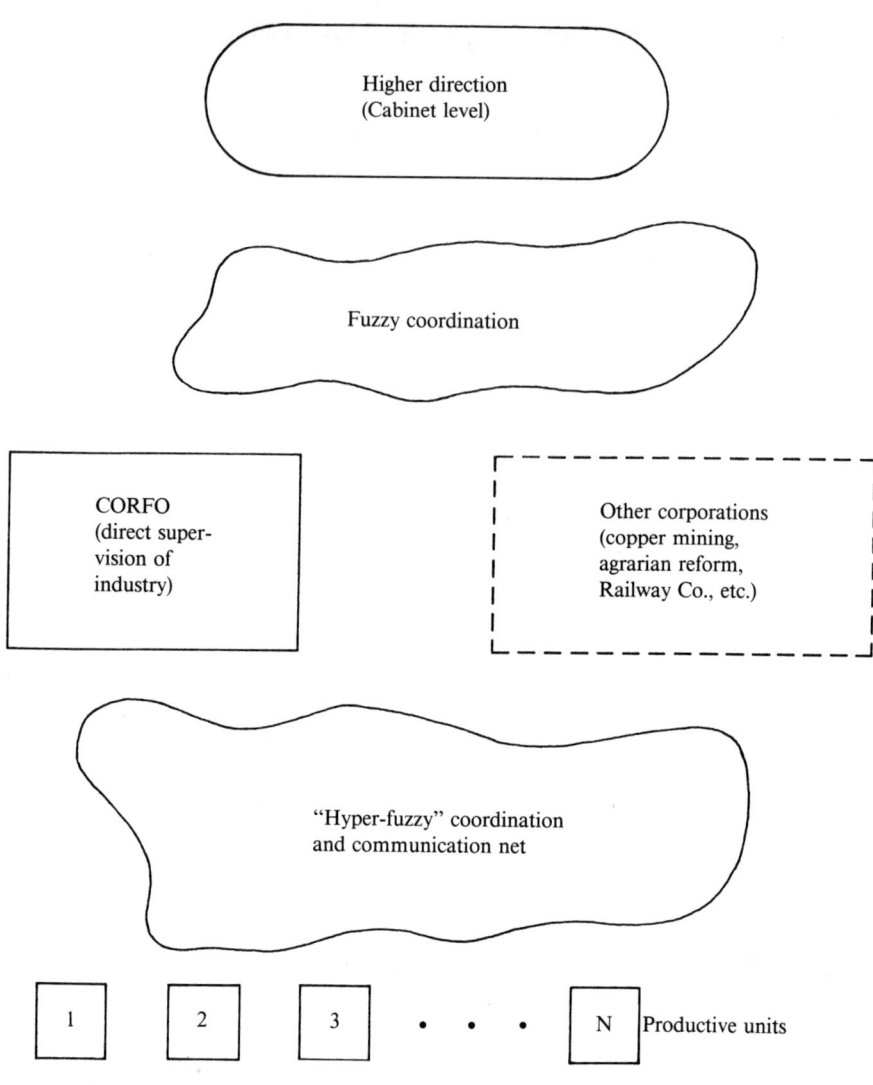

Figure 7/1: The nationalized sector of the Chilean economy before Project Cybersyn (according to Schwember 1976:83)

The main proportion of the effort we made in Chile was to install a regulatory system for the social economy. The project aimed to acquire the benefits of cybernetic synergy for the whole of industry, while devolving power to the workers at the same time. (Beer 1974:6)

It was specified that the system to be implemented should accept a high degree of relevant information for all the workers in the system, from top executives to production-line workers. Moreover, the design for information management should be such that relevant and effective participation of the workers in the decision-making process at the different niveaus of recursion[2] should be a practical possibility. (Schwember 1976:82)

The essential ideas on which Project Cybersyn was based are:
1. *The Brain of the Firm:* a neuro-cybernetic organization model
2. *Cybernet:* a real-time communication network, the "nervous system" linking the productive subsystems to the brain
3. *Cyberstride:* a computer program providing for variety attenuation
4. *The Operations Room:* an environment for computer-assisted decision making.

Let us now examine these crucial components of Cybersyn's design.

1.1. The Brain of the Firm

Beer's neuro-cybernetic organization model is based on the simple idea that management is about control of organizations, and that the basic difficulty of control in a complex and unstable world is that of handling *complexity* (cf. Section 1 of Chapter 6). Now, nature has given us a nearly perfect example of how the control of complexity can be organized, namely, the human brain, or more precisely, the central nervous system. In *Brain of the Firm* (1972), Beer draws on the central nervous system as a design model for the effective organization of social systems. He identifies three principles as basic to the organization of the central nervous system, and hence of Cybersyn: (a) the principle of viability, (b) the principle of recursion, and (c) the principle of autonomy.

The Principle of Viability

"Viability" is to Beer what purposefulness is to us: a guiding design ideal rooted in the underlying systems concept. Viability stands for the cybernetic ideal of organismic adaptation to a changing environment through intrinsic homeostatic control.[3]

---

[2] The concept of recursion is explained under 1.1. below; see also note 4.
[3] The concept of homeostasis was introduced by Walter B. Cannon (1932) to refer to the capability of organisms to keep certain crucial variables such as temperature and blood-sugar level within the limits required for the survival of the organism. Later Ross W. Ashby (1960:58) introduced the term "homeostat" to designate a machine with similar self-regulating properties, in particular his own technical construction of an "ultrastable system." Such a system can not only maintain certain variables within prescribed limits but also change its goal states when its self-regulative capabilities are insufficient to respond to environmental changes.

Purposefulness, on the other hand, contains the normative, political ideal of intrinsic motivation and responsibility in human action. Viability is taken to describe a value-neutral criterion of effective organization both in natural and in human systems, "value-neutral" because it allegedly embodies the universal and scientific principle that governs all processes of complexity control and adaptation in nature – Ashby's "law of requisite variety" (see Section 2 of Chapter 6).

Beer does not mention the fact (noted earlier) that this "law" is defined in the syntactic terms of information theory only and hence cannot simply be substituted for a pragmatic criterion of good management. As a substitute criterion of this sort, viability implies that the survival or homeostasis of the system under consideration is the purpose. In contrast, the design ideal of purposefulness was introduced in Chapter Six as calling for the explicit and critical consideration of the question: "whose purposes?" This brief comparison makes it already apparent that Beer relies on the contemporary "organic" systems paradigm: "viability" means intrinsic control, but extrinsic motivation (cf. Table 6/2 above).

Now, the principle of viability says that in order to be viable, *any* system – artificial, organic, or social – must have at its disposition five organizational functions which constitute the structural prototype of any viable system (cf. Beer 1972: Ch. 9). *Figure 7/2* shows this prototype in an illustration by Schwember (1976:87). The five functions are hierarchically arranged. For instance, if a manufacturing plant is to be designed as a viable system, the three lower levels stand for the classical functions of production management. Level 1 represents the basic centers of command in the productive subunits A, B, and C. Level 2 provides for information aggregation and filtration of upward communication, or translation and amplification of instructions coming down from level 3 to level 1. Level 3, the operations management, coordinates all the activities at levels 1 and 2; it is in charge of the whole "present" of the system (Schwember 1976:91). It is also responsible for routine reports to the next higher socioeconomic niveau (super-system level), in this case a sector of industry; and from the managerial committee there it receives routine feedback instructions. Levels 4 and 5, finally, represent the levels of "strategic" planning. Level 4, the development management, is a staff function responsible for monitoring environmental changes and for preparing the system's future, e.g., through market research and marketing, R & D, planning, etc., within the framework of the overall strategies determined by level 5. Level 5, the top management, can be interpreted as representing the "portfolio" level of strategic planning; it determines the overall policy and balances different strategies with respect to risks, resource generation vs. deployment, growth possibilities, etc. It keeps the ultimate decision authority in determining the system's goals; it balances "the conservative pulls of level 3 and the progressive pushes of level 4, [it is] the conscience of the system" (Schwember 1976:92).

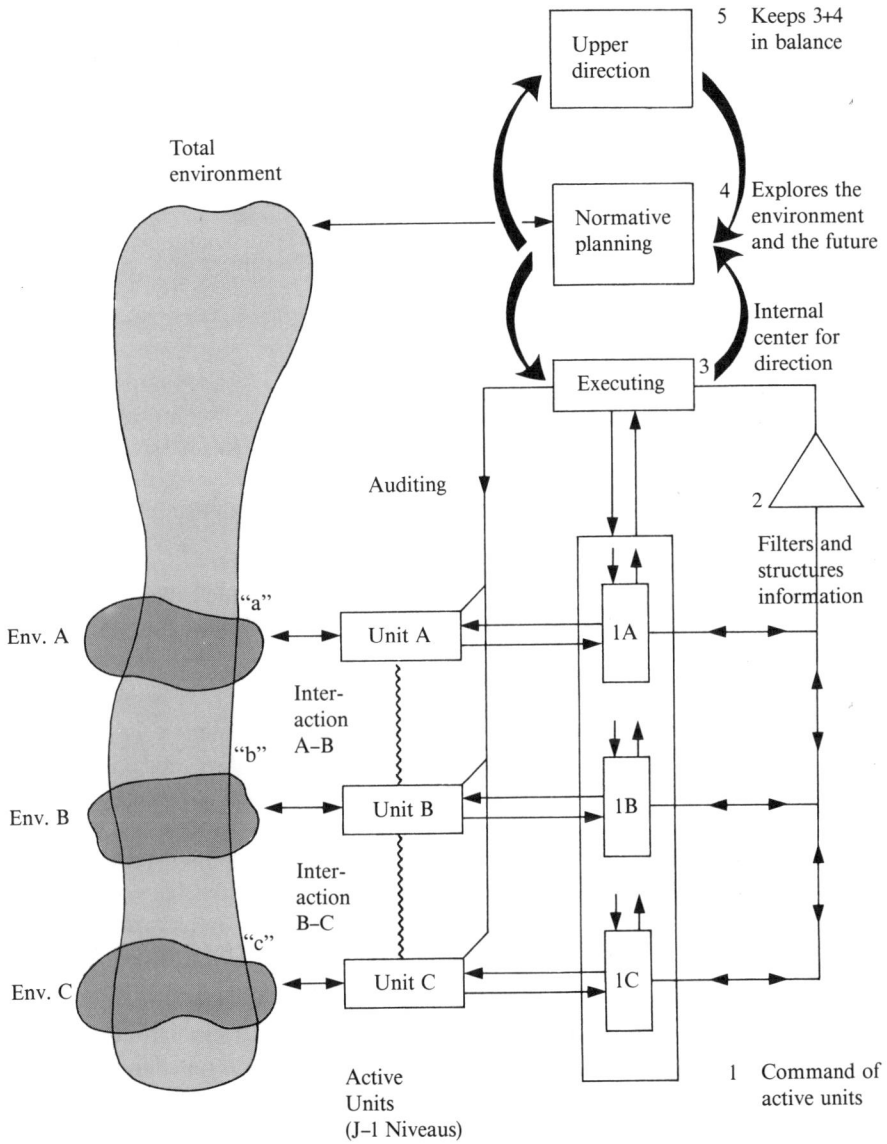

Figure 7/2: Prototype structure of any viable system according to Schwember 1976:87 (= internal hierarchy of viable systems, not to be confused with the external hierarchy shown in Figure 7/6)

349

It is significant of the underlying systems concept that the lower levels that are to be supported in becoming "viable," i.e., more self-regulating, are thus completely separated from the source of normative planning. The top level alone has the "ontological function" (F. Flores), that is, it defines what the system is, its purposes, its relevant environment, its future. There is a clear internal hierarchy of planning and decision making between levels 5-3-1; levels 2 and 4 are staff functions mediating between the others without authority over them. From this *internal* hierarchy of "any" viable system we have to distinguish the *external* hierarchy of socioeconomic niveaus.[4] The latter – which of course overlaps with the former – is the subject of the principle of recursion.

The Principle of Recursion

This [principle] says that all viable systems contain viable systems, and are contained within viable systems. Then if we have a model of *any* viable system, it must be recursive. That is to say, at whatever level of aggregation we start, then the whole model is rewritten in each element of the original model, and so on indefinitely. (Beer 1975:427)

Beer first formulated this principle for the organization of a viable "firm" in analogy to that of the "brain" (1972: Ch. 15). Relying on the assumption that the principle describes a universal "law," he now extends it to an entire socioeconomic system such as Chile:

If we model the state, then one element is the economic system; if we model the economic system, then one element is an industrial sector; if we model that industrial sector, then one element is a firm. The model itself is invariant. See what happens if we go on with this recursion. An element of the firm is a plant; an element of the plant is a particular shop; an element of the shop is a section; an element of the section is a man. And the man is assuredly a viable system – as a matter of fact, the model started from the cybernetic study of man's effective neurophysiological organization in the first place. (1975:427f)

The principle is meant to legitimize the application of the structural prototype of a viable system to all socioeconomic niveaus, be it national government, CORFO, a branch or sector of industry,[5] or a firm. Each niveau, if it is to function effectively, must be organized as a viable system. At the same time – in correspondence to the underlying extrinsic motivation concept – the external hierarchy of socioeconomic niveaus provides the basic structure of command. The result is a structure of over-

---

[4] In order to avoid confusion between the internal and external hierarchies, the term "level" will be used to refer to the former, while "niveau" refers to the latter.

[5] The nationalized part of the Chilean industry was divided into four branches or "ramas": heavy industry, light industry, consumer industry, and materials supply industry. Each branch was further subdivided into sectors. Cf. the second edition of *Brain of the Firm*, 1981:249.

lapping groups very much like that in Likert's (1961) well-known linking-pin model, but with the refinement that the link function is differentiated: routine reports and feedbacks are transmitted via the level-3 managements, while important reports and policy instructions are passed from one socioeconomic niveau to another via the level-5 directions (cf. Schwember 1976: 91, 93). In this way, the management (levels 3 and 5) of a branch of industry is at the same time level 1 within the viable system CORFO and as such receives instructions from CORFO's management; and so on.[6] In the case of the government (cabinet), the democratic process is supposed to fulfill the normative higher-level functions.

The Principle of Autonomy

This third principle, according to Beer (1974:6), is a cybernetic answer to the conflict between centralization and decentralization in organizations, and hence to the problem of participatory management. It is clear that effective control of complex systems requires a certain degree of centralization as well as decentralization (autonomy of subsystems versus top-down coordination). The principle claims that the maximum feasible autonomy of subsystems can be exactly determined as a function of the minimal hierarchical control required to maintain the overall system's performance within defined limits. To this end, Beer measures the "autonomy" of a subsystem by the *possible* number of states that it can assume (its "horizontal variety") minus the *actual* number of states excluded by hierarchical intervention ("vertical variety"). (The underlying conception appears to be Management by Exception.) In this way, he arrives at the following definition:

> *Definition:* If a system regulates itself by subtracting at all times as little horizontal variety as is necessary to maintain the cohesion of the total system, then the condition of autonomy prevails. (1974:7)

Applied to the Chilean situation, this principle of autonomy (together with the principles of viability and recursion) meant the following: At each niveau of the nationalized economy, the responsible decision committees were to be designed as homeostats that would receive all the feedback information necessary for them to control their activity, i.e., to keep certain output variables within prescribed limits. Only if a homeostat at one niveau (e.g., a firm) was not able to control its situation, an exception signal should go to the next higher niveau which would then observe the situation and eventually intervene. This is why Beer claims that his model does not mean centralization, but rather a "scientific way" to effective workers' participation in the control of the economy (e.g. 1975:425).

---

[6] As I have argued at another place (1975a:168ff), Likert's much-celebrated group model does not really overcome the rigidly hierarchical departmentalization which makes classical line organization so inimical to truly self-organizing, self-responsible, internally motivated groups with little internal hierarchy.

351

1.2. Cybernet: Real-Time Communication

How effectively the homeostats at each niveau of the economy work depends not only on what feedback information they receive, but also on how and how fast the information is received. Economic feedback information normally takes the form of statistics and reports that reach the decision maker with a considerable time-lag. In distinction to this, Cybersyn included a real-time communication network, called *Cybernet,* that was to reach all the nationalized firms of the Chilean economy.

Because of the lack of on-line teleprocessing equipment, Telex and microwave connections were used to simulate a true real-time system. Each unit (firm, sector, branch, total industry = CORFO) had to send a daily report on the state of its crucial variables. It would then receive a daily feedback which presented an analysis of the implications of all this information input. Beer reports that by the end of the project some 75% of Chile's nationalized industry was reached by Cybernet, with a switching center in Santiago where the data were processed by a special program, *Cyberstride* (1974:11).

1.3. Cyberstride: Variety Engineering

Fast information is meaningless if it is not well understood by the recipient, or if the recipient is overwhelmed by too much data. This becomes especially important when the recipients are not experienced managers but relatively unskilled workers, as was the case in Chile's nationalized firms.

Cyberstride was designed by Beer so as to reduce the large variety of data that the workers would have to handle. It is at this point that the computer assumes an important role as a tool for "intelligent" filtration, testing, aggregation, and presentation of data. As Beer says:

Above all, we would use our cybernetic understanding of filtration to deploy computers properly as quasi-intelligent machines, instead of using them as giant databanks of dead information. (1975:431)

In *Brain of the Firm,* Beer had developed some interesting approaches to this fundamental task of "variety engineering":
(a) *Iconic representation:* the quantified flowchart
(b) *A measure of performance:* capability, latency, and performance
(c) *Bayesian short-term forecasting:* testing for significance
(d) *Autonomic exception reporting*
(e) *Algedonic regulation*

Iconic Representation: The Quantified Flowchart

In search for an easily seizable form of information presentation – i.e., one that does not require any expertise in statistics or operations research on the part of the recipient, and one that attenuates variety – Beer developed an iconic (= visual) type of model that represents the relevant quantities of interesting variables as boxes of corresponding size, and the relation between these variables as linking flows of corresponding thickness *(Figure 7/3)*.

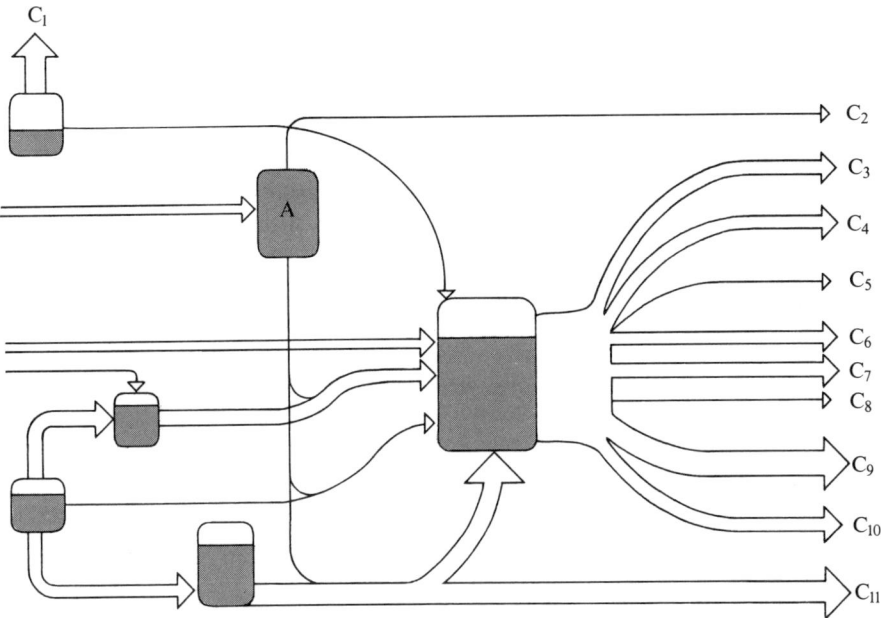

Figure 7/3: Quantified flow chart according to Beer 1975:434 (thickness of lines is proportional to rate of flow; size of process boxes proportional to productive capability; productivity indicated as a level in boxes; bottleneck process high-lighted at A; customers listed C_1 to C_{11})

The size of a box stands for the *capability* of a pertaining process (a measure that we shall define in a moment); its shaded part shows the actual utilization of the capability, i.e., *actuality*, at a given time and thus is a measure of "goodness" with respect to potential output. Clearly, this type of visualization of quantitative information makes it quite easy to recognize crucial bottlenecks that may be sources of problems. It is an effective variety attenuator because it permits suppression of words and numerical data; and it allows for whatever aggregation of details is wanted (cf. 1975:435).

353

In Chile, several teams were trained in the use of Beer's neurocybernetic organization model and then sent to each firm where they established such iconic models of the crucial operations in the plants. Because of the simplicity of these models, the workers were able to understand them and to join the operations reserarchers in determining the crucial operations. Some of the variables routinely identified in every plant were the size of stocks, inputs, outputs, bottleneck operations, and – as a measure of social unease – the level of absenteeism (cf. 1974:8). In addition, the workers were invited to enrich the models by whatever variables they wanted to be measured and reported to them; for *they* were going to be the users.

A Measure of Performance

As a measure of performance for any subsystem or single variable, Beer developed a triple index of economic achievement containing the three indices "latency," "productivity," and "performance." Each index ranges between 0 and 1. The three indices in turn are defined in terms of three measures of capacity called "potentiality," "capability," and "actuality," as *Figure 7/4* shows.

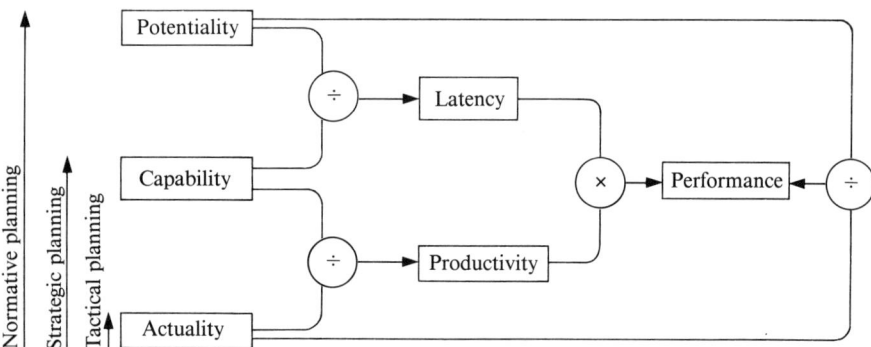

Figure 7/4: Three measures of capacity defining three indices of achievement and three concepts of planning, according to Beer 1975:437

Capability is an *estimated* measure of the performance that a variable or production unit can reasonably be expected to attain, considering the constraints exerted on it by other variables or production units of the same overall system (bottlenecks!). In contrast to "capacity," which measures the possible performance of a separate system, "capability" is a systems concept: it takes into account that the full use of capacity is rarely possible for a system that is not separate, but coproduces the outcome of a larger system and hence is dependent on its coproducers. Thus, a subsystem's systemic capability is normally smaller than its theoretical capacity as a separate system (cf. 1972:207, 1975:435).

354

Potentiality stands for the *anticipated* better performance than capability that a subsystem might produce in order to meet socioeconomic needs, "if only" some crucial bottlenecks among all its constricting coproducers in the overall system were reasonably improved. Potentiality thus indicates a potential for improvement of capability by means of investment (cf. 1975:435). (The definition of "latency," "productivity," and "performance" is seen in Figure 7/4.)

What then does the Cyberstride program do with all these measures of economic performance? (See *Table 7/5* for the basic program sequence as reported in the following.) As already said, Cyberstride receives the daily actuality figures for all measured variables of a system (e.g., a firm). It will then , after examining these figures for

	Step	Purpose
1	Read a figure with its code of origin	Daily input of measured variables of a viable system
2	Convert it to a non-dimensional value	*Index calculation* for the purpose of variety attenuation
3	Apply to it the statistical filter	Plausible?
4	Check whether it remains inside band of normality	Exception?
5	If yes, report it as normal and go to 13	
6	If not, check the trend with previous values	Important Change? *Bayesian forecasting*
7	If trend is transient, report it as transient and go to 13	
8	If trend is slope or step change, continue	
9	Report change and trend to original niveau	*Automatic Exception Reporting*
10	Check if time for correction at that niveau is exhausted	Alarm clock
11	If not, go to 13	
12	If yes, report fact to upper niveau and go to 10	*Algedonic reporting* (break of autonomy)
13	Check if indicator is used in other subroutines	
14	If yes, call subroutine for that niveau and go to 2; otherwise end	

Table 7/5: Basic Program Structure of Cyberstride (left half as reported by Schwember 1976:120; the interpretation on the right is my own)

plausibility, search for the pertinent capability and potentiality figures stored in the central files and compute the triple index for each variable. The indices of all units of one niveau of recursion (e.g., all firms) are also aggregated to overall indices for the next higher niveau (e.g., a sector of industry).

The program then faces an important question in respect to its task of information filtration (variety attenuation): Do the daily resulting new indices *matter* in comparison with the ones of the previous days, or can they be ignored as chance variations? In other words, what are the probabilities that the new indices stand for changes in trends important enough to deserve the attention of the responsible managers? The methodical means for computing such probabilities is Bayesian statistical theory.

A Bayesian Approach to Information Filtration

An index change, according to Harrison and Stevens (1971), may stand for a random variation, a transient change, a change of slope, or a step, the latter two being of significance to the manager. By means of Bayesian statistics, Cyberstride computes the posterior probabilities for each of the four events (cf. Beer 1975:439f). The program is sensitive to uncertainty: the more the posterior probabilities that are found point to a significant change, the more the time series considered will be extended so as to improve the basis of judgement.

Automatic Exception Reporting

Whenever a significant index change occurs, the responsible committee receives an automatic *exception report.* The task of the report is to focus the managers' attention on processes that need their intervention. The reports sent to one managerial committee are not available to any other, a precaution designed to further the envisaged devolution of control. The higher niveaus of recursion, including the government, are provided with aggregated data only, *so long as* – and here is the snag – things run smoothly.

Algedonic Regulation

So far, Cyberstride's organization is quite consistent with its purpose of devolving control to the managerial committees at each niveau. But now comes the crux: namely, the technical implementation of the underlying concept of autonomy. "Autonomy" is granted only so long as a subsystem successfully (or better, mechanically) acts as a homeostat with respect to the measured variables. Thus, whenever Cyberstride sends a negative exception report to a firm (or a sector, or a branch of industry), it also computes an acceptable delay time for the concerned system to react. The delay time is a function of the (estimated) reaction time required by a variable, and its importance within the system. The program then starts a clock, and if it does not record a recovery of the critical variable within delay time it will break the autonomy of the system and send a special alarm signal to the next higher niveau (cf. Beer 1975:442). The alarm consists in a so-called "algedonic" signal, i.e. literally, a "cry of pain" designed in analogy to the function of pain in the human nervous system: it will provide the higher niveau with the information that a subsystem has failed to perform properly with its curcial variables as a homeostat. To be fair, it should be noted that "the delay factors are discussed with the managers concerned, and they are informed if the algedonic signal is transmitted. Indeed, they may be very relieved – if the problem is seen as beyond their control – to know that the signal has automatically gone." (Beer 1975:422). Though this interpretation of Beer's appears somewhat one-sided, it must be recognized that there is at least an attempt at democratically handling the delicate determination of delay times which actually define the degree of autonomy given to each subsystem.

According to the principle of recursion, the same procedure of vertical reporting is then applied to the responsible management at the higher niveau: a clock is started as soon as it receives an algedonic report, and if it fails to produce a change for the better within *its* allotted delay time, another alert signal will be sent to the next higher niveau. Eventually, an unsolved detail problem of a single firm will thus reach the government (in Chile, the Secretary of Economics, Flores). The government is then free to decide whether or not it wants to react, for there is no higher controller.

We are now able to understand the organization of the entire design as given in *Figure 7/6.*

1.4. The Operations Room

The operations room is an "environment for decision" specifically designed for optimal visual presentation of the data produced by Cyberstride. The users were to be a group of people from levels 3 and 4 of any viable system under the guidance of a level-5 director; this arrangement was intended to secure a balance between internal and environmental perspectives, present and future, in the light of given socioeconomic priorities. There were special screens for the quantified flowcharts and for the reception of exception reports or algedonic signals. There was also an additional data bank called "Datafeed," and simulation equipment based on a System Dynamics-type simulation program, so as to provide the users of the room with an immediate experimental experience of what might be the consequences of their envisaged decisions (level-4 function!). The details of the technical equipment are not of importance for our assessment attempt; cf. Beer's own account and the photographs on the inside cover of *Platform for Change.*

Beer's mastery of the techniques of variety presentation is certainly noteworthy, but as Schwember acknowledges, "gadgets will help only if the overall concept is sound." (1976:108) This is the question to which we can now return.

357

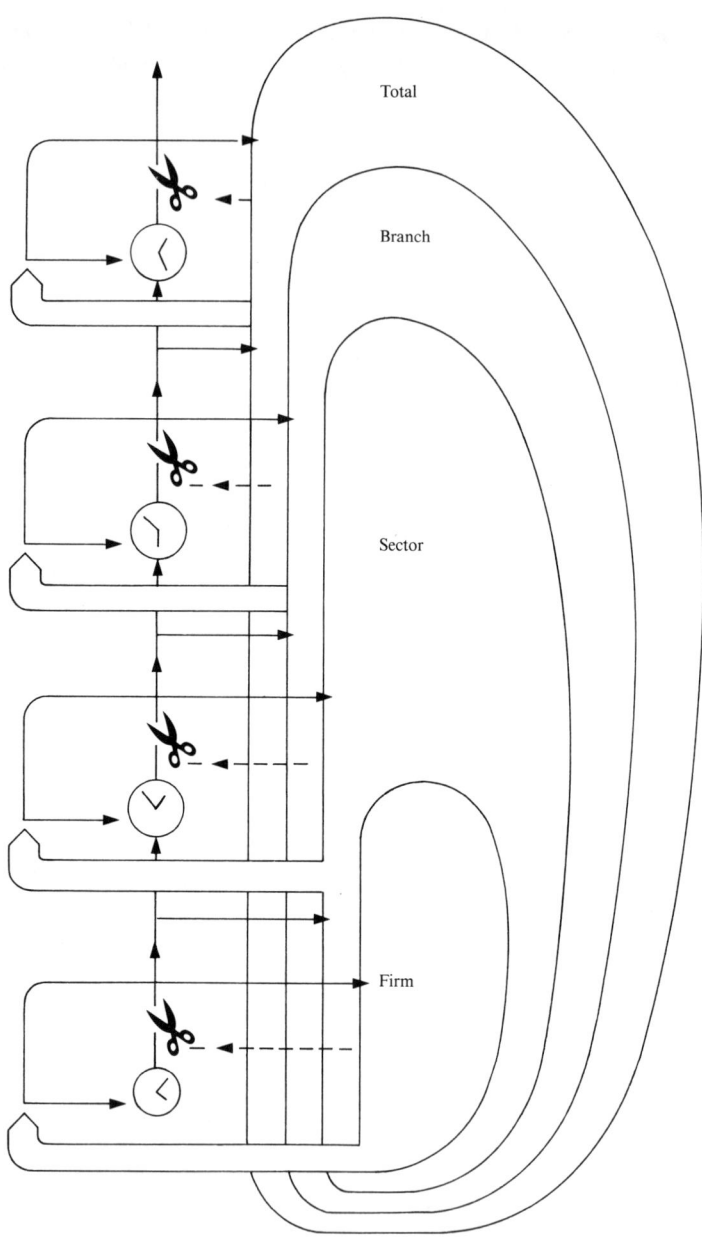

Figure 7/6: Cyberstride operating at four "autonomous" niveaus of recursion (= external hierarchy of viable systems), with algedonic reporting according to Beer 1975:443

2. Is Cybersyn a Design for a Purposeful System?
An Assessment Attempt

If Cybersyn is a design for a purposeful system, this ought to show itself with respect to the three earlier-mentioned, complementary problem-solving dimensions of any purposeful system: inquiry, action, and valuation.

In respect to the first dimension, we must now examine the question: Is Cybersyn a design for a purposeful inquiring system? More precisely: Is Cyberstride, the computer program, adequately designed for Cybersyn, the socioeconomic system, to become a purposeful inquiring system? The second and third (pragmatic and ethical) dimensions shall then be considered together by asking: Is Cybersyn adequately designed to become a purposeful social system? That is to say, what is its built-in *anatomy of purposefulness* as an action and valuation system? Since the first question is examined here mainly as a preparation for dealing with the second, we shall begin with some general considerations and then use the second question to illustrate our critically-heuristic categories.

2.1. Is Cybersyn a Design for a Purposeful Inquiring System?

In order to give concrete meaning to our design ideal of a purposeful inquiring system, we shall normatively stipulate that Cybersyn ought to distribute both information and decision power in such a way as to strengthen the autonomous decision-making capability of the relatively unskilled managerial committees at all niveaus and to improve self-coordination between them.[7] Of course, the underlying ideal is not only to improve the workers' effectiveness but also to democratize the nationalized sector of the economy and to enrich the workers' jobs. This stipulation comes close to Beer's own ideal of securing effective economic planning in the service of Allende's goals by means of a cybernetically based "devolution of power" (Beer 1975:428); but it shifts the focus from scientific definition to openly normative determination of Cybersyn's anatomy of purposefulness, and to corresponding provisions for critically reflected purposefulness *within* the social system concerned.

One of the main themes of Stafford Beer's cybernetic theory of organization is what he calls the *intelligent use of the computer.* A computer, he argues, is wasted if it is employed merely for more and more data production and data storage. Instead, the computer should be used for condensing and analyzing information, or, in Beer's terms: it ought to be used for the purpose of variety attenuation rather than for increasing the existing variety of data (cf. 1975:431, 435). Assuming that Beer is right,

---

[7] For reasons of space, this general formulation must stand here for a more detailed discussion of the "ought" questions parallel to the "is" questions chosen. Our second case study (Chapter 8) will illustrate the task of ideal mapping for each of the assessment questions considered.

the question must be: What kind of knowledge can a variety-attenuating computer program produce? That is, what kind of "intelligent" inquiry can the computer perform, and how should a human inquirer make use of it? Our answer to these questions should provide us with a standard of comparison for another question: What use of its data does Cyberstride impose on its users? Thus – to make it quite clear – we are not dealing in the following discussion with Stafford Beer's personal concept of knowledge, but with the one actually built into Cybersyn.

The key to variety attenuation in Beer's model is filtration of information so as to discriminate between significant and insignificant data. Although this assumption seems to be correct, the implication on which Cybersyn relies is not: namely, that filtration of information is a statistical problem. All the variety attenuators built into Cyberstride are based on statistical procedures such as index calculation and time series analysis, with the partial exception of the quantified flowchart which is a visual variety attenuator but nevertheless relies on index calculation. This focus on statistics is not of course due to Beer's inclination for (and his acknowledged mastery of) statistical procedures, but rather to the computer's restricted potential for inquiry. The point is simply that the computer's language leaves no choice but to apply statistical procedures. Hence, if one claims that the computer is capable of recognizing what is important and what is not, one must also assume that it can be told in its own formal language what it has to consider as important. Beer does assume this:

> The idea is to create a capability in the computer to recognize what is *important,* and to present only that very little information. (1975:431)

And:

> People do not really think out what is involved, because they conceive of the computer as a fast adding machine processing a data bank – instead of seeing in the computer, quite correctly, the logical engine that Leibniz first conceived. The computer can do anything that we can precisely specify; and that includes testing hypotheses by calculating probabilities. (1975:431)

Beer tacitly implies that we *can* precisely specify to the computer what "important" means, and specifically, that Bayesian statistics is a tool for just that. But his implication is not justified. The main point is a rather subtle one: while Cyberstride's design implies that the importance of data can be measured by statistical significance, the more correct position would be to say that statistical significance is a *heuristic* tool for discovering potentially important data but does not tell us anything about the real importance of data – "real" importance in the sense of *pragmatic* meaning.[8] The computer (and thus Cyberstride) works at a purely *syntactic* level, operating on

---

[8] E.g., long-term vs. short-term consequences, consequences for the involved firm or industry vs. consequences for affected third parties, etc. On the definition of the term "pragmatic" cf. section 3.1. of Chapter 4.

incoming symbols according to given syntactic (formal) rules and not bothering at all about their semantic and pragmatic meaning. It is important to recall that *syntactic truth does not necessarily imply semantic or pragmatic truth;* the computer produces syntactic truth nets (i.e., syntactically well-formed fact nets) but has no conception of semantic or pragmatic truth.[9] This is what Leibniz's logical engine invoked by Beer can be and what we understand with Churchman (1971:29ff) as a Leibnizian inquirer, or, in the terms of our taxonomy (Table 6/3), as a fact finding system.

Now, if Cyberstride is capable of performing the job of a fact finding system, it is only a second, human inquirer who by means of purposeful interpretation can yield semantic and pragmatic meaning to the syntactic truths produced by Cyberstride. That is to say, if we correctly understand the fact nets (indices) produced by Cyberstride as heuristic means for finding pragmatically meaningful information among abundant data, then we must make certain that there is a competent and free human inquirer who is in a position to bridge the heuristic gap between syntactic and pragmatic significance. In doing so, other heuristic sources such as personal experience and intuition, feelings and attitudes, and both purposeful (e.g., political) and purposeless (e.g., religious) values are as important as syntactic truth nets. Finally, there is yet another heuristic source that is not accessible to a Leibnizian inquirer: namely the *dialogue* between sensitive and reflective human inquirers. One might object that a great deal of "exact" science has ben practiced as Leibnizian inquiry and indeed produced pragmatically meaningful knowledge in spite of its disregard for feelings and values. But this holds true only because scientific knowledge had always been required to be *community knowledge* rather than personal knowledge, i.e., it acquired its status as scientific knowledge only because it was subject to critical dialogue among producers and clients (scientists, professionals, politicians, managers, technicians); and this dialogue makes sense exactly because it fulfills the role of closing the heuristic gap mentioned before. This is different from Cyberstride: because its hierarchical organization does not allow its clients the liberty of disregarding, modifying, or rejecting data (exception reports!), its results immediately become imperatives of action for the concerned managers.

Clearly, Cyberstride is more than a fact finding system: it is a Leibnizian inquirer which, through the crucial definition of autonomy on which it is based, has some kind of built-in executive power. The intention of its designer may have been to strengthen the autonomy of the lower-level decision makers in Chile's industry by providing them with an effective fact finding system; in reality, he appears to have implemented

---

[9] The semantic and pragmatic truth of the syntactically well-formed fact nets produced by a fact finding system is contingent upon the semantic and pragmatic validity of the original definitions and models of the "real world" given to the fact finder. All the fact finding system can do is to compare incoming well-formed formulae (WFF's, i.e., sentences that are neither tautological nor self-contradictory) with previously memorized formulae; if the new WFF is either implied by or implies a previous WFF, it is accepted as a "contingent truth" – contingent with respect to the previously established fact net. See the excellent account in Churchman 1971:29ff, esp. 31.

an *operating system* (cf. Table 6/3) that has been given its own autonomy, as if it were a purposeful action system. As an action system, Cyberstride can impose its autonomy on the allegedly autonomous decision makers by sending them exception reports and setting up pressures in the form of time allowances and algedonic alerts.

Thus, our question of whether Cybersyn is a design for a purposeful inquiring system leads us to the following answer:

(a) Cybersyn is not adequately designed to become a purposeful inquiring system, for its underlying concept of knowledge is purely syntactic. This means that Cybersyn is a *fact finding system* with a restricted ability to test the logical or statistical plausibility and significance of data, but not their pragmatic meaning.

(b) Cybersyn is an action system insofar as it is given an additional capability of controlling the use that is made of its results by its users. Cybersyn is not adequately designed, however, to become a purposeful action system, for it ignores the heuristic gap between syntactic truth nets and purposeful action. We must conclude that Cybersyn is a design for an *operating system* that is falsely substituted for a design for a social system. As a technical design for an operating system, it cannot internalize a purposeful orientation, while as a design for a social system it leaves no room for purposeful reflection on the part of its users. There is only one user to which this restriction does not apply, namely, the government; a consequence which seems to imply that not the workers but the government alone represents the client actually served.

(c) As a consequence of (a) and (b), Cybersyn does not function as a purposeful *valuation system* except at the niveau of the government; at all other niveaus, viability has been substituted as a criterion of good valuation for moral and political responsibility and reflection.

The question thus presents itself: What unreflected purposes will Cybersyn tend to serve, and who will have control over them? This is the issue with which our second basic assessment question is concerned.

2.2. Is Cybersyn a Design for a Purposeful Social System?

In order to unfold the normative content of Cybersyn as a design for a social system, let us concentrate on those of our critically-heuristic categories (cf. Table 4/4) which most directly cover the basic issues of social cybernetics according to Table 6/2:

(a) Who is (ought to be) Cybersyn's client?
(b) What is (ought to be) Cybersyn's purpose?
(c) Who is (ought to be) Cybersyn's decision maker?
(d) What is (ought to be) the role of expertise in Cybersyn?
(e) What is (ought to be) the guarantor of Cybersyn's success?

Referring to *Table 6/2,* questions (a) and (b) deal with the concept of motivation built into Cybersyn, (c) with the concept of control built into it, and (d) and (e) with the presupposed problem-solving perspective. The other categories are either implied in the above questions (e.g., Cybersyn's measure of improvement will be considered under the purpose question) or their content and significance has already become sufficiently apparent in the previous description of Project Cybersyn. For example, the key witnesses ought to be the workers to whom "devolution of power" was promised, and on whom Cybersyn now imposes its statistical interpretation of the significance of data, its exception reports, delay times, and algedonic alerts.

As far as space permits, each of the above questions will now be unfolded; we shall focus on the task of actual mapping rather than that of ideal mapping. The main heuristic purpose of this unfolding process will not be to reach a "final" judgement, but to illustrate the heuristic power and critical significance of our categories in tracing the normative content and the sources of deception built into a design.

Who Is Cybersyn's Client?

Stafford Beer's declared client were the Chilean workers whose alienation from the process of government he wanted to reduce:

> In Chile, I know that I am making the maximum effort towards the devolution of power. The government made their revolution about it; I find it good cybernetics. But the tools of science are not anywhere regarded as the people's tools; and people everywhere become alienated from that very science which is their own. Hence we are studying all these matters with the workers. Hence the systems I have to tell you about so far are designed for workers as well as ministers to use. Hence we are working on feedback systems to link the people to their government. (1975:428f)

We have no reason to doubt that devolution of power was Beer's sincere intention; but is this intention confirmed by Cybersyn's *design?*

To begin with the positive aspects, the fact that the workers were free to determine any additional variables they wanted to be measured and reported by Cyberstride gives evidence that they were indeed among Cybersyn's intended clients. Likewise, there is some democratic potential in the idea that Cyberstride's reports (including exception reports) were not available to recipients other than the committee concerned, not even to higher-niveau committees (however, the algedonic alerts and the potential abuse of the system bring this point into question).

Secondly, it must be recognized that President Allende's problem was in fact to guide the unexperienced workers' committees towards becoming more effective, better informed, in controlling their operations; in this sense, Cybersyn might well have contributed to creating the conditions of future, true participation. Particularly the educational potential of Cybersyn appears quite promising. Both Flores (personal communication) and Schwember (1976:108) report positive experiences with seminars held for workers:

> It is feasible to teach in a short period enough about the principles of organization of viable systems and their basic mechanisms to workers, even if their general education is very low. This was tested through the several experiences and seminars made with semi-skilled and specialized workers. They can effectively understand the process of decision-making and the importance of the ancillary tools. They would even become easily confident in strange environments such as the operation room." (1976:134)

The operations room itself might serve a useful training purpose as a simulator of decision-making situations.

On the other hand, objections need to be raised to which Cybersyn's design cannot give a satisfactory response:

1. Education of workers is no substitute, but only a prerequirement to giving them an active part in decision making. The internal hierarchy of the viable systems hardly supports the workers in becoming truly self-organizing and forming autonomous working groups; it is the level-3, 4 and 5 committees who via level 2 give instructions to the workers at level 1. It appears here that *"intrinsic control" is not realized in the original sense of ubiquitous distribution of control within a system,* nor is "autonomy" realized in the sense of self-responsibility. The underlying reason is clear: intrinsic control is in conflict with purely extrinsic motivation such as is built into Cybersyn. Even if one assumes that a productive unit may choose its own internal distribution and rotation of functions, those who are, at any given time, performing the upper-level functions are still subject to the external hierarchy of recursion, and so are not free to respect "their" lower-level coproducers as intrinsically motivated and responsible partners.

2. The *purely extrinsic concept of motivation* built into Cybersyn appears clearly whenever there is a real (nonroutine) decision to be made. We have seen that the workers' committees are granted "autonomy" as long as things run smoothly; but as soon as Cyberstride discovers a problem that really calls for decision making, the program also acts as a controller of the committee's decision making. This is a typical case of *inadequate application of the technical design ideal of purposiveness to social systems design* where the true ideal should be purposefulness; the result is extrinsic motivation rather than internal autonomy. Even this surrogate autonomy can at all times be broken by "algedonic" vertical reporting which represents not only a "cry of pain," as its name implies, but also a complete takeover of control by the alerted higher-niveau committee. Thus, the internal autonomy of each viable system below that of the government is completely dependent on the superior socioeconomic niveaus of recursion; what distinguishes Cybersyn from a traditional state bureaucracy is not a less hierarchical structure but the greater speed at

364

which vertical communication and control take place. In Chile, this fact may have corresponded to the best democratic interests of the people at that time; but it does not correspond to Beer's claim that his design secures devolution of power to the workers.

3. In addition, the fact that even a minor problem will take its way up through the entire hierarchy of government if by some reason it is not solved within allotted time spans points to the *centralizing effect* inherent in any strongly hierarchical organization. Let us assume that a workers' committee really takes seriously its responsibility and hence, in a certain situation, finds that it cannot responsibly act in accordance with Cyberstride (e.g., that it ought to ignore an exception report, or improve a variable other than the one indicated by an exception report). Such a decision should be expected from a truly responsible manager who is aware of both his given autonomy and the fact that no computer program is responsible, that only its users are. Indeed, we could even take the occurrence of such managerial decisions as evidence for true autonomy. However, in Cybersyn's organization, a workers' committee deciding *against* Cyberstride would subsequently have to defend its responsible decision against all the quasi-automatically acting "homeostats" at the upper niveaus, including the government; its decision would be effective only if it could persuade all higher niveaus of the need for an exception.[10] It is sufficiently clear from examples of strong hierarchies such as governmental bureaucracies or the military how difficult it is, under such conditions, to act effectively according to both the requirements of the situation and the expertise of the lower niveaus. It is also well known that such organizations largely prevent the lower niveaus from learning and from developing self-control – indispensable conditions of truly democratic participation.

These few considerations (others could easily be added) seem to lead to but one conclusion: Cybersyn's alleged goal of devolving power to workers is *not* confirmed by its design. Instead, its strongly hierarchical organization and its concept of "autonomy" one-sidedly serve the top decision maker, the government. The government is the main client who can

(a) use Cyberstride's reports autonomously, i.e., without any control by a higher homeostat (it has not to fear any algedonic reporting to the democratic "basis" if it fails to respond to an exception report);

(b) change the overall goal, by changing the measure of performance, the Cyberstride program, or Cybersyn's organization in general;

(c) control all the information potential of Cyberstride, be it by means of complete aggregation or disaggregation of data, be it by modifying data;

---

[10] Stafford Beer, in his comment on the draft of this paper, has denied this point. However, it seems to me that this is what Cybersyn's design implies *if* its concept of viability is not halfway abandoned.

(d) employ the communication potential of Cybernet for other than the original purposes.[11]

What is Cybersyn's Purpose?

Cybersyn's actual purpose – without questioning the sincerity of its designer's ideal of creating "systems that were intended to be devolutionary, popular, and pluralistic" (Beer 1974:3) – can be traced from two aspects of its design:
(a) its built-in measure(s) of improvement, and
(b) its underlying model of the social economy to be monitored.

As to (a), Cybersyn uses the triple index of economic achievement introduced earlier: "latency," "productivity," and "performance." These three main indices are interesting measures of economic production, but by no means do they consider such vital socioeconomic issues as quality of production, economic distribution, management of resources, quality of working life, or the socioecological quality of life in general. Especially, Cybersyn's focus on economic production will leave virtually no room for considering such goals as "devolution of control" and "pluralism." Whenever a problem arises, all the managerial attention is directed to the state of the critical production variables causing an exception report. It is an old objection against the so-called Management by Objectives that all purposes that are not quantified by some measure of improvement will tend to be neglected – an objection that fully applies to Cybersyn's alleged devolutionary and pluralistic orientation.

Cybersyn's built-in purpose thus appears to be a one-sided *efficiency of production*. With respect to this purpose, Cybersyn may indeed help the workers maximize their effectiveness, as Beer claims. But this goal again *reflects mere tool design* that does not consider its own normative content, the missed opportunity for true democratization of the working place, and for social reform in general: the workers are "helped" to be better tools of industrial production, that's all. True, the overall political purpose of improved productivity was democratic socialism. The tool, unfortunately, is closer to what Illich (1973:109) would call managerial fascism.

As to (b), it was explained above how the quantified flowcharts at all niveaus of the economy were based on "crude, but effective" operations research models (Beer 1974:433). It seems at least questionable whether the operations and goals of an entire sector of industry, for instance, can be described by some few indices in any meaningful way (cf. Grosch 1973:627). Knowledge of the development of some crucial production variables such as outputs, stocks, or bottlenecks does not tell the decision

---

[11] This actually happened during the "October Crisis" of 1972, when a CIA-instigated truckers' strike was successfully counteracted by the Allende government with the help of Cybernet (communication by Mr. Flores, see also Chapter 13 of the second edition of *Brain of the Firm*, 1981:312–314). Via Cybernet, real-time information on the developing situation was transmitted to the government and thus provided it with the requisite control variety to counteract the strike's effects. The use of Cybernet in this case was in the true interest of the country, but the potential for abuse is clear – "abuse" meaning that the actual client is not the one proclaimed.

makers much about the roots of the problem, and hence the range of effective countermeasures (e.g., is the problem caused by the economic blockade, by lacking skills, by a bad working climate, or by other, nonquantifiable factors?). That means, Cyberstride and with it the operations room merely serve a *real-time location of internal symptoms, but not real-time explanation of problems nor real-time decision making.* Traditional reports by staff members are necessary to clarify problems and alternative countermeasures – the procedure actually employed by CORFO (communication by Mr. Flores).[12]

Who Is Cybersyn's Decision Maker?

This question has largely been answered by the reflections on the client question; only one additional comment is required here.

Earlier we mentioned that whoever is in a position to control Cyberstride's input will have control over its functioning as an (unreflective) valuation system. This observation points to a *problem of potential manipulation.* Where control over inputs is the only way of controlling a system's quasi-autonomy, the distribution of control over inputs will inevitably be subject to a political struggle for power among all users. The chances are that increasing centralization, corruption, and sabotage will occur. Ultimately, it is the top controller, the government, which is in a position to change Cybersyn's design according to its political purposes, and thus also to manipulate the inputs coming in by Cybernet so as to produce the desired feedback reports. This is not meant to cast suspicion of any such intention on Allende's government, but merely to point to its built-in potential of control. It is of course another question whether or not in a democracy the government's autonomy is in turn controlled by the people; there is at least no evidence that Cybersyn could contribute anything to truly democratic control of the government on the part of the workers. Beer was probably aware of this fact when he outlined his idea of an "algedonic meter" (1974:21) that would give the government immediate feedback on the public's feelings about its decisions or plans when announcing them. Such a device might set the government under a sort of visualized public opinion pressure; but apart from other problematic aspects, it cannot secure public control over the potential manipulation of Cyberstride's input by the government.

The basic danger is always the same: more centralized tools not only increase the government's potential for pursuing democratically legitimate purposes, but also add new *problems of technology control* to those already existing. History teaches us that tools that can be abused sooner or later will be abused, be it under a socialist or a capitalist government.

---

[12] An exception might be seen in the attempt to include a measure of "social unease" in the models, by measuring the level of absenteeism in each subsystem. But this is only one internal source of difficulties, and its measure may represent an attempt to control absenteeism by means of vertical reporting rather than to secure decision making in view of a better quality of working life.

What Is the Role of Expertise in Cybersyn?

At issue here is the model of the relationship between science and politics built into Cybersyn: What importance does Cybersyn give to the tools of expertise (in this case, cybernetics and statistics) in government, compared to those of the politician? We have earlier discussed the three basic models of expert consultation according to Habermas (1971b:62ff), the decisionistic, the technocratic, and the pragmatistic model (see Section 2.3 of Chapter 1).

In accordance with the classical researcher-client relation in operations research, Cybersyn's presupposed consultation model appears to be a *decisionistic* one. The resulting practice is likely to tend toward a technocratic model, which is always a close, if not consequent next step. The decisionistic model is reflected in Cybersyn's extrinsic concept of motivation and in the corresponding *external* hierarchy of viable systems; means and ends are assumed to be separable in such a way that once the top niveau (the government) has determined the ends, the other niveaus can then function as means without introducing a normative content of their own. The technocratic model is partly evident in the *internal* hierarchy of the viable systems: the normative functions of levels 3, 4 and 5 are separated from the actually productive functions at level 1 and entrusted to expert-managers and expert-planners. Significantly, the Cybersyn team of operations researchers was given a level-4 position within the viable system of CORFO, the top niveau. The question of whether Cybersyn's design implies a predominantly decisionistic or rather a technocratic concept of expertise may not be very easy to decide on the basis of the design alone; nor is it very important. What is more clear, and more important, is that Cybersyn is *not* based on the one concept of expertise that seems appropriate to a political – and particularly to a democratic-socialist – undertaking of the importance of Cybersyn: namely, a critically-normative or *pragmatistic* one. In distinction to both the decisionistic and the technocratic models, the pragmatistic model does not presuppose strict separability of purposive-rational choice of means and purposeful selection of purposes; quite the contrary, it requires openly and critically normative debate on the value content of *all* decisions on tools and means, scientific or not, and their possibly counterproductive effects with regard to legitimately chosen purposes. Cybersyn, the social system, cannot live up to that demand because Cybersyn, the technical design, leaves no room for true self-organization and participation in government on the part of the workers. The basic reason for this is that no rational discourse on values is possible *within* the theoretical framework of Cybersyn, that is, within its syntactic-cybernetic language and rationality criteria (measures of performance). Instead values are "given" to Cybersyn, the social system, by the government and handed down through the external hierarchy of command called "niveaus of recursion." Whether or not this type of government runs counter to the intended and legitimate purpose of democratic and socioeconomic reform is not considered, and cannot be considered by those affected – the workers. For them, the experts have decided on what socioeconomic progress and democratization means, what kind of "socialism" is good for them. Beer expresses this in an amazingly overt way:

> I will go so far as to suggest a redefinition of liberty for our current technological area. It would say that *competent information is free to act* – and that this is the principle on which the new Liberty Machine [Cybersyn?] should be designed.
> ...
> Who are *we* to say that we know best and everyone else is wrong? ... It is that we are *responsible*. We are not responsible because we have been elected to govern affairs; we are responsible because cybernetics, that science of effective organization, is our profession. Such understanding of this subject as there is, we have. Therefore we must speak out. (1970:319 and 320)

Nobody will deny Stafford Beer his right to speak out. But perhaps we would do well to recall the important lesson to be learned from Charles P. Snow's famous account of the role of scientific advisors in British government during World War II, *Science and Government:* "If you are going to have a scientist in a position of isolated power, the only scientist among nonscientists, it is dangerous *whoever he is."* (1962:118) What Sir Charles meant is that no matter how good the scientific judgement of an advisor to government may be, the implication that there can be such a thing as value-neutral, quasi-objective advice or tool design in political affairs, and moreover "that intelligent and highplaced nonscientists should believe that it exists," is in itself dangerous. (1962:119)

What Is Cybersyn's Guarantor?

What source of guarantee for its effectiveness does Cybersyn's design imply? The question has nearly been answered by the previous reflections: *The rational designer who regards himself as a scientist will quite naturally tend to take his science as the best guarantor he can hope for.* This is exactly the danger meant by Sir Charles in his warning quoted above: the danger that nonscientists will take the science of their experts as a guarantor because the experts themselves do so and have become experts in doing so.

To be a bit more specific, Cybersyn seems to assume two scientific guarantors. The one is *cybernetic modelling* which by definition describes "universal" structural properties of the world's functional organization. What is wrong with this position? It is simply the neglect of an important idea discussed before: namely, that cybernetic modelling, in relying on structural analogies between the "brain," the "machine," and the "firm," is nothing more than a *heuristic* tool but should never be taken for a scientific guarantor of appropriate social system design.

The second scientific guarantor of Cybersyn is the *computer* with its absolute guarantee for logical truth. (The fact that all the statistical procedures involved can be handled without computer, on principle at least, does not contradict this assertion:

369

the important point is the belief in the quasi-objectivity of *syntactic truth nets.)* The computer, or the syntactic truth nets that it produces, replaces the unreliable judgement of Cybersyn's human partners by an absolutely reliable control of some crucial variables. More precisely, the allegedly autonomous decision making on the part of the workers will always be "homeostatically" kept within certain modest limits of human error. That does not seem too grave a thing to a rationalist designer because no "rational" manager will ever have the wish to ignore the results of computer-based anlaysis, given *the manager's own need for certainty.* Erich Fromm has convincingly argued that the manager's need for certainty makes it difficult for him to refuse a method of planning that is "free from the arbitrariness of the human will and entrusted to a computer system." (1974:50f) This is not to say that the manager may not be well aware of the uncertainty and potential deception in such computer-based decisions, due to the heuristic gap between syntactic truth and pragmatic meaningfulness; "but if disaster does happen after the decisions are made on the basis of unquestionable 'facts,' it is like an act of God, which one must accept, since man cannot do more than make the best decision he knows how to make." (1974:51)

What is basically wrong with this guarantor has been apparent throughout this case study: an approach to social systems design that takes syntactic criteria such as Ashby's law of requisite variety and statistical indices as guarantors of practical reason eliminates the only (though imperfect) possibility of avoiding hidden political values and social irrationality: namely, the consciously normative *dialogue* between purposeful and responsible humans.

2.3. A Personal Afterthought

In Chile, disaster *did* happen to Project Cybersyn against which Cybersyn's design was not and could hardly be expected to be a guarantor. The control of the country was taken over by a military regime which, because it was friendlier than Allende's government to the capital interests of the Western democratic nations, did not have to struggle with many of the difficulties that economic blocade and social-democratic reform had caused to the Allende government. Project Cybersyn was dead before we could learn about its weaknesses and its potential for being improved. Stafford Beer himself should be given allowance for not getting a chance of gradually improving his design, so that it could serve the democratic and social values to which he was personally committed.

Cybernetics and "systems science" was saved the trouble of accepting a challenge to practical reason from within. Few other systems scientists have shown the degree of ethical and political engagement that distinguishes Beer's view of cybernetics. In this respect, I regret that my critique of Cybersyn falls upon one of the very rare efforts undertaken by systems scientists in the service of democratic values. This is the eternal dilemma of the critic: that in order to advance his cause he needs to criticize not those whose work is irrelevant, but those who try most to do something relevant to that cause. It is precisely because I have no doubt about Stafford Beer's as well as the Allende Government's sincere democratic and social concern that I find it important to reflect on the sources of deception in the cybernetic tools they employed. As long as these tools are understood as scientific and value-neutral, it will be deceptive to expect any significant contribution to social and democratic progress from them.

In my opinion, "systems science" should finally start employing the systems idea as an inescapably value-laden concept, or else it should admit that it cannot meet the challenge to practical reason – for dealing with value-laden issues in openly and critically normative terms *is* the challenge to practical reason.

Chapter Eight
Health Systems Planning:
The Case of the 1976 Areawide Health Systems
Plan for Central Puget Sound

*I cannot be pessimistic about America. It is not a tenable
position for the United States to be that country among the
rich countries that has the most and the worst slums, the
highest rate of unemployed and unemployables, and the least
developed health services, and that is the most niggardly
toward its old people and its poor children who are so many,
as well as being the country that leads the whole Western
world in violence, crime, and corruption in high places.*
Gunnar Myrdal (1975:284)

Introduction

Gunnar Myrdal's statement, though not written with special regard to health planning, captures the basic dilemma and challenge of health planning: health planning cannot be about health services only. Almost no other problem of social concern so well illustrates the basic tenet of the systems approach: *no problem can be solved simply on its own basis* (cf. Churchman 1979:5). Whether there will be meat in the kitchen is not a problem to be solved in the kitchen. Whether the American people will be healthy is not a question determined in the health care system. The U.S. Congress has implicitly acknowledged this fact with the labels it gave to its health planning legislation: "Comprehensive Health Planning" (CHP Amendments of 1966, Public Law 89–749) and "Health Systems Planning" (National Health Planning and Resources Development Act of 1974, P.L. 93-641).

However, the law is not reality, but at best a plan for it. The real tenet of health planning has been: *more medical care = more health.* Wildawsky (1976:1, 1977:105, in 1979:284) has aptly called it "the great equation"; and it is not by mere coincidence that it is reminiscent of another "great equation" to which the U.S. Congress subscribes: *more private business = more public wealth.* Health planning in the United States has long been mainly an affair of private actors, whether profit or nonprofit-oriented. It has been dominated by providers who quite naturally thought and acted more in terms of the second and third tenet than in terms of the first one: private practitioners, the American Medical Association (AMA) and other professional health organizations, hospitals, insurance companies, the medical-pharmaceutical industry, and governmental agencies at the Federal, state and local levels (for a short overview of the history and the fragmented state of private and public health planning in the USA see Stebbins/Williams 1972 and Ardell 1970).

The CHP Amendments of 1966 for the first time brought about a concentration of coordinating responsibility at the state and areawide levels (CHP agencies) with significant participation of "consumers" (as opposed to providers). Though some of these CHP bodies undoubtedly did good work (examples: the California State Plan for Health, 1971, and the Bay Area CHP Council's Health Systems Plan of 1975), they were facing an "almost limitless task" for which their resources and authority were, according to the former Executive Director of the Bay Area CHP Council, Donald B. Ardell (1973:49), "dramatically inadequate." But unclear purposes and functions, continuing domination by vested interests with little eagerness for systems change, the lack of "planning for planning," lacking support by regional and national agencies, a lack of public involvement, dependence on private funds, and many other reasons, prevented CHP bodies from assuming the leadership role they were intended to play for innovative health planning (cf. Ardell 1971:29f, Waters 1976:141ff). The label of comprehensiveness alone could not stop the continuing focus on the "great equation."

The National Health Planning and Resources Development Act of 1974 (P.L. 93–641) brought about the transition from the CHP bodies to the *Health Systems Agencies* (HSAs). Along with more than 200 federally monitored and funded HSAs – each responsible for a "Health Service Area" – P.L. 93–641 also provides for stronger state level planning by the so-called "State Health Planning and Development Agencies".

Will the HSAs be able to assume the leadership role in health planning that the CHP bodies could not realize? More precisely: does P.L. 93–641 provide for the HSAs to overcome the focus on the "great equation" and to achieve what it claims to be its purpose; securing a "comprehensive, rational approach" to health planning?

Of course, only time and experience can give us the definite answer to that question. Our task is not to forecast the Health Systems Agencies' actual impact on health, but rather to give a prognostic assessment of the planning potential and probable failures that are built into HSA's design by P.L. 93–641. Is it possible to do so? In this case study, we assume that the tenet of the systems approach gives us a sensible criterion for this purpose. To the extent that HSA's design ignores the fact that no social problem can be solved simply on its own basis, this design is likely to fail in its purpose because of built-in sources of deception.

Contrary to Wildawsky's (1973:129) assertion that actual planning success is the only sensible criterion for identifying and evaluating "rational" planning, we maintain that rational planning cannot rely on *post hoc* evaluation only. Wildawsky's assertion barely hides his incrementalist, if not anti-planning, stance. Renouncing an anticipatory evaluation of plans in regard to built-in purposes and sources of deception is to relinquish the idea of planning altogether, for planning means just that: to anticipate the normative implications of designs and actions so as to make sure that the right goals are achieved. As Henrik Blum (1978) observes with an eye to the predominantly incrementalist mode of U.S. health planning, "we shuck tangible goals for [incrementalist] methods, a total denial of the purpose of planning, which is to achieve goals." Planning that is not openly and critically normative is no planning at all. In the terms of the present study, health systems planning must be understood as design for purposeful social systems.

In the following discussion, the case of the *Areawide Health Systems Plan for Central Puget Sound,* adopted by the Puget Sound Health Planning Council (Seattle, Washington) in 1976, will serve as a touchstone for assessing HSA's planning potential and the sources of deception built into it by P.L. 93–641. We will understand P.L. 93–641 as a publicly legislated metaplan for health systems planning in the designated health service areas (e.g. Central Puget Sound). This perspective is different from the traditional understanding of public law. Traditionally the function of public law, as exemplified by classical civil law, has been understood to be that of a "watchdog" against impingements on constitutionally guaranteed personal freedoms and civil rights. Increasingly, however, the function of new legislation is not so much that of a "watchdog" as rather that of a catalyst in securing improvement of societal conditions. Public law is thus assuming the function of a public metaplan and ought to be assessed as such: How well does it plan for future planning? It is true that much of contemporary social legislation such as worker protection, minimum wages, environmental protection, etc. still takes the form of "positive" law, i.e., a single-stage practical decision which rarely fulfills the function of a plan, and indeed often prevents adequate planning. But as Churchman (1968 b:150) emphasizes, "planning is concerned with multistage decision making." From a planning point of view, a public law will not fulfill its function unless it is a design for future multistage decision processes which, because of their political and technical complexity, cannot be reduced to a single-stage decision.

Table 8/1 contrasts the suggested planning perspective to the traditional "positive law" perspective of legislation. For instance, the Endangered Species Act of 1973 (P.L. 93–205) should serve as a metaplan organizing a multiplicity of future problem-solving and decision-making processes in view of changing preservation needs; similarly P.L. 93–641 should be a design for purposeful systems called HSAs that ought to be capable of performing a range of complex, future, multistage decision processes called "health systems planning."

A last introductory remark concerns the Health Systems Agency chosen for our case study, the Puget Sound Health Planning Council. It was formed in 1971 as a merger of the former Puget Sound Comprehensive Health Planning Board and the Regional Health Planning Council. When publishing its 1976 *Health Systems Plan* (quoted in the following as HSP), it had not yet been designated as an HSA, but it had

Perspective	Traditional perspective: stipulation of positive law	Metaplanning perspective: design for purposeful systems
Main function of public law	Law and order: preserving the given order of society and the personal freedoms it guarantees	Societal guidance: providing impetus and guidance for societal processes so as to facilitate social change
Examples	1. Civil law 2. Criminal law	1. Endangered Species Act of 1973 2. Health Planning and Resources Development Act of 1974?
Standard assessment	The Legislator cannot anticipate social change	The legislator must anticipate social change necessary to secure improvement of the whole social system
Basis of legitimation	Commonly acknowledged social values; response to the call for law and order (constitution state)	Democratic input to and control of deliberate social change; response to the need for improvement (social intervention state)
Planning approach	Single-stage decision process: formulating "positive law" and enforcing it (legislator = watchdog)	Multistage decision process: planning and organizing for purposeful problem-solving processes (legislator = metaplanner)

Table 8/1: Two perspectives of public legislation

applied for federal designation as an HSA and its 1976 HSP was in fact intended to qualify it for such designation. The Introduction to the HSP explains:

> This first Areawide Health Systems Plan for the Central Puget Sound Region of Washington State... closely resembles a Health Systems Plan as described in the National Health Planning and Resources Development Act of 1974 (P.L. 93–641). The new law, which specifies broad health goals and health priorities for the nation, requires preparation of an annual "Health Systems Plan" which is
>> "a detailed statement of goals (A) describing a healthful environment and health systems in the area which, when developed, will assure that quality health services will be available and accessible in a manner which assures continuity of care, at reasonable cost, for all residents of the area; [and] (B) which are responsive to the unique needs and resources of the area." (P.L. 93–641, Section 1513(b)(2))
>
> The Areawide Health System Plan which follows is a statement of goals, specifications for the health system, findings, and recommendations aimed at achieving these goals.
>
> As envisioned by the Puget Sound Health Planning Council, the areawide plan will link previous planning with the "next generation" planning called for in P.L. 93–641. The council ... has applied for designation as the health systems agency for the ten-county northwest Washington region. In the work program included in the application for designation, the council proposes using this areawide plan, in combination with the planning products of North Puget Sound, as the transition to publication of an enlarged Health Systems Plan early in 1977.
>
> Thus the National Health Planning and Resources Development Act of 1974 will not bring a new program to northwest Washington. Rather, the new federal Act offers a welcome opportunity to expand a planning philosophy already well established in this region. (HSP 1976:1f)

On the basis of this statement it seems fair to consider the case available to us as at least partly representative of the normative content and the sources of deception built into P.L. 93–641's design for HSAs. Although we will keep in mind that we deal with a particular planning agency rather than with a standard HSA, I shall take this particular case as providing us with an opportunity to reflect on the potential of HSAs to become purposeful systems, without any claim to do justice to the involved planners of Puget Sound's Health Planning Council. Our purpose is not to give a balanced evaluation of the Council's Health Systems Plan but rather to illustrate the critical relevance of our critically-heuristic categories.

1. What Is/Ought to Be the Purpose of Health Systems Planning?

Let us begin the mapping process with the purpose category, for it offers an opportunity to clarify the value basis for the unfolding of the other categories.

1.1. Ideal Purpose Map

There is no question that the function of health planning should be to improve health. The question is: What does "health" mean in terms of human needs to be planned for? At this place, we could simply stipulate a definition of health as a guiding ideal. However, for the mapping process intended it will be more helpful to recall – very briefly – the historical background of what "health" has meant to a changing society, and what it might mean again.

For the Greeks and Romans, health meant "mens sana in corpore sano," i.e., full and equal development of both spiritual and physical needs. They did not possess the idea of isolable "disease entities," the removal of which should be possible by purely physical intervention in the human body. It was only with the medieval body-mind dichotomy and then, later, with the advent of industrial society that health became more and more identified with the absence of disease entities. As Ivan Illich writes in *Medical Nemesis,* in a chapter with the significant title "The Invention and Elimination of Disease":

> We tend to forget how recently disease entities were born. In the mid-nineteenth century, a saying attributed to Hippocrates was still quoted with approval: "You can discover no weight, no form nor calculation to which to refer your judgement of health and sickness. In the medical arts there exists no certainty except in the physician's senses." Sickness was still personal suffering in the mirror of the doctor's vision. (1977:156)

Nineteenth century positivism definitively fostered a medical epistemology that reduced health to a value-free, operational concept, and sickness to a technical problem of removing material disease entities that people somehow "caught" or "got." As Illich comments,

> within this mechanized framework, pain turned into a red light and sickness into mechanical trouble. A taxonomy of diseases became possible. As minerals and plants could be classified, so diseases could be isolated and categorized by the doctor-taxonomist. The logical framework for a new purpose in medicine had been laid. Instead of suffering man, sickness was placed in the center of the medical system and could be subjected to (a) operational verification by measurement, (b) clinical study and experiment, and (c) evaluation according to engineering norms. (1977:156f)

The main consequences of positivist medical epistemology are still operative today:

(a) The spiritual component of health could no longer be dealt with in the positivist epistemological framework. Mental illness thus became an "unscientific" entity referred to the psychiatrist; health care became limited largely to controlling physical sickness insofar as it could be "objectively" observed and measured by trained professionals.

(b) The sociopolitical and socioecological conditions that created health or sickness – implicitly acknowledged in all the social protection legislation of the nineteenth and twentieth centuries – became something beyond the legitimate concern of health care. Health care was to be something that was "delivered" in hospitals, and its implicit function was to repair and maintain people's fitness for the given social conditions of industrial society. The political value implications of the underlying health concept were hardly ever recognized; instead, comprehensive health concepts advocated by social reformers, psychiatrists, humanitarian philosophers, and more recently by the environmentalists and by the holistic health movement, were criticized as being "normative" and hence "scientifically useless."

Many physicians and health care administrators have only recently begun to realize that the shortcomings of the present health care system – "our unacceptable health status... inequitable access to health care... continuously escalating costs," as Henrik Blum (1976 a:3) summarizes the situation in the United States – might be due to a crisis of "value-free" medical epistemology, and particularly to a crisis in its apolitical, inherently apologetic concept of disease. By excluding sociopolitical value considerations from the concept of health, public health planning is bound to ignore the fact that health and disease are *socially* created conditions and hence must be understood as problems of social change rather than as merely technical problems that could be solved by professional expertise. The same fallacy has dominated other areas of public planning; for instance, the deteriorating quality of urban life has been coproduced by professional city planners oriented toward positivist, apolitical measures of quality of life; the persisting poverty of the developing countries has been coproduced by developmental strategies based on positivist economic theory; and so on. In these areas, as in public health planning, scientism has demonstrated its inability to deal with problems of social concern. The implication is clear: key concepts of social planning such as "health," "quality of life," or "economic growth" will become sources of deception if they are defined without critical reflection on the epistemological and political assumptions that inevitably flow into them.

Any normative stipulation of what "health" ought to mean has, moreover, not only political and epistemological but also metaphysical implications. Metaphysically speaking, our concept of health will have to be compatible with the nonobjectivistic and nonreductionistic metaphysics of design on which our critically-heuristic approach relies. Our concept of health must take into account all aspects of the whole that constitutes health – let us not forget the common etymological origin of the concepts "health", "whole," and "holy" in the Old-English word *"hal"* = sound, whole, happy; similarly the German word *"heil"* (= sound) has the same root meaning as "whole" and *"heilig"* (= holy).

Politically speaking, such a holistic concept of health must avoid the one major pitfall of the holistic health movement, its frequently one-sided focus on the subjective-spiritual and cultural dimensions of health (right attitudes, relaxation, balanced diet, etc.); this focus tends to neglect the socioeconomic and political dimension of health. Health planning must always be understood as a political act with redistributive effects, and is hence in need of a collective basis of legitimation. Health planning should also be understood as having ethical implications; an "ethics of whole systems" (Churchman 1968a) rather than an individualistic ethics is required as a basis for health planning. For instance, a progress in health that creates or maintains social inequity, dependence, or arbitrariness ("Who shall play God?" cf. Howard/Rifkin 1977) may be no progress at all from an ethics of whole systems standpoint. The recent "advances" in terminal care and genetic engineering are just two prominent cases in point.

Let us now consider some definitions of health that come close to a truly holistic, i.e., cultural-socioeconomic-political-ecological-psychosomatic concept of health (though unfortunately they do not all explicitly mention the socioeconomic, political, and cultural dimensions, Illich's definition excepted). The best known and most widely accepted of all holistic definitions of health is certainly that of the World Health Organization (WHO):

> Health is a state of complete physical, mental and social well-being, and not merely the absence of disease or infirmity. (WHO-Constitution 1946)

Henrik Blum similarly proposes a definition that emphasizes the relation of health to individual self-realization and purposefulness:

> Health is a state of being in which the individual does the best with the capacities he has, and acts in ways that maximize his capacities. (1974:93)

Leonard Duhl offers a definition that points to the developmental and problematic nature of health as a process of social interaction, a process that can never come to a perfect solution and that includes illness – in the sense of failure to command this process – as an inevitable experience offering new opportunities for development:

> Health [is] the ability to command events (internal and external) that affect our life. The issue is to have choice and the freedom of movement... the faculty for mutual synthesis... the mediation between all aspects of "I" and all aspects of "Us." (1976:33, ellipsis dots original)

Similarly, Erich Fromm's definition sees health as a continuous process of birth, of becoming fully born, fully alive for creatively relating to one's outer and inner world, in close analogy to Zen Buddhism's concept of becoming "wide awake":

Health means to be born entirely and to become what one has the potential to be...
to be wide awake... to see the world as it is... to experience oneself in *being* rather
than in *having*. (1960, my simplified transl. from the German version, 1972:118f)

Finally, Ivan Illich suggests a definition that stresses the importance of self-reliance,
along with culturally (and implicitly, politically, socioeconomically) shaped patterns
of coping with suffering; he sees health as a balance between adaptation and autonomy, as "autonomous coping" rather than "heteronomous (i.e., administered) maintenance and management" (1977:xvii):

> Health designates a process of adaptation. It is not the result of instinct, but of an
> autonomous yet culturally shaped reaction to socially created reality.... Health
> designates a process by which each person is responsible.... Health is a task.
> (1977:270f)

and:

> To a large extent culture and health coincide. Each culture gives shape to a unique
> *Gestalt* of health and to a unique conformation of attitudes toward pain, disease,
> impairment, and death, each of which designates a class of that human perfor-
> mance that has traditionally been called the art of suffering. Each person's health is
> a responsible performance in a social script. (1977:122f)

It is especially Illich's concept of health which not only corresponds to our normative and metaphysical-epistemological perspective[1] but also offers a basic purpose to
impose on our ideal map for the Puget Sound Health Planning Council. This will be
our ideal purpose for health systems planning: "to secure cultural, political, socioeconomic, and ecological conditions that foster the will to, and the potential for,
self-reliance and mutual self-care on the part of the client community in dealing with
human suffering."

In Illich's own terms, we will assign the following ideal *task description* to the Puget
Sound Health Planning Council:

> The level of public health corresponds to the degree to which the means and
> responsibility for coping with illness are distributed among the total population.
> This ability to cope can be enhanced but never replaced by medical intervention or
> by the hygienic characteristics of the environment. That society which can reduce
> professional intervention to the minimum will provide the best conditions for
> health. The greater the potential for autonomous adaptation to self, to others, and
> to the environment, the less management of adaptation will be needed or tolerated.
> (1977:271)

---

[1] Cf. the pertinent remarks in the last paragraph of Chapter Six.

It becomes clear, then, that our *ideal avenues to health* are basically these two:

1. Minimizing the need for, and dependency on, professionally delivered health care on the part of the client community. This purpose clearly requires a change not only of sociocultural patterns (passive-dependent consumer life style, "fast food" diet, etc.) but also of socioeconomic inequities (poverty, unemployment, exploitation, meaningless working life), of socioecological sources of suffering (decay of cities, environmental pollution of every kind), and of the underlying political-institutional conditions (externalization of social costs in the cost accounting of "free enterprise," collective paralysis in securing collective goods). This *social change avenue* to better health in turn can be broken down to two basic, complementary purposes:

    (a) Planning for *quality of life,* e.g., for the quality of working conditions and recreation opportunities as experienced by all members of the client community. Especially with regard to improving the health status of the socially disadvantaged segments of the population, sick-making societal conditions will have to be overcome (prevention in a wide, socioecological sense of the term).

    (b) Insofar as human suffering and illness is an inevitable part of human life even under the best possible conditions, ideal planning must aim at forstering self-care and "share-care" (Blum 1976:Ch. 6). The essential purpose here is to plan for the *emancipation* of those in need from dependence of institutionalized health care. Such emancipation can be fostered relatively easily (and cheaply) through elementary education in primary care and sound, self-reliant life-style patterns. As a step in this direction, the World Health Organization has begun to advocate the deprofessionalization of primary care as the most promising way to improving the general health status of the population both in industrialized and in developing countries (cf. Newell 1975).

2. However, there will always remain a need for professionally managed health care delivery for those who cannot themselves cope with their needs. Therefore, a second, *health care avenue* to health has to be planned for: an effective health care delivery system that is compatible with the self-care approach, that is, does not undermine people's will to and freedom for self-reliance. Henrik Blum's model of a Primary Well-Being Center (PWC) as core of an Overall Well-Being or Health Care Delivery System (1976:Ch. 7) is an example of what is meant here by the health care avenue. Such a system will be called effective if it makes sure that the services delivered to those in need are
    (a) reliable (minimal production of iatrogenic disease)
    (b) reasonably accessible to everyone
    (c) equitably distributed among concurring needs
    (d) whenever feasible under full control of the client (no creation of new dependence or passivity), and

(e) affordable (reasonably cheap for both the individual client and the client community as a whole, in terms of marginal utility and lost opportunities for alternative improvements).

Again, planning for an effective health care delivery system must include an effort at emancipating clients from dependence on the very services provided. As Illich states so forcefully:

> If concern with equity [in the delivery of health services] is not linked to constraints on total production, and if it is not used as a countervailing force to the expansion of institutional medical care, it will be futile." (1977:240)

As a reminder of what has been said so far, we may add a list of progress criteria to the stipulated multiple purposes, which gives us the following *ideal purpose map:*

> *Ideal purpose:* "to secure cultural, political, socioeconomic and ecological conditions that foster the will to, and the potential for, self-reliance and mutal selfcare on the part of the client community in dealing with human suffering."
> *Ideal avenues to health, and corresponding progress criteria for health systems planning:*
> 1. *Social change avenue to health:*
>   (a) *Design for quality of life*
>   "Ethical" (ethics of whole systems)
>   "Environmental" (healthy socioecological conditions)
>   (b) *Design for self-care and share-care*
>   "Emancipatory"
>   "Educational"
> 2. *Health care avenue to health:*
>   (c) *Design for health care services*
>   "Effective" (reliable, not counterproductive)
>   "Equitable" (distribution)
>   "Emancipatory" (client in control)
>   "Efficient" (affordable, marginal utility)

It may be worthwhile to note that contrary to what one might believe, there is no built-in conflict between such progress criteria as "effective" and "efficient" or "equitable" *if* the emancipatory orientation is understood as a necessary component of both reduced institutional service production and also better health for all. Our ideal purpose map is thus truly an ideal map. Let us now see what the reality looks like in its light.

1.2. Actual Purpose Map

What planning purposes does P.L. 93–641 actually assign to HSAs? There are two ways in which HSAs might have been given a chance of working toward an ideal map such as the one suggested: they might have been directly assigned a corresponding ideal purpose map, or they might have been given the basic task and opportunity of developing their own ideal purpose map. The second strategy would seem particularly sensible if HSAs are first of all to be purposeful inquiring systems, i.e., planning bodies that ought to map out problems and produce data but are not solely responsible for implementation.

These are the tasks assigned to HSAs by P.L. 93–641:

Sec. 1513 (a) For the purpose of –

(1) improving the *health* of residents of a health service area,

(2) increasing the *accessibility* (including overcoming geographic, architectural, and transportation barriers), acceptability, continuity, and *quality* of the health services provided by them,

(3) restraining increases in the *cost* of providing them health services, and

(4) preventing unnecessary *duplication* of health resources,

each health systems agency shall have as its primary responsibility the provision of effective health planning.... To meet its primary responsibility, a health systems agency shall carry out the functions described in subsections (b) through (g) of this section. [italics added]

Subsection 1513 (b) prescribes the following tasks of inquiry:

(1) The agency shall *assemble and analyze data* concerning –

(A) the status (and its determinants) of the health of the residents of its health service area,

(B) the status of the health care delivery system in the area and the use of that system by the residents of the area,

(C) the effect the area's health care delivery system has on the health of the residents of the area,

(D) the number, type, and location of the area's health resources, including health services, manpower, and facilities,

(E) the patterns of utilization of the area's health resources, and

(F) the environmental and occupational exposure factors affecting immediate and long-term health conditions.

...

(2) The agency shall... establish, annually review, and amend as necessary a *health systems plan*... which shall be a detailed statement of goals.... [cf. the quotation of this section from HSP 1976:1f in the Introduction to the present chapter.]

(3) The agency shall establish, annually review, and amend as necessary an *annual implementation plan* (AIP) which describes objectives which will achieve the goals of the HSP and priorities among the objectives.... (italics added)

In addition to these functions as an inquiring system, subsection 1513(c) assigns HSAs the function of an action system: "(c) A health systems agency shall implement its

HSP and AIP." Nothing is said, however, as to how HSAs are to achieve the implementation of their plans. Let us now see how the Puget Sound Health Planning Council, in order to become a federally designated HSA, actually conceived its purpose. In its 1976 Health Systems Plan we read:

> In June of 1973, starting with *Health Goals for the Community* established the previous year, the council conceived an areawide plan that would have three components:
> - primary care
> - hospital care
> - long term care.
> ...
> Hospital care was the starting point because one of the council's predecessor agencies was concerned mainly with facilities planning and because the State Certificate of Need law requires the council to review and make recommendations about proposed hospital and nursing home construction.
> ...
> Planning to date has concentrated on the delivery of medical care services; planning of the future, as outlined in the new legislation, must also concentrate on other factors which influence the health status of people: the environment, personal lifestyle, and human physiology (heredity). (HSP 1976:3)

The plan then offers definitions of these factors adapted from Lalonde's pioneering report, *A New Perspective on the Health of Canadians* (1974), but fails to mention the broader implications of the underlying health field concept. This concept has been suggested by Blum (1969 and 1974:2f) and by Lalonde (1974:5 note, 35, 55) to refer to the totality of conditions affecting health, as opposed to the usual restriction of the "health care system" to the institutional facilities by which health care is provided (cf. *Figure 8/2*). It would certainly have been a good idea to put Blum's figure at the beginning of the plan, as a helpful reminder of the scope and principal approaches of health systems planning. Some quotations from Lalonde's report could also have served to remind the reader of the implications of the health field concept, e.g.:

> For these environmental and behavioral threats to health, the organized health care system can do little more than serve as a catchment net for the victims. (1974:5)

> Our goal will continue to be not only to add years to our life but life to our years. (1974:6)

> Difficulties in categorizing the contributing factors to a given health problem are no excuse for putting the problem aside; the problem does not disappear because of difficulties in fitting it nicely into a conceptual framework. (1974:36)

384

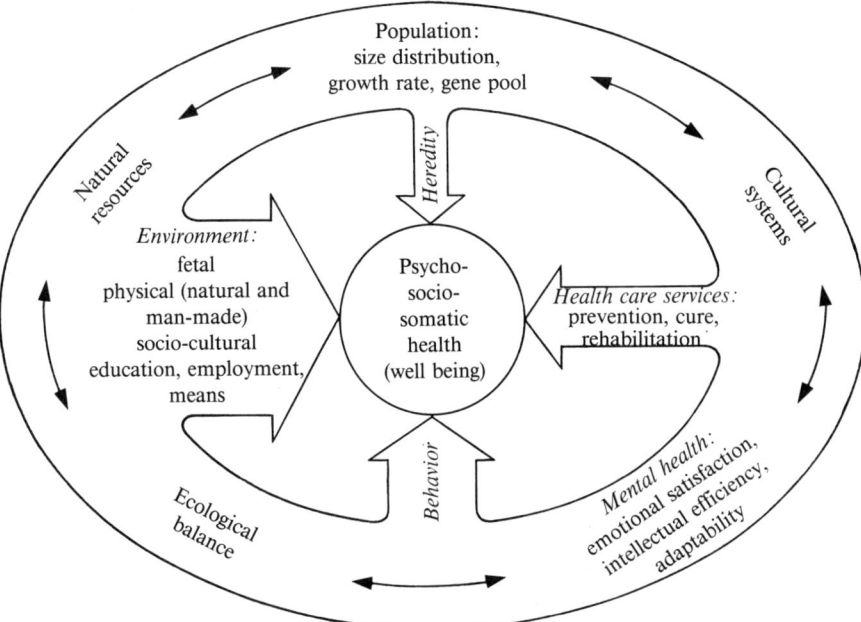

Figure 8/2: The health field concept

"The width of the four huge input-to-health arrows indicates my assumptions about the relative importance of the inputs to health. The four inputs are shown as relating to and affecting one another by means of an encompassing matrix which could be called the 'environment' of the health system." (Blum 1974:3)

Instead of discussing the implications of the health field concept, the plan quickly retreats to the traditional focus on a better organization of the health care delivery system, after paying lip service to the health field concept in the Preamble:

Health Goals for the Community

Preamble: The Health Council views health as influenced by four major components: human biology, environment, health services, and life style or health habits.... The component of most concern now is health services....

Goal I: Human biology, environment and life style/health habits shall all be given due consideration in endeavors to improve community and individual health.

1. Develop health plans with and for the community which recognize and will influence all components of health.

2. Plan with the many environmental organizations so that the health of man is as important an environmental consideration as asthetics and economy.
3. Assist the community to recognize the dependence of the individual or his/her surroundings and hence the importance of the many environmental factors which influence health.
4. Encourage organizations and institutions to promote awareness and understanding of life style (health habits) as a component of health.
5. Encourage organizations and institutions to promote awareness and understanding of heredity as a component of health.

Goal II: The Health Service System shall promote good health through education, research and preventive services.

1. Encourage an emphasis on Prevention and Education in all health service programs.
2. Stimulate effective professional, school, and community health education programs.
3. Stimulate effective communications between people and the health care community to increase knowledge and understanding.
4. Pursue activities which will decrease morbidity and mortality as a result of accidents.

Goal III: Services for diagnosis, treatment, and rehabilitation shall be organized to minimize the effects of ill health.

1. Promote educational programs which will enable patients and their families to become partners in the health care process.
2. Encourage mechanisms to assure continuity of care, including exchange of records and appropriate follow-up, in all diagnostic, therapeutic and rehabilitative services.

Goal IV: High Quality health care shall be available, accessible, and acceptable to all.

1. Develop ways to assess the quality of care which include professional standards and community values.
2. Plan for clearly identified, geografically convenient entry points to health care, available to all people.
3. Plan for health services to be located and coordinated to meet the needs of consumers as effectively as possible.
4. Promote equality in health services; i.e., race, creed, age, sex, national origin, economic status, or funding source, physical, mental, or sensory hardships shall not affect the quality of care.
5. Develop methods to assess the health care needs of the community and encourage the provision of needed services; i.e., outreach services.

6. Pursue means within the community, using all possible resources – government, private and voluntary – to finance health care and prescribed medications for persons without adequate funds.

7. Stimulate development of the health service potential of resources such as schools, health departments, and industry.

Goal V: The Health Service System shall promote the efficient and economical delivery of appropriate services.

1. Plan for needed health resources at the lowest cost consistent with high quality.

2. Stimulate development of incentives to eliminate unnecessary duplication of resources.

3. Stimulate development of incentives to assure the utilization of the least expensive resources that will appropriately meet the needs of the people served.

(HSP 1976:9–11)

Let us briefly discuss the five stated goals in the light of P.L. 93-641. In order to keep our discussion within reasonable space limits, we have to restrict it to one or two comments on each goal.

Goal I expresses the Health Council's will to consider the entire health field as component rather than as environment of the health care system. The trouble with this goal is its vague formulation; what is "due consideration"? As a general guideline this goal statement is unobjectionable, but if it is to have any meaning, it must be complemented by specific provisions that make sure that the health field will not remain environment to HSA's decision maker. The stated subgoals do not appear to be sufficiently specific to fulfill this purpose. Nothing is said about how the Council's planning staff is to "develop health plans with and for the community which will recognize and will influence all components of health" (Subgoal 1). Nor is there anything said about how an effective cooperation with environmental organizations (Subgoals 2) and with the client community (Subgoal 3) is to be secured, or how life style and health habits (Subgoal 4) are to be changed. This deficiency reflects the fact that P.L. 93-641 pays only lip service to the health field concept. There is only a vague mention, in Section 1513 (b) (2), that a Health Systems Plan should contain "goals describing a healthful environment." No provisions for an effective cooperation between HSAs and environmental planning bodies are made, and there is no provision for the support and legitimization of planning efforts that would really go to the heart of the matter and include efforts at deliberate social change. The only noteworthy authorization that HSAs are explicitly given is the power to "review and approve or disapprove each proposed use within its health service area of Federal funds" (Section 1513 (e) (1)); a purely negative function that cannot secure adequate unfolding of problems and coordinated planning for the entire health field. As Wildawsky comments on this point,

The HSAs will issue orders but these orders will not be obeyed. HSAs can say "no" but they cannot mandate "yes." They cannot command, so they will have to bargain. What will they give up to get what they want? (1976:10)

Goal II emphasizes the need for "research," "preventive services" and "education." Regarding the goal of *research,* the 1976 Health Systems Plan for Central Puget Sound makes no specific provisions at all. According to P.L. 93-641, HSAs are charged with narrowly conventional requirements of data collection (cf. Section 1513 (b) quoted above), as if adequate planning were above all a matter of "more" (supposedly objective and value-free) data. The requirement of basic data collection is not bad in itself, of course; but if it is not complemented by provision for the adequate unfolding of alternative problem views and value orientations, as is the case here, data collection tends to divert time and attention from the more important task of developing a normative and heuristic framework for the mapping of problems and for the design of solution approaches. No amount of data can tell the planner what he ought to consider as a planning problem (boundary judgements!). There is also a danger that the annual presentation of updated collections of data will become a major *surrogate purpose,* for data can be presented as a tangible result of scientific inquiry, in contrast to the tedious work of ideal mapping and bounding of problems.

Regarding the goal of *preventive services* and *education,* we need to consider the dangers of what Illich (1977:83) calls the *"medicalization of prevention."* As long as no major changes in the health services away from professional delivery and towards self-reliance on the part of the client are realized, more preventive services are likely to extend the dependence of people on managed sick-care to managed prevention-care: regular check-ups, eventually linkage of insurance payments to them, reduction of the will and freedom to self-care through indoctrination about an alleged need for early consultation of the physician, etc. Illich not only reminds us of the fact that there is no evidence for the effectiveness of large-scale professional prevention services, but he even gives a strong argument for their counterproductivity.

Along with sick-care, health care has become a commodity, something one pays for rather than something one does.... People are turned into patients without being sick. The medicalization of prevention thus becomes another major symptom of social iatrogenesis. It tends to transform personal responsibility for my future into my management by some agency. (1977:83)

Among the major unreflected hazards contained in a prevention strategy that follows classical patterns of regular check-ups and "mass hunt for health risks" (1977:85), Illich mentions:

1. The *bias* of medical check-ups toward detection of some disorder that turns a previously healthy person into an anxious and dependent consumer of diagnostic (and very soon also therapeutic) services:

Through a form of failsafe principle [the physician] usually acts as if imputing a disease to the patient were better than disregarding one. The medical-decision rule pushes him to seek safety by diagnosing illness rather than health. The classic demonstration of this bias came in an experiment conducted in 1934. In a survey of 1,000 eleven-year-old children from the public schools of New York, 61 percent were found to have had their tonsils removed. "The remaining 39 percent were subjected to examination by a group of physicians, who selected 45 percent of these for tonsillectomy and rejected the rest. The rejected children were examined by another group of physicians, who recommended tonsillectomy for 46 percent of those remaining after the first examination. When the rejected children were examined a third time, a similar percentage was selected for tonsillectomy so that after three examinations only sixty-five children remained who had not been recommended for tonsillectomy." This test was conducted at a free clinic, where financial considerations could not explain the bias. (Illich 1977:87, with quotation from Bawkin 1945).

2. Frequent *diagnostic error* is another iatrogenic risk in routine diagnostic test on large populations (cf. Illich 1977:87). The diagnostic procedures used in professionally managed preventive services often involve direct health risks of which clients are not fully aware and which are not warranted except in cases of clear evidence of need for such tests.

3. Even in the absence of diagnostic error, preventive services may cause harm:

Diagnosis always intensifies stress, defines incapacity, imposes inactivity, and focuses apprehension on non-recovery, on uncertainty, and on one's dependence upon future medical findings, all of which amounts to a loss of autonomy for self-definition. (Illich 1977:90)

All of this amounts to saying that professionally delivered preventive services on a broad base may not only have little impact on the health status of people, but may even cause clinical, social, and cultural iatrogenesis. Rather than freeing people from the need for institutionalized health care services, large-scale prevention services may make them dependent consumers of "prevention." Planning for prevention therefore needs careful reflection on the sources of deception and the lost opportunities for emancipation that it entails. Such critical reflection, had it been provided for, would have constituted a significant improvement of Puget Sound's Health Systems Plan of 1976.

Goals III, IV and V: These three purposes focus on the classical objectives of making quality services available to all and, at the same time, controlling the fast rising cost of these services. The focus on these three goals corresponds to the thrust of P.L. 93-641 which assigns health systems planning the purpose of improving the quality and equality (availability and acceptability) of health services along with better cost control (efficiency). Two comments seem indicated.

First, there is no explicit consideration of the fact that *equal access* to quality health services is at least partly a deceptive ideal so long as these "quality" services remain what they have been, professionally "delivered" medicine causing clinical, social, and cultural iatrogenesis. Apart from the obvious fact that "health can be delivered only in small part; it must largely be lived" (Wildawsky 1976:2), the iatrogenic risk in professionally delivered medicine is much higher than commonly thought. Even the American Medical Association (AM), the stronghold of established medical practice and privilege, acknowledges the magnitude of the problem. In January, 1972, an editorial of the *Journal of the American Medical Association* admitted that "so-called iatrogenic disease is unfortunately a medical commonplace." Most recently, William A. Silvermann (1980) has given a shocking insider report on the iatrogenic harm imposed on premature infants as a consequence of unwarranted reliance on the "expert opinions" of medical authorities and careless adoption of unproven treatment innovations.[2] His detailed report is likely to become a classic with regard to the dangers of contemporary notions of expertise, and the uncritical acceptance of authoritative opinion not only by laymen but also by trained professionals themselves.[3]

As a second comment, leaving apart the issue of equal access to institutionalized iatrogenesis, one might argue that a limited focus on conventional health services is not without merits. Although a holistic approach to health planning is desirable, one cannot do everything at once; it is not necessarily inconsistent to maintain a holistic health perspective and, at the same time, to recognize that "small is beautiful." From this point of view it might be unfair to criticize the Puget Sound Health Planning Council for concentrating its first Health Systems Plan on Goals III, IV, and V. Given an almost unlimited task and very limited possibilities, it is certainly a reasonable idea to start small in the sense of concentrating one's means upon one or two basic tasks such as improving the accessability and efficiency of services. Only so, one might argue, can an HSA secure some minimal level of achievement which will then provide it with the public recognition, the experience, and the continuous funding necessary for undertaking broader planning tasks. However, if one takes this viewpoint, one ought to establish some explicit criteria of what would constitute a minimal "arrival level of performance" (Ardell 1973:49). No such criteria can be found in Puget Sound's Health Systems Plan, and this deficiency brings into question the usefulness of its starting small.

---

[2] To mention but one tragic example from Silvermann's report, about ten thousand infants were affected since the early 1950's by Retrolental Fibroplasia (RLF), a form of blindness associated with the use of supplemental oxygen in the treatment of premature infants during their first days of life.

[3] Empirical evidence for the hypothesis that even a highly trained and experienced group of listeners (e.g. professional medical educators) tend to be seduced by prestigious speakers and by an impressive lecture format into uncritically accepting unsubstantiated and inconsistent "expert opinions" was found by Naftulin et al. (1973). The phenomenon has become known as the "Doctor Fox Effect" and has been confirmed in other fields (e.g. Williams 1976, Armstrong 1980).

What might such minimum norms be? Ardell, relying on the conjecture that "the debate on [planning] priorities cannot reasonably begin in earnest until the areawide agency has already accomplished a base set of criteria related to 'arrival' or a modestly advanced stage of development and sophistication" (1973:49f), suggests seven "arrival elements," as he calls such minimum norms:

1. *Becoming operational:* "The first element is that the agency be operational." (1973:50) By this Ardell means that basic organizational and funding questions have been settled; "planning for planning" should be finished so that these issues no longer distract the planning staff's attention from planning itself.

2. *Established guidelines for action:* "A second element is that the agency have or be in the process of producing a comprehensive health plan document that contains actions recommendations with both geographic and quantitative specifics." (1973:50)

3. *Established review mechanism:* "A third element of performance is a fully developed and tested review mechanism." (1973:51) Criteria for the evaluation of project proposals should be published and project review committees should be organized.

4. *Work program:* "A fourth element in arrival is seen in the agency's work program. ...It should, for each major work task, identify who is the responsible staff person, how the task will be undertaken (methodology), what outcomes are expected, when specified works products are due, and how assessment of the task will be conducted." (1973:52)

5. Provisions for cooperation among agencies: "One or more well developed 'common effort' relationships with other functional or multi-functional regional agencies qualifies as an indicator of basic performance." (1973:52) The idea here is that only a coordination of efforts with other governmental or private planning bodies will permit the accomplishment of the agency's work program.

6. and 7. *Attracting qualified personnel* and *earning a favorable image in the client community:* "The two final elements concern staffing and community regard; more than the other five elements, these are intangible dimensions which cannot so easily be set out or measured." (1973:52) Ardell nonetheless includes these two arrival elements in his list because without qualified personnel and/or without community regard, a planning agency "is an unlikely agent to promote constructive change, provide leadership, or otherwise fulfill public expectations." (1973:52) It is evident that the first five elements are key determinants of "arrival" in respect to these two less tangible requirements.

In order to conclude this critical discussion of the Puget Sound Health Planning Council's actual purpose map, let us briefly consider the question of whether there are actual purposes that are unintentionally built into its purpose map but that tend to become *surrogate purposes.* We have already noted "data collection" as a likely candidate. Secondly, the goal of providing more and more easily accessible quality care might easily serve as a rationalization for the creation or maintenance of *jobs* in extending health care delivery system. As positive a side-effect as this may be from a socioeconomic viewpoint, the danger is that jobs become a major surrogate purpose in deciding on "more," "better" or "less duplicated" facilities and services, a criterion that of course will be hidden behind some quality or equality-related goal. Thirdly, the goal of equal access, unless it is linked to the goal of emancipating the client from the health care provider, is easily perverted into the surrogate purpose of expanding the control of the health care system by the medical-industrial complex; the goal of improving the health status of underserved groups may then in fact serve as a rationalization for serving the purposes of vested interests.

Let us break off the mapping process at this point and venture a brief summary assessment of the Puget Sound Health Planning Council's *actual purpose map*:

(a) In comparison to our ideal purpose map, the actual purpose map contained in Puget Sound's Health Systems Plan appears very limited and conventional. This narrow focus corresponds to the fact that P.L. 93-641 does not assign HSA's decision maker any specific authority to control some of the health field factors outside the health care delivery system itself; the health field remains, to a large extent, environment for HSAs.

(b) In spite of its apparent "starting small" philosophy, the Health Council's plan does not establish any specific "arrival elements" and time limits that would permit later evaluation of its achievements.

(c) The central heuristic task of clarifying the methodological and normative framework for the unfolding and bounding of planning problems and for the tracing of the sources of deception in plans should be included in the actual purpose map. In the absence of such provisions, the Health Planning Council is likely to remain a conventional data collector (a fact finding system) rather than to become a truly purposeful inquiring system.

(d) The Health Council's potential for becoming an effective and purposeful action system is limited not only by the lack of provision for the adequate unfolding of problems but also by the lack of mandating power (and hence, democratic legitimation) for enforcing deliberate social, institutional, or environmental change. "When knowledge is missing and power is absent, planning becomes a word for the things we would like to do but do not know how to do or are unable to get others to do." (Wildawsky 1976:8)

(e) Hidden and unintended surrogate purposes are likely to influence the actual purpose map and should be critically examined.

2. Who Is/Ought to Be the Client?

2.1. Ideal Client Map

Ideally, all citizens who are living within the Health Service Area of Central Puget Sound and whose health status needs improvement ought to be clients. Given the broad definition of health underlying our ideal purpose map (health as the potential for autonomous coping with changing personal needs), and given the actual dependence of people on professionally delivered health care, the ideal client might indeed be identical with "everybody."

However, such an answer begs the client question. The client question aims precisely at critical reflection on the fact that *not everybody can be the planner's client* and that no conceivable plan will ever serve everybody's needs. Any plan inevitably has redistributive effects (some benefit, others pay), and this is what the client question is all about. If those who most urgently need support are to get significant help, we must accept the fact that not everybody can equally benefit.

A truly ideal client map would neither simply pass over the issue of redistribution nor impose any significant disadvantages on those who are not among the chief clients, at least not without fully compensating them. This ideal is implicitly presupposed in our ideal purpose map; for our ideal purposes, such as emancipating the client from institutional health care delivery and reducing his need for care via healthy socioecological conditions, are indeed oriented toward serving a key client group without hurting other community members – indeed, these ideal purposes are likely to serve everybody, though not to the same extent.

The key client implied in our ideal purpose map is obvious: those who actually are the most helpless in coping with suffering and illness, and those who suffer the most from the poor quality of life which societal conditions impose on them – the poor, the old, the uneducated, the working class, the unemployed, and the unemployables. At the same time it is clear that those who are lucky enough not to be among the socially disadvantaged are just as much in need of emancipation and more healthful patterns of life, though for quite other reasons (consumer life style, stress, poor diet, clinical iatrogenesis, etc.). The choice of the socially disadvantaged as client by no means excludes the well-off from benefiting, and in fact it may require them to do so, as, for example, whenever the social change avenue to health is indicated, or when medical counterproductivity is to be reduced, or when environmental pollution is to be fought. However, whenever there *is* an inevitable conflict among different client groups, our ideal client map stipulates as chief clients those who are the most disadvantaged in broader societal terms.

The guiding criterion for determining the ideal client of each singular plan or program should always be: Does this plan contribute to a socially more just distribution of the potential for health (autonomous coping, environmental quality) within the entire health service area (ethics of whole systems standpoint)? Our earlier-stated task description for the Puget Sound Health Planning Council contains an excellent reminder that we shall integrate with our *ideal client map:*

> The level of public health corresponds to the degree to which the means and responsibility for coping with illness are distributed among the total population.... The greater the potential for autonomous adaptation to self, to others, and to the environment, the less management of adaptation wil be needed or tolerated. (Illich 1977:271)

Understood in such distributional terms, the client question becomes an instrument for reflecting on the sources of deception contained in two often ignored facts:

(a) There is no such thing as a plan without redistributive, i.e., politically relevant, impacts. "To plan is to make decisions that affect others." (Wildawsky 1973:133) The implication is not that no planning is the best planning, as Wildawsky means to suggest, but rather that the witnesses representing all those who are affected but do not belong to the chief client must become the planner's partners in the process of unfolding.

(b) There is no such thing as a society without class structure; the socially disadvantaged tend not to be the actual client even where programs are designed to help them.[4] By "class structure" I mean here those socioeconomic and political-institutional patterns which, without regard to individual needs and personal merits, determine the actual client map of public planning both in the health sector and in other domains. What then is the actual client map implied in Puget Sound's Health Systems Plan of 1976?

2.2. Actual Client Map

Who is likely to benefit from the plan under consideration, and who is likely not to be served or to be negatively affected? Vicente Navarro gives a basic argument which may guide us in reflecting on the sources of deception in the client map. He reminds us of the fact that "the shape and form of the health sector – the tree – is determined by the same economic and political forces shaping the entire political and economic system of the United States – the forest." (1975:199) Experts on trees do rarely question the forest; the medical-industrial complex, i.e., the vested interests in control of the health care system, cannot be expected to question an economic system that serves them well. This economic system – the "advanced" capitalist state, as it is often

---

[4] For a forceful description of the class structure of the United States and its importance to health planning see Navarro 1975 and 1976.

designated – has an inherent orientation toward "capital realization" (securing of return on investments by the owners and managers of the economic capital stock) rather than toward noneconomic values such as health or quality of life; that is to say, it tends to make itself the surrogate client wherever noneconomic values are to be served.

Clause Offe's (1972:Ch. 3) earlier-mentioned theory of *institutional selectivity* is relevant in this context (cf. note 33 to Chapter Two above). Offe defines as selectivity any nonincidental, i.e. systematic, restriction of a range of possible decisions in public policy making and administrative planning (cf. 1972:78). He distinguishes three leverage points for tracing such systematic restrictions, in our own terms:

(a) *Input selectivity:* What external interests take influence on the administrative system and thus lead to an "external" determination of government and public planning by organized private interests, a source of influence that is not provided for by the constitutional model of the democratic process?

(b) *Internal selectivity:* What are the sources of selectivity located within the administrative system, i.e., internally generated influences that may explain why certain external influences are successful while others are not?

(c) *Output selectivity:* What effective restrictions governing the decision-making process of the administrative system become visible in its decision output? For instance, what are the unresolved steering problems resulting from these decisions? (cf. Offe 1972:66ff)

The first approach (a) will be necessary and sufficient to the extent that administrative selectivity is explained by an *"influence theory of selectivity."* (1972:66) Among the more common ways in which vested interests influence the public administrative apparatus are threats of "investment strike" and close-down of factories by corporations, control of mass media by private interests, economic dependency of communities on major industries or employers (jobs, taxes), and others. All these external influences point to input selectivity in favor of "capital realization." Exerting political pressure on the administrative system apparently is one important way for private capital to "resolve" rationality conflicts between public and private interests (e.g., ecological vs. economic rationality, "health" versus "jobs"). Theodore J. Lowi's theory of "interest-group liberalism" (in *The End of Liberalism,* 1969) can be cited as a major example of an influence theory of selectivity.

The second approach (b) is needed because the influence theory cannot fully account for administrative selectivity. As a rule, there is competition among vested interests for consideration by the administrative system; hence we need a second approach, a *"constraint theory of selectivity"* (1972:67), to explain why some of these competing influences are more successful than others. Galbraith's concept of the *"bureaucratic symbiosis,"* i.e., the frequent exchange of expertise, information and personnel, between the public administration and vested interests such as trade unions, multinational corporations, the banking system, political parties, etc. (1975:139) is a good example of this approach. Bureaucratic symbiosis is especially important to understand the actual client map of public planning in the domains of defense policy ("military-industrial complex"), economic policy (the "free market" as a surrogate planner, collective paralysis in securing noneconomic public goods), energy policy (exchange of nuclear experts between public regulatory commissions and the nuclear industry), environmental industry ("eco-industrial complex"), and foreign policy, especially vis-à-vis the developing countries (preference for right-wing dictatorships over democratic-reformist governments that offer a less stable "investment climate" for U.S. corporations, e.g. in Brazil, Chile, Dominican Republic, Indonesia, Iran, South Korea, Uruguay, etc., cf. Chomsky/Herman 1977 and 1979).

Apart from bureaucratic symbiosis, the very *structure of bureaucratic organization* as it is characteristic of administrative planning (hierarchy, preservation of comfortable routines, securing of public funding, re-election concerns of publicly elected top officials) is also a source of selectivity, especially with respect to information filtration and distortion. Harold Wilensky's *Organizational Intelligence* (1967) is a widely known study relying on this leverage point for tracing institutional selectivity. As he shows, information that throws critical light on the prevailing doctrines of the administration, or on the vested interests on which it depends for its political survival, are easily filtered out on their way up through the hierarchy by officials or subordinates "playing it safe" (1976:43); in addition, the sociological and political background of bureaucratic elites may also account for internal selectivity, as well as other structural features of the administrative system.

The third approach (c), finally, is to trace selectivity in terms of *visible decision outcomes* rather than in terms of its internal or external root causes. Do these decisions reflect a *systematic neglect of steering problems* (e.g., environmental pollution control, worker protection, internalization of social costs into the cost accounting of free enterprise, affirmative action in favor of underprivileged ethnic or socioeconomic groups, etc.), a neglect that serves vested interests better than the general public? Is there a corresponding need for stop-gap measures and "crisis management" to come to grips with the effects of these untackled problems? And so on. To the extent that such restrictions can actually be demonstrated it is justifiable to speak of a *"selectivity theory"* of governmental and administrative decision making in general. The Chomsky and Herman study referred to above would thus allow us to speak of capital-oriented selectivity in the domain of foreign policy. However, it is obvious – and Offe himself points to this – that such a "theory" will never be a full-fledged empirical theory, for complete empirical demonstration of effective restrictions would require evidence of *"non-decisions"* or *"non-events,"* i.e., of the deliberate suppression of generalizable or publicly recognized minority needs (cf. Offe 1972:74, 83).[5]

Apart from untackled steering problems, there is another phenomenon that is symptomatic of such non-decisions or non-events; namely, efforts on the part of the government or the administration to suppress public knowledge of non-decisions, i.e., of the ways in which necessary decisions or actions are suppressed. These efforts can take the form of counterselective proclamations, i.e., deliberate attempts to create an impression of responsiveness towards effectively neglected needs (e.g., human rights proclamations in the face of a foreign policy with a clear preference for right-wing dictatorships over democratic-reformist governments). Offe designates this latter phenomenon as *complementary selectivity* (1972:77); it represents selectivity intended to cover output selectivity. It is certainly tempting, from a critical point of view, to consider the following heuristic principle: whenever the administrative system exerts selectivity of information in the form of one-sided proclamations, one should suspect that this selectivity represents in fact complementary selectivity designed to cover output selectivity. Such a simple heuristic principle might do much to increase public awareness of institutional selectivity in public planning, if only it would be part of each citizen's training in citizenship; unfortunately, such critical political education is still a non-event in the public school system, or by all means cannot match the high degree of selectivity exerted daily by the administrative system and by the mass media reporting on its activity. *Figure 8/3* summarizes our discussion of Offe's framework for tracing institutional selectivity with regard to the client of public planning and policy making; some typical symptoms of selectivity are listed for each leverage point.

Let us now return to the task of mapping the actual client of Puget Sound's Health Systems Plan of 1976. What does the concept of institutional selectivity mean for this task?

1. At least so long as no evidence to the contrary is found, it might be a good idea to assume that the chief client of P.L. 93–641's design for HSAs is the medical-industrial complex. In this hypothetical sense we will enter Navarro's observation into *our actual client map:*

> The inner logic of the [health care] system – which is a product of the pattern of economic and political power as previously explained – determines that the distribution of benefits brought about through state interventions [in the form of public planning] is likely to benefit some groups more than others. Because I believe that the system functions this way, I am skeptical.... (1975:227)

---

5 Cf. in this context the critical comment by Nelson W. Polsby, to whom Offe himself refers: "It has been pointed out to me that sometimes decisions that are *not* made are every bit as significant in determining policy outcomes as decisions that are made.... It has been suggested that non-events make more significant policy than do policy-making events. [But] which non-events are to be regarded as most significant in the community? Surely not *all* of them. For every event... there must be an infinity of alternatives." (Polsby 1963:96) This objection seems to rely on a concept of value-free political science, however; for as soon as one traces the sources of institutional selectivity from an openly and critically normative point of view, it is obvious that the number of desirable but suppressed decisions is far from infinite. There is a very definite number of socio-economically disadvantaged classes or groups; if their basic needs remain neglected by public planning over a certain period of time, one can surely speak of empirical evidence for non-decisions.

398

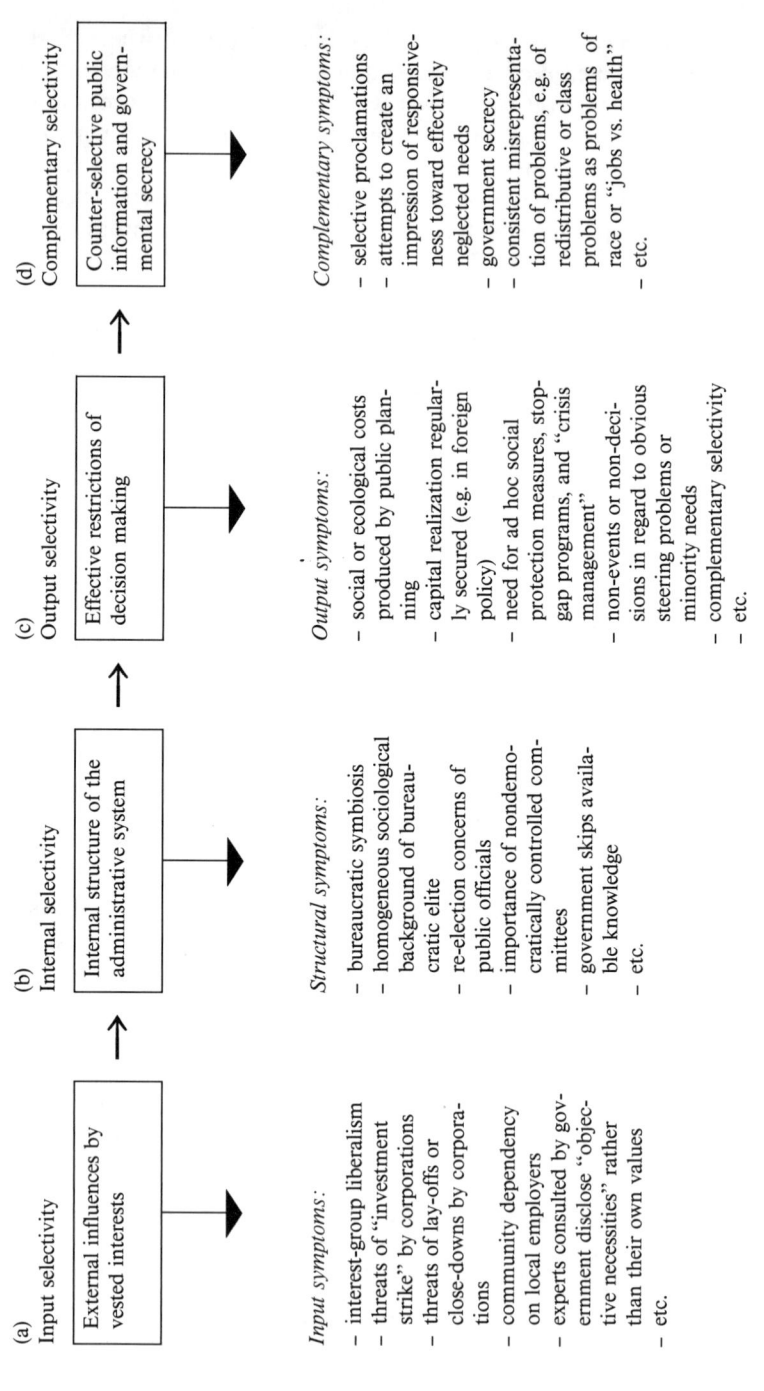

Figure 8/3: Leverage points for tracing institutional selectivity with regard to the actual client map of public (administrative) planning

Being skeptical is indeed important in mapping out the actual client of any plan. Being skeptical not only requires that we ask whose needs are actually served and whose needs are not so well served as intended or pretended, but also requires that we question the supposed needs themselves. Both as planners and as citizens (clients, witnesses) we must learn to recognize the fact that our beliefs about what are legitimate needs and who is legitimately the client tend to reflect the interests of surrogate clients rather than those of the socially disadvantaged who are in need (cf. Galbraith's concept of "emancipation of belief," 1975:Ch. 22). For instance, our earlier discussion of the iatrogenic harm involved in extending the established health care system to previously underserved population groups suggests that the call for "equal access" on the part of these groups may reflect the interests of the surrogate client "medical-industrial complex" rather than the authentic needs of the supposed clients, and that their real need is "emancipation of belief."

2. A second symptom corroborates the suspicion that the actual client of HSAs is the medical-industrial complex rather than the underserved, or in other words, that the actual client is to be found among those who are involved in the established health care system rather than among those who are affected by its shortcomings. This symptom consists in the fact that P.L. 93–641 does not make the fundamental distinction of the involved and the affected but instead employs the distinction of "providers" and "consumers." Section 1512(b)(3)(C) determines that a majority (but no more than 60 percent) of the members of an HSA's governing body "shall be residents of the health service area served by the entity who are *consumers* of health care and who are not (nor within the twelve months preceding have been) *providers* of health care." (my italics)

This distinction between providers and consumers does not adequately reflect the socioeconomic class structure of a health service area, although class structure is by far the major factor determining who is likely to benefit and who is likely to be negatively affected only. The distinction of the involved vs. the affected would have been much more relevant than that of providers vs. consumers for tracing the influence of class structure upon the actual client map. For instance, "consumers" who are appointed by the involved rather than being elected by the affected are more likely to represent the upper middle, professional, and corporate class than to represent the working class. Conversely, "providers" who are members of the working class and who happen to work in the health care system are more likely to be among the affected than among the involved. We must conclude that P.L. 93–641's provisions for making consumers the actual clients are a probable source of deception, for they do not adequately consider the question of what class interests have the major influence on the decision-making process within the public health sector, i.e., who is likely to control the actual client map. Under these circumstances, "consumer participation" and "pluralism" in health systems planning become mere covers for continuing institutional selectivity in favor of the privileged classes.

The problem is well exemplified by the composition of the Puget Sound Health Council's policy board (cf. HSP 1976:iif). Among the four "consumers" on its ten-member board, one finds a retired business executive and a city councilman who is a trained legislative assistant. The two remaining (female) consumers are identified as "volunteers." Even if one assumes that they do represent the under-served and socially disadvantaged, they are facing a majority of eight professionals on the board who are clearly closer to the medical-industrial complex than to the alleged client.

3. Another symptom of institutional selectivity is the widely-held belief that the pro-fessionals who are to serve the client should rightly be surrogate clients. That is to say, it is assumed that in order to serve the client well, the involved need to be well-served in the first place. (Similarly, in universities the faculty becomes the surrogate client to be served in order that the ideal client, the students, be served.) This assumption is not entirely mistaken, but we should not presuppose a near-automatic transfer of benefits from the surrogate clients to the intended clients. There are apparently no provisions in P.L. 93–641 (nor in Puget Sound's Health Systems Plan) that would exclude the health establishment from remaining the preferred surrogate client, as has been the case in the past. The belief that what is good for the health care system is good for health is alive and well and codetermines the actual purpose map of health systems planning.

4. As a last consideration in this context, let us look at the concept of knowledge built into HSAs as inquiring systems. P.L. 93–641's emphasis on conventional "value-free" data collection and the complete avoidance of the problem of the underlying normative and epistemological framework suggest that as inquiring systems HSAs are likely to produce knowledge with an inherent bias toward presently acknowl-edged values. Inquiry into social concerns which is not openly and critically polit-ical is more likely to serve the status quo than to foster deliberate social change. Significantly, Puget Sound's Health Systems Plan of 1976 does not at all mention the importance of class structure, vested interests, institutional counterproductiv-ity, regressive funding systems, etc. as factors that determine the actual client map. Whoever the actual client is, he is hardly to be found among those who do not benefit from institutional selectivity in favor of the medical-industrial complex.

3. Who Is/Ought to Be the Decision Maker?

3.1. Ideal Decision Map

The question of the ideal decision maker has two aspects, an internal and an external one:

(a) What internal structure would make the decision maker a purposeful and effective controller of the system under consideration (HSA)?

(b) What external factors that determine the performance of the system ought to be under the control of the decision maker, and what other factors ought to be part of his decision environment?

We shall have an opportunity to discuss some basic issues regarding the second question below, where we deal with the category of the "environment." At this point let us focus on the first question and simply assume that HSAs' decision maker ought to be able to control as many health field factors as possible.

Given this assumption, what basic requirements should the internal structure of an ideal decision-making body for HSAs (designated "governing body" in P.L. 93–641) fulfill? Two requirements seem fundamental: the body should be *competent* in respect to the complex task of health systems planning, and it should be *representative* with regard to the composition of its client community (the Health Service Area of Central Puget Sound). Earlier in this study (Chapter 5, Section 3.1) we have found that the two requirements conflict at least partly: "competence" implies expertise and a certain capability of conceptualization and cogent argumentation, while representativeness implies that all affected citizens have an equal chance to participate in the decision-making process, regardless of expertise.

There are two major – complementary – approaches to resolving the dilemma. The first consists in the *institutionalization of practical discourses* between representatives of the HSA (members of its governing body and of its planning staff) on the one hand, and representatives of the affected on the other (witnesses). In Chapter Five we have outlined the basic premises of a model of practical discourse that makes both demands compatible, "competent" or "cogent" argumentation and democratic representativeness or legitimation. Applying this model to the case at hand, practical discourses might be institutionalized for the public review of and vote on project proposals, for the periodic discussion and revision of Health Systems Plans and Annual Implementation Plans, for the election of members of the governing body, and for other purposes. In distinction to "public hearings," such practical discourses would indicate public votes on the matters under consideration, i.e., these discourses would be organized according to the principles of direct democracy, a concept that does not preclude the use of local television or radio stations and sophisticated elec-

401

tronic equipment for instant feedback and analysis of responses by a large audience.[6]

The second approach relies on the conventional idea of "adequate" *representation* of the affected *within* HSA's governing body, although the traditional criterion for adequate representation, "consumer" versus "provider," should be replaced by our category of the *witness*. Before considering the social actors qualifying as witnesses, let us ask what contributions we ought to expect from witnesses sitting on HSA-boards. Henrik Blum has summarized the expected planning functions of lay participants according to various authors in the health planning field:

1. Identifying and articulating health needs as seen from outside the viewpoint of medicine.
2. Providing clearer pictures of the inadequacies of the health care delivery system.
3. Providing perspectives on use of resources for living in general, versus those earmarked for health services.
4. Shortening reaction time between patients and doctors.
5. Improving the realism of expectations on both sides.
6. Bringing diverse brands of expertise to bear.
7. Forcing improved communication between subsectors of the biomedical sector.
8. Reorganizing centralized decision making in the health industry by injection of political, social, and economic know-how.
9. Offsetting both narrow-minded and self-centered professionalism and many racist attitudes.
10. Providing a meaningful feedback to consumers about inappropriate usage of health care.
11. Improving the scope of support and capacity, and thereby, [helping bring about] growth and change in the health industry.
12. Providing reassurance to consumers about the integrity of the system.
13. Providing access to a community power base for social action which no trade or profession can mobilize. (1974:455 and 458)

In the light of our earlier-stipulated ideal purpose and client maps, the main thrust of these expected functions of the witnesses can be condensed to three essential tasks:

(a) Challenge the "objective necessities" of the involved professionals and providers so as to secure critical reflection on the normative content of plans and programs (polemical employment of boundary judgements)

---

[6] An interesting experiment in this direction was undertaken by C. West Churchman, Helmut Krauch, Horst Rittel and others at the University of California, Berkeley, in 1967; see Churchman 1971:Ch. 8 and especially Krauch 1972.

(b) Provide impetus and direction for social and institutional change toward "autonomous coping"

(c) Improve communication between the health care establishment and consumers, translate the needs, concerns and knowledge of each side into the language of the other.

Turning now to the identification of "adequate" witnesses, let us again be guided by Henrik Blum, who has given much thought to this matter and who has arrived at an interesting list of what he calls *"the new lay participants"* (as opposed to traditional consumer participants, cf. 1974:452f):

1. the *victims* of the present health care system, e.g., those who are underserved and those who are suffering from the effects of clinical, social, or cultural iatrogenesis; their experiences and concerns are quite different from those of traditional consumer participants;

2. the *have-nots,* i.e., the victims of the overall class structure of the client community who are not so much interested in equal access to quality health care (which they can't afford) as in, first of all, job opportunities and other benefits they expect from adequate planning on their behalf;

3. the *ancillary health personnel* who represent the "have-nots" within the health care system (e.g., the nurses, orderlies);

4. and 5. in some health service areas the members of the *counter culture* and of *emancipatory movements* who have different *Weltanschauungen* relating to health and who want their health needs satisfied in innovative ways (the holistic health movement, women's liberation movement, environmentalists, etc.); they deserve representation as major marginal groups providing for innovative impetus (all social progress starts from marginal groups);

6. the *average consumer* of the lower and lower-middle classes whom Blum describes as "the typical Americans of modest education, means, aspirations, and politics" (1974:453), a group which includes a majority of the working population (but not the traditional uppermiddle class consumer participants) and which is anything but homogeneous.

At present, only a small fraction of the "consumers" sitting on the boards or executive committees of the HSAs come from any of the six groups of new lay participants, as Blum notes; the majority represents either the "middle-class, volunteer-agency type" or the "upper-class business and community leader, who is at last the social peer of the professional" (1974:454).

There are two main reasons why the new lay participants ought to be given a majority among the "consumers":

(a) The world-views and needs of the two groups – new lay participants versus traditional consumer participants – differ widely and there is a "remarkable potential for conflict" between them (Blum 1974:454). In this situation, the traditional consumer participants, whose *Weltanschauung* is, in many respects, closer to that of the "providers" than to that of the new lay participants, tend to collude with the providers and thus cannot fulfill their function of challenging the providers. The entire exercise of "pluralism" and "representation" is pointless if the majority of those who supposedly represent the views of the uninvolved and affected collude with the providers to preserve the *status quo*.

(b) The function of the witnesses sitting on HSA boards is not only one of representing their constituency but also one of representing the public in general. That is to say, *the ideal is not "interest-group liberalism" (Lowi 1969) with just one new interest group added; the ideal is public transparency and public control of HSAs*. Bruce C. Vladeck, in his discussion of "Interest-Group Representation and the HSAs" (1977), remainds us of this issue and emphasizes that we should not substitute the "representational hocus-pocus" for the crucial issue: "How does one go about controlling an elite group?" (1977:27) Assuming that "what has been wrong with the health care system... is that it has been dominated by an elite group – call them 'providers' – who have run the system pretty much in their own interest" (1977:27), Vladeck suggests three main strategies for making the elite responsive and responsible to the general public:

> The first is to guarantee that conflicts of interests are built into the elite. If the providers are the elite, creating conflict among them is one way to insure that they will control one another. Assigning them a fixed pool of money or patients and then leaving them to split it up among themselves is one possible approach.
>
> The second way is to internalize within the elite, through education or acculturation, the values that are to be promoted. One can teach physicians Community Medicine, for example, and then hope that over 20 or 30 years their outlooks will come to be more in conformance with the public interest.
>
> The third strategy is to make the elite accountable. In theory, they can be made accountable through some kind of electoral mechanism. Or they can be made accountable to a hierarchical authority, say the state, through a system of legal regulation that defines, with the force of the law, what they may do and what they may not, and what will happen if they fail to obey. (1977:27)

Before turning to the actual decision map of HSAs, the map which is built into them by P.L. 93–64 and exemplified by the Puget Sound Health Planning Council, let us attempt a synopsis of our *ideal decision map:*

1. The ideal decision maker not only has control over relevant health field factors (decision environment) but also has an internal structure that secures purposeful and effective health planning.
2. The two main elements of such purposefulness and effectiveness are "competence" and "representativeness," the latter being intended to secure democratic input; the institutionalization of practical discourses between the involved (HSA

board and staff) and the affected (witnesses) is desirable to resolve the partial conflict between the two elements.

3. As ideal witnesses, we have identified the following new lay participants who should be given a majority among the "consumer" participants:
    3.1. victims of the status quo in the health sector
    3.2. have-nots
    3.3. ancillary health personnel
    3.4. counter culture
    3.5. emancipatory movements
    3.6. lower-middle class consumer (working population)
4. We have assigned three essential tasks to these new lay participants, the underlying ideal being public transparency and democratic control of HSAs rather than "interest-group liberalism":
    4.1. Challenge the "objective necessities" of the elite (polemical employment of boundary judgements)
    4.2. Provide impetus and direction for change toward "autonomous coping"
    4.3. Improve communication between HSAs and population
5. Three strategies ought to make sure that "pluralism" and "representation" is not substituted for democratic control and institutional change:
    5.1. Built-in structural conflicts of interests within the health care establishment
    5.2. Raising the consciousness of the elite
    5.3. Making the elite accountable.

3.2. Actual Decision Map

Who is actually part of the decision maker of HSAs does not only depend on who is formally designated as a member of the governing body and of the body's executive committee (if there is one) and the planning staff; it also depends on the power of vested interests to influence the formally designated decision maker via input selectivity. Let us make some brief comments in response to both our above ideal map of the formal decision-making body and our earlier discussion of the problem of institutional selectivity (cf. Figure 8/3).

1. There are no provisions in Puget Sounds' Health Systems Plan of 1976 for the inclusion of *new lay participants* among the members of the governing board. The Health Systems Plan itself was apparently established without input from these groups, or at least there are no new lay participants – especially no victim-type consumers – among the list of "consumers" and "providers" that was responsible for the plan. This is hardly surprising since P.L. 93–641 contains no provisions regarding the role of new lay participants but instead relies on the dichotomy of "providers" and (traditional) "consumers" (see our earlier discussion in Section

2.2, where we assumed that mapping the actual decision maker is one way to trace the actual client).

2. None of Vladeck's above-mentioned strategies for controlling the elite ("providers") in control of the health care system is built into P.L. 93–641. We must conclude that *interest-group liberalism* rather than democratic control of HSAs has been the guiding idea of the U.S. Congress in adopting P.L. 93–641. In Vladeck's words,

> The philosophy Congress appears to have followed in this case, and in so many others, is under severe attack in other sectors just as it is gaining ascendancy in health planning. It might appropriately be called the theory of pluralist representation; Theodore Lowi, in *The End of Liberalism,* called it... interest-group liberalism. (1977:25)

As a result, Vladeck writes,

> providers and consumers will break bread together on the governing bodies, and distribute some of the crumbs to each of their members. Health planning will increasingly constitute an institutionalization and rigidification of what is, rather than a thrust toward what could be. (1977:27f)

3. Given the continuing reliance on interest-group liberalism, it seems likely that the vested interests of the medical-industrial complex will be successful in imposing *input selectivity* on HSA's actual decision map.

4. In addition to input selectivity, *internal selectivity* is built into HSA's decision map. According to P.L. 93–641, Section 1512(b)(2), the planning staff of HSAs who are doing the actual planning work consists entirely of hired professionals; there are no provisions that the planning staff include lay members, not even for the limited purpose of providing a training ground for the "consumer" participants on the governing body. The underlying epistemological assumption is deceptive: namely, that once the goals are defined by the governing body, the means for achieving them can be designed and implemented in a value-free, technical manner. This assumption, because it ignores the fact that all "means" have redistributive consequences and are, consequently, acceptable in varying degrees to alternative *Weltanschauungen,* is a major source of internal selectivity in favor of vested interests and the *status quo.*

5. There is a second way in which unquestioned epistemology reinforces the bent of the actual decision map toward the medical-industrial complex. *The "consumers" on the board, even if they do indeed represent the affected rather than the involved, cannot become important contributors of practical knowledge so long as "competence" and "expertise" are understood in the terms of positivist, "value-free" epistemology.* Ironically it is not only the "experts" (professional providers) but also the laymen themselves who all too often do not question traditional concepts of expertise and who distrust their own competence.

Puget Sound's thirty-year old *Group Health Cooperative* (GHC), which is a consumer-owned, nonprofit-oriented Health Maintenance Organization (strangely enough not mentioned at all in Puget Sound's Health Systems Plan of 1976), provides a significant example that even complete consumer domination is not really effective so long as the involved consumers follow traditional patterns of nonencroachment into the "professional affairs" of the medical staff. There has been a persistently low degree of active consumer participation in GHC's management, as Parker (1970:2141) and Polsgrove (1978:47) report. Consumer apathy is both a consequence and a cause of GHC's continuing "medicalization" (Illich) and bureaucratization, a process that more and more undermines GHC's original advantages, e.g., built-in incentives for cost control and quality care, a reduction of the client's "consumer" attitude, and a new potential for grass-roots democracy in health care systems. Only the involvement of new lay participants who do not succumb to professional elitism, and professionals who are ready to accept and support such lay decision makers, can bring a change. Critically-heuristic training is the key to making both groups aware of the significance of lay input, and of the fact that expert judgement is no less value-laden than lay judgement. (Cf. the discussion of this issue in Section 3.3 of Chapter Five.)

The fact that the actual decision map of planning agencies is not only a matter of organization (funding, executive power, representation) but also a matter of epistemology, is probably one of the most neglected considerations in health systems planning. In the case at hand, this neglect can only strengthen the impression that there is a strong bias of HSA's actual decision map toward the provider side, in spite of the emphasis that P.L. 93–641 puts on consumer representation.

6. A sixth consideration is the virtual *lack of executive authority* on the part of HSAs. This holds true in respect to all levels of government on which HSAs need to operate in order to fulfill their tasks of leadership and coordination, the regional or metropolitan level, city or county, and the local and neighborhood levels. The metropolitan and neighborhood levels are especially important for effective health planning, for it is at these levels that many health field factors are located. At these levels there is clearly an "authority vacuum" in that there is no organized authority from which HSAs might derive executive power. Regarding the other levels, we have mentioned earlier that the major authority given to HSAs is a merely negative one, a mere review and licensing function. HSAs, and thus the Puget Sound Health Council, have no positive authority to mandate state, city/county or local executive bodies to initiate health planning activities or health services.

7. Finally, even if HSAs were given specific mandatory powers, the fact remains that HSAs' decision maker would still have little control over most of the *health field factors* that coproduce its success in fulfilling its legal mission – improving the health status of the population. This consideration leads us to the mapping of HSAs' environment.

4. What Is/Ought to Be the Environment?

As a preliminary remark, let us remind ourselves of the meaning of our "environment" category: it does not refer to "everything that does not belong to the problem-relevant system" or to what is irrelevant, but rather to "everything that coproduces the system's performance but is not controlled by the system's decision maker." In other words, "environment" is what is relevant but is not component.

To be very precise, we should distinguish the "decision environment" (to which our category refers) both from the "problem environment" and also from the "natural environment." The natural environment may be regarded as a part of the decision environment insofar as it coproduces a system's performance, but the decision environment is *not* a part of the problem environment.

4.1. Ideal Environment Map

Ideally, the decision maker serves the true purposes of the ideal client and includes the witnesses representing the concerns of all the affected. In this case, the ideal environment would be an *empty class,* that is, the decision maker would control all the environmental factors that coproduce the system's performance in serving the client.

The ideal of the decision environment being an empty class is dangerous, however, in that it makes the system under consideration (and its actual client) the only point of reference for judging the rationality of a design. This presupposition presents no problem so long as the actual client is identical with the ideal client, for in this case systems rationality and social rationality converge. But as soon as systems rationality and social rationality do not converge, the ideal of a zero-environment becomes perverted into a source of social irrationality: for, as we have seen in Chapter Five (Section 2.4), if the system's own purposes remain the only point of reference, increasing control of the system's environment by its decision maker does not increase but rather decrease its social rationality (fallacy of the "open systems" approach).

Let us therefore enter the following reminder into our *ideal environment map:*

"The ideal environment is an empty class if and only if the system in question serves the true purposes of the ideal client. In all other cases, the ideal environment is not an empty class."

What then should be the content of the ideal environment? Basically, all the coproducers of the system's performance should remain part of the environment, so that the decision maker cannot control them for his purposes but is, to some extent, controlled by them. This stipulation applies not only to resources, e.g., socioecological and socioeconomic conditions, know-how, public law, public opinion, financial and political power, and to the democratic process in general, but also to human agents, e.g. politicians, public officials, and all the affected who do not become involved with the decision maker as lay participants. The affected, for instance, ought to remain "environment" for the decision maker in the sense that the decision maker needs to take into account their needs and interests but is not able to manipulate or control them.

Regarding the case at hand, what we have designated as "health-field factors" encompasses both resources and human agents. Whether or not these health-field factors ought to be controlled by the decision maker depends entirely on his actual client and purpose maps. Assuming that Congress had the right purposes and the right client in mind – improving the health status of those who most need it – did it succeed in designing an appropriate environment for HSAs?

4.2. Actual Environment Map

Since the answer to the above question is obvious, we can be rather brief.

1. There is a radical gap between the ideal of an HSA in control of all major health-field factors and HSA's actual inability to control any health factors outside the health care delivery system itself. Virtually all major health factors are coproducing environment for HSA's decision maker: environmental pollution, poverty, the low quality of working life for a large portion of the population, consumer life style, as well as the underlying social and political conditions. We must conclude that the health-field concept is *not* implemented in P.L. 93–614.

2. The salient feature of HSA's environment is its domination by commercial interests and governmental bureaucracies, both of which serve the same surrogate client: the medical-industrial complex and the vested interests in control of it.

3. Given the fact that the actual purpose and client maps built into P.L. 93–641, and into the Puget Sound Health Council's Health Systems Plan of 1976, are biased toward the medical-industrial complex rather than toward the ideal client, the task of assessing its actual environment map poses a dilemma: It seems desirable neither to implement the health-field concept (zero-environment ideal) nor to leave matters as they are. *Not* implementing the health-field concept is counterproductive because the health care system is design-nonseparable from the environment, or, as we have said in the beginning: whether or not the American people will be healty is not a question which is determined in the health care system. On the other hand, implementing the health-field concept implies an extension of the control of HSA's decision maker over its environment, and this extension of control cannot secure socially rational planning so long as the actual client of HSAs is bound to be a surrogate client. The only way to overcome the dilemma, it seems to

me, its to emancipate health planning from the vested interests that control its coproducing environment, and at the same time, as we have already said, to emancipate the true client from health systems planning on his behalf. This consideration leads us quite naturally to the last of our categories that we want to unfold here, the guarantor category. Where can public health planning find guarantee for its serving the right needs, and what is the concept of guarantee actually built into HSAs?

5. What Is/Ought to Be the Guarantor?

5.1. Ideal Guarantor Map

The question to be considered is: How can we ideally cope with the fact that a *lack* of guarantee is inevitable? It is precisely because we are looking for guarantee that we need to assume just the contrary: namely, that there is no guarantor on which to lay the burden of responsibility for our system's performance.

The appropriate ideal might be to free ourselves from the need for a guarantor rather than to "find" a guarantor. Or, to reformulate this a little: an ideal guarantor concept, unless it is to become a source of deception, can conly be an emancipatory one, i.e., the idea of autonomous coping that would free us from dependency on the very systems design for which we seek guarantee.

Transferring this guarantor hypothesis to the field of health planning, our ideal guarantor of health systems planning is the client's emancipation from the health care system and from being planned-for altogether. We have been relying on this guarantor assumption all along, and it also corresponds to the implicit guarantor concept underlying Illich's critique of the "expropriation of health" through the health care system. One of the main reasons why Illich puts emancipation toward "autonomous coping" (as opposed to heteronomous management) on his ideal guarantor map, as it were, is his clear awareness that the domination of the medical-industrial complex over the health care system is unlikeley to be overcome in a society whose goals, attitudes, and institutions are dependent on the industrial mode of production. This awareness comes to the fore in forceful statements such as the following:

> Iatrogenesis will be controlled only if it is understood as but one aspect of the destructive dominance of industry over society, as but one instance of that para-doxical counterproductivity which is now surfacing in all major industrial sectors. (1977:207)

and:

> Attemps to exercise rational political control over the production of medical health care have consistently failed. The reason lies in the nature of the product now called "medicine," a package made up of chemicals, apparatus, buildings, and specialists, and delivered to the client. The purveyor rather than his clients or political boss determines the size of the package. The patient is reduced to an object – his body – being repaired; he is no longer a subject being helped to heal. If he is allowed to participate in the repair process, he acts as the lowest apprentice in a hierarchy of repairmen. (1977:232)

These statements should not, however, be read as a call for the complete and indiscriminate abandonment of the industrial, heteronomous mode of production.

411

Autonomous production of health and other goods does not exclude heteronomous production altogether, but only that overreliance on heteronomous production which impinges on the autonomous mode and thus becomes counterproductive, a source of decreasing health and happiness (cf. our definitions of health in Section 1.1 above). Nor is "autonomy" to be understood in the perverted sense of "free-enterprise" liberalism: autonomous coping may very well presuppose restrictions on the freedom of anyone to impose "external" (social) costs upon others or to overuse the ecological capital stock on which the potential for autonomy of all others (including the future generations) depends. Autonomous creation of health thus must not be misunderstood as a purely individualistic ideal. On the contrary, fostering the client's will and capability to rely on himself is a *political* ideal, for it requires political-institutional change which only collective action can bring about. This implication should be seen as a quite positive challenge: it means that health systems planning may become a major leverage point for initiating social change – change toward *lived,* rather than consumed, quality of life.

Restoring self-reliance is not, however, the only conceivable nor a sufficient guarantor of health planning. It would be all too easy for the planner to tell the client that he must become his own guarantor, and then to leave matters as they are.

At least three co-guarantors appear to be necessary on our ideal map to make emancipatory health planning possible and democratically legitimate: planners, witnesses, and the general public.

1. *Health planners* ought to consider *themselves* as necessary co-guarantors, insofar as it is they who must *create impetus for change* (cf. Blum 1974:20f). Impetus for deliberate social change comes from a publicly perceived discrepancy between what is the case and what might be. This is why the planner needs to turn to the witnesses and to the public as co-guarantors of his own effort.

2. The *witnesses* represent here those citizens who are affected in the sense of not being given a chance for autonomous coping. Be it because of personal experience of iatrogenic harm or of the "expropriation of health," awareness of the distributive failures of the established health care system, concern about the counterproductive effects of the overreliance on the industrial mode of production, or whatever other reason, the witnesses are likely to be critical of the present health care system and thus represent for the planner an indispensable source of impetus for change.

3. The *public* as a guarantor of emancipatory planning – this is one of Jürgen Habermas' central answers to the deficit of rationality and legitimation in administrative planning. He observes that the ever-expanding need for public planning to compensate for the social evils produced by the industrial system has led to a growing politicization of originally private affairs. As examples he mentions the expansion of planning into "cultural affairs that were taken for granted" (1975:71), such as health planning or family planning. As he writes:

Administrative planning produces a universal pressure for legitimation in a sphere that was once distinguished precisely for its power of self-legitimation. (1975:71)

This view corresponds to Henrik Blum's observation quoted earlier, that

health care is moving into the public sector because the parties to what once was purely a private transaction could find no way to deal happily with one another. ...Decision making as a private matter is now further giving way to the public arena. (1974:496, cf. note 17 to Chapter 5)

In view of this factual politicization, a functioning public domain, as a marketplace of political ideas to which everybody has equal access, becomes an indispensable guarantor for democatically legitimate planning. Illich's "cultural iatrogenesis" is a prime example of what a legitimation deficit in terms of a depoliticized (nonfunctioning) public domain means: namely, the manipulation of cultural patterns of coping with disease by vested interests which make themselves the surrogate client of public, but apolitical, planning.

Finally, not only the absence of a functioning public domain but also the public's *anti-planning credo* is an obstacle that the planner must try to overcome. He can do so by his "play on impetus" (Blum 1974:21), and by modest but visible planning successes within the present institutional framework. "Start small and earn public recognition," or, as Blum (1974:487) says, "earn intrinsic authority": this is another reminder to be entered in our ideal guarantor map. Another strategy for finding co-guarantors among the public is suggested by Leonard Duhl (1976:55ff). His key concept in this context is *network building* as a form of power modification "from within" rather than from outside (through planning success). In order to initiate social change toward a healthier society, he suggests "a need for a network of people concerned with the problems of re-creation [of a healthy society], an informal, invisible college" (1976:55, cf. also Duhl/Volkman 1970). Although the idea of an invisible college may be in partial conflict with that of a functioning (= transparent) public domain as a guarantor, its potential for becoming an actual guarantor seems high, so much the more as it is a working strategy of the vested interests (e.g., Galbraith's "bureaucratic symbiosis" is a typical network building strategy of the medical-industrial complex, cf. Galbraith 1975:138f). This strategy appears especially suited to create impetus among the affected, who rarely form a well-organized, homogeneous interest group; it is not however a guarantor for democratically legitimate change and so can serve only a complementary function. With this reservation, let us add "network building" as another co-guarantor to our ideal map.

This then is what our *ideal map regarding the guarantor problem* looks like:

1. There is no ideal guarantor of health systems planning.
2. Relying on any singular guarantor thus implies deception. It is because we are looking for guarantee that we must assume that there is no guarantor.
3. The ideal guarantor is found when there is no need for a guarantor at all!

4. Hence, look for emancipatory guarantors that will free us from dependency on the very systems design for which we seek guarantee.
  4.1. the *client:* emancipate the client
     – autonomous coping rather than heteronomous management
     – emancipation of belief
  4.2. the *planner:* "play on impetus"
     – publicly perceived discrepancies
     – overcome anti-planning credo by earning intrinsic authority
     – network building
  4.3. the *witnesses:* "new lay participants" within the health care system and on HSA's governing boards
     – polemical employment of boundary judgements
  4.4. the *public:* restore a functioning public domain
     – emancipation of the state ⎫
     – emancipation of public planning ⎭ from vested interests

5.2. Actual Guarantor Map

After having drawn up such a marvelous ideal map, it is urgent to recall that the actual guarantor map is more likely to be dominated by surrogate guarantors than by ideal guarantors.

Let us now consider HSAs' design in the light of our ideal guarantor map. Are there any true guarantors designed into HSAs? Of course the intent of this question is not to demand the impossible, or to reject the good in the name of the best; its intent is to make us reflect on the sources of deception contained in the surrogate guarantors that are likely to dominate HSAs' actual guarantor map. What surrogate guarantors have been substituted for true guarantors?

Is the client likely to become an actual guarantor, or what surrogate guarantors have been substituted for him?

Hardly any provisions for the emancipation of HSA's client from heteronomous management in favor of autonomous coping can be found in P.L. 93-641. (The same observation applies to the Puget Sound Health Systems Plan of 1976. The emphasis it puts on "preventive services" (Goal II) might be thought to be an exception, but we have found that this goal is more likely to create new dependencies so long as no basic institutional change occurs.) Institutional and social change is clearly not the guarantor concept adopted by Congress in designing HSAs. In the terms of Chapter Six of the present study, "tool design" (facilities, services) has been substituted for social systems design (emancipation of belief, away from heteronomous management toward autonomous coping). P.L. 93-641 appears to "convert the desire for health into demands for equal access to medical facilities." (Illich 1977:234) The widely echoed call for "equal access" becomes a surrogate guarantor that actually serves the interests of the medical-industrial complex more than those of the alleged client.

Is the planner likely to become an actual guarantor?

This question is less easy to decide than the preceding one. On the one hand, "play on impetus" for deliberate social change is clearly not the role assigned to the planner by P.L. 93-641. As we have seen, the only specific description of his task, in Section 1513 (b) of the law, establishes narrow and conventional requirements of data collection, rather than providing for the purposeful unfolding of problems and of the normative content of designs. The crucial task of developing a heuristic and normative framework for planning is completely ignored, as if there were such a thing as an established and value-free methodology of planning. We must conclude that the inappropriate design ideal "fact finding system" has been substituted for the ideal "purposeful inquiring system" (cf. Table 6/3). Because "data" seemingly represents a more tangible result of inquiry than does problem unfolding, data collection is likely to assume the role of a surrogate guarantor for HSAs' effectiveness.

Another likely candidate for surrogate guarantor is the provision in Section 1502 (6) according to which the identification of needs related to the improvement of the quality of health services is entrusted to the so-called *Professional Standards Review Organizations* (PSRO) that were established under Section 1152 of the Social Security Act. In 1973, P.L. 92-603 established mandatory cost and quality controls by PSROs for Medicaid and Medicare; P.L. 93-641, Section 1513(d)(1), extends the reach of PSROs to HSAs and requires them to coordinate their activities with the PSROs. The name "Professional Standard Review" is a euphemism for what in other fields – e.g., in the evaluation of research proposals by the National Science Foundation or in the refereeing of academic papers submitted for journal publication – is called peer review. The effects of peer review are well demonstrated in these other domains; innovative and critical work that does not conform to established paradigms is filtered out, fundamental issues are withdrawn from public discussion, the involved become their own watchdogs. PSROs effectively give professional providers the authority to determine what is "good" health care for the affected, as if the pilot of a plane were the only person competent to judge where the plane should fly. Considerations of professional prestige and competition, together with purely technical and perhaps economic considerations, are likely to dominate social and political concerns such as equity, affordability for the client, emancipation from institutionalized dependency, etc. (for a detailed critical discussion of PSROs see White 1974 and Sidel 1976).

Many other aspects ought to be considered which bring into question the potential of HSAs' planners to become (co-)guarantors of purposeful health systems planning, e.g., the lack of any provisions that would give them control over major health field factors; the lack of executive authority except a negative review and licensing function; the mandatory reliance by planners on generally promulgated standards issued periodically by the Secretary of Health (Section 1501(b)(1)), standards which in fact represent a substitute for locally derived standards of expectations for the particular Health Service Area concerned and which tend to preclude thinking about ill-structured problems (standards assume that problems are well-defined and admit of general solutions, cf. for a detailed critique Blum 1974:222ff); etc.

But let us focus on one potential guarantor that seems to be designed into HSAs. I mean the "start small" philosophy that is implicit in many of P.L. 93-641's provisions.

First of all, in view of the deeply skeptical attitude of the American public toward public planning, and especially toward openly normative planning, the "start small" strategy might temporarily serve as an actual guarantor of HSAs' political survival. Second, "small" is also an actual guarantor in a sense that was certainly not intended by the legislator but that is nevertheless important: it is an effective guarantor against too much counterproductive expansion of the control by the health care establishment over health field factors not yet under its control. Third, and linked to this effect, "small" might also become a guarantor of equity, insofar namely as the present inequities are due to the control of the health sector by vested interests. Equity, unless it is to mean "equal exposure to counterproductive health care delivery" (iatrogenic risks at the clinical, sociopolitical, and cultural levels), must be understood as "equal opportunity for autonomous coping." As Illich argues in this context,

> the idea of health-as-freedom [autonomous coping] has to restrict the total output of health services within subiatrogenic limits that maximize the synergy of autonomous and heteronomous modes of health production. In democratic societies, such limitations are probably unachievable without guarantees of equity – without equal access. In that sense, the politics of equity is probably an essential element of an effective program for health. Conversely, if concern with equity is not linked to constraints on total production, and if it is not used as a countervailing force to the expansion of institutional medical care, it will be futile. (1977:240)

That is to say, "equity" and "small," as incompatible as they may seem to the conventional wisdom of liberal thinking, may well require each other within a framework of emancipatory health planning and in this sense become mutual co-guarantors. As a fourth and last conjecture, within such a framework "small" will also be a guarantor of cost control *without* loss of effectiveness.

This somewhat optimistic guarantor judgement must not of course become merely an excuse for ignoring the health field factor concept, i.e., for not dealing with the environmental and sociopolitical conditions that are crucial to health. Let us thus enter the following note into our actual guarantor map:

416

"small" – an effective guarantor against counterproductivity, but otherwise ineffective within the present framework of health systems planning; has a high potential for becoming a true guarantor within an emancipatory framework.

Are the witnesses likely to become actual guarantors?

As we have seen, P.L. 93-641 makes no provisions for the participation of "new lay participants" (as witnesses of the affected) on the governing boards of HSAs. Instead, a majority of traditional consumers over providers is taken for a guarantor of HSAs' serving the intended client, and of democratically legitimate planning. The underlying philosophy of interest-group liberalism, as well as the unquestioned reliance on traditional positivist epistemology, make it seem likely that consumer participation is an ineffective guarantor at best. More probably, however, it will become a surrogate guarantor serving the vested interests that are in control of the health care sector (cf. our earlier discussion in Section 3.2 above).

Is the public likely to become an actual guarantor?

There are no provisions at all in P.L. 93-641 to restore a functioning public domain in the health care sector. There is no institutionalization of practical discourses or of other means to make HSAs, and the health care system in general, accountable to the public. P.L. 93-641 conceives public health planning as a matter of administrative and expert planning rather than as an overtly political, democratic process directed toward deliberate social change. But as long as there is no emancipation of the state (of the administrative apparatus) from vested interests, *apolitical public planning is bound to function as a surrogate guarantor for these vested interests.*

The message of P.L. 93-641 to planners is "fix our problems" but "create no basic change" (cf. Blum 1978). The interest groups in control of Congress have determined the shape of HSAs, and they appear to have designed out of HSAs all guarantors that might secure the interests of the alleged client – the underserved, the poor, the general public – whenever these interests conflict with their own. Instead of offering any guarantee for innovative and emancipatory health planning, P.L. 93-641 relies on surrogate guarantors that promise us "more of the same" – and that clearly is not good enough.[7]

[7] Postscriptum (after termination of the manuscript): Since the present assessment of P.L. 93–641 was written before the 1979 amendments and the subsequent authorization of HSAs, in 1980, to undertake "appropriateness review" of selected areas of patient care, I should like to refer the reader to the first issue of the *Bulletin of the New York Academy of Medicine* of Vol. 58, 1982. This issue of the *Bulletin* provides an overview of recent efforts for assuring the appropriateness of medical care by means of HSAs, PSROs, and other quality assurance efforts. Of particular interest is Helen Darling's paper, "The Health Systems Agencies: Their Origins, Directions and Changing Assumptions." Her post-hoc evaluation of HSAs for the most part appears to confirm my prospective assessment. In the meantime, I have myself become professionally involved in post-hoc evaluation of public health planning; I have formulated some basic conjectures regarding a critically-normative approach to evaluation research in a paper in German language (Ulrich 1982).

Epilogue

"Perhaps the sentiments contained in these pages are not yet sufficiently fashionable to procure them general favor; a long habit of not thinking a thing wrong, gives it a superficial appearance of being right, and raises at first a formidable outcry in defense of custom. But the tumult soon subsides. Time makes more converts than reason."
Thomas Paine, in Common Sense *(1776)*

Bibliography

Abbott, Thomas Kingsmill, 1898: *Kant's Critique of Practical Reason* and Other Works on the Theory of Ethics, translated by Thomas Kingsmill Abbott, London-New York-Bombay: Longmans, Green & Co., 5th ed. (1st ed. 1873).

Ackoff, Russell L./Emery, Fred E., 1972: *On Purposeful Systems,* London: Tavistock, and Chicago: Aldine-Atherton.

Adorno, Theodor W., 1957: "Soziologie und empirische Forschung," in: K. Ziegler (ed.), *Wesen und Wirklichkeit des Menschen,* Festschrift für Helmut Plessner, Göttingen, Germany: Vandenhoeck & Ruprecht, pp. 245–260; reprinted in Topitsch 1965:511–525 and in Adorno et al. 1969:81–101.

Adorno, Theodor W., et al., 1969: *Der Positivismusstreit in der deutschen Soziologie,* Darmstadt and Neuwied-Berlin: Luchterhand (Sammlung Luchterhand edition, 1972). (Transl.: *The Positivist Dispute in German Sociology,* New York: Harper 1976.)

Albert, Hans, 1962: "Probleme der Wissenschaftslehre in der Sozialforschung," in: René König (ed.), *Handbuch der empirischen Sozialforschung,* Vol. 1, Stuttgart, Germany: Enke.

Albert, Hans, 1964 a: "Der Mythos der totalen Vernunft; dialektische Ansprüche im Lichte undialektischer Kritik," *Kölner Zeitschrift für Soziologie und Sozialpsychologie* 16:225–256 (reprinted in Adorno et al. 1969:193–234).

Albert, Hans (ed.), 1964 b: *Theorie und Realität,* Ausgewählte Aufsätze zur Wissenschaftslehre der Sozialwissenschaften, Tübingen, Germany: J.C.B. Mohr (2nd ed. 1972).

Albert, Hans, 1965: "Wertfreiheit als methodisches Prinzip," in Topitsch 1965:181–210.

Albert, Hans, 1969: *Traktat über kritische Vernunft,* Tübingen: J.C.B. Mohr, 2nd ed. (1st ed. 1968).

Albert, Hans, 1971: "Theorie und Praxis; Max Weber und das Problem der Wertfreiheit und der Rationalität," in: Hans Albert and Ernst Topitsch (eds.), *Werturteilsstreit,* Darmstadt, Germany: Wissenschaftliche Buchgesellschaft, pp. 200–236.

Albert, Hans, 1978: *Traktat über rationale Praxis,* Tübingen: J.C.B. Mohr.

Apel, Karl-Otto, 1967–70: Introductions to Charles S. Peirce, *Schriften* (German transl.), 2 vols. , ed. by K.O. Apel, Frankfurt am Main: Suhrkamp, Vol. I 1967, Vol. II 1970.

Apel, Karl-Otto, et al., 1971: *Hermeneutik und Ideologiekritik,* Mit Beiträgen von Karl-Otto Apel, Claus v. Bormann, Rüdiger Bubner, Hans-Georg Gadamer, Hans Joachim Giegel und Jürgen Habermas, Frankfurt am Main: Suhrkamp.

Apel, Karl-Otto, 1972: "The A Priori of Communication and the Foundation of the Humanities," *Man and World* 5:3–12, 14–16, 22–37 (reprinted in Dallmayr/McCarthy 1977:292–315).

Apel, Karl-Otto, 1976 a: "Sprechakttheorie und transzendentale Sprachpragmatik – zur Frage ethischer Normen," in Apel 1976 b:10–173.

Apel, Karl-Otto (ed.), 1976 b: *Sprachpragmatik und Philosophie,* Frankfurt am Main: Suhrkamp.

Ardell, Donald B., 1970: "Public Regional Councils and Comprehensive Health Planning: A Partnership?" *Journal of the American Institute of Planners* 36:393–404.

Ardell, Donald B., 1971: "CHP, Regional Councils and the Public Interest: A Case for New Leadership," *Inquiry* 8 (Dec.):27–35.

Ardell, Donald B., 1973: "Limitations and Priorities in CHP," *Inquiry* 10 (Sept.):49–56.

Arendt, Hannah, 1978: *The Life of the Mind,* Vol. I: *Thinking,* New York and London: Harcourt Brace Jovanovich.

Argyris, Chris, 1971: "Management Information Systems: The Challenge to Rationality and Emotionality," *Management Science* 17:B 275–292.

Armstrong, J. Scott, 1980: "Unintelligible Management Research and Academic Prestige," *TIMS/ORSA Interfaces* 10 (No. 2):80–86.

Ashby, W. Ross, 1956: *An Introduction to Cybernetics,* London: Chapman & Hall, and New York: Wiley.

Ashby, W. Ross, 1960: *Design for a Brain,* 2nd ed. New York: Wiley (1st ed. 1952).

Austin, John L., 1962: *How to Do Things With Words,* Cambridge, Mass.: Harvard University Press (2nd ed. 1975).

Bachelard, Gaston, 1978: *Die Philosophie des Nein,* Versuch einer Philosophie des neuen wissenschaftlichen Geistes, Wiesbaden, Germany: Heymann (French orig.: *La philosophie du non,* Paris: Presses Universitaires de France 1940, 6th ed. 1973).

Baier, Kurt, 1958: *The Moral Point of View:* A Rational Basis of Ethics, Ithaca, N.Y.: Cornell University Press.

Bateson, Gregory, 1972: *Steps to an Ecology of Mind,* New York: Ballantine Books.

Bawkin, Harry, 1945: "Pseudoxia Pediatrica," *New England Journal of Medicine* 232:691–697.

Bay Area Comprehensive Health Planning Council, 1975: *Health Systems Plan 1975,* San Francisco: Bay Area Comprehensive Health Planning Council, April 22.

Beck, Lewis White, 1949: *Immanuel Kant, Critique of Practical Reason and Other Writings in Moral Philosophy,* translated and edited with an introduction by Lewis White Beck, Chicago, Ill.: University of Chicago Press.

Beck, Lewis White, 1951: *Immanuel Kant, Prolegomena,* a revision of the transl. by Paul Carus (Open Court Publishing 1902), with an introduction by L.W. Beck, New York: Liberal Arts Press.

Beck, Lewis White, 1975: *The Actor and the Spectator,* New Haven, Conn., and London: Yale University Press.

Beer, Stafford, 1959: "What Has Cybernetics to Do With Operational Research?" *Operational Research Quarterly* 10:1–21.

Beer, Stafford, 1966: *Decision and Control,* The Meaning of Operational Research and Management Cybernetics. New York: Wiley.

Beer, Stafford, 1970: "The Liberty Machine," Address to the Conference on Ecological Systems, organized by the American Society for Cybernetics, Washington, D.C., Oct. 8, 1970; reprinted in Beer 1975:307–321.

Beer, Stafford, 1972: *Brain of the Firm,* The Managerial Cybernetics of Organization, Harmondsworth, England: Allen Lane The Penguin Press; 2nd ed. Chichester, England, and New York: John Wiley 1981.

Beer, Stafford, 1973a: "Fanfare for Effective Freedom: Cybernetic Praxis in Government," Third Richard Goodman Memorial Lecture, Brighton, England, Feb. 14, 1973; reprinted in Beer 1975:421–452.

Beer, Stafford, 1973b: "Beer replies," *New Scientist* 57:449.

Beer, Stafford, 1973c: "Beer to Grosch," *New Scientist* 57:685–686.

Beer, Stafford, 1974: *Cybernetics of National Development,* The Zaheer Lecture, Dec. 5, New Dehli, India: Zaheer Science Foundation.

Beer, Stafford, 1975: *Platform for Change,* New York: Wiley.

Bendix, Reinhard, 1970: "Concepts and Generalizations in Comparative Sociological Studies," in: Reinhard Bendix, *Embattled Reason,* Essays on Social Knowledge, New York: Oxford University Press, pp. 175–186.

Bendix, Reinhard, 1975: *Science and the Purpose of Knowledge,* Berkeley, Calif.: University of California, Institute of Industrial Relations, Reprint No. 397 (German orig.: Der Glaube an die Wissenschaft, Konstanz, Germany: Konstanzer Universitätsreden No. 48, Konstanz University Press).

Berlinski, David, 1976: *On Systems Analysis:* An Essay Concerning the Limitations of Some Mathematical Methods in the Social, Political, and Biological Sciences, Cambridge, Mass.: MIT Press.

Bierce, Ambrose, 1958: *The Devil's Dictionary,* New York: Dover Publications (orig. Neale Publishing Co., 1911).

Bloch, Ernst, 1977: *Subjekt-Objekt, Erläuterungen zu Hegel,* Frankfurt am Main: Suhrkamp (reprint of the 2nd ed. of 1962, 1st ed. 1951).

Blum, Henrik L. and Associates, 1969: *Health Planning 1969,* San Francisco: American Public Health Association, Western Regional Office.

Blum, Henrik L., 1974: *Planning for Health,* Development and Application of Social Change Theory, New York: Human Sciences Press (2nd ed. 1981).

Blum, Henrik L., 1976a: "From a Concept of Health to a National Health Planning Policy," *American Journal of Health Planning* 1 (No. 1):3–22.

Blum, Henrik L., 1976 b: *Expanding Health Care Horizons,* From a General Systems Concept of Health to a National Health Policy, Oakland, Calif.: Third Party Associates.

Blum, Henrik L., 1978: "Does Health Planning Work Anywhere, and if so, Why? Thoughts Provoked by Participation in an International Health Planning Study," *American Journal of Health Planning* 3 (No. 3):34–47.

Blümle, Ernst-Bernd/Ulrich, Werner, 1972: "Der internationale Vergleich als Hilfsmittel der Prognose im Handel, dargestellt am Beispiel der Entwicklung der Selbstbedienung in der Bundesrepublik Deutschland, Österreich und der Schweiz," in: E. B. Blümle/F. Fleck (eds.), *Festgabe für Professor Joseph Schwarzfischer,* Freiburg i. Ue., Switzerland: Freiburg University Press, pp. 293–321.

Braybrooke, David/Lindblom, Charles E., 1963: *A Strategy of Decision,* New York: Free Press.

Bryer, R. A., 1979: "The Status of the Systems Approach," *Omega,* The International Journal of Management Science, 7:219–231.

Bryer, R. A., 1980: "Some Comments on Churchman and Ulrich's 'Reply' to 'The Status of the Systems Approach'," *Omega,* The International Journal of Management Science, 8:280.

Bubner, Rüdiger, 1969: "Was ist kritische Theorie?" *Philosophische Rundschau* 16:213–249; reprinted in Apel et al. 1971:160–209.

Bubner, Rüdiger, 1974: "Zur Struktur eines transzendentalen Arguments," *Kant-Studien* 65, Sonderheft (Akten des 4. Internat. Kant-Kongresses, Mainz, 6.–10. April 1974, Teil I, ed. by Gerhard Funke and Joachim Kopper), pp. 15–27.

Bubner, Rüdiger, 1975: "Eine Renaissance der praktischen Philosophie," *Philosophische Rundschau* 22:1–34.

Bubner, Rüdiger, 1976: *Handlung, Sprache und Vernunft;* Grundbegriffe praktischer Philosophie, Frankfurt am Main: Suhrkamp 1976.

Buckley, Walter (ed.), 1968: *Modern Systems Research for the Behaviorial Scientist,* Chicago: Aldine.

California State Office of Comprehensive Health Planning, 1971: *California State Plan for Health,* Sacramento, Calif.: California Department of Public Health, Task Force for the Development of the State Plan for Health.

Campbell, Donald T., 1960a: "Blind Variation and Selective Retention in Creative Thought as in Other Knowledge Processes," *Psychological Review* 67:380–400.

Campbell, Donald T., 1960b: "Blind Variation and Selective Survival as a General Strategy in Knowledge-Processes," in Yovits/Cameron 1960:205–231.

Campbell, Donald T., 1965: "Variation and Selective Retention in Socio-Cultural Evolution," in: Barringer, H./Blanksten, G./Mack, R. (eds.), *Social Change in Developing Areas:* A Reinterpretation of Evolutionary Theory, Cambridge, Mass.: Schenkman 1965, pp. 19–49.

Campbell, Donald T., 1974: "Evolutionary Epistemology," in Schilpp 1974:413–463.

Cannon, Walter B., 1932: *The Wisdom of the Body,* New York: Norton.

Chamberlain, Neil W., 1973: *The Limits of Corporate Responsibility,* New York: Basic Books.

Checkland, Peter B., 1972: "Towards a System-Based Methodology for Real-World Problem Solving," *Journal of Systems Engineering* 3 (No. 2):1–30.

Checkland, Peter B., 1978: "The Origins and Nature of 'Hard' Systems Thinking," *Journal of Applied Systems Analysis* 5 (No. 2):99–110.

Checkland, Peter B., 1981: *Systems Thinking, Systems Practice,* Chichester, England, and New York: John Wiley.

Chestnut, Harold, 1966: *Systems Engineering Tools,* New York: Wiley, 2nd ed. (1st ed. 1965).

Chomsky, Noam, 1957: *Syntactic Structures,* The Hague, Netherlands: Mouton.

Chomsky, Noam, 1965: *Aspects of the Theory of Syntax,* Cambridge, Mass.: MIT Press.

Chomsky, Noam/Herman, Edward S., 1977: "The United States Versus Human Rights in the Third World," *Monthly Review* 29 (No. 3):22–45.

Chomsky, Noam/Herman, Edward S., 1979: *The Political Economy of Human Rights,* Boston, Mass.: South End Press.

Churchman, C. West, 1948: *Theory of Experimental Inference,* New York: Macmillan.

Churchman, C. West, 1968a: *Challenge to Reason,* New York: McGraw-Hill.

Churchman, C. West, 1968b: *The Systems Approach,* New York: Delacorte Press and Dell Publishing (rev. ed. Dell Publishing 1979).

Churchman, C. West, 1970a: "Kant – A Decision Theorist?" *Theory and Decision* 1:107–116.

Churchman, C. West, 1970b: "The Artificiality of Science," a review of Herbert A. Simon's *The Sciences of the Artificial, Contemporary Psychology* 15:385–386.

Churchman, C. West, 1971: *The Design of Inquiring Systems,* Basic Concepts of Systems and Organization, New York: Basic Books.

Churchman, C. West, 1974: "Philosophical Speculations on Systems Design," *Omega,* The International Journal of Management Science 2 (No. 4).

Churchman, C. West, 1979: *The Systems Approach and Its Enemies,* New York: Basic Books.

Churchman, C. West, 1981: *Thought and Wisdom,* Seaside, Calif.: Intersystems Publications.

Churchman, C. West/Ackoff, Russell L., 1950: "Purposive Behavior and Cybernetics," *Social Forces* 29:32–39 (reprinted in Buckley 1968:243–249).

Churchman, C. West/Cowan, Thomas A./Ulrich, Werner, 1983: "The Systems Approach and Its Enemies: A Dialogue," *Journal of Enterprise Management* (forthcoming).

Churchman, C. West/Mason, Richard O. (eds.), 1976: *World Modelling: A Dialogue,* New York: American Elsevier, and Amsterdam: North-Holland Publishing.

Churchman, C. West/Nelson, Harold G./Eacret, Kreg, 1977: *Value Distribution Assessment of Geothermal Development in Lake County, CA,* Report prepared for the U.S. Department of Energy under Contract No. W-7405-ENG-48, Berkeley, Calif.: University of California, Lawrence Berkeley Laboratory.

Churchman, C. West/Ulrich, Werner, 1980: "The Status of the Systems Approach, A Reply to R. A. Bryer," *Omega,* The International Journal of Management Science 8:277–280.

Collingwood, Robin G., 1946: *The Idea of History,* Oxford, England: Clarendon Press.

Dahl, Robert A./Lindblom, Charles E., 1953: *Politics, Economics and Welfare,* New York: Harper 1953 (2nd ed. with a new preface 1976).

Dallmayr, Fred R., 1972: "Habermas' *Knowledge and Human Interests* and its Aftermath," *Philosophy of the Social Sciences* 2:211–229 (Review Symposium on Habermas, Part II).

Dallmayr, Fred R./McCarthy, Thomas A. (eds.), 1977: *Understanding and Social Inquiry,* Notre Dame, Ind., and London: University of Notre Dame Press.

Dallmayr, Winfried, 1974: *Materialien zu Habermas' "Erkenntnis und Interesse,"* Frankfurt am Main: Suhrkamp.

Darling, Helen, 1982: "The Health Systems Agencies: Their Origin, Directions and Changing Assumptions," *Bulletin of the New York Academy of Medicine,* second series, 58:19–27.

Davidoff, Paul, 1965: "Advocacy and Pluralism in Planning," *Journal of the American Institute of Planners* 31:331–338.

Davis, Gary A., 1973: *Psychology of Problem Solving,* New York: Basic Books.

Dewey, John, 1938: "Means and Ends," in: Leon Trotsky/John Dewey/George Novack, *Their Morals and Ours,* Marxist vs. Liberal Views on Morality, New York: Pathfinder Press 1973, pp. 67–73 (orig. published as a reply to Trotsky's essay "Their Morals and Ours"; the two essays appeared in the June and August issues of *The New International,* 1938).

Dickson, Gary W./Senn, James A./Chervany, Norman L., 1977: "Research in MIS: The Minnesota Experiments," *Management Science* 23:913–923.

Dingler, Hugo, 1923: *Die Grundlagen der Physik,* Synthetische Prinzipien der mathematischen Naturphilosophie, Berlin and Leipzig: de Gruyter, 2nd ed. (1st ed. 1919).

Doyle, Arthur Conan, 1892: "A Study in Scarlet," in: *The Complete Sherlock Holmes,* Vol. 1, Garden City, N.Y.: Doubleday, n. d.

Duhl, Leonard J., 1976: "The Process of Recreation – The Health of the 'I' and the 'Us'," *Ethics in Science and Medicine* 3:33–63.

Duhl, Leonard J./Volkman, Janice, 1970: "Participant Democracy: Networks as a Strategy for Change," *Urban and Social Change Review* 3 (Spring): 11–14.

Eccles, John C., 1970: *Facing Reality,* Berlin and Heidelberg, Germany, London and New York: Springer.

Emery, Fred E. (ed.), 1969: *Systems Thinking,* Harmondsworth, England: Penguin Books.

Emery, Fred E./Thorsrud, E., 1969: *Form and Content in Industrial Democracy,* London: Tavistock.

Erasmus, Desiderius/Luther, Martin, 1961: *Discourse on Free Will,* transl. and ed. by Ernst F. Winter, New York: Ungar 1961.

Ewing, A.C., 1974: *A Short Commentary on Kant's Critique of Pure Reason,* Chicago: University of Chicago Press (orig. 1938).

Feyerabend, Paul, 1970: "Against Method, Outline of an Anarchistic Theory of Knowledge," *Minnesota Studies in the Philosophy of Science* 4:17–130.

Feyerabend, Paul, 1975: *Against Method,* Outline of an Anarchistic Theory of Knowledge, London: New Left Books, and Atlantic Highlands: Humanities Press.

Feyerabend, Paul, 1980: *Erkenntnis für freie Menschen,* veränderte Ausgabe, Frankfurt am Main: Suhrkamp (improved German version of *Science in a Free Society,* London: NLB 1978).

Findlay, J(ohn) N., 1958: *Hegel: A Re-examination,* London and New York: George Allen & Unwin; Oxford University Press paperback reprint 1976.

Forrester, Jay W., 1969: *Industrial Dynamics,* Cambridge, Mass.: MIT Press, 6th ed. (1st ed. 1961).

Forrester, Jay W., 1971. *World Dynamics,* Cambridge, Mass.: Wright-Allen Press.

Frank, Helmar, 1969: *Kybernetische Grundlagen der Pädagogik,* Baden-Baden, Germany: Agis-Verlag, and Paris: Gauthier-Villars (1st ed. 1962).

Fromm, Erich, 1941: *Escape from Freedom,* New York: Holt, Rinehart & Winston.

Fromm, Erich, 1947: *Man for Himself,* An Inquiry into the Psychology of Ethics, New York: Holt, Rinehart & Winston.

Fromm, Erich, 1960: *Zen Buddhism and Psychoanalysis,* New York: Harper & Brothers (German edition: Zen-Buddhismus und Psychoanalyse, Frankfurt am Main: Suhrkamp 1972).

Fromm, Erich, 1974: *The Revolution of Hope,* Toward a Humanized Technology, New York: Perennial Library (orig. 1968).

Galbraith, John Kenneth, 1975: *Economics and the Public Purpose,* New York: Signet (New American Library); orig. Boston, Mass.: Houghton Mifflin 1973.

Gomez, Peter, 1977: "Organic Problem-Solving in Management: Systems Methodology Applied to the Design of Viable Systems," in: *The General Systems Paradigm:*

Science of Change and Change of Science, Proceedings of the 21st Meeting of the Society for General Systems Research, J. Whyte, ed., Washington, D.C.: Soc. f. Gen. Sys. Res.

Gomez, Peter/Malik, Fredmund/Oeller, Karl-Heinz, 1975: *Systemmethodik,* Grundlagen einer Methodik zur Erforschung und Gestaltung komplexer sozio-technischer Systeme, 2 vols., Bern, Switzerland: Paul Haupt.

Gordon, William J.J., 1961: *Synectics,* The Development of Creative Capacity, New York: Harper & Row (also Collier Books, Macmillan 1968).

Grosch, Herbert R.J., 1973: "Chilean Economic Controls," *New Scientist* 57:626–627.

Habermas, Jürgen, 1957: "Literaturbericht zur philosophischen Diskussion um Marx und den Marxismus," *Philosophische Rundschau* 5:165–235, reprinted in *Theorie und Praxis* (but not in the Engl. transl., 1973a), pp. 387–436.

Habermas, Jürgen, 1962: *Strukturwandel der Öffentlichkeit,* Untersuchungen zu einer Kategorie der bürgerlichen Gesellschaft, Darmstadt and Neuwied, Germany: Luchterhand.

Habermas, Jürgen, 1963: "Analytische Wissenschaftstheorie und Dialektik, Ein Nachtrag zur Kontroverse zwischen Popper und Adorno," in: Max Horkheimer (ed.), *Zeugnisse, Festschrift für Theodor W. Adorno,* Frankfurt am Main: Europäische Verlagsanstalt 1963:473–501 (slightly modified versions in Topitsch 1965:291–311, in Adorno et al. 1969:155–191, and in Habermas 1970:9–38).

Habermas, Jürgen, 1964: "Gegen einen positivistisch halbierten Rationalismus," *Kölner Zeitschrift für Soziologie und Sozialpsychologie* 16:636–659 (reprinted in Adorno et al. 1969:235–266, and in Habermas 1970:39–70).

Habermas, Jürgen, 1965: "Erkenntnis und Interesse," Inaugural lecture, University of Frankfurt, June 28, 1965, orig. publ. in *Merkur* (Munich) 19 (No. 231): 1139–1153, reprinted in Habermas 1968:146–168; Engl. transl. as Appendix in Habermas 1971a:301–317.

Habermas, Jürgen, 1968: *Technik und Wissenschaft als "Ideologie,"* Frankfurt am Main: Suhrkamp.

Habermas, Jürgen, 1970a: *Zur Logik der Sozialwissenschaften,* Materialien, Frankfurt am Main: Suhrkamp.

Habermas, Jürgen, 1970b "Der Universalitätsanspruch der Hermeneutik," in: Rüdiger Bubner, Konrad Cramer and Reiner Wiehl (eds.), *Hermeneutik und Dialektik I, Festschrift für H.-G. Gadamer,* Tübingen, Germany: J.C.B. Mohr 1970, pp. 73–104; reprinted in Apel et al. 1971:120–259.

Habermas, Jürgen, 1970c: "Summation and Response," *Continuum* 8:123–133.

Habermas, Jürgen, 1970d "Towards a Theory of Communicative Competence," *Inquiry* 13:360–375.

Habermas, Jürgen, 1971a: *Knowledge and Human Interests,* Boston, Mass.: Beacon Press (orig.: *Erkenntnis und Interesse,* Frankfurt am Main: Suhrkamp 1968).

Habermas, Jürgen, 1971b: *Toward a Rational Society; Student Protest, Science, and Politics*, Boston, Mass.: Beacon Press.

Habermas, Jürgen, 1971c: "Vorbereitende Bemerkungen zu einer Theorie der kommunikativen Kompetenz," in Habermas/Luhmann 1971:101–141.

Habermas, Jürgen, 1971d: "Theorie der Gesellschaft oder Sozialtechnologie? Eine Auseinandersetzung mit Niklas Luhmann," in Habermas/Luhmann 1971:142–290.

Habermas, Jürgen, 1973a: *Theory and Practice,* transl. by John Viertel, Boston, Mass.: Beacon Press (partial transl. of *Theorie und Praxis,* Sozialphilosophische Studien, 4th ed. with a new introduction, Frankfurt am Main: Suhrkamp 1971, orig. Neuwied-Berlin: Luchterhand 1963).

Habermas, Jürgen, 1973b: "Nachwort (1973)," in Habermas, *Erkenntnis und Interesse,* 2nd ed., Frankfurt am Main: Suhrkamp 1973:367–416 (Postscript to Habermas 1971a, not contained in the English ed.); transl. published as "A Postscript to Knowledge and Human Interests," *Philosophy of the Social Sciences* 3 (1975):157–189.

Habermas, Jürgen, 1973c: "Wahrheitstheorien," in: Helmut Fahrenbach (ed.), *Wirklichkeit und Reflexion, Walter Schulz zum 60. Geburtstag,* Pfullingen: Neske, pp. 211–265 (partly reprinted in Riedel 1974:381–402).

Habermas, Jürgen, 1973d: *Kultur und Kritik,* Verstreute Aufsätze, Frankfurt am Main: Suhrkamp.

Habermas, Jürgen, 1975: *Legitimation Crisis,* Boston, Mass.: Beacon Press (orig.: *Legitimationsprobleme im Spätkapitalismus,* Frankfurt am Main: Suhrkamp 1973).

Habermas, Jürgen, 1976: *Zur Rekonstruktion des Historischen Materialismus,* Frankfurt am Main: Suhrkamp.

Habermas, Jürgen, 1979a: "What is Universal Pragmatics?" in Habermas 1979b:1–68 (orig. "Was heisst Universalpragmatik?", in Apel 1976b:174–272).

Habermas, Jürgen, 1979b: *Communication and the Evolution of Society,* Boston, Mass.: Beacon Press.

Habermas, Jürgen, 1981: *Theorie des kommunikativen Handelns,* 2 vols., Frankfurt am Main: Suhrkamp.

Habermas, Jürgen/Luhmann, Niklas, 1971: *Theorie der Gesellschaft oder Sozialtechnologie – Was leistet die Systemforschung?* Frankfurt am Main: Suhrkamp.

Hanlon, Joseph, 1973a: "The Technological Power Broker," *New Scientist* 57:347.

Hanlon, Joseph, 1973b: "Chile Leaps Into Cybernetic Future," *New Scientist* 57:363–364.

Harrison, P.J./Stevens, C.R., 1971: "A Bayesian Approach to Short-Term Forecasting," *Operational Research Quarterly* 22:341–342.

Hartmann, Nicolai, 1924: "Diesseits von Idealismus und Realismus," *Kant-Studien* 29:160–206.

Hartmann, Nicolai, 1949: *Grundzüge einer Metaphysik der Erkenntnis*, Berlin: de Gruyter, 4th ed. (1st ed. 1921).

Hegel, Georg Wilhelm Friedrich, 1807: *Phänomenologie des Geistes*, Bamberg und Würzburg 1807; Vol. 3 of the Theorie-Werkausgabe, Frankfurt am Main: Suhrkamp 1970. English transl. by J.B. Baillie: *The Phenomenology of Mind*, 2 vols., London and New York 1910, 2nd rev. ed. in 1 vol. London: George Allen & Unwin, and New York: Macmillan, 1931. (A transl. of the important Preface has been published by Walter Kaufmann, cf. Kaufmann 1977).

Helmer, Olaf, 1968: "Analysis of the Future: The Delphi Method," in J.R. Bright (ed.), *Technological Forecasting for Industry and Government*, Englewood Cliffs, N.J.: Prentice-Hall.

Hempel, Carl G./Oppenheim, Paul, 1948: "Studies in the Logic of Explanation," *Philosophy of Science* 15:135–175.

Hill, Melvyn Alan, 1972: "Jürgen Habermas: A Social Science of the Mind," *Philosophy of the Social Sciences* 2:247–259 (Review Symposium on Habermas, Part IV).

Höffe, Otfried, 1979: *Ethik und Politik*, Grundmodelle und -probleme der praktischen Philosophie, Frankfurt am Main: Suhrkamp.

Hoggatt, Austin C./Balderston, Fred E. (eds.), 1963: *Symposium on Simulation Models:* Methodology and Application to the Behavioral Sciences, Cincinnati, Ohio: South Western Publ.

Holling, C.S., 1976: "Resilience and Stability in Ecosystems," in Jantsch/Waddington 1976:73–92.

Holzkamp, Klaus, 1968: *Wissenschaft als Handlung*, Versuch einer neuen Grundlegung der Wissenschaftslehre, Berlin: de Gruyter.

Holzkamp, Klaus, 1971: "Kritischer Rationalismus als blinder Kritizismus," *Zeitschrift für Sozialpsychologie* 2:248–270, also reprinted in Holzkamp 1972: 173–205.

Holzkamp, Klaus, 1972: *Kritische Psychologie*, Vorbereitende Arbeiten, Frankfurt am Main: Fischer Taschenbuchverlag.

Hoos, Ida R., 1972: *Systems Analysis in Public Policy: A Critique*, Berkeley and Los Angeles: University of California Press.

Horkheimer, Max, 1937a: "Traditionelle und kritische Theorie," *Zeitschrift für Sozialforschung* 6:245–294.

Horkheimer, Max, 1937b: "Philosophie und kritische Theorie," *Zeitschrift für Sozialforschung* 6:625–631.

Horkheimer, Max, 1941: "Notes on Institute Activities," *Zeitschrift für Sozialforschung* (Engl. title: *Studies in Philosophy and Social Science*) 9:121–123.

Horkheimer, Max, 1967: *Zur Kritik der instrumentellen Vernunft*, Frankfurt am Main: Fischer.

Horkheimer, Max/Adorno, Theodor W., 1947: *Dialektik der Aufklärung,* Philosophische Fragmente, Amsterdam: Querido, new ed. Frankfurt am Main: Fischer 1969.

Howard, Ted/Rifkin, Jeremy, 1977: *Who Should Play God?* New York: Dell Publishing.

Hull, Clark, 1952: *A Behavior System,* New Haven: Yale University Press.

Husserl, Edmund, 1970: *The Crisis of European Sciences and Transcendental Phenomenology,* transl. by David Carr, Evanston, Ill.: Northwestern University Press.

Illich, Ivan, 1973: *Tools for Conviviality,* New York: Perennial Library.

Illich, Ivan, 1977: *Medical Nemesis,* The Expropriation of Health, New York: Bantam Books (orig. London: Calder & Boyars 1975).

Jantsch, Erich, 1966: *Technological Forecasting in Perspective,* A Framework for Technological Forecasting, Paris: OECD.

Jantsch, Erich, 1980: *The Self-Organizing Universe,* Scientific and Human Implications of the Emerging Paradigm of Evolution, Oxford, England, and New York: Pergamon Press.

Jantsch, Erich/Waddington, Conrad H. (eds.), 1976: *Evolution and Consciousness,* Human Systems in Transition, Reading, Mass.: Addison-Wesley.

Jay, Martin, 1973: *Dialectical Imagination: The History of the Frankfurt School and the Institut für Sozialforschung 1923–50,* Boston, Mass.: Little, Brown & Co.

Jung, C.G., 1953: "The Relations Between the Ego and the Unconscious," in *Collected Works Vol. 7, Two Essays on Analytic Psychology,* New York: Pantheon Books, Bollingen Series.

Kambartel, Friedrich (ed.), 1974: *Praktische Philosophie und Konstruktive Wissenschaftstheorie,* Frankfurt am Main: Suhrkamp.

Kamlah, Wilhelm/Lorenzen, Paul, 1967: *Logische Propädeutik,* Vorschule des vernünftigen Redens, Mannheim, Germany: Bibliographisches Institut.

Kant, Immanuel, 1770: *De Mundis Sensibilis Atque Intelligibilis Forma et Principiis/ Von der Form der Sinnen- und Verstandeswelt und ihren Gründen,* Inaugural Dissertation, orig. ed. (A₂), in: Wilhelm Weischedel (ed.), Kant Werkausgabe Vol. V, Schriften zur Metaphysik und Logik 1, Frankfurt am Main: Suhrkamp 1968.

Kant, Immanuel, 1781/87: *Kritik der reinen Vernunft,* first ed. (A) 1781, second ed. (B) 1787, ed. by Wilhelm Weischedel, Frankfurt am Main: Suhrkamp 1968. (Quoted *KrV* or "first Critique".)

Kant, Immanuel, 1781/87: *Critique of Pure Reason,* transl. by Norman Kemp Smith, New York: St. Martin's Press 1965 (orig. Macmillan 1929). (Quoted *KrV* or "first Critique".)

Kant, Immanuel, 1783: *Prolegomena zu einer jeden künftigen Metaphysik, die als Wissenschaft wird auftreten können,* first ed. (A), ed. by Wilhelm Weischedel, Werkausgabe Vol. V: Schriften zur Metaphysik und Logik 1, Frankfurt am Main: Suhrkamp 1968. (Quoted "Prol.")

Kant, Immanuel, 1783: *Prolegomena to Any Future Metaphysics,* a revision of the transl. by Paul Carus (Open Court Publishing 1902), with an introduction by L. W. Beck, New York: Liberal Arts Press. (Cf. Beck 1951.)

Kant, Immanuel, 1784: "What Is Enlightenment?" In Beck 1949:286–292 (orig. "Zur Beantwortung der Frage: Was ist Aufklärung?" in *Berlinische Monatsschrift,* Dec. 1784).

Kant, Immanuel, 1786: *Grundlegung zur Metaphysik der Sitten,* second ed. (B), (first ed. [A] 1785), ed. by Wilhelm Weischedel, Frankfurt am Main: Suhrkamp 1968. (Quoted *GMS* or "Foundations".)

Kant, Immanuel, 1786: *Groundwork of the Metaphysic of Morals,* translated and analyzed by H.J. Paton, New York: Harper Torchbooks 1964. (Transl. of the *Grundlegung,* second ed. (B), quoted *GMW* or "Foundations".)

Kant, Immanuel, 1788: *Kritik der praktischen Vernunft,* first ed. (A), ed. by Wilhelm Weischedel, Frankfurt am Main: Suhrkamp 1968. (Quoted *KpV* or "second Critique".)

Kant, Immanuel, 1788: *Critique of Practical Reason* And Other Writings in Moral Philosophy, Translated and Edited with an Introduction by Lewis White Beck, Chicago, Ill.: University of Chicago Press, 1949. (Cf. Beck 1949.)

Kant, Immanuel, 1790: *Kritik der Urteilskraft,* ed. by Wilhelm Weischedel, Frankfurt am Main: Suhrkamp 1968 (transl.: *Critique of Judgement,* transl. by T.H. Bernard (1892), New York: Hafner 1951).

Kaufmann, Walter, 1966: *Hegel: A Reinterpretation,* Garden City, New York: Anchor Books.

Kaufmann, Walter, 1977: *Hegel, Texts and Commentary,* Translation of the Preface to the *Phenomenology* and of "Who Thinks Abstractly?", Notre Dame, Indiana: University of Notre Dame Press 1977 (orig. Garden City: N.Y.: Anchor Books 1966).

Keller, Donald A., 1980: *On Intercultural Transfer, and the Adaptation of, Planning Methodology,* unpubl. Ph. D. Thesis, Cambridge, Mass.: MIT, Dept. of Civil Engineering.

Kleinmuntz, Benjamin (ed.), 1966: *Problem Solving: Research, Method, and Theory,* New York: Wiley.

Klir, George J./Valach, Miroslaw, 1967: *Cybernetic Modelling,* London: Illiffe.

Klix, Friedhart, 1971: *Information und Verhalten,* Aspekte der organismischen Informationsverarbeitung, Berlin-East: VEB Deutscher Verlag der Wissenschaften, and Bern, Switzerland: Huber.

Kohlberg, Lawrence, 1969: "Stage and Sequence," in: D.A. Goslin (ed.), *Handbook of Socialization Theory and Research,* Chicago: Rand McNally.

Kohlberg, Lawrence, 1971: "From Is to Ought," in: Theodore Mischel (ed.), *Cognitive Development and Epistemology*, New York: Academic Press, pp. 151–236.

Korzybski, Alfred, 1958: *Science and Sanity; An Introduction to Non-Aristotelian Systems and General Semantics*, 4th ed., Lakeville, Conn.: The International Non-Aristotelian Library Publishing Co., distributed by the Institute of General Semantics (1st ed. 1933).

Krauch, Helmut, 1972: *Computer-Demokratie*, Düsseldorf, Germany: Econ.

Kuhn, Thomas S., 1962: *The Structure of Scientific Revolutions*, Chicago: University of Chicago Press, 2nd ed. 1970.

Lakatos, Imre, 1970: "Falsification and the Methodology of Scientific Research Programmes," in: I. Lakatos and A.E. Musgrave (eds.), *Criticism and the Growth of Knowledge*, Cambridge, England: Cambridge University Press.

Lalonde, Marc, 1974: *A New Perspective on the Health of Canadians*, A Working Document, Ottawa: Government of Canada, Dept. of National Health and Welfare, n.d. (April 1974).

Landau, Martin, 1969: "Redundancy, Rationality and the Problem of Duplication and Overlap," *Public Administration Review* 29:346–358.

Laporte, Todd R. (ed.), 1975: *Organized Social Complexity*, Princeton, N.J.: Princeton University Press.

Lenhardt, Christian K., 1972: "Rise and Fall of Transcendental Anthropology," *Philosophy of the Social Sciences* 2:231–246 (Review Symposium on Habermas, Part III).

Liddell, Brendan E.A., 1970: *Kant on the Foundation of Morality*, A Modern Version of the *Grundlegung*, translated with commentary, Bloomington, Ind., and London: Indiana University Press.

Likert, Rensis, 1961: *New Patterns of Management*, New York: McGraw-Hill.

Lindblom, Charles E., 1959: "The Science of 'Muddling Through'," *Public Administration Review* 19:79–88.

Lobkowicz, Nikolaus, 1972: "Interest and Objectivity," *Philosophy of the Social Sciences* 2:193–210 (Review Symposium on Habermas, Part I).

Locke, John, 1690: *An Essay Concerning Human Understanding*, ed. by J.A. St. John, The Philosophical Works of John Locke, Vol. I, London: George Bell and Sons 1902 (orig. London 1690).

Lorenz, Kurt, 1972: "Der dialogische Wahrheitsbegriff," in: *Neue Hefte für Philosophie*, No. 2/3: *Dialog als Methode*, Göttingen, Germany: Vandenhoeck & Ruprecht, pp. 111–123.

Lorenzen, Paul, 1969: *Normative Logic and Ethics*, Mannheim, Germany: Bibliographisches Institut.

Lorenzen, Paul, 1974: *Konstruktive Wissenschaftstheorie*, Frankfurt am Main: Suhrkamp.

Lorenzen, Paul, 1977: "Das Begründungsproblem politischen Wissens," in: Günther Patzig, Erhard Scheibe and Wolfgang Wieland (eds.), *Logik, Ethik, Theorie der Geisteswissenschaften,* Proceedings of the 11th German Congress on Philosophy of 1975, Hamburg: Meiner (reprinted in Lorenzen 1978:119–139).

Lorenzen, Paul, 1978: *Theorie der technischen und politischen Vernunft,* Stuttgart, Germany: Reclam.

Lorenzen, Paul/Schwemmer, Oswald, 1975: *Konstruktive Logik, Ethik und Wissenschaftstheorie,* Mannheim, Germany: Bibliographisches Institut.

Lowi, Theodore J., 1969: *The End of Liberalism;* Ideology, Policy, and the Crisis of Public Authority, New York: Norton.

Lübbe, Hermann, 1962: "Zur politischen Theorie der Technokratie," *Der Staat* 1:19–38, reprinted in Lübbe 1971:32–53, and in Lübbe 1978:35–60.

Lübbe, Hermann, 1971: *Theorie und Entscheidung,* Studien zum Primat der praktischen Vernunft, Freiburg i. Br., Germany: Rombach.

Lübbe, Hermann, 1976: "Dezisionismus – eine kompromittierte politische Theorie," *Schweizer Monatshefte* 55:949–960, reprinted in Lübbe 1978:61–77.

Lübbe, Hermann, 1978: *Praxis der Philosophie, Praktische Philosophie, Geschichtsphilosophie,* Stuttgart: Reclam Universal-Bibliothek.

Lucas, H.C., Jr., 1975: *Why Information Systems Fail,* New York: Wiley.

Luhmann, Niklas, 1971a: "Moderne Systemtheorien als Form gesamtgesellschaftlicher Analyse," in Habermas/Luhmann 1971:7–24.

Luhmann, Niklas, 1971b: "Sinn als Grundbegriff der Soziologie," in Habermas/Luhmann 1971:25–100.

Luhmann, Niklas, 1973: *Zweckbegriff und Systemrationalität,* Über die Funktion von Zwecken in sozialen Systemen, Frankfurt am Main: Suhrkamp (orig. Tübingen, Germany: J.C.B. Mohr 1968).

Malik, F./Gomez, P./Oeller, K.H., 1977: "Organic Problem-Solving in Management: A Systems Methodology," in: *Proceedings of the 3rd European Meeting on Cybernetics and Systems Research,* Vienna, Austria, 1976; Washington, D.C.: Hemisphere Publishing.

Mao Tse-tung, 1968: "On Contradiction," in: Mao Tse-tung, *Four Essays on Philosophy,* Peking: Foreign Languages Press, pp. 23–78 (orig. written in 1937, published in the *Selected Works of Mao Tse-tung,* Vol. I, Peking Foreign Languages Press 1967).

Marcuse, Herbert, 1964: *One-Dimensional Man,* Studies in the Ideology of Advanced Industrial Society, Boston, Mass.: Beacon.

Maruyama, Magoroh, 1963: "The Second Cybernetics: Deviation-Amplifying Mutual Causal Processes," *American Scientist* 51:164–179, 250–256, reprinted in Buckley 1968:304–313.

Maruyama, Magoroh, 1976: "Toward Cultural Symbiosis," in Jantsch/Waddington 1976:198–212.

Marx, Karl, 1953: *Die Frühschriften,* ed. by Siegfried Landshut, Stuttgart: Alfred Kröner Verlag.

Maslow, Abraham H., 1969: *The Psychology of Science,* A Reconnaissance, Chicago: Henry Regnery (1st ed. 1961).

Mason, Richard O./Mitroff, Ian I., 1973: "A Program for Research on Management Information Systems," *Management Science* 19:475–487.

Maurer, Reinhard K., 1977: "Jürgen Habermas' Aufhebung der Philosophic," *Philosophische Rundschau* 24: *Beiheft 8* (special issue, Tübingen, Germany: J.C.B. Mohr).

McCarthy, Thomas, 1978: *The Critical Theory of Jürgen Habermas,* Cambridge, Mass., and London, England: MIT Press.

Meadows, D.H./Meadows, D.L./Randers, J./Behrens III, W.W., 1972: *The Limits to Growth,* A Report for the Club of Rome's Project on the Predicament of Mankind, New York: Universe Books.

Mesarovic, Mihajlo/Pestel, Eduard, 1974: *Mankind at the Turning Point,* The Second Report to the Club of Rome, New York: E.P. Dutton.

Mittelstrass, Jürgen (ed.), 1975: *Methodologische Probleme einer normativ-kritischen Gesellschaftstheorie,* Frankfurt am Main: Suhrkamp.

Mittelstrass, Jürgen (ed.), 1979: *Methodenprobleme der Wissenschaften vom gesellschaftlichen Handeln,* Frankfurt am Main: Suhrkamp.

Mitroff, Ian I., 1974: *The Subjective Side of Science,* A Philosophical Inquiry into the Psychology of the Apollo Moon Scientists, Amsterdam: Elsevier, and New York: American Elsevier.

Morris, Charles W., 1938: *Foundations of the Theory of Signs,* International Encyclopedia of Unified Science, Vol. I, No. 2, Chicago: Chicago University Press.

Morris, Charles W., 1946: *Signs, Language, and Behavior,* New York: Prentice-Hall.

Myrdal, Gunnar, 1933: "Das Zweck-Mittel-Denken in der Nationalökonomie," *Zeitschrift für Nationalökonomie* 4:305–329; Engl. transl.: "Ends and Means in Political Economy," in: Gunnar Myrdal, *Value in Social Theory,* A Selection of Essays on Methodology, ed. by Paul Streeten, London: Routledge & K. Paul, and New York: Harper & Brothers, 1958, Ch. 10, pp. 206–230.

Myrdal, Gunnar, 1975: *Against the Stream,* Critical Essays on Economics, New York: Vintage Books (Swedish orig. 1973).

Naftulin, Donald H./Ware, John E., Jr./Donnelly, Frank A., 1973: "The Doctor Fox Lecture: A Paradigm of Educational Seduction," *Journal of Medical Education* 48:630–635.

Narr, Wolf-Dieter, 1972: *Theoriebegriffe und Systemtheorie,* 3rd ed., Stuttgart, Germany: Kohlhammer (1st ed. 1969).

National Commission on Community Health Services, 1966: *Health Is a Community Affair,* Report, Cambridge, Mass.: Harvard University Press.

Navarro, Vicente, 1975: "Social Policy Issues: An Explanation of the Composition, Nature, and Functions of the Present Health Sector of the United States," *Bulletin of the New York Academy of Medicine*, second series, 51:199–234.

Navarro, Vicente, 1976: *Medicine under Capitalism*, New York: Prodist.

Newell, A./Shaw, J.C./Simon, H.A., 1958: "Elements of a Theory of Human Problem Solving," *Psychological Review* 65:151–166.

Newell, A./Shaw, J.C./Simon, H.A., 1960: "Report on a General Problem-Solving Program for a Computer," in: *Information Processing, Proceedings of the International Conference on Information Processing*, Paris: UNESCO, and London: Butterworths, pp. 256–264.

Newell, Allen/Simon, Herbert A., 1972: *Human Problem Solving*, Englewood Cliffs, N.J.: Prentice-Hall.

Newell, Kenneth W. (ed.), 1975: *Health by the People*, Geneva, Switzerland: World Health Organization (WHO).

Nichols, Christopher, 1972: "Science or Reflection: Habermas on Freud," *Philosophy of the Social Sciences* 2:261–270 (Review Symposium on Habermas, Part V).

Nicolis, Grégoire/Prigogine, Ilya, 1977: *Self-Organization in Non-equilibrium Systems*, From Dissipative Structures to Order Through Fluctuations, New York: Wiley-Interscience.

Nordhofen, Eckhard, 1976: *Das Bereichsdenken im Kritischen Rationalismus; Zur finitistischen Tradition der Popperschule*, Freiburg i. Br. and Munich: Alber.

OECD-CERI (ed.), 1971: *Educational Technology*, The Design and Implementation of Learning Systems, Paris: OECD, Center for Educational Research and Innovation.

Offe, Claus, 1972: *Strukturprobleme des kapitalistischen Staates*, Aufsätze zur politischen Soziologie, Frankfurt am Main: Suhrkamp.

Ogilvy, James, 1979: *Many Dimensional Man*, Decentralizing Self, Society, and the Sacred, New York: Harper Colophon Books (orig. Oxford Univ. Press 1977).

Osborn, Alex F., 1953: *Applied Imagination*, Principles and Procedures of Creative Problem Solving, New York: Charles Scribner's Sons (3rd rev. ed. 1963).

Paine, Thomas, 1776: *Common Sense*, Philadelphia.

Papanek, Victor J., 1969: "Tree of Life: Bionics," *The Journal of Creative Behavior* 3:5–15.

Parker, Alberta W., 1970: "The Consumer as Policy-Maker – Issues of Training," *American Journal of Public Health* 60:2139–2153.

Pask, Gordon, 1958: "Organic Control and the Cybernetic Method," *Cybernetica* 1:155–173.

Paton, H.J., 1964: *Immanuel Kant, Groundwork of the Metaphysic of Morals,* translated and analyzed by H.J. Paton, New York: Harper Torchbooks (orig. publ. under the title *The Moral Law,* London: Hutchison 1948, 3rd ed. 1956).

Peirce, Charles S., 1878: "How to Make Our Ideas Clear," in *Collected Papers,* Vol. V, ed. by Charles Hartshorne and Paul Weiss, Cambridge, Mass.: Harvard University Press, 1931ff, 2nd ed. 1960; together with German transl. and commentary reprinted in Klaus Oehler (ed.), *Über die Klarheit unserer Gedanken/How to Make Our Ideas Clear,* Frankfurt am Main: Klostermann 1968.

Pepper, Stephen C., 1942: *World Hypotheses,* Berkeley and Los Angeles: University of California Press.

Piaget, Jean, 1965: *The Moral Judgement of the Child,* New York: Free Press (1948).

Piaget, Jean, 1970: *Genetic Epistemology,* New York and London: Columbia University Press.

Piaget, Jean, 1971: *Biology and Knowledge,* An Essay on the Relations Between Organic Regulations and Cognitive Processes, Chicago: University of Chicago Press.

Polsby, Nelson W., 1963: *Community Power and Political Theory,* New Haven, Conn.: Yale University Press.

Polsgrove, Carol, 1978: "A Co-op Way to Health," *The Progressive* 42 (No. 3): 46–49.

Poole, Roger, 1972: *Towards Deep Subjectivity,* New York: Harper & Row (Harper Torchbook, orig. London: Allen Lane, The Penguin Press 1972).

Popper, Karl R., 1940: "What Is Dialectics?" orig. published in *Mind,* N.S. 49 (1940), now in Popper 1963:312–335 (German transl.: "Was ist Dialektik?" in Topitsch 1965:262–290).

Popper, Karl R., 1957: *The Poverty of Historicism,* London: Routledge and Kegan Paul, and Boston, Mass.: Beacon (3rd ed. New York: Harper Torchbooks 1961).

Popper, Karl R., 1961: *The Logic of Scientific Discovery,* New York: Basic Books (London: Hutchison 1959, German orig. *Logik der Forschung,* Wien: Springer 1935; a revised ed. has been published as a Harper Torchbook, New York 1968).

Popper Karl R., 1962: "Die Logik der Sozialwissenschaften," *Kölner Zeitschrift für Soziologie und Sozialpsychologie* 14:233–248; reprinted in Adorno et al. 1969: 103–123.

Popper, Karl R., 1963: *Conjectures and Refutations,* The Growth of Scientific Knowledge, London: Routledge & K. Paul (4th ed. 1972; also New York: Basic Books 1968).

Popper, Karl R., 1964: "Die Zielsetzung der Erfahrungswissenschaft," in Albert 1964b:73–86 (orig. in *Ratio* 1, 1957, No. 1).

Popper, Karl R., 1966: *The Open Society and Its Enemies,* 2 vols. Princeton, N.J.: Princeton University Press, 5th ed. (1st ed. 1945; German version: *Die offene Gesellschaft und ihre Feinde,* 2 vols., Bern, Switzerland: Francke 1958).

Popper, Karl R., 1972: *Objective Knowledge,* An Evolutionary Approach, Oxford, England: Clarendon Press.

Popper, Karl R., 1974: "Intellectual Autobiography," in Schilpp 1974: I, 3–181.

Popper, Karl R./Eccles, John C., 1977: *The Self and Its Brain,* Berlin and Heidelberg, Germany, London and New York: Springer.

Prince, George M., 1970: *The Practice of Creativity,* A Manual for Dynamic Group Problem Solving, New York: Harper & Row.

Quade, E.S./Boucher, W.I. (eds.), 1968: *Systems Analysis and Policy Planning:* Applications in Defence, New York: American Elsevier.

Rawls, John, 1971: *A Theory of Justice,* Cambridge, Mass.: Harvard University Press (Belknap Press).

Reichenbach, Hans, 1938: *Experience and Prediction,* An Analysis of the Foundation and the Structure of Knowledge, Chicago, Ill.: University of Chicago Press.

Riedel, Manfred (ed.), 1972: *Rehabilitierung der praktischen Philosophie,* Band I, Freiburg i. Br.: Rombach.

Riedel, Manfred (ed.), 1974: *Rehabilitierung der praktischen Philosophie,* Band II, Freiburg i. Br.: Rombach.

Riedel, Rupert, 1975: *Die Ordnung des Lebendigen,* Systembedingungen der Evolution, Hamburg and Berlin, Germany: Paul Parey.

Rittel, Horst W.J./Webber, Melvin M., 1973: "Dilemmas in a General Theory of Planning," *Policy Sciences* 4:155–169.

Rivett, Patrick, 1977: "The Case for Cybernetics, A Critical Appreciation," *European Journal of Operational Research* 1:33–37.

Rosenblueth, Arturo/Wiener, Norbert, 1950: "Purposeful and Non-Purposeful Behavior," *Philosophy of Science* 17:318–326.

Rosenblueth, Arturo/Wiener, Norbert/Bigelow, J.H., 1943: "Behavior, Purpose, and Teleology," *Philosophy of Science* 11:18–24.

Royce, Josiah, 1913: "The Principles of Logic," in: *Encyclopedia of the Philosophical Sciences,* Vol. I, *Logic,* ed. by A. Ruge, W. Windelband et al., London and New York: Macmillan, pp. 67–135.

Runciman, Walter G., 1963: *Social Science and Political Theory,* Cambridge, England: Cambridge University Press (2nd ed. 1969).

Russell, Bertrand, 1938: *Power: A New Social Analysis,* New York: Norton.

Sarlemijn, Andries, 1975: *Hegel's Dialectic,* Publications and Monographs of the Institute of East-European Studies at the University of Fribourg/Switzerland, Vol. 33, Dordrecht (Holland) and Boston, Mass.: D. Reidel (German orig.: *Hegelsche Dialektik,* Berlin and New York: de Gruyter 1971).

Scharpf, Fritz W., 1973: *Planung als politischer Prozess,* Aufsätze zur Theorie der planenden Demokratie, Frankfurt am Main: Suhrkamp.

Schilpp, Paul A. (ed.), 1974: *The Philosophy of Karl Popper,* 2 vols., LaSalle, Ill.: Open Court.

Schrader, George, 1967: "The Thing in Itself in Kantian Philosophy," in Wolff 1967:172–188.

Schumacher, E.F., 1975: *Small Is Beautiful,* Economics as if People Mattered, New York: Perennial Library (orig. London: Blond & Briggs 1973).

Schwember, Hermann, 1976: "Cybernetics in Government: Experience With New Tools for Management in Chile 1971–73," in: Hartmut Bossel (ed.), *Concepts and Tools of Computer-Assisted Analysis,* Basel, Switzerland: Birkhäuser, pp. 81–138.

Schwemmer, Oswald, 1971: *Philosophie der Praxis,* Versuch zur Grundlegung einer Lehre vom moralischen Argumentieren in Verbindung mit einer Interpretation der praktischen Philosophie Kants, Frankfurt am Main: Suhrkamp.

Searle, John R., 1969: *Speech Acts:* An Essay in the Philosophy of Language, London: Cambridge University Press.

Sidel, Victor W., 1976: "Quality for Whom? Effects of Professional Responsibility for Quality Health Care on Equity," *Bulletin of the New York Academy of Medicine,* second series, 52:164–176.

Silvermann, William A., 1980: "Medical Inflation," *Perspectives in Biology and Medicine* 23:617–637.

Simon, Herbert A., 1945: *Administrative Behavior,* New York: Free Press (2nd ed. 1957).

Simon, Herbert A., 1957: *Models of Man,* New York: Wiley.

Simon, Herbert A., 1960: *The New Science of Management Decision,* New York: Harper & Row.

Simon, Herbert A., 1962: "The Architecture of Complexity," *Proceedings of the American Philosophical Society* 106:467–482.

Simon, Herbert A., 1969: *The Sciences of the Artificial,* Cambridge, Mass.: MIT Press.

Singer, Edgar A., Jr., 1959: *Experience and Reflection,* ed. by C. West Churchman, Philadelphia: University of Pennsylvania Press.

Singer, Marcus G., 1961: *Generalization in Ethics,* New York: Knopf.

Skinner, B.F., 1966: "An Operant Analysis of Problem Solving," in Kleinmuntz 1966:225–257.

Skinner, B.F., 1968: *The Technology of Teaching,* New York: Appleton-Century-Crafts.

Smith, K.V./Smith, M.F., 1966: *Cybernetic Principles of Learning and Educational Design,* New York and London: Holt, Rinhart & Winston.

Smith, Norman Kemp, 1962: *A Commentary to Kant's 'Critique of Pure Reason'* 2nd ed., New York: Humanities Press 1962 (Macmillan 1923).

Smyth, David S./Checkland, Peter B., 1976: "Using a Systems Approach: The Structure of Root Definitions," *Journal of Applied Systems Analysis* (formerly J. of Systems Engineering) 5 (No. 1):75–83.

Snow, Charles P., 1962: *Science and Gouvernment,* The Godkin Lectures at Harvard University, With a New Appendix, New York: New American Library.

Sommerhoff, G., 1969: "The Abstract Characteristics of Living Systems," in Emery 1969: 147–202.

Spaemann, Robert, 1972: "Die Utopie der Herrschaftsfreiheit," *Merkur* (Munich) 26 (No. 292): 735ff.

Spinner, Helmut, 1974: *Pluralismus als Erkenntnismodell,* Frankfurt am Main: Suhrkamp 1974.

Stebbins, Ernest L./Williams, Kathleen N., 1972: "History and Background of Health Planning in the United States," in: William A. Reinke/Kathleen N. Stebbins (eds.), *Health Planning: Qualitative Aspects and Quantitative Techniques,* Baltimore, Md.: Waverly Press, pp. 3–19.

Strawson, Peter F., 1964: "Truth," in: George Pitcher (ed.), *Truth,* Englewood Cliffs, N.J.: Prentice-Hall, pp. 32–53.

Swanson, E. Burton, 1974: "Management Information Systems: Appreciation and Involvement," *Management Science* 21:178–188.

Tarski, Alfred, 1956: *Logic, Semantics, Metamathematics,* Oxford, England: Clarendon Press.

Thorndike, Edward L., 1898: "Animal Intelligence: An Experimental Study of the Associative Processes in Animals," *Psychological Review Monograph Supplements* 2 (No. 4), New York and London: Macmillan.

Topitsch, Ernst (ed.), 1965: *Logik der Sozialwissenschaften,* Köln and Berlin: Kiepenheuer & Witsch.

Toulmin, Stephen, 1964: *The Uses of Argument,* Cambridge, England: Cambridge University Press (orig. 1958).

Ulrich, Werner, 1975a: *Kreativitätsförderung in der Unternehmung,* Ansatzpunkte eines Gesamtkonzepts, Bern, Switzerland, and Stuttgart, Germany: Paul Haupt.

Ulrich, Werner, 1975b: "Sei die Spinne, nicht die Fliege!" Über einige Voraussetzungen des kreativen Denkens und Erkennens in Alltag und Wissenschaft," *Chemische Rundschau* 28 (Oct. 22, No. 41): 10–13.

Ulrich, Werner, 1975c: "Analyse und Gestaltung problemlösender Systeme: Ein Konzeptualisierungsversuch," *Die Unternehmung* 29:197–217.

Ulrich, Werner, 1976a: "Procès-verbal d'une séance de Synectique," *Revue d'Economie d'Entreprise Coop* 9 (No. 3/4):28–32.

Ulrich, Werner, 1976b: "Einführung in die heuristischen Methoden des Problemlösens (I): Abgrenzung, Systematisierung und verhaltenswissenschaftliche Grundlegung," *Das Wirtschaftsstudium* 5:251–256.

438

Ulrich, Werner, 1976c: "Diskursive Heuristik als Systemmethodik und Systemanalyse" (Einführung in die heuristischen Methoden II), *Das Wirtschaftsstudium* 5:401–406.

Ulrich, Werner, 1977a: "Intuitive Heuristik: Einführung in die gruppendynamischen Methoden des Problemlösens; das Brainstorming" (Einführung in die heuristischen Methoden III), *Das Wirtschaftsstudium* 6:51–56.

Ulrich, Werner, 1977b: "Intuitive Heuristik: Die Synektik, 1.Teil" (Einführung in die heuristischen Methoden IV), *Das Wirtschaftsstudium* 6:199–204.

Ulrich, Werner, 1977c: "Intuitive Heuristik: Die Synektik, 2.Teil" (Einführung in die heuristischen Methoden V), *Das Wirtschaftsstudium* 6:247–253.

Ulrich, Werner, 1977d: "The Design of Problem-Solving Systems," *Management Science* 23:1099–1108.

Ulrich, Werner, 1977e: "Intuitive Heuristik: Schöpferische Entwicklung" (Einführung in die heuristischen Methoden VI), *Das Wirtschaftsstudium* 6:395–401.

Ulrich, Werner, 1977f: "Produktivitätsziel und Qualität des Arbeitslebens: Tendenzen der Organisationsentwicklung in den USA – Folgerungen für Europa," *Industrielle Organisation* 46:317–323.

Ulrich, Werner, 1978: "Human Systems Management: Overcoming the Irrelevance Syndrome," *HSM Co-Enzyme,* Communicator of the Circle of Human Systems Management, No. 10 (February):4–6.

Ulrich, Werner, 1979: "Zur Metaphysik der Planung. Eine 'Debatte' zwischen Herbert A. Simon und C. West Churchman," *Die Unternehmung* 33:201–211.

Ulrich, Werner, 1980: "The Metaphysics of Design: A Simon-Churchman 'Debate'," *TIMS/ORSA Interfaces* 10 (2):35–40. (An expanded version of this article, entitled "The Metaphysics of Social Systems Design," will appear in van Gigch 1984.)

Ulrich, Werner, 1980/81: *Epistemological Foundations of a Critical Systems Approach for Social Planners:* From "Critical Rationalism" and "Critical Theory" to "Critical Heuristics," Ph. D. Thesis, University of California, Berkeley, Ad Hoc Interdisciplinary Ph. D. Program of the Graduate Division, November 13, 1980. Published on Microfilm by University Microfilm International, Ann Arbor, Michigan, 1981.

Ulrich, Werner, 1981a: "Systemrationalität und praktische Vernunft – Gedanken zum Stand des Systemansatzes," Translator's Introduction to C. West Churchman, *Der Systemansatz und seine "Feinde,"* Bern, Switzerland: Haupt 1981.

Ulrich, Werner, 1981b: "On Blaming the Messenger for the Bad News: Reply to Bryer's Comments," *Omega,* The International Journal of Management Science 9 (No.1):7.

Ulrich, Werner, 1981c: "A Critique of Pure Cybernetic Reason: The Chilean Experience With Cybernetics," *Journal of Applied Systems Analysis* 8:33–59.

Ulrich, Werner, 1982: "Wissenschaftliche Evaluation als Aufgabe der Gesundheitsdirektion: Kanton Bern," in Felix Gutzwiller/Gerhard Kocher (Hrsg.), *Die Qualität medizinischer Leistungen,* Konkrete Möglichkeiten der Qualitätsmessung,

-kontrolle und -förderung, Zürich, Switzerland: Schweizerische Gesellschaft für Gesundheitspolitik, SGGP.

Ulrich, Werner, 1984: "Systemtheorie der Planung," to be published in Norbert Szyperski (ed.), *Handwörterbuch der Planung (HWPlan)*, Stuttgart, Germany: Poeschel.

U.S. Congress, 1966: "Comprehensive Health Planning and Public Health Services Amendments of 1966," *Public Law* 89–749, 87th Congress, S. 3008, Nov. 3.

U.S. Congress, 1974: "National Health Planning and Resources Development Act of 1974," *Public Law* 93–641, 93rd Congress, S. 2994, Jan. 4.

U.S. Congress, 1975: "Endangered Species Act of 1973," *Public Law* 93–205, 93rd Congress, S. 1983, Dec. 28.

Vaihinger, Hans, 1924: *The Philosophy of "As If,"* a System of the Theoretical, Practical and Religious Fictions of Mankind, London: K. Paul, Trench, Trubner & Co., and New York: Harcourt, Brace & Co. (German original: *Die Philosophie des Als Ob*, System der theoretischen, praktischen und religiösen Fiktionen der Menschheit aufgrund eines idealistischen Positivismus, Berlin: Reuther & Reichard 1911).

van Gigch, John P. (ed.), 1984: *Metamodels and Metasystems*, Turnbridge Wells, Kent, England: Abacus Press (in preparation).

Varela, F. G./Maturana, H. R./Uribe, R., 1974: "Autopoiesis: The Organization of Living Systems, Its Characterization and a Model," *Bio-Systems* 5:187–196.

Viehweg, Theodor, 1954: *Topik und Jurisprudenz*, Ein Beitrag zur rechtswissenschaftlichen Grundlagenforschung, München: Beck (5th ed. 1974).

Vladeck, Bruce C., 1977: "Interest-Group Representation and the HSAs: Health Planning and Political Theory," *American Journal of Public Health* 67:23–29.

von Foerster, Heinz, 1960: "On Self-Organizing Systems and Their Environments," in Yovits/Cameron 1960:31–50.

Walter-Busch, Emil H., 1970: *Soziologie und das Ende der Geschichtsphilosophie*, Studien zum historischen Situationsverständnis neupositivistischer deutscher Soziologie, Diss. Frankfurt am Main 1970, München: Ressy Dissertationsdruck.

Waters, William J., 1976: "State Level Comprehensive Health Planning: A Retrospect," *American Journal of Public Health* 66:139–144.

Weber, Max, 1947: "Science as a Vocation," in H. H. Gerth and C. W. Mills (eds.), *From Max Weber, Essays in Sociology*, New York: Oxford University Press 1947, pp. 129–156. (German orig.: "Wissenschaft als Beruf," 1919, reprinted in Max Weber, *Gesammelte Aufsätze zur Wissenschaftslehre*, ed. by J. Winckelmann, Tübingen, Germany: J. C. B. Mohr, 3rd ed. 1968).

Weber, Max, 1949: "'Objectivity' in Social Science and Social Policy," in Edward A. Shills/Henry A. Finch (eds.), *The Methodology of the Social Sciences*, New York: Free Press, pp. 72–111. Partly reprinted in Dallmayr/McCarthy 1977:24–37

440

(German orig.: "Die 'Objektivität' sozialwissenschaftlicher und sozialpolitischer Erkenntnis," *Archiv für Sozialwissenschaft* 19 (1904):22–87, reprinted in Max Weber, *Gesammelte Aufsätze zur Wissenschaftslehre,* ed. by J. Winckelmann, Tübingen: J.C.B. Mohr, 3rd ed. 1968).

Weber, Max, 1968: *Economy and Society,* ed. by Günther Roth and Claus Wittich, New York: Bedminster Press, reissued Berkeley and Los Angeles: University of California Press 1978 (based on the 4th ed. of *Wirtschaft und Gesellschaft,* Tübingen, Germany: J.C.B. Mohr 1956, orig. 1921).

Wellmer, Albrecht, 1967: *Methodologie als Erkenntnistheorie,* Zur Wissenschaftslehre Karl R. Poppers, Frankfurt am Main: Suhrkamp.

Wellmer, Albrecht, 1970: *The Critical Theory of Society,* New York: Herder & Herder (also New York: Seabury Press 1974).

White, Kerr L., 1974: "Caveats for PSRO's," *The Western Journal of Medicine* 120:338–343.

WHO, 1946: *Constitution of the World Health Organization of the United Nations,* Geneva, Switzerland: WHO.

Wiener, Norbert, 1948: *Cybernetics,* or Control and Communication in the Animal and the Machine, New York: Wiley, 2nd ed. 1961.

Wild, Jürgen, 1970: "Probleme der theoretischen Deduktion von Prognosen," *Zeitschrift für die gesamte Staatswissenschaft* 126:553–575.

Wildawsky, Aaron, 1973: "If Planning is Everything, Maybe it's Nothing," *Policy Sciences* 4:127–153.

Wildawsky, Aaron, 1976: "Can Health Be Planned? Or, Why Doctors Should Do Less and Patients Should Do More: Forecasting the Future of Health Systems Agencies," *The 1976 Michael M. Davis Lecture,* Chicago: Center for Health Administration Studies, University of Chicago.

Wildawsky, Aaron, 1977: "Doing Better and Feeling Worse: The Political Pathology of Health Policy," *Daedalus,* Journal of the American Academy of Arts and Sciences 106 (No. 1):105–123, reprinted in Wildawsky 1979:284–308.

Wildawsky, Aaron, 1979: *Speaking Truth to Power,* The Art and Craft of Policy Analysis, Boston: Little Brown & Co.

Wilensky, Harold L., 1967: *Organizational Intelligence,* Knowledge and Policy in Government and Industry, New York: Basic Books.

Williams, R.G./Ware, J.E., 1976: "Validity of Student Ratings of Instruction Under Different Incentive Conditions: A Further Study on the Dr. Fox Effect," *Journal of Educational Psychology* 68:48–56.

Winner, Langdon, 1975: "Complexity and the Limits of Human Understanding," in Laporte 1975: 40–76.

Wolff, Robert Paul (ed.), 1967: *Kant, A Collection of Critical Essays,* Garden City, N.Y.: Anchor Books.

Yeang, Ken, 1974: "Bionics: The Use of Biological Analogies for Design," *Architectural Association Quarterly* 6 (No. 2):48–57.

Yovits, Marshall C./Cameron, Scott (eds.), 1960: *Self-Organizing Systems,* Oxford, England, and New York: Pergamon Press.

Zmud, Robert W., 1979: "Individual Differences and MIS Success: A Review of the Empirical Literature," *Management Science* 25:966–979.

Zwicky, Fritz, 1961: *Entdecken, Erfinden, Forschen im Morphologischen Weltbild,* Munich, Germany, and Zurich, Switzerland: Droemer Knaur (transl.: *Discovery, Invention, Research Through the Morphological Approach,* New York: Macmillan 1969).

Name Index

Flores, Fernando 16, 344f, 350, 357, 363, 366n, 367
Forrester, Jay W. 22n, 94
Frank, Helmar 94
Freud, Sigmund 111
Fromm, Erich 107, 370, 379f

Galbraith, John Kenneth 119n, 150n, 254, 314n, 395, 399, 413
Gomez, Peter 94, 327n
Gordon, William J.J. 22n
Grosch, Herbert R.J. 344, 366

Habermas, Jürgen 15, 23, 26f, 29f, 32–36, 42, 61–64, 75, 77–79, 84f, 100, 106–172, 175–177, 193, 223, 252, 261, 265, 278, 285, 295n, 297f, 302, 311, 326, 330f, 343, 368, 412
Hanlon, Joseph 344
Harrison, P.J. 356
Hartmann, Nicolai 105, 208, 280, 286–288, 293
Haupt, Max 17
Hegel, Georg Wilhelm Friedrich 30, 36, 65n, 68n, 109f, 266, 268–277, 285, 338
Helmer, Olaf 22n
Hempel, Carl G. 56, 138
Herder, Johann Gottfried von 65
Herman, Edwards S. 396
Hill, Melvyn A. 152n
Hippocrates 377
Hobbes, Thomas 69,72, 118
Höffe, Otfried 23, 68n, 165n, 166, 289n, 302n
Hoggatt, Austin C. 94
Holling, C.S. 339
Holzkamp, Klaus 54, 66n, 80n
Hoos, Ida R. 22n
Horkheimer, Max 27, 30, 107
Howard, Ted 379
Hull, Carlk 90
Hume, David 28, 44, 46, 53, 56, 57n, 99, 105n, 109, 181–183, 185, 194, 196n
Husserl, Edmund 219

Illich, Ivan 340f, 365, 377, 380, 382, 388f, 407, 411, 415f

James, William 240
Jantsch, Erich 17, 22n, 183, 326
Jay, Martin 107n
Jung, Carl Gustav 263

Kambartel, Friedrich 27, 31, 148
Kamlah, Wilhelm 31, 132n, 148n
Kant, Immanuel 5, 15, 20–30, 35, 44, 46, 51n, 64n 105n, 106–110, 112f, 129n, 131, 142f, 146, 153f, 158–165, 175–269, 271, 276n, 279–291, 295n, 301–306, 309-312, 338–340
Kaufmann, Walter 270f (esp. 270n), 275, 277
Keller, Donald A. 226n
Kleinmuntz, Benjamin 437
Klir, George J. 94
Klix, Friedhart 331
Kohlberg, Lawrence 159f
Korzybski, Alfred 185, 202, 226, 298
Krauch, Helmut 402n
Kuhn, Thomas S. 290n

Lakatos, Imre 60n, 88
Lalonde, Marc 384
Landau, Martin 324
Landshut, Siegfried 110n
Laporte, Todd R. 441
Leibniz, Gottfried Wilhelm von 109, 181, 183, 338, 360f
Lenhardt, Christian K. 152n
Lenk, Hans 74n
Liddell, Brendan E.A. 179
Likert, Rensis 351
Lindblom, Charles E. 224
Lobkowicz, Nikolaus 152n, 170n, 272
Locke, John 42, 109, 181f, 338
Lorenz, Kurt 166n
Lorenzen, Paul 26f, 30–32, 132n, 146n, 148, 302
Lowi, Theodore J. 127, 395, 404, 406
Lübbe, Hermann 69, 74n, 76–78, 297n
Lucas, H.C.; Jr. 332n
Luhmann, Niklas 117, 326, 330
Luther, Martin 180

Malik, Fredmund 94, 327n
Mao Tse-tung 272, 274
Marcuse, Herbert 30, 62n, 107
Maruyama, Magoroh 196n
Marx, Karl 30, 65n, 81n, 109–111, 163, 171, 268, 277
Maslow, Abraham H. 317
Mason, Richard O. 22n, 332n
Maturana, H.R. 326
Maurer, Reinhard K. 152n, 156n, 165, 172
McCarthy, Thomas 69f, 73, 107n, 117n
Meadows, Dennis L. 22n

Subject Index

polemical 305, 308
reasonable (as defined by Lorenzen) 31f
quasi-transcendental, see quasi-transcendental
Argumentation
  a priori of, see a priori
  cogent 120, 137, *138f,* 140f, 143–146, 297n, 301
    and consensus (conflicting demands of) 301–303, 305, 309
    and democratic participation (conflicting demands of) 302, 309f, 312f, 401
    and the polemical employment of boundary judgements 305, 310, 312f
    pragmatic structure of 120, 139, 143
  levels of 137, 140f (*cf.* discourse, levels of)
  unity of (Habermas) 132–135, 137
Aristotelian
  logic 291 (*cf.* logic, classical)
  thinking (as opposed to non-Aristotelian thinking) 274 (*cf.* non-Aristotelian thinking)
  tradition of thought, and systems science 320
Arrival level of performance (Ardell) 390
Art
  of judgement 19
  of making "the problem" the problem 22
  of "never thinking dialectically, never learning to philosophize" (Bloch) 272
Artificial intelligence 21, 324
"As if"
  in Bachelard's philosophy of the "no" 290f, 294
  in Critical Heuristics 260–262, 294, 304
  in Kantian a priori science 197, *232,* 260, 290, 304
    and the merely heuristic status of Kant's "transcendental" a priori concepts and ideas 232
  in rational discourse 126
Assessment of systems designs, see design and assessment of purposeful systems
Asymmetry between verification and falsification by experience (Popper) 46
"Attention to the concept" (Hegel) 271
"Auctoritas non veritas facit legem" (Hobbes) 69, 72, 118, 144
Autonomous
  coping (Illich) 340, 380, 393f, 403, 411f, 414, 416
  work group 337, 339, 364

Autonomy
  of subjects, as understood by Illich 412
  of subsystems, as defined by Beer *351,* 356, 361, 364
  maximum feasible 351
  principle of 347, *351*

B

Bayesian
  forecasting 352, 355
  statistics (or statistical theory) 356, 360
Behavior
  feedback-monitored 328
  purposeful 328
Behavioral science 35n, 62, 127n, 332n, 334n
Behaviorism 90, 101
"Big bang" theory of the origin of the universe 219
Bionics 22n
Bottleneck operation or process (in Project Cybersyn) 353n
Boundary criterion (in systems thinking) 191, 226
Boundary judgements *191,* 215f, *225–230,* 235, 240, 244f, 247–258, 263, 274, 282f, 296, 299, 301–310, 312f
  and expertise 305–309, 312
  and immanent metaphysics 227
  and Kant's problem 282f
  and systems science 226f, 299
  and the affected 227f, 245, 248f, 251f, 256–258
  and the critical significance of the systems idea, see systems idea
  as being constitutive of (the normative content of) social maps or designs 226, 229f, 235, 240, 244f, 247, 253, 259f, *283,* 302, 305f (*cf.* normative content of boundary judgements; whole systems judgements)
  as being presupposed in the exercise of expertise 306
  as being understandable to laymen 306
  "as if" character of 304 (*cf.* "as if")
  dogmatic assertion of (the objectivity of) 302–305, 307
  forms of 245, 264 (*cf.* a priori judgements, synthetic, forms of)
    and actors in planning 245, 247–258
  normative content of, see normative content

450

transcendental deduction of, *see* transcendental

validity of

in Kantian a priori science 209

in Critical Heuristics 234f

Causality

category (or concept) of 28, 160, 182, 202, 208, 237

mutual, as distinguished from linear 196 (esp. 196n)

principle of universal, *see* principle

Central nervous system (as a design model in managerial cybernetics) 347

Centralization vs. decentralization (in organizations) 351

Challenge to practical reason, *see* practical reason

Chile, Stafford Beer's "Project Cybersyn" in, *see* Cybersyn

CHP Amendments, *see* "Comprehensive Health Planning Amendments of 1966"

Citizen(s)

and administrative planning 314n

and communicative competence, *see* communicative competence of the affected

and expert(ise) 78, 167–169, 263, 290, 306, 308, 312, 314, 369 (*cf.* the affected, as emancipating themselves from the premises and promises of the experts)

and planner, or systems designer 169f, 279n, 309f, 312

and "rational attitude" (Popper) 82

and rational discourse 37

and systems rationality 169f, 292, 295f, 309, 312

as affected by planning, *see* the affected

as emancipating themselves from the experts, *see* the affected, as emancipating themselves from the premises and promises of the experts

democratic participation of 290, 296, 302, 309

democratic sovereignty and equality of 168, 266, 295 (*cf.* democratic idea; democratic principle)

"irrational" (as seen from the viewpoint of the systems approach) 169

veto of free (Kant) 310

Citizens'

initiatives 314

movements 314n

training in citizenship 397 (*cf.* critically-- heuristic training)

Civil

law 374f

liberties, and discourse 126

Class structure (of society) 394, 400

Client (of planning) 228, 290, 334, 414

actual vs. ideal 393–395, 397, 399f (*cf.* client, ideal; ideal client map)

and advocacy planning 171

category of *245f, 250,* 252–254, 256–258, 264, 306, 342, 363, 393, 414

ideal 393f, 408 (*cf.* ideal client map; client question)

is- vs. ought- 250

question 393f

surrogate c. 250, 254, 307, 325, 395, 399f

Clue

for a critically-heuristic reformulation of Kant's transcendental ideas 257

to the a priori validation of critically-heuristic categories 235, 247

to the systematic discovery (or introduction) of relative a priori concepts (in Critical Heuristics) 216, 232, 234, 240, 244f, 247, 253

to the systematic discovery of a priori concepts (in Kantian a priori science) 206f, 235

Cogency of argumentation

as a pragmatic rather than syntactic modality 137, 302 (*cf.* argumentation, cogent)

Cognitive developmental psychology (Piaget) 159

Cognitive interest(s) (Habermas)

emancipatory 63f, 111f, 126, 132, 261 (*cf.* knowledge-constitutive interest in emancipation; emancipatory self-reflection)

object domains of, *see* object domains

practical 63, 73, 111f, 132, 155, (*cf.* knowledge-constitutive interest in mutual understanding and consensus)

quasi-transcendental function (or status) of 112, 152

technical (or theoretical) 63, 111f, 132, 155 (*cf.* knowledge-constitutive interest in technical, or instrumental, control; instrumental control)

theory of 108f, 111, 113–115, 155 (*cf.* knowledge-constitutive interests, theory of; knowledge and interest)

Common good 150, 171
Communication
a priori of (Apel) 113, 115
community 119
distorted *122*, 125
pure 130n, 158, 164, 167
semiotic levels of 241, 327
undistorted (theory of) 33, 125f, 158
Communicative
action 111, 115, 117n, 136, 155
as distinguished from discourse *130f*, 134, 137, 140
as distinguished from strategic action 131, 140
pure 125, 163f
competence 25, *124*, 128, 168, 302f, 305
as presupposing rather than producing discursive rationality 168, 311 (*cf.* rationality, ideal conditions of)
as subverting the purpose of practical discourse 311
of the affected (citizens, witnesses) 32, 34, 167f, 237, 267, 296f, 310f, 313, 406 (*cf.* witnesses, testimony of; witnesses, as not having to pretend to be objective; subjectivity of discourse participants)
theory of (Habermas) 32, 108, 125, 172
ethics, *see* ethics
experience, *see* experience
Community
ecological 333, 337, 339
of agreement 43
of competent speakers (Habermas) 128
of scientific investigators (Peirce) 128
political 337, 340 (esp. *340*) *(cf. polis)*
Competence
communicative, *see* communicative
linguistic, *see* linguistic
Competent speaker (Habermas) 124, 128, 265, 302 (*cf.* ideal speaker; ideal speech situation; communicative competence)
Complexity 319, *320f*, 323-325, 328
management (or control) of 319-331, 343, 347
measure of 328, 330
models of, and systems concepts 319-325
Components (of a system)
as distinguished from a system's environment 255
category of 245f, *255,* 258, 264, 306, 342

design-nonseparability of (Churchman) 320, 322
near-decomposability of (Simon) 322, 325
Comprehend
two root meanings of the verb 271
Comprehensibility (as a speech-act-immanent validity claim) 123 (esp. *123n*), 130, 134 (*cf.* speech-act-immanent obligations; validity claims)
"Comprehensive Health Planning (CHP) Amendments of 1966" (Public Law 89-749) 372f
Comprehensive
rationality, *see* rationality
rationality of reason that becomes transparent to itself (Habermas), *see* reason, the comprehensive...
Comprehensiveness
and comprehension 271
in social maps and designs (or in our understanding of social systems)
ideal of 260-262, 298, 305 (*cf.* systems idea)
inevitable lack of 21, 224f, 230, 235, 260, 262, 293, 296, 301 (*cf.* totality of relevant conditions, inevitable lack of knowledge in respect to; rationality, comprehensive, inevitable lack of)
"look for c. (on the side of the conditions)!" 260, 262
Compromise
as distinguished from rational consensus 147, *149f,* 171
pseudo- *149f*
Computer 337, 365 (*cf.* information processing machines; fact nets; syntactic truth nets; fact finding system; inquiring system; information system)
and "intelligent" filtration of data (Beer) 352 (*cf.* information filtration)
and manager 370
as a (false) guarantor of design 369
as a logical engine (Leibniz) 360 (*cf.* syntactic truth nets; Leibnizian inquirer; variety attenuation; information filtration)
"intelligent use of" (Beer) 359
Conceptual framework(s) 19, 33, 36, *114f*, 132, 139f, 143, 155f, 158-162, 205, 207, 227
of Critical Heuristics 216, 231, 235, 240-264 (esp. 258, 262, *264*), 329, 341f
the three levels of 216, 231, 239f

Conceptualization of the planning situation as a social system (or social process) 244f, 247n (*cf.* planning situation; actors in planning)

Concerns

moral (of the affected), and ideal speech situation 164

role-specific, of actors in planning, *see* actors in planning

Conjectural character

of all observational statements and theories 48f

of knowledge 49, 51

Conjectures and refutations, method of (Popper) 48, 60, 90

Consciousness

technocratic 73

Consensus

about basic statements 59

and cogent argumentation (conflicting demands of) 301–303, 305, 309

and mutual understanding (as constitutive interest of adequate social inquiry), *see* knowledge-constitutive interest in mutual understanding and consensus; cognitive interest, practical)

factual, as distinguished from rational 26, 33, 114, 118, 138, 158, 176, 302

false 125

rational (or rationally-motivated) 26, 33, *114*, 123, 125, 127, 129f, 143–145, 158, 162f, 165, 167, 170f, 176, 252, 265, 302

theory of truth, *see* truth

true 26, 114, 116, 118–125, 166, 302

Consequences and side-effects of norms, prediction of 144f

Consistency

condition 48, 60, 283 (*cf.* principle of excluded contradiction)

trap of (Churchman) 276, 285

Constructivist Logic, Ethics, and Science-Theory (Lorenzen) 26, 30f

Constructivism 32, 148n

Constructivists 27, 31f, 34

Consultation model 256, 261, 368 (*cf.* theory-practice model; expert and politician; expertise and politics; reason-practice mediation)

"Consumers" vs. "providers" (in health systems planning) 399f, 402–407, 417 (*cf.* "new lay participants"; the affected, and the distinction of "consumers" vs. "providers" in health systems planning)

and epistemology 406f

and expertise 406f

Context

of application 20n, 60, 67, *74,* 83, 101, 104, 112, 134, 198

of argumentation 129

of discovery 26, *46,* 55, 58, 60, 86, 88, 93, 100, 112, 193, 195

of experience and action 115, 130–132, 164

of justification 46, 60, 67n, 74, 193, 195

of meaning 61f, 66, 294 (*cf.* meaning)

and system boundaries 330

Contradiction (in Hegelian dialectics) 272, 274

antagonistic (Mao) 272

as contradictory opposition (in the realm of thought) 273f, 276

as contrary opposition (in the realm of being) 272–274, 276

dialectical principle of universal 272–274

formal, as distinguished from material 273

"Maintain the …!" (Churchman) 275f, 285

non-antagonistic (Mao) 273

principle of excluded 48, 193, 208, 272, 277, 283, 285 (*cf.* consistency condition)

Contrary opposition, *see* contradiction as contrary opposition

Contravalence (in symbolic logic) 272

Control

concept of 333, 335, 363

extrinsic (in cybernetics) 327n, 333

homeostatic 327, 347

instrumental (or technical), *see* instrumental; knowledge-constitutive interest

intrinsic (in cybernetics) 261, *327*–329, 331, 333, 339, 348, 364

of complexity, *see* complexity

of technology 367

organic (in cybernetics) 326, *327n,* 328, 333

problem, as taken for the crucial problem in systems design (in distinction to the boundary problem) 323

question of 327

sources of (in the conceptual framework of Critical Heuristics), *see* sources

Controller (in cybernetics)

extrinsic 331

intrinsic 340

Conventionalism (in epistemology) 49, 59f

Copernican

hypothesis of Kant, *see* Kant's

revolution of metaphysics, Kant's *see* Kant's

CORFO (Chile) 345f, 351f, 367f
Correspondence theory of truth, *see* truth
Corroboration (of hypotheses, in Critical Rationalism) *49,* 57, 61
Cosmological
  idea (in Kantian a priori science) 189, 213, 221, 232f, 259f
  question of reason (Kant) 181, 219
Cosmology
  as not being able to emancipate itself from Kant's cosmological question 219
Cost-benefit analysis 22n
Creative Development 22n
Counterproductivity (Illich) 340f (esp. *340n*), 411, 417
  institutional 340, 400
  sources of (in systems design) 341
Counter-theories (Feyerabend) 60
Critical *19f,* 27, 42, 45, 49, 107f, 187, *285, 288*
Critical Heuristics (of social planning) 15, 19–*23,* 35, 107f, 132, 151f, *157f,* 172, *177,* 192, 280, 289, 305, 334
  and Kant's principle of reason 218–220, 225, 227, 260f
  and the dogmatic assertion of the objectivity (or rationality) of boundary judgements 304 (cf. boundary judgements)
  and the need for at least a critical solution to Kant's problem (of the "unavoidable questions of reason") 5, 176, 192
  and the systems idea 222–230, 260, 262–264 (*cf.* systems idea)
  and uncritical heuristics 22
  as depending on Kant's work for clarifying its own position 193
  as distinguished from Critical Theory (of society) 23, 152, 154
  conceptual framework of 216, 231, 235, 240–264 (esp. *258, 262, 264*), 205, 207, 227
  the three levels of 216, 231, 239f
  its reformulation of Kant's problem *198f,* 282f
  transition from Kantian a priori science to, *see* transition
Critically-heuristic
  approach 23, 30, 161, 222, 229
    and the systems idea 222–230
    overall structure of 341f
  categories (of pragmatic mapping) 37, 231, 234f, 239f, 242–258, 260, 342, 362, 376

(*cf.* quasi-transcendental concepts or categories; pragmatic mapping, categories of; a priori categories, relative; a priori concepts, relative)
  of control 264, 342
  of expertise, 264, 342
  of legitimation 264, 342
  of motivation 264, 342
concepts 231–240
  and the complementary view of theoretical and practical reason 222, *233n*
ideas 231–234, 240, 247, 257, 259–264
  (*cf.* quasi-transcendental ideas)
  and corresponding heuristic principles, *see* heuristic principle(s)
  and immanent metaphysics *257,* 259–262
  dialogical (or discursive) employment of 263
  "dynamic" interpretation of 263f
  monological employment of 263
  mapping dimensions 231, 236–240
  principles standing for the three quasi-transcendental ideas, *see* heuristic principles
  purpose of systems thinking, as opposed to a mere heuristics of systems purposes 299
  training 407 (*cf.* citizens' training in citizenship)
  turn (of practical philosophy) 36, 152f, 155, *157f,* 162, 177f, 215, 293
Critically-normative *25*
  systems thinking *25,* 332
Critically oriented sciences (Habermas), *see* science; social inquiry and design, critical; social science, critical
Critically-rational discussion (Popper) 30, *49f,* 52, 56, 59, 64, 67, 74, 104
Critical path (Kant) 183, 217
Critical Philosophy (Kant) 19, 26
Critical Rationalism (Popper) 21, 24, 26, 30, 35, 44–107, 109f, 129, 175, 281
  as having been adopted by the German Social-Democratic Party 81n
  as having lost its originally critical function 45
  Popper's claims about, as distinguished from what its methodological rules imply 58
  the originally progressive role of 51
Critical rationalists 27–30, 34, 62, 67, 72, *74n,* 77, 79, 81, 103, 135, 156n, 175, 297n
Critical social inquiry, *see* social inquiry and design, critical; social science, critical;

metaphor of 317f, 331 (cf. systems concept, mechanistic)

organicist (or "organic") paradigm or root metaphor of 317 (cf. systems concept, organic)

social 20, 103, 169, 326, 330, 332n, 362

Cyberstride (Beer) 347, 352f, 355–365, 367

Cybersyn (Beer) 37, 326, 343–371

D

Dadaism 34, 60

Data

basis of the planner, see planner

collection, as tending to become a surrogate purpose of planning 388, 391, 400, 415

"intelligent" filtration of (Beer) 352 (cf. information filtration; variety attenuation)

measuring the importance of 361

Deception

and discovery 22, 157, 162

sources of, see sources

theory of (Churchman) 57n

Decision

and "objective" knowledge 59, 61

and rational discourse or inquiry 29, 59, 69, 76

and vote 76

environment, see environment

its reduction to rational argument 33, 117

maker

actual vs. ideal 401, 404–407

and ethics of whole systems 340 (cf. the involved, as arguing the case of the affected; planner, as placing himself in the position of the affected)

and expert(ise) 228, 255, 406f

category of 228, 246, 250, 252, 255, 258, 264, 306, 335, 342, 367, 401, 408

ideal (in health systems planning) 404 (cf. ideal decision map)

making

administrative (or governmental), selectivity theory of, see selectivity of administrative planning

multistage (Churchman) 374f

political 75, 77

programmed (Simon) 323

map, see ideal decision map; actual decision map

on ends, as opposed to means 29, 71f, 75f

on means, as opposed to ends 71–75

political 69, 75, 77, 127

subjective, as mere (irrational) belief act (in Critical Rationalism) 29, 71, 77, 80, 104, 143, 297n, 329 (cf. psychological context; decisionism)

theory 28, 75

Decisionism 29, 30, 32, 67, 69, 71, 76f, 79, 102, 117f, 127, 143, 152, 269, 297n, 298

and Max Weber's means-end schema 71f

and rationalism 32f

and practical reason 73, 85, 148, 171, 297n, 298

as immunizing normative validity claims against the efforts of practical reason 148, 171, 297n, 298, 300

critical (Lübbe) 76, 297n

historical rise of 67

moral 82, 143, 146–149, 165, 167, 170, 298, 300

Decisionistic

act of entering into a rational discussion or discourse 32, 165

introduction of the moral principle (or the generalization principle) 33, 146, 148, 165

model of the relation of science (or expertise) to practice (or politics), see theory-practice model

Decomposability principle (in systems science) 321f (cf. near-decomposability; design-non-separability; "divide et impera!")

Deductive

-empirical method of testing hypotheses (in Critical Rationalism) 45, 59, (cf. deductive logic, as organon of criticism)

logic 46, 153

and objectivity (in Critical Rationalism) 46, 48f

and the principle of (intersubjective) transference 46

as organon of criticism (Popper) 24, 28, 48f, 80, 104, 110

Delphi technique 22n

Demarcation

call to (in the positivistic Kant interpretation) 213

criterion (Popper) 47f

problem of (Popper) 47, 59, 213n

Democracy

and discourse 127, 167f, 311, 314, 401

Discursive
  approach to practical philosophy, *see* practical philosophy
  principles 36
  rationality, *see* rationality
Discussion
  rational 83, 172 (*cf.* discourse; critically-rational discussion)
"Divide et impera!" (Caesar) in systems science 320, 323
Doctor Fox Effect (Naftulin) 390n
Dogmatic
  assertion of (the objectivity of) boundary judgements 302–304, 307
  slumbers (of Kant) 105n, 183
Dogmatism
  as understood by Kant 181, 183, 304

E

Eco-industrial complex 396
Ecological
  community 333, 337, 339
  costs or risks of planning, as being transferred to third parties or to future generations 144, 237, 251, 256f, 304, 398
Economics 63
Ecosystem 337, 339
  resilience of (Holling) 339
Einsteinian physics 291
Emancipation
  and socially rational planning 257, 263
  category of *257f,* 264, 342
  from domination of men over men 127
  from expertise, *see* the affected, as emancipating themselves from the premises and promises of the experts
  from institutionalized health care 381 (*cf.* autonomous coping; health, heteronomous maintenance of)
  from natural constraints 127
  from oppression 111f
  from the objectivist illusion 50 (*cf.* objectivist illusion)
  of belief (Galbraith) 399, 414
  of (public) planning from vested interests 410, 414 (*cf.* interests, vested)
  of politically relevant planning from special interests 314n (*cf.* governmental selectivity, theory of)

of the state (Galbraith) 119n, 314n, 414
Emancipatory
  interest, *see* cognitive interest; knowledge-constitutive interest in emancipation
  movements (in health planning) 403
  planning 382, 412, 416f
  self-reflection, *see* self-reflection; knowledge-constitutive interest in emancipation
  utopia 126f
Empirical analysis (as distinguished from formal, or reconstructive, analysis) 160, 162
Empirical-analytic science, *see* science
Empirical basis
  of practical discourse 267, 282, 289
  of the planner, *see* planner, his basis of experience
  of truth claims 49, 57, 236
  problem of *49,* 58–65, 67, 74, 86, 102
  (theory of) the objectivity of 59, 61, 64, 102
Empirical content
  of concepts or categories (in Kantian a priori science) 190f, *193f,* 197f, 204, 208f, 229
    as distinguished from metaphysical content 193
  of relative a priori concepts or judgements (in Critical Heuristics) 229, 231
  of social maps and designs 231
  of statements (in Critical Rationalism) *47f,* 51, 55, 62n, 133, 147
    and truth 53f, 102, 116, 194
Empirical falsification attempts 48f, 58, 64 (*cf.* falsification)
Empirical illusion (as distinguished by Kant from the transcendental illusion) 213
Empirical reality (of space and time) 201f, 243, 288
Empirical science(s), *see* science
Empirical social research 35n
Empirical, the
  critical concept of 106
Empiricism 106, 183, 274, 277, 281
  as being dependent on an induction principle 44
  British 42–44, 109, 181f
  contemporary (as distinguished from classical British empiricism) 281
  "critical" (Popper) 42
  inductivist 45, 51
  Kant's opening up of 291
  logical (or logical positivism) 21, 44, 46, 51, 106, 109n, 110, 129, 281
  naive 42

deductive model of (Hempel/Oppenheim) *56, 138*

in formal pragmatics, *see* speech-act-immanent obligations; facts, recourse to; norms, recourse to

"No objective science explains or ever can explain anything in a serious sense" (Husserl) 219

teleological, as distinguished from causal-mechanistic 334n (*cf.* teleonomy; teleology)

Expropriation of health (Illich), *see* health

Extension

as distinguished from intension and intentionality 202, 241

as the essence of spatiotemporal mapping 202

Extrinsic

control 327n, 333

motivation (in cybernetics) 328, 331, 333, 336–341, 348, 368

F

Fact

net (Churchman) 338

syntactically well-formed 361 (*cf.* syntactic truth nets)

questions of 71, 74, 76

Facts

as defined by Strawson *132*

assertion of 114–116, 132, 135

of human suffering 83

recourse to (in theoretical discourse) 135f, 139

"Facts" 59f, 61, 106f, *114,* 116, 168, 234

and a priori concepts 117, 197

and boundary judgements 308

and "decisions" (dualism of) 76, 79

and knowledge-constitutive interests 64

and moral argument 145

and sources of expertise 250

and the a priori of argumentation 132

and "values" (dualism of) 72, 76, 274

as distinguished from objects 132

as distinguished from theoretical propositions or statements 61n, *132*

autonomy of (or autonomous) 60, 87, 110, 286 (*cf.* "facts", universe of)

hypostatization of 116

meaning of 61f, 64, 139

of nature, and the idea of physical determinism 237

of social reality, and the idea of mental determinism 237f

of the social life-world 62

universe of (autonomous, or established) 60, 87, 210, 276, 279, 285

and social mapping and design 242, 286, 304

reason's transcendence beyond 210

Faculty

of concepts (Kant) 204, 206

of judgements (Kant) 204

of principles (Kant) 204

of rules (Kant) 204

Faith

Kant's denial of knowledge "in order to make room for f." 210

Falsifiability (of statements) 47

condition 48

Falsification

and the problem of the empirical basis, *see* problem

attempts 48f, 58, 64

method 28, 80

principle 46f, 59, 64, 66n, 74, 80, 86

theory 45–52, 54f, 64, 67, 86, 92, 116

Falsificationism

naive 60n

sophisticated (Lakatos) 60n

Falsifier *48*

Falsifiers, class of potential 47

Federal Aviation Agency 150n

Formal

analysis (Habermas), see reconstructive analysis

design ideal 335 (*cf.* design ideal)

pragmatics (Habermas), *see* pragmatics

systems properties (Checkland) 247n

Formalistic thinking (Hegel) 270–272

Frankfurt School 30, 107, 163

Free

market, as a surrogate planner 325, 296

will, see will

Freedom

and mental determinism 237

and the moral idea 222

as defining feature of the practical (Kant) 221

of choice 221

of the will, *see* Man, the freedom of his will; free phenomenal expressions of 211

practical idea of 210
transcendent idea of 210
Future generations
and the categorical imperative 146
as being affected by, but not possibly involved in, planning 146, 237, 298
as the equivalent in Critical Heuristics to Kant's "unavoidable" idea of Man's immortal soul 262
intergenerational transfer of social costs to 228, 251, 412

G

Generalization
as a bridge principle (in formal pragmatics) 147
of basic (observational) statements, see induction; nomological hypotheses; problem of the empirical basis
of needs (or interests) 145, 150
of norms 145–148, 165
principle of 32, 144–148, 164, 170f, 340
and moral decisionism 146–148, 170
and practical discourse 144–151 (esp. 145–147), 170f
as an a priori concept of practical reason 171
as located within the formal properties of practical discourse (by Habermas) 33, 146, 164
General Systems Theory 20, 37, 223, 324 (cf. systems theory)
Genetic
engineering 379
epistemology (Piaget), see epistemology
Gentlemen's agreement 150n
German Social-Democratic Party 81
Goal
planner (Churchman) 263
-seeking 334n (cf. systems, goal-directed; systems teleology; teleology; teleonomy; purposefulness; purposeful systems)
God
as an unavoidable idea (and problem) or reason (Kant) 180–182, 184, 189, 200n, 210, 217, 218, 222, 232, 259, 262, 287
"Government of the people, by the people, for the people" (Lincoln) 296
Government secrecy 398

Governmental selectivity, theory of (Offe) 119, 149, 150n, 314n (cf. selectivity)
Grassroots democracy 314
Gravitational law (of Newton, in Kantian a priori science) 196
"Great equation" in health planning (Wildawsky) 372f
Group-dynamic techniques of problem solving 22n
Growth of knowledge (in Critical Rationalism) 48, 55, 58, 90
Guarantee
inevitable lack of (in design) 262, 411
sources of, see sources
Guarantor
assumptions 293
built into a design 256, 262, 293
category 246, 247n, 256, 258, 264, 342, 369, 410f, 414–417
as distinguished from the guarantor idea 261
emancipatory 411, 414 (cf. autonomous coping)
false 261
idea 261–264, 293
and Kant's principle of reason 261, 296
and the democratic principle 296
and the process of unfolding 263f
as distinguished from the guarantor category 261
heuristic principle standing for 262
ideal 411–414 (cf. ideal guarantor map)
of comprehensive rationality 292
of democratically legitimate planning 413
of design 261f
of emancipatory planning 412
of generalizability (of norms) 148
of impetus for change 412
of implementation 263
of socially-rational planning 170, 312

H

Health
care (delivery) 378, 381, 388, 390, 393
as moving into the public sector 314n, 413
care (delivery) system 340, 372, 378, 381f, 394, 399, 403f, 409, 411f, 417
and representation of consumers, see "consumers" vs. "providers"; lay participants

464

465

468

mathematical (in Kantian a priori science)
202
positivist classification of 194
synthetic (in Kantian a priori science) 188,
193, 194–196, 205, 207f, 235, 283, 285
(*cf.* a priori judgements, synthetic)
a priori 193–198, 215, 225, 235, 240, 244,
282, 284, 304, 312
as distinguished from a posteriori judgements *195, 285*
as implying both synthetic a priori and
a posteriori judgements 194, 235
highest principle of, *see* highest
whole systems, *see* whole systems judgements
Justification
as a pragmatic rather than syntactic notion
117n
as being substituted by the idea of criticism
(in Critical Rationalism) 51, 54, 105

K

Kant
as a critical idealist 185–187, 199 (*cf.* idealism, critical; idealism, problematic; idealism, transcendental)
as a positivist against his will (in the positivist Kant-interpretation) 199
– Laplace theory of the origin of the solar
system 181
literature on 188n
Kantian a priori science 23, 25, 34–37,
175–215, 230, 234, 265
and planning 186f, 198f, 211, 306
and the cybernetic principle of mutual causality 196n
and the planner's quest for (or challenge to)
practical reason 199, 276n
architectonic of 188f, 264
as dealing with a limiting case 183, 197
as going right to the heart of the crucial
issues in today's social
inquiry and design 199
historical roots of 180–187
inherently dialectical character of 202
program of 209
systematic structure of 187–214 (esp. 189)
Kantian program of practical reason 33
Kantian rationalism 291

Kant's
Analogies of Experience 195
call for enlightenment 64n, 129n
categorical imperative, *see* categorical imperative
classification of judgements 194f
correct (i.e., non-positivist) reading of 195
clue to the systematic discovery of a priori
concepts (esp. categories) 206f, 235
(*cf.* clue)
Copernican hypothesis 183f, 208, 282, 287
Copernican revolution of metaphysics 180, 183
critical intent regarding the distinction between reason and the understanding 204,
217f
critical intent regarding the distinction of
phenomena and noumena, *see* phenom-
ena-noumena distinction, critical intent of
critical (or critically-idealist) standpoint 185f,
202, 209, 212, 217, 236, 282–288
"critical path" 183, 217
distinction between knowledge and thought
(or between knowing and thinking) *210,*
213, 225, 229, 232, 233n
distinction between reason and the understanding *203f,* 212f, 217–220, 225, 271f, 281
distinction between theoretical and practical
reason 23f, 29, *220*–222, 233n
distinction between theory and practice,
see theory-practice
distinction between totality and system,
see totality (of relevant conditions) and the
systems idea
doctrine of the two standpoints (of agent
vs. spectator) 221n, 334n
metaphysics of experience 189, 193, 264
moral philosophy 221 (esp. 221n)
positivistic shortcut in the Transcendental
Analytic 211f, 237
postcritical writings 183
precritical writings 182f
principle of reason 214f, 217–220 (def. *219*),
222, 231, *232,* 234
and Critical Heuristics 218–220, 225, 227,
260f
and heuristic necessity of critically-heuristic ideas 232–234, 239, 257
and internal standards of criticism 295
and systems rationality 295f, 301
and the guarantor idea 261, 296
and the moral idea 221f, 233n, 260f, 296

L

as distinguished from pragmatic cogency 302

Needs
 and norms *145*–147
 and the common good 171
 as the starting point for the construction of linguistic norms (Lorenzen) 31
 generalizable 146f, 396
  suppression of 396 (*cf.* interests, generalizable, suppression of; selectivity)
 non-generalizable 164
 particular, generalization of 145f, 164

Negotiation (as distinguished from discourse) 147

(Neo-)Marxists 27, 30

(Neo-)Positivists 27 (*cf.* logical positivists; logical empiricists; positivism)

Network building (Duhl) 413f

"New lay participants" (H. Blum), *see* health systems planning, "new lay participants" in

Newtonian physics (or science) 107, 181, 195, 197, 202, 207, 236, 237n, 290f

Nihil est in intellectu quod non fuerit in sensu (Locke) 42, 182

Niveaus of recursion, *see* recursion

Nomological hypotheses *56,* 58, 61, *62n,* 71, 194, 138f, 144

Non-Aristotelian
 logic 291
 thinking 273f, 321

Non-decisions 396, 398 (*cf.* non-events)

Non-Euclidian geometry 291

Non-events 150n, *396*–398 (*cf.* selectivity of administrative planning)

Non-objectivistic
 concept of rationality 109
 correspondence theory truth, *see* truth, non-positivistic or non-objectivistic correspondence theory of
 theory of knowledge 158

Normal, the (as being elevated to the norm) 126, 224, 230

Normative content *20n*
 of any standard or concept of rationality 176, 294, 298
 of boundary judgements, or whole systems judgements 21, 224, 226–228, 230, 244, 247, 252, 258, 266, 308
 of empirical propositions 198
 of expert judgement 407 (*cf.* expertise and boundary judgements; experts and "objec-

tive necessities")
 of maps, *see* maps
 of means (as distinguished from ends) 72n
 of planning (or plans) 20, *20n,* 24f, 37, 244f, 329, 362f, 402
 of rational discussion 29
 of relative a priori concepts or judgements 229, 231
 of social (systems) maps or designs 229, 231, 235, 240, 259, 266, 293, 300, 328, 362f
 as rooted in boundary judgements (or whole systems judgements) 226, 229f, 235, 244f, 247, 258, 302
 of speech acts, *see* speech acts
 of systems concepts and judgements 280
 of systems rationality, *see* systems rationality
 of (theoretical) statements, or theories 28, 56, 89, 133, 135, 137f, 144f, 222
 of the systems concept (in every application) 191, 223
 of tool design (as distinguished from social systems design) 25
 of whole systems judgements, *see* normative content of boundary judgements; normative content of social maps or designs, as rooted in boundary judgements

Normative context (of meaning), *see* meaning

Normative foundation
 of communicative understanding (Habermas) 126
 of theoretical discourse, *see* theoretical discourse

Normative presuppositions
 flowing into our maps of social reality, *see* maps
 of social inquiry, and metaphysical presuppositions 198n

Normative validity basis of rational discourse (or of speech) 33, 123, 125, 134

Normative validity claims 33, 114, 164, 175, 278, 285 (*cf.* validity claims; speech-act-immanent obligations)
 discursive redemption of 115, 148 (*cf.* validity claims, discursive redemption of)
 of boundary judgements, or whole systems judgements 227
 of social maps and designs 216, 263
 rational treatment of 143

Norms
 and needs (or interests) *145*–147
 assertion of 114–116

and assessment of purposeful systems)
and Kantian a priori science 186f, 198f, 211
and "objective necessities" as disclosed by
    experts, *see* "objective necessities"
and the dialectic of a priori and a posteriori
    concepts of practical reason, *see* dialectic;
    process of unfolding; practical discourse;
    dialectics; dialogical approach
and the dialectic of expertise and emancipa-
    tion, *see* dialectic; process of unfolding;
    expert; expertise; the affected, as emanci-
    pating themselves from the premises and
    promises of the experts; emancipation;
    self-reflection, emancipatory; emancipa-
    tory interest)
and the dialectic of standpoint and problem,
    see dialectic; process of unfolding
and the dialectic of systems rationality and
    social rationality, *see* dialectic; systems
    rationality; planning, socially-rational;
    process of unfolding
and the institutionalization of discourse 127
    (*cf.* discourse, institutionalization of)
and the reason-practice dialectic, *see* dialec-
    tic; dialectics
and the systems idea 180, 260–262 (*cf.* sys-
    tems idea)
apolitical 127n
as advocacy planning (Davidoff) 171
as defined by Ambrose Bierce 37
as social systems design *24f,* 329 (*cf.* social
    systems design; tool design)
as societal guidance 375
democratization of 127 (*cf.* participation;
    democratic planning; democratic princi-
    ple; citizens, democratic participation of)
ecological side-effects (costs or risks) of 144,
    186, 237, 251, 256f, 304, 307, 398
effectiveness vs. efficiency in 382
emancipatory 412 (*cf.* emancipation; the af-
    fected, as emancipating themselves from
    the premises and promises of the experts)
ethics of, and ecological concepts 339
for the common good (of for the "public in-
    terest") 171
generally promulgated standards of 416
incrementalist (approach to, or mode of)
    224, 324, 374 (*cf.* incrementalism)
legitimation of 257
    deficit of 296
normative (in Project Cybersyn) 349f

normative content of, *see* normative content
paradigms of 317 (*cf.* systems paradigms; sys-
    tems concepts)
political (or politically relevant), as distin-
    guished from private 24, *297n,* 314n
public *24,* 171, 378, 395, 397n, 398, 412, 416
    actual client map of 398
    apolitical, and vested interests 417
    ever-expanding need for 412
    legitimation deficit of 413 (*cf.* legitimation)
rational 19, *20,* 23, 32, 37, 278, 290, 292,
    296f, *342* (*cf.* planning, socially-rational;
    "rational")
    non-objectivist approach to 305
    redistributive effects of 171, 186, 251, 279
    and client question 393
scientific (as understood by Popper) 57
situation
    as seen from a Kantian viewpoint 305
    its conceptualization as a social system
        (or social process) 244f, 247n
    its resisting complete rational penetration
        from the systems standpoint of the plan-
        ner 293f (*cf.* dialectic of standpoint and
        problem; metaphysics of problems)
social, *see* social planning; social inquiry and
    design; social mapping and design; social
    systems design; design and assessment of
    purposeful systems
social costs of 144, 186, 211f, 237, 251, 256f,
    300, 304, 307, 398, 412
    as phenomenal expressions of human in-
        tentionality 238
    intergenerational transfer of 228, 251, 412
socially rational 15, 24, 34, 81, 151, 164, 167,
    170, 237, *263,* 290, 312 (cf. planning, ratio-
    nal; "rational"; social rationality)
    and emancipation 257, 263, 409f
"start small" philosophy of 390, 392, 413,
    416f
strategic 348
    portfolio level of 348
synoptic 274 (*cf.* systems design; comprehen-
    siveness; holism; incrementalism)
systems p., *see* systems design
systems-scientific approach to 21
technocratic 127
theory 28, 242, 319
Platonic dialogues 268
"Play on impetus" (H. Blum), *see* impetus; so-
    cial change, providing impetus for; planner)

and the principle of generalization 144–151 (esp. 145–147), 170, 340
as a process of unfolding the dialectic of a priori and a posteriori concepts of practical reason 169, 262, 266, 289, 342
as discourse *on* practice vs. becoming a piece of practice 142, 166f, 277
as not being able of location within the boundaries of reason 163, 167, 178f, 311
as validating relative a priori concepts or judgements 229
contemporary models of 26, 30, 32f, 35, 169, 302
inherently elitist charakter of 302, 313
dialectical approach to (the problem of) 265
dialectical model (or framework) of 171, 295n
genuinely decisionistic moment in 76, *297n*
ideal of 296
institutionalization of, *see* discourse, institutionalization of
logic of 135, 137–141 (*cf.* discourse, logic of; discourse, pragmatic logic of)
model of 26, 32f, 36, 117, 142f, 152–154, 158, 162f, 172, 175f, 179, 252, 265, 311, 314
practical status of 143, 152
problem of 36f, 177, 227, 263
critical solution to, *see* critical solution
employment of pure reason (as distinguished from its speculative employment) 211, 221f
and boundary judgements 309
and ideas 221f
and the burden of proof 309f
employment of the understanding (as distinguished from its theoretical understanding) 212
knowledge *210f,* 222, 282, 289
philosophy 15, 25, *26f,* 172, 314, 334n
contemporary schools of 27
dialogical approach to, *see* practical philosophy, discursive approach to; ethics, dialogical approach to; ethics, communicative; process of unfolding
discursive approach to 26 (*cf.* ethics, dialogical approach to; ethics, communicative; practical discourse)
monological approach to 26, 229, 281, 302, 311 (*cf.* ethics, monological approach to)

of Aristotle 27, 67f, 73, 289n (*cf. polis;* virtue)
of Kant 27, 221, 269
questions and expertise 168 (*cf.* politics and expertise)
statements 26, 30, 84, 132
understanding 210 (*cf.* practical knowledge)
Practical reason *23f,* 27, 29, 30f, 33–35, 50, 67, 104, 112, 142, 163, 171, *175, 220*–222, 264f, 277f, 289, 295n, 311, 343
and decisionism 73, 85, 148, 171, *297n,* 298
and expertise 255f
and social rationality vs. systems rationality 295n, 297n, 298 (*cf.* dialectic of systems rationality and social rationality)
and social systems design vs. tool design 329
and the agent's point of view vs. the spectator's point of view 221n
and the moral idea 221f, 298
and the negative result of Kant's Transcendental Analytic 211
and the principle of generalization 170f, 298
a posteriori concepts of, *see* a posteriori
a priori concepts of, *see* a priori concepts of practical reason
as distinguished from theoretical reason *23f,* 29, 142, *220*–222, 269, 274, 277
as exercising causality in respect to the will 221
as having "causality in respect to the will" (Kant) 221
as understood by Aristotle 68, 269
challenge to 23–25, 27, 84, 105, 163, 168, 199, 328, 335, 370
and Kantian a priori science 199, 276n
complementary view of theoretical and 222, 233n
critical solution to the problem of, *see* critical solution
dialectic between a priori and a posteriori concepts of, *see* dialectic
dialogical (or discursive) approach to, *see* practical philosophy, discursive approach to; ethics, dialogical approach to; ethics, communicative; practical discourse; process of unfolding
ideal of 298
ideal of a self-justifying 33
ideas of, as related to ideas of theoretical reason (in Critical Heuristics) 233n (*cf.* practi-

cal reason, complementary view of theoretical and; reason, "unavoidable" ideas of)

its reduction to instrumental (or theoretical) reason 27–29, 50, 58, 71, 74, 82n, 143, 226n, 269

its reduction to rational discourse *on* practice, or to rhetorical skill 31, 34, 172 (*cf.* sophistic shortcut)

monological approach to, *see* practical philosophy, monological approach to primacy of (Kant) 269

principles of, as distinguished from laws of nature 221

problem of 15, 20, 26, 34–37, 109, 140, 158, 165f, 175–177, 198, 216, 233n, 265, 276n, 311, 326, 334n

critical solution to, see critical solution

heuristic approach to 23, 113, 156f (*cf.* critically-heuristic approach; critical solution to the problem of practical reason)

in Critical Rationalism 28, 50, 311

theoretical solution to 23

pure 164 (*cf.* pure)

"unconditioned" character of the principles of 221 (esp. *221n*)

unity of theoretical and 222

Practice

as distinguished from production (*poiesis*), *see praxis*

as distinguished from theory, *see* theory-practice distinction

as object domain of social planning, *see* social practice; social reality; *praxis;* lifeworld

discourse on, as distinguished from practice itself 31, 153, (*cf.* sophistic shortcut)

Pragmatic

as defined in pragmatism (Peirce, Dewey, James) 240

as defined in semiotics (Morris) *240f*

aspect of communication processes 241, 327f

dimension of historical-hermeneutic and critically oriented inquiry 161, 242f

level of communication of speech 137f, 143–145, 241, 302, 327

logic of discourse, *see* discourse

mapping

as distinguished from semantic mapping *241*

as related to social mapping and design *241*

as related to spatiotemporal mapping 241–244 (esp. 242)

categories of 207, 216, 239, 244–258, 264, 342 (*cf.* critically-heuristic categories)

clue to the systematic discovery (or introduction) of the categories of 216, 240, 244f (*cf.* clue to the systematic discovery of relative a priori concepts)

dimension *202,* 216, 239–244 (*cf.* mapping dimensions; critically-heuristic mapping dimension)

and the "teleological fallacy" 243

quasi-transcendental definition of 242f

means and ends in 243

maxim (of Peirce) 240n

meaning, *see* meaning

reality (of purpose, in Critical Heuristics) 243

significance

as distinguished from signification (in semiotics) 241

as distinguished from statistical, or syntactic, significance 361

truth, as distinguished from syntactic truth 361

Pragmaticism (as distinguished by Habermas from American pragmatism) 111 (esp. *111n*), 240n (*cf.* theory-practice model, pragmatistic; pragmatics)

Pragmatics

as a branch of semiotics (Morris) 111n, *241* (*cf.* semiotics, pragmatic aspect of; pragmatic level of communication; pragmaticism)

universal, or formal (Habermas) 33, 108, 125, 132, 152, 154, 157f, 161, 163

Pragmatism, American (Peirce, Dewey, James) 111n, *240*

Pragmatistic model of the theory-practice relationship, or of expert consultation, *see* theory-practice model

Praxis (Aristotle) 67f, 73

Prediction 56–58, 63, 71

and explanation 56f

and practical discourse on moral issues 144

of the consequences and side-effects of normative validity claims 144f

Preference

pragmatic (for theories, in Critical Rationalism) 53, 55, 58, 67n, 84n

empirical (or pragmatic) reality of 243
heuristic ideality of 243
surrogate p. 382, 391
transcendental ideality of 243
"We can never assume the absence of p.
    from our maps of social reality" 242
Purposeful
    action 362
    action system 336–339, 342, 362, 392
    behavior 328
    inquiring system 336–338, 342, 359, 362, 415
    social system 359, 362
        design for, see design (cf. purposeful sys-
            tems)
    systems 37, *334*–342
        assessment 329, 333
        complementary problem-solving dimen-
            sions of (or processes in) 335f, 359
        concept 326, 333, 334n (cf. purposeful sys-
            tems paradigm)
        design and assessment of 333–337,
            340–342
        critically-heuristic approach to (over-
            view) 341f
        guiding question of *334*, 339, 341
        taxonomy of problem-solving dimen-
            sions for 335–337, 342
        design for 373, 375 (cf. design for purpose-
            fulness; design *for* social systems)
        paradigm 37, 318, 326, *332f*, 335
        polis as a root metaphor of 335 (cf. *polis*)
    valuation system 336, 340, 342, 362
Purposefulness 70n, 90, 92, 102, 242, 261, 294,
    326, 336
    anatomy of 342, 359 (cf. systems teleology,
        anatomy of)
    and laws of nature 294
    and rationality 294
    and the charge of a "teleological fallacy" 328
    as a concept of practical philosophy rather
        than behavioral science 334n
    as a design ideal for social systems 331, 333,
        335, 337, 364
    as being grounded in contexts of meaning
        294
    as distinguished from purposiveness *328,*
        332f
    as distinguished from viability (in systems
        science) 347f
    sources of 327 (cf. sources of motivation)
Purposiveness (as distinguished from purpose-

fulness) 328, 332f, 364
Purposive-rationality, see rationality, purpos-
    ive; action, purposive-rational;
    ideal type of purposive-rationality

Q

Quality of life 167, 251, 290, 306, 366, 378,
    381, 395, 412
    indicators 255 (cf. social indicators)
Quantified flowchart (Beer) 353, 357, 360, 366
Quantity
    category of (in Kantian a priori science) 202,
        206
Quasi-metaphysical
    as distinguished from metaphysical *156,* 291,
        293
    as distinguished from quasi-transcendental
        156f, 293f
    concepts 156, 293 (cf. quasi-metaphysical
        reflection)
    criticism 156f (def. *157*), *293f*
    reflection 280, 290, 293f
    understanding of heuristic concepts, critical
        purpose of 156 (cf. quasi-metaphysical crit-
        icism)
Quasi-transcendental 36, 156, *162, 177*
    approach (to the problem of practical reason)
        35f, 153, 156, 158f, 232, 285
    arguments 36, *215f,* 230–240 (def. *233*), 264,
        293
        for critically-heuristic categories 231, 234f,
            239f, 244
        for critically-heuristic ideas 231f, 234, 239f
        for critically-heuristic mapping dimensions
            231, 236–240
        Kant's transcendental ideas admit only of
            233
        structure of (or forms of) 230–232, 235,
            239, 240
    as distinguished from quasi-metaphysical
        156f
    as distinguished from transcendental *36,* 156,
        162
    concepts (or categories) 156, 162, 166, 293
        (cf. quasi-transcendental reflection)
    criticism 156f (def. *157*), *293f*
    ideas 215, 231, 293f, *257,* 259–264 (esp. 262),
        293, 342

issues, or questions, the two (Apel) 35f, 177f
  critical solution to 177
reflection 162, 280, 290, *293f,* 301f
  and the principle of reason 293–295, 301
  status
    of cognitive (or knowledge-constitutive)
      interests 112, 152, 155
    of relative a priori concepts 216, 247
    of the moral idea (as distinguished from
      the moral testimony of the witnesses)
      296
    of the planner's basic categories 177, 247
    of the principle of generalization 170f
    of universal pragmatics (Habermas) 159
  understanding of heuristic concepts, critical
    purpose of 156, *162* (cf. quasi-transcendental criticism)

R

Radicalization of discourse, *see* discourse
Rama (branch of the nationalized part of Chilean industry) 350n
RAND-systems analysis, *see* systems analysis
"Rational" (as a claim calling for the question:
  "*whose* rationality?") 15, 19, 21, 23, 32, 34,
  56, 67, 75, 80f, 83, 104, 119, 169, 266, 289,
  292, *294,* 299, 312
Rational
  attitude (Popper) 52, 81f, 84, 96, 168, 265,
    302, 311
    and social rationality 82
  cybernetically 328
  discourse, *see* discourse
  motivation (Habermas) *129,* 167f (*cf.* discourse, rationally-motivated; consensus,
    rationally-motivated)
  planning, *see* planning, rational; planning,
    socially rational; rationality, comprehensive; social rationality; systems rationality
  purposive- 70 (*cf.* purposive-rationality; ideal
    type of purposive-rationality; action, purposive-rational)
"Rationalistic" 278
Rationalism 34, 36, 274, 277, 281
  and decisionism 32f
  contemporary (as distinguished from classical
    German rationalism) 281
  German 109, 181
  Kantian, opening up of 291

Rationality 19, 24, 28f, 32, 34, *42,* 56, 65, 75,
  82, 104f, 108, 112, 162, 266, 277, 289f, 294,
  408
  and criticism 42
  and morality (or the moral idea) 142f, 148
  and puposefulness 294
  and the principle of generalization 170
  as a process of mediation between a priori
    and a posteriori concepts of practical reason 278, 297n, 301
  as being presupposed, rather than produced,
    by contemporary models of practical discourse 22f, 168, 311 (*cf.* rational attitude;
    rational motivation; communicative
    competence; competent speaker; ideal
    speaker)
  as defined by Ambrose Bierce 19
  as equated with purposive-rationality 78
    (*cf.* action, purposive-rational, as an ideal
    type of rational action)
  as understood by Churchman 34
  as understood by Popper 56, 62, 81f, *96, 104,*
    175
  bounded (Simon) 224
  comprehensive 25, 33f, *109,* 112, 143, 167,
    278, *292,* 297n, 298
    and social practice 112, 295
    as referring to two dialectically opposed
      contexts of meaning (i.e., systems concepts vs. social practice) 295 (*cf.* dialectic
      of system rationality and social rationality)
    inevitable lack of 298 (*cf.* comprehensiveness, inevitable lack of)
  the quest for (or ideal of) 34, 109, 111, 265
  decisionistic concept of, *see* decisionism;
    theory-practice model, decisionistic
  dialectical concept of 35
  discursive (concept of) 26, 35, 51, 143, 150,
    163, 168, 175, 177, 278, 298
  ideal (or utopian) conditions of 126, 148n,
    149, 152, 154, 157, 176, 265
  instrumental 25, 29, 70, 74f, 79 (*cf.* reason,
    instrumental; instrumental control)
  monological concept of 163, 170, 298
  non-objectivist concept of 109
  non-rationalistic concept of 34, *278*
  normative content of any concept or standard of 176, 294, 298
  of boundary judgements 226
  dogmatic assertion of 302–304

in any design for inquiry (or for an inquiring system) 338
in consensus 117, 176, 261
in Critical Rationalism 101–105
in democratic decision-making processes 150
in empiricism 106, 281f
in expertise 256, 261
in heuristic categories 154, 162
in our (the planner's) concepts of social reality 176
in "rational" design 266, 363
in "rational" discourse 126, 151
in relative a priori concepts 182
in social cybernetics 371
in social maps and designs 235, 260, 263, 301, 392
in the a priori component of all knowledge and thought 157
in the assumed (or built-in) guarantor of design 256 (*cf.* guarantor)
in the "induction gap" (in prediction) 57
in the objectivistic (or scientistic) approach to social inquiry and design 35
reflection on, and Kant's principle of reason 220
of discovery 157
of expertise (in conceptual framework of Critical Heuristics) *250,* 255f, 258
of guarantee 256, 261 (*cf.* guarantor)
of implementation 258
of knowledge 281f, 284
of legitimation 256, 258
of motivation (in the conceptual framework of Critical Heuristics) *250,* 253, 256, 258, 327, 336f
of purposefulness 327
of selectivity (in administrative planning) 395f (*cf.* selectivity; institutional selectivity)
of suppression of generalizable interests 149f
Space
as a mapping dimension in Critical Heuristics 242
as a pure form of intuition in Kantian a priori science 189, *201f,* 212, 216, 236, 239f, 242–244, 288
Spatiotemporal mapping, *see* mapping
Spectator's point of view, as opposed to agent's point of view (Kant) 221n, 334n
Speech
disciplination of 31

situation, ideal, *see* ideal
three semiotic levels of, *see* semiotics, three levels of
validity basis of 123, 134
Speech-act-immanent
obligations 123f, 135–137, 139f, 143
obligation to provide grounds 123, *124,* 136, 139
obligation to provide justification *124,* 136, 139
obligation to prove trustworthy 123, *124,* 136
validity claims, *see* validity claims
Speech acts *120,* 125, 137–139
constative *121,* 124, 132, 136
expressive *121,* 124, 136
mutual imputation of accountability 122
normative content of 121, 123, 134f, 138, 144
propositional content of 132, 134f, 138, 144
regulative 121, 124, 136
representative 121n
three modes of employing 124 (*cf.* speech acts, three pragmatic functions of)
three pragmatic functions of *120f,* 134, 136
Standards
of criticism, *see* criticism
of rationality, *see* rationality standards
Standpoint 185f, *287f,* 292
absolute (of Kant's knowing subject) 107
and choice of system boundaries 230, 244
and problem, dialectic of, *see* dialectic
-dependent character of knowledge 220
"No s. is ever sufficient to validate its own implications" 285
"One's s. is one's blind spot" 185
selective character (and implications) of any 185f
State Health Planning and Development Agencies (in U.S. Health Systems Planning) 373
Statements
and "facts" 132, 135
basic *58f,* 61, 138f
objectivity of, *see* empirical basis, (theory of) the objectivity of
conjectural character of all 48
empirical *47f*
expressive content of 135, 138 (*cf.* speech acts, expressive)
metaphysical, *see* metaphysical statements; metaphysical presuppositions, two defining characteristics of
normative content of, *see* normative content;

494

as not serving any critical purpose 222
distinction 28f, 221, 269
mediation 30, 76, 103, 172
model 74
  decisionistic 29, 72–78 (esp. *75*), 103, 167, 255, 329, 368
  expanded decisionistic (Lübbe) 75f, 78
  pragmatistic (Habermas) 75, 77–*78,* 329, 368
  technocratic 75–77, 368
problem 69, 152
relationship 29, 67, 72–74, 143
  Aristotle's view of 67f
Thesis–antithesis–synthesis (dialectical triad of Fichte) 268–270 (esp. 270), 275
The Systems Approach and Its Enemies (Churchman) 15, 27n, 34, 169f, 230n, 246, 292, 325
"The true is the whole" (Hegel) 275, 278
Thing in itself (Kant) 184, 209, 211, 243, 287n (*cf.* noumenon; noumena)
Thinking
  Aristotelian 274
  complementary 274
  critical
    and the dialectic of standpoint and problem 288
    as being standpoint-transcendent rather than standpoint-free 288
  dialectical 68n
  dualistic 274
  non-Aristotelian 273f
  "on pense comme on se frappe" (Valéry) 287
  self-reflective 271 (*cf.* self-reflection; reason, self-reflective)
  subject
    in Kantian a priori science 189, 218, 259, 262 (*cf.* knowing subject; transcendental subject)
    in Hegelian dialectics 271, 276
  "Thinking that comprehends" (Hegel) 271f. 274
Thought
  a priori component in 202
  as separated by Kant from knowledge *210,* 213, 225, 229, 232, 233n
Three Mile Island, Harrisburg/Penn. 325
Time
  as a mapping dimension in Critical Heuristics 242
  as a pure form of intuition in Kantian

a priori science 189, *201f,* 208n, 212, 236, 239f, 242–244, 288 (*cf.* mapping, spatio-temporal)
  horizon (of planning) 228
Tool design (as distinguished from social systems design) 25, 75, 104 *329,* 331–333, 366, 369
Tools for rationalizing (political) decisions 75, 77
Topic (of Aristotle) 68, 269
Topical thinking 68
  as distinguished from dialectical thinking 68n
Totality (of relevant conditions) 21f, 191, *218*–220, 223–225, 228–230, 232, 259f
  and the systems idea 222–225, 227, 229f, 244, 260, 295f
  as being itself unconditioned 219, 227, 231
  inevitable lack of knowledge in respect to 220, 224, 230 (*cf.* comprehensiveness, inevitable lack of)
Trade-off principle 254
Training
  critically-heuristc 407
  methodical, of practical discourse (Lorenzen) 31
  of citizens, in citizenship 397
Transcendent
  as distinguished from immanent *200*
  as distinguished from transcendent *199f*
  employment of reason (or of the pure concepts of the understanding; of noumenal concepts) *200,* 209, 213, 217, 303f (*cf.* noumenal concepts, transcendent employment of)
Transcendental *153,* 159, *160–162, 199*
  Aesthetic 189, 199, *201*–203, 215, 240, 244, 288
  Analytic 27, 185n, 189, 199, 202-213, 215, 281
    Kant's main conclusion from 209, 211f
    Kant's main conclusion from, as restated in the terms of Critical Heuristics 212
    Kant's "positive" interpretation of its "negative" result 211
    negative result of 210, 217
    positivistic shortcut in 211f, 237
  Analytic of Concepts 205
  Analytic of Principles 205, 208, 283
  approach (of Kant) 35, 107, 114, 116, 158, 163, 201, 207, 215, 229, 285
  arguments, as distinguished from quasi-transcendental arguments 233

502

Visibilia (Plato) 87, 184n
Vote and decision 76 (*cf.* decisionism)

W

Well-formed
    fact nets 361 (*cf.* fact nets; syntactic truth nets)
    formulae, *see* WFF
    sentences, *see* WFF
Weltanschauung
    category of *257f,* 264, 342, 406 (*cf.* world-views)
Werturteilsstreit in German sociology 27, 69
Western
    medicine 168
    thinking (or thought) 273, 321 (*cf.* Aristotelian thinking; non-Aristotelian thinking)
WHO, *see* World Health Organization
WFF (well-formed formulae) 120, *241,* 284, *361n*
Whole
    "The true is the..." (Hegel) 275, 278
"Whole system" 21, 207, 224f, 227, 260, 262f, 324f, 340
    comprehensive understanding (or knowledge) of, as being impossible 224, 230
    process of unfolding the, *see* process of unfolding
    "We never know the..." 21, 224
Whole systems
    ethics of (Churchman) 323, 337, 339f, 379, 382, 394
Whole systems judgements
    and expertise 309 (*cf.* expertise and boundary judgements; boundary judgements, dogmatic assertion of; boundary judgements, polemical employment of; expert and "objective necessities")
    and Kant's principle of reason 225
    and systems rationality 309, 313 (*cf.* systems rationality)
    and the critical significance of the systems idea 21, 224, 227, 260, 293, 309
    and the map-territory relation 207, 226
    and the moral idea 261, 263
    and value transparency of social maps or designs 229, 306
    as being constitutive of the normative con-
        tent of systems maps or designs 229f, 235, 244, 258, 306
    as implied in social maps and designs 207, 226–229, 235, 263, 293, 306, 309
    normative content of, *see* normative content of boundary judgements or whole systems judgements
    understood as boundary judgements 226–229, 235, 244, 306, 309
"Who shall play God?" question in health planning (Howard/Rifkin) 379
"Who we are is how we understand and question Kant" 193
Will
    free 180f, 222, 242n, 287, 328
    moral 143
    rational 143
Wisdom, Greek 68
Witness(es)
    and cogent argumentation 302, 309f, 313, 401
    and experts 302, 305–309, 313
    and planners 265–267, 289f, 293–295, 301f, 307, 309f, 312f, 340
    and practical discourse (or the process of unfolding) 263, 265–267, 289f, 297n, 302f, 305–313
    and quasi-metaphysical reflection 293f, 301
    and the ideal environment map 408
    and the polemical employment of reason (or of boundary judgements), *see* reason, polemical employment of; boundary judgements, polemical employment of
    and the practical employment of reason 309
    as contesting the "objective necessities" of the experts 305 (*cf.* "objective necessities" as disclosed by experts; reason, polemical employment of; boundary judgements, polemical employment of)
    as "new lay participants" (in health systems planning) 402–405, 407, 414, 417
    as not having to pretend to be objective in order to contest the expert's "objective necessities" 305, 312
    category of *252, 256*–258, 261, 264, 306, 342, 402, 417
    communicative "competence" of 267, 302f, 310f (*cf.* communicative competence of the affected)
    essential functions in health systems planning of 402 (*cf.* "consumers" vs. "providers";